D0392450

CYRUS R. VANCE

'HARD

CHOICES,

CRITICAL YEARS
IN AMERICA'S FOREIGN POLICY

WITHDRAWI

SIMON AND SCHUSTER • NEW YORK

1 3 5 7 9 10 8 6 4 2

LIBRARY OF CONGRESS CATALOGING IN PUBLICATION DATA

VANCE, CYRUS ROBERTS, DATE.
HARD CHOICES.

INCLUDES INDEX.
1. UNITED STATES—FOREIGN RELATIONS—1977–1981.
2. UNITED STATES—FOREIGN RELATIONS ADMINISTRATION.
3. VANCE, CYRUS ROBERTS.   I. TITLE.
E872.V36   1983   327.73   83-592
ISBN 0-671-44339-9

Acknowledgments

I give special thanks to my friend and colleague Eric Newsom, who spent many long months organizing and interpreting mountains of material. His wisdom, determination, and energy were indispensable to the completion of this book.

Anthony Lake, Richard Holbrooke, and Harold Saunders were, as always, matchless counselors and friends. I benefited immeasurably from their sage advice and the many hours they so generously gave to reading the manuscript.

I am indebted to many other former colleagues and friends for their help, in particular to Warren Christopher, Marshall Shulman, Richard Moose, Paul Warnke, Leslie Gelb, David Newsom, Lloyd Cutler, Cyrus Ghani, and Sol Linowitz for their patient and invaluable assistance in sharpening my recollection and providing wise advice on particular aspects of this book.

I am most grateful to Elva Murphy, who faithfully and skillfully shepherded the typing of the manuscript through countless drafts. Her cheerfulness and willingness made my task much lighter and more pleasant than it might have been. I also wish to thank Joyce McDowell, Eric Newsom's assistant, for her unstinting help.

The encouragement and perceptive criticism of my editor, Alice Mayhew, were of inestimable help. I am immensely grateful for her clear and patient guidance and her unflagging optimism.

Finally, I wish to express my heartfelt thanks to my dear wife, Gay, who encouraged me to undertake this task and who assisted me every step along the way.

To my beloved wife, Gay,
without whom neither this book
nor much of what is in it
could have been accomplished.

CONTENTS

FOREWORD

This book is not a diplomatic history or even a memoir. It is simply a story of our country and those who led it during four critical and turbulent years. I have tried to describe a few key events that affected our lives and those of many others around the world. I have also sought to set down some of the choices we faced, the decisions we made or failed to make, and the lessons learned, in the hope that this may be of help to those who follow. Finally, I have put down my views on the foreign policy goals and priorities that we should fix for ourselves over the next ten to fifteen years if we are to cope with the changing times. The path ahead will undoubtedly be uneven and strewn with obstacles. But we must not be daunted. We have the power to choose and to help shape our future. The choice is ours.

CYRUS VANCE

January 1983
New York City

AUTHOR'S PREFACE

We all desire a strong and effective foreign policy but there are structural and human constraints that hobble us in achieving this objective. Perhaps the most important of these is the president's four-year term. From experience in the making of foreign policy in several administrations, I have concluded that a four-year presidential term has serious drawbacks, especially when it comes to foreign affairs. It takes each new president from six to nine months to learn his job and to feel comfortable in the formulation and execution of foreign policy. For the next eighteen months the president can operate with assurance. But during the last year or so, he is running for reelection and is forced to divert much of his attention to campaigning. As a result, many issues are ignored and important decisions are deferred. Sometimes bad decisions are made under the pressures of months of primary elections. And at home and overseas, we are frequently seen as inconsistent and unstable.

We should, I believe, change the current four-year term to a single six-year term in which the president would be free from the pressures of campaigning and would have more time to carry forward the public business. This step would produce more timely and better decisions. In short, the six-year term would provide a needed matrix of continuity and stability for our foreign policy.

Another problem affecting the execution of foreign policy is the necessity, for every recent secretary of state, to contend with a multitude of issues simultaneously. This is a heavy burden that hampers the effective discharge of his duties. I remember Secretary Dean Rusk saying ruefully that one of the burdens that a secretary of state must shoulder is the fact that at any given moment in the day at least two-thirds of the people around the world are awake and some of them are making mischief.

One example of this compression of events can be seen in the events of a single day—the day after the Camp David accords were signed. That morning, after two weeks of round-the-clock negotiations at Camp

David, the president and I met with the Chinese ambassador to discuss a critical issue about normalization of relations with China. At that point we were still enmeshed in the problems of the Middle East, as we had not yet received Prime Minister Menachem Begin's letter confirming our agreement for a freeze on construction of new settlements in the West Bank. Moreover, that afternoon I had to return again to urgent matters pertaining to the SALT negotiations, which were entering a crucial phase, and to grapple with negotiations relating to southern Africa that demanded immediate attention. A day like this was not unusual.

Each secretary of state finds his own way of coping. Mine was to appoint as my deputy a man in whom I had complete confidence, a man who could act as my true alter ego. I had had such a relationship with my great friend and former colleague Robert McNamara when I served as his deputy in the Pentagon, and I sought to duplicate that relationship with Warren Christopher when he agreed to serve as my invaluable deputy at the State Department. There are, however, numerous issues that a secretary cannot delegate, and the problem of controlling one's agenda remains exceedingly difficult.

All sorts of demands impinge on the life of the secretary of state and restrict his ability to set his own agenda: the exigency of events overseas, over which we may have little, if any, control; time spent with the president and the Congress; weeks of foreign travel; and meetings with the press. The hours a secretary spends with the president at the White House or talking to him on the telephone take precedence. Also important is the time spent with individual members of Congress and in testifying on Capitol Hill. Congress cannot be neglected without serious repercussions. I estimate that close to a quarter of my time was spent on congressional matters. For every hour of testimony, it took five to six hours of preparation.

During the budget season, which lasts for several months, the pressure of appearances on Capitol Hill was particularly intense. During the Iranian hostage crisis, it was necessary for Warren Christopher and me to spend up to two hours each day in meetings with the congressional leaders or briefings of groups of senators and congressmen. This was essential to keep the Congress informed and to retain its support of our policy.

I have often asked myself what can be done to lessen the time spent on these necessary meetings with the Congress. Two possibilities especially appeal to me. One is to lighten the burden by having more joint hearings of the relevant Senate and House committees. This should be possible at least in ordinary matters, such as the annual review of the budget. A second is the practice in parliamentary democracies of having a weekly session when the minister of foreign affairs comes to the floor of the parliament to defend the government's policy and to answer questions which the members may raise.

Next to congressional hearings, the most time-consuming obligation is overseas travel. When I came to office I announced that I was going to travel infrequently. I soon found that this was impossible. First, there were matters which the president and foreign leaders expected me to handle personally. This was especially true in the Middle East, where I was expected to conduct face-to-face discussions with heads of government and their foreign ministers. This was also common in Europe, where, unlike the situation of the U.S. secretary of state, the short distances between capitals make it easy for foreign ministers to travel back and forth. On several occasions, I felt that it was unnecessary for me to travel abroad and that others could take my place, but the president thought otherwise. I still believe that it would be best if the secretary of state could spend more time at home and use resident ambassadors or special emissaries when possible.

The secretary of state is the president's spokesman on international affairs, and there is no way that he can properly shed this responsibility. Not only making speeches is involved, but also numerous meetings on- and off-the-record with the press. Each word of a secretary of state is examined microscopically by every country around the world, and a badly chosen word or phrase can create serious problems at home and abroad. On looking back, perhaps I did not spend as much time as I should have with the press, as some have suggested. I had complete confidence in the department's superb spokesman, Hodding Carter, and I felt I could devote the time saved to other important matters. Even so, much time was spent on speeches, press conferences, and other public appearances.

Each day the secretary of state must manage his department, guiding the making and execution of foreign policy. At the same time he must be sensitive to the problems and morale of his several thousand colleagues and provide the leadership that will weld them into a confident service which will best serve our country. On top of this, the secretary must carry out the normal duties of administering a complex organization located around the world.

Finally, the secretary has the responsibility of meeting with visiting senior officials from other countries on an almost daily basis. This is not a matter which can be casually delegated to others without danger of offending other nations. Each head of government, opposition leader, and cabinet minister expects the same courteous treatment that would be extended to our president and his cabinet abroad.

I have set down these reflections on the constraints and demands that affect the conduct of foreign policy to give a sense of the range of events and competing pressures which face the president and the secretary of state. This should help the reader better to understand the narrative that follows.

1

OUR LEGACY

THE BLACK CHAIKA sped down Kutuzovsky Prospekt leaving a wake of pedestrians. The heat was oppressive inside the car. Moscow was in the grip of an unusual heat wave in June of 1981, with the temperature near 90 degrees. I was on my way to the Foreign Ministry to meet, once again, with Andrei Gromyko, the Soviet foreign minister, this time as a private citizen. I was there to attend a meeting of the Independent Commission on Disarmament and Security Issues, which rotated its meetings among the countries of its members.

As we slowed and made a U-turn at the entrance of the Foreign Ministry, I reflected on how much had changed since Gromyko and I had last met, a little over a year before. There had been the Soviets' brutal invasion of Afghanistan; U.S. failure to ratify the SALT II agreement; the progressive erosion of our countries' relations; the release of the U.S. hostages from Iran; the threatened invasion of Poland; and the election of a new American president. I wondered whether the events of the past year had aged Gromyko and how frank he could be in discussing the wrenching issues that divided our countries.

The huge Moscow Gothic Foreign Ministry Building had not changed. The cathedral-like entrance hall is cavernous and depressing. I entered the elevator, which moved slowly up to the seventh floor. As the door opened, I saw two familiar faces, Victor Sukhadrov and Victor Komplektov. We greeted each other cordially, for we had become well acquainted over the last several years. Sukhadrov, a handsome man with a friendly manner, had for many years served as interpreter for President Leonid Brezhnev and other senior Russian officials and their American counterparts. Komplektov, solemn and intelligent, formerly a specialist on the United States and arms control, was then the head of the American section of the Foreign Ministry, and is now a deputy foreign minister.

We went into a nearby waiting room and were soon joined by Foreign Minister Gromyko. I was genuinely pleased to see him again. Gromyko

had been foreign minister for over twenty-five years, making him the
senior in length of service of all foreign ministers. Highly intelligent, a
tough and stubborn negotiator with a sharp and sometimes acerbic
tongue, but with a dry sense of humor hidden behind a stern face,
Gromyko is a talented diplomat with his material at his fingertips. This
comes, in part, from his long years of experience. I remember my wife
telling me that on a drive from Andrews Air Force Base to downtown
Washington, when she was accompanying Mrs. Gromyko, Gay asked if
the Gromykos weren't weary after the tiring trip and said that she hoped
the foreign minister didn't have work to do that night. "Oh, no," Mrs.
Gromyko replied, "he has been foreign minister for twenty years and he
already knows everything there is in all those papers."

Gromyko guided me down the corridor to a brightly lit conference
room crowded with photographers. As we stepped into the glare of the
klieg lights, I thought of the many times he and I had faced the press
together during the difficult and delicate SALT II negotiations in Geneva, in Moscow, in Washington, and in New York. We sat across from
one another at the green-baize-covered table, with Victor Sukhadrov at
Gromyko's side. The foreign minister soon dismissed the press and the
three of us were left alone.

Gromyko welcomed me and sent his and Mrs. Gromyko's best wishes
to my wife, which I reciprocated. He said he was prepared to discuss any
matters.

I asked how he saw the future of the strategic arms negotiations. His
reply was sprinkled with homely metaphors and an occasional Russian
proverb. What he had to say was clear. The Soviet Union considered the
ratification of the SALT II Treaty to be of cardinal importance. The
Soviets were prepared to discuss some adjustments to the SALT II Treaty
signed in 1979 in Vienna with the new American administration, but
would under no circumstances substantially change the key elements of
the treaty or accept a policy of nonratification. I pressed him on whether
the Soviets were prepared to negotiate further reductions in the numerical ceilings contained in the treaty. Gromyko thought for a moment and
replied that the Soviets were prepared to make further cuts—indeed,
substantial cuts. He added that all of this would be conditional on a
sincere effort by both sides to bring about ratification of the SALT II
Treaty. I was struck by his comment on further cuts: I remembered the
Soviets' abrupt and harsh turndown of the deep-cut proposal I had
brought to Moscow in 1977. The wheel had turned.

I asked Gromyko how he saw the development of negotiations on
theater nuclear forces (intermediate-range nuclear weapons), which had
not yet started. He thought for a moment, and replied that the Soviets
were prepared to discuss these issues in parallel with the discussion of
the SALT issues. He added quickly that he wanted to make it clear that
there could be no final agreement on theater nuclear forces until there

was also an agreement on the ratification of SALT II. He said that the two were intertwined, that so far there had been no serious discussion on theater nuclear forces and he wondered whether there was any real intention on the part of the United States to move forward with these discussions. I said that I believed that the United States would move forward with the theater nuclear force negotiations and, although I was not privy to the current thinking in Washington, I hoped it would be soon.

Our conversation turned to antiballistic missiles. I noted that the antiballistic missile treaty was coming up for review next year, and asked him what the Soviet position was. It is essential to maintain the treaty, he said, since it is the underpinning for both SALT I and SALT II. He then added emphatically, "The Soviets will not be the first to abrogate the treaty."

Gromyko said he wanted to ask me a question that was troubling him and a number of his colleagues: what does the future hold for U.S.-Soviet relations? There are some in the Soviet Union, he said, who would write off any hope for progress in the foreseeable future. I replied that that would be a grave mistake and a self-fulfilling prophecy. I said that I did not believe the final word has yet been said on the shape and texture of our bilateral relations, and it would be wrong to conclude now that the current rhetoric foreshadowed a total freeze in U.S.-Soviet relations. I said I hoped that would not be the case and counseled patience.

Gromyko remained silent for almost a minute and his face clouded. He said he wanted to raise another matter that was extremely serious. He spoke slowly, choosing his words with great care. China, he said. Secretary Haig* is on his way to Peking and the Soviets will watch very carefully. If the United States should decide to sell offensive weapons to China, this will be seen as an act hostile to the national interests of the Soviet Union. It would be a grave matter and could have international consequences extending beyond our bilateral relations. He assumed that I would be talking to my government about our meeting. I replied that I would certainly report our conversation on my return to the United States.

We then turned to other matters and when I looked at my watch almost two hours had gone by. I decided it was time to leave. I thanked him and said I would be expecting him to come to the United Nations General Assembly meeting in the fall and I hoped we would have a chance to meet. We walked back to the elevator, where an assistant was waiting to escort me to my car.

The air was still heavy and oppressive but the sky had cleared and a slight breeze stirred. As I rode to a reception for the members of the commission at the Praha restaurant, I reflected on our conversation and

---

* Secretary of State Alexander Haig.

my thoughts turned to the course of U.S. foreign policy since World War II. The relationship between the United States and the Soviet Union had been a major factor in that policy and would continue to be. There had been times when our relations were strained and tense, and there had been occasional periods of grave danger—the confrontation on the Berlin autobahn in 1961, the Cuban missile crisis in 1962. There were also periods of thaw, as in the early and mid-1970s, when important new bilateral agreements and treaties were signed and increasing cooperation seemed possible where our mutual interests coincided. I hoped that we could avoid another cold war and find a way to maintain a working relationship and avoid blundering into a nuclear war.

In a moving speech at American University in June 1963, President John F. Kennedy said some things that were to infuse his own efforts (and to be carried on by succeeding administrations) to break through the wall of fear and mistrust between us and the USSR and to bring nuclear weapons under control before they destroy us:

> . . . Total war makes no sense in an age when great powers can maintain large and relatively invulnerable nuclear forces and refuse to surrender without resort to those forces. It makes no sense in an age when a single nuclear weapon contains almost 10 times the explosive force delivered by all of the allied air forces in the Second World War. It makes no sense in an age when the deadly poisons produced by a nuclear exchange would be carried by the wind and water and soil and seed to the far corners of the globe and to generations yet unborn.

> • • •

> I speak of peace, therefore, as the necessary rational end of rational men. I realize that the pursuit of peace is not as dramatic as the pursuit of war, and frequently the words of the pursuer fall on deaf ears. But we have no more urgent task.

> • • •

> I am not referring to the absolute, infinite concept of universal peace and good will of which some fantasists and fanatics dream. I do not deny the value of hopes and dreams, but we merely invite discouragement and incredulity by making that our only immediate goal.

> Let us focus instead on a more practical, more attainable peace, based not on a sudden revolution in human nature but on a gradual evolution in human institutions—on a series of concrete actions and effective agreements which are in the interest of all concerned. There is no single, simple key to this peace, no grand or magic formula to be adopted by one or two powers. Genuine peace must be the product of many nations, the sum of many acts. It must be dynamic, not static, changing to meet the challenge of each new generation. For peace is a process, a way of solving problems.

I had urged Gromyko not to draw premature conclusions about the direction of American foreign policy from the confrontational posture of the Reagan administration because there were strong currents of pragmatism at work that propelled us to the broad middle of the stream, away from the extremes of Right and Left. I hoped these forces could draw President Reagan and his advisers from their initial preoccupation with ideology and confrontation toward the main lines of postwar American foreign policy generally followed by all presidents from Truman to Carter. During those years, those in the political center essentially shaped American foreign policy. And there had been continuity in U.S. policy, each administration building on the work of its predecessor. The record shows us that when we have stayed in that center, we have had the support of our citizens and the understanding of our friends and allies. When we have drifted off the center, we have lost their essential support at home and abroad, with painful consequences, as we saw in the era of Senator Joseph McCarthy.

During the first Nixon administration, as the long-drawn-out disengagement from Vietnam took place, the primary task of American foreign policy was to move U.S.-Soviet relations away from an unbounded rivalry and to guide the strategic relationship into channels that would improve American and Western security and reduce the risk of nuclear conflict.

The logical starting point for this effort, as President Johnson and Secretary of Defense Robert F. McNamara had recognized, was the strategic nuclear relationship, for arms control is inevitably coupled with general East-West relations. In the late 1960s, when the Soviets attained rough equality with the United States in strategic nuclear weapons, both opportunity and necessity (in the mutual interest in national survival) for a cooperative effort to maintain the emerging nuclear balance were born.

Technical advances in satellite and photographic reconnaissance, and other forms of intelligence monitoring during the 1960s, gave each side reliable means to observe the strategic forces of the other without the necessity of physical inspections on national territories. On November 17, 1969, the first phase of the Strategic Arms Limitation Talks (SALT) began. It culminated in two momentous agreements at the 1972 Moscow summit: the Interim Agreement on the Limitation of Offensive Weapons, a five-year freeze on numbers of strategic ballistic missiles; and the Anti-Ballistic Missile Treaty (ABM), a stringent limitation of indefinite duration on deployment of antiballistic missile defenses. Negotiations for a longer term SALT Treaty on strategic offensive weapons began quickly thereafter.

The SALT process was the centerpiece of the Nixon-Kissinger-Rogers* strategy of "détente" to engage the Soviet Union in a coopera-

* Henry Kissinger, national security adviser, secretary of state; William Rogers, secretary of state.

tive effort to avoid military confrontation, and to establish an international framework within which the U.S.-Soviet political competition could be contained. There were other elements of the strategy: increased U.S.-Soviet and East-West trade; greater Soviet access to U.S. technology and capital; and mutual agreement on some general principles of international conduct, a kind of "rules of engagement" to reduce the risks of direct U.S.-Soviet confrontation in the increasingly volatile Third World regions.

With the familiarity brought about by the continuing SALT process over more than a decade, it is easy to forget the enormous political and strategic significance of the 1972 agreements, and the negotiations that produced the 1979 SALT II Treaty. For the first time, the superpowers were negotiating and reaching agreements on the limitation of the supreme weapons of the modern era, exchanging information that had been of the highest secrecy. They were beginning a long, arduous road toward *controlling, managing* the nuclear balance out of their mutual interest in avoiding nuclear holocaust. This was a more limited goal than the grand disarmament schemes of the 1950s, but a much more realistic and attainable one that, in a step-by-step process, could lead to deep reductions in the levels of nuclear weapons. In all of this, Ambassador Gerard Smith, our SALT negotiator, played a key and often unsung role.

Politically, the counterpart of the strategic arms limitation process was the Conference on Security and Cooperation in Europe (CSCE)—the acceptance by the West of the political status quo in Europe and the creation of mechanisms for an ongoing East-West contact on the political issues that continued to divide the continent. At the same time the Mutual and Balanced Force Reductions (MBFR) negotiations began the process of attempting to equalize and stabilize the military balance in central Europe in recognition of the overarching need for political stabilization.

It must be remembered that these measures, brought to fruition by President Nixon and his advisers, were the result of policies that had been pursued since Truman, and with increasing emphasis since Kennedy. As the international environment evolved, the relative emphasis in U.S. strategy gradually had shifted from military and political containment of the Soviet Union toward a more balanced and flexible mixture of Western military strength together with careful efforts to engage Moscow in cooperative, mutually beneficial measures.

This more balanced approach toward the Soviet Union, merely labeled "détente" or relaxation of tensions, was not easy to define or to defend to the American public. Although it was the logical outcome of the basic American approach to the Soviet Union since the Second World War, conceptually it required an acceptance of the Soviet Union, our adversary for thirty years and more, as a partner in certain limited but vital respects. The Right and, oddly, some liberals were unable to make this adjustment.

Nixon and Kissinger made a conceptual breakthrough in strengthening the international equilibrium in beginning the process of normalization of relations with the People's Republic of China (PRC). One of the costs of the polarization of the early 1950s, and the U.S. preoccupation with Vietnam in the 1960s, was our slowness to recognize the depth of the hostility between the Soviet Union and China. This impaired the prospects of drawing China into playing a positive role in preserving the global equilibrium. Strategically and politically, it made good sense for the United States to precede the May 1972 Moscow summit, at which the SALT I agreements were concluded, by the president's historic trip to China. Wisely, he did not cast the opening to China as an anti-Soviet move, but as the beginning of a relationship that took account of the reality of China's world and regional role.

I fault our foreign policy during these years for not understanding the explosive forces of change in the developing world. All through the 1960s and early 1970s, new forces and actors appeared in areas of the world that had been on the periphery. It required a broader American conception of U.S. security interests and of the scope of our foreign policy than merely the U.S.-Soviet or the East-West geopolitical competition. Historically, our interest in peace in the Middle East, for example, had been predicated largely on our moral commitment to the security and survival of Israel, and on our strategic interests in matching Soviet political and military footholds in the region. The explosion of the 1973 Arab-Israeli War, the Arab oil embargo, and the staggering escalation of OPEC oil prices, however, gave a new dimension to U.S. interests in peace and stability in the Middle East and to our relations with Arab states. The energy crisis had begun, and we became acutely aware of the perilous dependence of the West on Middle East oil.

The oil embargo and price increases had even more far-reaching significance. Beyond driving home the reality of energy vulnerability and our stake in the stability and policies of fragile regimes, OPEC oil policy epitomized the postcolonial awakening of the developing world and the decline of Western political influence in Africa and Asia. It also brought home the importance of the southern half of the globe to the wealthy industrialized North. The ominous Indian "peaceful" nuclear explosion of 1974, signaling the continuing spread of nuclear technology into the developing world, was another demonstration of the urgent need to pay greater attention to the sources of discontent and conflict in the Third World. Yet another was the growing danger of conflict in southern Africa, with the likely radicalization of much of black Africa and the expansion of Soviet influence in this important area. After 1973, the United States had to shift much of its attention to grappling with these problems, both in the East-West context and as manifestations of what was coming to be recognized as an increasingly diverse and interdependent world. The polarized world of the 1950s, already giving way to diversity and the diffusion of power in the 1960s, became the interdependent, multipolar world of the 1970s.

In the mid-1970s, Secretary Kissinger, recognizing these far-reaching changes, sought to exert U.S. leadership. But his preoccupation with the problem of managing the increasingly complex and multifaceted strategic equilibrium among the United States, the Soviet Union, the PRC, western Europe, and Japan distorted his initial view of the problems of the Third World conflict and change. This caused him to misjudge the Angola crisis of 1975, which he interpreted almost entirely in terms of the East-West rivalry. His failure to focus on the local causes of the Angolan civil war, the profound nationalism of the Angolan forces of whatever ideological coloration, his insistence on viewing the struggle (indeed, the whole complex political and racial situation in southern Africa) as a battle in the larger East-West geopolitical competition, led him to take actions and positions that reduced our ability to maneuver. In the end, the strongest nationalist faction was left with no alternative but dependence on Soviet, and eventually Cuban, assistance for survival.

In my judgment, the Angolan crisis of 1975, following the Middle East events in 1973–74, brought home to Kissinger the need to look at Third World problems on their own terms and not through the prism of East-West competition. In April 1976, he made a speech in Lusaka, Zambia, which signaled a new U.S. attitude toward African nationalism, racial injustice in southern Africa, and more fundamentally, toward the whole constellation of the forces of political change in the developing world. On the same trip to Africa, he reiterated in Nairobi the U.S. commitment, made the year before, to a positive U.S. role in the dialogue between the industrialized North and the developing South.

Unfortunately, his attempts to broaden U.S. foreign policy to take account of the changed global environment were undermined by international and domestic perceptions of the administration's earlier preoccupation with East-West competition. Moreover, by that time the United States was in the throes of the Watergate crisis, which weakened the executive branch's authority. This was compounded by a period of intense congressional activity which limited the president's freedom of action in foreign affairs.

However, aside from relations with the Third World, real progress had been made in the first half of the 1970s in strengthening strategic stability, limiting the nuclear arms race, improving political relations with the Soviet Union and the People's Republic of China, and intensifying U.S. cooperation with Europe and Japan. Two of the tasks before us in the Carter administration would be to continue to strengthen the processes for managing the ongoing East-West competition and to develop a more effective and progressive strategy for shaping change in the rapidly evolving world.

It was against this backdrop that we came to Washington.

2

THE ADMINISTRATION
TAKES OFFICE

IN 1969, after being in and out of government for nearly eight years, in various positions in the Defense Department and as the special representative of the president in Cyprus and Korea and during the riots in Detroit and Washington, D.C., as well as a negotiator in the Paris peace talks, I was glad to return to private life and to my New York law practice. The 1960s had been turbulent. I looked forward to a more normal life where I could reflect on what I had learned and have a chance to develop and clarify my thinking about the future directions our foreign policy should take.

In the course of the next eight years, much in foreign affairs and national security policy developed that demanded critical thought. During the administrations of presidents Nixon and Ford, the international scene became increasingly complex and impervious to the simple black and white solutions of earlier years. Ambiguity, contradiction, and change surrounded America's foreign policy choices in the 1970s.

During the 1960s and the 1970s, events occurred that significantly affected the character of the U.S.-Soviet relationship. The Soviet Union had attained a level of military capability and political influence that transformed it from a major Eurasian power into a global superpower. It was the recognition of this change that led Johnson, Nixon, and Ford and their secretaries of state to move beyond a largely unbounded political and military competition to a more balanced relationship. American military strength alone, although fundamental to U.S. and Western security, was no longer a sufficient guarantee of nuclear stability. It became necessary for the United States to intensify its efforts to ease the political tensions and to establish new concepts and procedures for regulating the East-West competition.

I supported a policy of regulated competition coupled with reciprocity

—what was to become known as "détente." But unfortunately expectations for détente were unrealistically inflated while the competitive nature of the relationship with the Soviet Union was underplayed. In addition, the two sides had different understandings of what détente meant. When the Soviets continued to expand their power and influence in the Middle East and Africa, an overly optimistic American public became disillusioned. The public mood swung toward fear and suspicion, and the concept of détente became suspect. The need to move toward greater cooperation, even though limited—particularly in regulating military competition with the Soviet Union—became urgent, and the policy required a fresh and hardheaded examination.

A flaw in our foreign policy during this period was that it was too narrowly rooted in the concept of an overarching U.S.-Soviet "geopolitical" struggle. Obviously, such a conflict did exist and it was of major dimensions. But our national interests encompassed more than U.S.-Soviet relations. New crises unrelated to competition with the Soviet Union had and would occur around the globe with increasing frequency. We were living in a rapidly changing world. Many developments did not fit neatly into an East-West context. I was convinced—as I believe Henry Kissinger was by the end of his tenure—that not only had the bipolar focus of the postwar period given way to a more complicated set of relationships in which power was more diffuse, but also it had become essential for the United States to grapple with the North-South issues—the interwoven problems of the industrialized and nonindustrialized nations. Global interdependence, once a fashionable buzzword, had become a reality, and our future was inextricably entwined with the economic and political developments of a turbulent Third World.

• • •

There had always been an interplay between American domestic politics and foreign policy. This reciprocal relationship had become increasingly important. There were a number of reasons for this. They included the impact of the Vietnam War and Watergate on the attitudes of Congress and the American people. Congress was determined to play a larger role in the formulation and execution of foreign policy. This would force a change in the conduct of foreign affairs. No longer would the executive branch have the power to formulate its policy without greater consultation and support of the Congress. And the government would have to take the American people into its confidence to a greater extent if it was to win their needed support.

I concluded that in the future, a realistic American foreign policy should rest on four principles:

First, our foreign policy should be understood and supported by the American people and the Congress. Our recent experience had shown that without a broad base of support in the Senate and the House and among the American people, policies were vulnerable to misunderstanding, public disillusionment, and repudiation. Congress would have to be a partner in the formulation of our broad objectives if the executive branch was to pursue effectively long-range goals.

Second, a program should be formulated for managing East-West relations, particularly U.S.-Soviet relations. I believed that we faced in the Soviet Union a powerful potential adversary with growing global interests and a compelling stake in avoiding military conflict with the United States. In my view, it was doubtful that there was a Soviet master plan for world domination, but rather an unceasing probing for advantage in furthering its national interests. The need to temper political and military competition between the two countries stemmed from our mutual interest in avoiding nuclear war, not from weakness on our part or a willingness to compromise our values. I believed that a more realistic explanation of our policy toward the Soviet Union should be offered to the American people.

1. The scope and prospects for cooperation were modest. The Soviet Union would continue to try to expand its influence when possible. Competition was, and would continue to be, the principal feature of the relationship. Our task was to regulate it.

2. Patience and persistence in the pursuit of American long-term objectives were essential, and we should strive to reduce the swings in mood and attitude that had made a consistent policy difficult in the past.

3. We had to remain militarily strong and determined in the defense of our vital interests and our values without being bellicose. And we had to be firm and resolute, but pragmatic, in identifying American interests so vital that they would justify recourse to military force.

4. There existed areas, especially in nuclear arms control, where cooperation with the Soviet Union was possible because our interests coincided with theirs. When cooperation could enhance our security, as in limiting the nuclear arms race, it should be pursued without attempting to link it to other issues.

Third, there should be a recognition of the changes taking place in global political, economic, and social conditions and the need to understand the process of change. In addition to managing the problems of the U.S.-Soviet relationship, American foreign policy had to address a wide range of problems that affected the well-being and development of Third World nations, such as human rights, economic development, energy, population growth, environmental damage, food, nuclear proliferation, and arms transfers.

Practical self-interest would compel us to pay heed to these problems. If we neglected them, they would threaten not only disorder and suffering but perhaps uncontrollable conflicts that could draw the nuclear powers into potentially disastrous military action.

The fourth element of a new American approach should be the harnessing of the basic values of the Founding Fathers to our foreign policy. Historically, our country had been a force for progress in human affairs. A nation that saw itself as a "beacon on the hill" for the rest of mankind could not content itself with power politics alone. It could not properly ignore the growing demands of individuals around the world for the fulfillment of their rights. I believed that these aspirations were producing new or strengthened democratic institutions in many nations, and that America would flourish in a world where freedom flourishes.

· · ·

In 1976 I was working with my old friend Sargent Shriver, who was making a bid for the Democratic presidential nomination. I received a call from Professor Richard Gardner, a longtime friend, who was a foreign policy adviser to Governor Jimmy Carter. Dick asked if I would consider joining the Carter foreign policy team. I explained that I was helping Shriver. Dick said he was very sorry and hoped that if the situation changed I would be willing to reconsider.

Sarge's bid failed and he withdrew from the race. Shortly thereafter, Governor Carter called me at home one evening to ask if I were now in a position to join his group of foreign policy advisers. I said that I was flattered to be asked and would let him know promptly. I then began to examine his views seriously. I had met Carter briefly on two occasions, once in Atlanta in 1971 and once at a meeting of the Trilateral Commission, of which we were both members. We were little more than casual acquaintances.

The next day I talked with Gardner, Anthony Lake, and Richard Holbrooke—all old friends who were members of the Carter foreign policy staff—and a few others. What I learned impressed me. Carter was intelligent and hardworking. He had a set of values that I found attractive. His thinking reflected a principled approach to foreign affairs, which I believed essential for the reestablishment of a broad base of domestic support for a more comprehensive foreign policy. His views on specific issues, although still largely unformed, were in the centrist mainstream in which I felt comfortable. I concluded that this intense and energetic man had a real chance to become the next president of the United States. After further reflection and discussing the matter with my wife, I sent word to Governor Carter that I would be pleased to help him as a foreign policy adviser.

During the next several months, I gave Carter my advice on a number of occasions. As the weeks passed, it became increasingly clear that we agreed philosophically about the main elements of a fresh approach to foreign policy. In the early fall of 1976, at his request, I prepared a memorandum setting out specific goals and priorities for a Carter foreign policy, should he be elected.* I sent the memorandum to him in late October. I was told that Carter had asked two or three others, including George Ball and Zbigniew Brzezinski, also to prepare memoranda. My own was to become a kind of foreign policy road map and a standard against which I measured our success and failure in attaining the goals we ultimately set for ourselves.

Throughout most of 1976 Carter tapped a wide range of sources for views and advice, educating himself on the issues and perhaps trying to get a feel for potential candidates for secretary of state.

In addition, his foreign policy staffs, headed by Dick Holbrooke and Tony Lake in Atlanta, prepared more detailed position papers on specific issues. It was clear that Carter was deeply interested in foreign affairs and that he intended to master the details as well as the broad outlines of policy issues, and to play an active and leading role in foreign policy if he were elected.

*   *   *

On election night, Dick Gardner, Zbig Brzezinski and I and our wives, Daniele, Mushka, and Gay, gathered for dinner at Dick's apartment in New York. The evening was filled with drama as the returns came in bringing moments of elation and gloom. It was not until the early hours of Wednesday morning that Mississippi put Carter over the top. All of us were thrilled. As we left Dick's apartment and walked out into the chilly November morning, Zbig and I speculated about what the future might bring and whether we both might be asked to play a role on the new president's team.

During the early afternoon of November 29, I received a telephone call at my office from the president-elect asking me to come the next day to his home in Plains, Georgia, and to spend the night. He didn't say what he wanted to talk about, but I had a feeling it might be an invitation to join his cabinet. At home that night, I talked late into the evening with my wife about what Carter might ask me to do, and whether, if asked, I should give up my law practice and go back to Washington. I was excited at the prospect of being part of a new government, but I knew all too well the long hours and vicissitudes of serving in high office.

Just before that trip to Plains, I had read in the newspapers that some of Carter's staff was opposed to my becoming a member of his cabinet on the grounds that I was a member of the eastern "establishment." Hamilton Jordan was the most outspoken of the group, saying that "if, after the inauguration, you find a Cy Vance as secretary of state and Zbigniew Brzezinski as head of National Security, then I would say we failed. And I'd quit." Subsequently, Hamilton and I became good friends and worked closely and well together. There were rumors in the press

---

* See Appendix I.

that I was being considered for secretary of defense, but after nearly seven years in senior positions in the Defense Department during the Kennedy and Johnson administrations, I did not find that prospect appealing. I hoped that I would be asked to become secretary of state because I had strong views about what should be done in foreign policy, and because I believed that the next four years could be a period of intense and creative diplomacy. With a strong Democratic president and Congress, I felt that progress could be made in several major areas—the Middle East, the strategic arms negotiations, normalization of relations with China, the Panama Canal negotiations, East Asia and southern Africa.

I arrived at the airport in Columbus, Georgia, in the late afternoon of November 30. It was a beautiful fall evening. The evening light on the Georgia pines and the gently rolling hills reminded me of holidays I had spent in this part of Georgia during college years. Only the president-elect and his daughter, Amy, were at home when I arrived in Plains. It was already getting late and Carter invited me into the kitchen, where he fixed us soup and sandwiches. After supper, we cleaned up and did the dishes. Amy began her homework. Carter and I made ourselves comfortable, and began to talk.

My recollection is that we covered virtually every aspect of foreign affairs, generally following my October 24 memorandum. We talked for over five hours, stopping only briefly while Carter put his daughter to bed, and then continuing on into the night. If my October paper had been the written examination, this was the oral comprehensive.

Carter shared my belief that we should continue to work for a reduction in tensions with the Soviet Union, while vigorously defending our global interests and maintaining an unquestioned military balance. We both believed in the necessity of continuing détente, but we agreed that it must be reciprocal—the Soviets must understand that political, economic, and trade cooperation with us entailed obligations that they act with restraint. But Carter made clear that one of his highest priorities would be to conclude a new SALT agreement, and without linking it to other aspects of U.S.-Soviet relations. We expected the Soviet leadership to continue to pursue the SALT negotiations and to follow their own version of détente, which meant that they would continue to exploit opportunities to expand their influence, especially in the Third World. In general, we expected Soviet behavior to be characterized by the same mixture of assertiveness and caution that we had seen since the inception of détente.

We did not discuss the details of a possible SALT approach, but it was obvious that Carter felt strongly that we must begin cutting deeply the nuclear arsenals of both sides. In this, as in other foreign policy matters, he was always to prefer a bold, "comprehensive" approach rather than a more modest "incremental" building on past agreements.

We agreed that we must join a strong and clear policy toward the Soviets with concrete actions to improve our political and economic relations with Europe and Japan. We also agreed that our allies were hoping we would provide clear and consistent American leadership. We both felt confident that for the first time in years, the United States was politically, psychologically, and materially capable of offering leadership.

As to defense policy, I said that while the overall strategic balance was roughly equal, we needed to do more to strengthen NATO's conventional forces. Carter agreed that the alliance needed strengthening and stressed that we would have to give high priority to restoring mutual confidence and to improving the military balance in central Europe.

I outlined my thinking on the growing importance of Third World issues, and cautioned that we must not become so preoccupied with U.S.-Soviet and East-West relations that we failed to give Third World problems proper attention. I favored giving a high priority to the Arab-Israeli question and to reviving the Middle East negotiations. We agreed that U.S. leadership in promoting peace in the Middle East was essential, and that a rare and possibly fleeting opportunity existed for genuine cooperation among the key actors. The energy crisis gave a special urgency to finding a settlement in the Middle East and to improving relations with the Arab states. Carter and I agreed that we should be prepared to furnish military equipment to key moderate Arab nations, provided that we did not upset the military balance in the Middle East.

On China, we were in complete agreement that normalization of relations should be one of our principal objectives. For several years I had felt that it made no sense for us not to have normal relations with a nation of close to one billion people. I believed we should proceed promptly but carefully. We first needed a better understanding of the internal political situation in China and the opportunity to meet their leadership face to face. We also had to work out plans for preserving the security and well-being of the people of Taiwan. We knew this would be a thorny problem, whoever were the leaders in Peking. We hoped, however, that all of this could be achieved by midpoint in the president's first term.

I felt that a special problem for our Asia policy would be the president-elect's campaign commitment to pull American ground forces out of South Korea. I urged that we do nothing without the closest consultation with Seoul and Tokyo, and that in any event, troop withdrawals should take place only in carefully planned stages, making sure before each stage that it was militarily and politically feasible to go forward. Another difficulty I foresaw in our relations with Korea was the application of our human rights policy. Given the importance of South Korea for the security of Japan and for our political and military position in East Asia, I recommended that we continue to press hard on this issue, but not to tie it to our economic or military assistance.

I had been Lyndon Johnson's special representative during the 1964 Panama Canal crisis and the 1965 Dominican civil war. One of my specific concerns was that we should forge a sounder, more equal relationship with Latin America. I recommended that we drop the notion of a "special relationship," which smacked of paternalism, and deal with each Latin American and Caribbean nation as a sovereign power with differing problems, except when it came to multilateral issues. The first step toward a mature Latin American policy, I believed, was the successful completion of the stalled Panama Canal Treaty negotiations. Carter was aware of the political sensitivity of this issue, but he agreed anyhow that we should continue the negotiating path begun by Johnson and carried on by Nixon and Ford. The conventional wisdom was that it would be better politically to delay the Panama issue. I did not agree with this view and neither did Carter. The Panama situation was pressing, the negotiations were far advanced, and we could not shape a more realistic and lasting hemispheric policy until this obstacle was removed.

I was also deeply concerned with the so-called "global issues," that array of complex problems that transcend bilateral and regional relations. Carter shared my feeling that we should redefine and give higher priority to nuclear proliferation, international arms transfers, human rights, and international economic development and cooperation. He felt particularly strong about the need for the United States to make human rights a central theme of its foreign policy. I was in accord. I pointed out, however, that we had to be flexible and pragmatic in dealing with specific cases that might affect our national security, and that we had to avoid rigidity.

I cannot recall that during this long and at times detailed discussion Carter and I had any significant disagreement. I did not find the president-elect's lack of familiarity with the intricacies of some of the complex foreign policy issues unusual, since in the past he had neither held national office nor been deeply involved in foreign affairs. He was obviously highly intelligent and had firm principles. I felt that he could be a leader in foreign policy, and that I could function effectively as his chief lieutenant.

About midnight, the *tour d'horizon* drew to a close. I cannot claim that any special bond of closeness sprang up between us at that time, although I believe that such a relationship did emerge subsequently. Our exchange had been warm and friendly, and I felt a growing rapport with this earnest, intelligent man who grasped the necessity of basing his leadership and policies on the support and common sense of the American people.

Shortly before we retired for the evening Carter asked me to serve as his secretary of state. It was a deeply moving moment. I accepted with gratitude and a sense of optimism.

The next morning, after meeting his mother, who stopped by the

president-elect's house, Carter and I took a walk. We discussed how the
administration's foreign policy and national security coordination system
would be organized. I told the president-elect that I would like to follow
the procedure of the Kennedy administration in staffing the State Department. I would pick my own team; he could veto any selection; he
would suggest any names he wished, which I too could reject. As it
turned out, the president did not turn down any of my recommendations, and the only suggestion I recall him making was that of W. Hodding Carter III as departmental press spokesman. It was a superb choice.

In keeping with his declared intention to make greater use of the
cabinet, and to keep his personal staff out of the line between them and
himself—a sentiment I shared—Carter chose his cabinet officers before
he named his White House team. He asked whether I had any objection
to Zbigniew Brzezinski, whom he had worked with at the Trilateral Commission, as White House adviser for national security affairs. I said that
I did not know Brzezinski well, but I believed we could work together. I
asked two conditions: first, that it be made clear that I would be the
president's spokesman on foreign policy; second, that I had no objection
to Brzezinski's offering Carter independent foreign policy advice—in fact
I encouraged the president to seek a variety of views—but that I must be
able to present to him my own unfiltered views before he made any
foreign policy decision. Carter readily agreed, and we turned to other
subjects, including other names for cabinet posts.

I returned to New York that afternoon to break the momentous news
to my wife, Gay, and to let my law partners know that I would soon be
leaving the firm. On December 3, Carter announced my nomination.

ORGANIZING THE ADMINISTRATION'S
FOREIGN POLICY SYSTEM

One of our most pressing tasks during the transition period was to establish a mechanism for the review, coordination, and implementation of
foreign and national security policy that would suit the preferences of
the new president. The 1947 act establishing the National Security
Council (NSC) created a formal body of senior officials under the direction of the president. Over the years each president had organized the
structure of the NSC to suit his personal style. Under Eisenhower, there
had been considerable delegation of authority to subordinate committees, reflecting Eisenhower's military background. At the other end of
the spectrum, John Kennedy preferred an informal system, consisting of
ad hoc groups of trusted advisers on specific issues.

The problem, as I saw it, was to devise a system that would permit a
thorough airing of key policy issues without engaging the senior foreign

policy and national security advisers in time-consuming debate to no useful end. We needed a structure that would enable the president and his senior advisers to set policy and oversee its implementation by subordinates without the senior officials becoming enmeshed in tactical considerations. There were some issues that were more pressing than others, and I believed we should husband our time and energy for those key issues without slighting other concerns. The difficulty was how to remain in control of the organization and the flow of events and not to be at the mercy of others' agendas.

• • •

In the Carter foreign policy apparatus, the personal dimension would be unusually important. The president's manner of dealing with his senior officials was unpretentious and open-minded. He listened carefully and wanted the fullest discussion before making decisions. He was, if anything, willing to permit debate to go on too long and to try to absorb every detail and nuance before making his decision. The president encouraged frankness and accepted disagreement on policy from his advisers. He did not want to be shielded from unpleasant facts, hard options, or difficult decisions. His policy coordination and review system would therefore have to provide for frequent face-to-face meetings with his chief advisers.

The president's use of the nickname "Jimmy" rather than the more formal "James" as his official signature epitomized his conception of himself and his presidency. He could not abide pomposity and inflated egos. He emphasized his desire for a "team spirit" among his advisers. He looked for personal compatibility in every candidate for a cabinet-level post. The president made clear he did not want a repetition of the morbid backbiting and struggling over real or imagined bureaucratic prerogatives that often prevailed. "Collegiality" was to be the rule among his principal advisers. Carter wanted his cabinet to be composed of friends and equals, sure enough of themselves that they would not feel compelled to squabble about who should take the lead on any particular issue.

I supported the collegial approach with one critical reservation. Only the president and his secretary of state were to have the responsibility for defining the administration's foreign policy publicly. As time went on, there developed an increasingly serious breach of this understanding. Despite his stated acceptance of this principle, and in spite of repeated instructions from the president, Brzezinski would attempt increasingly to take on the role of policy spokesman. At first, his public appearances, press interviews, and anonymous "backgrounders" to journalists were simply a source of confusion. Eventually, as divergences grew wider between my public statements and his policy utterances, Brzezinski's practice became a serious impediment to the conduct of our foreign policy. It also became a political liability, leaving the Congress and foreign governments with the impression that the administration did not know its own mind. I warned the president of this danger and of the confusion it was causing.

• • •

In late December, Brzezinski, now the designated national security advisor, sent Carter a draft memorandum for an NSC structure that largely retained the previous system of specialized committees but that returned the leadership role to the departments. A "Policy Issues Committee" would be chaired by the secretary of state, for example, while a "Defense Issues Committee" would have the defense secretary in the chair. Other committees would deal with intelligence, international economic policy, and so on. In the previous administration such committees had been chaired by Kissinger or, after he became secretary of state, his deputy and successor as national security advisor, General Brent Scowcroft.

I was less concerned about the precise structure of the NSC system than I was about the relative distribution of responsibility within it. I favored a paramount role for the secretary of state on all foreign policy and some national security matters on the principle—as I had stated in my October 24 memorandum—"Nothing is more central than that military instruments be always seen as means of, and not ends of, foreign policy."

Carter did not accept Brzezinski's proposal. He found it overly elaborate and too similar to the preceding structure. He ordered that a simpler system be devised in keeping with his desire to streamline government and to emphasize the authority of the department heads. In early January, after consultation with other foreign policy advisers, Brzezinski proposed a plan for the NSC that provided for only two committees: the Policy Review Committee (PRC), usually to be chaired by the secretary of state, and the Special Coordination Committee (SCC), to be chaired by the assistant for national security affairs. The president approved it on Inauguration Day.

The Special Coordination Committee, chaired by Brzezinski, would "deal with specific cross-cutting issues requiring coordination in the development of options and the implementation of Presidential decisions." The SCC was also to be the focus of crisis management, and would coordinate arms-control issues and oversee sensitive intelligence activities. I had no problem with placing the focus of crisis management in the SCC as long as my views of crisis issues went directly to the president and my communication lines were full and open. I did not want to get bogged down in the minutiae that attended crisis management problems.

In addition to these two main committees, there would be lower-level interdepartmental groups, chaired by senior agency officials, to deal with matters not requiring the attention of the SCC or PRC.

About a week later, Brzezinski proposed and the president approved a procedure for recording the views and recommendations emerging from the SCC and PRC. When no conclusion was reached on an issue, the national security advisor, drawing on the notes of a member of his staff, would prepare a summary report for the president. If a meeting of agency principals arrived at recommendations for policy actions, Brzezinski would submit a presidential directive (PD) to Carter for signature. In neither case were the summaries or PDs to be circulated to the SCC or PRC participants for review before they went to the president. This meant that the national security advisor had the power to interpret the thrust of discussion or frame the policy recommendations of department principals.

I opposed this arrangement from the beginning, and I said so to the president. He told me he preferred this procedure because he was afraid of leaks if these sensitive documents were circulated before they reached his desk. Unhappily, it was true that deliberate leaking to the press had become a widespread tactic in government to promote or discredit a certain course of action, and was a serious constraint on frankness.* Carter said that naturally I or any other head of a department could come to the White House and review the summaries or PDs in draft if we wished. Given the enormous pressure on our time, this was not realistic.

In retrospect, I made a serious mistake in not going to the mat on insisting that the draft memoranda be sent to the principals before they went to the president, whatever the risk. The summaries quite often did not reflect adequately the complexity of the discussion or the full range of participants' views. The reports were too terse to convey the dimensions and interrelationship of issues. Sometimes, when the summaries or PDs—with the president's marginal notes, or his initials or signature— arrived back at the State Department by White House courier (often marked for my "eyes only"), I found discrepancies, occasionally serious ones, from my own recollection of what had been said, agreed, or recommended. This meant that I had to go back to the president to clarify my views and to get the matter straightened out.

(When my successor, Senator Edmund Muskie, asked my advice about what changes he should seek, I told him that one of the most important was that he must insist on the right to review NSC-prepared

* Moreover, as time passed and the president became more angry about leaks of sensitive policy discussions, he demanded tighter and tighter control, even of signed final documents. This inhibited the use of knowledgeable subordinates and the institutional memories of the State Department's career staff. It reached the point where I had to ask my closest aides and assistants to come to my office to read materials relating to critical policy issues within their area of responsibility.

summaries and presidential directives in draft form before they went to
the president.)

•   •   •

The formal mechanism for policy coordination and implementation
was now in place. It was tolerably effective for debating policy options
and securing presidential decisions, especially early in the administration
when there was broad agreement among the president and his principal
advisers on the main outlines of our policy. Later, as the president was
faced with sharp policy differences the system functioned less well. Increasingly, I also found the tedious and often aimless SCC discussions
unproductive. I found it simpler and quicker to deal directly with the
president, Brzezinski, Secretary of Defense Harold Brown, or others on
policy issues, to avoid wasteful and often inconclusive formal meetings.

In an effort to reduce the drain on the time of harried senior agency
heads in attending too frequent SCCs and PRCs, I urged greater use of
the assistant-secretary-level interdepartmental groups. I had found in my
earlier years in government that such forums were very effective. These
lower-level officials could refine the issues and narrow the range of policy
options to genuinely realistic ones. But the tendency of the departments'
staffers to dig in on their departments' positions has always had to be
resisted. The collegiality and the relative absence of interdepartmental
jealousies which (at least at the beginning) prevailed among the cabinet
members were not always shared by our staffs.

I do not wish to be unfair. It is also true that as U.S.-Soviet relations
eroded and policy differences began to spill over, more issues began to
be drawn upward for debate at the political level. This is one reason why
senior officials increasingly found themselves monitoring the details of
policy implementation. One notable exception was the highly effective
use of the so-called "mini-SCCs," assistant-secretary-level meetings
chaired by an NSC official, to develop, coordinate, and monitor implementation of certain national security policies, especially in the areas of
NATO and SALT.

•   •   •

A parallel system of informal channels within the administration existed that reduced the pressures on the formal structure. The most important of these was my nightly report to the president. This document
(usually two to five pages) went directly to Carter for his evening reading,
and contained a brief report on and an analysis of important foreign
events and policy developments. In addition to keeping the president
informed, I used this document to raise policy issues directly and quickly.

I worked intensively each evening to make this report as pointed and
concise as possible. Unlike most documents, it bypassed the NSC (and

its customary "cover memo" which interpreted, summarized, or added to the department's presentation).

Two other important devices for communicating were the "President's weekly breakfast" and the weekly lunch that Zbig, Harold, and I held. The foreign policy breakfast included at first only the president, Vice-President Walter Mondale, Brown, Brzezinski and myself. Later on, others attended from time to time, including Press Secretary Jody Powell, Hamilton Jordan, Hedley Donovan, Lloyd Cutler, and Warren Christopher, my deputy at State. It was a valuable forum for frank discussion. Issues were aired thoroughly and we were able to consider the interaction between domestic and foreign policy matters.

The lunch, referred to by our staffs as the "VBB luncheon" (Vance, Brown, and Brzezinski), proved to be an especially useful means for the three of us to make decisions and settle policy differences. It permitted us to have free-ranging discussions of current and forthcoming issues without the constraints of formal agendas, agency positions, and bureaucratic infighting. For that reason, as with the presidential breakfasts, there were no notetakers or aides present.

To a large degree, the VBB luncheon continued to serve its original purpose of providing a forum for an unfettered exchange of views among the president's top three foreign policy and national security advisers. It did, however, become somewhat routinized, with a complex and too-lengthy agenda negotiated in advance by the staffs. To the annoyance of nonparticipating agencies, the VBB increasingly became a place where agreement could be quickly reached on a broad range of national security issues, followed either by a direct recommendation to the president or by a common position arrived at in a Policy Review Committee or SCC meeting. Obviously, if the secretaries of state and defense and the national security advisor came to an interagency meeting in agreement on a particular course of action, it would be extremely difficult for another point of view to prevail.

ORGANIZING THE STATE DEPARTMENT

At State, I found myself faced with a difficult organizational problem: how to make effective use of one of the most talented and important departments. Although it is small in number of personnel and budget, the State Department contains probably the most able and dedicated professional group in the federal government. It is worth noting that the department has fewer personnel than it did a decade ago, despite the increase in its responsibilities. I do not wish to suggest that I do not have a very high regard for the countless other dedicated and able civil servants and military personnel in other departments. Our government is peopled with extraordinarily able and devoted men and women who are not adequately appreciated by many of our citizens. Too few people are aware of the countless hours, days, months, and years that are given, without proper recognition, by our public servants to the well-being of our nation and its people. I consider myself fortunate to have spent a good part of my life working with them.

It seemed to me, as I took over, that there had been a growing tendency in recent times to ignore the problems of the Department of State as an institution and to fail to use adequately the full resources of the department. The large body of foreign and civil servants who staffed the labyrinthine hierarchy of geographic and functional offices was left to occupy itself with the conduct of the routine business of U.S. foreign relations, while the secretary too often relied on a small hand-picked group of trusted aides and assistants. This practice was especially damaging to the professional diplomatic corps, the Foreign Service officers, a rigorously selected and highly motivated group with a strong sense of corporate identity. As it struggled to cope with the vastly expanded scope of postwar American foreign policy, the department was haunted by widespread doubt concerning its primacy and role in the management of foreign affairs.

Within the limits of the possible, I wanted to counteract this growing remoteness of the secretary from the career services and the immense resources spread throughout the department. As President Johnson's special representative in several international crises, I had observed the skill and ability of people in the State Department, and I knew that these men and women constituted an invaluable source of expertise, insight, ideas, and memory that was often not adequately used.

I was determined to bring the department and the Foreign Service more fully into the process of developing and implementing policy. I believed deeply in the necessity of "institutionalizing" foreign policy. To be enduring, our policies have to be rooted in the institution charged with implementing them. However skilled, a diplomacy that depends on the talents of a single individual is bound to be ephemeral. The United States needs a firm, consistent foreign policy, understood and supported by its professionals, if we are ever to bridge the gap that exists between the formulators of policy at the political level and the professional executors of that policy in the Foreign Service.

I was convinced from the outset that a key to successfully managing the State Department was to have an outstanding deputy secretary who could, in every sense, act as my alter ego. I had learned from Robert McNamara, a superb executive and a man for whom I have the greatest affection, when I was his deputy at Defense, the importance of such an organizational arrangement.

The first step I took after my nomination was to call Warren Christopher, a splendid man, an outstanding lawyer, and a former deputy attorney general, to ask him to be my deputy. I knew Warren from our years together in the Johnson administration, and particularly from our work during the Detroit riots in 1967 and the Washington riots in 1968. I had also known him as a trial lawyer. He was strong and imperturbable under pressure, with a keen, analytic mind and a selflessness all too rare in government. Warren agreed to serve, provided his wife and the president agreed.

I wanted Warren to have the same relationship of mutual trust and confidence that I had enjoyed with Bob McNamara, and he did. He was truly my alter ego, and his decision on any issue was the equivalent of mine. When I traveled, Warren was fully in charge of the department. I did not want to try to manage the State Department from an airplane in the middle of hectic travels and intense negotiations.

In day-to-day activities Warren was to play a leading role in many areas, including human rights policy, ratification of the Panama Canal Treaties, passage of legislation governing our relations with Taiwan after we normalized relations with China, critical Central American issues, and, of course, the Iran hostage crisis, when he finally received the long-overdue recognition of his great skills.

• • •

In organizing the department I set several long-term objectives.

First, to assign greater responsibility and authority to senior subordinates in Washington and to ambassadors in the field. I felt this would give these officials a greater personal and institutional stake in the policies of the administration, and would reduce the workload placed on recent secretaries of state.

Second, to draw regularly on the career service for advice on major foreign policy matters as well as for the conduct of routine business. Of course, I intended to supplement the career officials with individuals drawn from outside the department, but I wanted to avoid creating a small closed group around my office that would screen me off from the rest of the department.

Third, to start a process of internal reform and modernization of the State Department and the Foreign Service which would make the Foreign Service both a more attractive and rewarding career to able people and at the same time more representative of American society. The white, male Foreign Service was already on its way out, and I intended to hasten the transformation.

Sharing authority was to prove an extremely difficult matter, perhaps indicating an underlying institutional problem requiring major structural reforms. Even working twelve to fourteen hours a day, secretaries of state are hard pressed to discharge their responsibilities effectively. In a memorandum on March 14, 1977, I asked the assistant secretaries, ". . . to assume more responsibility in the running of the State Department. You should also know that I find myself anxious to delegate a greater measure of responsibility to you, in part, because of the confidence I have acquired in your talents and ability to anticipate my needs and policy concerns."

I also urged ambassadors in the field to play a larger role in formulating and implementing policy. One of the more unfortunate consequences of the speedup in modern communications had been the diminishment of the role of our ambassadors as personal representatives of the president. The tendency to override or ignore ambassadors had become most pronounced during periods of crisis when, because of the speed of communications, Washington had assumed direct control. But even in the conduct of day-to-day foreign policy matters, initiative had become more concentrated in Washington. I told the ambassadors that I wanted to rely more heavily on their personal advice and recommendations. I urged them to use personal messages to me if necessary, to communicate their unvarnished views. In order to obtain the views of those below the rank of ambassador, I welcomed greater use of the existing special "dissent channel" which permitted junior officials to send their views directly to me if they were not shared—even if they were opposed—by their superior officers.

To achieve the second objective, we retained or appointed career officials in a large number of senior positions. They included Philip Habib * as undersecretary for political affairs, later succeeded by David D. Newsom, another career Foreign Service officer; Arthur Hartman, and later George Vest as assistant secretary for European affairs; Alfred Atherton as assistant secretary for Near East and South Asian affairs; Terence Todman and later Myron P. Viron as assistant secretary for international American affairs; and William Schaufele as assistant secretary for African affairs. Harold Saunders headed the Bureau of Intelligence and Research and later replaced Atherton as the assistant secretary for Near East and South Asian affairs. William Bowdler followed Hal Saunders as head of the Bureau of Intelligence and Research and later became assistant secretary for InterAmerican affairs. Another superb career officer, Peter Tarnoff, was the executive secretary of the department and my special assistant. These and many other able career officials too numerous to mention justified my hopes.

We complemented the career structure with a number of outstanding assistants from outside government. These included Anthony Lake, whom I placed as head of the policy planning staff; Richard Holbrooke, assistant secretary for East Asian and Pacific affairs; Richard Moose, deputy undersecretary for management affairs and later assistant secre-

---

* I had first worked with Phil Habib years before, during the Paris conference on Vietnam in 1968. He is an extraordinary man, blunt, strong, warmhearted, and immensely gifted. It was a great comfort to know that he would be my strong right arm once again. I shall forever be grateful for his help, and for his friendship.

tary for African affairs; Leslie Gelb, director of political military affairs; Matthew Nimitz, my law partner, who served as counselor of the department and general troubleshooter and later as undersecretary for security assistance; Marshall Shulman, special adviser on Soviet affairs; William Maynes, assistant secretary for international organization; Hodding Carter, Jr., assistant secretary for public affairs; Patricia Derian, assistant secretary for human rights; Andrew Young, our permanent representative at the UN; Donald McHenry, who went to the UN as Young's deputy and later successor; Lucy Benson, undersecretary for security assistance; Richard Cooper, undersecretary for economic affairs; and Benjamin Read, undersecretary for management affairs. They were all creative and imaginative in helping to develop and carry out the administration's overall foreign policy. Another key appointment was that of director of the Arms Control and Disarmament Agency (ACDA). One candidate stood out above all the rest—Paul C. Warnke. The president agreed to appoint Paul and to give him dual responsibilities, that of director of ACDA and the principal negotiator for SALT II. Paul, a brilliant lawyer and former assistant secretary for international security affairs, was admirably suited for these difficult tasks. He was a tough and skillful negotiator and an expert in arms control matters.

I am proud of our accomplishments in beginning the long process of making the Foreign Service and the department's career structure more modern and representative of American society. There was much to do.

I strongly endorsed and supported the affirmative action program developed by Dick Moose and his successor, Ben Read. At the beginning of the administration, there were a total of 3,528 Foreign Service officers. Of that total, 217 (6.3 percent) were minorities, and 349 (9.9 percent) were women. By January of 1981, the number of minority Foreign Service officers had risen to 384 (10.5 percent) and women to 512 (14 percent). We devised programs to locate and recruit talented women and minorities for the midcareer levels of the Foreign Service and to increase their numbers in senior career and political positions in the department. These efforts caused concern among some of the professionals that we might dilute the quality and competitiveness of the career services. I believe the results justified our programs and have provided solid answers to those concerns. We still have a considerable way to go, but we are moving toward a more representative and a stronger State Department.

The Foreign Service was suffering one of its perennial crises of morale when we took office. Foreign Service officers, from top to bottom, knew that something had to be done to prevent a steady erosion of the sense of identity and purpose of this small but distinguished service. Laboring under antiquated personnel practices, some dating from the 1920s, and attempting to carry out reporting and representational functions designed for a slower, less complicated era, the Foreign Service was in danger of becoming stultified. The growing reluctance of Foreign Service officers to serve abroad—the very raison d'être of the Foreign Service—had many causes, among which were the declining value of the dollar and the reluctance of spouses to forgo their careers. But it was also symptomatic of the spreading conviction that our posts abroad were becoming peripheral to the process of making and carrying out foreign policy.

Ben Read began a long and courageous struggle to reform the Foreign Service and make it a more attractive occupation, better able to hold its own against competing careers. These efforts culminated in the Foreign Service Act of 1980, which overcame a number of the inequities and disabilities of the career service. Although the act did not go far enough, it was a major step forward in what must be a continuing search for a more substantive and significant role for Foreign Service officers.

• • •

In those early days, I was optimistic that we were on the threshold of an important period in American diplomacy. We had the confidence and support of the American people. The president, the vice-president, Brown, Brzezinski, and I agreed on the shape and direction of our foreign policy. Our priorities were clear to us: a stable military balance; a stronger, more confident NATO; a new SALT agreement; progress toward peace in the Middle East; a Panama Canal Treaty; a settlement of the racial and political crises in southern Africa; an improving and positive relationship with the People's Republic of China; a strong and involved East Asian policy; a sensible energy policy; and a principled yet pragmatic defense of basic human rights.

Our approach was to be determined, principled, firm, and flexible. We would naturally disagree on specific objectives and tactics, but we had many assets. As long as we could hold together on our broad approach to foreign policy, I believed we could leave office having launched our country on a bold new course.

3

MANAGING
THE GLOBAL COMPETITION

STRATEGICALLY, our main problem as the administration came to power was to contain Soviet expansion while reinvigorating the long-term American effort to moderate U.S.-Soviet tensions. As in all post-World War II administrations, the backbone of our policy would be the maintenance of strong American defenses and alliances so that we could manage our relationship with the Soviet Union from a position of equivalent strength.

I was convinced, as was President Carter, that in addition to military strength, successfully negotiating a fair and verifiable SALT Treaty was central to our strategy as we faced a period of international turbulence and perhaps a change of leadership in Moscow. A SALT agreement would also be important in maintaining the confidence of our western European allies. Moreover, stable U.S.-Soviet relations would help to create an international climate favorable to our other foreign policy objectives. A SALT agreement would not guarantee U.S.-Soviet cooperation and mutual restraint, but it was difficult to imagine a balanced relationship without it.

The strengthening of our political and military bonds with our NATO allies was integral to our security policy. Our relationships with our allies had undergone subtle and significant change as a result of developments affecting the strategic balance, shifts in global relationships, and a greater European assertiveness in foreign policy matters. The security ties between the United States and western Europe remained vital, but we could not ignore the insistent European desire to share more actively in the political and security decisions that directly affected their future.

As to the People's Republic of China, I had concluded that we should move promptly toward full diplomatic relations. As long as we maintained a realistic appreciation of the limits of Sino-American cooperation, especially in security matters, and carefully managed the complex interrelationships between China, the Soviet Union, and ourselves, better U.S. relations with China would contribute to strengthening the balance of power both in Asia and globally. This was a goal shared by Japan, the anchor of our Asian policy, and other allies and friends in East Asia.

. . .

In early 1977 the most pressing issue in U.S.-Soviet relations was how to proceed in the SALT II negotiations, which had been stalled for almost a year during the American presidential election campaign. The Soviets, always edgy when confronted by a new American administration, were uneasy about Carter's well-publicized desire for sharp reductions in nuclear weapons and uncertain about his intentions regarding détente. They also were concerned about Carter's outspoken defense of the rights of Soviet dissidents, in particular his sympathetic letter to Andrei Sakharov and his meeting at the White House with Vladimir Bukovsky.

My preference in dealing with human rights issues was to emphasize quiet diplomacy, saving public pressure for those occasions that called for a strong and forthright public statement. I stated my views in a press conference in late January of 1977:

> We will speak frankly about injustice both at home and abroad. We do not intend, however, to be strident or polemical, but we do believe that an abiding respect for human rights is a human value of fundamental importance and that it must be nourished. We will not comment on each and every issue, but we will from time to time comment when we see a threat to human rights, when we believe it constructive to do so.

I shared fully the president's commitment to weave the defense of human rights throughout the fabric of American foreign policy. Soon after the new administration took office, I took the opportunity in a speech at the Georgia Law School to define the elements of a sound human rights policy. There was considerable confusion about human rights resulting from the fact that the issue served different purposes for different groups. Some saw the issue primarily as a powerful instrument in the political offensive against the Soviet Union, whereas others saw it as having universal application. I spelled out the considerations we would take into account, on a country-by-country basis, in deciding the extent to which human rights concerns would influence other aspects of our relations with a particular country. I wanted to make clear the shape and substance of our human rights policy, and the fact that it was universal in application, yet flexible enough to be adapted to individual situations.

THE SALT NEGOTIATING BACKGROUND:
THE VLADIVOSTOK ACCORDS

The negotiating situation we inherited was quite far advanced. At Vladivostok, in November 1974, presidents Ford and Brezhnev had agreed to replace the SALT I Interim Agreement on offensive weapons (which was to expire in October 1977) with a SALT II Treaty lasting until 1985.* Unlike the interim agreement, which permitted the Soviets a numerical advantage in numbers of land-based (ICBM) and sea-based (SLBM) ballistic missile launchers but excluded strategic bombers, in which the United States had a huge lead, SALT II was to have an equal aggregate ceiling of 2,400 for all launchers of strategic nuclear delivery vehicles (SNDVs) and a subceiling of 1,320 for launchers of "MIRVed" missiles (rockets carrying a cluster of warheads, each capable of attacking a separate target).

To attain the Vladivostok agreement, the United States had dropped its insistence on reductions in the Soviet modern heavy ICBM force. In return, the Soviets had given up their demand for limitations on the so-called U.S. forward-based nuclear systems (FBS), our land- and carrier-based aircraft stationed in western Europe, and had accepted the principle of equal aggregate ceilings for missiles and bombers.

Despite repeated valiant attempts, especially in January and February of 1976, Henry Kissinger was unable to translate this accord into a final agreement, primarily because of a stalemate over whether and how to limit the nascent U.S. cruise missile program, and the development of the Soviet Backfire medium-range bomber, which some in the U.S. defense community believed had a limited capability to attack the United States.

The Soviets believed that substantial agreement on cruise missile limits had been reached in early 1976. However, our review of the negotiating record showed that the limits under discussion were never agreed to by the Ford administration. The Soviets refused to agree to formal treaty limits on the Backfire on grounds that it was not a strategic system, and the United States had not pressed too hard for including it in the treaty for fear the Soviets would insist on reopening the FBS issue, which our allies were anxious to keep out of the talks. However, it was believed that the Soviets would agree to limit the Backfire in a parallel "understanding" once an acceptable agreement emerged on other issues.

Since the SALT I Interim Agreement was due to expire in October 1977, it was desirable either to have a new agreement in place by then, or at least to have made substantial progress toward a treaty. Basically,

* An executive agreement required approval of a majority of both houses of the Congress. A treaty required approval of two-thirds of the senators present when the vote on the treaty took place.

we had two major options: (1) to reach substantial agreement on the basis of Vladivostok (which offered the best chance for early agreement on a treaty, assuming the Soviets would give up or moderate their demands for stringent cruise missile limits); or (2) to take a bold step which would move us beyond the simple numerical limits of Vladivostok to deep cuts in the number of launchers and to limitations on qualitative improvements of strategic weapons. The second approach would clearly take longer to negotiate.

My preference was to take advantage of the political strength and momentum of a new administration, and the traditional honeymoon with Congress, to attempt to conclude an agreement based essentially on Vladivostok, which would postpone the cruise missile and Backfire issues until SALT III. We recognized that it might be necessary to negotiate some loose cruise missile constraints, but this would not materially impede our ultimate ability to use cruise missiles to strengthen our strategic forces. As I saw it, in SALT III we could immediately begin to negotiate deep cuts and other limitations. Paul Warnke, our extremely able chief SALT negotiator and head of the Arms Control and Disarmament Agency, shared this view.

Others in the administration, calculating that our long-term arms control and security objectives justified the risks of pressing at once for deep reductions and qualitative restraints on weapons modernization, argued for the comprehensive deep-cut approach, rather than waiting for a SALT III negotiation that might take place under uncertain international and domestic political conditions. The comprehensive approach envisioned substantial reductions in the Vladivostok overall missile launcher ceilings, as well as in the number of Soviet heavy missiles. As for cruise missiles, the United States could accept only high range limits because we wanted to protect our option to fire them from our aging B-52 bombers as stand-off weapons.

My view was that we could agree to a mix of range limits that would not interfere with the effectiveness of the cruise missiles, should we eventually decide to deploy them. I was not particularly concerned about short-range limits—600 km—on the ground- and sea-launched versions (GLCM and SLCM), since at that time we had no plans to deploy them. However, for the air-launched cruise missile (ALCM), I agreed we must insist on the right to much greater range capabilities—1,500 km to 2,500 km—since we intended to deploy them on our B-52 bombers to strengthen the bomber leg of our strategic forces. We would be prepared to accept limits on the Backfire bomber outside the treaty text, for example, the Soviets could not employ the Backfire for intercontinental missions or increase its production rate.

I did not disagree in principle with those who favored the comprehensive approach. In the long term, this was clearly where we had to go. Where I differed was in the assessment of negotiating difficulties. I had

strong doubts that the comprehensive approach could succeed without extremely difficult negotiations involving substantial compromise on both sides. In my view, the modest alternative—accepting the Vladivostok framework—offered the best prospect for a rapid conclusion of a SALT II Treaty that would limit Soviet strategic forces and provide a more stable foundation for U.S.-Soviet relations in what could well be a rough period ahead.

After substantial debate, which Paul Warnke and I summarized in a memorandum on March 17, the president decided that despite the political and negotiating risks, he wanted to go beyond Vladivostok and seek deep cuts in a comprehensive proposal. I knew that the president's attempt to "jump over SALT II" was a long shot. I disagreed with the decision but I was determined to give it my best. It might be that the Soviets, confronting a new president and the prospect of having to deal with him for at least four and perhaps eight years, would be willing to take a bold step. We could not know unless we tried. And success would mean a dramatic breakthrough in turning around the arms race.

• • •

Though the comprehensive proposal was rejected by the Soviets in the March meeting, as I shall later describe, a number of the elements of that proposal were ultimately contained in the SALT II Treaty. Thus, it is important to understand the strategic rationale that underlay the comprehensive proposal.

Since at least the late 1960s, there was growing concern on the part of some in the U.S. national security community about two interrelated problems: the continuing deployment and increasing accuracy of the Soviet "heavy missiles"; and the possibility that by the mid-1980s the Soviets would have enough ICBM warheads of sufficient accuracy to threaten our ICBM force sheltered in hardened underground silos. It is important to note that in contrast to the Soviets, our military leaders had decided in the early 1960s to forgo heavy missiles in favor of the smaller, more versatile, solid-fueled Minuteman ICBM. Since that time our military leaders have shown no interest in developing or deploying heavy missiles.

Because of its enormous lifting power or "throwweight," the newest Soviet heavy ICBM, the SS-18, was capable of carrying a massive "payload" that could be divided (or "fractionated") into a large number of warheads, eventually enough, theoretically, to destroy most of our ICBMs in their concrete silos. I use the term "theoretically"; the threat was predicated on the assumption, made by those who held this view, that Soviet missiles would perform with predicted accuracy and reliability and that the Soviets could actually coordinate the simultaneous arrival on widely dispersed targets of hundreds of missiles and thousands of warheads. This was and remains a highly questionable assumption.

The Soviets, of course, could never test such a capability to be sure that an attack of such magnitude and complexity could actually be carried out. Moreover, the flight paths of attacking missiles would be along axes that were subject to geophysical forces whose influence on statistically derived accuracy estimates was highly uncertain. Some experts believed that such uncertainties made a Soviet attempt to destroy our ICBMs highly doubtful. Former Secretary of Defense James Schlesinger, for instance, took this view in testimony before the Senate Foreign Relations Committee, stating: "I can publicly state that neither side can acquire a high confidence first-strike capability. I want the President of the United States to know that for all the future years, and I want the Soviet leadership to know that for all the future years."*

In any case, the theoretical vulnerability of our ICBMs would not inevitably expose the United States to nuclear coercion. In the 1960s the United States had wisely chosen a strategic triangle or triad of land-based missiles, sea-based missiles, and bombers, so that the vulnerability of any one leg would not undermine nuclear deterrence. Even in the remote event that the Soviets should attempt a first strike on our ICBMs, we could retaliate with many of our bombers and SLBMs, which carry some two-thirds of our total warheads, more than enough to devastate the Soviet Union.

Thus, fundamentally, the ICBM vulnerability question and the suggested "special" threat posed by Soviet heavy ICBMs were largely political problems. Should SALT be unable to check the theoretical vulnerability of our silo-based ICBMs, the United States would be compelled to take countermeasures, leading to a new cycle in the nuclear arms race.

It was because of these concerns that the Nixon and Ford administrations had tried to gain Moscow's agreement in SALT I and II to cut back its heavy missile program. The Soviets had adamantly refused, asserting that their heavy land-based missiles were the mainstay of their nuclear forces and their counterweight to the large U.S. lead in the number of strategic warheads and to our technological superiority. They did agree in SALT I, however, to freeze the number of launchers of heavy missiles at 308.

A major question confronting us was whether we should renew the previous administration's attempt to reduce the number of Soviet heavy missiles in SALT II. If we did not do so, it would be necessary to retain the option to adopt mobile basing for some of our ICBMs to reduce their theoretical vulnerability to a Soviet attack.

However, our technical analysis showed that reductions in Soviet heavy missiles alone would no longer suffice to hold Soviet ICBM warhead numbers below the number defense planners believed necessary to

* Hearing before the Subcommittee on Arms Control, International Law and Organizations of the Committee on Foreign Relations, United States Senate, March 4, 1974, p. 17.

launch an attack. Since SALT I the Soviets had begun to put "multiple independent reentry vehicles" on their missiles (MIRVs) and to improve the accuracy of their "light" ICBM forces as well (SS-17s and SS-19s). We found that unless the increase in the number and accuracy of these missiles was also sharply curtailed, they would eventually be able to threaten our ICBMs even if all the Soviet heavy SS-18s were eliminated. To meet the ICBM vulnerability problem, therefore, SALT II would have to hold the total Soviet MIRVed ICBM level well below what we believed they planned to deploy, and severely restrict the number of test flights, which would be required for improving the accuracy and reliability of their missiles.

This was asking a lot of SALT, particularly in light of our determination to retain the freedom to deploy large numbers of long-range, air-launched cruise missiles on our strategic bomber force. We could not accede to Soviet demands for significant limitations on either the numbers or range of these weapons. This would surely toughen the Soviet position on other issues. Obtaining restrictions on cruise missiles, an area of U.S. technological advantage greatly feared by Moscow, had been a major Soviet objective in the post-Vladivostok negotiations.

In addition to these strategic considerations, there were important political reasons for trying to achieve deep cuts now, rather than waiting for SALT III. Shortly after we took office, Senator Henry Jackson sent the president a memorandum opposing Vladivostok and calling for deep cuts, especially in heavy missiles, which he continued to regard as the most threatening element of Soviet strategic forces. Jackson would be a major asset in a future ratification debate if he supported the treaty, and a formidable opponent if he opposed it. And the strength of the potential opponents to a SALT II Treaty was demonstrated in the Senate vote on March 9 that confirmed Warnke as SALT negotiator by a vote of only 58 to 40. Since a SALT Treaty would need two-thirds of the Senate for ratification, the 40 votes against Warnke were a warning of the difficulties we might face in ratifying an agreement that did not have the support of such senators as Jackson.

There was another factor at work which pushed the president toward deep cuts. It was his profound commitment to reversing, not simply curbing, the upward spiral of nuclear weapons. As much as any other president since World War II, Carter was repelled by the irrationality of piling up thousands upon thousands of unimaginably destructive nuclear weapons in both sides' arsenals. He never shrank from the political and strategic realities of the nuclear age; he stated he could order nuclear retaliation if necessary, and unquestionably he meant it. He also clearly understood the perceptual and political importance—in the foreign policy sense—of American strategic equivalence with the Soviet Union. But he was convinced that rational men should start moving seriously and at once toward reducing the terrible danger of nuclear weapons. The president (and virtually all his senior security and foreign policy advisers) believed that despite our fundamental political and military rivalry with the Soviet Union, the Soviet leadership was composed of men who also understood that nuclear weapons pose a unique threat to our survival and that of civilization as we know it.

· · ·

Once the president had made his decision for deep cuts, I was determined to do my utmost to bring it to fruition. But I also believed we should be prepared for a Soviet refusal to move away from the Vladivostok agreements.* I felt we must have a backup approach that could permit the negotiations to continue. I urged Carter to allow me to take in my pocket a second proposal that accepted the Vladivostok ceilings and deferred the cruise missile and Backfire issues. Carter was determined not to miss the chance for a major breakthrough, but he also recognized the risk of Soviet rejection of the comprehensive approach. He agreed I could present the deferral proposal, but he warned me it must be made crystal clear to the Soviets that he personally preferred deep cuts now. In addition, although I could not reveal it to them without further authorization, I had higher fallback numbers for the various ceilings contained in the comprehensive proposal.

Although I was not sanguine that the Soviets would agree to defer cruise missile consideration, I believed there was a chance they would take the cruise missile elements out of the comprehensive proposal and fold them into the deferral proposal.

Preparing for the Moscow meetings with Brezhnev and Gromyko, I called Soviet Ambassador Anatoliy Dobrynin to my office a few days before my departure and outlined the comprehensive deep-cut proposal. His reaction was negative, reflecting the hardening mood in Moscow. I told him to tell Moscow that I would be prepared to listen to and discuss Soviet responses or questions. I stressed this point because much was

---

* The essential elements of the comprehensive proposal were as follows: First, reductions in the Vladivostok ceilings and subceilings: the total of strategic launchers from 2,400 to between 2,000 and 1,800; the total of MIRVed launchers from 1,320 to between 1,200 and 1,100. A new subceiling of 550 was proposed for MIRVed ICBMs. A further subceiling of 150 was proposed for heavy missiles, a reduction from the 308 Soviet heavy missiles agreed to at Vladivostok. In addition, the proposal contained a ban on the construction of new ICBMs; a ban on the modification of existing ICBMs; a limit on the number of flight tests for existing ICBMs; a ban on the development, testing, and deployment of mobile ICBMs; and a limit on all cruise missiles to a range of 2,500 km. Finally, the Backfire bomber would not be counted as a strategic bomber, provided that the Soviets complied with a number of measures that would have limited its range. These deep cuts were a radical departure from Vladivostok and would be very hard for the Soviets to swallow. However, they might be accepted by them as a starting point for negotiation of numbers between those proposed and the Vladivostok ceilings. Insofar as United States programs were concerned, the ban on mobile missiles and new ICBMs would have required cancellation of the MX missile, but that was still on the drawing boards.

written at the time about our alleged failure to notify the Soviets in advance of the trip of our deep-cut proposal.

The already charged atmosphere surrounding my trip, our first encounter with the Soviet Union, was intensified by the president's decision to outline the objectives of the comprehensive proposal in a speech to the UN General Assembly before I left for Moscow, and by a high level administration backgrounding of the press. Until then both sides, at least in public statements, had adhered to the confidentiality of the negotiations. This had helped insulate the talks from excessive political or ideological posturing. The administration's "openness" violated that canon of the SALT process and may have contributed to Moscow's suspicions.

• • •

I arrived in Moscow on March 27, after first stopping in Brussels to brief the North Atlantic Council. My first meeting was at 11 A.M. on March 28 in the Politburo meeting room in the Kremlin. A visibly aging Leonid Brezhnev greeted us. He was a powerfully built man with beetling eyebrows and a mobile lined face. One could feel that this man was used to exercising power. He was accompanied by Foreign Minister Andrei Gromyko, Deputy Foreign Minister Georgi Kornienko, Ambassador Anatoliy Dobrynin, and Victor Sukhadrov. With me were Paul Warnke, Ambassador Malcolm Toon, Philip Habib, Marshall Shulman, Leslie Gelb, William Hyland, an NSC SALT expert, and Walter Slocombe, an assistant to Harold Brown, and William Krimer, interpreter. After a cordial greeting and the inevitable round of picture taking, we seated ourselves on opposite sides of a long green-baize table. The room was paneled in white oak. It had a high ceiling and two large chandeliers. It was functional in appearance and lacked the charm of other rooms in the Kremlin.

I had hoped we would move directly to SALT, but Brezhnev immediately launched into a diatribe in which he cataloged alleged human rights abuses in the United States. I responded sharply to his charges and stressed the importance of making progress in our talks. We needed concrete progress, not polemics.

The first substantive discussions took place at a second meeting, held at 5:30 that afternoon, without Brezhnev. Gromyko opened by pushing strongly for an agreement based on Vladivostok and what he claimed were subsequent agreements with the Ford administration on cruise missiles. I disputed the latter assertion, and I then presented both the comprehensive and deferral proposals, strongly emphasizing that the comprehensive approach was the president's preferred position.

Gromyko said he would study the proposals and give me the official Soviet response before I left Moscow. He then devoted a great deal of time to reviewing the Soviet interpretation of the Vladivostok agreement.

We also discussed a number of other matters concerning the limitation of armaments. We agreed to set up bilateral working groups to talk about these questions.* A number of international issues, including the Middle East, Cyprus, southern Africa, and the preparatory conference on the Helsinki accords to be held in Belgrade, were also discussed.

I expected that after a day of study and discussions in the Politburo, the Soviets would come back with objections to specific aspects of our proposal and to our numbers and possibly with counterproposals. This could provide a basis for serious negotiations. Consequently, when I next met with Brezhnev on the evening of March 30, I was angered at the vehemence and finality with which he rejected our SALT proposals. There was not even a hint of a counterproposal. He called our position "unconstructive and one-sided," and "harmful to Soviet security." It was evident there was no point in attempting to pursue serious negotiations on this trip.

Despite the harshness of Brezhnev's response, the Soviet leadership did not want SALT to founder. At their suggestion we agreed that Gromyko and I would meet again in early May in Geneva.

Gromyko saw us off at the airport and soon thereafter held an extraordinary press conference. It was long and harsh and out of character with Gromyko's usual style. Obviously, a decision had been made to take a tough line, probably in an attempt to throw the blame for lack of progress on the United States and to counter the strong statement which had been made by Brzezinski criticizing the Soviet rejection of our proposals. It was, unfortunately, effective as a propaganda device. It created widespread fear that the the the U.S.-Soviet relationship was in jeopardy.

The March 1977 meetings have been portrayed as a serious setback for SALT. I do not wish to understate the damage caused by the flat rejection of our proposal and Gromyko's press conference. It was substantial. The Soviets' categorical rejection without any counterproposal was a bad mistake on their part (which they have subsequently acknowledged) and a disappointment to all of us in the administration. At home, the American press overreacted, attacking our human rights policy and calling us "naive" and inconsistent.

Much of their reaction can be attributed to an understandable anxiety that an important component of the U.S.-Soviet relationship was in jeopardy. I do not believe our human rights policy was the cause of the failure of the Moscow negotiation, although it did affect the general atmosphere in which our talks took place. Our position on human rights

* The working groups covered the following matters: (1) negotiations looking to a comprehensive ban on the testing of nuclear weapons; (2) a chemical weapons treaty; (3) an agreement providing for prior notification of missile test firings; (4) an agreement restricting antisatellite weapons; (5) civil defense; (6) an Indian Ocean agreement; (7) a radiological weapons treaty; (8) an agreement limiting arms transfer to Third World countries; (9) steps to strengthen the Non-Proliferation Treaty.

matters had undoubtedly irritated the Soviets, but it did not cause them to reject our proposals. The Soviets were much too pragmatic to let their deeper security interests be jeopardized by matters that were only an irritant.

Obviously, time would have been saved had the Soviets reacted positively and negotiations had begun in March on ways to combine elements of both our proposals. That, in essence, was the negotiating path that we followed two months later in Geneva.

In retrospect it is clear that a prolonged negotiation was inevitable. The fact is, the Soviets considered stringent cruise missile limits integral to the Vladivostok framework, which we did not. The United States was not going to accept limits on cruise missiles, even loose ones, without improvement of the Vladivostok accords in areas of security important to us, quantitative and qualitative limits on MIRVed land-based missiles.

This judgment after the fact does not explain the severity of the Soviet reaction to our March proposals. I believe a combination of factors produced it. First, before the Vladivostok negotiations, the Soviet leadership had thrashed out compromises that enabled Brezhnev to make significant concessions in his discussions with Ford and Kissinger. Brezhnev and others of like mind did not want to reopen a harsh debate within the Politburo and with the military on new and more extensive Soviet compromises, as they would have been required by the comprehensive proposal. For the Soviet government and for Brezhnev personally, Vladivostok had become politically sacrosanct. Moscow may have concluded the the new administration felt no commitment to Vladivostok and to what the Soviets regarded as the commitments of the previous administration. The Soviets misunderstood our seriousness and our flexibility in March 1977.

Second, the Soviets may have seen the comprehensive proposal as an unacceptable attempt to reduce Soviet numerical advantages in land-based missiles, which constituted the bulk of their strategic forces. Unlike the United States, the Soviets do not have a balanced strategic triad. About two-thirds of their total nuclear weapons are carried on land-based ICBMs.

Third, the Soviets were suspicious that the Carter administration was more ideologically oriented than its predecessors, and that it had put forward the comprehensive proposal as a propaganda ploy to capture world opinion.

Perhaps the most serious cost of the Moscow discussions was to be felt later in the domestic battle over SALT ratification. The comprehensive proposal gave a weapon to anti-SALT and antidétente hard-liners, who held up the deep-cuts proposal as the only standard against which to measure the success of the ultimate agreement. A SALT Treaty that contained limitations less stringent than the comprehensive proposal would be attacked as falling short of "real arms control."

• • •

On my return to Washington, our first step was to take stock. By early April we reached agreement on a strategy that was shortly to get negotiations back on the track. We would stress the need for perseverance and patience in achieving an agreement. There had been too much undisciplined talk before the Moscow trip, which had resulted in inflated expectations that the talks would produce a breakthrough. This intensified the shock and anxiety over the outcome. Henceforth, we would try, not always successfully, to avoid excessive optimism. I would continue to emphasize to the Soviets, through Ambassador Dobrynin, our preference for the comprehensive approach. Finally, we would see how the elements of the comprehensive approach might be repackaged to achieve our basic objectives: the achievement of numerical reductions and qualitative limits on strategic weapons in SALT II, and a joint commitment to even more substantial steps in SALT III. Our aim at my next meeting with Gromyko, scheduled for May 18–20 in Geneva, would be to reach agreement on our proposed repackaging and the initiation of serious negotiations.

We wanted to give the Soviets more time to digest our ideas in advance. Warnke and I met with Dobrynin in late April to suggest that we should think about a three-part package: a treaty lasting until 1985, with weapons ceilings appreciably reduced from Vladivostok; an interim agreement for two or three years on difficult issues, such as cruise missiles; and a commitment to negotiate deeper cuts and limitations on qualitative improvements in SALT III. This idea was developed mainly by Leslie Gelb and William Hyland. Dobrynin responded favorably, suggesting that the third part be called a "declaration of principles," and he undertook to report my informal thoughts to Moscow as ideas for exploration, not as a U.S. proposal.

With this advance preparation, Gromyko and I met in Geneva in a businesslike atmosphere. The Soviets were ready to negotiate. I formally proposed and he quickly agreed on the three-part structure. Gromyko wanted the separate interim executive agreement on "thorny" issues, which we had suggested, to be a protocol* to the treaty and integral to it. He was familiar with American legislative process, and wished to avoid the possibility that the Senate, which has sole jurisdiction over treaties, might ratify the treaty—thus locking the Soviets into the limits on their ICBMs—while the House might reject the executive agreement—on which *its* approval would be required—thus leaving cruise missiles with no limits.

To meet Gromyko's valid point, I agreed to a protocol. We also agreed that the treaty would contain the Vladivostok ceilings of 2,400 and 1,320

_____
* A separate agreement annexed to the treaty.

on strategic delivery vehicles, but I insisted that these numbers merely be starting points for further reductions to be specified in the treaty. We were prepared to accept a 600-kilometer-range limit on ground- and sea-launched cruise missiles—but not less than 2,500 km on air-launched cruise missiles for our heavy bombers—in the protocol (which we had already decided must expire *before* our cruise missile programs were actually ready for deployment). Our reasoning was that the short-term protocol was simply a method of deferring the cruise missile issue to subsequent negotiations, since these nominal limits would have no significant impact on our programs.

Aside from concurrence on the three-part framework, there was little agreement on specifics. Gromyko stolidly rejected a new proposal we put forward that Soviet heavy missiles be limited to 190, down from the 308 agreed at Vladivostok, in return for acceptance of a ceiling of 250 on the number of heavy bombers carrying air-launched cruise missiles (ALCMs). He took the position that heavy bombers carrying ALCMs must be counted within the 1,320 ceiling, as if they were MIRVed missiles. We rejected that position. We were not prepared to accept his proposal unless the Soviets accepted a reduction in the 308 ceiling on heavy missiles.

I was satisfied with the Geneva talks. We had moved beyond charge and countercharge and had begun the practical business of identifying the issues and negotiating our differences. Although I was confident that ultimately an agreement would be reached, I knew there would be difficult bargaining ahead. I hoped that the major issues could be resolved in principle at the ministerial level by October 3, the expiration of the SALT I Interim Agreement. But the painstaking process of translating agreements in principle into precise and binding treaty language made actual conclusion of a formal agreement by that date virtually impossible.

CANCELLATION OF THE B-1: A POLITICAL BLOW

On June 30, President Carter announced one of the most courageous and politically costly defense decisions of his presidency. He cancelled the B-1 strategic bomber program in favor of modernizing and arming the B-52 bomber force with thousands of highly accurate long-range air-launched cruise missiles. Persuaded by the technical analysis, the president made his decision on cost-effectiveness grounds. The B-1 bomber was proving to be inordinately expensive, and he had concluded that B-52s armed with cruise missiles could do the job as well at much lower cost. However, defense hawks, anti-SALT hard-liners and political opponents of the administration seized on the decision as evidence that the president was "soft" on defense and was practicing "unilateral" arms control. This charge was repeated throughout the administration's term and into the 1980 political campaign. It was in this way that the Reagan administration became politically locked into attempting to resuscitate this obsolescent bomber.

I believe the president was right about the B-1. However, given the growing political sensitivity of defense issues and concerns about the long-term strategic trends, more attention should have been given to finding ways to soften the impact of this decision on congressional and public attitudes about the administration's commitment to a strong defense. One option might have been to seek some Soviet concession in SALT in return for canceling the B-1. Another might have been to announce that the administration intended to design a more advanced follow-on bomber for the 1990s, using ALCM-armed B-52s simply as a stopgap. A third might simply have been to postpone the decision until we could determine the impact of a SALT II agreement on our defense requirements.

Regrettably, this correct and courageous decision became a millstone around the administration's neck and hurt us in the ratification debate.

• • •

Over the summer we continued preparations for the next SALT meeting, which was to be held in Vienna in early September. During this period, concern over Soviet and Cuban activities in Africa increased. I told Dobrynin in late August that since the two sides were still far apart on the major SALT issues, I did not think a Vienna meeting would be good for either of us. Obviously relieved, Dobrynin suggested we wait until Gromyko came to New York in late September to attend the UN General Assembly session. We would then meet in Washington, where Gromyko could also see the president. I was satisfied with this arrangement.

With no chance of an agreement by October 3, I was apprehensive that SALT opponents, in Congress and out, would use the Vienna postponement and the expiration of the interim agreement to undermine public support for SALT. To prevent this, we decided to issue a statement saying that we were prepared to continue to observe the interim agreement during the SALT II negotiations, so long as the Soviets also did so.

On September 10, I gave Dobrynin a proposed U.S. statement to this effect, which we would make public after Gromyko's September visit. Dobrynin and I also agreed that a joint statement could be issued during the visit, reaffirming the SALT I Anti-Ballistic Missile (ABM) Treaty, which was due for a five-year review toward the end of the year. This would remind the public of the continued existence of one of the most important arms control agreements ever signed.

In the first two weeks of September, the president and his advisers worked out our negotiating strategy for the Gromyko visit. It was agreed that the Soviets must make the next major move. We had taken the initiative in developing the three-part framework in May, but the Soviets had shown little flexibility on the specific limitations. We felt the ball was in their court.

On September 9, we conveyed to the Soviets, through Dobrynin, three major U.S. concerns on which we expected Soviet movement: reductions in the Vladivostok ceilings, limits on heavy missiles, and a subceiling on the number of MIRVed ICBMs. We also made clear that with Carter's decision to cancel the B-1 bomber, a SALT agreement must permit the United States to deploy a substantial number of bombers armed with long-range air-launched cruise missiles without cutting into our own force of MIRVed missiles. I met with Dobrynin the next day and asked him to press Moscow to respond in time for us to take the answer into account in our forthcoming discussions with Gromyko.

Dobrynin gave us Moscow's reaction a week later and it did not raise my spirits. The Soviets refused to consider our proposal to reduce heavy missiles in return for a subceiling on ALCM-carrying heavy bombers. An unhappy Dobrynin said that we should give up trying to link these two issues since Moscow considered the heavy missile issue closed. He rehashed the Soviet position that the Ford administration had agreed to count ALCM-carrying heavy bombers in the 1,320 total. As evidence, Dobrynin cited an inaccurate statement attributed to Brzezinski, in a press conference held after the March talks, that the Carter administration accepted this alleged commitment. I pointed out that U.S. positions were not formulated in press conferences, and I told him that further arguments by Gromyko about Vladivostok would not be productive. At the end of this unsatisfactory exchange, Dobrynin handed me a copy of a proposed Soviet unilateral declaration stating in essence that the Soviets would observe the SALT I Interim Agreement after October 3.

On September 22, at 10 A.M., Gromyko and I and our respective delegations met in my conference room on the seventh floor of the State Department. It is a functional room, slim on amenities, and it fitted the mood perfectly. Gromyko responded dourly to my opening presentation —in which I had reiterated our demand for a sublimit of 220 on heavy missiles and proposed a new ceiling of 800 on MIRVed ICBMs, in return for which we would accept a limit of 250 on ALCM-carrying heavy bombers—with a long defense of the Vladivostok accords and a critique of our negotiating positions which had been relayed through Dobrynin.

In a second session that evening, however, Gromyko made two positive moves that convinced me, despite the sterile opening round, that he had come prepared to make substantial progress. Referring to our proposal to limit MIRVed ICBMs to 800, he suggested that if we would drop our demand for reductions in Soviet heavy ICBMs (and agree to count ALCM-carrying heavy bombers in the 1,320 ceiling), the Soviets would be prepared to accept a new subceiling of 820 on deployments of

MIRVed ICBM launchers. He also read a proposed Soviet assurance outside the SALT Treaty. The declaration said that the Backfire bomber did not have the range to strike the United States, and that the Soviets would not give it the capability of operating at intercontinental distances. Without indicating the figure, Gromyko said the Soviets would not increase the present production rate of the aircraft. Although neither of these proposals was adequate, they were important steps forward and I reported them as such to the president immediately after this meeting.

Carter agreed that Gromyko's proposals represented significant movement, although we knew that giving up the long-standing objective of reductions in the Soviet heavy missile force would be politically difficult for us. Strategically, however, we had long recognized that a cutback in heavy ICBMs could not, by itself, do much to meet the issue of ICBM vulnerability. We had concluded after very careful study that a ceiling on the overall Soviet MIRVed ICBM force would be strategically as advantageous to us as a subceiling on heavy missiles alone.

Working late into the night, we developed a counterproposal which the president could put to Gromyko the next morning. The counterproposal dropped the separate heavy ICBM and ALCM-carrying bomber subceilings. Instead, it proposed that the Vladivostok 1,320 ceiling be converted into a hybrid ceiling covering both the MIRVed ballistic missile launchers and ALCM-carrying heavy bombers. Finally, drawing from our Moscow comprehensive proposal, we proposed a 1,200 ceiling on land- and sea-based launchers of MIRVed missiles.

Since our total planned MIRVed missile deployments would not exceed 1,200 during the term of the treaty, this would allow us 120 ALCM-carrying heavy bombers under the 1,320 ceiling before the United States would have to dismantle any MIRVed land- or sea-based intercontinental ballistic missiles. The Soviets, without a comparable ALCM program, would be unable to make use of the differential between the 1,200 and 1,320 ceilings. We were prepared to accept Gromyko's proposed number of 820 for launchers of MIRVed ICBMs. This figure was substantially higher than the 550 figure from the comprehensive proposal, but at least 100 launchers below what they could have deployed under the Vladivostok agreement. If accepted, this would constitute an important step toward curbing this most destabilizing element of the Soviet strategic forces.

Our meeting with Gromyko on the morning of September 23 was encouraging, apart from a sharp exchange over human rights. When the president described our counterproposal to Gromyko, Carter added a demand that the Soviets agree to a strict application of the already agreed to "MIRV launcher type rule," which provided that any launcher of a type used for MIRVed ICBMs be counted in the ceilings applying to such launchers, even if the launchers actually contained single-warhead missiles. The Soviets had two missile fields (at Derazhnya and Pervomaisk) containing a total of 120 such launchers which the Soviets contended contained only ICBMs with single warheads.

Gromyko and I met again that afternoon in my office to review where we stood. Gromyko said he wanted to be certain he understood accurately the president's proposals, because he believed they contained important new elements. In diplomatic language this meant that the Soviets were genuinely interested. Since Gromyko was to remain in the United States for some time in order to attend the UN General Assembly, we expected that several days would pass as the Politburo mulled over our proposals. Instead, Gromyko asked to see the president again soon.

Clearly Moscow had decided to settle many of the major issues. We met again during the evening of September 27 in the cabinet room. Gromyko quickly got down to business. He told us that the Soviets would agree to a reduction in the overall launcher ceiling of 2,400 contained in the Vladivostok accord. He proposed an overall launcher ceiling of 2,250 against our suggestion of 2,160. He said that they accepted our hybrid ceiling of 1,320 for launchers of MIRVed missiles and ALCM-carrying heavy bombers, as well as a separate ceiling on launchers of MIRVed missiles (he proposed 1,250 to our proposed 1,200). He concluded by stating that the Soviet Union would agree to a limit of 820 on MIRVed ICBMs, and that they accepted our insistence on applying the MIRV launcher-type rule to the 120 ambiguous launchers at Derazhnya and Pervomaisk.

Except for the numbers in the ceilings, which obviously could be settled in subsequent negotiations, we had reached agreement on most of the main outlines of the treaty. There were still some tough issues ahead—particularly the handling of cruise missile limitations, the introduction of new types of ICBMs, and restraints on the improvement of existing missiles—but I was heartened and optimistic.

•   •   •

Opponents of SALT, set back by our progress in late September and by some incautiously optimistic public statements by the administration, began to step up their criticisms of the emerging agreement. Since the negotiations were still in progress, and since we had to respect the confidentiality of the proposals made by both sides, we were compelled to conduct our discussions with Congress behind closed doors. Similarly our public defense of the agreement had to be cast in general terms.

Many SALT critics, on the other hand, felt no compunction about confidentiality. They released classified materials; they made false charges about U.S. "concessions"; they published unsubstantiated and incorrect allegations about Soviet cheating on the SALT I agreement; and they attacked the administration for not solving fundamental strategic problems, such as the alleged ICBM "window of vulnerability," through the SALT process.

Motives varied. Doubtless, some genuinely feared that the course we were following would lead to a "cosmetic" agreement that did little to alleviate what they regarded as an increasingly adverse strategic situation for the United States. Some argued, in my judgment incorrectly, that the United States should use the Soviet interest in SALT as a club to compel Moscow to act with greater restraint in the global competition— to "link" progress in SALT to Soviet behavior around the world.

Others opposed SALT on ideological grounds. The Right feared any negotiation with the Soviets on the theory that nothing the Communists would agree to could possibly be in our interest. No negotiable SALT agreement would satisfy them. Others criticized SALT for political reasons. By the end of 1977, some politicians had concluded that with a growing national mood of suspicion, particularly suspicion about Soviet adventures in Africa, and a concern over perceived adverse trends in the U.S.-USSR military balance, defense issues and "being tough on the Russians" would be good politics.

These disparate groups had not yet formed themselves into a coalition advocating linkage of SALT with other issues and generally opposing a SALT Treaty. But the outlines of a coalition were becoming visible.

I did not want us to surrender the initiative to SALT's opponents, who were making an impression on some well-disposed but worried members of Congress. In an effort to take the criticisms head-on, I appeared several times that fall before the Senate Foreign Relations and Armed Services committees and Senator Jackson's Armed Services Subcommittee on Arms Control to argue our case in closed sessions.

Jackson and some others disagreed with virtually every aspect of the emerging agreement, but especially with our dropping the demand for reductions in heavy missiles in favor of the subceiling on MIRVed ICBMs. I explained the strategic rationale for the change in our position, including the fact that Secretary Brown and the Defense Department had concluded that limiting Soviet MIRVed ICBMs to 820 was as beneficial to our strategic posture as placing sublimits on heavy Soviet missiles alone.

On November 3, I went to the Senate Foreign Relations Committee to make a major statement on the political and strategic rationale for SALT. I wanted to get the senators to look beyond the technical details and to examine the agreement and the SALT process as a whole. I tried to give them a sense of what we could expect SALT to do and not do. It seemed to me that people were asking too much of the SALT Treaty.

I told the senators that SALT could help keep the strategic competition within bounds and make our force planning easier, but it could not become a substitute for adequate defense capabilities and for modernizing our strategic forces. A good SALT agreement, I said, could enable us to focus a larger share of our defense expenditures on strengthening our conventional forces, which were the main instrument for protecting our interests in critical Third World regions. I reminded the committee members, who would play a crucial role in the ratification process, that in addition to helping us manage our strategic relationship with the Soviets, a SALT Treaty would also play an important political role in U.S.-Soviet and East-West relations by lessening the chance that dangerous competition would escalate.

Brown, Warnke, and others also appeared frequently on Capitol Hill. The congressional hearings helped, but SALT was a complex set of issues filled with technical terms and acronyms. It was easy to get lost in a jungle of technical detail. But there was a reservoir of support for arms control and for a balanced policy of competition and cooperation with the Soviets, and I was sure we were succeeding in putting SALT into a clearer perspective. I was also convinced that once we had an agreement in hand, SALT's supporters would come forward. Our security policies and programs were sound. Politically and economically we were much stronger than the Soviet Union; militarily we were at least equal.

Nevertheless, some of the president's political advisers were worried about the attacks from the Right, and were concerned about the SALT head count in the Senate. They recommended that we deliberately slow down the negotiations and toughen our positions. It was suggested that this was necessary to undercut the opponents who were claiming that the administration was in too much of a hurry.

I disagreed emphatically. We should be under no artificial sense of urgency in the negotiations, and we should not compromise our security interests for the sake of an agreement. But I wanted to keep moving steadily ahead without any self-imposed delay. A responsible administration could not allow so fundamental an objective to be sidetracked. I need not have been concerned about the president. He rejected all such advice. Even so, some of those around him who were offering this advice did succeed in slowing down the process, partly by making adjustments in U.S. negotiating positions more difficult. They did so by exacerbating public concerns over Soviet activities in Africa and elsewhere, and by creating a de facto political linkage between SALT and worsening U.S.-Soviet relations.

4

THE CHALLENGE
OF LEADERSHIP

NATO

In NATO, cornerstone of Western security, the administration faced a critical test. The alliance needed a comprehensive effort to strengthen its political cohesion and its defensive capabilities. For a decade there had been disturbing trends in the East-West military balance which could eventually threaten Western security. The Soviets were expanding and modernizing their conventional capabilities in eastern Europe. They were also testing a new intermediate-range ballistic missile, the mobile MIRVed SS-20 with three warheads.

NATO's theater nuclear forces (TNF), virtually all American, were large and diverse, but heavily concentrated in aging short- and medium-range tactical weapons. NATO had only a limited capability to threaten nuclear retaliation with intermediate-range weapons based in western Europe. Unless countered by modernization of NATO's theater nuclear forces, deployment of the SS-20 would erode the alliance's long-standing advantages in TNF, which it had relied upon since the 1950s to offset the larger Soviet conventional forces. The Soviets might gain a conventional and theater nuclear advantage in Europe that might embolden them to try to intimidate our NATO allies if they believed that the United States would not dare threaten nuclear retaliation to defend western Europe under conditions of strategic parity. Such a grave miscalculation of Western will and our determination to defend our allies might have dangerous consequences.

A major task of the Carter administration would be to help lead the alliance in developing practical programs to preserve the political and military balance in Europe. The military aspect would be only one element in strengthening NATO security and political unity. The alliance was strongly committed to a policy of easing East-West tensions and expanding political and economic contacts with eastern Europe and the Soviet Union. For our Western allies, effective U.S. leadership in managing East-West relations—including bringing the SALT negotiations to a successful conclusion—was as important as steps to preserve the military balance.

• • •

In May 1977, at President Carter's initiative, after months of intensive preparations, the leaders of the alliance met in London to consider specific steps to reverse the negative trends in the conventional and theater nuclear balance. Carter stressed that the alliance as a whole, not just the United States and one or two of the larger allies, should improve the structure and composition of its military forces. The United States was shouldering a very heavy share of the defense burden; we wanted to establish firmly the principle that all must do more. In the past there had been much talk and little action. We were determined not to settle for another praiseworthy declaration of alliance unity. What was needed was a concrete plan to overcome the conventional and theater nuclear force deficiencies both in individual allied forces and the collective defense structure.

The response was encouraging. A long-term defense program to strengthen conventional and theater nuclear force capabilities was adopted unanimously by the assembled heads of government. Ten working groups of defense experts were established to coordinate implementation of the program. Eventually, the politically sensitive task of increasing the capability of NATO's long-range TNF was assigned to a special group, the High Level Group, under the chairmanship of U.S. Assistant Secretary of Defense David McGiffert.

The most controversial action taken at the summit was an agreement that each member state would increase its defense spending by 3 percent per year above its inflation rate.* Considering the financial difficulties and the inflation all of us faced, this was a remarkable step. It reflected the shared concern about the Soviet buildup.

The 3 percent defense spending standard has been criticized as unrealistic, inadequate, politically divisive. There were considerable political and economic difficulties, but the alliance needed a common benchmark. The long-term defense program and the 3 percent commitment, together with the 1979 decision to modernize long-range theater nuclear forces, represented a concrete, comprehensive program to

---

* Harold Brown and I recommended to the president a 3 percent increase in military spending, after inflation, for all NATO countries.

strengthen NATO's military capabilities and maintain a stable balance in Europe.

• • •

At the time of SALT I, the allies were concerned primarily that U.S. forward-based aircraft capable of carrying nuclear weapons, as well as British and French nuclear forces, not be included in negotiations. NATO relied on its superiority in TNF to compensate for the Soviets' conventional force advantage. As the Europeans began to worry about the impact that further limitations in the Salt II Treaty might have on their security, particularly constraints on cruise missiles, their interest in the military implications of the negotiations grew.

After the March talks in Moscow the allies were deeply concerned that the SALT negotiations and détente were in jeopardy. Repeatedly, they stressed a fervent desire that the talks get back on track. This may have contributed to our failure to appreciate the depth of their interest in avoiding any significant limitations on ground- and sea-launched cruise missiles. Up to then, we had not given our allies adequate information about the state of development of these new weapons, nor had we made clear to them our strategy in negotiating short-term limits on the deployment of cruise missiles at the May talks in Geneva. In fact, it would be five years before missiles would be ready to be deployed.

The U.S. objective at Geneva had been to use a protocol lasting only two to three years to defer the cruise missile issue. Our view was that this strategy would give us time to examine with our allies various options for future cruise missile deployments and their arms control implications while the development and testing of the missiles went forward. We did not anticipate allied objection to the 600 km range restrictions on ground- and sea-launched cruise missiles during the protocol. We were insisting on the right to test and deploy the air-launched version of the cruise missile at ranges up to 2,500 km.

The allies (and for that matter the Soviets) did not for a time seem to grasp the point that ground- and sea- and air-launched cruise missiles were all basically the same missile, but launched from different platforms. Once the Soviets recognized the insignificance of the range constraint—all one had to do was add more fuel for the missile to fly farther than 2,500 km—they were willing to drop even the 2,500 km limit on ALCMs. After the protocol had expired, all ground- and sea-launched cruise missile range limits would terminate and we would then be free to deploy them with whatever range capability we believed necessary.

When we briefed the allies after the May talks in Geneva, we found them concerned about our decision to include ground- and sea-launched cruise missiles in the protocol. Some allied leaders felt that this decision indicated that we placed a higher priority on SALT than on alliance security. They felt that we were perhaps more concerned about protecting ourselves by limiting Soviet intercontinental weapons in SALT, while ignoring the threat of shorter range missiles aimed at Europe. In October 1977, Chancellor Helmut Schmidt, whom I regard as an outstanding statesman and for whom I have the greatest respect, delivered a speech in London emphasizing the German conviction that parity in intercontinental strategic weapons and the prospect of further strategic limitations in SALT II without any constraints on the SS-20 would have a negative effect on what he called the "Eurostrategic" balance of nuclear forces. We had hoped to conduct a study of NATO nuclear requirements in the 1970s and beyond out of the limelight, free from the pressures generated by intense public interest and scrutiny. After the Schmidt speech this was no longer possible.

The most immediate problem facing us was to alleviate allied concerns about SALT II. Beginning in mid-1977, we began intensive consultations that transformed the nature of SALT discussions in NATO. Previously, consultations had been carried out by routine briefings. Now, under the Carter administration, no SALT issue of importance to European security (such as the transfer of nuclear weapons technology to our allies) was resolved without advance consultations with all members of the alliance. The consultations were not limited to those issues that were regarded as NATO concerns, and the discussions were not simple briefings. They included a full exchange of views in which the allies' opinions were sought. These steps—especially the prior clearance of our negotiating positions on "NATO issues"—greatly complicated the negotiations; but we accepted these willingly because we knew that vital European security interests were involved. More direct participation by the allies was a necessity. We understood that the United States did not face, as some had tried to suggest, a choice between European security and SALT: the interests went hand in hand.

By the end of the year, our consultations had succeeded in reassuring the allies, in particular West Germany. The British and Germans remained concerned about how the details of cruise missile constraints would be resolved, how we would protect our freedom to transfer nuclear weapons technology to our allies, and how and on what terms we might negotiate reductions in theater nuclear weapons in SALT III. But we had done a lot to put to rest a great number of allied concerns.

NEUTRON BOMB

An issue that was to have a damaging impact on U.S.-European leadership began almost unnoticed. On April 22, the House Appropriations Committee released classified testimony about the funding for production of the "enhanced radiation warhead" (ERW). This warhead was designed for U.S. nuclear artillery and short-range tactical missiles deployed in Europe. The testimony didn't get much attention until the *Washington Post* began a series in June of 1977 that sensationalized the ERW, calling it the "neutron bomb." It was called a weapon that killed people by increased radiation while protecting property through suppression of blast and heat.

The articles, quickly picked up in the European press, set off an explosive political and public reaction. Antinuclear groups described the weapon as more "immoral" than the thousands of other Soviet, American, British, and French nuclear warheads already deployed in Europe. There were arguments that the development of the ERW demonstrated that the United States intended to wage a nuclear war in Europe while escaping damage to itself.

Stripped of the imagery, the ERW was a weapon that was designed to counter the Warsaw Pact advantage in tank warfare by knocking out enemy tank crews with intensified radiation, reducing blast damage to troops and civilians in the neighborhood.

Many Europeans were ambivalent about the role of any nuclear weapons. Looking east at the array of Soviet power, some feared that the United States might not live up to its nuclear guarantee in the event of a massive Soviet attack. Looking west at the enormous U.S. strategic and theater nuclear arsenal, there were those who feared that if the Soviets did attack and seemed to be winning, the United States would use nuclear weapons and invite Europe's destruction.

Since the flexible response strategy was put in place in the early 1960s, NATO had dealt with this understandable European attitude by a calculated ambiguity concerning the role of nuclear weapons in NATO strategy, and by the most careful and nuanced handling of any changes in American nuclear doctrine or deployments in Europe. Such subtlety was not possible in dealing with the ERW. The public uproar made production and deployment of the weapon a test of the administration's will to carry out its stated intention to strengthen NATO's defense. The president turned back efforts in Congress to block funding for the ERW so that we would retain the option to go ahead with production if our allies would agree on a deployment program.

The crux of the deployment issue was that the Germans, on whose territory the use of the ERW was most likely, faced severe domestic problems with it. Chancellor Schmidt had his hands full keeping the left wing of his own party from coming out in open opposition to deployment. He wanted the United States to make a unilateral decision on production, and only then to consult with the allies about whether and where to deploy it. Schmidt warned us that there would be very strong opposition within West Germany if it were the only European country to accept it.

The administration was facing a dilemma. In our minds, the decisions on production and the deployment were linked. There was no sense in producing the ERW unless it could be deployed in Europe, and that was not possible unless the allies agreed. Yet if it were to appear that the allies were being pressured by the United States to accept the weapon, European political opposition could become unmanageable.

With the ERW issue a bone of contention, the realistic course was to consult quietly with our allies and, to the degree possible, defuse the clamor, which was being exploited by Soviet propaganda. Quietly we shelved an October target date for a decision and conferred with our allies on whether, and under what conditions, they would accept deployment if we decided to produce it.

But by the end of the month, these discussions had failed to produce a consensus. The Germans wanted to extend the consultations, hoping the furor would die down. I was dismayed by this prospect since the shadow of ERW hung over every NATO discussion. I concluded that the only way to reach an alliance position was for the United States to make a tentative decision and then consult with key allies to see whether they were prepared to support it. Once they were in agreement, we would hold a formal meeting of NATO and announce the decision.

The president accepted this strategy. He sent a letter to Schmidt in November indicating that he was prepared to make a decision on the ERW if the allies were ready to share the political consequences. Carter told Schmidt that we would consider his proposal to link ERW deployment to an arms control initiative. It would take about two years from a production decision to have the weapon ready for deployment. During that interval we might be able to negotiate arms control restraints with the Soviets that would enable the alliance to limit or even forgo deployment. The response was that Germany favored an early U.S. decision to produce the ERW to be used as a bargaining chip to reduce Soviet tanks. The Germans refused to accept a tie between production and deployment.

By year's end, the ERW controversy had become a test of the alliance's ability to make hard and politically sensitive decisions. Worse, for many allies, the issue was becoming a test of the president's ability to lead the alliance.

AFRICAN ISSUES

As had been true during the Nixon and Ford administrations, our ability and determination to pursue a balanced policy toward the Soviet Union was most severely tested in the Third World. We had reached a consensus within the administration on NATO and SALT, but Soviet activities in Africa caused sharp differences among us. What we did in Africa in the early months of 1977 would have a major effect on Third World perceptions of our policy toward the developing nations, and would set the tone for the remainder of the administration.

• • •

In March of 1977, a force of Katangan opponents of President Mobutu Seko of Zaire launched an incursion from Angola into the Shaba province (formerly Katanga) of Zaire. The regime of Angolan President Agostinho Neto, with whom we had no diplomatic relations, apparently permitted this attack in retaliation for Mobutu's covert support of antigovernment groups in Angola. Since the postcolonial Angolan civil war had ended in victory for Neto's Soviet- and Cuban-supported MPLA (Popular Movement for the Liberation of Angola) faction, a low-level insurgency had continued in several parts of the country.

The tangible U.S. interests in Zaire were primarily economic. In addition, Mobutu was a source of consistent, if sometimes embarrassing, political support to the United States. We had supported the territorial integrity of Zaire since its troubled birth as the Congo in the early 1960s. We had small economic and military aid programs but sought to avoid linking ourselves too closely with Mobutu's political position.

Belgium, the former colonial power, and France, with important interests in francophone Africa, had more substantial security relations with Mobutu and provided his army with military supplies and advisers. While we were limited legally and politically in helping Zaire, we wanted to cooperate with the French and Belgians, and others who might decide to aid Mobutu in fighting off this challenge. None of us wished to face the uncertain consequences that might flow from the collapse of his regime and the consequent disintegration of Zaire into unstable segments open to radical penetration.

I wanted the crisis resolved before it provided an opportunity for Soviet or Cuban meddling in Zaire, which could turn the affair into an East-West "test of strength." The Soviets and Cubans present in Angola would hold most of the cards in that case. I also wanted to improve relations with Angola to get its help in attaining acceptable solutions to the conflicts in Rhodesia and Namibia. I believed as well it would be in our long-term economic and political interests to establish normal relations with Angola as most other Western nations had already done. These objectives, I feared, would be jeopardized by a negative outcome in Zaire or by escalation of the Shaba crisis into open hostilities between Zaire and Angola.

The strategy I urged to contain the incursion and restore political stability was to deal with the Shaba invasion as an African—not an East-West—problem. We and a number of our European allies strongly supported the mediation effort of the very able Nigerian president, General Olusegun Obasanjo, and his capable and tireless foreign minister, Joseph

Garba. At the same time, we gave limited support to Zaire to help it through the crisis, and held out to the Angolans the prospect of talks on normalization of relations, provided the Shaba problem was satisfactorily resolved.

There were problems, though, in dealing with Angola. One was the legacy of hostility and fear resulting from the abortive American support for the UNITA (National Union for the Total Independence of Angola) faction and other opponents of the MPLA in 1975. Another was our identification with the South African military intervention against the MPLA during that same period. But we also had significant leverage in Angola, which desperately wanted a solution to the Namibia issue and an end to South African military strikes into southern Angola. In February, before the Shaba incident began, we had already responded to Angolan overtures by agreeing to discussions in early April. In late March, however, we notified officials in Luanda that the talks would be delayed because of Shaba.

On April 11 I met with congressional leaders to discuss our plans to supply nonlethal military equipment and further economic assistance to Zaire. By this time, Morocco, with French encouragement and assistance, had sent a combat unit to Shaba to help repel the invaders. To other African nations, this move by an African nation was infinitely preferable to Western military intervention. After a spirited discussion, the legislators agreed that we must avoid making the Shaba conflict an East-West confrontation or a test of American will.

By summer, the Shaba conflict had begun to wind down, although there were signs that the Katangan secessionists were regrouping in Angola. Concerned that fighting might resume, we approved the shipment of some rifle ammunition for the Zairean Army. Zaire survived this test, but it appeared likely that we had not heard the last of the Katangan secessionists.

In the meantime, my hope of increasing our leverage in Angola had disappeared with the administration's decision not to recognize the Neto government as long as Cuban forces remained in Angola. Some proponents of this move believed that U.S. support for the UNITA insurgency in the south, led by Jonas Savimbi, would provide a way to drive the Cubans out of Angola. On the contrary, I believed that the reason the Angolans kept the Cubans in Angola was because they feared further incursions by South Africa and South African support of UNITA. I felt that the solution lay in removing these Angolan concerns that, in African opinion, legitimized the Soviet and Cuban presence.

As to the suggestion that we support Savimbi, this would have been illegal under the Clark Amendment of 1974. In any case, I was convinced that even if we could legally help UNITA, it would be neither wise nor expedient. To do so would confirm Angola's suspicions of our ideological hostility and would drive the Angolans into greater reliance on the Soviets and Cubans. Further, support of the South African-supported UNITA forces against a legitimate African government would have had a devastating effect on our African policy.

I was confident that our interests would be best served by working with Angola to bring about an end to the Namibian and Rhodesian conflicts and the consequent removal of the South Africans from Angola's southern border. At the same time, we would have to try to reverse the negative decision on recognizing Angola. Ultimately we were to succeed in achieving a Rhodesian breakthrough, but regrettably we failed to establish normal diplomatic relations with Angola. This was and remains a serious error.

•   •   •

The Carter administration inherited a complex and shifting political situation in the Horn of Africa. Somalia, which had irredentist claims on the Ogaden region of Ethiopia, had for several years permitted the Soviets to use a substantial naval facility at Berbera on the Gulf of Aden in return for arms and political support. At the same time, Somalia was heavily involved in supporting a guerrilla war waged by its kinsmen in the Ogaden. Ethiopia was caught in a bloody civil war and had much of its army tied down fighting a secessionist movement in its Eritrean province. The ancient empire of Ethiopia, led by a Marxist military junta under President Mengistu Haile Mariam, was hostile to the United States and had begun to turn to the Soviet Union for help. In December 1976, the Ethiopians signed their first arms-supply agreement with the Soviets.

For a while, the Soviets attempted to ignore the bitter antagonism between Ethiopia and Somalia and hold on to their position in Somalia while supplanting us in Ethiopia. But this was a difficult balancing act, and after a period of hesitation, the Soviets chose Ethiopia, presumably because of its Marxist government, large population, and strategic position on the Red Sea.

Examination of this problem indicated it was in our interest to prevent the Soviets from increasing their political influence in the Horn of Africa. Our strategy should be to retain a presence and as much influence as we could in Ethiopia, while strengthening our relations with Somalia. I was not persuaded by arguments that we should adopt a position of open hostility to the government in Addis Ababa, or that we should uncritically support Somalia. Both suggestions seemed short-sighted and somewhat naive. I felt strongly, and persuaded the administration to agree, that we should coordinate our strategy with France, West Germany, Great Britain, and Italy, all of whom had experience and weight in the region, and with regional friends such as Egypt, Saudi Arabia, and the Sudan. This we did.

We approached our relations with Somalia with caution, for there was a growing probability that the regime in Mogadiscio would send its army into Ethiopia to attempt to seize the Ogaden. If we became too closely linked with Somalia while it was involved in a blatant invasion of the Ogaden, we would find ourselves inadvertently on the wrong side of one of Africa's most cherished principles—the territorial integrity of the postcolonial states. In addition, aggression against Ethiopia would provide in African eyes the same justification for Soviet and Cuban military presence in Ethiopia as South African intervention in Angola in 1975 had done.

For several months, early in 1977, the Somalis probed our attitude on replacing the Soviets as their arms supplier and as a source of political support. When in May 1977, the Soviets signed a second arms agreement with Ethiopia, the Somalis recognized that the Soviets had begun to shift away from them. Their overtures to us grew increasingly pointed, culminating in a direct and urgent request in the early summer of 1977 for arms and economic aid. The wily Somali leader, Siad Barre, frustrated by the Soviet tilt toward Ethiopia, decided to turn to us.

The temptation to agree at once to Siad Barre's request—and perhaps to replace the Soviets in Berbera—was strong, but my reaction was to act with caution. I recommended to the president that we refuse to supply even defensive military equipment or to permit our allies and friends to transfer U.S. arms to Somalia until the Ogaden affair was settled. I also urged that we keep our lines open to Colonel Mengistu, letting him know that we would not supply the Somalis with arms while they were involved in the Ogaden. There was some evidence that Mengistu was unhappy with the Soviets and was still willing to maintain contact with us. The president approved this suggestion.

In mid-June, the Somali ambassador met with President Carter with an urgent new request from Siad Barre for military assistance. The president replied that it would be difficult for us to provide military assistance, but we would see whether our allies could help Somalia maintain its defensive strength. The Somalis interpreted this as a "forthcoming attitude," and on July 9 made a specific request for arms. After considerable discussion, we concluded that "in principle" we would help other countries to meet Somalia's needs for defensive equipment. The Somalis were informed of this decision in mid-July.

A week later, Somali regular forces were identified in the Ogaden and within a matter of a few more weeks the Somali Army was driving full tilt toward the main population centers in the northern Ogaden. As we feared, despite the rejection of its territorial claims by the Organization of African Unity (OAU), the Somalis had not been able to resist the temptation to seize the Ogaden. On August 4, Richard Moose, our wise and skillful assistant secretary for African affairs, called in the Somali ambassador and told him that although our agreement in principle to provide defensive arms to Somalia still stood, their involvement in the Ogaden prevented its implementation. On August 18, Philip Habib told the Somali ambassador that we also would not approve transfers to Somali of U.S.-manufactured arms in the hands of third countries while Somalia was involved in the Ogaden. The Somalis denied that their regular army was in the Ogaden and painted in vivid colors the threat posed by the Soviet Union and the growing Cuban presence in Ethiopia.

In October, the Somalis informed us that in return for our cooperation and friendship, they would abrogate their treaty with the Soviets and end all military ties with Moscow. We responded that although we wished to cooperate in meeting legitimate Somali defense needs, we could not do so while they were fighting in the Ogaden. We told them that we would be prepared to supply defensive arms if they would withdraw.

In November, the Somalis expelled their Soviet military advisers, renounced their treaty with the Soviets, and broke relations with Cuba. They then returned to us with a new appeal for arms. We advised them to accept OAU mediation of their dispute with Ethiopia, to seek a negotiated peace, and to offer their neighbors (Ethiopia and Kenya) assurances of respect for their territorial integrity.

As long as Somalia continued its invasion of Ethiopia, neither we nor our Western and African friends, with whom we had been cooperating closely, could do much to help. We had to direct our efforts to limiting the conflict and getting Somalia out of the Ogaden so we could provide assistance without serious damage to our African policies.

On November 10, we met in London with the British, French, and Germans, who agreed with us that Soviet aid to Ethiopia, coupled with the recent appearance of several hundred Cuban military advisers, would probably lead to expulsion of the Somalis from Ethiopia within the coming months. There was a consensus that none of us was willing to assist Somalia as long as its forces were fighting in the Ogaden. Nor had the moment yet arrived for a Western mediation effort or for taking the matter to the UN Security Council. By mid-December a major Soviet airlift of arms and military personnel to Ethiopia was in full swing, and even with a major diplomatic effort, we were unable to persuade other African and Middle Eastern states to condemn the Soviet and Cuban role.

Until the Somalis withdrew or were driven out—which, with the influx of Soviet arms and advisers and Cuban troops, appeared to be just a question of time—there was little we or our allies could do. We did maintain diplomatic pressure on Somalia to withdraw, and kept our lines of communication open to Ethiopia so that we would be ready to launch a mediation effort when the time was ripe.

In Washington, we in the State Department saw the Horn as a textbook case of Soviet exploitation of a local conflict. In the long run, however, we believed the Ethiopians would oust the Soviets from their country as had happened in Egypt and the Sudan. Meanwhile we should continue to work with our European allies and the African nations to bring about a negotiated solution of the broader regional issues. We believed that in the long run Ethiopian-Soviet relations undoubtedly would sour and Ethiopia would again turn to the West. Some of the president's political advisers, on the other hand, believed the Horn offered an opportunity to damage the Soviets by tying them down in a costly and endless struggle and even forcing them to back down in a confrontation. This difference of view was to sharpen in the months ahead.

NORMALIZING RELATIONS WITH THE PRC

From the very outset, normalizing relations with the People's Republic of China was my goal and that of President Carter, but I did not expect that diplomatic recognition could be achieved before the second year of the administration. Our first priorities were to strengthen NATO, to move toward a second SALT agreement, and to restore momentum to the Mideast and Panama negotiations. Before the administration decided how and when we would pursue normalization, I wanted to review the overall political-military situation in Asia and to analyze how U.S.-Chinese relations would weigh in the strategic and regional balances. I expected that the Chinese, who were still preoccupied with an internal political realignment, would also want to proceed with caution and watch how we handled ourselves. They seemed concerned that we would place too high a priority on our relations with the Soviets, and they were skeptical about détente and arms control.

But there were significant interests on both sides that would keep us moving on the course set by President Nixon and Chairman Mao in 1971–72. Peking wanted to end the long period of hostility and to modify the balance of power, which it feared was tilting toward the Soviets. This was a major factor in my own thinking. I believed that better relations with China would help to stabilize post-Vietnam East Asia. Although there was useful "parallelism" on geopolitical problems, I felt we were a long way from security cooperation with China.

Because of the importance to the Chinese of visible continuity, I had recommended to Carter during our foreign policy discussion in Plains that at an early date we publicly reaffirm the Shanghai Communiqué of 1972 in which the United States and the People's Republic of China had declared that their goal was to normalize relations. In the communiqué the United States acknowledged "that all Chinese on either side of the Taiwan Strait maintain there is but one China and that Taiwan is a part of China," and stated our interest in a peaceful resolution of the Taiwan question. In December of 1976, I reaffirmed the communiqué to Ambassador Huang Chen, chief of the Chinese liaison office in Washington, at a luncheon Henry Kissinger arranged.

Also in December 1976, I set up a small team of China specialists, including Dick Holbrooke, Tony Lake, Deputy Assistant Secretary of State William Gleysteen, and Michel Oksenberg, the NSC expert, to study the normalization question. I gave the group full access to the carefully guarded Nixon-Kissinger papers on China, including the minutes of the negotiations. I told them I wanted analyses of the case for normalization and of the political, legal, and strategic issues. I also instructed them to develop a fallback strategy for maintaining the status quo should we fail to make progress. The early work preceded the formal agencywide review of U.S. policy toward China which began shortly after the administration took office in January.

On April 15, 1977, I sent President Carter a memorandum that laid the basis for his decision, in the summer of 1977, to seek normalization on acceptable terms. I told the president that:

> The principal condition for good relations with the PRC will be to convince the Chinese that this Administration has a mature and realistic view of the world situation and the strategic balance. We will need to demonstrate our determination to remain strong and to stand up to the Soviets.
>
> The Chinese must also be made to understand that we do not perceive our relations with them as one-dimensional (i.e., vis-à-vis the USSR), but that we also look at our relationship in the context of key bilateral and international issues.
>
> With normalization itself, I do not believe we should feel so compelled to establish diplomatic relations with Peking that we jeopardize the well-being and security of the people of Taiwan. Neither should we place ourselves under artificial deadlines.

At the time this memorandum was being prepared, work was going forward on an interagency study on China, Presidential Review Memorandum 24 (PRM-24). Defense Department participants tended to look at U.S.-Chinese relations primarily in terms of the U.S.-Soviet strategic competition, and some were arguing that we should forge a de facto security relationship with the PRC before, or instead of, diplomatic relations. In my April memorandum I told the president that:

> This approach could be quite dangerous and going very far down the road would pose real risks. The Chinese might be receptive, but I would be concerned at the Russian—and Japanese—reaction. Nothing would be regarded as more hostile to the Soviet Union than the development of a U.S.-Chinese security relationship . . . right now the U.S. has a closer relationship with each Communist superpower than either has with the other. We must continue to maintain that fragile equilibrium, recognizing always how dangerous it is, but recognizing also that some other relationship between

the three nations could be more dangerous. . . . Normalization is the best way to move our relations with Peking forward.

The negotiating issues of the normalization question were rather straightforward—which is not to underestimate the potential difficulties we would face. The Chinese had three conditions for normalization: cessation of diplomatic relations with Taipei; withdrawal of U.S. military forces and installations from Taiwan; and abrogation of the U.S.-Taiwan defense treaty. Since we were determined not to jeopardize the security of Taiwan, I did not feel we could simply accept these conditions. They could, however, provide a framework for our discussions. Holbrooke began an intensive series of consultations with key members of Congress. It was apparent there was broad understanding of the value of and support for diplomatic relations, but Congress felt strongly that we should continue to assist Taiwan in defending itself.

On the central issue of an American link to Taiwan after normalization, I believed we should retain unofficial relations with Taipei, including the provision of "carefully selected defensive weapons." Few China experts believed Peking would acquiesce to this, but I took this to be a sine qua non for congressional acceptance. We had a moral obligation not to jeopardize the well-being and security of the people on Taiwan. In addition, the continuation of the U.S.-Taiwan arms-supply relationship would, in my judgment, be necessary for maintaining the confidence of other countries. The Israelis were particularly concerned about how we would handle this issue.

I was strongly opposed to the suggestion that the United States should abrogate its defense treaty with Taiwan. The State Department's legal advisers held the view that the treaty would automatically cease to exist upon derecognition of the government in Taipei. I concluded we should insist that the treaty ultimately be terminated in accordance with its provisions—that is, upon one year's notice. Finally, I felt that we should make clear that the United States was interested in a peaceful resolution of the Taiwan question. Therefore, the Chinese must abandon their rhetoric about "liberating" Taiwan by force. For the Chinese to agree to these three requirements, especially the arms-supply relationship, would be extraordinarily difficult. I would have to be clear and firm on these positions in internal policy discussions, for some of the president's advisers, particularly Zbig, were so anxious to move rapidly toward normalization that they seemed ready to compromise the well-being of the people of Taiwan.

In June, a preliminary draft of PRM-24 was completed under Holbrooke's direction. It reflected the judgments I had offered the president in April. The memorandum concluded that full diplomatic recognition of Peking would reinforce positive trends in Asia and would improve the environment for achieving our goals in South Korea and Southeast Asia.

The president agreed that after we finished the review and he had made his decision on our recommendations, I would go to Peking in August.

On June 27, a Policy Review Committee agreed to recommend to Carter that we should seek normalization in the "near term," but only if we could be confident that it would not damage Taiwan's security. We also agreed that I would tell the Chinese leaders in August that the administration wished to establish full diplomatic relations, but that we must also be able to maintain economic and cultural relations with Taipei and continue to provide them with carefully selected defensive weapons.

On this occasion the first of what was eventually to become a major difference of opinion between Brzezinski and, to a lesser degree, Brown, and me over the question of security relationships with Peking surfaced. Brzezinski was interested in China primarily because of mutual strategic concerns about the Soviet Union. Both Brzezinski and Brown wanted to consider—even before normalization—various "security enhancements," such as exchange of military attachés, Chinese access to U.S. and Western "dual-use" (civilian or military) technology and equipment, acquiescence by the United States in third-country sales of military equipment to China, and other forms of security cooperation. Their view was that such measures might persuade Moscow to be more careful in their dealings with us and our interests for fear of pushing us into substantial security cooperation with China.

I disagreed with their reasoning but not with each of the actions they proposed. In my judgment, as far as economic development and military strength were concerned, China was not a major strategic power. I was persuaded that any assistance we or our allies could feasibly provide would be limited and would make little difference in China's overall military capabilities. Because of the Soviets' excessive fear of China, however, any U.S. security cooperation with Peking would have serious repercussions on U.S.-Soviet relations. To me, the suggestion of a U.S.-PRC security relationship was an unwise notion that posed substantial risks for our relations with Moscow and for our relations with Tokyo and other Asian allies. Although my views on this issue largely prevailed throughout 1977, we were to debate this issue again during the remainder of my term as secretary of state.

Although everyone in the administration agreed that normalization would serve U.S. interests, we had different reasons for reaching this conclusion. Brzezinski looked at normalization largely in light of the impact it would have on the U.S.-Soviet geopolitical competition. Brown emphasized the contribution that improved relations with Peking, including a modest security relationship, could make to our ability to counter Soviet military power. Others were intrigued by the drama of having closer relations with a nation that contained a quarter of the world's population.

I believed that China constituted a political, economic, and cultural weight in the world that the United States could not ignore. Better relations would help our foreign policy across the board—by producing increased regional stability and, in the long run, a more stable global order. As I saw it, China was a great country that had an important role to play in the final quarter of the twentieth century, not simply one that might be a useful counterweight to the Soviet Union.

The president made his basic policy decision on normalization in late July. A group of us—Brown, Brzezinski, Holbrooke, Oksenberg, and I—met with him in the cabinet room of the White House for nearly three hours. We discussed the strategic and domestic political implications of normalization. At the end the president said he wanted to complete normalization and he was prepared to face the political criticism of those who would claim we were abandoning Taiwan. He asked me to prepare a draft communiqué to be issued in Peking if the Chinese responded favorably to our presentation. Carter approved the draft in early August.

• • •

As I prepared to leave for Peking, the Panama Canal Treaties were about to be signed and sent to the Senate, after six months of intensive negotiations. A political battle of epic proportions was about to begin, and it would require an all-out effort by everyone in the administration to get the treaties ratified.

I left Washington believing it would be unwise to take on an issue as politically controversial as normalization with China until the Panama issue was out of the way, unless—and I did not expect it to happen—the Chinese were to accept our proposal across the board. For political reasons, I intended to represent a maximum position to the Chinese on the Taiwan issue. U.S. government personnel would have to remain on Taiwan after normalization, under an informal arrangement, for the purpose of rendering practical assistance to U.S. citizens in Taiwan. Peking's position, which it regarded as a concession to the Ford administration, was that it would tolerate a continued U.S. relationship with Taiwan along the lines of the Japanese model—a nonofficial presence through an ostensibly private organization. Accordingly, I did not expect the Chinese to accept our proposal, but I felt it wise to make it, even though we might eventually have to abandon it. This strategy was agreed to by the president and my colleagues.

We arrived in Peking in the middle of the August heat at a remarkable moment in the history of modern China. We were met at the airport by Foreign Minister Huang Hua, his wife, Mme. Ho Liliang, Ambassador Woodcock, and a number of officials from the American Embassy and the Chinese Foreign Ministry. Our welcome was correct and friendly.

It was Monday, August 22, the last day of the Eleventh National People's Congress—the final spasm of Maoism and the consolidation of the pragmatists. As we drove through the streets of Peking, we passed hundreds upon hundreds of thousands of demonstrators setting off firecrackers, beating drums, and chanting slogans celebrating the last day of the party congress, at which Chairman Hua Guofeng was elected premier.

This boisterous outpouring of self-confident enthusiasm contrasted sharply with the tentative mood of our flight into Peking. Our pilots had never been there and were uncertain about the location of the airport. Chinese English was very hard to understand, as our English must have been for them. We found ourselves at 31,000 feet, 80 miles from Peking, traveling at 495 mph and unable to obtain permission to descend to a lower altitude to prepare for our approach. The Chinese were extremely reluctant to allow us to start down. The pilots wondered if it was feared that we would see forbidden military sights.

When permission finally came we were told to come down to 15,000 feet—still very high for a landing in two minutes or so—and it seemed as though we might overfly our destination. Not knowing where the airport was, and seeing a large one off to the right, we made for it, only to discover a few seconds before our approach that the planes neatly lined up in rows on the runways were military. So we veered off and fortunately spotted another airfield which turned out to be the right one.

Our arrival at the official guest house complex and the Great Hall, where a banquet in our honor was held that night, was recorded in my wife's diary as follows:

> We arrived at Guest House Number 5, situated in a pleasant enclave of similar guest houses. They bore an uncanny resemblance to the guest houses of Lenin Hills in Moscow. There were the same proportions—a large entrance hall, high ceilings, square rooms, yellow oak woodwork and furniture. A pretty curving staircase rose from the front hall to the second floor. It was the most graceful feature of the interior.
>
> We were assigned a bedroom, living room, and cavernous bathroom. It had a tile floor and enormous tub. The bedroom provided a large double bed, oak bureau and dressing table, two oak chairs, and two bluish upholstered chairs with antimacassars.
>
> On our dressing table, as in Moscow, were nail polishes and beauty aids of various kinds, a hairbrush with strong bristles, and an oversized comb. On the bureau was an assortment of hard liquor and liqueurs.
>
> In our living room, besides the desk, was an upholstered chaise longue with wooden arms, a large round central table laden with candy and fruit, surrounded by four armchairs, a mirror-backed cabinet displaying modern china and enameled objects and an icebox filled with carbonated water and orange drink. It was all very

comfortable, but disappointing to find ourselves in such an un-Chinese house.

Foreign Minister Huang Hua and Mme. Ho gave us a dinner at the Great Hall of the People that evening. The Great Hall is the all-purpose government building. It has several huge dining and reception rooms and thirty province rooms, including one for Taiwan. It also has a small theater and a vast meeting hall where the Eleventh National People's Congress delegates had gathered for the preceding days.

We drew up to the bottom of the wide, high staircase that led, under the large picture of Mao bordered by quotations from his thoughts written on red panels, to the two-storied entrance of the hall. It was a very belittling entrance—humans shrink like Alice in Wonderland in its scale.

Welcomed by the foreign minister and Mme. Ho, we were ushered without further ado into dinner.

There were one hundred and eighty people at the banquet. The foreign minister gave a pleasant, firm, but polite toast. Cy did the same. After each toast, the proposer goes around each table toasting the nationals of the other country. Huang Hua only raised his glass once at each table. Cy raised his to *each* Chinese at *each* table, which took a while. Mme. He said he was very conscientious. There were some jokes about his ability to get back to our table, as mao tai, the liquor, is China's strongest.

Our first formal meeting was with Foreign Minister Huang Hua the next morning in our guest house. We were seated across from each other at a long green-baize-covered table. I was flanked by Phil Habib, Leonard Woodcock, and Dick Holbrooke. After an exchange of courtesies, I came quickly to the point. The president had authorized me to explore how the United States and China might normalize relations. "Provided we can find a basis that will not lessen the prospects for a peaceful settlement of the Taiwan question by the Chinese themselves and which would enable informal contacts to continue," I said, "the president is prepared to normalize relations." In accordance with the Shanghai Communiqué, which acknowledged the existence of only one China, we were prepared to recognize the PRC as the sole legal government of China. I stated that our defense treaty with Taiwan would "lapse" (we would not use the word "abrogate"), and we would complete the withdrawal of our military forces and installations from Taiwan.

I stated carefully that we had concluded that, "It would be necessary for U.S. government personnel to remain on Taiwan under an informal arrangement." I stressed that such representation would be neither diplomatic in character nor have any of the characteristics or appurtenances of an embassy, such as flags or a government seal. I pointed to the negative reaction in the United States to Chinese statements about liberating Taiwan by force, and said that at the appropriate time we would make a public statement of our interest in a peaceful settlement. I stressed that it would be essential that China not contradict such a statement or make any new statements about liberation by force.

The next morning we met in the Great Hall of the People to hear Huang Hua's not unexpected response. My presentation had been too much for him to accept. He reiterated the three Chinese conditions and said our position simply gave "lip service" to them. After tough words about liberating Taiwan, the foreign minister concluded that normalization would be further delayed.

After lunch, Habib, Holbrooke, Oksenberg, Gleysteen, other China experts from the State Department, and I discussed what to do about the draft communiqué I had in my pocket. To avoid being overheard, we strolled about in the guest house's exquisite ornamental garden, stopping on a beautiful bridge that arched over a pond and leaning against the railing to talk. I decided we would stick with our maximum position, and that I would not put forward the communiqué for discussion. I still believed that with the Panama debate beginning, the time was not right. In any case, the Chinese did not seem ready to negotiate seriously.

I met Vice-Premier Deng Xiao-ping that afternoon. We had last seen each other in 1975 in Peking. He jokingly reminded me that the last time we met was just before he was demoted for the second time. He quipped, "You know I am the only man who was twice resurrected." After an exchange of pleasantries we turned to serious business. I briefly outlined our position again, stressing that I offered it as a starting point for discussion. Deng, an embodiment of Chinese courtesy, calmly termed my comments a retreat from the Shanghai Communiqué. He read me portions of a memorandum of a conversation in which Henry Kissinger had allegedly agreed that the United States owed a debt to China and that normalization would be in conformity with the Chinese conditions. He referred to a discussion with President Ford in December 1975, in which the president had stated he would be in a better position to normalize relations in accordance with the so-called Japanese formula after the 1976 elections. Deng omitted to note, though, that Ford had added a qualifying "if"—if the Taiwan issue was worked out. Deng characterized my proposal to Huang Hua as a retreat from the previous state of affairs.

Deng said that the most China could accept was the "Japanese formula." He described what I had proposed as an embassy that would not have a sign or a flag at its door.

After we left Peking, I stopped in Tokyo to brief the Japanese government. As we were boarding the plane, Hodding Carter came to me, visibly disturbed. Among the "playbacks"—the telegraphic reports of world press coverage that were relayed to me by the State Department whenever I traveled—was an article written by John Wallach, the diplomatic correspondent for the Hearst chain. Writing from Washington, he reported that members of the National Security Council staff, reading my reports to the president on my trip, had seen signs of "progress." I was angry. I had reported no such thing. Normally, such inaccurate articles do not set off international repercussions, although egos are bruised and tempers flare with monotonous regularity. But this article had the potential to cause serious problems. If the Chinese were to believe that we thought they were being flexible when, in fact, they had not been, or even that we were playing propaganda games, I knew they would feel impelled to correct the record publicly. A few days later Deng issued a critical statement, as I had feared.

Although I was not surprised by Chinese unhappiness with our firmness, I was annoyed by the uncharacteristic airing of Chinese displeasure in the press. But despite the public rhetoric, the Chinese made it clear in private that they wanted to keep talking. For my part, I was determined to avoid a pointless public debate. I recommended to Carter that we should stick to our course, and that we should not imply that we would move any faster on normalization than we actually could.

We marked time over the next several months as we concentrated on the Panama Canal Treaties and other matters. Nevertheless, we continued to prepare for what I was confident would be the eventual realization of our goal. I asked our able legal adviser, Herb Hansell, to work closely with Holbrooke on the arrangements that would govern our relationship with the Taiwanese after normalization. Hansell assembled a handful of talented lawyers who, over the next year, produced a voluminous study of alternatives. This study provided the framework for the Taiwan Relations Act, and was done independently of the negotiations.* I also turned to one person outside the government to give us his view of the legal issues involved in normalization. I chose a man of great ability and integrity in whom I had complete confidence, Herbert Brownell, who had been the attorney general under Eisenhower and was now practicing law in New York. In the fall of 1978, Brownell met with me and our ambassador to China, Leonard Woodcock, and Dick Holbrooke in New York. Brownell forthrightly reported that he had completed his analysis and could support normalization, but only if we terminated the defense treaty with Taiwan in accordance with Article 10, that is, after one year's notice. He added that he believed Congress would take a similar position. I agreed that abrogating the treaty was unsound, and I indicated I would so recommend to the president.

* The final text of the act was developed by the Congress after extensive hearings.

5

BALANCED POLICY
UNDER PRESSURE

THE LINKAGE ISSUE ARISES IN AFRICA

BY THE BEGINNING of 1978, the first serious disagreements had broken out within the administration over Soviet and Cuban actions in the Horn and how we should respond. These differences were primarily between Brzezinski and me.

The disagreement centered on how to interpret Soviet actions in the Horn and in the Katangan invasion of the Shaba province. Zbig was increasingly convinced that Soviet actions were part of a larger, well-defined strategy. He argued that Soviet behavior was incompatible with our policy of balancing competition with cooperation. We and our allies, he thought, should take what I felt were ill-defined measures to make Soviet adventurism more "costly." Zbig was convinced that others would perceive us as failing to counter Soviet expansionism, and that this perception would weaken international confidence in the United States and damage the administration politically. It is true there was growing public and congressional concern about Soviet international behavior. But I felt that much of it arose from background press sessions held by staff members of the national security advisor and was self-inflicted.

I did not believe Soviet actions in Africa were part of a grand Soviet plan, but rather attempts to exploit targets of opportunity. It was not that Soviet actions were unimportant, but I felt realism required us to deal with those problems in the local context in which they had their roots.

The critical question was what politically and militarily feasible strategy would most effectively counter Soviet actions while advancing our overall interests. This was in keeping with the president's intention, which I shared, that we not allow ourselves to become so preoccupied with the Soviets that we lose sight of our basic policy objectives in Africa. I remained convinced that the heart of our strategy must be to combine diplomacy, negotiations, concerted Western actions, and the powerful forces of African nationalism to resolve local disputes, and to remove ostensible justification for Soviet involvement.

I did not rule out the careful application of military pressure as in the Shaba. Still, I was convinced it was wrong to threaten or bluff in a case where military involvement was not justified, or where Congress and the American people would not support it. It made no sense to attempt to bluff when we were not prepared to carry out the threat. In my judgment, the Horn of Africa was precisely such a case.

• • •

Our position on the Horn at the beginning of 1978 was unchanged. We were prepared to support Somalia in a limited way, including the supplying of defensive arms, but only after the Somalis withdrew from the Ogaden. Most of our NATO allies and other friends in the area had adopted a similar policy, for providing military aid to Somalia was unlikely to be successful and would probably lead to an even larger Soviet and Cuban presence.

In late January, a five-power group (Britain, France, Italy, the United States, West Germany) met to coordinate policy for the Horn. We agreed that all of us should press more vigorously for a negotiated settlement of the Ogaden crisis. The avenues available were the ongoing mediation effort of the OAU, discussions with the Soviets to secure their cooperation in ending the fighting, and pressures on Somalia and Ethiopia to reach a negotiated solution.

A diplomatic strategy would take time. Meanwhile, political pressures were growing, both inside and outside the administration, to counter Soviet and Cuban assistance to Ethiopia by calling into play other aspects of the U.S.-Soviet global relationship. The suggested linkage included slowing down the SALT and other arms control negotiations, and limiting economic relations and high-level visits and exchanges.

I favored making it clear to the USSR that its behavior was undermining our ability to follow a balanced policy. Hostility in the United States was being stimulated which would make ratification of a SALT II Treaty very difficult. But carrying the linkage idea far beyond that had serious drawbacks. First, most of the suggested actions would adversely affect American interests. Second, these steps would probably have little or no effect on Soviet actions in the Horn.

Meanwhile, the Cubans shifted from an advisory to a combat role in Ethiopia. With this change our problem became the prevention of an Ethiopian-Cuban invasion of Somalia and an attempt to overthrow Siad Barre. In private we warned Moscow sharply about the damage that

Soviet and Cuban involvement was causing, and urged our NATO allies to press home the same point. If Moscow would hold back the Ethiopians and Cubans while we pressured the Somalis to get out of the Ogaden before their army was completely destroyed, we might rescue Somalia from its obsession with the Ogaden and improve our own position in the Horn as well. High-level information from the Soviets indicated that restraining the Ethiopians and ending the crisis was the course they were trying to follow.

Our own ability to stay on course was being severely tested. Among the NSC staff there was talk of exercising some sort of vague "military option." Among the actions discussed were large-scale U.S. naval deployments to the area; providing U.S. air cover for Somali forces if the Ethiopians and Cubans crossed the border in pursuit; and funneling military aid to Somalia (and even the Eritrean rebels) through proxies, to tie down the Soviets and Cubans in a bloody and inconclusive struggle. This last notion was particularly dangerous, for it would have isolated us from the rest of Africa and NATO and destroyed any chance of a negotiated settlement. Our long-term policies in Africa would have been damaged, perhaps irredeemably, and our larger foreign policy goals undermined. Fortunately, there was virtually no support for such ideas.

A cohesive strategy began to take shape in early February after intensive Special Coordinating Committee deliberations, discussions with our NATO allies, and quiet contacts with the Soviets. This approach had five components:

• First, to work with our NATO allies to achieve agreed Western goals: a negotiated settlement; preventing an invasion of Somalia; preventing an increase in Soviet and Cuban influence in the area.

• Second, to ensure that other friends in the region—Egypt, Iran, Saudi Arabia, and Sudan—also understood and supported these goals and would urge them on Siad Barre.

• Third, to obtain Somali agreement to withdraw from the Ogaden.

• Fourth, to lay the diplomatic and political groundwork to help Somalia defend its territory, including supplying defensive arms after it withdrew from the Ogaden.

• Fifth, to keep pressure on the Soviets to stop the Ethiopians and Cubans at the Somali border and to support a negotiated resolution.

Steps were taken immediately to implement this strategy. The second week of February we met with British, French, and German representatives in New York. We agreed that we would all tell the Somalis that they must withdraw from the Ogaden and that we would seek a cease-fire that would protect their forces and the Somali inhabitants of the province as they withdrew. On February 16, President Carter obtained Mengistu's agreement to receive David Aaron, the deputy national security advisor, as the president's personal emissary. In his talks, Aaron was to seek Mengistu's assurance that Ethiopia would respect Somalia's border.

On February 14, I met with Ambassador Dobrynin and outlined our proposals for ending the conflict. I emphasized the necessity for a firm commitment that neither Ethiopians nor Cubans would cross into Somalia. Dobrynin replied that the Ethiopians had given the Soviets such an assurance. Further, Raul Castro had said during his recent visit to Moscow that the Cubans had no intention of moving into Somali territory. Moscow also said it would support a cease-fire in conjunction with Somali withdrawal, peace negotiations, and the territorial integrity of both states. The Soviets made clear, however, that a Somali withdrawal was an essential precondition.

The administration's senior foreign policy and national security officials met on February 21. Brzezinski again raised the idea of U.S. military countermoves. He suggested the deployment of a carrier task force to the region and the encouraging of friendly states to supply Somalia with non-U.S.-origin weapons. He argued that it was important that the United States not be perceived as passive in the face of Soviet and Cuban actions.

Every other member of the committee opposed the idea of deploying a carrier task force. Brown argued that if we were to do so, and Somalia were invaded or Siad Barre overthrown—distinct possibilities—it would be perceived as a defeat for the United States. Neither Brown nor I wanted to engage in a bluffing game. If our bluff were called and we were not prepared to use our planes, the credibility of future carrier task force deployments in crises would be compromised. The meeting closed with agreement that there would be no linkage between the Soviets' and Cubans' activities in the Horn and other bilateral issues between the United States and the USSR.

The Somalis were increasingly desperate. Repeatedly, they appealed for U.S. military help as Cuban and Ethiopian pressure mounted. Each time we asked whether they were prepared to withdraw from the Ogaden. Their answer was no. We also refused, but told them we were prepared to ask Congress for authorization for third-country transfers of defensive weapons of U.S. origin, *if* they would announce publicly they would withdraw from the Ogaden and do so promptly. The Somalis continued to bluster about the need for U.S. commitments before they would withdraw, but it was hollow talk; they were facing imminent defeat.

On February 22, I reported to the president that Ethiopia had given assurances that Ethiopian forces would not cross the Somali border. We were reasonably confident that the Ethiopians would prefer restraint if they could achieve Somali withdrawal short of an Ethiopian invasion. The Ethiopians had many other problems, not the least of which was the growing civil war in Eritrea.

These developments increased the likelihood that we would ultimately be successful in preserving the territorial integrity of Somalia. But on March 1, Brzezinski stated publicly that Soviet actions in the Horn would complicate the SALT talks. The president immediately denied that we intended to link the SALT negotiations to other issues. He did acknowledge, though, that Soviet behavior was jeopardizing the chances of getting a SALT agreement approved in Congress. After noting that he had received assurances from the Soviets and the Ethiopians that the Somali border would be respected, Carter added, "The Soviets' violating these principles would be a cause of concern to me, would lessen the confidence of the American people in the word and peaceful intentions of the Soviet Union, and would make it more difficult to ratify a SALT agreement or comprehensive test ban agreement if concluded, and therefore the two are linked because of actions by the Soviets. We don't initiate the linkage."

Brzezinski's public statement implied that he would deliberately slow down the SALT negotiations unless the Soviets showed more restraint in Africa. The president, on the other hand, was simply describing political reality.

We were shooting ourselves in the foot. By casting the complex Horn situation in East-West terms, and by setting impossible objectives for U.S. policy—elimination of Soviet and Cuban influence in Ethiopia—we were creating a perception that we were defeated when, in fact, we were achieving a successful outcome. Our African policies were sound and, I was convinced, would protect our interests as long as we kept a clear sense of what was attainable. We needed to be more consistent in explaining the purposes of our policies or we would end in creating public uncertainty and confusion.

On March 8, as his forces were being driven from the Ogaden, we finally received from Siad Barre his long-awaited agreement to withdraw. By March 14, the withdrawal of the Somali Army was virtually complete. The Ethiopians and Cubans, as the Soviets had assured us, did not cross the border. We immediately began consultations with Congress on providing economic aid and defensive arms to Somalia as we had promised. The reaction on Capitol Hill was favorable.

Even so, we were not able to assist Somalia militarily at that time because Siad Barre reneged on his assurances that he would leave Ethiopia alone. He told us what he thought we wanted to hear, but he was determined to integrate the Ogaden into a Greater Somalia. Siad Barre was perfectly willing to treat the Horn crisis as an East-West confrontation in order to gain American political and military support. Our interest lay in preventing the resumption of Soviet influence in Somalia either by force or by a new Somali turnabout (and either was possible) with the limited diplomatic means at our disposal. We could not in the short run expect a break between the Soviets and the Marxist regime in Addis Ababa. To allow that to be regarded as a realistic objective by the public and Congress ensured that the outcome would be seen as administration weakness in the face of Soviet challenge.

• • •

At the end of 1977, the Angola-Zaire border problem flared up again. In mid-December, the Katangans began to cross again into Shaba. This time the Zairean forces, supported by the Moroccans, were more successful in resisting the incursion, and by late March Mobutu had not only blunted the attack of the invaders but also launched retaliatory raids into Angola. He was convinced the Katangans were acting with the authorization of the Angolan government.

Despite the differences with President Neto over the presence of Soviet advisers and Cuban troops in Angola, we had a mutual interest in the maintenance of a secure border between Angola and Zaire and an end to the support each was giving to opponents of the other. In addition, we shared with Angola an interest in getting the South African troops out of Namibia. Removing the threat to Neto's regime in Luanda would remove the raison d'être for the Soviet and Cuban involvement in Angola and would open the door for normalization of relations between us and Angola.

Simplistically blaming the situation on Moscow and Havana was pointless. Because of legal constraints and congressional opposition to U.S. involvement, we could do little beyond what we had done. But disregarding these realities, some in the administration persistently argued that we should "increase the cost to the Cubans" by helping UNITA. I disagreed. There was no prospect that we could gain the legally required congressional approval for aid to UNITA. In any case it would not serve our national interests to do so.

By late spring the Zairean counterattack began to falter. Americans and other foreign nationals were evacuated from the danger zone around the mining town of Kolwezi, although a few Americans and a larger number of Belgians remained. We warned Angolan representatives in Brussels that the safety of foreign nationals in Shaba must be respected, and we began contingency planning with the Belgians, French, and British for a possible rescue mission. In mid-May a number of Europeans in Kolwezi were killed. The French and Belgians, with the help of our transport aircraft, sent paratroops to the Kolwezi area to protect their citizens. We briefed members of Congress on our limited aid and their reaction was positive.

On May 22, I reported to the president that although the fighting had died down, tensions in Zaire remained high and there was a widespread loss of confidence in Mobutu. The Belgians had decided to leave one of their battalions in Shaba, and had requested U.S. participation in a predominantly Western international force to provide internal and external security for Mobutu. This would permit the reopening of the copper mines around Kolwezi. The president's response was an emphatic no. He believed that additional military forces on the ground should be predominantly African. The French, with our support, then took the lead in assembling an African security force to protect Zaire. The force was drawn from several African states. This was a far better solution than one composed primarily of Western units.

On May 25, the president announced that the carefully limited, one-time deployment of U.S. transport aircraft in support of the Belgian and French rescue operation had come to an end. He laid stress on the limited nature of the U.S. role because of congressional fears of further U.S. support of Mobutu. At the same time, he blamed the Angolan government and the Cubans for the Katangan attack, noting that the Cubans had played a role in arming and training the Katangans. He said the Cubans had known of the Katangan plans to attack and had done nothing to restrain them, thereby assuming part of the responsibility.

That evening I was in New York for the meeting of the UN General Assembly. I met with the Cuban vice-president, Carlos Rafael Rodriguez, at Ambassador Andrew Young's residence at the Waldorf. Rodriguez was angered by the president's public dismissal of Castro's assurances that the Cubans were not involved, which had been conveyed to us through our diplomatic representatives in Havana. He asserted that the Cubans had had no part in the Shaba incident and had had no connection with the Katangans for more than two years. He claimed that Cuba did not like Mobutu but wanted no trouble between Angola and Zaire because the real danger for Angola was the South African forces in Namibia. I told him our information indicated that the Cubans had supported the Katangan incursion. Indeed, we did have some ambiguous and, as it turned out, not very good intelligence to this effect.

The United States and several European allies were meeting in Paris on June 5 to prepare for further meetings in Brussels on June 13 and 14 to discuss economic aid to Zaire, whose economy was on the verge of collapse. In a press conference on May 30, I tried to counter the impression that the Katangan invasion was an East-West conflict, pointing out that both we and our allies agreed that the dispute should be solved by peaceful means. I noted that the roots of the conflict went far deeper than East-West differences. I denied that there was any linkage between the SALT negotiations and the Zairean situation, although I recognized that the Soviet and Cuban activities in Africa could have an effect on the eventual SALT ratification process. As for the importance of SALT, I stated, ". . . As I have said on so many occasions that you must all be sick and tired of hearing it, it is our view that a SALT agreement should be negotiated on its own merits."

Congress was firmly behind our policy in Zaire. The limited actions we had taken with our allies were widely supported. But there was concern that we were in danger of drifting away from the main thrust of our African policy: to maintain contacts with the key actors in southern Africa, and to promote moderate solutions to the political and racial conflicts in the area. I told the president that even those members of Congress who accepted as fact that the Soviets and Cubans were involved in training and equipping the Katangans believed that we must prevent Africa from becoming an arena for East-West confrontation.

• • •

The internal divisions over Africa's place in our global strategy of managing U.S.-Soviet competition were becoming increasingly difficult. The lurching back and forth in public about linkage, about the significance of Soviet and Cuban activities in Africa, and the impact of the Shaba and the Horn on U.S.-Soviet relations and SALT was hurting the president politically. It was also undercutting our ability to conduct a consistent and coherent foreign policy.

When the success of our Horn policy failed to restore the internal administration consensus on U.S.-Soviet relations, I recommended to the president that we undertake a broad review of our African policy. I wanted to test our basic assumptions.

This exhaustive governmentwide study led most participants to reject the "grand design" interpretation of Soviet behavior. It concluded that Soviet policy in Africa could best be described as an exploitation of opportunity, an attempt to take advantage of African conflicts to increase Soviet influence. This view did not, of course, make Soviet behavior any more tolerable, but it did suggest that we should deal with each problem in its own context and not as a local battle in a global East-West geopolitical struggle. Most participants also agreed that African nationalism was strong enough to preclude permanent Soviet domination and that the best strategy for protecting our interests was to help bring about peaceful solutions to African conflicts. There was widespread agreement that neither political nor economic pressures were likely to force out the Soviets or Cubans, and that so-called punitive actions, such as delaying the SALT Treaty, might damage our own interests.

On October 6, the president convened the first National Security Council meeting on Africa since early 1977. At this critical meeting, evidently unpersuaded by the analysis in the Africa study, Brzezinski challenged the approach we had been following in Africa, arguing that it had not proved successful. He contended that under the circumstances we had two options: Either we should make Soviet-Cuban actions a major issue in our relations with Moscow or we should reduce our involvement. Thus the African moderates would learn the hard way the harm that the Cubans and Soviets were doing, and the need for concerted action to oppose them.

The debate was essentially between Brzezinski and me. I responded that there was a third option, and that was to pursue our current policy. I argued that the best tools we had to combat the Soviets and Cubans were our superior political, economic, and diplomatic strengths. Like

Andy Young, I was convinced that the continuation of the political and racial problems of southern Africa increased the frustration of African nationalists and made possible the deeper entrenchment of the Soviets and Cubans. As we had concluded in our review, a policy of confrontation was not a winning strategy: Congress and the American people would not support direct U.S. military involvement (providing limited military aid to Zaire had been hard enough). By posing the issues in terms of an East-West controversy, we would be avoiding the underlying causes that produced these local conflicts.

After everyone had had his say, the president reaffirmed the approach we had been following. Just the same, he was growing increasingly worried about the domestic political impact of Soviet and Cuban activities in Africa, for it was giving rise to a view that he was not dealing firmly enough with the Russians.

Despite the reaffirmation of our policy, I was concerned about administration disunity during the previous year. In the face of adverse conditions our policies in the Horn and in Shaba had been remarkably successful. Yet, a large segment of Congress and the public saw confusion and weakness, not only regarding Africa, but more significantly, in our ability to manage our relations with the Soviet Union. There was an important lesson for the administration in this: good policies would not ensure public support and understanding if we tolerated diverse and discordant voices who made us appear to be the loser.

U.S.-NATO: Political Crisis and Recovery

U.S.-NATO security relations during 1978 were dominated by two major issues. One, the neutron bomb, was to cause a crisis of confidence in the alliance. The second, consultations on SALT II and theater nuclear force modernization, restored allied faith in the fundamental U.S. commitment to European security.

By early 1978, we had concluded that the only way to forge a NATO policy on the enhanced radiation weapon (ERW)—the neutron bomb—was for the United States to develop a firm position around which the allies could rally. In January it was decided that we would inform our allies that we were prepared to produce the ERW and to deploy it when ready, in about two years. We would offer to forgo deployment of the ERW if the Soviets would agree not to deploy the SS-20 missile. Before announcing this position, we would require an alliance statement of agreement with our proposed plan, including acceptance of deployment of the ERW on European soil if our arms control proposal proved unsuccessful.

In high-level exchanges, conducted by senior NSC officials, key allied leaders were told that the president had personally decided to go forward with the ERW package as I have described it. Alliance support was cast in terms of NATO confidence in the president's leadership. I had urged that we sound out the British, Germans, and one or two other allies about a tentative U.S. position to see if it could serve as the basis of an alliance position, for in the State Department we were uneasy about the risks of staking the president's personal prestige on this extremely sensitive issue.

Between January and March, key State, Defense, and NSC aides worked to build allied support for the U.S. approach, hammering hard on the theme that the president had personally decided that NATO should go forward with the production and deployment of the ERW. The Germans shared our judgment that it was essential from a political standpoint for the alliance to support deployment, while holding open the possibility that this might not be necessary if we made sufficient progress in arms control negotiations with the USSR. Bonn was adamant that Germany could not be the only continental ally to accept deployment. For the Germans, it was essential that ERW deployments take place as part of an overall alliance agreement, and not as a bilateral arrangement between the United States and Germany. The fact that the British—now also thoroughly alarmed about the political damage the ERW was causing to NATO—had privately indicated their willingness to accept deployment was insufficient, since Britain was already a nuclear power. The Germans wanted the Belgians and the Dutch to share the political burden by accepting deployment of the ERW on their soil, but both were governed by fragile coalitions and were faced with powerful internal antinuclear movements.

We, with the British and Germans, worked energetically through February and early March to pull together an alliance consensus around the basic U.S. position. To make this possible we did not require that individual countries declare for the public record that they would accept the ERW two years hence if the arms control approach failed. On March 8, the Dutch Parliament passed a resolution opposing production of the ERW. By mid-March, after strenuous efforts, we had gained agreement from the Dutch, Belgians, and Scandinavians not to object to an alliance statement of collective support for the arms control approach and for deployment, if necessary, when this decision would be announced. The NATO consensus would have to be formed from positive statements by the United States, the United Kingdom, and the Federal Republic of Germany, with the tacit support of France. The remaining allies were peripheral to the issue, no doubt to their great relief.

By Saturday, March 18, after a nerve-racking week of nonstop consultations, the United States, with the Germans and the British, had worked out a phased plan for a preliminary North Atlantic Council meeting on March 20. There the prearranged consensus would be given a dry run, and a final meeting would be held on March 22 at which an agreed statement of alliance support for the U.S. position would be issued. A public announcement of the NATO policy on the ERW would be made on March 23.

George Vest and Leslie Gelb, who were handling the ERW issue for the State Department, reported to me on the afternoon of March 18 that the final arrangements for the two NATO meetings were completed. Throughout the discussions with our allies, the president had been kept continuously informed by the NSC staff, and had checked all of the appropriate boxes on the papers that went to him. Still, since the president was in Georgia, I felt vaguely uneasy about whether he was fully in accord. I asked that a memorandum from Harold Brown and me be prepared so that we could send it to the president.

I was startled on Sunday when the president instructed me to cancel the Monday, March 20, meeting of the North Atlantic Council and instead to meet with him. The president apparently had not focused on how far down the road we were. We prepared an excuse for the delay, which we dispatched immediately to NATO headquarters in Brussels and to the allied capitals.

Harold Brown, Zbig Brzezinski and I met the president on Monday. Carter was angry that he was essentially committed to produce and deploy the ERW. He felt that the burden and political liability for this weapon, which as far as he could see no ally really wanted, was being placed on his shoulders instead of being shared by the whole alliance. He appeared not to appreciate the enormous damage to his prestige and U.S. leadership that would result from backing away from the alliance consensus that had been worked out in his name.

Brown, Brzezinski, and I argued strenuously that it was imperative for the cohesion of the alliance and for his political standing that he go ahead as planned. His standing as a leader of NATO, both in Europe and at home, was at stake. Allied leaders had gone out on very shaky political limbs to support the March 18 scenario on the understanding that they were following his lead. Although the president was moved by the strength of our arguments, he leaned strongly against production unless the Germans publicly committed themselves to deployment.

The allies were understandably anxious to know what was going on. The press had caught wind of the delay and sensed a story in the making. Brown, Brzezinski, and I struggled to prevent the allies from breaking away from the March 18 consensus while we went back to the Germans. Warren Christopher was dispatched to see Chancellor Schmidt on March 30 to explain the president's views. Schmidt was restrained but deeply upset. He was unyielding that Germany could not be alone in accepting deployment of the ERW on its soil.

Back home, word had already begun to spread that the Germans had made it impossible to secure allied support, which was why the president could not go ahead. Foreign Minister Hans-Dietrich Genscher, a splendid man and a staunch friend of the United States, sped to Washington to restate the German position that the ERW should be deployed only after arms control negotiations had failed. Brown, Brzezinski, and I continued to urge the president not to decide against the ERW and to leave open the option of producing it in the future, depending on Soviet actions. The president accepted these arguments.

The leaders on both sides of the Atlantic were under extremely heavy domestic pressure. It appeared that the only sensible thing to do, since the president would not go forward with production without a German commitment to deployment, was to close off the issue. We attempted to do this on April 7 when the president announced that he would defer production of the ERW, and that his final decision would be influenced by what the Soviets did to show restraint in their conventional and nuclear arms programs.*

. . .

The impact of the neutron bomb decision at home and abroad was very damaging. The president's name had been invoked heavily to build the alliance consensus of late March. How had we reached this unfortunate end?

As someone later said, there was plenty of blame to go around. The initial consultations in the summer of 1977 failed to achieve agreement among the allies on whether the military value of the ERW outweighed its political liabilities. The issue drifted inconclusively through the summer and fall of 1977, with allied uneasiness and uncertainty continuing to build. During those crucial months we missed a chance to draw the allies quickly around a clear U.S. position before Soviet progaganda and antinuclear sentiment had had a chance to build strong political opposition in Europe.

By early 1978, when we decided to come forward with a preferred U.S. plan and sought to rally the allies around it, the domestic political problems for most of the allies had become acute. No ally wanted the burden of blocking a measure to strengthen the defense of western Europe, but none of the critical countries (Germany, Belgium, and the Netherlands) dared break the logjam by coming out openly for deployment. To overcome allied reluctance to take a public position, we turned to an ambiguous alliance statement of support in which individual countries were not required to commit themselves. On March 18, we sent a memorandum to this effect to the president.

Because I was preoccupied with the Middle East, SALT, Africa, China, and Panama in late 1977 and early 1978, I did not monitor the ERW issue closely. It is painful to recall, but tragically, none of us

---

* To strengthen this position, in October the president ordered that warheads be built for U.S. nuclear artillery and tactical missiles that could be converted to enhanced radiation weapons, and approved the production, but not the installation, of critical components.

recognized or took seriously enough continuing signs of the president's uneasiness with the progress reports he was receiving on the course of our ERW strategy and consultations with the allies.

Up to the point of the March 18 memorandum, the president had followed the unanimous advice of all his senior advisers, had signed all the letters and checked all the right boxes on decision memoranda. But evidently, in his mind, all these actions had been steps in a consultative process, not a final commitment to a particular outcome. When he saw the March 18 memorandum spelling out in detail the scenario for the alliance statement of support and for the public announcement, it may have hit home that the last step was at hand, that he was essentially committed to producing and deploying a nuclear weapon that his allies —for whose security it had been developed—would not request. At that moment, I can only surmise that the president's innermost self rebelled and he rejected the logic of the previous six months of arduous negotiations within the alliance.

On the allied side, the Germans, who were the key to the issue, were caught between their desire not to block a NATO defense measure and their political sensitivity on all nuclear matters. Their demand that the weapon also be deployed in another country, although politically understandable, placed too great a burden on the fragile Dutch and Belgian coalition governments. The most sustained pressure by the Germans, the British, and the Americans was necessary to keep the Dutch and Belgians, as well as the Scandinavian allies, from openly opposing the ERW decision. It would have been better had the Germans told us in secret that they would take the ERW if necessary, but that it was politically vital for them to have another continental ally.

•   •   •

Militarily, little was lost by the postponement of the ERW decision. Politically, the costs were extremely high. The president's standing in the alliance received a strong blow. Political opponents of the administration linked the ERW with the B-1 to charge wrongly that the administration was engaged in unilateral disarmament. The incubus of the ERW haunted subsequent alliance consultations on the far more significant issue of modernization and enhancement of NATO's long-range theater nuclear capabilities.

Brown, Brzezinski, and I with our staffs immediately began a series of intensive political and military studies on theater nuclear forces. U.S. and allied officials alike understood instinctively that after ERW it was especially important to NATO that the theater nuclear force issue be dealt with firmly, but with a united alliance and under visible American leadership. These studies and consultations were to lead to the December 12, 1979, alliance decisions to deploy new intermediate-range U.S. cruise and ballistic missiles in Europe capable of striking targets in the

Soviet Union, and to seek negotiations with the Soviets on the limitation of their intermediate-range nuclear weapons.

SALT II ISSUES IN THE ALLIANCE

Early in 1978, we successfully concluded consultations with the allies on how to deal with the delicate issue of "nontransfer/noncircumvention" in the SALT negotiations. As I have said, the Soviets wanted the treaty to include a clause prohibiting the transfer to any other country of weapons systems on which limitations were placed in the SALT Treaty and the technology relating to them. Since cruise missiles were included in the protocol to the SALT II Treaty, from the Soviet point of view a nontransfer prohibition would include cruise missiles. The Soviet nontransfer position was aimed at changing the long-standing pattern of U.S. defense cooperation with its allies in the nuclear area, for example, the sale of Polaris missiles to the British and the provision of nuclear delivery systems (under a dual-control "two-key" arrangement) to several other allies.

There was no question of our accepting a nontransfer provision. To have done so would have driven a wedge between ourselves and the NATO allies in perhaps the most sensitive aspect of our security relationship. We could agree to a general commitment not to circumvent the provisions of the treaty. This would add no new legal obligation, since we, as well as the Soviets, were prohibited from doing so by international law. Before proposing it, in February we cleared the wording of a general noncircumvention clause with our allies. To allay fears that the Soviets might use this clause to challenge future transfers, we also told our allies we would make a public statement of interpretation to the alliance and to the U.S. Senate after the SALT II Treaty was signed. This statement would make clear that the SALT II agreement would not interfere with U.S. defense cooperation with the allies.

In bilateral consultations held during the summer and fall of 1978 with the British and Germans (the two allies most concerned about the noncircumvention provision), and later with the whole alliance, we worked out the wording. The statement indicated that we would consider any future request for weapons systems or technology limited by SALT II on a case-by-case basis (as we would have done even in the absence of SALT), but the agreement would not interfere with existing patterns of defense cooperation or preclude U.S. assistance in the modernization of alliance nuclear forces.*

---

* In addition, we gave private assurances to the British, who at that time were studying options for modernizing their strategic forces, that the SALT II Treaty would not necessarily preclude us from transferring air-launched cruise missiles to Britain, or even numerically limited systems such as Trident I sea-launched ballistic missiles (SLBMs)—as in fact the

To ensure that Moscow could not misunderstand our position, Warnke and I repeatedly told the Soviets that the noncircumvention clause was not a nontransfer provision in disguise, and that we intended to continue traditional defense cooperation with our allies after SALT II was signed. The theater nuclear force modernization decision and our decision to sell Trident I to the British are unequivocal demonstrations that we would not allow SALT to hobble traditional defense cooperation with our NATO colleagues.

We also made a commitment to our allies not to accept future limitations on cruise missiles or other U.S. missiles designed for theater uses, such as the Pershing II missile, unless the Soviets agreed to appropriate limitations on their own theater nuclear forces. This commitment for SALT III represented a radical departure from NATO policy in SALT I and II, when the allies opposed the inclusion of theater systems in the SALT negotiations and placed the United States in the position of negotiating on their behalf on matters of the most direct and immediate importance to European security.

I was pleased with the support we received from our allies as we moved toward a SALT II agreement. At the NATO foreign ministers meeting in December 1978, even before the SALT negotiations were concluded, several allied officials assured us privately that their concerns about SALT II had been met and that their governments would firmly support the treaty. We had had a long, uphill struggle after the ERW episode to restore allied confidence in our leadership on security matters. The consultations we conducted throughout late 1977, 1978, and 1979 on SALT II issues, the status of theater nuclear forces in SALT III, and theater nuclear force modernization overcame the crisis of confidence brought on by the ERW issue. They put the alliance back on the track we had mapped in the summit of May 1977 and reaffirmed at the May 1978 summit in Washington.

Carter administration ultimately agreed to do when the British decided in 1980 to modernize their SLBM force.

6

SALT II
AND U.S./USSR

U.S.-Soviet Tensions

DURING 1978, I was increasingly involved in the struggle to halt the growing polarization of U.S.-Soviet relations. Despite repeated top-level decisions not to link Africa and other Third World issues to our bilateral relationship with the Soviets or to the SALT negotiations, political pressures were building for the president to appear tougher. Although Carter refused to slow down the negotiations, some of his advisers were less concerned about progress in SALT than in sending signals to the Soviets that their international activities were damaging U.S.-Soviet relations and that the administration was responding firmly.

The next SALT session with Brezhnev and Gromyko was planned for April 20–22 in Moscow. Early in April, I stressed to Dobrynin the political importance of making progress. He replied that the Soviets viewed this trip as crucially important. The Soviets had reacted badly to the president's March speech at Wake Forest University when he had warned them to show greater restraint. In Moscow, the Soviets were taking stock of U.S.-Soviet relations. I hoped to use the April talks to pave the way to resolving the remaining issues in the SALT negotiations. Warnke and I wanted to map out a negotiating strategy that would lead to a summit on SALT, perhaps as early as the summer. Before I left for Moscow, Warnke described our positions to Dobrynin and probed for areas of Soviet movement.

Despite our efforts and some Soviet flexibility, the Moscow talks did not produce a major breakthrough. The escalating public rhetoric and the talk about linkage were having a political impact on the negotiating climate, as well as on the willingness of the administration to consider adjustments in U.S. positions in return for Soviet concessions. However, important progress was made. The Soviets agreed to our proposal of 1,200 for the MIRVed missile launcher ceiling, while we accepted their proposed 2,250 strategic nuclear delivery vehicle ceiling. We also made some progress on limiting new types of ICBMs. Most important, especially in light of the recent ERW shock to NATO, we settled the noncircumvention issue on our terms. The Soviets dropped their demand for a prohibition on the right to transfer systems and technology limited by the treaty in favor of our general clause prohibiting circumvention of the obligations of the treaty "through any other state or states."

Ironically, the April Soviet acceptance of a reduction of the Vladivostok ceiling and the new ceiling on MIRVed missiles was characterized by SALT opponents as a U.S. compromise, which was nonsense. To reach 2,250, the Soviets would have to eliminate over 250 systems; we would not have to eliminate any American systems. The same was true of the 1,200 figure: we would not have to dismantle any U.S. systems to stay within that number, and the 1,320 combined ceiling on the MIRVed missiles and ALCM-carrying heavy bombers gave us 120 "free" bombers so equipped. In contrast, the Soviets, without a comparable cruise missile program, would be unable to make use of the 1,320 combined ceiling and would be limited to 1,200 MIRVed missile launchers.

Despite such a favorable outcome, several Republican senators issued a statement on May 3 attacking the administration for "a frightening pattern of giving up key U.S. weapons systems for nothing in return." They claimed the emerging agreement represented a retreat from the March comprehensive proposal, and described as U.S. concessions what in fact were Soviet moves toward our own positions. I did not want to write off any senators, but the president was probably right when he told me that many Republicans, as well as Democratic Senator Henry Jackson, were going to oppose the treaty no matter what was in it.

My own soundings of pro-SALT senators revealed mixed feelings. Many hoped that a SALT ratification fight could be postponed until after the November congressional elections. This was not a good sign. It suggested that these potential supporters would feel compelled to take a hard line on U.S.-Soviet relations, and by extension, on the SALT negotiations, for their own political survival. A few, however, believed that the sooner we could get the treaty before the Congress, the sooner the gloves would come off and the pro-SALT forces could take the offensive. I was convinced that this latter view was right.

On May 25, after saying he did not favor a direct linkage between SALT and other issues in U.S.-Soviet relations, the president said that Soviet human rights abuses and their involvement in Africa were harming the chances that a SALT agreement would be ratified. Moscow seemed unable or unwilling to grasp the political message the president was sending, or the responsibility it bore for domestic hostility toward the Soviets.

I was troubled by the continuing erosion of U.S.-Soviet relations and the prospect of a further deterioration in the coming months. I felt that I must go directly to the president. I sent him a long letter outside the regular bureaucratic channels, warning him that an intense mood of hostility toward the Soviet Union was building in the United States. This mood, I believed, arose at least in part from domestic impatience with the complexity and intractability of international problems. It was heightened by the high level of Soviet involvement in Africa and perceptions that the United States had become militarily weaker and less resolute and that the administration seemed divided and uncertain. I recommended strongly that we prepare and circulate clear guidelines on our policies and that all members of the administration use them to dispel these perceptions.

I observed that the Soviets too seemed to be increasingly disturbed by the direction of the U.S.-USSR relationship. They were displaying a deepening mood of harshness and frustration at what they saw as our inconsistency and unwillingness to deal with them as equals. They purported to believe their actions in Africa were within the bounds of acceptable competition; they felt our human rights efforts were aimed at overthrowing their system; they saw our behavior as unpredictable; and they were growing uncertain whether we still wanted a SALT Treaty. I believed that the hostility could lead to new Soviet hard-line actions to which we would be compelled to respond, imperiling our relations at a critical period when a leadership change in Moscow seemed possible in the near future. The increase in U.S.-Soviet tensions might set the tone and direction of U.S.-Soviet relations for a long time to come.

I urged the president not to accept the counsel of those who wanted to intensify the tensions for domestic political reasons or for transitory foreign policy gains. I conceded that there might be a favorable political boost in doing so in the short term, but pointed out that in the long run, the president's natural center constituency would react negatively to an intensified arms race, renewal of cold war tensions, and a diversion of resources from domestic social programs.

I suggested that the administration needed to take several steps to maintain a coherent strategy:

1. As Harold Brown was recommending, we should undertake a prudent increase in our defense spending and continue our efforts to strengthen NATO to preserve the military balance.

2. As a complement, we should conclude the SALT II Treaty to stabilize the strategic competition. I was convinced that with proper preparation and a major effort by the entire administration, the agreement would be ratified.

3. We should review the application of our human rights policies toward the Soviet Union. It was clear there was a critical point beyond which our public pressure was causing the Soviets to crack down harder on Soviet dissidents.

4. We should be careful how we managed the U.S.-PRC-USSR triangular relationship and should avoid trying to play China off against the Soviets.

5. We should accept the fact of competition with the Soviets, and we should not link Soviet behavior in the Third World to issues in which we had so fundamental an interest as SALT.

6. With respect to Soviet and Cuban activities in Africa, we should strive to deter further Soviet and Cuban adventures, using our many instruments of influence: diplomatic pressure; strengthened ties with Third World states; and increased economic and military aid to key countries.

7. In our public statements, we should project a sense of confidence and consistency, and give greater emphasis to our strengths. We held most of the cards in the East-West competition.

I recommended finally that the president give a major speech on U.S.-Soviet relations in which he would realistically describe our policy for regulating a basically competitive relationship with the Soviet Union.

I believe my advice coincided with the president's inclinations. He had said consistently and from the beginning of his administration that one of his first priorities was to improve U.S.-Soviet relations. Although he had skirted close at times, Carter had resisted the politically easy way out of linking the SALT negotiations to overall U.S.-Soviet relations or to Soviet actions in Africa. But the political pressures on him to be harder on the Soviets were intense and growing more so.

The president agreed to give a major address. He planned to deliver it at the Naval Academy commencement on June 7. I sent him a draft of a speech that emphasized the complex nature of the U.S.-Soviet relationship and the need for lowering political tensions on a reciprocal basis. Brzezinski also gave him a more confrontational draft. Carter drew from both, splitting the difference between the two poles of advice he was receiving. The end result was a stitched-together speech. Instead of combating the growing perception of an administration rent by internal divisions, the image of an inconsistent and uncertain government was underlined.

Our next talks with Gromyko took place in late May, when our relations with the Soviets were at their lowest point in several years. Gromyko and I had serious talks in New York on SALT issues, followed by stiff exchanges over African affairs. Gromyko met with the president and his senior advisers in Washington on May 27. Again, we concentrated on SALT. Almost unnoticed by the public, the Soviets made one of their most important concessions in SALT II: Gromyko agreed to accept a freeze on the number of warheads that could be deployed on existing types of ICBMs. This meant that the Soviets could deploy no more than ten warheads on each SS-18 ICBM during the term of the SALT II Treaty, rather than the twenty to thirty warheads the missile was capable of lifting. This so-called "fractionation" freeze would also apply to the SS-17 and SS-19 intercontinental missiles.

Gromyko and Carter, however, had acerbic exchanges over Africa and human rights. The president underlined Soviet and Cuban involvement in Shaba and the Horn and pointed to the fact that our information indicated Soviet personnel were directing military operations. Gromyko rejected them as "myth." The president, he said, was being given "fantastic" information. Carter was furious; he felt he was being deceived by Gromyko.

I met again with Gromyko in New York on May 31. We discussed at length the reasons for the deterioration in U.S.-Soviet relations. Gromyko began by asking about the "explosion" of anti-Soviet rhetoric in the United States and said that what Moscow feared was a return to a cold war atmosphere. I told him there were three reasons for the downturn: the Soviet arms buildup, Soviet and Cuban actions in Africa, and human rights abuses in the Soviet Union. I also said that we did not seek a return to cold war tensions, and that the most important way to get back on the track was to make progress in SALT.

Gromyko's response, particularly on Africa, was unyielding. He rejected our claims of Cuban involvement in Shaba, and adding a new entry on the list of U.S.-Soviet irritants, he strongly protested Brzezinski's briefing of the Chinese on SALT when he had been in Peking earlier that month.

In July, Gromyko and I met again, this time in Geneva. Once more, our discussions were clouded by Soviet human rights abuses. On May 30 we had canceled the proposed visit to Moscow of Joseph Califano, secretary of health, education and welfare, to protest the harsh sentence given to Yuri Orlov. Since then the Soviets had put the dissident Anatoly Shcharansky on trial and had arrested two American journalists and a businessman on trumped-up charges. I protested these actions vigorously. To underline our seriousness, the president had ordered the cancellation of visits to Moscow by two U.S. scientific delegations. Senator Jackson urged me to postpone my trip to Geneva to show our disapproval. Carter, though, had agreed with me that the Geneva SALT talks should not be delayed.

In spite of the tense mood, the foreign minister and I managed to make some further progress on the excruciatingly technical issue of limiting improvement of modernization of strategic missiles. In May, Gromyko had indicated the Soviets might accept either a flight-test and deployment ban on all new ICBMs or a ban on new ICBMs, except that each side could have one new ICBM but armed only with a single warhead. These proposals were unacceptable. Both would have blocked our new MX program and the second would have permitted the Soviets to deploy the new single-warhead ICBM they had on the drawing boards. But now in July, Gromyko revised the proposal to ban flight-testing and deployment of all new ICBMs for the treaty period, except that each side could have one exception, MIRVed or non-MIRVed, as it chose. Again the Soviets had moved toward our position.

After further interagency analysis, we decided that the United States could accept a ban on flight-testing and deployment of new ICBMs with a single exception for each side. This would allow us to go ahead with the MX as our answer to the problem of ICBM survivability, while blocking all but one of the next generation of Soviet ICBMs. We decided to give up on trying to negotiate a similar ban on new sea-launched ballistic missiles (SLBMs) with one exemption for each side. The Soviets wanted to make the Trident I SLBM, which was on the verge of deployment, our excepted missile, while theirs would be one that had still not even been flight-tested. This would have permitted them to continue their most advanced SLBM program, while ours, the Trident II, would have been prohibited. We could not agree.

The ICBM vulnerability issue arose again in the summer of 1978, this time because of our desire to ensure that the Soviets would have no basis in SALT to challenge the "multiple aim point" (MAP) basing modes we were considering for the MX. The Defense Department was analyzing various basing systems for the MX missile which depended in part on deceptive movement of the missile and cannister launcher among a large number of shelters. As an aid to our ability to monitor Soviet compliance, we had insisted on a verification rule prohibiting "deliberate concealment" activities that would make satellite observation more difficult. In addition, the emerging SALT II agreement continued the SALT I ban on the construction of new fixed missile launchers. Thus, unless we established in advance that the mobile basing schemes we had under study were consistent with the provisions of the treaty, the Soviets might have a basis to raise a legal challenge.

When Paul Warnke met with Ambassador Dobrynin in July, he had said that the mobile basing schemes the United States was considering for MX were not precluded by SALT. However, in Geneva, the chief Soviet negotiator, Ambassador Vladimir Semenov, made an ambiguous statement that suggested Soviet reservations about our position. It was decided that I should restate our position in Moscow. To demonstrate that this was not a negotiating issue, Harold Brown also made a speech in late July to the American Legion Convention, stressing that the proposed treaty would allow mobile ICBM basing schemes of the kinds we were studying.

• • •

As was his custom, Gromyko would be coming to the United States in September to attend the fall session of the UN General Assembly and he planned to visit Washington to meet with the president. I hoped that with proper preparation we might be able to repeat the progress made during Gromyko's previous visit. Carter hoped so too, and he authorized me to present a comprehensive negotiating package. This package, which Warnke described to the Soviets in a quick trip to Moscow on September 7–8, contained proposals to resolve virtually all the remaining major issues. Warnke told the Soviets we were ready for what negotiators call the "endgame," the final stage of negotiations in which the last remaining issues are resolved. He found Moscow skeptical.

The key elements of the package were: each side could test and deploy one new type of ICBM, MIRVed or non-MIRVed, during the term of the treaty (thus protecting the nascent MX program); no limits would be placed on SLBM testing and deployment (this would permit us to go ahead with the Trident II missile if we chose); there would be a freeze on the number of warheads carried on each type of existing MIRVed ICBM (which would prevent the Soviets from loading more warheads on their SS-17s, 18s, and 19s); and there would be a limit of ten warheads on the one new ICBM permitted under the new treaty (the maximum number we planned for the MX missile). The package also contained a limit of fourteen warheads on SLBMs (the maximum that Trident II could carry); a ban on mobile heavy missiles (in which we had no interest); and a number of highly technical constraints and definitions relating to cruise missiles. As to the Backfire bomber, Warnke was to make clear the political importance of a satisfactory resolution of two key issues: adequate Soviet assurances concerning the limits on its capabilities, and the rate of its production.

Our proposal for a ban on the testing and deployment of mobile launchers of heavy ICBMs was significant. There had been criticisms by SALT opponents during the hearings in the summer of 1977 that we had allowed the Soviets a unilateral right to heavy missiles. Up to September 1978, there was no prohibition against the deployment of heavy missiles on mobile launchers—only on the construction of new fixed silos for heavy missiles. Thus, had we wished, we could have retained the right under the SALT II agreement to test and deploy a heavy missile on mobile launchers. We asked the Joint Chiefs of Staff whether they wished us to protect this option in the negotiations. Their answer was that they had no interest in a mobile heavy missile for U.S. forces, but they wished us to close off this loophole to prevent the Soviets from exercising it.

On the eve of Gromyko's visit, there were modest grounds for hope that the erosion in U.S.-Soviet relations could be halted. African issues had receded, and the Soviets had taken several steps that suggested they wished to reduce the strain between us. The U.S. businessman who had been jailed was released; Jewish emigration levels rose to the highest number in five years; recent trials of Soviet dissidents ended in relatively light sentences; and restrictions on U.S. newsmen in Moscow were eased. The Soviets also indicated through various channels that they expected and would not object to our establishment of diplomatic relations with China, so long as normalization was not portrayed as a move against the Soviet Union.

The administration had also taken some positive steps. We had approved a long-stalled license for high-technology oil drilling equipment, permitted the resumption of Soviet trade visits to the United States, and had indicated that Secretary of the Treasury Michael Blumenthal would go to Moscow in December.

Gromyko and I met in New York on September 27 and 28. I told him that I was speaking on behalf of the president and myself, and that we wanted to use his visit to the United States to resolve the remaining major issues. I reminded him that he knew what our proposal was from Warnke's visit to Moscow earlier in the month. Meeting privately, with only our interpreters present, I asked him to be prepared to remain in Washington after his meeting with the president so we could make full use of this negotiating opportunity.

We reviewed the state of negotiations on the outstanding issues. It was clear that the Soviets were still disturbed by our stance on cruise missile limits. In particular, the Soviets were upset by our proposal that an allowance be made for the fact that cruise missiles follow an evasive and circuitous flight path from the launching site to the target. The allowance was so large that it would have rendered the 2,500-km range limit on air-launched cruise missiles and the 600-km limit on ground-launched cruise missiles and sea-launched cruise missiles valueless. Gromyko offered to drop the 2,500-km range limit on ACLMs if we would agree to a strict (i.e., straightline) range limit on ground (GLCM) and sea-launched (SLCM) cruise missiles.

I concluded from these preliminary discussions that Gromyko might be flexible on the remaining issues if we would meet his government's concerns on ground- and sea-launched cruise missiles. I recognized that agreeing to tighter constraints on GLCMs and SLCMs in the protocol could raise problems with our allies, but I felt they would be manageable since we had made clear to both the Soviets and our allies that any cruise missile limitations would expire with the termination date of the protocol. We had also assured our allies that upon the signing of the SALT II agreement we would make a statement to the Soviets that we would not accept further limitations on U.S. systems designed primarily for deployment in Europe—including GLCMs—without appropriate limits on comparable Soviet theater nuclear weapons systems. I therefore concluded that we could agree to the proposed Soviet GLCM and SLCM range definitions without jeopardizing our allies' security interests.

On September 28 I sent a personal message to the president from New York saying that Gromyko's proposals confirmed my assessment that the Soviets were ready to resolve most of the remaining problems and complete a SALT II agreement. I asked the president to authorize me to develop a counterproposal he could put to Gromyko in Washington. "The actual conclusion of the SALT II agreement," I wrote, "will do more to build support for SALT II in the country and reduce the political divisions on this issue within Washington than a negotiation which would continue to drag on inconclusively, and thus raise doubts among the American people and with the Soviet leadership about the importance we attach to SALT." The president approved my recommendation.

The meeting between Gromyko and Carter produced some movement. The USSR agreed to drop the range limit on air-launched cruise missiles, permitting us to test and deploy them at unlimited ranges. (Later the Soviets dropped the 2,500-km limit on testing of ground- and sea-launched cruise missiles as well.) In return, we accepted a strict definition of the 600-km range limit on GLCMs and SLCMs in the protocol of the treaty. However, the Soviets would not give us the assurances against upgrading the Backfire bomber that we had proposed and refused to specify its exact production rate. As a counter, Carter told Gromyko that the United States reserved the right to deploy an aircraft comparable to the Backfire during the term of the SALT II Treaty.

To our disappointment, Gromyko did not remain in the United States to follow up on these talks as he had the previous fall. He returned immediately to Moscow.

• • •

In late October, I went to Moscow. I told Gromyko bluntly that the Soviets had missed an opportunity to conclude a SALT Treaty. I said that the Russians did not seem to understand that Carter had made a serious attempt at the last meeting in Washington to make an agreement possible, particularly with our movement on cruise missiles. Cruise missile limits were politically and militarily difficult for us, but we had tried to meet Soviet concerns and had gone as far as we could, consistent with our security interests and those of our NATO allies. The Soviets should have understood the importance of this move, as well as our proposal of a comprehensive negotiating package.

The October Moscow talks produced little movement and resulted in a setback on the so-called "telemetry encryption" issue. The Soviets encoded some of the electronic signals from their missile tests. These signals contain information about the characteristics and performance of the missile. Our ability to collect some (but not all) of these signals or "telemetry" would be necessary for monitoring Soviet compliance with certain provisions of the treaty. Therefore, we had sought to ban encryption of telemetry which impeded our ability to verify Soviet compliance with the SALT II agreement. The issue was intertwined with the highly sensitive area (for both sides) of intelligence collection on Soviet strategic forces. Given the traditional Russian obsession with secrecy, it was psychologically and politically painful for them to agree to accept our monitoring of Soviet missile tests.

Whatever Soviet military practices might be, the United States could not accept any ambiguity regarding our right to monitor missile telemetry, which was essential if we were to verify that the Soviets were living up to their obligations. There was too much mistrust of the Soviet Union to rely on Soviet good faith. We could not defend a treaty in the Senate that depended on unverifiable Soviet compliance with an important element of the treaty. There had to be a binding agreement that the ban on deliberate concealment contained in the SALT I agreement applied to the encoding of telemetry that was relevant to the SALT II Treaty. Before I arrived in Moscow, Paul Warnke had worked out in Geneva such an understanding with Vladimir Semenov, his opposite number as the chief SALT negotiator.

Stansfield Turner, director of the CIA, was dissatisfied with the understanding Warnke had reached with Semenov. He was afraid the Soviets were agreeing to what some called "an empty set"; that is, that they were merely saying that they would not encrypt telemetry relevant to the agreement, but that they did not actually concede that *any* telemetry related to provisions of the treaty. Turner preferred an outright ban on all telemetry encryption. But we could not tell the Soviets precisely what kinds of telemetry encryption actually interfered with our ability to monitor compliance with various SALT limitations. To do so would reveal too much about our intelligence capabilities.

On the other hand, I personally was convinced that a total ban was unfeasible and in some respects undesirable. The Soviets were correct in arguing that telemetry related to missile tests included considerable data not relevant to SALT limitations, and there was no prospect, in my judgment, that the Soviet military would provide information on its strategic forces that did not relate to SALT provisions. There was also the possibility that we ourselves might wish to encrypt non-SALT-related telemetry at some future date.

Because of the concern about the understanding worked out between Semenov and Warnke, it was decided that I should raise the telemetry encryption issue directly with Gromyko. I was reluctant to do this, partly because I believed Warnke had established a satisfactory negotiating record for challenging in the Standing Consultative Commission (a permanent SALT mechanism set up in SALT I precisely to deal with such compliance issues) any subsequent encrypted telemetry we believed impeded our ability to verify compliance.

I raised the matter at my next meeting with Gromyko. I reviewed the

Semenov-Warnke understanding, pointing out that we were not seeking to ban all encoded telemetry, but only encrypted telemetry that impeded verification. Semenov, who was sitting across the table, interrupted and reneged on his understanding with Warnke. I can only assume that he had been repudiated by his superiors in Moscow. Gromyko sharply denied that telemetry had anything to do with the treaty.

The problem was that Moscow did not understand what we were proposing. Despite repeated attempts to explain that we were proposing to ban only encryption of telemetry that impeded verification, the Soviets evidently believed we were attempting to get them to agree to a vaguely worded understanding that would allow us to challenge *any* Soviet telemetry encryption. They had concluded that this was what we were in fact after, and Semenov was made to recant. The negotiating record was now clouded, and the telemetry encryption issue was wide open again.

The next morning, while I met with Brezhnev and Gromyko, Warnke met with Deputy Foreign Minister Kornyenko to underscore the critical importance of this issue to us and to put back together the earlier understanding. The discussion showed that what the Soviets wanted was an understanding that telemetry encryption was permitted *unless* it impeded verification. Both sides were groping toward the same end, except that the Soviets wanted to emphasize the permissibility of encryption, whereas we were trying to stress its restriction. It was a question now of finding precise language to bridge these two positions satisfactorily.

Before I left Moscow, I met with Brezhnev and conveyed to him Carter's personal wish for an early summit meeting. Brezhnev said that as much as he wanted to talk with the president, a summit was not possible until Gromyko and I had settled all the remaining issues on SALT.

Despite the slow progress in the September and October meetings and the continual discovery of additional technical issues, I still believed that there was a chance we could resolve most of the remaining "big" issues by the end of the year and hold a summit early in 1979. According to Dobrynin, the Soviet leadership also thought this would be possible. In Washington, we began to do some general contingency planning for a summit.

In the midst of preparations for the next SALT meeting, scheduled for late December 1978 and while I was in the Middle East, the president called me in Jerusalem. He told me that negotiations with the Chinese had been successfully concluded. He planned to make an announcement shortly that we had reached agreement with Peking to normalize relations and to receive a visit from Vice-Premier Deng at the end of January. Before I had left for the Middle East, we had agreed that if the negotiations in Peking were successful—as we were confident they would be—the announcement would be made on January 1, that is, one week after my discussions with Gromyko in Geneva.

I asked the President if it would be possible to hold up the announcement until January 1, as we had planned. While the Soviets anticipated that we would be normalizing our relations with China soon, I thought it sensible to avoid this extra distraction in Geneva. It was certain to upset the Soviets. The president replied that he was concerned that the negotiations might become unraveled and said that he would go ahead with the announcement within the next forty-eight hours. I said I would return to Washington immediately to be present for the announcement.

•   •   •

On December 15 the normalization announcement was made. With mixed feelings of hope and concern, we left for Geneva on December 20. Gromyko and I met between December 21 and 23 in Geneva. On the first day, our discussions centered on the outstanding major issues, especially telemetry encryption. I offered a draft of a common understanding that we believed reflected the essence of both sides' positions, but which began with language stressing the impermissibility of telemetry encryption whenever it got in the way of verification. Gromyko countered with language that stressed the right of each party to use telemetry encryption "provided that" it did not deliberately interfere with verification.

Gromyko wanted to remand the two proposals to the expert level for resolution. I opposed this because I was concerned that the issue would then drag on indefinitely. I wanted to crack this nut then and there. I told him I wanted to reflect on the issue overnight and would return to it the next day.

Later in the afternoon, when Gromyko raised for the first time in the negotiations the question of including remote pilotless vehicles (drones) in the treaty, my colleagues and I became uneasy. This was clearly a red herring, as these slow-flying reconnaissance vehicles were not a potential military threat. The very fact that they had not been mentioned before indicated the triviality of the matter. On the way back to the hotel from the meeting, Ralph Earle, Paul Warnke's successor, noted presciently that the incident might mark the beginning of an effort to drag out the negotiations.

December 22 was difficult. Gromyko's businesslike demeanor had changed; he was testy and showed none of his customary sardonic wit. He began our 10 A.M. session in the U.S. delegation building by reviewing in exhaustive detail a host of issues we had considered secondary and technical, best handled at the expert level. Then, when we had gathered again in the afternoon at the Soviet mission, Gromyko turned to the reason for his stiffness. It was China. As the Soviet leaders had been telling us for some time, he remarked, Moscow was not opposed to the establishment of full diplomatic relations between China and the United States. They were angered, however, by a reference in the U.S.-PRC joint communiqué to mutual opposition to "hegemony." ("Hegemony" is a Chinese code word for describing Soviet global ambitions.) He was also angry about the announcement of normalization "at this time," just as he and I were about to conclude a SALT Treaty and arrange a U.S.-Soviet summit. The foreign minister asked me to tell the president that, "In the view of the Soviet leadership all this resembled some sort of political game on the broadest possible scale."

I replied that the president had repeatedly told the Soviet leadership that one of his central goals was to improve relations between the United States and the Soviet Union. I reiterated the president's personal assurance that normalization with the PRC was not aimed at the Soviet Union or anyone else. We did not intend to change our policy of refusing to sell weapons to either China or the Soviet Union, and we would be even-handed regarding the transfer of nonmilitary technology to the Soviet Union or China. For the moment, this ended the discussion of China.

Gromyko's lecture on China was not unexpected, but the emphasis he put on *how* normalization was taking place was troubling. The Soviets felt that the timing and the characterization of normalization were deliberately provocative and intended to be publicly perceived as such. On SALT III, we made some progress and appeared to be on the verge of resolving the telemetry encryption issue. At noon that day, Ralph Earle had given Ambassador Victor P. Karpov, chief of the Soviet delegation, suggested compromise language on telemetry encryption. I asked Gromyko for his reaction to our language. After a brief recess he said that with the addition of a phrase emphasizing the right to encrypt telemetry whenever it did not impede verification, the Soviets could accept the new language we had proposed.

I sent the text of the proposed understanding back to Washington that night with a request that I be authorized to resolve the issue on the basis of the compromise language. I felt we were about to break the back of the single biggest issue remaining.

Reports from Washington reflected optimism. Preparations were being made for a possible announcement the next evening that agreement had been reached on all significant remaining SALT issues, and that a Carter-Brezhnev summit would take place early in 1979. In our own contacts with reporters in Geneva we tried to curb any excessive optimism, but press reports from Washington reflected high-level back-grounding that agreement was near.

The morning of December 23, I received from Washington the response to my request for further instructions on the issue of telemetry. It was relayed to me by Brzezinski at the meeting site in the Soviet Embassy on an open telephone line. Apparently a heated debate had gone on through much of the night, with Turner finally and reluctantly agreeing to the compromise language—though with a stipulation. I was instructed to inform Gromyko that telemetry encryption as practiced in certain recent Soviet missile tests would violate the ban on deliberate concealment. Still, because it might reveal too much about our own intelligence capabilities, I could not explain what it was that was objectionable. Moreover, I was instructed to inform Gromyko that the president would reiterate this statement to Brezhnev at the summit. We were now demanding that the Soviets accept a compromise that would give us the right to challenge telemetry encryption under the treaty. We were also insisting that the Soviets concede, even before the treaty was in force, that past encryption practices would be in violation of it. Gromyko refused to respond to my statement.

By the time the Geneva talks ended we were close enough that I could tell the press we had agreed in principle to a summit. But because the Soviets had raised the secondary issues on December 22, and because of my statement on telemetry encryption on the twenty-third, we were far enough apart for Gromyko to state that there were still too many issues to resolve to set a date. Once again agreement had eluded us.

· · ·

The Geneva talks, because there had been reason to believe beforehand that we were close to agreement, raise difficult questions. Why did Gromyko toughen the Soviet position in Geneva, and why did it take another six months of almost weekly negotiating sessions with Dobrynin in Washington to settle the remaining issues?

I think that those of us at the political levels on both sides failed to appreciate how difficult and politically sensitive the so-called secondary issues would be, particularly in the incredibly complex area of cruise missiles.

Also, because of the erosion of U.S.-Soviet relations and the looming domestic political struggle over the SALT Treaty, virtually every remaining issue, however technical or abstruse, had to be considered by the Special Coordinating Committee and often by the president himself. Adjustments in the U.S. position had to be weighed in terms of how we could defend it against claims that what was in fact a rational negotiating compromise was a political "concession," made for the sake of getting a treaty.

The sudden surge of Soviet inflexibility in the winter of 1978–79 was due primarily to developments relating to China. It was not the substance of normalization, but the manner and timing of the announcement. The use of anti-Soviet code words such as "hegemony" in the language of the U.S./PRC communiqué, as well as some of the backgrounding of the press, stimulated visceral Soviet fears of a de facto U.S.-PRC alliance.

Soviet suspicions were exacerbated by stories in the Washington press at the beginning of the December Geneva talks which reported Gromyko had suggested we were planning a Carter-Brezhnev summit in mid-January—that is to say, about two weeks before Deng was to make a historic visit to the United States. It was unlikely that the Soviets would agree to a U.S.-Soviet summit that would be upstaged, and they were predictably upset that we seemed to be taking for granted that Brezhnev would allow himself to be fitted into our schedule. Almost certainly, one of the main reasons Gromyko uncharacteristically raised the secondary issues at Geneva was to make sure that the negotiations would go on long enough to cause a considerable delay between Deng's visit and Brezhnev's attendance at a summit.

I do not believe that the completion of normalization of relations with China and the concluding of a SALT Treaty at about the same time was unwise or unfeasible, from either an international or domestic political standpoint. To the contrary, I believe that accomplishing these two fundamental objectives in close juxtaposition could have greatly strengthened both foreign and domestic perceptions that the administration was managing a balanced and stable triangular relationship among the United States, the PRC, and the Soviet Union. The problem arose from announcing normalization on the eve of a critical SALT meeting and the backgrounding which accompanied it.

NORMALIZATION WITH CHINA: COMPLETING THE PROCESS

For the first few months of 1978, Harold, Zbig, and I focused on defining administration policy on the transfer to China of advanced "dual-use" equipment and technology which could have either civilian or military uses. We also continued to discuss what the U.S. attitude should be regarding the sale of arms by our allies to China.

Because many allied weapons systems contained American parts or technology, and because the major Western powers had agreed to cooperate through a Western consultative committee ("COCOM") in controlling the sale of weapons and defense-related technology to Communist countries, our approval would be sought in the case of virtually any significant proposed Western transfer. The long-standing prohibition on the sale of U.S. arms to the PRC had been reaffirmed by the president in 1977. However, the question of whether we would encourage, tolerate, or discourage allied weapons transfers to China remained unsettled at the highest levels of the administration, and debate on it intensified as U.S.-Soviet relations worsened. The same was true of the gray area of dual-use technology. Discussions of these issues were carried on in great secrecy, with the assistance of only a few key aides.

The issue of allied arms sales to the PRC had become active in early 1978. The British and the French were contemplating sales to Peking and were probing our attitude. Because of increasing disagreement within the administration over how to respond to Soviet activities in Third World countries, the allies had become uncertain about our position, and suspected that we might be prepared to relax American opposition to such sales.

My view was that we should be neutral, and certainly we should not encourage allied arms sales. The declared administration policy opposed the transfer of U.S. military equipment to China. However, my argument did not prevail with the president. In January 1978, in a meeting with President Giscard d'Estaing, Carter said that while we would not try to influence French decisions, we would not be concerned if they went ahead. I was worried that the French, as well as the British and other allies, would interpret the president's remarks as signaling a "benevolent" attitude on allied arms sales to the PRC. The allies wanted our support against what would be a sharp Soviet reaction to any major weapons sales to China, as well as criticism from within their own countries for exacerbating East-West tensions.

We were then in the midst of a highly sensitive review of administration policy on the sale of dual-use equipment and technology to the PRC. I was concerned that we continue the existing policy, begun by the previous administration, of evenhandedness in considering requests for sophisticated dual-use equipment or technology. Under this policy, we applied both to China and Russia equally strict restraints on the transfer of any high-technology items that could be used for military purposes.

Brown and Brzezinski wanted, in varying degrees, a stronger security component in the evolving relationship with Peking. I thought we should continue to consider requests for transfers on a case-by-case basis, and avoid any tilt toward China. If we abandoned or relaxed our policy of evenhandedness, we would jeopardize our long-term interests in developing more stable and predictable relationships with both Moscow and Peking.

●   ●   ●

At the beginning of 1978, along with the discussions of U.S. policy on arms sales and technology transfers, we had begun work on a strategy for normalizing relations with China. In March the president told me that he wanted either the vice-president or Brzezinski to go to Peking soon, and that I should go to Moscow. Since at least the end of 1977, Zbig had been seeking permission to go to China. I was opposed to the trip on several grounds, the most important of which was my concern that such a highly publicized trip would bring into sharp relief the question of who spoke for the administration on foreign policy. As I have said, I felt very strongly that there could only be two spokesmen, the president and the secretary of state. I was also concerned that Zbig might get into the issue of normalization before we had finished formulating a detailed position and had consulted Congress adequately. Timing was crucial, and the issue was filled with nuance and complexities that it would have been premature to address.

Zbig, very anxious to make the trip, agreed to limit himself to a statement confirming that Leonard Woodcock would begin making our normalization proposal in the month of June and that the president "was serious" about normalization.

Mondale, who hoped to go to China himself, also opposed Zbig's trip. But Carter overruled us and sent Brzezinski to Peking. (Later, in August 1979, Mondale was to make one of the most important and successful trips ever made by an American official to China.)

With the ratification of the Panama Canal Treaties in March and April, I concluded that it was time to set the normalization process in motion. In early May, I sent a memorandum to the president outlining a negotiating plan that would lead to agreement with the Chinese by the end of the year. Since this memorandum was to form the basis of the administration's normalization strategy, I had asked Brown and Brzezinski to join me in sending it to the president. The president, then, could be assured that his three principal foreign policy and national security aides were in agreement on what might well be one of the most politically difficult steps he could take.

Because of the importance of the May 10 memorandum for the events that follow, I will summarize the key points:

• *U.S. terms for normalization.* We were prepared to "close down our embassy in Taipei, terminate the U.S.-ROC [Republic of China] mutual defense treaty, and withdraw our remaining military personnel and installation." We would insist on continuing selective arms sales to Taiwan for defensive purposes, terminate all official relations with Taiwan, and remove all U.S. government representation; we would insist that we retain economic, cultural, and other unofficial ties with Taipei, and would also publicly reaffirm the American interest in a peaceful resolution of the Taiwan issue.

• *Negotiating scenario.* We proposed to the president that if he decided to move ahead, Brzezinski would tell the Chinese during his trip to Peking that Ambassador Leonard Woodcock, the chief of our liaison office in Peking, would begin in June a series of presentations that would outline the formal American position. If the Chinese responded favorably, Woodcock would begin negotiations during the summer. In addition to presenting the U.S. terms for normalization, Woodcock would also discuss the mode and timing of a joint communiqué establishing diplomatic ties, the necessary legislation for implementing the arrangement, and the visit of a very high Chinese official to Washington at or shortly after the announcement of normalization.

• *Balancing SALT*. We did not believe normalization should be delayed until the SALT II Treaty was concluded. In fact, as far as Congress was concerned, our judgment was that normalization could strengthen our hand in securing ratification of SALT II. However, we did not want SALT and normalization to come to Congress at the same time, for this would greatly overload the political circuits and strain the administration's ability to guide these two great issues safely through public and congressional debate. At that time we considered it too early to foresee which would be concluded first.

• *Impact on Asia*. Although recognizing that the move would be a shock to Taiwan, we believed Taipei had the political and economic strength to adjust. We expected that the long-term impact of normalization on the political and economic situation in the region, as well as the military balance, would be beneficial.

We concluded by recommending a prompt effort to complete the normalization process, although we warned that because of our firm position on Taiwan, success in the negotiations could not be guaranteed.

The president approved our negotiating strategy and told Brzezinski and me to bring into the Washington end of the negotiations one aide each. I chose Dick Holbrooke and, as with all other matters, I kept Warren Christopher fully informed. Zbig chose Michel Oksenberg, his China expert on the NSC staff. Later Vice-President Mondale joined the small group. This tight compartmentalization was successful in preventing leaks.

Although Brzezinski followed his instructions in the private talks with the Chinese in May, he made provocative remarks in public about Soviet international actions. In general, he allowed his trip to be characterized as a deliberate countermove by the United States at a time of worsening relations with Moscow over the Horn of Africa and other issues. This disturbed me. Along with my most senior and experienced advisers, I was convinced that loose talk about "playing the China card," always a dangerous ploy, was a particularly risky move at a time when we were at a sensitive point in the SALT negotiations. Further, we were also at that time seeking a measure of Soviet cooperation and restraint in protecting Somalia from the consequences of its invasion of the Ogaden.

On June 13, I sent Woodcock's detailed negotiating instructions to the president for approval. I recommended to him that SALT and the normalization process be handled so that Congress would act on normalization first in early 1979. I stressed the fundamental importance of advance consultations with Japan and Taiwan and with the top congressional leadership before it was announced.

In July, Woodcock began the secret negotiations with the Chinese. To lessen the risk of leaks, all messages to and from Woodcock were sent in special communications channels controlled by the White House rather than through the usual State Department facilities. Ironically, as it turned out, the idea of using the special White House channel was Holbrooke's and mine. We had agreed that a single copy of all traffic through this channel would be sent immediately to my office in a sealed envelope; it would be brought at once to my attention or, in my absence, to Warren Christopher, and in his absence, to Dick Holbrooke.

The decision to use Woodcock as negotiator instead of undertaking highly publicized shuttle diplomacy proved a sound one. Shuttle diplomacy would have received so much attention, every nuance being examined for signs of progress or setback, that it would have inevitably invited strong opposition to normalization before the Chinese had had a chance to react. The Chinese decision-making process is a methodical, careful one, which requires extensive consultations among the leadership after each proposal. Trips by senior American officials, bathed in the glare of publicity, would not have left the Chinese enough time to go through the difficult process of adjusting their positions.

In Woodcock we had an outstanding ambassador. Although he had no previous international experience until Carter had asked him to head a special mission to Hanoi to discuss American servicemen missing in action, Woodcock drew on his extensive experience as the president of the United Automobile Workers of America and proved an instinctive and brilliant diplomat. He had a photographic memory, discretion, and a verbal precision critical in these negotiations. We all came to rely on his wisdom. I have long been in favor of using ambassadors in place to conduct negotiations whenever possible, rather than relying on pyrotechnics and acrobatics. In this case, Woodcock proved to be the ideal ambassador/negotiator.

Woodcock completed the preliminary negotiations by late October, and in early November we sent the Chinese the draft of a joint communiqué announcing the establishment of diplomatic relations. The Chinese asked for clarification of several points. At virtually the same time, on November 6, we announced that we would offer to sell F-5E interceptor aircraft and munitions to Taiwan, but would not approve Taipei's request for more advanced aircraft that could attack the mainland. This was a clear demonstration to both Taipei and Peking that we meant what we said about supplying defensive weapons to Taiwan.

We felt that the Chinese were prepared to face the "realities" on the Taiwan question. At the same time, the president decided that we would not object to a French sale to China of a nuclear reactor that contained significant U.S. technology, subject to satisfactory assurances on peaceful uses and controls over the retransfer of technology to other countries. Positive signals on both sides were thus exchanged.

On December 4, Woodcock met Chinese foreign ministry officials again to respond to questions Peking had raised about our position. At that meeting, the Chinese said that Deng wished to meet Woodcock soon. When I received this message I had a feeling in my bones the Chinese had decided to meet our essential terms. A historic breakthrough was near. We authorized Woodcock to propose January 1 for the joint announcement of normalization. As I have indicated, I had wanted the announcement of normalization to come after my Geneva meeting with Gromyko.

On December 13 Woodcock had a decisive meeting with Deng. Vice-Premier Deng indicated that the PRC was prepared to conclude the negotiations on terms acceptable to us. The deal was set, almost to the letter of our May memorandum to the president.

When Woodcock's report of the critical December 13 meeting arrived, I was in the Middle East. I had gone there reluctantly, at the president's request, to try to push the Israelis and Egyptians into meeting the December 17 goal that had been set at Camp David for the conclusion of a peace treaty. Holbrooke had urged me to remain in Washington during the critical final days of the Woodcock negotiations, but I could not refuse the president's personal request to try to keep the Middle East process on schedule.

Before I left, I had a final meeting in my office with Christopher, Holbrooke, Brzezinski, and Oksenberg to go over Woodcock's instructions for the crucial December 13 meeting. During that session, we also had an intense debate about whether we were at this point required under a sense of the Senate resolution, which had just passed by an overwhelming vote, to consult with Congress in secret about the negotiations in Peking. Supported by Christopher and Holbrooke, I argued that although the Senate resolution was not legally binding, we would be risking a political backlash if we did not consult Congress, given the advanced stage of the negotiations. Brzezinski and Oksenberg argued the contrary, and the president subsequently sided with them. I regret to this day the failure to talk to Congress. I believe the leadership would have respected our confidence. In any case, the risk of offending the Congress exceeded the risk of leaks in this delicate process. The backlash that did come affected the debate during the long process of enacting the necessary implementing legislation.

I was not at that point overly concerned about leaving Washington, for I assumed then that there would be more than two weeks to take critical preparatory steps after I got back. It was then that the president called me in Jerusalem to say we had an agreement, and to my surprise told me that he wanted to move the date of the announcement up to December 15.

This news came as a shock. At a critical moment, Brzezinski had blacked Christopher and Holbrooke out of the decision making for about six hours, and they had been unable to inform me of what was taking place.

I arrived in Washington the afternoon of December 15 just in time to rush to the White House for the announcement. As we had feared, several key members of Congress, including critically important ones, such as Frank Church, John Glenn, Jacob Javits, Howard Baker, and Clem Zablocki, were irritated by the lack of consultations and by the fact that they had been called to the White House one hour before the announcement to be informed, not consulted.

However, everyone was caught up in the drama of the event. The day was chaotic, as we attempted to manage the proceedings on short notice. But the muddle typical of such occasions was unimportant. A historic step was being taken for which we had been preparing the groundwork for two years. It will remain one of the enduring achievements of the Carter years.

7

STEERING A BALANCED COURSE

CHINA

MY GREATEST CONCERN after the December 15 announcement of the beginning of diplomatic relations between the United States and the People's Republic of China on January 1, 1979, was that the administration keep a sense of proportion and realism and avoid exaggerating the possibilities of mutual opposition to the Soviet Union.

Right after the announcement, Moscow stressed to us and to key NATO allies its profound concern about any sales of Western arms to China. I believed their apprehensions were genuine, not simply a tactic to divide us from our allies. The president agreed to make clear to the Soviets, and also to Callaghan, Giscard d'Estaing, and Schmidt at the January 6 four-power summit in Guadeloupe, that we intended to pursue our interests with China in a positive way, and not as an anti-Soviet gambit. However, our "hands off" stance on the sale of defensive weapons by the allies, reaffirmed in internal debates in November and widely reported in the press, tended to offset these assurances. The Soviets feared a tacit NATO-PRC encirclement.

At State we believed that Deng would use his January visit, which would be a media event, to try to influence us to take a harder public line against the Soviets. Both we and the Chinese were concerned about the growing ties between Moscow and Hanoi—a Soviet-Vietnamese "friendship treaty" had been signed on November 3—and the risks of a major confrontation sparked by Vietnam's widening conflict with Cambodia and the genocidal Pol Pot regime. In a sense, the roles of 1977 and 1978 were being reversed; now it was the Chinese who wanted to play the "American card" as a counterweight to Soviet influence in Vietnam. I strongly recommended to the president that he make it clear to Deng that we would not permit any disruption of our policy toward the Soviet Union.

Carter was well aware of the pitfalls. Even before he arrived in the United States, Deng was calling for greater Sino-American efforts to oppose the Soviet Union and was issuing warnings to Vietnam. The president told me to inform the Soviets that we were discouraging the Chinese from attacking Vietnam. Holbrooke had met several times with the Chinese ambassador to discuss the escalating tensions in Southeast Asia and to make clear our opposition to a conflict between Peking and Hanoi. The Chinese continued to tell us they could not show restraint much longer. At the same time, we were warning Moscow not to exploit the situation to obtain military or naval bases in Vietnam.

Deng's visit was an extravaganza, and understandably so. It symbolized the attainment of one of our fundamental goals. Normalization of relations with the PRC with the full support of our friends in Japan, ASEAN (Association of Southeast Asian Nations) and ANZUS (Australia, New Zealand, and the United States) had opened a new chapter in American policy to promote stability in Asia and to overcome the debilitating legacy of the Vietnam War and the "Nixon shock" of 1972. In my view we had accomplished normalization in a way that met all of our objectives.

● ● ●

The euphoria of normalization and the Deng visit was marred by the vice-premier's insistence on publicly opposing our policy toward the Soviet Union, which the president described to him in talks in the White House. His public anti-Soviet statements questioned the value of the SALT agreement and threatened Vietnam. The threats were real. On February 17, anxious, as Deng put it, to "teach Hanoi a lesson," China launched a substantial border attack in northern Vietnam. Inevitably, Moscow interpreted the attack, coming on the heels of Deng's visit to the United States, as having received at least our tacit blessing.

The Chinese immediately informed us the "pedagogical war" was a limited action that would last only two weeks or so. They professed to be unconcerned about the Soviet reaction, believing that at most the Soviets might provoke incidents on the Sino-Soviet border.

We convened the Special Coordinating Committee on February 19 to discuss our policy on the conflict. The president approved our recommendations, including steps to minimize the effects of the war on our relations with both China and the Soviet Union, to secure the withdrawal of China from Vietnam and Vietnam from Cambodia, and to deter the Soviets from escalating the conflict. I met with Dobrynin on February 24 to caution the Soviets about becoming militarily involved or stationing military or naval units in Vietnam. Dobrynin refused to rule out the possibility of Soviet assistance to Vietnam if China did not soon desist. He also made clear that many in Moscow believed "our anti-Soviet, pro-China attitude" had encouraged Peking to attack.

In this tense atmosphere, when American calm and prudence were essential to avoid any misinterpretation by Peking that we supported their adventure or by Moscow that we were colluding with the Chinese, we in the State Department were told by reporters that they were being briefed in the White House about a Soviet buildup taking place on the Sino-Soviet border. In fact, we had no such evidence, and I told the president that there was no extraordinary military movement on the Soviet side of the border.

Fortunately, the Chinese withdrew as they had said they would. However, large Chinese and Vietnamese forces continued to confront each other across the border, and tensions remained high.

VIETNAM

One of the great inhibitions on our ability to offset Soviet influence in Southeast Asia was the lack of an American diplomatic presence in Hanoi. Early in the administration, we had agreed that we would be prepared to establish normal relations with Vietnam. I felt that normal diplomatic relations with Hanoi, strongly supported by our Asian friends, could increase our influence with Vietnam and offer it alternatives to excessive political, economic, and military dependence on the Soviet Union or China. During the Paris peace talks, the Vietnamese often spoke wistfully about being free to have normal relations with the United States, thus freeing them from this dependence, once the war was over.

Hopes of early progress were blocked by Vietnamese preconditions that had been advanced in talks with Holbrooke in the summer of 1977, especially the demand that the United States provide economic assistance as a matter of obligation, "reparations." We refused to discuss normalization on that basis and contacts languished until the summer of 1978, when we received indications that Hanoi was prepared to talk without reference to reparations. In September 1978, in a meeting with Holbrooke in New York, Vietnamese Vice-Foreign Minister Nguyen Co Thach dropped all the Vietnamese preconditions. Political conditions in late 1978, however, were considerably different from early 1977. Intelligence reports indicated that Vietnam was preparing for a massive invasion of Cambodia. Moreover, the boat people, refugees deliberately and callously encouraged by Hanoi, were streaming into the South China Sea, adding a new dimension to the massive human tragedy of the Vietnamese people. Vietnamese apprehensions over China's intentions were growing, and in November 1978 Hanoi signed a friendship treaty with Moscow. This doomed the hope of normalization. The president agreed that we should not respond to the Vietnamese, even when they approached us again in December. How different events might have been if the Vietnamese had taken a less intransigent position in 1977. Thousands of lives might have been saved, and the course of history in Southeast Asia radically changed.

Political considerations at the beginning of 1979 were obviously against renewed contact with Hanoi. However, while diplomatic relations with Hanoi were impossible under existing circumstances, I believed that direct discussions with Vietnamese representatives in New York could still serve our interests in deterring an attack on Thailand, where Cambodian guerrillas had taken refuge, and in reducing Hanoi's dependence on the Soviet Union. We had had no dialogue with the Vietnamese since Holbrooke's talks in New York in September 1978. Our allies in ASEAN and ANZUS, as well as Japan, were intensely concerned about the reestablishment of greater stability in Southeast Asia and were looking to us to play a leading role. They were concerned that in our preoccupation with China, we were allowing our Asian policy to become skewed, that we were failing to play our natural role, one that could counterbalance the influence of both Communist giants and offer an alternative source of political, diplomatic, and economic support to all of the states of the region, including Vietnam. They feared the consequences of renewed Sino-Vietnamese hostility, possibly with direct Soviet military involvement.

In May 1979, after the situation in Southeast Asia had calmed somewhat, I recommended to the president that we reopen communications with Vietnam through their UN delegation in New York. My aim was to warn Hanoi to act with restraint in Southeast Asia, especially regarding Thailand, and to caution them about the long-term implications of the growing Soviet military presence in Vietnam.

On May 30, Carter authorized the resumption of quiet talks with Vietnamese representatives. The talks began in July between Robert Oakley, Holbrooke's senior deputy, and Ambassador Ha Van Lau, the Vietnamese permanent representative to the UN. I had known Ambassador Lau from the Paris peace talks in 1968–69. He was a tough, able, and skillful negotiator with extensive experience, and I respected him. Lau told us the Vietnamese still wanted to establish normal relations with us and that they blamed China for all the tensions in Southeast Asia. We responded that normalization was impossible while they were invading Cambodia and threatening other neighboring countries. In August, in a public relations ploy, the Vietnamese told the press that we were conducting secret negotiations. In response, I authorized a statement that the normalization talks had been halted by Hanoi's attack on Cambodia and could not proceed under existing circumstances. Hanoi was made to understand that we meant to stand by Thailand, but the chance for normalization was dead for the time.

CAMBODIA

There are times when your obligations as a senior government official force you to take a position which, although essential for our national interests, is at the same time extremely distasteful. Fortunately, such dilemmas are rare, but when they arise they are wrenching, even when there is little choice in the matter.

This was especially true in 1979 when the United Nations struggled with the question of which of two rival delegations to accredit as the Cambodian (or Kampuchean) representative to the UN.

One claimant was the People's Republic of Kampuchea (PRK), the government headed by Heng Samrin and installed by the Vietnamese during their December 1978 invasion of Cambodia, and backed by the Soviet Union. The other claimant to the seat was the regime ousted from the capital of Phnom Penh by the Vietnamese, Democratic Kampuchea (DK). It was supported by the PRC.

Choosing between these two regimes was not the sort of decision which on its face seemed to matter much to the United States. Both claimants had fought against the United States only a few years earlier. One regime, sponsored by Hanoi, was imposed by external force and would undoubtedly conduct itself with ruthlessness. The other, headed by the notorious Pol Pot, had earned a unique place in the annals of terror. Estimates ranged as high as two million Cambodians killed by Pol Pot and his Khmer Rouge army since they had taken over the country in the spring of 1975.

From intelligence, we knew that the Vietnamese, striking at Phnom Penh in late December of 1978, had succeeded easily in taking the capital city and the other major towns. They had, however, failed to destroy the Khmer Rouge military structure or capture its leadership. And the internationally recognized symbol of the Cambodian state, Prince Norodom Sihanouk, had slipped out of his confinement in a villa in Phnom Penh just ahead of the Vietnamese and reappeared dramatically in Peking.

The first challenge to the DK seat came almost immediately in the Security Council. With Sihanouk making a dramatic reappearance on the world scene to denounce the Vietnamese invasion of his homeland, the issue was deferred until the fall and placed on the agenda of the General Assembly.

The battle lines were now being drawn for a significant test of alliances and friendships throughout the world. On one side were the Vietnamese, the Soviet Union and its allies, Cuba, and a few other countries. On the other side were China and, most important to us, the five countries that form the Association of Southeast Asian Nations (ASEAN).

The five ASEAN nations—Indonesia, Malaysia, the Philippines, Thailand, and Singapore—in 1967 had formed an economic organization that by the mid-1970s had begun to show effectiveness in both economic and political areas. In the 1970s, ASEAN had achieved the highest sustained real growth rate of any region outside the oil states of the Mideast, and a relative political stability had settled over the area. Once regarded as the fragile dominoes that would topple one by one if the United States lost in Vietnam, the five ASEAN states had survived the traumatic events of 1975 and greatly strengthened their political cooperation. The Carter administration had reversed the previous policy of ignoring ASEAN and dealing with its members only on a bilateral state-to-state basis; I had chaired the first significant U.S.-ASEAN discussions in August of 1978 in Washington, which fourteen ASEAN ministers from all five countries had attended.

One of the building blocks of our post-Vietnam policy, not only in East Asia but throughout the world, was support of regional economic or political organizations that could bear an increasing role in maintaining stability in the world. New regional security arrangements along the lines of SEATO (which was formally disbanded in July 1977) and CENTO were unlikely, given the mood in the United States after Vietnam, but we felt that we could gain substantial support for a policy in which we supported and encouraged—but did not necessarily join—the regional organizations. ASEAN was perhaps the outstanding example of such an organization. And our change of policy had been greatly appreciated in the region, although fears of a post-Vietnam American retreat from the Pacific persisted.

As Sino-American relations flourished, we also recognized that our old friends in Southeast Asia, with their long-standing fear of being dominated by their giant neighbor, would be greatly concerned if we did not attempt to match Sino-American progress with special attention to their concerns. Now, in 1979, with the Vietnamese Army for the first time on the border of Thailand, with Pol Pot's remaining forces scattered in the countryside, ASEAN came to us and asked for our support in three critical ways.

Two forms of material support were immediately forthcoming. We had already been increasing aid to most of the ASEAN states, especially Thailand. Now we again accelerated our military assistance to the latter. Second, we also led a massive international rescue and refugee resettlement effort to save the beleaguered peoples of Indochina fleeing the chaos of the area. Some, setting out from Vietnam in small and often unseaworthy ships, threatened to swamp the resources of the ASEAN nations onto whose shores they drifted; but these now-famous "boat people," who caused crises in Malaysia, Thailand, Singapore, and Indonesia, were only part of the problem; an even larger number of Laotians and Cambodians were fleeing by land into Thailand. "Our house is full," the Bangkok government pleaded in official statements, and turned to us for help.

I am proud that our nation responded as it did. During the Tokyo Economic Summit in June 1979, President Carter authorized us to double our intake of Indochina refugees to 17,000 per month—an annual total of 168,000. A month later, Vice-President Mondale led our delegation—and the world—in a historic conference in Geneva that, I believe, forced changes in Vietnamese policy, saving countless lives and forcing open the doors of other countries to larger resettlement efforts. Mondale's moving speech in Geneva brought tears to the eyes of many in the audience; the policy he outlined that day will long stand as one of the most significant acts of the Carter administration.

The third ASEAN request was quite different. Recognizing clearly the odious nature of the DK regime, the ASEAN nations nonetheless asked us to join them in supporting the DK claim to continue to occupy the Cambodian seat at the UN, even though by now the DK was reduced to a 30,000-man guerrilla force struggling for survival against a 200,000-man Vietnamese Army.

We faced a difficult choice. We were being asked to vote for the continued seating in the UN of one of history's most barbaric regimes, one that had fought us and that now controlled none of the cities of Cambodia. Yet there were compelling reasons to consider the vote carefully. ASEAN had the full support of Japan, Australia, New Zealand, and China, which, of course, saw Hanoi as Moscow's surrogate in Southeast Asia. A majority of the European Community, including both France and the United Kingdom, was prepared to back ASEAN unless we broke ranks.

From Bangkok, our brilliant ambassador, Morton Abramowitz, who had played such a vital role in refugee policy, argued the strategic consequences of not siding with ASEAN. From Peking, Leonard Woodcock, a humane and wise man, came down on the same side. Dick Holbrooke, collecting views from the entire region, concluded that a vote not to seat the DK would gain us nothing and cost us much. It would isolate us from our friends, and appear to legitimize a forcible takeover of one country by another.

Other voices were heard. Patricia Derian, representing the human rights viewpoint, argued passionately for a strong vote against Pol Pot. Several junior officers expressed their concern, as did Don McHenry in his first General Assembly session as our permanent representative to the United Nations. And on the day before the vote, McHenry and Tony Lake forwarded to me in the DISSENT channel * an eloquent cable from a junior officer at the U.S. Mission to the UN arguing that a vote by the United States in favor of the DK retaining the Cambodian seat was inconsistent with American values.

I had weighed the pros and cons of this issue for weeks. Days before

---

* The uncensored DISSENT channel was established to allow officers to present to the secretary of state objections to policy, whatever the view of their superiors might be.

the final vote, I had come to the conclusion that, unpleasant as it was to contemplate voting, even implicitly, for the Khmer Rouge, we could not afford the far-reaching consequences of a vote that would isolate us from all of ASEAN, Japan, China, our ANZUS treaty partners, and most of our European allies, and put us in a *losing* minority with Moscow, Hanoi, and Havana. I had instructed McHenry to make sure that in all his statements he stress our total opposition to seeing the DK ever return to power in Phnom Penh; our vote would also be explained on "narrow technical grounds," the "superior claim" of the DK. I declined to cosponsor or lobby for the ASEAN resolution, but told my ASEAN colleagues in a series of private meetings that we would not let them down. The Chinese, still emotionally committed to the Khmer Rouge, were upset at our insistence on criticizing the DK even while voting for them.

The evening before the vote, I called Holbrooke up to my office for one last review of the issue. I had long since made up my mind, but my own distaste with the course I felt necessary had been focused by the DISSENT channel cable from New York. I knew, of course, that many whose support was important to us would not understand the vote, even after explanations.

We went over the ground once more, and then, with night settling in over Washington, I called Don in New York and repeated my instructions. We made the only decision consistent with our overall national interests, although, as expected, the vote soon became a subject of criticism from both the Left and the Right.

KOREA

Almost every administration in the last generation has had, in one form or another, a "Korea problem." We were no exception. The anachronistic cold war stalemate along the 38th parallel, and the continuing face-off between heavily armed North Korean troops and American forces combined with South Koreans, has been a troubling reminder that in some places in the world, we must live at all times with potential flash points.

Our Korean problem was partly inherited, partly self-inflicted. Inherited was the legacy of bitterness, political scandal, and congressional backlash arising out of the so-called Koreagate affair—a seamy saga of influence-peddling by some Koreans that involved a few members of Congress in the mid-1970s. The bad taste that this left whenever votes on security assistance to Korea came up was a major problem for us as we constructed a policy toward the perennially embattled peninsula.

Then there was the human rights situation, a subject that always arose when Korea was discussed. While the situation in the south fell far short of what most of us felt was desirable, we constantly had to weigh the fact that only thirty-five miles to the north of Seoul was a nation in which control of the population was absolute and freedom nonexistent. The contrast could not be ignored, and although some critics felt that we were not vigorous enough in advocacy of human rights in South Korea, I felt that a careful balance was essential, and made sure that it was maintained.

Against this background came a serious difficulty immediately upon inauguration. During the campaign Governor Carter had said that he wanted to withdraw American combat troops from Korea if he was elected. Upon his election, he reaffirmed this objective in one of his first press conferences. Americans paid his comments little attention. Asians reacted in shock.

To them, coming on the heels of Cambodia and Vietnam and the withdrawal by the Ford administration of our remaining troops from Thailand, Carter's policy seemed to signal the beginning of a final with-drawal from East Asia. Although this was not the case—in fact, our strategic position was to be strengthened substantially throughout the region during the Carter years—the Asian reaction was understandable, for nothing had been done either to prepare them for this position or to take their concerns into account.

Japanese Prime Minister Fukuda was the first to react, telling Vice-President Mondale during his February 1977 visit to Tokyo that the withdrawals would be a serious mistake. Mondale, despite private sym-pathy for the Japanese position, was under instructions from the presi-dent simply to inform the Japanese of our position, not to entertain the possibility of reversing it. This only compounded the problem.

Thus began a difficult two-and-a-half-year period during which the policy came under increasing attack from inside and outside the govern-ment. The Koreans themselves behaved with surprising restraint, given their concern, but they made clear their fear of the withdrawals. I di-rected Dick Holbrooke to oversee the Policy Review Memorandum pro-cess carefully, but he was not permitted to offer as one of the options that of *not* withdrawing at all. His final submission, therefore, reflecting the views of every element of the government, offered a series of differ-ent withdrawal rates, and recommended the slower, more cautious ones. Withdrawals would be limited only to ground combat and support troops, and the U.S. Air Force in Korea would be increased significantly. In addition, we would ask Congress to authorize us to transfer over $800 million worth of equipment to the Koreans to beef them up. Finally, he recommended linking our withdrawals to the overall situation in Korea, a considerable departure from Carter's campaign rhetoric. Harold Brown supported these important modifications.

Even this did not quell the growing opposition. Senator Charles Percy, a strong supporter of every other aspect of our East Asian policies, told Holbrooke, banging his fist on the table, that he would forge a united

Republican opposition to the withdrawals. He was joined by such key Democrats as Senators John Glenn, the new chairman of the East Asian Subcommittee, and Sam Nunn, the powerful Georgian on the Armed Services Committee. Senators Henry Jackson and Daniel Inouye, and ultimately, Senator Gary Hart joined the opposition.

Within the executive branch opinion was also running strongly against the withdrawals. Almost all of us had serious misgivings, but the president, having made such strong public commitments so early, still felt strongly about it. In the Pentagon, civilians and generals alike were totally opposed, of course, as were most of my own associates in the East Asian Bureau, including Holbrooke. From my own experience in Korea when I was secretary of the army, and later as a special troubleshooter for President Johnson, I knew how delicate the situation was. But each time Harold Brown or I tried to raise the subject with the president, we found him adamant. Only Zbig, among the president's senior advisers, continued to favor the withdrawals. Luckily, the depth of the disagreement within the executive branch never became public, although there were a few flurries.

With the president dug in, we had no choice but to wait for an opportunity to reargue the case. This presented itself when the president agreed to visit South Korea after the 1979 economic summit in Tokyo. All further discussion of the issue within the executive branch was now deferred, although the Congress continued to hammer home warnings of a political explosion if the withdrawals actually proceeded.

As the trip approached, the CIA came up with a revised estimate of North Korean strength. Using new methods, they said that they had now found their earlier estimates to be about 30 percent too low; the North Koreans were stronger than expected and capable of attacking with almost no warning. It will come as no surprise to the student of Washington politics that this new intelligence estimate, prepared in great secrecy on the eve of the president's trip, found its way into the press within hours after it had been disseminated within the government and briefed to the Congress. The president was not happy, feeling that his hand was being forced.

Indeed it was. When he reached Seoul, he found to his intense annoyance that President Park intended to raise the issue with him directly. He asked us to prevent this from happening, since he already knew Park's views. However, despite our warnings, Park began the first meeting between the two men with a forty-five-minute statement on the dangers that the troop withdrawal policy created for his country and the region. We could almost feel the temperature in the room drop as Park continued, through an interpreter, his assault on the policy. Sitting between the president and Harold Brown, I could feel the contained anger of the president, but there was nothing to be done but let the drama play itself out.

As soon as the meeting ended, the president made clear to me in no uncertain terms what he thought of what he had just heard. (He had not responded at all to Park's presentation when it was made, only asking to meet alone with him to discuss other matters, primarily human rights.)

Driving back in the president's limousine with our splendid ambassador in Seoul, William Gleysteen, and Brown, Brzezinski, and me, the president unburdened himself. He felt isolated, opposed by all his advisers except Zbig. Gleysteen carried a heavy burden as we sat in the parked car in front of the entrance to the ambassadorial residence with a long and puzzled motorcade stalled for blocks behind us. Harold and I joined Ambassador Gleysteen in pointing out the vast difficulties that we faced in carrying out the policy as originally announced and the benefits that would accrue from its suspension, especially in light of the new intelligence figures.

That afternoon, our Korean policy hung in the balance. While the president rested, Gleysteen, Holbrooke, and I raced around Seoul, working with key Korean officials, especially Korea's discreet and effective ambassador to the United States, Kim Yong Shik, to get the message to Park that when he next saw Carter that evening, he must say certain more positive things to the president in order to avoid a personal rupture so serious that it would leave substantial scars. Above all, we told the Koreans, Park must not continue to press the president for an answer on the troop issue. Rather, the best chance for salvaging the situation lay in Park's showing appreciation for the vast array of positive elements in the Korean-American relationship. The troop issue simply could not be decided in Seoul during the trip; perhaps upon our return to Washington it could be reopened.

During that afternoon of hectic meetings and telephone calls, the message got through. The state dinner was a success, and some of the tension was removed from the air. When we parted company in Seoul the next morning—the president to return to Camp David for what was to prove to be the beginning of a difficult period in his presidency marked by the speech on "national malaise" and the traumatic departure of several cabinet officers, I to the ASEAN foreign ministers meeting in Bali—nothing more was said about the troop withdrawal issue.

Three weeks later, on July 20, the president agreed to suspend the troop withdrawals in light of the new intelligence estimates and other factors. A long and difficult policy dispute had been resolved satisfactorily. No permanent damage had been done, although it had been a close call. And three months later when Park Chung Hee, who had ruled his nation with an iron hand for seventeen years, was killed by his own intelligence chief during a private dinner, we immediately redeployed an aircraft carrier into Korean waters to show our support for the security of South Korea.

U.S.-SOVIET RELATIONS

At the beginning of 1979, there seemed a chance that the downward slide in U.S.-Soviet relations might be slowed, or at least cushioned, by the conclusion of a SALT II agreement. However, the international and domestic political climate continued volatile. Attention shifted from Africa to Southeast and Southwest Asia and the Caribbean, where new issues simmered that threatened to undermine our aim of maintaining a balanced policy toward the Soviet Union.

At home, we faced a number of difficult decisions on defense issues, including the controversial MX missile program and a substantial increase in defense spending. The domestic debate on U.S.-Soviet relations became more politicized, as opponents of the administration sought to manipulate public concerns about adverse trends in the military balance and alleged softness in opposing the expansion of Soviet influence.

At this time two bilateral issues arose in U.S.-Soviet relations that ultimately were to have a major negative impact on efforts to achieve ratification of the SALT II agreement—Cuba and Afghanistan.

• • •

At the outset of the administration, we had sought to improve relations with Cuba. In my confirmation hearing I signaled our willingness to open a dialogue with Havana. Although it was not our first objective, President Carter and I believed U.S. interests would be served by maintaining diplomatic relations with Cuba, as with others with whom we had political differences, such as Angola and Vietnam.

Improved relations with Havana, we felt, would help to increase our influence on a number of issues of considerable importance to us, specifically, the presence and destabilizing role of Cuban forces in Angola, the Horn, and elsewhere in Africa; reduction of the Soviet military presence in Cuba; and an improvement in the conditions of political prisoners of the Castro regime. Our objective was to see whether it might be possible slowly to change Castro's perspective on relations with the United States from one of fear and hostility to one in which he might see benefits in restraining his revolutionary adventurism and in lessening his dependence on the Soviet Union. I felt we had some significant leverage—the prospect of lifting the economic blockade; Castro's dislike of being perceived as a tool of the Soviets; his aspirations for international acceptability; and his fear of the corroding influence on his regime of the growing contacts between the Cuban people and the Cuban-American community in Florida.

The Cubans responded favorably to our initiative, and the first U.S.-Cuban official contacts in more than fifteen years took place in New

York on March 24–29, 1977. These formal talks continued in Havana in April, leading to agreements on fisheries and maritime boundaries, and on September 1, to the opening of diplomatic interest sections in both capitals.* However, this promising improvement died in the mood of intense hostility engendered by the Cuban presence in Africa. In addition, in late 1978, questions arose about the Soviet military role in Cuba itself.

In the fall of 1978, we became aware of the possible presence in Cuba of Soviet Mig-23 aircraft. Our intelligence community believed a version of this aircraft might be capable of carrying nuclear weapons. By mid-November, there was growing evidence that there were as many as a dozen Mig-23s with the Cuban forces, although we could not be certain whether or how many nuclear-capable models were present. Soviet delivery of nuclear-capable aircraft to Cuba would be a serious violation of the U.S.-Soviet understanding of 1962, after the Cuban missile crisis, in which the Soviets agreed not to deploy nuclear weapons or nuclear weapon delivery systems in Cuba.† Anything relating to the Soviet military role in Cuba is politically volatile in the United States. It is guaranteed to inflame domestic opinion and make a sensible resolution difficult. I felt that unless we could close off the issue quickly and satisfactorily, it would set back U.S.-Soviet relations and present us with a major domestic problem.

On November 14 I asked Ambassador Dobrynin whether the aircraft we had observed in Cuba were nuclear delivery systems—and therefore in contravention of the 1962 understanding. Moscow responded on November 19 that the Mig-23s were of "the same class as those which have already been there for a long time," and that they had nothing to do with the 1962 agreement.

This response was ambiguous and unsatisfactory. We demanded a direct Soviet confirmation or denial that the Mig-23s were nuclear-capable. In Moscow, on November 21, Foreign Minister Gromyko told our Ambassador Malcolm Toon that the aircraft in question were not capable of carrying nuclear weapons. This assurance was also relayed to us the same day through Ambassador Dobrynin in Washington.

On November 29 I sought further Soviet confirmation that the Mig-23s in Cuba did not have a nuclear capability. Referring to the Soviet assurances of November 19 and 21, I told Dobrynin that if our understanding of the facts was correct, that is, that there were no Mig-23D nuclear-capable aircraft in Cuba and only a limited number of non-

---

* An interest section is a small diplomatic presence usually housed in the embassy of another nation in a country with which the parent of the interest section does not have normal diplomatic relations.

† There were several types of Mig-23s. Ambiguous evidence indicated that at least some of the Mig-23s could be of a type that in Soviet forces was used for ground attack, and when deployed with Soviet forces, believed to be nuclear-capable. Other versions were used as interceptors and for air-to-air attack, and were clearly for defensive purposes only.

nuclear-capable ground attack models of the Mig-23, we would be prepared to consider the issue closed. I also warned Dobrynin that an increase in the number of ground attack Mig-23s, even without a nuclear
capability, would have a seriously adverse effect on U.S.-Soviet relations.
I asked for confirmation of our understanding and gave Dobrynin a copy
of a public statement we proposed to make to this effect if the Soviet
response were satisfactory.

Dobrynin's answer, after checking with Moscow, was that we were free
to make a public statement about the nonnuclear capability of the aircraft, but that we should not imply that the Soviets had agreed not to
increase the number of Mig-23s that could be supplied to Cuba. Their
position was that ground attack aircraft that had no nuclear capability
had nothing to do with the 1962 understanding. We repeated that an
increase in the number of such aircraft would have adverse consequences for U.S.-Soviet relations.

The Soviet explanation was in line with previous practice. The Soviets
had been modernizing Cuban armed forces for many years, and provision of sophisticated tactical aircraft was consistent with that pattern. We
had no reason to disbelieve the Soviet assurances. By their lights, the
Soviets had gone a long way in offering us private assurances which they
knew we intended to use publicly.

On November 30 and again on December 7, the president stated publicly that we had received assurances from the Soviets that they had not
violated the 1962 understanding, and that we had no evidence that there
were nuclear weapons in Cuba. He said we would continue to monitor
Soviet actions very carefully. I hoped this would settle the matter and
allow us to get on with the serious issues. But Cuba and the problem of
the Soviet military presence were to rise again in late 1979 in the midst
of Senate consideration of the SALT Treaty.

SALT: The Endgame

While in Geneva our SALT delegation worked diligently under the leadership of Ralph Earle on the technical aspects of the remaining issues,
Anatoly Dobrynin and I conducted in parallel the final phase of the
SALT negotiations in a series of almost weekly meetings in my office
between January and early May 1979. We chipped away at a number of
highly technical but important issues concerning the permissible
changes that could be made in modernizing existing ICBMs, the politically sensitive telemetry encryption matter, and the final set of limitations and definitions relating to cruise missiles. Progress continued
despite the tensions generated by the Chinese attack on Vietnam in
February and the public charges and countercharges between the Soviets and us over the worsening situation in Southeast Asia.

Most of the remaining issues of any consequence fell slowly into place, and after Dobrynin and I had reached agreement, were remanded to the U.S. and Soviet delegations in Geneva to be put into treaty language. One of the critical breakthroughs was Soviet acceptance of our proposal that key parameters of existing types of ICBMs could not be changed by more than 5 percent. This step, when coupled with our prior agreement to freeze the number of warheads that existing types of MIRVed ICBMs could carry, constituted a major breakthrough. We had finally achieved another of the basic objectives of our March 1977 comprehensive proposal—establishing significant restraints on the modernization of ICBMs. In return, during the term of the treaty, we gave up the right to test multiple warheads on long-range ALCMs—for which we had no plans—and on GLCMs and SLCMs during the term of the protocol. We made clear that after the protocol expired we would be free to test and deploy multiple-warhead GLCMs and SLCMs with ranges over 600 km.

During this period, the vexing telemetry encryption issue was raised to the top political level in an exchange of letters between Carter and Brezhnev. It was explicitly restated that both sides recognized that telemetric information relevant to the verification of the treaty could not be deliberately denied by encryption. This exchange, in my judgment, should have closed off the issue once and for all, but some of my colleagues, particularly Stan Turner, were worried about the verification issue during the ratification debate. They argued that the Soviets had not yet clearly accepted that some telemetry was relevant to the treaty. I finally agreed that the president should lay out our position once again at the summit.

These were legitimate political concerns, but my opinion was that we had already established an unequivocal right to challenge any encrypted telemetry that related to the treaty. We would be the judges of what could be challenged. I believed that anything more—short of a total ban on encryption, which was unattainable—would create impossible problems of definition as we tried to spell out what was permitted and what was banned. The need to protect our own intelligence sources and methods of collection would prevent us from identifying with real specificity what was objectionable in Soviet testing practices. As Paul Warnke wrote me early in the year, this was an instance when the United States seemed unable to take yes for an answer.

The issue of the Backfire bomber was not finally settled during the negotiations between Dobrynin and me. The Soviets continued to hedge about specifying the precise annual production rate, which we knew to be thirty. However, Dobrynin and I worked out an arrangement. When Brezhnev gave us the Soviet statement of Backfire assurances at the summit, Carter would respond with our understanding of the actual production rate. Brezhnev would not contradict the president's figure, and the production rate would then become part of the formal negotiating record.

To remove any doubts about the binding character of the planned exchanges on Backfire, the Special Coordinating Committee suggested that the president state to Brezhnev at the summit that, "any Soviet actions inconsistent with these statements would be treated in the same manner as actions inconsistent with the SALT II Treaty itself." Thus, although the Backfire limitations would be outside the treaty text, our formal position was that a violation of these assurances would be equivalent to a violation of the treaty.

By early May, all but technical drafting issues were resolved. On May 8, I reported to the president that Dobrynin and I had concluded our negotiations and the long, arduous SALT II negotiations were completed. On May 9, I announced to the press that agreement had been reached, and on May 11, that presidents Carter and Brezhnev would meet in Vienna on June 15–18 to sign the treaty.

• • •

The deep sense of satisfaction that all of us felt at reaching this goal after more than seven years of negotiations by three different administrations, Republican and Democratic, was tempered by a sober appreciation of the political struggles that lay ahead. The battle lines over SALT and, more broadly, over the very concept that the United States should attempt to moderate relations with the Soviets, had been forming for more than two years. Unlike SALT I, this time the Congress, the executive branch, and critical sectors of public opinion would be drawn into a prolonged debate over U.S.-Soviet relations, the military balance, and Soviet intentions. SALT would be the anvil on which the differences would be hammered out. The debate would have strong partisan overtones, which would increase as we approached the presidential election.

I was confident that the treaty could stand up well in an objective debate. It was a balanced, carefully wrought set of agreements that left us with virtually full freedom of action to modernize our strategic forces in every area of interest, while requiring a significant reduction in Soviet strategic forces. It placed quantitative and qualitative limitations on the Soviets that would be valuable to our long-term strategic force planning. It would also open the way to SALT III and to negotiations leading to much deeper reductions and increased qualitative constraints on intercontinental nuclear weapons, as well as limitations on Soviet theater nuclear forces.

In April, Zbig and Harold made strong speeches defending the SALT agreement on national security grounds. This unemotional, practical view of SALT—a candid recognition of its political and military contribution to Western security and of its limitations as a vehicle for moderating the U.S.-Soviet global competition—was what I had been urging since my earliest appearances before the Senate Foreign Relations and Armed Services committees. One of the problems of SALT, as well as of détente in general, was that it had been oversold in the early 1970s. The best argument for SALT was a tough-minded description of what it could do for United States and Western security, as opposed to unrealistic and unsustainable claims about a new era in U.S.-Soviet relations.

The political climate for SALT in mid-1979 was probably as good as it would ever be. The Sino-Vietnamese border clash had ended, Zaire and the Horn had receded as issues in bilateral U.S.-Soviet relations, and the crisis over Mig-23s in Cuba had been satisfactorily resolved. Although events in Iran were profoundly troubling, and there were worrisome signs of future problems for U.S.-Soviet relations in Afghanistan and in Central America, where Nicaragua was drifting into civil war, these issues had not yet inflamed U.S.-Soviet relations or provided fuel for the opponents of SALT.

The president's domestic standing had also improved, thanks in large measure to Camp David and the historic Egyptian-Israeli peace treaty, which had been signed in March. The polls continued to show heavy public support for SALT, though it was mixed with continuing unease about trends in the military balance and mistrust of Soviet intentions. To capitalize on a broad though amorphous support for SALT, we had to ensure that both the Senate and the American people understood and supported the administration's programs for maintaining our defense capabilities. We had also to dispel any significant concern about our ability to verify adequately, through our own unilateral means, Soviet compliance with the SALT agreement.

The problem of public confidence in the verifiability of the SALT II agreement had surfaced even before the negotiations were completed, as a consequence of the events in Iran. The fall of the shah lost us two CIA intelligence sites in Iran in January 1979. Among their functions, these sites collected data from Soviet ICBM tests which were important for monitoring compliance with some of the qualitative limitations on ICBM modernization. We were confident that over a relatively short period of time we could compensate for the reduction in our SALT monitoring capability with other intelligence sources and by acceleration of some of our new collection programs.

Despite our assurances in closed sessions to members of the Foreign Relations Committee and other senators that we had plans to make up for the lost monitoring capabilities from the Iranian facilities, concern in Congress was growing. In March, Senator Henry Jackson asserted in a speech that without the Iranian sites it would be impossible to monitor Soviet compliance. SALT opponents on Capitol Hill leaked classified testimony by CIA head Stansfield Turner in April that seemed to indicate it would require four or five years to recoup the capabilities lost in Iran.

On April 17, Harold Brown explained publicly that it would take only a year to regain the capability to verify adequately Soviet adherence to pertinent SALT limitations. This was well before the Soviets could complete any illegal testing program. Turner had been referring to the time needed to recover all of the lost intelligence capability; only part was related to verifying SALT. Despite our clarifications, the effect of this exchange was to stimulate fears that key portions of the SALT agreement would not be adequately verifiable. It was simply not true.

Another troubling development in this period just before the summit was a decision by certain senators, on whom we had counted to be among the staunchest advocates of SALT, to question the arms control value of the agreement. In March, senators George McGovern, Mark Hatfield, and William Proxmire announced that they had written the president that it might be impossible for them to support the treaty because it did not " 'curb' the arms race." Others who should have been defenders of SALT were lukewarm or silent in the difficult political climate.

Some of this criticism or silence may have been tactical, a way of setting the administration up to extract commitments on specific arms control goals in SALT III. It was a case of pushing on an open door if ever there was one. However, the hedging in mid-1979 by moderate senators as the debate gathered momentum helped the anti-SALT forces in ways I believe the moderates did not foresee. Hard-liners, who saw that it would be politically unwise to attack the goal of controlling strategic arms, were able to claim they were part of a broad consensus—that the treaty was not "real arms control," but rather a codification of the arms race.

On June 8, a week before we were to leave for Vienna, it was announced that the president had decided to approve full-scale development of a large, ten-warhead version of the MX ICBM for mobile deployment. For some time we had had a number of alternative mobile basing modes under consideration, but by then the one receiving the most serious attention was the so-called "Multiple Protective Shelter" (MPS) system. This system provided for enhancing the survivability of the MX by moving the missiles among a group of widely spaced shelters. The issues of missile size and type and the mobile basing alternatives were interrelated.

Of course, the bulk of the analysis of the ICBM options was done by the Defense Department and the air force. However, the kind of missile selected—and there were several variants under study—would have long-term strategic, foreign policy, and arms control implications. I had had my own staff, principally Leslie Gelb and his team of excellent systems analysts, carefully examine the various missile options so that I could offer the president and Harold Brown an informed foreign policy and arms control judgment on the issues.

Several meetings had been held in April and May to review the alternatives to put to the president. From these discussions it had become clear that the Joint Chiefs of Staff strongly favored the largest variant of the possible MX sizes and were strongly opposed to the smaller "common missile" sizes that could be used for both the air force's future ICBM and the navy's successor to the Trident I sea-launched missile. The Joint Chiefs were committed to retaining land-based ICBMs and feared that the smaller "common missile" alternatives would lead to abandonment or sharp curtailment of land-based ICBMs in favor of an enhanced sea-based missile force.

In the end, I decided to support production of the large version of the MX. This recommendation was accepted by the president. Since it had not been feasible in SALT to redress the theoretical vulnerability of our fixed-site ICBMs, it was necessary to move forward with our MX program. Politically, I believed the MX production decision, to be followed shortly by a basing decision, would relieve the Joint Chiefs' concern about the long-term trends in the strategic balance and strengthen their endorsement of SALT. The MX decision, when added to our planned growth in defense spending, would also reassure those senators concerned about trends in the military balance.

· · ·

The meeting between Carter and Brezhnev in Vienna, the first summit between the Soviet and American heads of state since President Ford had gone to Vladivostok in 1974, was a long-sought goal of President Carter. Like so many presidents before him, this president had seemed to feel that if only he could just sit down with the Soviet leadership, he could break through the political, cultural, and ideological differences and the accumulated crust of institutional and vested interests in both countries, to reach a mutual understanding on our respective responsibilities as superpowers in the nuclear age. Perhaps the men who have carried the terrible burdens of the presidency since Hiroshima have instinctively sensed that there must be a common ground between them and their Soviet counterparts, and that given the chance to meet face to face, that common ground could be found.

I doubt that by June 1979 President Carter still cherished such hopes. Too much had happened since January 20, 1977, for any of us to expect much at Vienna aside from the practical business at hand: to sign the SALT II Treaty and associated agreements. Moreover, President Brezhnev's health had been poor and it was uncertain how active a participant he would be.

This is not to underestimate the tremendous political and strategic importance of concluding the SALT Treaty at this juncture in U.S.-Soviet relations. A transition in leadership was ahead for the Soviets, and a SALT Treaty in place could strengthen the more moderate elements in the Soviet political establishment and ease what was almost certain to be a difficult period in the global competition.

The exchange between the two presidents was less extensive than would have been desirable. It was confined largely to winding up the final details on SALT II and a general exchange on the world situation. The discussion included a somewhat sharp exchange on our respective activities in the Third World. President Carter strongly criticized Soviet use of Cuban proxy forces in Africa and called for restraint in our political competition. Brezhnev responded by denouncing the propensity of some in the United States to blame the Soviets for every Third World problem.

Carter appealed for progress across the board in arms control and proposed that we anticipate SALT III by agreeing in advance to further cuts in nuclear weapons from the SALT II levels. President Brezhnev, foreshadowing political and strategic concerns the Soviets intended to address in the next phase of negotiations, said that it would be impossible to agree to new reductions until the sides had also dealt with U.S. nuclear systems based in Europe and with the nuclear weapons of our British and French allies. The Soviets were increasingly apprehensive at the prospect of significant deployment of new, highly accurate U.S. long-range cruise and ballistic missiles in Europe which could attack targets in the Soviet Union. They did not intend to go very far in a new round of strategic arms reductions until they could take into account the threat against them from Europe.

After some confusion over the acting out of the scenario Dobrynin and we had prearranged, Carter and Brezhnev registered the understanding that the Soviets were prohibited from encoding telemetry that we needed in order to verify the treaty. After handing us a letter of assurances on Backfire, Brezhnev confirmed that the annual production rate was thirty aircraft per year.

With that, the SALT II negotiations, which had begun in 1972 and had taken seven laborious years, were completed. The next day, June 18, presidents Carter and Brezhnev signed the treaty, the protocol, and the joint statement of principles for SALT III in a glittering ceremony in the Redoutensaal in the Hofberg Palace. I was deeply gratified that we had finally concluded this agreement, which was so clearly in our security interests, but subdued as I thought about the long and bitter ratification debate that lay ahead.

8

THE PANAMA CANAL
TREATIES

THE PANAMA CANAL ZONE problem was extremely complicated, bound up as it was with history, intense nationalism, and emotion. It involved far-reaching foreign policy and national security issues interwoven with sensitive political considerations in both Panama and the United States. The question demonstrated the increasingly close relationship between American domestic politics and the conduct of foreign affairs. It brought together, into a single explosive issue, contending ideological crosscurrents.

The debate over the canal treaties would reflect the political and philosophical differences brought about by the searing events of the last decade: Vietnam, Watergate, inflation, the energy crisis, accelerating social change, intractable international problems, loss of economic and military supremacy. Those developments shook American self-confidence and fed fears of national decline.

The president, as politician, and I, as someone who had spent many years in government service, were keenly aware of the deep emotions that were aroused by the idea that the United States would voluntarily relinquish the canal and zone. To many, they symbolized America's will to maintain its global predominance. The political and foreign policy risks of taking on an uphill ratification battle that might well be lost were great, and a less courageous president might have ducked the issue. Despite the risks, one of the president's earliest decisions, made during his first week in office upon my strong recommendation, was to make a real attempt to negotiate a new and more durable treaty with Panama.

. . .

I was familiar with the canal issue. As Lyndon Johnson's personal emissary during violent anti-American riots in 1964, I had witnessed firsthand the Panamanians' fierce resentment at what they saw as an island of American affluence and dominion in their midst. The anti-American events of 1964 led me to the conclusion that almost all Panamanians regarded exclusive U.S. authority over the canal and zone as an affront to their national dignity and sovereignty. There was little question in my mind that sooner or later Panama would resort to major violence, even to the point of destroying the canal.

Defending the canal would be an extremely difficult task. It could be closed by the simplest act of sabotage. We could and would defend it by force if necessary, but the cost in human life and the economic loss would be high for both countries, and the United States would be condemned by world opinion for perpetuating a morally objectionable "colonial" relationship. Therefore, I encouraged and supported President Johnson's 1964 decision to begin negotiating a new arrangement to replace the anachronistic 1903 treaty which gave the United States unilateral control in perpetuity over the canal and zone with all rights and powers, as though it were sovereign. A draft treaty placing the canal under joint control was negotiated by 1967 but was never submitted to the Senate for ratification. A military coup brought General Omar Torrijos to power in 1968, and he immediately rejected the agreement. Panama wanted an end to the American political and military presence on its territory, even if it had to wait.

Negotiations continued under the Nixon and Ford administrations, demonstrating that the desire to form a more equitable relationship with Panama represented a bipartisan consensus. A major breakthrough was achieved in February 1974 when Kissinger reached agreement with Panamanian Foreign Minister Juan Tack on the following principles that would guide further negotiations:

• A new treaty would be for a *fixed* term—thus satisfying the fundamental Panamanian request that the concept of perpetuity be abandoned.

• The United States would retain the right to operate and defend the canal during the life of the treaty, which the American side expected to be fifty years or more.

• The United States would return the Canal Zone to Panamanian jurisdiction during the treaty period. This principle reflected the growing agreement in our national foreign policy and defense community that our primary interest was the secure and efficient operation of the canal, not control of the zone.

Pursuant to the Kissinger-Tack principles, the chief American negotiator, Ellsworth Bunker, was able to reach agreement with Panama by the end of 1974 that the United States would have the primary responsibility for operating and defending the canal during the term of the treaty, although there would be increasing Panamanian participation to ensure that Panama would be able to manage the canal efficiently after Ameri-

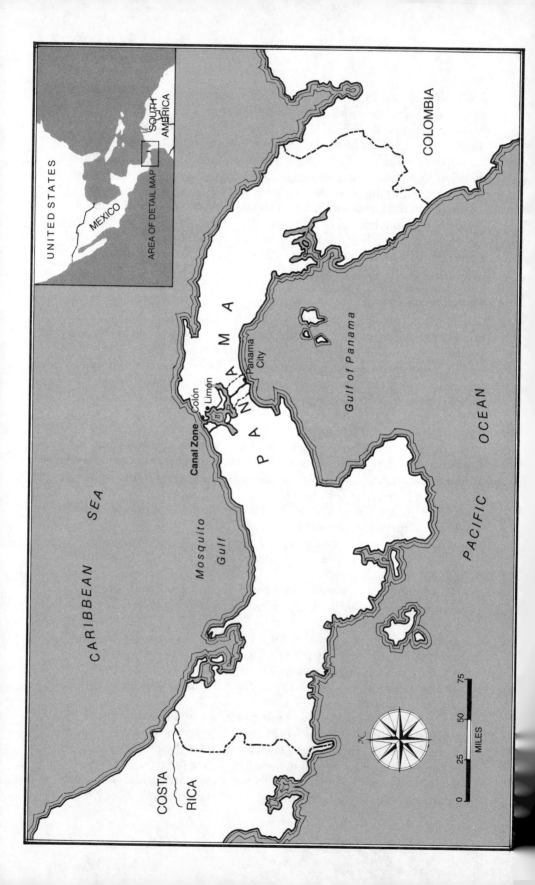

can administration ended. Jurisdiction over the Canal Zone would revert to Panama over a three-year transition period, thus allowing gradual adjustment to its changed status. However, Panama would give the United States the right to use the lands necessary for the operation and defense of the canal until the treaty expired. Of great importance, both parties committed themselves to maintain the permanent neutrality of the canal after the treaty expired. This principle was critical in gaining the firm support of our military leaders for the eventual relinquishment of the canal to Panama.

Because of domestic political considerations, particularly Governor Ronald Reagan's challenge to Gerald Ford in the 1976 Republican presidential nomination, the promise of the Kissinger-Tack breakthrough and of Bunker's effective negotiating skills was not realized. Public sentiment favored the Reagan position, and he narrowly missed seizing the nomination from Ford. Doubtless Ford intended to conclude a new treaty if he was reelected. But in 1975 presidential politics had taken precedence and negotiations were shelved. Panama grew ever more impatient.

· · ·

The Carter administration thus found itself facing serious and mounting dangers to the security of the canal, and an open sore in our relations with Latin America. As a signal of our determination to move forward, on my recommendation the president named our former ambassador to the Organization of American States, Sol Linowitz, as conegotiator with Ellsworth Bunker. I had met with Sol in December of 1976 to see if he would join us in seeking a solution to the canal issue. He agreed to join us for six months to see if an agreement was possible, but he would be willing to do so only as a conegotiator with Bunker. I wholeheartedly seconded this decision.

Linowitz had recently headed a private study commission that had published a report concluding that the canal dispute was the most urgent problem facing us in our relations with Latin America. The president, Zbig and I agreed that the security of the canal, as well as the possibility of improving U.S.-Latin American relations, required a serious effort to negotiate an agreement before time ran out. I also agreed with Sol that we could not hope to have a better relationship with our neighbors if we failed to work out a fair settlement with Panama.

Carter decided in the first week of his presidency that Linowitz and Bunker should be given broad authority to explore possible solutions with the Panamanians. The principal outstanding negotiating problems were the duration of the treaty and the defense of the canal after its expiration. I believed we should offer a treaty termination date of December 31, 1999, if Panama would satisfy us on arrangements to guarantee the permanent neutrality of the canal after that date. The crux of the problem, as it was to remain throughout the negotiations and the ratification debate, was to find a mutually acceptable way to reconcile two profoundly different points of view: On the one hand, our sine qua non was a permanent unilateral American right to maintain the neutrality of the waterway, with military force if necessary, after the treaty expired; Panama, on the other hand, was firmly opposed to a perpetual American right to take military action on its sovereign territory to protect the canal.

For Linowitz and Bunker, the formidable task would be to find the least abrasive way to state our right, so as to make clear that its only purpose was to keep the canal open and accessible—not to intervene in the internal affairs of Panama. Therefore, we wanted to give our negotiators as much latitude as possible to explore various formulations without being constrained by detailed instructions. Broad instructions had been of great help to me when I served as a presidential emissary in international crises, such as Cyprus in 1967 and Korea in 1968 after the seizure of the USS *Pueblo*.

During the Cyprus crisis, I had been called the day before Thanksgiving, just as Gay and I were leaving New York to visit one of our children, and asked to leave immediately for Turkey. I was told that Turkish troops were already at the embarkation port and were expected, according to our intelligence, to invade Cyprus the next morning. This would mean war between Greece and Turkey. My instructions from President Johnson were clear and simple: "Do what you have to to stop the war. If you need anything, let me know. Good luck." In Korea, my instructions were equally simple: "Do what is necessary to stop Park from invading North Korea." Nothing can be more helpful than such instructions and the confidence that they inspire.

As we formulated our approach to the canal negotiations, Carter accepted the recommendation that we consult on a continuing basis with the Congress, particularly the Senate, which has the constitutional responsibility to advise and consent to the ratification of all treaties. Normally, the executive branch negotiates treaties and presents them to the Senate for ratification. We knew, however, that we would need the support of both houses of Congress on a matter as sensitive as this one. We ultimately had to have specific legislation to implement the treaty, and this, of course, would require the affirmative vote of a majority of both houses. In the climate of the late 1970s, controversial foreign policy and national security issues could be dealt with constructively only in partnership with an activist legislative branch.

Although all of us, including the president, were involved, the brunt of the consultations was borne by Linowitz and Bunker, who met often with key senators, sometimes once or twice a week, to brief them on the state of the negotiations. In taking this course, we were risking a breach of confidentiality and serious political repercussions in Panama. But true to their word, the senators maintained the confidentiality of the information we gave them. This almost unprecedented consultation, which was similar to what we were doing on SALT, was vital in building Senate confidence in the treaty. This would serve us well once the bitter ratification debate began.

We also thought it important to conclude a treaty with the incumbent Torrijos government, which we judged to be strong enough to ratify it. The charismatic Torrijos' authority was solid, but Panama's internal political divisions and its serious economic difficulties would deepen if the canal issue dragged on. The canal dispute was the overriding issue in Panamanian politics, and leaders were judged by their stand on it. We felt Torrijos was anxious to find acceptable compromises in order to obtain a treaty rapidly. If he were rebuffed on the canal issue, a successor government might be either too weak or too radical to deal effectively with the treaty question. Our assessment was that once Torrijos obtained approval of the treaty, no future Panamanian regime would willingly renounce it.

With the president's approval, on January 31, 1977, I reaffirmed the U.S. commitment to the Kissinger-Tack principles in a meeting with Panamanian Foreign Minister Aquilino Boyd. I told Boyd that reaching agreement on a treaty termination date depended on his government giving the United States the right to defend the canal after the treaty expired. I stressed that while the new administration wanted to be fair, we would not jeopardize our national security interests in the canal.

• • •

The negotiations got off to a rocky start in February, when Boyd was suddenly removed as foreign minister. The new Panamanian negotiator, Romulo Escobar, probed for softness in our basic positions. We realized that the Panamanians were testing us. We were determined not only to stand firm, but to make it clear to the Congress that we were doing so. Torrijos was pleased that we were willing to have the treaty expire twenty or thirty years sooner than the Ford administration had proposed, but our unshakable insistence on maintaining a perpetual U.S. role in protecting the canal was politically difficult for him to accept. However artfully stated, any suggestion of a unilateral American right to set foot on Panama's soil to defend the canal after the treaty expired derogated from Panamanian sovereignty and evoked bitter opposition and resentment.

In early April, Bunker and Linowitz reported that Torrijos had recognized that we would not budge on our right to defend the canal's neutrality, and had concluded, therefore, that a treaty could be concluded promptly if both sides were prepared to move rapidly. Linowitz, who knew the temper of the Senate because of his frequent consultations, warned us that ratification would require a very hard fight, probably harder than we had anticipated.

Linowitz believed that success in the ratification debate would turn on our securing Panama's formal agreement to our right to protect the canal permanently. We had thought in terms of a single treaty with a definite termination date. This raised the problem of how to state our right to defend the canal after the treaty expired. In a brilliant stroke, Linowitz and Bunker suggested that we prepare two treaties, one assuring permanent neutrality of the canal and a second transferring the canal to Panama. A treaty of indefinite duration which gave us the right to defend the canal's neutrality—which would be negotiated first—would give us a clear answer to those who claimed that turning the canal over to Panama would threaten U.S. security. Carter and I saw the political importance of this suggestion, and immediately authorized Linowitz and Bunker to pursue this course.

Negotiations resumed in Washington in May. Bunker and Linowitz proposed, in addition to the basic Panama Canal Treaty which would last until December 31, 1999, a new neutrality agreement of indefinite duration that would give the United States the right to act to maintain the canal's neutrality even after Panama assumed full control on January 1, 2000. The negotiations progressed rapidly. By the end of May, the negotiators had begun to draft the two treaties. In an effort to allow a "decent ambiguity" in the Neutrality Treaty rather than insisting on formal language in the text, we stated to the Panamanians as part of the negotiating record that we would interpret our right to guarantee permanent neutrality to mean that the United States could take any steps necessary to defend the canal after we transferred it to Panama. The Panamanians accepted our interpretation.

However, a great deal of work remained in translating these broad agreements into precise treaty language. A serious problem soon arose when Panama demanded huge financial payments. We were told that these exorbitant demands reflected the conviction of a large number of Panamanians that the United States had exploited Panama's main economic asset for sixty years and that we owed them adequate compensation. Perhaps an equally important reason was their desire for a major U.S. concession to draw attention away from the permanent rights accorded to us under the Neutrality Treaty. Even had we agreed with the Panamanian arguments, which we did not, such massive payments were out of the question. We simply would not put ourselves in the position of appearing to pay for relinquishing our control over the canal.

The negotiations were essentially finished in August, but not before Panama made a final effort to extract further concessions. Bunker and Linowitz went to Panama for what they hoped was the final round of negotiations, just as Linowitz' six-month appointment was about to expire. To their dismay, the Panamanians tabled a new draft, which reopened many closed issues including tolls, revenues, the payment of a large annuity, rights of U.S. canal employees, the size of American military forces, and others. The new draft would have moved us back to square one. Linowitz telephoned us to suggest we prepare a statement announcing that there would be no treaty. The next day, however, the Panamanians, seeing that we could not be moved, dropped their new demands, including their proposal of a one-time payment of nearly half a billion dollars and a huge annuity. They accepted our offer of a $10 million annual payment to be drawn from canal revenues and a larger share of canal tolls.

When he returned, Linowitz, supported by General George Brown, chairman of the Joint Chiefs of Staff, briefed former president Gerald Ford. Ford spoke in favor of the treaties, as did former secretaries of state Dean Rusk and Henry Kissinger. These endorsements were important to demonstrating that the treaties were the product of both Republican and Democratic administrations and should not become a partisan issue.

The treaties were completed on August 29. The president decided to make the signing a major event. The ceremony took place in Washington on September 7. Carter and Torrijos signed the two treaties in the Pan American Union building in the presence of the assembled leaders of most of the nations of the Western hemisphere. Public opinion polls reflected strong opposition to the treaties and the president wanted to place his prestige fully behind them as we prepared for the ratification debate.

• • •

The administration made its case for the treaties in the fall of 1977. On September 26, I described the treaties before the Senate Foreign Relations Committee as ". . . a triumph for the principle of peaceful and constructive settlement of disputes between nations . . . a principle we seek to apply in all aspects of American foreign policy," and told the committee that ". . . the ratification and implementation of these treaties will be the single most positive action to be undertaken in recent years in our relations with Latin America."

American interests were fully protected. We retained the right to operate and defend the canal through the year 2000. Under the Neutrality Treaty the United States would have the right to ensure the canal's neutrality after the year 2000, which we had informed the Panamanians meant we would have the right to defend the canal if necessary. American warships would have the right of expeditious passage through the canal, ahead of other ships in case of need. The jobs, benefits, and rights of American canal employees were protected, a negotiating achievement that won us the support of the AFL-CIO.

Putting the central question squarely to the committee, I warned that " . . . if thirteen years of effort were lost, and these treaties rejected, our relations with Panama would be shattered, our standing in Latin America damaged immeasurably, and the security of the canal itself endangered."

The next day Harold Brown and General George Brown emphasized to the senators the importance of the treaties in providing for the security of the canal. The most serious threat to the canal was not foreign aggression—although the unilateral American right to protect the canal had been preserved—but sabotage and terrorist actions. Eliminating the Canal Zone as the focus of Panamanian nationalism would reduce the risks to the continued operation of the canal and ease the task of defending it.

It was apparent from these hearings that there was still serious concern in the Senate as to whether the United States had a clear right to act unilaterally to keep the canal open and operating. Linked to this concern was the less difficult problem of clarifying the right of U.S. warships to expeditious passage through the canal in time of war or emergency. The senators' concerns had been stimulated by Romulo Escobar's August 19 statements in Panama that the Neutrality Treaty gave the United States only an "assurance that the canal will be permanently neutral." On expeditious passage of U.S. warships, I had made clear to the Panamanians that we interpreted the treaty language to mean that our vessels could go to the head of the line, if necessary. They had agreed. Notwithstanding, Escobar denied that U.S. warships would be given "preferential rights."

We and the Panamanians had similar political problems on how to "sell" the treaties to skeptical constituencies. I am confident that there was no misunderstanding of the interpretations, which had been agreed to during the negotiations. Escobar was trying to deflect domestic criticism in Panama, but in doing so, he had created a major problem for us in the Senate. Opponents of the treaties seized on Escobar's statements as proof that the treaties did not adequately protect our interests. Senate Minority Leader Howard Baker and Foreign Relations Committee member Senator Richard Stone, both of whom acknowledged the importance of the treaties for U.S.-Latin American relations, argued that Panama should provide us with a written clarification to ensure that there was no disagreement about our right to defend the neutrality of the canal after the year 2000. Their votes, especially Baker's, would be crucial.

It was evident that ratification of the treaties would require one of two things: Either we had to renegotiate the Neutrality Treaty, or there must be a clarification of the disputed interpretations. Renegotiation was out of the question. It would have caused a political upheaval in Panama. Instead, on October 1, at the suggestion of Sol Linowitz, I recommended that we resolve the problem by issuing a joint interpretive note before Panama's October 23 national plebiscite on the treaties. It was imperative that we clarify the rights issue under the Neutrality Treaty before October 23 or a second Panamanian vote focusing exclusively on this question might be necessary. Carter approved, and Linowitz started work on an agreed interpretation.

The atmosphere worsened on October 4. On that day, Senator Robert Dole, a leading treaty opponent, released a classified cable from our embassy in Panama that reported continuing Panamanian differences of view over our defense rights under the Neutrality Treaty. The Panamanians were upset with statements allegedly made to the Foreign Relations Committee that the treaty gave the United States the right to "intervene" in Panama. They also disputed my statement that the right of expeditious passage meant that our warships could go to the head of the line. On October 5 we sent a letter to Senator John Sparkman, chairman of the Foreign Relations Committee, emphasizing that the administration stood firmly behind the interpretation we had given to the Panamanians during the negotiations, but stating that "The Treaty does not give the United States the right to intervene in the internal affairs of Panama, nor has it been our intention to seek out or to exercise such a right." Notwithstanding, Senator Byrd told the president that unless these differences were settled in a formal way, the Senate would not approve the treaties. The strength of the opposition dictated that a vote would have to be postponed until early 1978 to give us more time to build support.

I suggested to the president that he meet with Torrijos to see if a joint statement could be worked out. Carter agreed, and invited Torrijos to come to Washington. Carter then met with key senators on October 11 to explain the purpose of the Torrijos visit, which was kept secret. The president said he understood the importance of clarifying the U.S. right to take military action to preserve the canal's neutrality, and that later that week he and General Torrijos would discuss a joint statement. Carter then disclosed the contents of a draft to see if it met the senators' concerns, warning that Torrijos might insist on some changes. He told them we needed to issue the joint statement prior to the October 23 plebiscite.

Carter and Torrijos met on October 14, first privately in the Oval Office, then in the cabinet room with their advisers. The president told Torrijos straightforwardly that he thought we had only about 55 of the 67 votes needed for ratification, with 20 senators opposed and the rest undecided. He pointed out that we needed most of the undecideds and that the Escobar statements had made this task very difficult. Carter stressed that it was essential he and Torrijos clarify the crucial points of expeditious passage of U.S. warships and America's right to defend the neutrality of the canal.

Torrijos reluctantly agreed. Torrijos preferred a joint oral statement, but Carter insisted that it must be in writing. He explained that while he opposed amending the treaty, the Senate could be expected to add a condition to its resolution of advice and consent, embodying the language that he and Torrijos would agree upon. Carter and Torrijos then discussed the idea of an exchange of letters prior to October 23. Linowitz, who was listening to the two leaders, did not want to let Torrijos return to Panama without resolving the issue. There was no way to be sure of Torrijos' reaction once he was again exposed to domestic criticism. Linowitz said that in his opinion neither an oral declaration nor an exchange of letters would satisfy the Senate. What was needed was a written statement issued by both leaders that very day. Romulo Escobar continued to argue for an exchange of letters, although he was coming closer to our position.

To avoid the discussion petering out without a firm conclusion, Linowitz suggested that he and Romulo Escobar try to prepare a written understanding on the spot. Within an hour they had worked out a draft, which Escobar took to Torrijos. Torrijos agreed, both to the text and to issuing it as a joint understanding before he left Washington. Linowitz secured Carter's approval, then rushed to a hastily convened meeting of the Senate Foreign Relations Committee to review it with the members. The statement, released later that day, reflected the agreement reached on the three key points: The United States had the right to "defend the Canal against any threat to the regime of neutrality . . ."; although "this does not mean, nor shall it be interpreted as a right of intervention of the United States in the internal affairs of Panama"; and finally, U.S. and Panamanian warships and auxiliary vessels would receive expedited passage and would have the right "in case of need or emergency, to go to the head of the line of vessels in order to transit the Canal rapidly." I was delighted with this result, which was critical to ratification of the treaties.

On October 23, the Panamanian people approved the treaties by a two-to-one margin. However, the delays occasioned by the dispute over interpretation and the powerful surge of conservative opposition during the Senate hearings eliminated any chance of ratifying the treaties before early 1978. As debate resumed in the United States, treaty opponents focused their efforts on three fronts:

• persuading public opinion that "giving away" the canal was an act of weakness, symbolizing America's decline as a world power and stimulating a flood of antitreaty mail to make clear that senators who voted for the treaties would pay with their political lives;

• raising a constitutional challenge to the executive branch's power to dispose of federal property in the zone by treaty without the approval of the House of Representatives; and

• forcing a renegotiation of the treaties by attaching to the treaties "killer amendments" deliberately designed to be unacceptable to Panamanian opinion.

To counter this strategy, in late 1977 and early 1978 we intensified our campaign to explain the treaties to the American public. The struggle was not between the Democratic and Republican parties, but between the liberals/centrists and the Right, between those who believed America must live in the present and those who wanted to cling to the past. We needed to generate support to protect the political lives of those senators who were disposed to vote for ratification, but who feared it would cost them their jobs. Harold Brown, Warren Christopher, Sol Linowitz, and I, as well as other senior officials, stepped up our speaking engagements around the country. America's most distinguished diplomat, my dear friend and associate W. Averell Harriman, undertook at the age of eighty-seven to head up an important and effective national committee of private citizens who supported the treaties. I also urged Carter to give a televised "fireside chat" on the treaties, which he did very effectively on February 1. By then our efforts were paying off. Some polls began to show that a narrow majority of the American people now favored the treaties.

•   •   •

On January 26, the Senate Foreign Relations Committee began its consideration of the treaties, starting with the Neutrality Treaty. We agreed with the Senate leadership that it would be best to deal first with the issue of U.S. rights to defend the canal during the neutrality regime in order to gain the necessary two-thirds vote before we took up the treaty that would transfer the zone and canal to Panama. The key, we felt, was to integrate the Carter-Torrijos October 14 statement into the Neutrality Treaty.

The strategy we had worked out with the Senate leadership was to oppose amendments that would require reopening negotiations to secure Panama's agreement, and would probably result in a second Panamanian plebiscite. We hoped to deflect such proposals, which we recognized were central to the opponents' plan to defeat the treaties, by devising "understandings" and "reservations" that could be added to the resolution of advice and consent as the Senate's conditions for approving ratification. If Panama exchanged the instruments of ratification without objecting to these Senate understandings and reservations, they would be legally binding without any further Panamanian acquiescence. By January we knew that the Senate would not ratify the treaties without a number of prior conditions. We thus believed it crucial that these be in a form that Panama could accept without formal negotiations or a second plebiscite. Consultations with several Senate leaders made clear that the only way to garner the crucial dozen additional votes was to enable senators to "improve" the treaties by adding conditions so that they could justify a yes vote to their constituents.

Our expectation that this strategy would work was strengthened when, in early January, after a visit with Torrijos, Senator Baker told us he could support the treaties if the October 14 Carter-Torrijos understanding could be formalized. Baker stressed that although he believed some changes were essential if the Neutrality Treaty were to be ratified, he did not want to press for modifications intolerable to Panama. Baker's leadership was indispensable, and it was an act of statesmanship, for he intended to contest Reagan for the 1980 Republican presidential nomination. Later in January, Torrijos told visiting members of the Senate Foreign Relations Committee that since the October 14 understanding had been issued before the Panamanian plebiscite, he would agree to incorporating it into the Neutrality Treaty, but he warned that he could not accept amendments that would require another referendum.

As the Foreign Relations Committee began to draft the resolution of ratification, senators Baker and Byrd announced that they would offer a "leadership" amendment to add the language of the Carter-Torrijos statement to the treaty. With administration support, the committee, by a 13-to-1 vote, adopted a new article at the end of the treaty drawing on the October 14 understanding. Torrijos, however, shaken by a sharp outcry in Panama, quickly changed his mind and claimed that inserting a new article would necessitate a plebiscite. In some confusion, we and the committee leaders regrouped to search for a means to clarify our right to defend the canal without provoking a confrontation that would play right into the hands of treaty opponents.

When Torrijos agreed to keep working with us to find a suitable form for incorporating the October 14 statement, we were confident that the Foreign Relations Committee would ultimately report the Neutrality Treaty favorably to the Senate. But every vote was critical and our head counts showed the treaty was still several short of the necessary 67. If the committee sent the treaty to the floor by an overwhelming margin, this could help create a sense of momentum. We hoped to contribute to this result by persuading protreaty senators to coordinate their announcements of support so that every day or two another senator would come out in favor of the treaties.

On January 30, the Foreign Relations Committee voted 14 to 1 to send both treaties to the Senate with a favorable recommendation. After further discussions with the Panamanians, the committee had decided to insert language from the October 14 understanding into existing treaty articles rather than add it as a separate clause. Torrijos had informed us that, unlike adding a separate article, this procedure would not require a second plebiscite. Although it was difficult to perceive the difference, the important thing was that it was agreeable to Torrijos.

The Senate began to debate the Neutrality Treaty on February 8. A leading opponent, Senator James Allen of Alabama, indicated that he and others intended to introduce dozens of amendments in an effort to kill it. Warren Christopher represented the administration in our day-to-day dealings with the Senate, coordinating with Senate leaders on blocking the "killer amendments." We set up a direct channel from Warren through our ambassador in Panama, William Jorden, to discuss Senate proposals with the Panamanians as they were introduced. Torrijos designated several representatives to work with us, so we could determine whether the language and intent of any proposal was acceptable or whether it would require renegotiation or formal acknowledgment. Christopher worked closely with the managers on the Senate floor, senators Frank Church and Paul Sarbanes, as well as the Democratic and Republican leaders, senators Byrd and Baker. Sometimes we were able to help senators draft reservations and understandings that would achieve their purposes without provoking the Panamanians. In many cases, the senators who introduced proposals were out to destroy the treaty, not to clarify ambiguities or alleged deficiencies.

On February 23, Senator Allen introduced the first of many such amendments, a proposal that the United States be allowed to maintain military forces in Panama beyond December 31, 1999. The vote to set aside this amendment showed that protreaty forces were strong enough to block patently unacceptable amendments. However, as Byrd and Baker had warned, the real danger lay in proposals that seemed reasonable and that the uncommitted or wavering would find politically hard to oppose. Christopher suggested to the Senate leaders that one or two acceptable understandings and reservations be prepared that could be offered to influential, uncommitted senators at the appropriate moment. Thus they could "put their stamp" on the treaty and justify a favorable vote. Byrd agreed and Christopher drafted a reservation to the effect that the Neutrality Treaty did not preclude the United States and Panama's negotiating an agreement to allow U.S. military forces to remain in Panama after the expiration of the basic treaty. On March 13, Christopher met with Byrd, Church, Sarbanes, Nunn, Talmadge, and others to discuss tactics. It was agreed that the reservation should be introduced by Sam Nunn, a highly respected southern Democrat whose vote was certain to influence other conservatives, and who was up for reelection in Georgia. Joined by Senator Herman Talmadge of Georgia, he introduced the reservation Christopher had drafted just before the final vote on the Neutrality Treaty. The two senators were thus able to declare that this reservation allowed them, "reluctantly," to support the treaty.

Arizona Senator Dennis DeConcini, who was thought to be leaning against the treaty, had in late February begun pressing for an amendment to the Neutrality Treaty to state explicitly the right of the United States to take whatever measures "it deems necessary . . . in Panama" to keep the canal open and operating. An implication of his amendment was that this right could apply to internal threats, as well as to external threats. This proposal was extremely upsetting to Panama, and unnecessary as well, in light of the Senate's approval of the Byrd-Baker leadership amendment incorporating the language of the Carter-Torrijos understanding into the Neutrality Treaty. But DeConcini insisted that it was essential that he, too, be the main sponsor of a condition if he were to vote for the treaty. It was still unclear whether we would have the necessary 67 votes, and it appeared that at least two or three waverers would follow DeConcini. Therefore, despite the misgivings of some of his advisers, the president agreed that we should work with DeConcini. Christopher met with him several times to argue that his proposal should be in the form of a reservation to the Resolution of Ratification, rather than an amendment to the treaty, and to suggest improved language, in particular removing the words "in Panama."

By March 13, DeConcini had abandoned his insistence on a treaty amendment and agreed to put it in the form of a reservation. However, Christopher's best efforts to get him to modify his proposed language were only partly successful. Early on March 16, DeConcini telephoned Christopher to say he would not change the language asserting the U.S. right "to take such steps as it deems necessary, including the use of force in Panama, to reopen the Canal or restore the operations of the Canal, as the case may be." Carter called DeConcini to tell him that the administration would support his reservation as it stood if he would vote for the Neutrality Treaty. Earlier, on March 15, Carter had forewarned Torrijos that the DeConcini reservation would be adopted, and he had pleaded for Panamanian restraint. Torrijos' negotiating team had warned Jorden that the DeConcini reservation could cause Panama to reject the Neutrality Treaty. It nearly did. Torrijos came very close to calling it off. Only the greatest patience and pragmatism enabled the Panamanians to remain silent while the president did what was necessary to get the treaty through.

The morning of March 16 we briefly considered asking a treaty proponent to introduce a new understanding reasserting the principle of nonintervention contained in the October 14 joint statement. The idea was discussed with the Panamanians, who were initially inclined to allow us to go ahead. However, Senator Byrd and other treaty supporters, although supporting the concept, feared that it would undo what had been won through the DeConcini reservation. DeConcini himself objected to such a new understanding. To lose DeConcini and perhaps one or two votes that might go with him would mean the likely defeat of the Neutrality Treaty. When the Panamanians heard this assessment they agreed it would be better not to offer it. However, the idea of a counterbalancing understanding was to reappear in the debate over the second treaty.

After defeating a final flood of proposed amendments, the Senate, on March 16, by a vote of 68–32 (one more than the two-thirds needed), approved the Neutrality Treaty with the Byrd-Baker amendment, the DeConcini and Nunn-Talmadge reservations, and a number of uncontroversial reservations and understandings. The final vote was a scene of high drama I will never forget. I was in the vice-president's Capitol Hill office throughout the vote observing the action ebb and flow, as each senator cast his vote. We were not sure the treaty would pass until the last senator voted. There were many brave senators who paid a high price in the next election for the courage they showed that day.

• • •

Debate on the Panama Canal Treaty began the next day. The vote on the Neutrality Treaty had shown that the treaty proponents had the strength to defeat all challenges. Recognizing this, the opposition agreed to an early vote on the second treaty. The Federal District Court had rejected the contention that the executive branch could not dispose of the canal without the approval of the House as well as the Senate. In the first test vote on April 5, the Senate turned back a proposal by Senator Orrin Hatch that the Canal Treaty's entry into force should be conditional upon congressional approval of the disposition of U.S. property in the zone.* If the proposal were approved, the opponents would have a new battleground. The April 5 vote appeared to be a decisive indicator of Senate sentiment. Therefore, although we recognized that the debate on the second treaty would be as arduous as the first, we anticipated no unusual difficulties.

The Panamanians had acted with restraint during the debate on the first treaty in the face of severe provocation from its opponents. They had been outraged by the DeConcini reservation and at what they considered an insulting and demeaning assertion of an American right to intervene in their internal affairs. Torrijos had written Carter, protesting that the reservation altered the basic character of the Neutrality Treaty, and Panama had circulated a similar statement at the United Nations. Torrijos had telephoned Carter on March 21 to insist that some way be found to offset the DeConcini reservation.

Not only had DeConcini refused Carter's request, now he intended to offer a similar amendment to the Canal Treaty. The problem of reconciling the U.S. right to maintain the canal's neutrality with Panama's right not to suffer unilateral American intervention was wide open again. The credit for resolving this difficult problem and getting the treaty back on track goes to Warren Christopher, the Senate leadership, especially senators Byrd, Church, and Sarbanes, and the Panamanian leadership.

Out of his discussions with leading senators, Christopher had come to the opinion that a second DeConcini reservation might actually provide a vehicle for restating the principle of nonintervention. Working with Byrd, Church, and Sarbanes, Christopher developed a statement that could be integrated into the DeConcini reservation. However, while he appeared to accept the idea of a generalized declaration of nonintervention, DeConcini objected to Christopher's language, and for several days the leadership and Warren labored to produce something that would

---

* Entry into force means the time at which a treaty becomes effective.

satisfy DeConcini and Senate conservatives, yet speak to Panamanian sensitivities. By April 13 a version had been developed that the Panamanians found acceptable. However, DeConcini contended that this version still tended to undermine the intent of his original proposal. At this point, Byrd, Church, and other senators asked us to stand back from the debate and allow the Senate to try to resolve its internal disagreements.

The next day, the Senate leaders devised a new variation, one we could accept. On April 15, Christopher met with senators Byrd, Church, and Sarbanes and Panamanian representatives to discuss this draft reservation, and the language was again slightly modified. The revised reservation now declared that ". . . any action taken by the United States of America in the exercise of its rights to assure that the Panama Canal shall remain open, neutral, secure and accessible . . . shall be only for the purpose of assuring that the Canal shall remain open, secure, and accessible, and shall not have as its purpose nor be interpreted as a right of intervention in the internal affairs of the Republic of Panama, or interference with its political independence or sovereign integrity."

Panamanian leaders informed us that the draft reservation was both acceptable and desirable. The reservation was then introduced by senators Byrd, Baker, Church, Sarbanes, Javits, Leahy, Gravel, and DeConcini, and adopted on April 18. The Senate approved the Canal Treaty that day by the same 68–32 vote as the Neutrality Treaty.

Carter and Torrijos exchanged the instruments of ratification in Panama City on June 16, although the treaties did not enter into force until 1979. A prolonged and difficult struggle ensued in both houses of Congress to secure passage of the necessary implementing legislation (although the treaties would have gone into effect without it) as the opponents continued a strenuous, ultimately futile, rearguard action.

•   •   •

The Panama Canal Treaties were an indispensable part of the Carter administration's strategy to forge a new and more constructive relationship with the nations of the Western hemisphere and the Third World. Failure to resolve the decades-long dispute with Panama in a just and equitable manner would have made a positive American policy toward Latin America difficult, if not impossible, given the depth of hemispheric feeling about the Panama Canal as a symbol of American hegemony and intervention in the region. It is difficult to imagine how the United States could hope to deal in any affirmative way with the turbulence in Central America and the Caribbean today if, in addition to problems in Nicaragua and El Salvador, we also confronted Panamanian nationalism directed against the canal and the Canal Zone.

It is argued, even by some who served in the administration, that by putting the Panama Canal issue at the top of our agenda we dissipated political strength that should have been reserved for larger, more important issues. In my judgment, this argument is wrong on two counts. First, the Panama Canal issue was of great national importance in its own right. The resolution of this explosive issue was long overdue, and the time was ripe for settling it. The Torrijos government, which was willing and able to negotiate and ratify an acceptable treaty, was not immune to the forces of radicalism that fed on the canal dispute. It badly needed to settle this issue on terms acceptable to Panamanian opinion in order to stave off these pressures. Had we delayed negotiations for domestic political reasons, the Torrijos government might have been replaced by a weaker regime unable to gather support for any treaty that protected our interest in preserving the secure, efficient operation of the canal. Alternatively, Torrijos might have been forced to yield to ultranationalist pressures and to acquiesce to violent disruption of the canal operations. Such an outcome could easily have expanded into an international confrontation, with world opinion solidly united against the United States. Moving promptly to negotiate and ratify treaties that would guarantee secure and unimpeded operation of the canal was in our national interests.

Moreover, the president knew that negotiating a fair treaty with Panama would serve the cause of peace and stability in the region. As in the Middle East, Carter did what he thought American values and interests demanded, even though he was keenly aware of the political risks.

Second, to suggest that the president started his term with a stock of political "credits" which he depleted excessively in order to gain approval of the canal treaties is to take an overly simplistic view of the relationship between the executive and legislative branches. Panama was a discrete issue with its own particular set of emotional, political, and psychological baggage. The president and the sixty-eight senators who voted for the treaties all took political risks. Some paid a heavy price for their courageous action. But to conclude that the president's ability to work with Congress on difficult foreign policy issues was weaker because of Panama claims too much. The ratification of the treaties showed that the administration was able to take the most contentious foreign policy problem on the national agenda and build a coalition in Congress for its resolution.

In my opinion, the president's problems in dealing with Congress had much more to do with the rightward shift in the temper of the country, a shift that had been underway for some time and that began to accelerate in 1979 and 1980. But that shift was more a reflection of national frustration and anger at the growing complexity and intractability of political, economic, and security issues than it was the product of an anxiety generated by the Panama Canal Treaties that saw them as a symbol of national "decline."

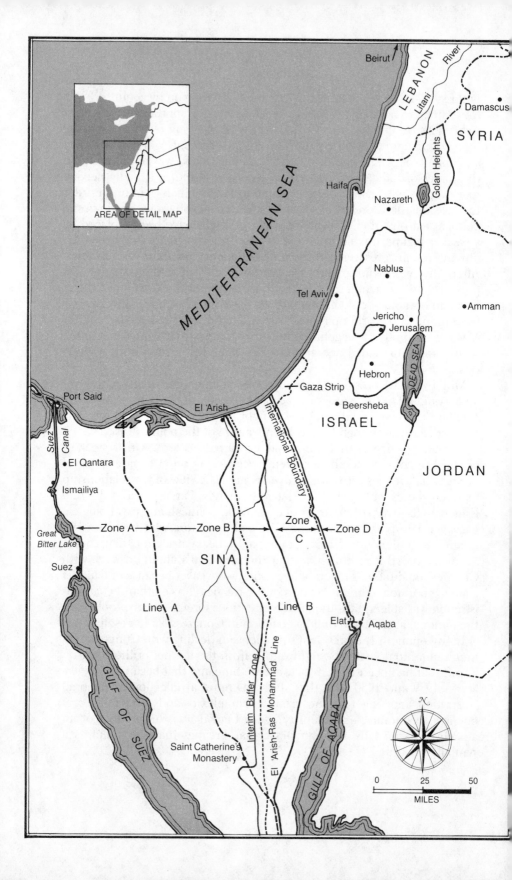

AREA OF DETAIL MAP

MEDITERRANEAN SEA

Beirut

LEBANON

Litani

River

Damascus

SYRIA

Haifa

Nazareth

Golan Heights

Nablus

Tel Aviv

Amman

Jericho

Jerusalem

Gaza Strip

Hebron

DEAD SEA

Port Said

El 'Arish

Beersheba

Suez Canal

ISRAEL

International Boundary

El Qantara

JORDAN

Ismailiya

Zone A

Zone B

Zone
C

Zone D

Great
Bitter Lake

SINA

Suez

Line A

Line B

GULF OF SUEZ

Elat

Aqaba

Interim Buffer Zone

El 'Arish-Ras Mohammad Line

Saint Catherine's
Monastery

GULF OF AQABA

N

0   25   50

MILES

9

THE ADMINISTRATION
AND THE MIDDLE EAST:
NEGOTIATIONS BEGIN

BACKGROUND

IN THE SIX DAY WAR OF JUNE 1967, Israel decisively defeated Egypt, Syria, and Jordan and gained complete military supremacy in the region. Of Egypt's territory, Israel occupied the Sinai peninsula up to the Suez Canal, including the Gaza strip. Jordanian forces were driven from the West Bank between the Jordan River and the 1949 Israeli frontier, including East Jerusalem. Finally, Israel seized from Syria the strategic Golan Heights, the hills from which Syrian artillery had shelled Israeli villages and farms in the Galilee Valley below.

After the 1967 war and after five months of negotiation, United Nations Security Council Resolution 242 was adopted. Resolution 242 called for recognition of the right of all states in the area to live in peace within secure and recognized boundaries, and for withdrawal of Israel from occupied territories. Resolution 242 represented the consensus of the international community that lasting peace would come only through a bargain between Israel and its Arab neighbors: Israel would relinquish land in exchange for Arab acceptance of Israel's right to exist in peace and security.

A major difference in interpretation of Resolution 242 existed between Israel and most of the rest of the world, particularly with respect to the phrase "withdrawal from territories." Israel ultimately interpreted the phrase to require withdrawal from *some*, but not substantially *all* occupied territories. Israel also ruled out withdrawal from East Jerusalem, which had been governed by Jordan since the war for Israel's independence ended in 1948–49. In July 1967, in an act of de facto annexation, Israel extended its law to that portion of the city as well.

The Arab states interpreted the phrase in question to require Israeli withdrawal from *all* the territories occupied in 1967. The United States understood the spirit of the resolution as requiring Israel's withdrawal from most of the territories, but accepted the necessity for minor border changes for security or humanitarian reasons and to allow for a sensible arrangement in Jerusalem. The United States also took the position that the final borders should be defined in negotiations. Israel shared that view, whereas the Arab states held that Resolution 242 required Israel's total withdrawal.

The ambiguous language of Resolution 242, which was necessary to secure Security Council approval of the resolution, was to become a source of sharp disagreement between Israel and the United States. First, while the Israeli Labor party governments between 1967 and 1977 accepted in principle that Resolution 242 required some withdrawal on all fronts, it became apparent that Israel intended a major redrawing of the boundaries for security reasons. Then under Prime Minister Menachem Begin, it became increasingly clear that his Likud coalition government intended to assert a claim of sovereignty over the West Bank and probably Gaza and would not accept the principle of withdrawal as applying to these areas.

Resolution 242 dealt with the Palestinian issue only as a refugee problem. Under the existing political circumstances the United States and others in Europe and the Arab world who supported Resolution 242 assumed that the territories from which Israel would withdraw would revert to the Arab authorities who controlled them before 1967. They did not, at that time, focus on the question of a Palestinian state. It was only in 1969 and 1970 that serious attention began to focus on the Palestinian people and their aspiration for a homeland in the West Bank and Gaza.

The opposition of Arab states and the main Palestinian political organization, the Palestine Liberation Organization (PLO), to negotiations and to recognition of Israel's right to exist dimmed any real hope of a peaceful settlement. The dependence of some Arab parties on the Soviet Union for arms and political support increased. American identification with Israel, on the other hand, reduced U.S. diplomatic flexibility in mediating between the sides. During the period between the 1967 and 1973 Arab-Israeli wars, the UN with U.S. support unsuccessfully attempted to bring the parties to the negotiating table.

Faced with a prolonged deadlock in the peace effort in October 1973, the Arabs again resorted to military force and economic pressure. The political and diplomatic stalemate in the Middle East was broken by the concerted Egyptian-Syrian attack on Israel and the selective Arab oil embargo against the United States, western Europe, and other supporters of Israel. Even though the Arab attack failed to dislodge Israel from the occupied territories, the entire atmosphere of the Middle East was dramatically changed. Limited Arab military gains and the oil embargo helped restore Arab self-respect and made them more aware of their economic leverage over the West, while Israeli military strength showed the moderate Arabs that their lands could not be regained by force. In fact, evidence indicates that President Anwar Sadat's purposes in going to war were mainly political and diplomatic. In accepting UN Security Council Resolution 338, which ended the war and called for negotiation, Egypt explicitly recognized the necessity of negotiating with Israel and implicitly conceded Israel's legitimacy as a state. Neither Egypt nor any of the other principal Arab actors, however, was yet willing to consider more than an end to the state of war with Israel. They were far from ready to contemplate full peace and normalization of relations.

The 1973 war and the oil embargo also marked a transformation of the U.S. role in the search for peace in the Middle East. No longer could the United States afford to leave primary responsibility for initiatives to achieve a settlement in other hands. Nor could the United States appear in Arab eyes as insensitive to the Palestinian problems and occupation of Arab lands. The interrelationship between Arab oil, the industrialized West's strategic and economic interests in Middle East stability, the sharpening focus of the U.S.-Soviet rivalry in the Third World, and the incalculable impact of a fifth major Arab-Israeli war on the United States fundamentally altered our stake in achieving a peaceful and lasting solution of the conflict. Without weakening its basic commitment to the existence of Israel, the United States began to move toward a position of active intermediary between the two sides.

Direct American involvement after October 1973 was feasible for several reasons. The Arabs had finally recognized that the Soviet Union could do little beyond providing military assistance. Because of Israel's fear of Soviet aims in the region, the USSR was unable to take the initiative in shaping a peace process. Moreover, conservative states, such as Saudi Arabia and the Persian Gulf sheikhdoms, and moderate leaders, such as President Anwar Sadat of Egypt and King Hussein of Jordan, shared American concerns that Arab radicalism, feeding on the Arab-Israeli confrontation, could provide a base for the expansion of Soviet influence. Feared by Israel, treated with caution even by its closest Arab friends, the Soviet Union was essentially limited to a secondary role in the post-1973 effort to start negotiations. Conversely, despite its long association with Israel, the United States had access to all sides, including the key Arab parties. Moderate Arab leaders understood they could not shake the U.S. commitment to the security of Israel, but they believed the clear American national interest in stability in the Middle East gave them significant leverage in seeking an acceptable political settlement.

Since Sadat's expulsion of Soviet military advisers in 1972, Egypt, with Saudi Arabia's financial and political support, had been turning away from the Soviet Union and the more radical Arab nations. After the 1973 war, Sadat increasingly began to look to the United States as the most likely catalyst for securing the return of Arab lands, an acceptable solution to the Palestinian problem, and a durable Mideast peace. Along with this shift in political orientation, President Sadat also embarked on an economic policy designed to bring Egypt's economy and development closer to the West.

In December 1973, the United States and the Soviet Union, acting under the auspices of the United Nations, invited Egypt, Syria, Jordan, and Israel to attend a Middle East peace conference in Geneva. The negotiations were to be based on the principles of Resolutions 242 and 338. Syria, angered by what it regarded as Sadat's betrayal in unilaterally stopping the October 1973 war, refused to attend. After two days of plenary discussions, the conference adjourned to consider specific issues in bilateral working groups. It was hoped that once they had made sufficient progress, the conference would be reconvened to conclude a comprehensive peace agreement. In fact, the sides were too deeply divided even to discuss the fundamental issues of peace, security, borders, and the Palestinian question. Nevertheless, at the beginning of the Carter administration, the conference still was widely regarded as the most appropriate forum for the negotiation of a comprehensive peace.

It was against this background that Henry Kissinger, in a dazzling diplomatic tour de force, negotiated the 1974 disengagement agreements in Sinai and the Golan Heights and the second Sinai agreement in September 1975, in which Israel withdrew from a further portion of the Sinai and returned it to Egypt. Kissinger felt that the distrust between Egypt and Syria, the intransigence of Arab radicals, and Arab disunity prevented a serious attempt to conclude an overall solution. He therefore developed the so-called "step-by-step" strategy of partial bilateral agreements to separate the parties, reduce the risk of renewed conflict, and begin the long task of building each side's confidence in the negotiating process.

Egypt's interests in negotiations were clear. Sadat understood that war could not regain the lost territory. The return of a portion of the Sinai gained Sadat time to strengthen his domestic political base and encourage the United States to play a more evenhanded role between the Arabs and Israelis. But Israel's price for the small Sinai withdrawal was high. Israel's perception was that it was surrendering territory, its security buffer and greatest bargaining asset, with little assurance that useful steps toward genuine peace and full normalization of relations would continue. Thus, it demanded that the Ford administration agree, among other things, to coordinate with Israel any future U.S. peace proposals and to refrain from recognizing or negotiating with the PLO until it acknowledged Israel's right to exist and accepted Resolutions 242 and 338. The Israelis interpreted the first commitment as giving them a veto over the presentation of U.S. ideas for peace to the Arabs. The second commitment, while it was essential for Israeli confidence in the United States as intermediary, was to make our task of finding a way to deal with the PLO close to impossible at a time when the Palestinian question had become a pivotal issue.

DEVELOPING OUR MIDDLE EAST POLICY

President-elect Carter and I first discussed the basic elements of his administration's approach to the Middle East at length during our foreign policy review at his home in Plains in late 1976.

There was substantial agreement between the Nixon-Ford assessment of U.S. political, strategic, and economic interests in Middle East peace and that of President Carter and myself. We concluded that the step-by-step approach had exhausted its potential and that it was time to renew the pursuit of a comprehensive peace. Without question, the bedrock of the Carter Middle East policy would continue to be our commitment to Israel's security. We agreed, however, that the critical importance of stable, moderate, pro-Western regimes in the Middle East and access to Arab oil meant that a return to a passive U.S. posture was not realistic. The United States would have to be a fair and active mediator between the parties if there was to be any chance of a genuine peace. Playing this role would necessarily require serious attention on the part of the mediator to both sides of the dispute and a sincere effort to address the Palestinian problem. Because of the intimate American association with Israel in previous Middle East peace efforts, for Carter to adopt an activist, balanced policy carried a significant political risk. He could be seen both at home and in Israel as tilting toward the Arabs and pressuring Israel to make dangerous territorial concessions. In this, as in many other decisions at the outset of his administration, Jimmy Carter unflinchingly refused to take the easy course on politically sensitive foreign policy matters.

Carter and I concurred that avoiding another major Middle East war was imperative for U.S. and Western interests. Despite overwhelming Israeli military superiority, we believed the possibility of a new Arab military gamble or an Israeli preemptive attack could not be dismissed. An element of our concern was the dangerous possibility that another war could lead to a U.S.-Soviet confrontation in the region—either directly or on behalf of friends—that might escalate into conflict.

There was an additional dimension to the Carter policy that sharply distinguished our Middle East approach from that of our predecessors. Peace in the region would be a critical element in a broader American strategy for shaping a more cooperative world order in the coming decades. To cope with the complex challenges of a prolonged period of widespread, turbulent upheaval, we believed we would have to work toward developing institutions and processes for the prompt and orderly resolution of conflicts and the accommodation of social, economic, and political change. I also felt that in addition to serving the people of the region, peace in the Middle East would give support to those at home and abroad who believed that resolution of potential or incipient conflicts could be resolved by peaceful means.

My sense was that the heart of the Middle East question was the intrinsic right of both Jews and Arabs to live side by side in peace and security. Ejected from their homes, embittered, radicalized, living in squalor and desperation, the Palestinians remained the central, unresolved, human rights issue of the Middle East. The president and I were convinced that no lasting solution in the Middle East would be possible until, consistent with Israel's right to live in peace and security, a just answer to the Palestinian question could be found, one almost certainly leading to a Palestinian homeland and some form of self-determination.

Neither of us was under any illusion that the search for peace would be easy or without daunting risks. Failure could lead to the overthrow of moderate Arab leaders, the strengthening of anti-Western Arab radicals, an increase in Soviet influence, a return to the brink of war. We recognized, however, that the peace process could be revived only if the United States provided the leadership. Only the United States commanded sufficient confidence and access to the participants to undertake a major initiative. Nevertheless, I advised President Carter in November of 1976 that as a practical matter the Soviet Union, with political interests in the region and as a patron of several Arab states, should be accorded a role in negotiations that would help to dissuade it from undermining our efforts. Without doubt Moscow would seek to augment its influence in ways we might oppose. But by any rational calculation, the Soviet Union had a fundamental interest in avoiding a superpower confrontation in this pivotal area.

President Carter and I agreed that his administration would take an immediate, leading role in breathing new life into the Middle East peace process, building on the foundations laid by our predecessors. Even before the president took office we made plans that I would go to the Middle East as early as February of 1977. In order to make this possible, I asked Brzezinski to accelerate the National Security Council policy review process for developing a cabinet-level consensus on our objectives.

• • •

My principal Middle East advisers were Roy Atherton, then assistant secretary for Near East and South Asian affairs (NEA) and subsequently ambassador at large for the Middle East negotiations, and Hal Saunders, at that time director of intelligence and research (INR) and later Atherton's successor. These two extraordinarily able diplomats possessed unparalleled understanding of Arab-Israeli issues, each of them having been involved with Arab-Israeli problems for over fifteen years. These qualifications were coupled with an inspiring ability to work together and with others in and outside the State Department without bureaucratic rivalry. Their disinterested, patient, and imaginative policy analysis and support were vital to our participation in the peace process over the next three years.

Together with Anthony Lake, the brilliant and invaluable director of policy planning in the State Department on whom I relied heavily on a host of matters, Saunders, Atherton, and their staffs undertook a thorough review of the Middle East situation at the beginning of 1977 and presented the broad policy options they believed were open to the Carter administration. They were joined in this enterprise by the particularly gifted and imaginative William Quandt, the Middle Eastern expert on the NSC staff. Bill Quandt worked in total harmony with his State Department counterparts. The cooperative effort of this interagency team was a model for others to follow.

The experts posed two alternative strategies for the president and the Policy Review Committee to consider. The first was a "damage-limiting" approach of minimal involvement in the face of apparently intractable issues and the steep political risks of failure. An activist approach intended to hold the initiative for the United States and convince the parties that the new administration was prepared to participate directly in reviving the negotiating process was the alternative. The experts laid out the first option to assure that the new administration faced squarely the heavy political weather a serious peace initiative would provoke. They strongly recommended that we start moving at once to break the political impasse that existed and to regain the momentum of 1974 and 1975.

They warned, however, that an activist approach was certain to lead to strains in our relations with Israel. As the president and I had already recognized, this risk was unavoidable. Israel, with its national existence at stake and suspicious of the Arabs' sincerity, feared rapid change, outside pressures, and confronting frightening decisions about its security. A serious negotiating effort, especially one aimed at a comprehensive settlement, would require actions by Israel that would be internally divisive. Clearly it would be difficult for Israel to make such decisions. Its leadership would have to be convinced through a careful process of dealing incrementally with specific, operational issues that the proposed actions were consistent with Israel's national interests. The cumulative effect of a series of individual decisions could eventually result in basic changes in Israeli positions, while maintaining their confidence that the process was under control and was headed in an acceptable direction.

There would, of course, also be severe strains on U.S.-Arab relations, as we sought to convince them that the occupied lands could be recovered and the Palestinian question resolved only through unreserved Arab acceptance of Israel in a full peace, with secure, yet open, borders and normal economic and political relations. The Arab nations, even those committed to a settlement, were still psychologically unready to accept real peace. They saw peace at most as a formal end of the state of war. But the key Arab states, Egypt, Syria, and Jordan, wanted U.S. mediation and would expect us to exert pressure on both sides to compromise their maximum demands.

The immediate question to be decided in those first hectic weeks was whether our basic objective should be a partial or comprehensive settlement. Again, the experts' analysis coincided with my own sense that a comprehensive settlement, rather than resumption of efforts to achieve new interim agreements, was the proper road to follow. Attempting to reach a comprehensive peace would not, of course, rule out falling back to additional partial agreements if that was all that appeared possible.

The decision to seek a comprehensive settlement dictated our first goal of getting the parties to agree to reconvene the Geneva conference on Middle East peace, which had been dormant since December 1973. This seemed within reach on the Arab side—at least in principle—since Egypt, Syria, and Jordan tended to equate a Geneva conference with negotiation of a comprehensive settlement. To the Arabs, a comprehensive settlement meant a resolution of the Palestinian question as well as the return of the occupied territories. The greatest difficulty was that Israel preferred to negotiate individually with each Arab state in order to obtain separate settlements. This was not acceptable to most of the Arabs, who saw strength in Arab unity. Notwithstanding, I thought it likely Israel would go to Geneva so long as the agenda and procedural arrangements did not compromise its positions in advance.

The apparent consensus in favor of reconvening Geneva masked a number of complex substantive issues. It was by no means certain that these matters could be resolved in time to get the parties together by our target date of the end of 1977. We had concluded that it was vital to have visible progress by that time if the moderate Arabs were to withstand internal and external pressures for renewed confrontation with Israel.

To avoid a repetition of the inconclusive 1973 conference, the Arabs insisted on a large measure of advance agreement on substantive issues, particularly Israeli withdrawal to the borders that existed in 1967. On the other hand, the Arabs were deeply divided on procedures for a conference, a reflection of internal suspicions and differing objectives. The Egyptians, with Arab "great power" status and more experience in negotiating with Israel, preferred to send a national Egyptian delegation and to deal bilaterally with Israel. The Syrians, feeling Sadat had left them in the lurch in ending the 1973 war and needing Egypt's weight on the negotiating scale, wanted a single pan-Arab delegation in order to prevent Egypt from concluding an agreement before Syria and Jordan could settle with Israel. Discussion of this issue took the form of debate over whether a conference should negotiate in plenary session or, as in 1973, break up into separate committees. Related to this was the question of whether such committees should be organized on a geographical (e.g., Egypt-Israel) or functional (e.g., borders, security, and so on) basis. Egypt favored a geographical and Syria and Jordan a functional approach.

Behind all these issues loomed the greatest procedural problem of all: how were the Palestinians to participate? Could the PLO, designated by the Arabs as the "sole legitimate representative" of the Palestinian people, yet the mortal enemy of Israel, attend a peace conference? Would it form a separate delegation or be integrated into a pan-Arab delegation? If national delegations were the rule, in which should it appear? Would the Israelis, viscerally opposed to any contact with the PLO, accept any device that would enable PLO representatives to be present?

Israel had strong views on all these questions. In addition, there were important constraints on U.S. flexibility in proposing solutions to any of these problems. The commitments of the Nixon and Ford administrations mentioned earlier gave us a rather narrow line to walk in discussing our ideas with Israel before trying them out with the Arabs.

Against this background, it became apparent that my first trip to the area must be devoted largely to exploring the issues and sounding out the ideas of the parties. Nevertheless, my aim was also to start discussion of American ideas for overcoming the obstacles that stood in the way of a conference. As I prepared to leave, the president determined that our objective would be a consensus that with active U.S. leadership, the common goal would be a new Geneva conference in the second half of 1977.

Finally, I was to begin the long, arduous task of showing the two sides that their goals were asymmetrical. The Arabs wanted a return of all the occupied territories in exchange for merely an end to the legal state of war. Israel wanted full peace, normalization of relations, and security in exchange for only a partial withdrawal from the occupied territories. As long as the parties held to these maximum positions, there was no chance for successful negotiations.

Looking beyond the February trip, the president and the Policy Review Committee agreed that the president should meet with the key Arab leaders and the Israeli prime minister during the spring and early summer. These meetings would demonstrate that the president was committing his personal prestige and influence to the peace process. The best way of bringing the sides, especially the Israelis, to face up to hard, dangerous choices was for Carter to intervene directly in the negotiating process at critical moments. Without his personal involvement, it was unlikely that the leaders, Arab or Israeli, would have sufficient confidence to take the necessary risks to achieve peace.

• • •

On February 14 I left for an eight-day trip to Israel, Egypt, Jordan, Saudi Arabia, and Syria. In what may have been the first exercise in shuttle diplomacy as Lyndon Johnson's emissary during the 1967 Cyprus crisis, I had shuttled back and forth among Ankara, Athens, and Nicosia until an agreement was reached avoiding war between Greece and Turkey. Now I was about to embark on the first of many visits to the Middle East over the next three years.

Shuttle diplomacy has both advantages and disadvantages. Its advantages are obvious. It demonstrates the importance attached to the mission, and it is usually conducted at a high level, which permits the making of decisions on the spot. It has become expected practice, particularly in the Middle East, where personal diplomacy is so important. Its disadvantages are serious. Shuttling at ministerial level invites the spotlight. Everything is done in a glare of publicity that inhibits concessions and compromises. It raises the political stakes for the mediating country because every mission is measured in terms of success or failure. It imposes enormous physical and mental strains on the participants, usually in a compressed time frame, and sometimes important decisions have been made by delegations that are on the point of exhaustion. Finally, it take the minister away from duties at home in running his department. Despite these difficulties, however, shuttle diplomacy is often essential to break through impasses that will not yield to more conventional diplomatic means.

From my discussions during this initial trip, there emerged four fundamental issues that would have to be addressed in varying degrees of specificity before we could get to the peace table: the nature of the peace to be negotiated; the ultimate boundaries between Israel and its neighbors; the question of a Palestinian homeland; and the procedural questions of how to organize and conduct a renewed Geneva conference, including representation of the Palestinians.

The nature of the peace. For the Israelis, the nature of the peace to be concluded was the ultimate test of Arab sincerity. In our discussions on February 16, Prime Minister Yitzhak Rabin, a dour and shrewd soldier-statesman, emphasized to me that peace did not mean the absence of a state of war; rather there must be full peace with normalization of relations, open borders, and Arab acceptance of Israel as a legitimate state. Rabin was profoundly skeptical of Arab intentions and adamant that

Israel would not trade territory for symbolic Arab gestures that could be withdrawn at any time.

Anwar Sadat showed more flexibility on the question of peace than the other Arab leaders I met. Although he was not prepared to agree in advance to normal relations with Israel, he indicated that he expected such relations to develop over time as the basic issues were resolved and as Arabs and Israelis became accustomed to peace. President Hafez al-Assad of Syria was adamant against full peace, insisting that the history of the Arab-Israeli conflict would not allow more than peaceful coexistence for a long time to come. King Hussein of Jordan, concerned about survival of his nation amid stronger powers on all sides, would go no further than Sadat and Assad. His protection against Palestinian and radical pressures on his kingdom was Arab unity.

Boundaries. Rabin told me that Israel was willing to compromise on borders, but would not return to the 1967 lines. For him the central problem was not sovereignty over territories, but security for Israel, which meant the presence of the Israeli Defense Forces (IDF), not United Nations or even U.S. forces, within defensible borders. Neither Rabin nor his successor saw security guarantees, including a defense treaty with the United States, as a sufficient inducement for withdrawal. For all Israelis, the status of Jerusalem was nonnegotiable. Nothing seemed to touch this sensitive chord more than assertion of the long-standing American position against the annexation of East Jerusalem.

All the Arab leaders insisted that Israel must withdraw to the 1967 lines, and King Hussein made an especially insistent demand for Arab sovereignty over East Jerusalem. While Sadat demanded total withdrawal from the Sinai and the Golan Heights, he recognized that certain rectifications in the border between Israel and the West Bank would be necessary, since the line had never been internationally recognized. He also accepted the reality of Israel's security concerns and was prepared to negotiate "secure" boundaries—although he defined secure boundaries in terms of demilitarized zones, international peacekeeping forces, and special monitoring arrangements. King Hussein was also willing to consider minor reciprocal changes in his border in the context of Israeli withdrawal from the West Bank. Sadat stressed that Israeli withdrawal from the occupied territories should not stretch out over a long period. With his experience in negotiating with Israel over the Sinai, he was convinced the Israelis would attempt to drag out withdrawal as long as possible.

Palestinian issues. As a negotiator, I sensed that there was room for compromise on the nature of the peace and even, with ingenuity and flexibility, on boundaries. But in the Palestinian question we faced the essence of the Arab-Israeli dispute. It was an issue rooted in history, passion, prejudice, fear, and hatred. Unless some means could be found to approach this explosive problem rationally, there could be no negotiation, no peace, and in the long run, no security for Israel or stability in the Middle East.

Rabin told me Israel could never accept an independent Palestinian state in the West Bank and Gaza because the real Arab aim was the reconquest of all Palestine. Pointing out that the Arabs had not created a Palestinian state when, before 1967, they controlled the West Bank and Gaza, Rabin insisted that the PLO would never accept a small independent state as a permanent solution and would use it as a base from which to continue its struggle to destroy Israel. He said Israel was willing to negotiate about the West Bank with Hussein, but there could be no independent state between Israel and Jordan. Rabin refused to be more specific, but the traditional Labor party position had been that Israel was prepared to negotiate a partition of the West Bank with Jordan.

Strikingly, some of the Arab leaders seemed willing to consider less than a fully independent Palestinian state in the West Bank and Gaza as part of a comprehensive settlement. However, all the Arab leaders were irrevocably committed to the principle that a comprehensive settlement must include resolution of the Palestinian problem. Sadat made clear that the Palestinian issue, not Sinai or the Golan Heights, should be at the top of the negotiating agenda. The solution he envisioned was a Palestinian state constitutionally linked with Jordan. At the Arab summit at Rabat in 1974, Hussein had been relieved of his role of representing the Palestinians in the West Bank and therefore refused to take a formal position. I gathered, however, that he also favored some form of federation or confederation between the kingdom of Jordan and a Palestinian state in the West Bank and Gaza. In 1970 he had fought the PLO in a bloody war to regain control of his own country, and he now seemed to be working to build a non-PLO political base in the West Bank as an alternative or counterweight to PLO domination of a future Palestinian state.

Surprisingly, Assad—on most issues the hardest of the three Arab leaders—also appeared ready to consider something less than a fully independent Palestinian state. His previous full support of PLO demands had moderated noticeably after bitter Syrian-PLO armed clashes in Lebanon. With some reticence, Assad acknowledged that he and the PLO were hardly on speaking terms. However, like Hussein, he was unwilling to be specific about the shape of a final settlement of the Palestinian homeland question, merely affirming that whatever was acceptable to the Palestinians would be acceptable to him.

Procedures. Of course, none of the foregoing issues could be settled unless the parties could be brought to the negotiating table. The issue of procedures thus sparked lengthy discussions, accompanied in the case of Israel by a high level of emotion.

Israel utterly refused to consider formal PLO attendance at Geneva, referring to the U.S. commitment made at the first Geneva conference to block the presence of any party not present in 1973 negotiations. Rabin told me, however, that at a Geneva conference Israel would not seek to inspect the credentials of the Jordanian delegation; I took this to mean that Israel would expect and tolerate Palestinians among the Jordanian delegation. Officially, however, Israel would not accept the presence of any PLO representative. Israeli Foreign Minister Yigal Allon also told us that "a PLO that accepts 242 would no longer be the PLO," which sparked further examination of how we could get the PLO to accept UN Security Council Resolution 242.

The Arab leaders had differing positions on the procedural issues. To deal with the Palestinian representation problem, Sadat suggested the Palestinians be represented either by the UN, by the Egyptian general heading the joint Arab military command, who had Palestinians on his staff, or that they be included in an Arab League delegation. Assad insisted that the PLO be invited to attend any conference. How the PLO manifested its presence was of less importance to him than that the PLO not be able to claim peace had been negotiated over its head. Hussein stated that Palestinians should be part of a single Arab delegation, which would include representatives of Syria, Egypt, and Jordan. He was adamant, because of the Rabat decision, that Palestinians could not be part of a national Jordanian delegation. We were informed that the PLO demanded a separate delegation, although it was not clear whether the PLO would accept an invitation without a prior Israeli commitment to a Palestinian state.

On the procedural problem of how to organize a Geneva conference to negotiate specific issues, Sadat and Rabin stood firm on their demand for a bilateral approach to the negotiating arrangements. Assad and Hussein were just as unyielding in insisting that the Arabs should attend as a single body, and negotiate "functional" rather than "geographical" issues together, as Egypt and Israel wanted. Except for the all-important Palestinian representation issue, Egypt and Israel were not very far apart on procedural matters. The real problem was disunity among the Arabs.

• • •

On my return from the Middle East, I believed that progress on convening a Geneva conference could be made before the end of 1977. We had shown the key parties that the Carter administration intended to play an active role in breaking the impasse. The very act of getting each of them to define its positions, to hear our account of the views of the others, and to recognize that the United States would seek compromise solutions was an important step in unfreezing the negotiating climate.

Everyone, even the Israelis, endorsed the goal of trying to convene a peace conference by the end of the year.

Our first problem was to work out acceptable conference procedures. Carter wanted to press the Arab leaders to reach a consensus on how to organize Arab, including Palestinian, participation before we entered the next phase of our approach—the president's meetings with the individual heads of government. I suggested that we should wait a short while to see if the Arabs could sort out this issue among themselves. I was very much aware that the Israelis were acutely nervous about our newborn activism and I did not want us to appear to be rushing things.

Over the next two weeks, my Middle East team and I worked with the president on preparations for his meetings, beginning with Rabin in early March. I believed we should not go into these meetings with the intention of offering an American peace plan. We still did not have a sufficient understanding of the positions of each party to see where the opportunities for compromise might lie. The Arabs, especially Sadat, were eager that we introduce our own proposals as quickly as possible, for they believed there would be no give in Israel's position unless we took the initiative. Clearly, there would come a time when we would have to put forward American proposals. For the time being, however, I believed we should proceed cautiously in order to avoid exacerbating Israeli apprehension and stirring unnecessary anxieties in Congress and the American Jewish community about American "pressure" on Israel.

I advised the president that another reason for continuing the "exploratory" phase through the spring meetings was that the United States "could live with a variety of outcomes in the Middle East provided they do not sow the seeds of future instability." We did not yet know what was feasible. My experience in difficult negotiations led me to maintain as much flexibility as we could at this early stage since we faced a long and rough road full of twists and surprises.

In our discussions before the beginning of the spring meetings, it was decided that at a minimum, we would try to determine:

• How far the Arabs were willing to go toward satisfying Israel's demand for full peace and normalization. We would make clear we stood firmly with Israel on this demand and that the Arabs could not expect the return of the occupied territories for anything less.

• Whether Israel would be prepared to withdraw to substantially the 1967 borders and what kinds of security guarantees and arrangements it would require in return. We would tell Rabin we did not believe Israel could have the peace it wanted without such a withdrawal.

• How far each side was prepared to go in devising an acceptable solution to the Palestinian question. We would explain our view that justice, stability, and peace demanded that some means be found for Palestinian self-determination without its leading to a radical, anti-Israel state on the West Bank. Without specifying a final outcome, we would probe how far the sides would go in relating the Palestinian question to the creation of a Palestinian "entity" or homeland.

• How much flexibility the parties were prepared to show on the procedural issues, including Palestinian representation.

THE SPRING MEETINGS

The Arab leaders approached the meetings with President Carter in a spirit of hope and cautious optimism. The Israelis, however, were preoccupied with forthcoming parliamentary elections and were anxious that we might be setting out on a dangerous course with unforeseeable consequences.

The Carter-Rabin talks in early March went badly. The chemistry between Carter and Rabin was poor, and the two appeared to grate on each other's nerves. By the end of the visit the president was angry at Rabin, regarding him as stubborn and unimaginative and unwilling to take positive steps or risks to achieve peace. Doubtless looking over his shoulder at Israeli domestic politics, Rabin was more rigid than when I had met him in Jerusalem. Pointing to the moderate Arabs' need for progress, he argued that the United States and Israel had an opportunity to extract concessions if we would take a tough stand together. He wanted us to seek advance Arab agreement that the principal purpose of a Geneva conference would be to negotiate "real" peace and normalization, with the "sequence" for implementing that peace to be the subject of detailed negotiations. He dismissed international or U.S.-Soviet guarantees of a settlement as meaningless; the only commitment Israel wanted from us was to supply arms. Nevertheless, Rabin did not retreat from his statements to me in February that Israel's primary concern was defensible borders, not sovereignty. Building on this, in a press conference on March 9 Carter carefully drew a distinction between internationally recognized borders and "defense lines," which might not be one and the same. Noting that the Israeli leaders also recognized this distinction, the president observed that "there may be extensions of Israeli defense capability beyond the permanent and recognized borders." He also stated our view that peace would involve Israeli withdrawal and "minor adjustments in the 1967 borders."

Sadat came to Washington a month later with one overriding aim: to learn whether President Carter was serious about providing leadership in seeking a Middle East peace. Sadat was risking everything in a gamble that Egypt could get a settlement that would enable him to turn his full attention to smoldering internal problems—political, economic, and social. He knew that without the president's leadership there would be no peace. Sadat wanted to be absolutely confident that Carter was committed to carrying through despite the domestic political problems he would have to face.

Anwar Sadat was a truly extraordinary man. A patriot, he was wise and visionary, bold and courageous, yet at the same time, private and sensitive. Above all, he valued loyalty and friendship. Once his trust was gained, he would stand with you unfailingly. From our first meeting in February, I was drawn to him by his warmth and charisma.

As he was to demonstrate repeatedly, Sadat had a flair for the dramatic, a strong sense of his role in history, and a broad strategic perspective. Intuitive rather than methodical, he preferred fluidity and mobility in his diplomacy, seeking to keep the parties to the Middle East dispute off balance, reacting to his initiatives. Bored by semantic wrangling, he had a strong proclivity for personal discussions by political leaders of what he considered the fundamental issues. The generosity of his nature made him impatient of details. Strong on principles, weak on implementation, he appeared to expect concrete solutions to flow automatically from political level agreement on the essentials and was frequently irritated by Israeli insistence on negotiating every issue to the last comma.

In their first meeting in April 1977, Carter and Sadat began developing a special bond of trust and confidence. Carter was frank about the political limitations on his freedom to act as an intermediary, and about the unwavering American commitment to the security of Israel. He was also blunt in stressing to Sadat the necessity for a public Arab commitment to full peace, the normalization of relations and acceptance of Israel as a legitimate nation if there was to be a durable settlement. Sadat halfheartedly resisted the idea of treaties with Israel and mentioned peace "agreements," out of which normalized relations would develop after Israel withdrew from Arab lands. However, before the summit ended, he said that full peace and normal relations might be possible within five years after a settlement; previously he had spoken of it taking a generation.

Before Sadat arrived we had decided to explore with him the feasibility of a continued Israeli military presence beyond its borders after a settlement. Sadat reiterated that he reluctantly accepted the necessity of security arrangements for Israel in return for withdrawal, and he was willing to agree to demilitarized zones, as well as U.S. or other international guarantees to Israel. He flatly refused, however, to accept a continuing Israeli military presence in any of the territories beyond the 1967 borders after withdrawal. He was also unenthusiastic about our suggestion of phased withdrawal of the IDF from the occupied territories in order to enhance Israeli confidence.

Sadat made it clear that he wanted to accelerate the pace of negotiations so he could point to some concrete progress before the end of the year. He confided to Carter that he was ready to be very flexible in order to get to Geneva if we could honestly assure him that Israel would seriously negotiate a comprehensive settlement. He did not disguise his fear that essentially Israel was satisfied with the status quo and was merely stringing us along in the exploratory talks.

The unique rapport between the two presidents added a special dimension to the Middle East peace process. How this bond developed between these two men—the systematic, precise, and logical Carter, and Sadat, who thought in broad, overall terms and shunned mere "detail"—remains something of a mystery. But the rapport was sincere and real. Because Sadat trusted Carter, he was repeatedly willing to take Carter's word that a given step was necessary; and because Carter truly believed Sadat wanted peace, he was willing to take repeated political risks to maintain the momentum of the negotiating process.

After the Rabin and Sadat visits we took stock. Despite serious problems ahead, the president agreed that reconvening the Geneva conference by year's end remained a high U.S. priority. The talks with Sadat reinforced our appraisal that he and the other moderate Arab leaders needed a Geneva conference to avoid a deterioration in their political positions. Carter decided that as soon as he completed his round of talks with Arab and Israeli leaders, I should return to the Middle East to try to work out agreement on the procedural issues. The president agreed that we would have to make American proposals on these matters to bridge the differences, even if this caused strains with Israel.

In late April, King Hussein came to Washington to meet with the president. He was accompanied by his very able and wise minister of court, Abdul Hamid Sharaf, who was later to become prime minister. The meeting went well and was illuminating for the president and his advisers.

King Hussein showed himself a thoughtful and highly intelligent leader with great personal charm and dignity. Charismatic, urbane, articulate, and well informed, he was at ease with substantive discussions of detailed issues. Because of the small size and location of his country, Hussein has long had to rely on supple diplomacy and careful alignment with stronger powers for survival. Since coming to the throne in 1953 at only eighteen years of age, he has governed with skill and courage. I have always been struck by his gracious and kind manner with strangers as well as friends.

We met in the cabinet room at the White House on April 25. After a warm welcome, the president invited Hussein to assess the attitudes of the different Middle Eastern countries to the question of peace and to give us his suggestions on what we might do to accelerate negotiations.

Hussein gave a helpful and clear analysis of the positions of the key countries and their approaches to the pivotal questions of withdrawal, the nature of peace, and the Palestinian question. He underscored the importance to the Arab nations of withdrawal to the 1967 borders with minor reciprocal modifications. He stressed the point, as did the presi-

dent, that peace was more than the absence of war and that the ultimate
bargain called for under Resolution 242 was the trade of withdrawal for
real peace. He also emphasized the importance of solving the problem
of East Jerusalem. He recognized the necessity to Israel of adequate
security, but reminded us of what he had said to me as we stood on the
porch of his home looking across the Jordan Valley at the lights of Jerusalem: "Security is less a matter of geography and borders than a state of
mind and a feeling of wanting to live in peace."

Hussein dwelt at length on the importance of the Palestinian issues
and offered suggestions as to how these issues should be addressed. As
to Palestinian participation at a reconvened Geneva conference, he favored a single pan-Arab delegation which could break into functional
committees to deal with each topic, although he recognized that both
Egypt and the PLO were against such an approach. He also walked
carefully through a discussion of what the links would be between Jordan
and a "Palestinian entity" to be established in the West Bank and Gaza.
Both the president and I favored individual Arab delegations, if possible,
with Palestinian representatives preferably in the Jordanian delegation; if
this were impossible, we would accept a pan-Arab delegation.

The meeting closed with a discussion of the need for a framework for
negotiations. Hussein was adamant that without such a framework the
conference would face enormous difficulties. Hussein and Sharaf both
emphasized that after listening to all of the parties, the United States
would have to come forward with its own proposals. Without this, progress could not be made, they said. The meeting closed on a friendly note,
with further discussions to take place the next day on matters of bilateral
interest, such as military and economic assistance. The president also
indicated that I would be returning to the Middle East when he had
completed his talks with the other leaders.

The next summit meeting took place on May 9 in Geneva with President Hafez al-Assad. President Assad was another strong and forceful
leader with a sharp and penetrating mind and an overriding concern for
Arab solidarity. He believed deeply that only if the Arab states hung
together could they have the strength to negotiate with Israel, yet he was
a realist who recognized the divisions and tensions that existed within
the Arab world. Assad has often been described as cautious, flexible, and
pragmatic. He is all of those and much more. He possesses great self-
confidence, a good sense of humor, a sharp and biting wit, and the
patience required of a good negotiator. He is an impressive leader and a
man whom I grew to respect and like.

We met with him in the Intercontinental Hotel in Geneva, taking
advantage of the NATO summit in London to arrange a central meeting
point in Europe for the two presidents. President Carter was impressed
by President Assad's candor and intelligence. The two men got along
well.

Assad opened the meeting with a long and perceptive historical analysis of the region beginning with the colonial period and extending up to the present. This was followed by a discussion of the three central issues, land, peace, and the Palestinian question. Although no new ground was plowed, the meeting gave the president a good picture of Assad's views on these critical matters. Particularly useful were Assad's views on the Palestinian issues and his emphasis on addressing the problem of refugees (of which there were 192,915 in Syria), as well as the question of a Palestinian state. The president drew Assad out on the latter's views on the relations between the parties, should there be a Palestinian entity, including the possibility of a larger confederation of Jordan, Syria, and the West Bank, and perhaps Lebanon. The president also raised the question of whether the PLO could be persuaded to accept Resolution 242, except for the part in which the Palestinians were dealt with only as refugees. Assad responded that it would depend on what the PLO could get in return. The president indicated it would be helpful if the PLO would accept Resolution 242 and thus recognize Israel's right to exist, and he asked Assad to feel out the Palestinians on this matter. Assad agreed, but said it would have to be tied to the complete presentation on Palestinians rights, i.e., the manner in which the question of Palestinian rights would be addressed. The president responded by suggesting that we leave the matter open, saying that while he was making no commitment, it might be important to be able to talk to PLO Chairman Yasir Arafat directly.

Assad asked the president his view on Palestinian rights. Carter replied that he was not in a position to put forward solutions, but that the Palestinians must have a homeland, and his preference was that it be tied to Jordan or a larger confederation.

The meeting closed with a discussion of the nature of the peace, in which Assad said that he saw peace coming in stages, with the first stage being merely the end of a state of belligerency. Carter made it clear that he did not agree with this.

The final meeting between the president and individual Arab leaders took place on May 24 in Washington. Crown Prince Fahd, who would later become the king of Saudi Arabia, had arrived in the United States the day before, accompanied by Prince Saud and several other important cabinet ministers. We were looking forward to this meeting with anticipation because of the range of the discussions and the fact that Saudi Arabia could play a significant role in the search for a solution to the Arab-Israeli conflict.

King Fahd is an astute ruler, who has managed the affairs of his nation and employed its vast wealth effectively. His role has not been an easy one because the economic power and influence of his country have placed upon it a disproportionately large burden. This problem has been aggravated by Saudi Arabia's limited military forces and small population. In addition, the Saudi leadership has had to cope with the dangers of rapid modernization that threaten the country's Islamic system of values. All of these difficulties have been compounded by the rise of fundamentalist Islamic forces.

President Carter opened the meeting by referring to his speech at Notre Dame University on the preceding Sunday, in which he had spelled out our position on the Middle East. He said that he understood the crown prince had read it and approved of this position. He further stated that the United States must retain positions that were acceptable both to the Arab nations and the Israeli people. He then emphasized our unshakable commitment to the security of Israel. He noted the statements recently made by the new prime minister of Israel, Menachem Begin, and asked Fahd for his thoughts on the steps that should be taken at this time.

Fahd said that he felt this was an especially auspicious year to find a comprehensive solution to the Arab-Israeli problem. He noted that for the first time he had a feeling that on the Arab side there was a deep desire for peace. Fahd reviewed the current situation in the region, including the talks recently held in Riyadh with Presidents Sadat and Assad and an emissary of King Hussein. As the meeting had taken place at the time of the Likud victory in Israel, it was noted that it was a time for steady nerves on everyone's part. Turning to the central issues, Fahd said that Israel wanted assurances of its existence and independence, and as far as the Arab people were concerned that was acceptable. The other side of the coin, however, was that the Palestinians also wanted their own home and were willing to have it in the West Bank and Gaza. He asked what then is required? Answering his own question, he said that Israel must withdraw to the 1967 borders and 1977 was the year for steady steps toward that goal. Fahd observed that perhaps Israel would find it too much to start the process by creating a Palestinian state. He believed, however, that it was inevitable that this step be taken, since it would open the way to a true peace in the region. This would lead to other elements of neighborliness that would fall into place.

The president pointed out that his own public and private comments had supported substantial withdrawal from the post-1967 lines and a Palestinian homeland. Carter then emphasized that acceptance by both sides of genuine peace was the most important question for Israel. He summed up by saying that flexibility was needed on both sides.

A discussion in depth about the question of a Palestinian entity and its relationship to its neighbors ensued. Fahd emphasized that Saudi Arabia strongly supported an independent Palestinian state and said he believed not one Arab state would agree to an immediate link between a Palestinian state and Jordan. This did not square with information we had received from other Arab states.

The next day the discussions ranged over a number of important bilateral matters, including oil and the sale of military equipment to Saudi Arabia. The talks ended on a warm and friendly note.

We had now completed all of the bilateral discussions with heads of government, with the exception of the new Israeli prime minister. The pieces were beginning to fall into place, and we had a much clearer view of where to start searching for the areas of compromise.

At their meeting, the president reaffirmed to Fahd the previous administration's commitment to sell Saudi Arabia the highly sophisticated F-15 fighter, an aircraft we had also agreed to sell to Israel and Iran. This proposed transfer was to become the focus of an intense debate with Congress over Saudi Arabia's role in the peace process and the administration's policy of strengthening the vital U.S.-Saudi relationship. Soon after the Carter-Fahd meetings, I began quiet consultations with key congressional leaders to build support for what was undoubtedly to be a controversial sale.

On May 17, the Israeli elections resulted in the victory of the rightist-religious Likud coalition that had become a possibility after political and personal events forced Prime Minister Rabin's resignation in the spring. Menachem Begin became prime minister, and the president immediately invited him to come to Washington in the summer. During June, the Policy Review Committee, under my chairmanship, mapped out our strategy for the critical Begin visit and beyond. On my return to the Middle East in August, I would offer American suggestions for resolving the procedural issues and for reaching agreement on general principles upon which peace negotiations would be based. Even though the Israelis had resisted the idea, I thought we should try to go to Geneva with as much advance agreement as possible on the basic principles of a settlement. I did not regard this as a move toward the Arab position, although this is how many Israelis interpreted our attitude. The decision reflected my judgment that the only way to get the parties to adjust their positions was to confront them with concrete ideas to which they could respond with counterproposals, and thus start narrowing the differences. I wanted to get the opposing sides to start addressing principles relating to the main substantive questions. Until this was achieved the parties would continue talking in generalities and taking maximalist positions.

The Policy Review Committee therefore concluded that during my August trip I should invite all parties to respond promptly to a set of U.S.-drafted general principles, and to send their foreign ministers to New York at the time of the General Assembly meeting in September for informal talks with us. During these discussions in New York, I would seek further reactions to the draft principles, which we would have revised to take into account the comments we had received on our initial draft. If these talks produced sufficient agreement on principles and procedural issues, we would then be in a position, together with the Soviet Union as cochairman, to issue invitations to a Geneva conference by November or December.

The Begin talks clearly would be crucial to this strategy. Unfortunately, we immediately had a falling out with the new Begin government when it reacted sharply to public statements—no different from what we had said before—that expressed the U.S. position that a settlement would entail full peace and normalization of relations, Israeli withdrawal to the 1967 borders "with minor modifications," and the establishment of a Palestinian homeland. The Begin government apparently thought we were trying to box it in before the prime minister and his advisers had fully shaped their positions. Simcha Dinitz, Israel's able ambassador, came to see me at the end of June and urged that we make no further public statements about American views on the core elements of a settlement. I responded that the president wanted to discuss specific issues with Begin and not simply to talk in generalities. We knew little about the positions the Begin government would take, except that we believed it would be less inclined to compromise on issues relating to the West Bank than had Rabin and the Labor party. As Rabin's parliamentary opponent, Begin had insisted on Israel's right to sovereignty over the West Bank (or Judea and Samaria, as he called it). He did not regard it as "occupied territory." However, in order to form a coalition government, which included Moshe Dayan as foreign minister, he had found it necessary to agree not to annex the West Bank except as part of a peace settlement and only after the approval of Israel's parliament. This was only a temporary accommodation; Begin believed deeply that Israel had a legitimate claim to sovereignty over biblical Judea and Samaria.

●   ●   ●

The visit of Prime Minister Begin and Foreign Minister Moshe Dayan to Washington in mid-July was preceded by tough public Israeli statements about withdrawal, continued Israeli control of the West Bank, and unbending opposition to a Palestinian homeland. Israel also declared its intention to continue increasing the number and size of settlements in the occupied territories, which we regarded as a policy of "creeping annexation." I immediately recommended to the president that he seek Begin's private agreement to a moratorium on new settlements while serious negotiations were underway. We recognized that it would be politically difficult for Begin to make such a commitment publicly, but for Israel to continue its settlement activities would harden Arab convictions that Israel would never withdraw from the West Bank.

The Carter-Begin talks on July 19–20 were a sharp contrast to the president's April meetings with Sadat. Although respectful and courteous toward each other, Begin and Carter did not seem to spark the same degree of mutual trust that Sadat and Carter so clearly felt.

Menachem Begin is a strong and determined leader. Although small in stature, he is a powerful man. To me he is a combination of Old Testament prophet and courtly European. He can be harsh and acerbic at one moment and warm and gracious the next. Like Sadat, Begin also has a powerful sense of history, of being a person shaping a moment in time. He is clear about his objectives and at all times relentless in achieving them. However, he is shrewd enough to know when he must adapt, and he can act with restraint when necessary.

A fervent Zionist, Begin was deeply influenced by his exposure to anti-Semitism as a youth in Poland, by his detention in a Siberian labor camp during the early 1940s, and above all by the Holocaust. From those experiences he developed an unshakable conviction that only the strong survive, that the Jewish people must have a secure and powerful state, and that the Jewish state should by right encompass the whole of biblical Israel. Begin is also dedicated to legal principles and the importance of the written word in embodying truth. (At times, however, he appears to believe more in the letter of agreements than in the spirit.) His precision with words, his superb, almost photographic memory, his tenacity and conviction of the rightness of his beliefs make him a formidable and, at times, difficult negotiator, as well as a master of parliamentary debate.

An odd mixture of iron will and emotionalism, Begin was capable of endlessly adhering to the same positions while castigating the motives of his negotiating partners for failing to agree. When formal negotiations ceased, he could become charming and relaxed, speaking lovingly of his family and grandchildren. Withal, he is a patriot, and a good friend of whom I became very fond.

In the White House cabinet room the morning of July 19, Carter outlined the U.S. position. Our goal was a comprehensive settlement—not a separate peace between Egypt and Israel (which we believed Begin and Dayan really preferred). We were prepared to mediate among the parties, but recognized that a settlement could not be imposed by the United States. Thus we tried to reassure Begin that we would not pressure Israel to accept an American, U.S.-Soviet or any other outside peace plan. Moreover, the basis for negotiations should be the peace-for-withdrawal equation of the two UN resolutions and direct negotiations between the parties. Carter said that peace must include open borders and diplomatic recognition—the full normalization of relations Israel was demanding. Furthermore, we believed the final territorial boundaries would have to be negotiated by the parties themselves and should be defensible from a military standpoint. The president told Begin that we were convinced the Palestinian question must be dealt with, but we did not think an independent state would be advisable and preferred a homeland linked to Jordan.

Begin responded with the Israeli position: readiness to negotiate territorial compromises with each of the parties in the context of full peace and recognition; a continued Israeli security presence beyond its final borders where necessary; refusal to accept international security guarantees as a substitute for secure borders; and total rejection of a Palestinian state, entity, or homeland on the West Bank. He then produced a procedural proposal for convening a Geneva conference. The proposal contained four main points: (1) The conference should be reconvened by the United States and the Soviet Union and should be conducted in accord with Resolution 338. Begin conceded that Resolution 338 included 242, thereby acknowledging by extension the principle of withdrawal, although, as we were to see later, not on *all* fronts. (2) The participants should be the sovereign states involved—no PLO, no Palestinian Arab delegation. (3) The conference should have no preconditions or prior commitments, that is, Israel would not commit itself in advance to any specific withdrawal as the price of Arab attendance. (4) Negotiations would be face to face, and the chairmanship of the working groups or commissions would rotate between each of the two national delegations involved—signifying that the Americans and the Soviets would not serve as intermediaries in the commissions where the actual negotiations would take place, and that participation in the committees would be bilateral, between Israel and each of the three Arab states. There would be no combined Arab delegation. After the committees had negotiated treaties, the conference would reconvene solely for the purpose of signing them. Begin also offered alternatives: if any "relevant party"—the United States, the Soviets, or the Arabs—balked at these arrangements, the United States should unilaterally convene three committees to negotiate treaties, or, failing that, act as go-between in proximity talks.

Although Begin's proposal had some positive elements, it was patently unacceptable to the Arabs. Carter pointed out some of the problems, especially the omission of any reference to the issue of a Palestinian homeland and to Palestinian participation in the negotiations. The president firmly restated our judgment that the status of the West Bank must be on the agenda, and there would be no negotiations if Begin really meant to rule out the Palestinian question as a topic for negotiations. Squarely facing the most explosive disagreement between us, Carter warned Begin that Israel's settlement activities in the West Bank and other occupied territories almost foreclosed the possibility of ever having a conference. Carter also made clear that if the PLO would publicly endorse Resolution 242 and acknowledge Israel's right to exist in peace, we would talk to them. There was nothing new about this statement, but by asserting that we would talk to the PLO if they met our conditions, Carter was signaling our view that the PLO must be brought into the process if at all possible.

Begin categorically ruled out contact with the PLO under any circumstances and denied that any predecessor Israeli government had ever agreed to PLO members in a Jordanian delegation. This was true. However, we had interpreted Rabin's undertaking not to inspect the credentials of a Jordanian delegation at a conference to imply a willingness to ignore the presence of low-level PLO members. Begin reiterated that Israel would not look for Palestinian Arabs in a Jordanian delegation, but there could be no PLO. Emotionally, he stressed that Israel would never agree to a Palestinian homeland or entity, because this would inevitably lead to a Palestinian state devoted to the destruction of Israel. As for settlements, Begin said we would just have to disagree. The existence of settlements, he said, would not determine the outcome of a final solution, and there was no way the Israeli government could prevent Jews from settling in Judea and Samaria, part of biblical Israel. The die had been cast. Both of us knew where the other stood and the problems that lay ahead.

Later in the day, I met separately with Begin to go over our peace conference draft principles. They contained in written form the elements of the American position Carter had outlined that morning. Afterward, I planned to review them in light of Begin's views before discussing them in Arab capitals. Begin had no difficulty stipulating a comprehensive settlement as the goal of a peace conference, except to ask that we specify that the results were to be embodied in peace treaties, not "agreements." This was a fine point, arising out of a past distinction between the binding nature of a treaty as contrasted with an agreement. We were to find that these apparent niceties were matters of real substance that could not be overlooked. He also agreed that the two UN resolutions would be the basis of the negotiations, and that a settlement naturally would require an end to the state of belligerency and the establishment of normal peaceful relations between Israel and its Arab neighbors.

The fourth principle, which called for phased withdrawal on all fronts to mutually secure and recognized borders with security arrangements and guarantees, stimulated prolonged discussion. Begin politely but firmly expressed disinterest in United States or other outside security guarantees, including a security treaty with the United States, which I suggested might be possible. I told him frankly that I did not believe there would be peace unless the final borders were quite near the 1967 lines. He asked in the strongest terms that the administration refrain from any more public statements about our position on borders, arguing that by doing so we only made the Arabs less willing to consider territorial compromise. Of critical importance, I thought, Begin did not object to the phrase "on all fronts" in the draft principle on withdrawal. However, this turned out to be only the first of many misunderstandings with Begin on exactly what had been agreed in our discussions.

Begin adamantly refused to discuss the fifth principle, which called for a Palestinian "entity," rather than a state, and for arrangements by which the Palestinians would determine their future status. He said that while he would put all the principles to his cabinet, he would oppose that one.

The next morning the president summed up the progress we had made. On the draft principles it was substantial. Begin had agreed to all but the principle on the West Bank. He had also indicated willingness to the opening of a Geneva conference in plenary session with a single Arab delegation, with prompt adjournment to bilateral working committees. He had, it seemed, accepted Resolutions 242 and 338 as the basis for negotiations, although he continued to insist this did not imply any prior Israeli commitment, such as withdrawal from occupied territories, in attending the conference. Begin also agreed that we should continue working to convene a peace conference before the end of 1977, preferably by October. He accepted my suggestion for informal talks in New York in September to prepare for the conference. In the meantime, we . told him, I would go to the Middle East in August to discuss with the Arab leaders the draft principles, revised to take into account our conversations. We would then rework them for further discussion during the informal talks in New York. I said I would present Begin's procedural proposals and alternatives and seek reactions from the Arab leaders.

• • •

As a result of the exchanges since February, we were reasonably confident that tenacious mediation could eventually lead to workable answers to the procedural problems. I also believed—mistakenly, as it turned out—that we had achieved a breakthrough with Begin in his acceptance of the proposition that Resolution 242 applied to all fronts. Although this would be a step forward, it was not the commitment to withdrawal to the 1967 borders that the Arabs were demanding. We realized that because of this it would be very difficult to move the Arabs closer to accepting full peace and normalization as the goals of a Geneva conference. Even more troubling was the Israeli refusal to consider any solution to the Palestinian question. Nevertheless, I hoped we could convince the Arabs that beginning negotiations, even without substantive agreement on all the basic principles, was the best means of revitalizing the peace process and regaining momentum toward an overall settlement. The strongest argument we had with the Arab parties was that on the issues of land and the Palestinian question, our views were closer to theirs than to Israel's.

The hope for a just and durable peace ultimately rested on the capacity of the Israeli political leadership to resolve its internal divisions and atavistic fears and mistrust of the Arabs. My Middle East advisers and I were concerned about timing and the pace of negotiations. Perceived American pressure on Israel to move too fast could provoke all Israeli political elements to rally around an uncompromising stance. We knew there were important forces within Israel ready to take risks for peace, and we did not want to hobble them by appearing to disregard Israel's legitimate security concerns. We concluded we should avoid gratuitous confrontation with Israel while pursuing three interrelated objectives:

• Continuing our role as a fair intermediary between the sides. There were powerful political pressures on the administration to return to a more pro-Israel posture. But we were committed to the evenhanded role we had undertaken, and I was confident the president would withstand the political heat.

• Developing a credible package of security arrangements and guarantees to ensure Israel's security after withdrawal to approximately the 1967 borders and to build strong congressional and domestic support for our Middle East policy.

• Intensifying efforts to persuade the Arabs that concluding full peace with Israel was indispensable to an overall settlement.

Unfortunately, U.S.-Israeli relations took a sharp drop as I prepared for the critical August trip. Hardly had Begin returned to Israel when his government announced plans for a large number of new settlements on the West Bank, ignoring the president's personal plea for a temporary halt to building any new settlements. Thus, on the eve of my departure, we issued a strong condemnation of the Israeli plan and repeated the long-standing American position that the settlements were illegal under international law. As a result, there was a sharp public exchange that accentuated the profound disagreement between the United States and Israel on this issue.

Compounding the problem was a disagreement over what Begin had said in our July 19 discussion in Washington about the fourth and fifth principles, as well as the ideas for Palestinian representation I planned to show to the Arab leaders. Simcha Dinitz came to my office on July 26 to discuss how I would proceed in these visits. I showed him the revisions we had made in the principles to take into account Begin's comments, and said I would submit all the revised principles to the Arab leaders, including the fifth principle on a Palestinian entity which Begin had totally rejected. I also discussed with Dinitz four alternatives we had developed concerning Palestinian representation at Geneva. They were: (1) Palestinians, including PLO members, would be included in a national Arab delegation, such as Jordan's; (2) Palestinians, including PLO members, would be included in a pan-Arab delegation; (3) prior Arab-Israeli agreement that when the Palestinian question arose at Geneva, Palestinian representatives would join the discussions; and (4) prior Arab-Israeli agreement that when the Palestinian issue arose at the conference, the terms of Palestinian participation would be negotiated.

The next day, Dinitz asked to see me "on instructions from Prime

Minister Begin and Foreign Minister Dayan." In an exchange that vividly illustrated the problems of interpretation that were to bedevil us in the future, Dinitz said that in agreeing to the principle on withdrawal from occupied territories, Begin had not intended his agreement to mean withdrawal on *all* fronts. What Begin meant, he explained, was that while Israel agreed that Resolution 242 "applied" to all fronts, it did not accept that this required *withdrawal* on all fronts. Begin, Dinitz said, planned to seek a solution other than withdrawal for the West Bank. I was furious at what I saw as a backsliding from an agreement we had reached.

Dinitz also told me that unless we changed the first of our suggested alternatives for Palestinian attendance to specify that Palestinians must be in a Jordanian delegation and dropped all references to the PLO, none of the alternatives would be acceptable to Israel. I replied that while we would, of course, make Israel's views known to the Arabs, the four alternatives would be presented as I had shown them to him. I also told him that I would tell the Arab leaders that the United States did not accept the Israeli position as the only way the Palestinian representation issue could be resolved. I believed it was possible to find a formula that would enable PLO members who were not "well known" to be among the Palestinians at a peace conference.

Hardly had I reported this conversation to the president when Dinitz returned with a new message from Begin. Dinitz reiterated that somehow there had been a misunderstanding: Begin had not agreed to the principle of withdrawal on the West Bank. Moreover, Dinitz said, Begin had again requested that I not tell the Arabs our views on the question of final borders in a settlement. Our position on this matter was, of course, public knowledge. However, to allay Begin's concern, Carter had assured him in their July meeting we would not make any further public statements but would continue to state our views in private conversations with Arab leaders. I informed Dinitz that the president had not changed his position on this matter.

The next day Begin sent directly to the president a personal message asking not only that I not be permitted to convey our position to the Arabs, but that I also refrain from presenting the two disagreed-upon principles and the procedural suggestions to which Israel objected. This was an unmistakable challenge of our intention to mediate fairly. We carefully drafted a response in which the president repeated courteously, but firmly, that if the Arabs asked our views on borders, I would respond with the official American position. The message emphasized that it was only proper for us to put the principles and other suggestions to the Arabs just as we had to Begin. The significance of this exchange was the president's underlying message that his administration was committed to evenhandedness in the search for peace and although we would consult closely with Israel, we were not going to concert with it against the Arabs.

THE AUGUST TRIP: ORIGINS OF THE
WEST BANK-GAZA TRANSITIONAL PROPOSAL

I left for the Middle East on August 1, traveling between Egypt, Syria, Jordan, Saudi Arabia, Israel, and back to Egypt and Jordan again. The most important aspect of this trip was not the progress on the tangle of issues blocking a peace conference, but rather gaining broad Arab agreement to consider a different approach to the Palestinian question. Over the previous several weeks, Atherton, Saunders, Quandt, and I had exhaustively studied all the parties' positions and statements about Palestinian self-determination and the status of the West Bank. We had come to the conclusion that solving this emotion-laden issue in a single negotiation was not feasible. Despite our differences with the Israelis on how to solve the Palestinian problem, the president and I shared their concerns about a radicalized Palestinian state. We concluded that some form of transitional arrangement was needed so that the Palestinians could demonstrate whether they were prepared to govern themselves and live peacefully beside Israel, while remaining under international supervision to ease Israel's fears. If a transitional arrangement worked, each side might come to accept the other.

Before I left Washington, I had obtained the president's blessing to suggest to the Arabs the concept of a transitional arrangement for the West Bank and Gaza. My initial idea was a UN trusteeship under joint Israeli-Jordanian administration, leading to a plebiscite and Palestinian self-determination after several years. This concept was to undergo considerable revision and development, but it was one of the roots of the Camp David arrangement for Palestinian autonomy during a transitional regime.

In each of the Arab capitals, I presented Prime Minister Begin's procedural proposals, which were rejected with varying degrees of specificity and heat. I also introduced the five draft principles, as well as our suggestions for dealing with the Palestinian representation issue. After explaining that Israel had rejected the principles on withdrawal on all fronts and on a Palestinian entity, I elaborated on our thinking about the nature of a transitional arrangement for the West Bank and Gaza. Sadat at once saw possibilities in the concept, although he ruled out Israeli participation in the UN trusteeship and insisted that the transition period be shorter than the several years I had suggested. Syrian Foreign Minister Khaddam objected to the term "trusteeship," reminding us of the Arabs' experience with foreign rule under League of Nations mandates. He was interested, however, in the idea of a transitional international agreement for the West Bank and Gaza that would lead to Palestinian self-determination. Encouraged, I put the idea to King Hussein in Amman, dropping the word "trusteeship." Hussein readily accepted the notion of such a transitional regime. When I arrived in Saudi Arabia, I was able to tell Prince Fahd that all the key Arab governments accepted our suggested approach.

Putting aside the all-important problem of securing Israeli approval, the biggest challenge in further developing the transitional arrangement concept was to convince the Palestinians that it offered a realistic way for them eventually to gain a homeland and to participate in determining their own future. For this reason, finding a way to bring the Palestinians into the process was a problem much on Fahd's mind, as well as my own. Before I left Washington the Saudis told me the PLO wanted to know what we meant by our suggestions to Arab leaders that we would talk to the PLO if they would accept Resolution 242 with a reservation that it did not deal adequately with the Palestinian issue. The Saudis were acting as a conduit and coordinator among the Arabs on this matter in the hope that through them we and the PLO might reach agreement on a formula that would open the way to direct contact.

When I got to Cairo, my first stop, the Egyptians asked what the PLO would have to say to satisfy us on this matter. I replied that the PLO should accept Resolution 242 with a reservation to the effect that in referring only to refugees it did not deal adequately with the Palestinian question. The Egyptians then produced what was doubtless a PLO-drafted statement. It was unacceptable because it demanded a Palestinian state and did not mention Israel's right to exist in peace and security.

The same question was raised in Syria and Jordan, and I gave the same response. When I arrived in Taif to meet with King Khalid, Crown Prince Fahd, and Foreign Minister Prince Saud, I had prepared specific language:

> The PLO accepts United Nations Security Council Resolution 242, with the reservation that it considers that the resolution does not make adequate reference to the question of the Palestinians since it fails to make any reference to a homeland for the Palestinian people. It is recognized that the language of Resolution 242 relates to the right of all states in the Middle East to live in peace.

I told the Saudis that if the PLO would accept this language and thus publicly acknowledge Israel's right to exist, we would have met our commitment under the Sinai II agreement and would be willing to meet with the PLO immediately. However, to avoid any misunderstanding, I stressed that only the parties themselves, including Israel, could decide who would participate at Geneva, and we were bound by previous commitments to support Israel on this point. King Khalid asked whether, if the PLO did as we requested, we could assure them they would get a homeland on the West Bank. I replied that this was our goal, but we could not guarantee it.

Prince Saud, a wise and skilled foreign minister whom I came to admire greatly, said that he would communicate the language I had given him and that he hoped we would get a positive response from Arafat before I left Taif. Saud was optimistic, saying that the Executive Committee of the PLO was meeting that night and would consider our proposed language and that I would have its response before I left for Israel.

The next morning, when I met Saud at the airport, his face was clouded with gloom. He told me that our suggestion had indeed been considered last night and had failed to muster the necessary votes for approval. The opposition was led by the extreme elements within the PLO. I departed Taif with a heavy heart as I felt that an important opportunity had been missed because of the deep division within the PLO.

I urged Saud not to let the matter drop and to continue to press the issue with Arafat and other Arab leaders. The matter was raised again on several occasions and remains, in my judgment, an unexplored avenue to a possible breakthrough in the Middle East tangle.

In hindsight, it appears that nothing came of our suggestion because the PLO would not use what it regarded as its chief bargaining asset, acceptance of the right of Israel to exist within secure and recognized boundaries, without an assurance that it would get a Palestinian homeland in return.

My discussions with the Arabs on this matter found their way into the press. Where asked I acknowledged willingness to talk to the PLO if they met our conditions. By the time I reached Jerusalem, the Israelis were thoroughly aroused at the effort we had made. Prime Minister Begin lectured me, referring again and again to the U.S. commitment not to recognize or negotiate with the PLO. Angrily, he read me passages from the PLO Covenant that called for the destruction of Israel, and he questioned the morality of our position. I stiffly reviewed the sequence of events and emphatically denied that we had violated any American commitment. I repeated what I had said throughout the trip: If the PLO met our essential conditions—acceptance of 242 with specific reference to the right of all states to live within secure and recognized boundaries—our requirements for beginning discussions with them would be satisfied. Our view was that a PLO reservation in acceptable language would not change Resolution 242 and would supersede the parts of the PLO Covenant that Begin had quoted to me.

I went through the rest of the agenda with Begin, explaining the Arabs' problems with his procedural proposals and their generally favorable reaction to our draft principles. I then turned to the concept of a West Bank-Gaza transitional international regime leading to a plebiscite and Palestinian self-determination. He completely rejected the concept, as well as the principles concerning withdrawal on all fronts and a Palestinian entity. However, as we were to see in talks with Begin in December, the idea either lodged in his mind or dovetailed with options being considered in the Israeli government for West Bank-Gaza solutions and ultimately bore fruit.

• • •

On my return to Washington, I met with President Carter to sum up the results of the trip and to map our next steps.

I told the president there were some positive elements in the talks despite continuing obstacles. The Arabs seemed finally to be coalescing in their views. I had sensed in Arab capitals that a solution to the procedural problem lay in agreement that the Arabs would be represented by a single delegation at an opening plenary conference, after which they would split into national delegations in working groups or committees. The Israelis still objected to certain aspects of this idea, but I believed their problems could be worked out. The Palestinian representation issue was still a serious impediment, and the August trip had produced no breakthrough. Nevertheless, I felt that ultimately the Israelis would not refuse to go to Geneva if there was to be only a limited PLO presence.

It seemed that our draft principles probably had achieved all that could be expected at this stage, which was to narrow the differences. Saunders, Atherton, and Quandt were working on the concept of a transitional arrangement, as well as the other elements of a comprehensive settlement. I recommended that henceforth, in addition to discussion of the general principles, we also begin the development and presentation of more specific U.S. proposals on the main issues. Carter agreed that the August discussions pointed the way to the next phase: informal talks with the respective foreign ministers in New York to work out the remaining issues before reconvening in Geneva by the end of the year. Each party had indicated it would participate and each had promised to send me, to be held in the utmost confidence, a draft peace treaty that I would meld into a single negotiating document. At the same time, we would use Foreign Minister Dayan's September visit to continue to explore the concept of an international transitional regime. Dayan was imaginative and creative, and we hoped he would stimulate serious consideration of the idea within the Israeli government.

As a result of the recent discussions we had reached a turning point in our strategy. We could not continue the pre-Geneva diplomatic track much past September without encountering serious problems. I was apprehensive that if the New York talks did not at least produce agreement to reconvene the peace conference, the moderate Arabs might conclude our strategy was not going to produce results. There were signs that Assad was running out of patience or was dragging his feet, and that in a short time he might revert to a more hard-line position. I told the president that Sadat and Assad could have serious political problems if we did not have more to show before the end of the year.

PRELUDE TO THE SADAT INITIATIVE: SEPTEMBER-OCTOBER 1977

Although the September and October negotiations did not lead to the long-sought Geneva peace conference, substantial progress was made. In fact, we appeared to be on the verge of reconvening the conference when Anwar Sadat, for reasons that I will attempt to analyze later, undertook his historic trip to Jerusalem in November.

Despite continuing U.S.-Israeli disputes over PLO representation and continuing Israeli settlements in the occupied territories, we managed in September to reach agreement with Dayan on a number of important issues. My meetings with the Arab foreign ministers also indicated progress toward the procedural solutions we thought most feasible: a unified Arab delegation, including Palestinians, at the plenary; and national delegations for the working groups, with Jordanians and Palestinians sitting together on one committee, to negotiate the Palestinian question.

In a meeting on September 19, the president obtained in our discussion with Dayan important movement on the critical issue of Israeli settlement activities. Dayan agreed that Israel would establish no additional settlements in the occupied territories for at least one year. Moreover, any new Israeli settlers would be required to join the Israeli armed forces and to locate in six existing military installations; no lands would be expropriated to enlarge these settlements. Dayan also confirmed that Israeli settlements in the occupied territories would not be allowed to determine final boundaries; settlements beyond the final agreed borders would be removed or allowed to remain only with the permission of the sovereign power. In welcoming these assurances, we were careful to stipulate that the United States continued to regard all the civilian settlements in the occupied territories as illegal under international law and contrary to Resolution 242.

After these productive talks with Dayan, we took a step which I hoped would help improve prospects for a Geneva conference, but instead proved to be controversial and jarring in our relations with Israel. This was the October 1 joint U.S.-USSR communiqué setting forth the views of the Geneva cochairmen on the objectives of a reconvened conference.

The need for a cochairmen's statement prior to a Geneva conference was first raised when I met Foreign Minister Gromyko on May 19, 1977. Since then I had kept the Soviets generally informed of progress in the negotiations to head off attempts by them to interfere. I had always felt, however, that at the appropriate time the Soviets would have to be involved. The October communiqué itself arose out of the August 29 meeting I had with Ambassador Dobrynin following my August Middle East trip. Dobrynin noted that Gromyko would, as customary, be coming to the United States in September for the UN General Assembly session and would like to discuss the possibility of a joint statement on the principles of a Middle East settlement. A U.S.-Soviet statement including some mention of the Middle East would be necessary when I met with Gromyko, and in any case, it made sense to start bringing the Soviets carefully into the process of preparing for a Geneva conference of which they would be one of the cochairmen. I invited Gromyko to send me his ideas on what he would recommend go into a cochairmen's statement. I said that I would be prepared to discuss a draft of such a statement in September.

Over the next several weeks Dobrynin and I discussed on several occasions a draft text, which steadily moved toward the basic American position on a comprehensive settlement. The final text was developed in a lengthy session with Gromyko on September 30 and released the following day. It received general approbation from the Arab nations and many other countries. The PLO, in particular, welcomed the statement and afterward frequently pointed to it as a significant step forward. Why this was so has never been clear to me, since the statement did not refer to the PLO or to a Palestinian state. I had carefully consulted with Egyptian Foreign Minister Ismail Fahmi while negotiating the statement with Gromyko, and he reported that Sadat welcomed the communiqué.

I, of course, also consulted with Foreign Minister Dayan on the content and purposes of the communiqué in the days before its release. He was not enthusiastic about the idea of a joint U.S.-Soviet statement, but seemed to understand the reason for it and the important concessions the Soviets had made in the text. Therefore, while we anticipated some Israeli unhappiness because the communiqué reflected the U.S. positions on withdrawal and Palestinian self-determination, we were surprised by the fierce denunciation of it by Israel, some members of the Congress, and by members of the American Jewish community. I believe that part of the reason was that the moderate expressions of Dayan in New York did not adequately convey the political sensitivity of Israel or Begin to a joint U.S.-Soviet statement. Israel's reaction was, in fact, a preemptive warning about U.S.-Soviet cooperation in the Middle East peace process, intended to make us step back from a course Israel opposed. It was a tactic we were to see many times.

On October 4, President Carter and I had a rather tense meeting with Dayan to discuss why Israel had created such a tempest about the statement. We pointed out that the position reflected in the communiqué was the one we had taken publicly and privately on a number of occasions. Moreover, we had succeeded in significantly moderating the Soviet position: Moscow had explicitly committed itself to the goal of normal relations among Israel and the Arabs and had agreed not to refer to its position in support of an independent Palestinian state. Contrary to usual Soviet statements, the document contained no reference to the PLO and was entirely consistent with Resolutions 242 and 338. With the prospect of a peace conference, which the Soviets must necessarily co-chair, it was important to have obtained this movement on the part of the Soviet Union.

Dayan said Israel was upset because the communiqué contained the phrase "the legitimate rights of the Palestinian people." I pointed out that we had rejected the phrase "the legitimate *national* rights of the Palestinian people," suggested by the Russians, and said that we saw nothing wrong about referring to the legitimate rights of the Palestinians. (Interestingly, those precise words were to be used in the joint statement agreed to at Camp David, and they appear in the Camp David accords.) The joint statement represented our conviction that a just solution to the Palestinian problem was morally and politically essential to any lasting Middle East settlement.

Dayan responded that the statement was "totally unacceptable to the Israeli government," and Israel would not go to Geneva on the basis of it. He argued that the existence of the cochairmen's statement would tilt the balance at a conference against Israel. Of course this patently was not our intention, and we explained to him that no government, Arab or Israeli, was being asked to accept the statement as a condition of attending Geneva. We reiterated that the basis for Geneva would be Resolutions 242 and 338. This appeared to satisfy him, and we agreed to issue a U.S.-Israeli public statement to that effect. This statement calmed the Israelis and their more vocal supporters in Congress, but upset the Arabs, who saw it as a U.S. retreat in the face of Israeli political pressure.

In meetings on October 4 and 5 I was able to reach agreement with Dayan on a working paper for convening the conference along the lines I had pressed with the Arabs during the September talks and which the Egyptians had indicated they would accept. The main points of this working paper, which was to be the subject of negotiations virtually to the moment of Sadat's trip to Jerusalem, were:

• The Arabs would attend the opening sessions in a single delegation which would include Palestinian Arabs.

• After the opening sessions the conference would break into bilateral committees to negotiate bilateral peace treaties.

• The basis for the negotiations would be Resolutions 242 and 338.

• The West Bank and Gaza issues would be discussed in a separate working group consisting of Israel, Egypt, Jordan, and the Palestinian Arabs.

Discussions on this working paper began with the Syrians, Jordanians, and Saudis, who pressed to include a commitment to address the Palestinian question and to give the West Bank-Gaza working group the same status as the bilateral committees. Dayan, however, sought to interpret the October 5 working paper as ruling out discussion of a Palestinian homeland or the participation of low-level PLO members. On October 11, the Israeli cabinet accepted the October 5 arrangement as interpreted by Dayan. The Syrians also continued to raise objections about the procedural arrangements, and refused to accept Egypt's positions, although Syria's position was slowly evolving toward a satisfactory resolution.

The haggling and maneuvering continued for another three weeks, and we continued to inch painfully toward a reconvened Geneva conference. Then, with surprising suddenness, Anwar Sadat altered the entire political and psychological atmosphere by announcing on November 9 that he was prepared to go to Jerusalem and address the Knesset on the questions of peace.

• • •

Contrary to rumors after the event, no advance consultations took place between Sadat and President Carter on Sadat's dramatic and historic decision to go to Jerusalem. He merely let the president know the day before he made his announcement that he was thinking of going. We were momentarily stunned by the decision, although we knew that he was intensely frustrated at the prolonged and tedious negotiations required to get agreement to convene the conference. We had asked him how he thought the deadlock might be broken. On November 3, Sadat replied that he was considering convening a Middle East summit of all relevant parties, including the Soviet Union, Britain, France, the People's Republic of China, and the PLO in East Jerusalem in order to give fresh momentum to the peace process and take some of the domestic political pressure off President Carter.

The idea of the Soviets, the Chinese, and the PLO, among others, attending a conference in East Jerusalem, or that Israel would permit them to do so, was farfetched and the president and I discouraged Sadat from attempting it. Nonetheless, he had decided somehow to seize the initiative. I tried to assure the Egyptians that we were getting close to a Geneva conference, and with patience and determination we would soon get over the remaining obstacles. But Sadat had become impatient with consultations, draft working papers, and alternative formulations of positions. He decided that the way to break out was to make a bold and unthinkable move—offering to go himself to Jerusalem and speak to the Israeli people about peace.

Once we had recovered from the initial surprise, we at once endorsed Sadat's initiative. I was worried, however, that this decision, which had been taken without consultations with his Arab partners, could leave him isolated and exposed and jeopardize the prospects for a Geneva conference. Evidently, Sadat believed he would be secure as long as his principal Arab supporters, the Saudis, did not join the Syrians, the PLO, and other hard-line Arabs in attacking the initiative. For the short run, this was a reasonable calculation. The Saudis, the Jordanians, and other moderate Arabs exercised public restraint while they awaited the results of his attempt to change political attitudes in Israel. It was clear, however, that the Saudis could resist pressures to denounce Sadat only if he achieved speedy and noteworthy results.

Nevertheless, although the president and I agreed that our broad objective continued to be a Geneva conference and a comprehensive peace, it was clear to us that the probable outcome of Sadat's initiative would be an initial peace agreement between Egypt and Israel. Thus, from early 1978 on, we followed two parallel paths toward peace: agreement between Egypt and Israel on the bilateral issues between them, and an interim solution to the problem of a Palestinian homeland in the West Bank and Gaza. Success on both paths was an indispensable precondition to engaging the other Arab parties and attaining our ultimate goal of a comprehensive and lasting settlement for all the parties.

Our immediate task was to ensure that Sadat gained positive results from his initiative. Once Sadat had taken this enormous political risk, his survival, and probably the pro-Western orientation of Egypt, depended on progress toward peace.

While Sadat's visit to Jerusalem on November 19–20 was a psychological and political breakthrough of historic importance, it did not produce the basic shifts in Israeli attitudes and positions that he was seeking. Of course, once Begin had absorbed the significance of Sadat's offer to come to Jerusalem, he welcomed the opportunity to talk directly with the leader of Egypt. But he did not greet Sadat's initiative with great optimism; it was exactly the kind of unpredictable act that caused Israel to worry whether it was in control of its own future.

On December 5, Syria, Libya, Iraq, South Yemen, Algeria, and the PLO formed the Arab "rejectionist bloc" and vowed to oppose Sadat. Sadat reacted by asserting that he would negotiate alone if the other Arabs refused to join him. Saudi Arabia and Jordan, torn between private hopes for Sadat's initiative, fears that he would fail, and intense desire to restore Arab unity, turned to us for help in building on Sadat's initiative before he was so discredited in the Arab world that they would be forced to break openly with him.

10

THE MIDDLE EAST: CAMP DAVID

WHILE SADAT'S BOLD MOVE had not produced the instantaneous and dramatic response he had hoped for, it had affected profoundly the political and negotiating climate. Following Sadat's trip and prior to the decision to convoke the Camp David summit in September 1978, our effort to build on Sadat's initiative was to pass through several phases.

In Jerusalem Sadat had emphasized to the Knesset his commitment to a comprehensive settlement. He had decided that the most effective means to reach that end was to negotiate with Israel a favorable settlement for Egypt and a solution to the Palestinian question that would persuade Syria, Jordan, and the PLO to follow his leadership and resume negotiations. The danger was that he might not achieve his aims rapidly enough to prevent the moderate Arabs from moving toward the rejectionists.

The task of turning Sadat's initiative into a concrete negotiating process fell largely to the United States. Sadat's first step was to invite all of the parties, the PLO, and the United Nations to meet in Cairo in mid-December as the analogue of the Middle East summit he had been considering in early November. However, even intensive American efforts failed to produce Arab interest in this meeting, and only American, Egyptian, and Israeli representatives and a UN observer attended.

Before the Cairo meeting, I returned to the Middle East from December 10 to 14 in order to coordinate plans for the future with Sadat and Begin, and in an effort to direct our joint efforts toward reconvening the Geneva conference. I went first to Egypt to meet with Sadat, who was staying at his house, the Barrages, a few miles north of Cairo on the Nile. Sadat was, as always, warm and forthright. I found him confident that Hussein and Assad would eventually have to follow his lead. He stressed the importance of securing Begin's assurance that Israel would withdraw virtually to the 1967 borders and would deal with the Palestinian problem in all of its aspects. He felt that his November trip had accorded Israel its fundamental requirement—acknowledgment of Israel's legitimacy by its major Arab neighbor. It was now up to Begin, Sadat said, to respond in a way that would make it possible for Syria and Jordan to join the Egyptian-Israeli talks. It was crucial for Sadat to show the Arab world that he was not seeking a separate peace. If Begin would commit Israel to withdraw to the 1967 lines and to negotiate seriously on the Palestinian question, Sadat was ready to be accommodating on the nature of peace, security arrangements, and the manner and timing of the resolution of Palestinian issues. He asked that I make these points to Begin and stressed the importance of early progress.

The next day I flew to Israel for meetings with Begin and Dayan. I was met at Lod Airport, outside of Tel Aviv, by Dayan and drove with him through the plains and rising hills to the beautiful and awesome city of Jerusalem. I had come to admire Dayan, whom I found to be a brilliant, imaginative, and honest man. The next morning I met with Prime Minister Begin. I was coming to like him as well. Although prickly and stubborn, he had a warm and gracious side which was appealing. After describing my meeting with Sadat, I turned to a discussion of the key substantive issues. Begin understood that it was up to him to respond to Sadat's initiative, but despite a personal plea from President Carter, which I brought in a letter, he was unwilling to make a clear statement on withdrawal to encourage Arab attendance at the scheduled Cairo conference. He explained that his response to Sadat would be to offer withdrawal from the Sinai and a plan for Palestinian "home rule," which he wanted to discuss first with President Carter in Washington after the opening of the Cairo meeting. Begin did not, it seemed to me, share Sadat's and our interest in trying to make the Cairo talks a stepping-stone to Geneva. Instead, his objective in proposing a withdrawal from the Sinai and an autonomy plan for the West Bank and Gaza appeared to be to use the Sadat initiative and the Cairo negotiations as the opening toward an Israeli-Egyptian peace treaty. Begin and Dayan stressed that the Cairo discussions should focus entirely on the nature of peace, diplomatic relations, and open borders, and declared that the Israeli delegation would have no authority to discuss final borders, the Palestinian issue, or other questions of concern to the Arabs.

After a short stop in Beirut, I met with President Assad in Damascus. He was as usual perceptive and incisive. Despite his anger at Sadat and his suspicions that the United States and Israel were maneuvering Egypt into a separate peace, I found Assad cautious about aligning himself completely with the Arab rejectionists. Our discussions led me to believe that he intended to remain on the sidelines for a time to see what developed.

King Hussein, whom I met with next in Amman, indicated that he was willing to join the negotiations if Israel would issue positive declarations on withdrawal from the entire West Bank and a solution to the problem of a Palestinian homeland. Both he and the Saudi leaders, whom I met in Riyadh, stressed that time was of the essence. All of them were concerned about the political consequences for Sadat if Israel did not respond promptly and positively. And they were profoundly skeptical that Israel would meet Sadat's political requirements.

BEGIN VISIT TO WASHINGTON: DECEMBER 1977

Carter and Begin, with their senior advisers, met in the cabinet room of the White House on the morning of December 16 to discuss Israel's response to Sadat. I had urged the president to press Begin to focus on the central issues necessary to revive the Geneva conference and not to let ourselves be drawn into a debate over specific aspects of Begin's West Bank home-rule plan, nor to endorse his proposals until we had discussed them with Sadat. It was important for the prime minister to understand that although our support for Israel was unswerving, we would not underwrite an Israeli policy that would destroy the chance for peace.

President Carter began by emphasizing the vital importance of making Sadat's initiative a success and asked how Begin intended to respond. Begin said he had two peace proposals to describe:

1. In the Sinai, Israel would withdraw in two stages to the 1967 international border. For a transitional period of three to five years, Israel would retain some military positions in the Sinai along a line running from El Arish in the north to Ras Muhammad in the south. The second stage of withdrawal to the 1967 borders would coincide with the establishment of diplomatic relations, both of which could proceed in phases.

2. Israel would grant home- or self-rule to the Palestinian Arabs in Judea and Samaria (the West Bank) and Gaza. An administrative council would be established through free elections to deal with the problems of daily life. Israel would retain reponsibility for public order, as well as security, and would maintain military camps in the area. For five years Israel would hold in abeyance its claim to sovereignty over Judea and Samaria, and at the end of that period Israel would review the arrangement to see how well it had worked.

Carter observed that the Sinai proposal seemed reasonable, although he stressed he did not yet understand all of the details. On the self-rule plan, we asked several crucial questions: Was Israel willing to commit itself in principle to withdrawal from the West Bank, except for minor adjustments? Would Palestinian Arabs be permitted to immigrate to the West Bank? How would the question of sovereignty be dealt with at the end of five years?

Begin answered that Israel did not believe Resolution 242 required withdrawal on all fronts and that the 1967 line in the West Bank did not constitute a secure border. He repeated that Israel would not claim sovereignty beyond the 1967 line during the five years, although its "security border" would be the Jordan River. This was further limited by his insistence that the powers of the self-governing authority, or administrative council, would derive from the Israeli military government in the West Bank, which could revoke any powers delegated to the council. It appeared that Israel intended to retain military and, ultimately, political control over the West Bank and Gaza even under the self-rule plan.

Begin and his colleagues pressed hard for American approval of these proposals. Vice-President Mondale interjected that it was not the purpose of the talks to agree to a plan or to negotiate. Mondale stressed that we were friends consulting together, not parties negotiating a text. Mondale's intervention was important because subsequently Begin was to claim the president had endorsed his proposals.

Begin's self-rule proposal fell far short of what we believed necessary for an interim solution for the West Bank and Gaza. It appeared to be designed as a substitute for Israeli withdrawal and Palestinian self-determination, not as a first step toward these goals as envisaged in our concept of an international transitional regime. Nevertheless, the fact that Begin was prepared to make an autonomy proposal was a significant development. In offering it, Begin implicitly conceded that there was a Palestinian problem, that the Palestinian Arabs should participate in governing themselves, and that autonomy was an acceptable concept. We now had a basis for beginning to narrow the differences between Begin's plan and a transitional international regime which we believed preferable.

There were four important differences between what Begin proposed and what we believed essential if there were to be an agreement:

• Begin's plan provided no role for the Arab states during the autonomy period. We believed the Arabs, especially Jordan, had to participate in negotiating the transitional arrangements and assume a share of the responsibility for their success.

• The Begin proposal would confer ultimate authority for the West Bank during the five years on an Israeli governor general. We believed an international authority, an Israeli-Jordanian authority, or some arrangement other than unilateral Israeli control over the Palestinian autonomy council was essential.

• We foresaw an international peacekeeping force as the guarantor of order and security, whereas Begin would reserve this function entirely to Israel.

• We saw the five years as a transition period ending in a plebiscite and a peace treaty negotiated between the Palestinians and Israel. Begin apparently saw his plan as an experiment in local autonomy that *might* be permanent *if* it worked out.

A significant element of the Israeli proposals that struck us was that, although Begin was proposing to give the inhabitants of the West Bank and Gaza only an administrative role, he accepted the 1967 borders, except in Jerusalem, to define the area of their authority. The Arabs never fully grasped the significance of this point. On the other side of the coin, however, the self-rule plan provided that the administrative council's jurisdiction would extend only to Arab residents of the West Bank and Gaza, not to those inhabitants who were Israeli citizens. Moreover, it gave all Israelis the right to acquire land and to settle in the West Bank and Gaza, whereas Arab inhabitants who did not choose to accept Israeli citizenship would not have similar rights in Israel. Arab immigration into the area would be controlled by the *unanimous* decision of a committee composed of representatives from Israel, Jordan, and the administrative council.

If there was to be any chance of Arab agreement, the Begin self-rule plan would have to be brought much closer to genuine autonomy. And we would have to involve at least Jordan and, we hoped, other Arabs in the process of setting up the transitional arrangements. In detailed discussions the next day, I suggested that the authority of the administrative council should be derived from agreement between Israel and Jordan, with each reserving its legal rights and sovereign claims. This would at least allow an Arab voice in defining the powers of the council. The suggestion was well received by Begin, who agreed to consider it.

• • •

After the unproductive Cairo conference, Sadat and Begin, accompanied by their advisers, met face to face in Ismailia (near the Suez Canal) at Christmastime. Before substantive issues were discussed, they agreed to establish a dual-track negotiating process: a political committee would meet at the foreign-minister level starting in Jerusalem in mid-January; a security committee of defense ministers would convene in Cairo at about the same time. This agreement reflected Sadat's recognition that protracted negotiations were going to be necessary.

Sadat received with satisfaction Begin's proposal to withdraw from the Sinai to the 1967 border, but totally rejected any continuing Israeli presence, civilian or military, beyond that line after withdrawal. Begin's West Bank-Gaza self-rule plan received little attention, as the two leaders spent much of their time discussing a profound disagreement stemming from Sadat's demand for an Israeli declaration on withdrawal and Palestinian self-determination.

After the Cairo and Ismailia meetings, the euphoria of the Sadat visit diminished, and the two sides faced the harsh reality of profound disagreement on key issues. A disappointed Sadat and a defensive Begin engaged in strident public exchanges, and the atmosphere between Egypt and Israel became strained.

At this difficult moment, President Carter was scheduled to visit Iran and Saudi Arabia as part of a larger trip, which was to include summits in India and Europe. He used the trip to try to draw the moderate Arab states behind Sadat's peace policy. In Tehran we met with the shah and with King Hussein, who came to Iran especially to see the president. After a visit to New Delhi to meet with Prime Minister Desai we flew to Riyadh for discussions with King Khalid and the Saudi leaders. Both the Jordanians and the Saudis were unyielding in their refusal to support either Sadat or the negotiations until Israel explicitly accepted the principles of full withdrawal to the 1967 borders and Palestinian self-determination. When we arrived in Aswan, Egypt, on our way back to the United States, Carter publicly stated after meeting with Sadat that all parties must recognize the "legitimate rights of the Palestinian people" (as we had said in the United States-Soviet communiqué in October), and that means must be found to "enable the Palestinians to participate in the determination of their own future." This formulation, developed by Atherton, Quandt, the president, and me on the plane flight from Riyadh to Egypt, was meant to come close to support for Palestinian self-determination without using the phrase itself, which had become, in Israeli minds, a code word for "an independent Palestinian state." The Aswan statement implied that an "interim" solution might be found in a joint Israeli-Jordanian-Palestinian administration of the West Bank during a transitional period, at the end of which there could be a referendum to determine whether the inhabitants wanted to continue that arrangement or establish a confederacy with Jordan. The stop in Aswan was aimed at helping Sadat and bolstering his initiative, as well as nudging Begin in the direction of our concept of a transitional regime.

On January 17, 1978, I attended the first political committee meeting between Foreign Minister Muhammad Kamel—Foreign Minister Ismael Fahmi had resigned over Sadat's trip to Jerusalem—and Foreign Minister Dayan. I hoped the Jerusalem discussions would move Begin's self-rule plan toward an interim arrangement that did not foreclose eventual Israeli withdrawal from most of the West Bank and Gaza. The first day principally was spent in arguing over the agenda, and I finally had to work out a compromise that would enable each side to address its central concerns.

That night our Israeli hosts gave a large dinner for all of the participants at the Hilton Hotel, where we were staying. They also invited a visiting congressional delegation from the House Foreign Affairs Committee. When it came time for the after-dinner speaker, Prime Minister Begin unfortunately and, I believe, unwittingly used offensive words in describing Foreign Minister Kamel. As a result Kamel was deeply wounded, feeling that the remarks were a conscious affront to Egypt.

Both I and members of the congressional delegation were upset by the incident and conveyed our unhappiness to our hosts. The first day of the meeting ended on a negative note.

The next day each side tabled widely differing draft declarations of principle and Dayan presented the Israeli self-rule plan. The Israelis also indicated that they wished to keep some settlements in the Sinai and refused to discuss either the West Bank or Gaza. Thereafter my American colleagues and I began a shuttle between the rooms of the two sides in an effort to probe for common ground. When we broke for lunch, Kamel called Cairo to report on what had taken place. Not long thereafter the Egyptians told me that they had received instructions from Sadat to break off the talks and to return to Cairo immediately. I told Kamel that this was a serious mistake and urged him to call Sadat and seek a reversal of his instructions. I offered to speak to Sadat to tell him that I felt he was making a major mistake, but to no avail. The orders were affirmed and Kamel and his party prepared to leave for Cairo in the late evening. Everyone was stunned by this volte-face, including the Egyptians. We were to learn later that Sadat was dismayed by the reports he received, which led him to conclude that the Israelis were "haggling" over what he considered to be small issues and refusing to address matters that were important to him. I also believe that his decision to recall the delegation was affected by the events of the dinner on the first day of the meeting. The opening round of the political committee talks had gotten off to an inauspicious start and it was with sadness that Dayan and I said good-bye to our Egyptian colleagues that night. The next morning to relieve my flagging spirits, Sam Lewis, our superb ambassador to Israel, and I had two vigorous sets of tennis with Israeli friends. This helped to dispel some of the gloom we all felt.

In the aftermath of the Jerusalem talks, I met with Sadat and Begin separately in an effort to get negotiations back on the track. Begin was upset at being castigated by the Egyptians as intransigent, and he asserted that, inasmuch as Carter had "endorsed" his December peace proposals, we should be supporting him against Egypt's criticisms. Begin and I had a sharp and painful exchange over what Carter had said in December. I pointed out that it had been made clear at the time of the December meeting, as well as later, that although Begin's proposals were seen as positive steps, they were never endorsed. I also pointed out that subsequent to December the Israelis had made changes in the proposals that decreased their attractiveness. I concluded our discussion by offering to say publicly that the proposals were a fair basis for negotiations, but would not endorse them, and would continue to affirm our position that Israeli settlements were illegal.

On January 20 I flew to Cairo to try to persuade Sadat that withdrawing Kamel from Jerusalem had been a bad mistake. After our talk, Sadat agreed as a goodwill gesture to continue the military committee talks with Israel. The Israelis then responded by threatening to postpone the talks in retaliation for the recall of Kamel, but Roy Atherton stayed behind and managed to get Begin's and Dayan's agreement to resume these talks on January 31. The situation remained precarious as I returned to Washington to find a new and serious U.S.-Israeli "misunderstanding."

In early January, before I left for Jerusalem, the president had written to Begin referring to the commitments Dayan had made in September regarding Israeli restraint on settlements. Begin replied that he had checked the record and Dayan had agreed only that *during 1977* just six more settlements, all in military camps, would be established. This was definitely not what our records showed. On February 1 Dayan publicly rejected our interpretation of what had been agreed. There was nothing we could do but restate our position and try to minimize the damage on the eve of Sadat's second visit to Washington.

*   *   *

The Egyptian-Israeli military talks resumed on January 31, owing to Atherton's skillful diplomacy, but only to adjourn sine die the next day. With that, the last direct Israeli-Arab negotiating channel was closed. Although we did not yet fully recognize it, the events in December and January foreclosed the possibility of any further movement toward Geneva. The reversion to American good offices and shuttle diplomacy was now to lead toward Camp David.

SADAT VISIT TO WASHINGTON: FEBRUARY

When Sadat came to the United States from February 3 to 8 he was disappointed with us and angry at Begin. He realized that in the Cairo and Jerusalem meetings he had allowed much of the momentum gained from his November initiative to dissipate in sterile debates over the language of a proposed declaration of principles. He was convinced that Israel would move only if confronted by firm American proposals. Sadat now realized that he could not deal alone with the Israelis, and he wanted to get the United States into the center of the peace process once more.

I felt that we should not give up on the possibility of a declaration of principles, but at the same time, we must start moving ahead at once on a solution to the West Bank-Gaza problem. In order to do this we had to know how far Sadat was prepared to go on the Palestinian question. At the same time it must not be the separate peace that would deepen his isolation in the Arab world.

For several months, Hal Saunders, Roy Atherton, Atherton's deputy Pete Day, Bill Quandt, and I had been working on a plan for an interim solution in the West Bank. If this plan would satisfy Sadat's minimum objectives, I wanted to discuss it first with the Israelis and then the other Arabs. The features of what came to be called the "nine-point" West Bank-Gaza approach were: (1) a five-year transitional period during which the inhabitants of the West Bank-Gaza would have self-rule; (2) authority for the self-rule would derive from Israel, Jordan, and Egypt, the arrangements to be negotiated by these three states and the Palestinians; (3) members of the self-governing authority would be elected by the inhabitants of the West Bank and Gaza; (4) Israel and Jordan would refrain from asserting sovereignty over the area during the five-year transition period; (5) Israeli forces would withdraw to limited and specified encampments; (6) during the transition period, the self-governing authority and Israel, Jordan, and Egypt would negotiate Israeli withdrawal to the 1967 borders, with minor modifications, the security arrangements to accompany Israeli withdrawal, and the terms and conditions of the long-term relationships between the West Bank and Gaza and Israel and Jordan; (7) the long-term relationships would require the express consent of the inhabitants of the West Bank and Gaza; (8) the parties also would negotiate arrangements for reciprocal rights for Israelis and the inhabitants of the area; and (9) a regional economic development plan would be established.

The nine-point approach was a composite of our transitional international regime/plebiscite concept of the previous August, the December Begin self-rule plan, and our growing recognition that any solution would have to be limited, leaving open the final status of the West Bank and Gaza during the transitional period while reserving the rights of all the parties. Under existing political conditions, more could not be expected from Israel. But if successful, the plan might set in motion a process that could, under the right circumstances, lead to Palestinian self-determination consistent with the security of Israel.

In the conversations with Carter, Sadat refused our plea to reopen direct negotiations with Israel. Taking a hard line, he argued that Israel had done nothing that it would not have done had he not gone to Jerusalem. He said that in return for his offer to give Israel what the Israelis had always claimed they must have, they continued to argue about agendas and words and refused to return the Arab lands. He said he would not negotiate directly with them until they were ready to meet his basic demands on withdrawal and a solution to the Palestinian question.

It soon became clear that Sadat had one overriding question for us, which he put directly to the president: Would the United States put forward its own positions? Carter assured him that we would, and we talked about the timing and strategy for doing so, including the need for a more concrete Egyptian proposal. Carter told Sadat we did not endorse the Begin self-rule plan as proposed and were thinking of reshaping it to serve as a key element of an interim arrangement at the end of which the Palestinians would have a voice in their own future. We believed that Sadat would accept such a solution as part of a larger framework. He was determined not to let other Arab leaders block his peace policy, even if it meant he would have to proceed without them. However, there had to be an arrangement for the West Bank that he could defend as providing the means for Palestinian self-determination and Israeli withdrawal. We were sure that if that could be achieved, he was ready to conclude a genuine peace treaty with Israel.

DAYAN VISIT: FEBRUARY

Just before Moshe Dayan was scheduled to arrive in Washington for further talks, the president approved the sale of 75 F-16s and 15 F-15s to Israel, 60 F-15s to Saudi Arabia and 50 F-5Es to Egypt. I announced this decision on February 14. We planned to submit the package formally to Congress for approval later in the spring, although we anticipated considerable congressional resistance to the sales to Egypt and Saudi Arabia. We had concluded, nevertheless, that the package was realistic and viable, since it would maintain the existing military balance in the Middle East while strengthening the confidence of all parties in the peace negotiations. Israel immediately voiced strong opposition to the sales to both Saudi Arabia and Egypt. Begin called on the administration to separate the package and seek approval of the Israeli sale first. This almost certainly would have ensured the defeat of the sale of F-15s to Saudi Arabia and perhaps even the less sophisticated F-5Es to Egypt. I told Congress that all parts of the package were interrelated and that if any were rejected, we would have to withdraw all of it.

Thus, on February 16, Dayan, a flexible pragmatist whose driving ambition was a peace treaty with Egypt, arrived during a period of strained relations, exacerbated by another dispute over settlements. Angered by my public statement about the illegality of Israeli settlements in the Sinai on February 10, Begin asserted that the president had not objected to settlements during their December discussions. The White House denied Begin's interpretation and reiterated the well-known American position that the Israeli settlements were contrary to international law.

Dayan obviously had got himself into trouble with Begin on settlements the previous fall, and he was cautious on this subject in the February discussions. He was worried that lack of progress could cost Israel the chance for a bilateral peace with Egypt, and his primary aim was to try to learn how much Sadat would have to have on the West Bank issue to conclude a peace treaty with Israel. He feared Sadat would demand an understanding that would have to satisfy Jordan and Saudi Arabia, and he felt sure the Israeli cabinet would be unwilling to give the advance commitment to withdrawal that Jordan would require to join the negotiations.

I wanted to make sure that Dayan understood clearly that we would not support Israel in pushing Sadat to make a bilateral agreement with Israel that failed to deal with the West Bank and Gaza. I also wished to underline that we regarded a solution to this issue as essential to the achievement of peace. In addition to explaining our ideas for an interim regime for the West Bank, I felt it important to learn precisely what security arrangements Israel would require in order to have confidence that such an interim solution would not pose a threat to it.

When we met with the president, he outlined our nine points to Dayan, who as usual proved open-minded in discussing them. Dayan said Israel was prepared to accept the right of Palestinian Arabs to participate in determining their future, but there could never be negotiations if Israel was required to agree in advance to withdrawal and self-determination. The president also emphasized the essentiality of a moratorium on settlements. Dayan evaded the issue. He was operating under heavy constraints in that the Israeli government was deeply divided over the issues of settlements, its peace policy, and the tone of its relations with the United States. Israeli moderates—Dayan among them—were pressing for a temporary halt in settlement activities to ease strains in U.S.-Israeli relations and provide a better climate for peace negotiations. Hard-liners in the cabinet were urging full speed ahead on settlements to further entrench Israel in the occupied territories.

Although emotionally Begin leaned toward the hawks on settlements and territories, as leader of a coalition government and a statesman trying to find a way to peace, he was caught in the middle of this fierce debate—which helps explain some of the "misunderstandings" we kept having. Begin did not want the peace process to fail, and tried to show as much flexibility as he could, given his intense concern for Israel's security, his convictions about Israel's right to be in the West Bank, and the necessity to take account of the political realities in Israel. Politically it would be risky for him to appear to have bowed to American pressure for a freeze on settlements or advance commitments to territorial withdrawal.

While Dayan was in Washington, a new issue surfaced that was to become a point of acute disagreement with Begin. We already had forewarning of it from Begin's rejection of our draft principle relating to withdrawal on all fronts. Now, as the West Bank issue was becoming pivotal, Dayan said that the position of the Begin government was that Resolution 242 only required withdrawal "from territories," not necessarily including the West Bank and Gaza. Dayan stated that the Israeli view was that since there was no universally agreed interpretation of this resolution, each side was entitled to adhere to its own interpretation and resolve the issue of the West Bank in negotiations. This was a repudiation of the official Israeli position dating back to 1968 that Resolution 242 required withdrawal on *all* fronts, and Begin's own undertaking in June 1977 to honor the commitments of previous governments.

BEGIN VISIT: MARCH

Begin's trip to Washington in March took place in a period of extreme tension. We faced the prospect of even greater tension since we planned to reiterate our view that the basic elements of any settlement were withdrawal of Israeli forces on all fronts in exchange for full peace and security for Israel. Moreover, our refusal to acquiesce in Israeli urging that we withdraw the proposed Saudi and Egyptian aircraft sales would have further exacerbated the existing strains. To counter an anticipated barrage of criticism of administration "favoritism" toward the Arabs, we had embarked upon a program of intensive consultations with Congress over the coming weeks to explain the issues and how we planned to address them. In those contacts with Capitol Hill just before Begin's arrival, one of the central subjects was a discussion of the negotiating history of Resolution 242 and the American position that it required withdrawal on all fronts.

On the eve of Begin's arrival our assessment was that Israel hoped to conclude a bilateral peace treaty with Egypt which would include as little as possible on Palestinian-related issues. We believed that Israel would not shift its existing position on the West Bank and Gaza unless it was convinced that Sadat would not sign a peace treaty without such changes. As we prepared for the talks, I suggested to the president that if, as I anticipated, the talks did not produce the necessary progress, we should present to the Israelis written questions on the West Bank and Gaza in an effort to obtain definitive answers.

To minimize the friction, I recommended that we offer Begin several assurances if he would unequivocally agree that Resolution 242 required withdrawal on all fronts including the West Bank. If he would do so we would state that our support for withdrawal would be conditional on working out satisfactory arrangements for protecting Israeli security. Second, we would oppose an independent Palestinian state or the presence of any hostile military force in the West Bank and Gaza. Third, we would support minor modifications in the final borders necessary for Israel's security. Further, we would again attempt to persuade Sadat to resume direct negotiations, draw Hussein into the negotiations, gain Saudi support for them, and work for a transitional regime that would permit the retention of some Israeli Defense Forces presence in the West Bank.

The Begin talks were preceded by preparatory discussions on March 9–10 among Israeli Defense Minister Ezer Weizman, Harold Brown, and me. Weizman warned us that if we did not ease up on our positions on settlements and Resolution 242, we were headed for a major clash with Begin which might even lead to a breakdown in the peace effort. Weizman urged us to reduce the tension by giving Israel new military assistance commitments and by separating the sale of aircraft to Israel from the Middle East arms package. When I refused to break up the package, Weizman suggested we provide Israel with additional advanced aircraft to "balance" the situation. I asked him whether Israel would alter its opposition to the Saudi and Egyptian aircraft sales if we worked out such an arrangement. He replied it would not.

Begin initially was scheduled to meet with the president on March 14–15. However, as Begin was about to leave, Palestinian terrorists operating out of Lebanon staged a murderous attack in Israel, killing a number of civilians. Begin sent Carter a message informing him that the Israeli Defense Forces were moving into southern Lebanon to destroy PLO bases and that his arrival in Washington would accordingly be postponed for several days. In fact, the Israeli counterstrike was far more than a retaliatory raid; it was a massive operation that brought most of Lebanon south of the Litani River under temporary Israeli control. The incursion gave Israel the opportunity to consolidate an enclave in southern Lebanon held by Christian militiamen under the command of Major Saad Haddad as a buffer zone along the Israeli border. After intense diplomatic efforts in the Security Council, a UN peacekeeping force was put into southern Lebanon, and Israel technically withdrew—although it continued to support the Christian militia. Lebanon was to return to the Middle East stage again and again, demonstrating that the Lebanese problem was inextricably intertwined with the larger Arab-Israeli peace process.

The Lebanon crisis did provide an important demonstration that Begin would respond when he understood the president was determined that a particular Israeli course of action detrimental to American interests should not continue. The case in point was the Israeli attempt, after its withdrawal from Lebanon, to strengthen clandestinely the friendly Christian forces in the south.

On April 5, as the conflict in Lebanon was subsiding, a seemingly small but important event occurred. In response to queries from congressmen Paul Findley and Charles Whalen, I sent a letter to Congress stating that Israel's use of American military equipment in its invasion of Lebanon may have violated the Arms Export Control Act. That act states that defense articles may be provided by the United States only if foreign recipients agree that they will use military items transferred by the United States only for self-defense and certain other purposes and not to retransfer those items to another country or party without the permission of the United States. If the letter stated a violation *had* occurred, the president or Congress could have automatically suspended all military assistance to Israel. The fact was that we had little doubt Israel's use of U.S.-origin military equipment had gone beyond the requirements of self-defense. However, since our principal interest was in Israel's compliance with the UN withdrawal order—and Israel was doing so—we did not want to trigger a counterproductive crisis. At the same time, we protested Israel's use of cluster bombs in Lebanon in violation of its agreement with the United States that it would use this antipersonnel weapon only when attacked and only against military targets. On April 20, Defense Minister Ezer Weizman conceded using the cluster bombs had been a mistake.

Israel continued its staged withdrawal through April and May. But after Israel had allegedly completed the withdrawal of all its forces on June 13, we received information that it had left behind, in the hands of Major Saad Haddad, a small number of armored personnel carriers and artillery pieces. Haddad was blocking the entry into southern Lebanon of the UN peacekeeping forces. If this report was true, we would face a blatant violation of the Arms Export Control Act. Through Sam Lewis in Tel Aviv, we asked the Israeli government whether it had transferred U.S. equipment to Major Haddad. The response was a flat denial and an assertion that the Israeli Defense Forces had removed all American-made military equipment from southern Lebanon.

We ascertained that contrary to the Israeli denials, the armed personnel carriers and artillery pieces were of U.S. origin. They could only have come into Haddad's hands from the IDF. With the peace process at a critical stage, it was imperative that this matter be dealt with promptly and forcefully.

The issue—a handful of APCs and artillery pieces—was small, but the principles at stake were large. The president acted immediately and decisively. We sent a terse, blunt message to Begin saying that unless the equipment were removed at once, we would report to Congress immediately that a violation of the Arms Export Control Act had taken place. Begin could not fail to recognize that the president meant business. Carter sent the message to Begin personally, rather than to the government, thereby giving him a chance to handle the matter quietly, but his intentions and firmness were unmistakable. Begin removed the equipment at once.

The terrorist raid and the Israeli military response changed the political atmosphere for our talks with Prime Minister Begin. Before March 14, Begin had been on the defensive on both settlements and withdrawal, as American and important segments of Israeli opinion were critical of Israel's positions on these issues. The terrorist attack greatly strengthened Begin's position and, as I put it to Carter, "refocused the attention of Israel's supporters in the U.S. from the peace process to concern for Israel's security." The possibility of getting Begin to alter his positions on the West Bank and Palestinian questions was virtually eliminated.

Sadly, the March 21–22 discussions with Begin were confrontational and unproductive. He rejected our arguments on Resolution 242 and insisted that the resolution did not require withdrawal on all three fronts. He blamed Sadat for the breakdown of negotiations in January. The president explained his understanding of the Egyptian position, stressing that Sadat was not insisting on either a withdrawal to the 1967 border on the West Bank without any modifications, or upon the establishment of an independent Palestinian state in the West Bank and Gaza. The president's exasperation was evident as he remarked sharply that he could not understand why the sides continued to quibble over semantics while the chance for peace was slipping away. He underscored again that Sadat was prepared to negotiate peace with Israel even if Jordan stayed out, provided that Israel would agree to withdraw on all fronts and to negotiate seriously on the Palestinian question. The first day's talks ended when Carter declared bluntly that in his opinion the obstacle to peace was Israel's obvious intention to retain perpetual control over the West Bank. He warned Begin that if he did not seize the opportunity for peace, it soon would be lost.

On March 22, Carter outlined to Begin our thinking on the elements for an interim regime in the West Bank and Gaza and the form of a Palestinian self-rule arrangement under Israeli, Jordanian, and perhaps Egyptian authority. He suggested that the area should be demilitarized, although Israel could retain limited forces in a small number of strategically located encampments. Carter emphasized that during the negotiations for self-rule there should be no new or expanded Israeli settlements. He warned that unless Begin was prepared to meet Sadat's essential political needs, there was little hope that talks could be resumed.

Begin responded sharply that our views about Israeli policy were all negative and that we failed to appreciate how far Israel had come since its refusal even to talk about the West Bank. He denied again that Resolution 242 required withdrawal on all fronts, adding that not only did Israel oppose withdrawal in the West Bank, it was not committed to total withdrawal from any territories, including the Sinai. Begin then repeated Israel's willingness to withdraw from the Sinai to the previous international border in two stages. He said, however, that Israeli settlements in the Sinai would remain and would be protected by an Israeli military contingent.

Begin reviewed his December plan for the West Bank and Gaza, emphasizing that by "self-rule" he meant an administrative council that could deal with the problems of daily life. Although the Israeli military governor was the only existing source of authority for the administrative council, Begin said he was prepared to abolish the military administration. He reiterated his willingness to consider my suggestion of an agreement between Israel and Jordan providing for the devolution of authority to the self-governing authority. He left the door slightly ajar for restraint on settlements during negotiations, but only at the discretion of the Israeli government.

· · ·

By the end of Begin's visit it was apparent that he did not share our sense of urgency in capitalizing on Sadat's initiative. Sadat, however, was reassured by Carter's firmness during the Begin meetings. Regrettably, Sadat did not seem to grasp the damage he had done by breaking off the political talks and by his continuing refusal to engage in direct discussions with Israel. He was convinced that his standing in the Arab world required a tough posture until Begin moved.

We decided that we should continue our present strategy for at least the next several months:

• We would hold to our current positions on the basic issues, try to avoid the trap of harsh public debate with Israel, continue working closely with Congress to build understanding of our views, and wait to see if the forces in Israel that wanted improved relations with the United States would stimulate Begin to adjust his policies.

• We would keep up our bilateral consultations with all the negotiating parties on the specific issues. These consultations would serve a useful purpose as we continued to explore possible compromises on political, legal, and military issues that eventually would have to be addressed. At a minimum, the consultations would keep the negotiating process alive while the crucial struggle for public and congressional support continued.

Roy Atherton, having become ambassador at large for the Middle East negotiations in early April, carried much of the burden in the bilateral consultations through the spring of 1978. In late April, Atherton met with Sadat and Foreign Minister Kamel to convey President Carter's assurance that with the Panama Canal Treaties finally ratified, we intended to redouble our efforts in the Middle East. He told them our overriding aim was to ensure that Sadat's November initiative led to a successful outcome. At the appropriate time, Atherton promised, we would come forward with our own proposals in the hope of narrowing the differences between the parties.

Atherton used his April talks with Sadat and Kamel to explain in detail how our thinking had evolved on the critical Palestinian issue. We had concluded that the gap between Israel and the Arabs on this problem was so great that no final settlement could be negotiated as part of the current peace effort. Israel, he said, could only make decisions on initial questions affecting its security in the context of steady negotiations. Atherton explained our conclusion that the only feasible solution was a transitional regime in the West Bank and Gaza of sufficient duration to provide a "time buffer" during which the parties would attempt to negotiate a final settlement. He stressed that although it was unrealistic to expect that Israel would commit in advance to withdraw on all fronts and accept Palestinian self-determination, we believed that an interim arrangement could start a process that would change the status quo. Atherton reiterated our concern that so far the only proposal on the table for the West Bank was Begin's self-rule or administrative autonomy plan; he emphasized to Sadat the political disadvantages of such a state of affairs. Until Egypt responded with a specific counterproposal, Israel would feel no need to consider any changes in its position. Atherton reviewed the elements in the U.S. nine-point approach and urged the Egyptians to produce their own plan. As the president and I had told Sadat in February, we wanted to be confident when we put forward an American proposal that it would encompass Sadat's essential requirements.

Sadat and Kamel agreed to prepare an Egyptian proposal giving emphasis to the "transitional" aspects of the plan. They asked in return that we take into account their proposal and their comments on our nine points in preparing a formal American proposal. They also urged that we agree to consult again with them before we introduced our revised proposal. Sadat was extremely worried that our plan might not go far enough; he felt that if it did not, he would have lost a major asset in dealing with Israel—substantial agreement between Egypt and the United States on the issue of the West Bank and a homeland for the Palestinians.

Fortuitously, Moshe Dayan asked to come to Washington at the end of April. Taking advantage of this, I planned to use our private conversations to discuss offering American compromise proposals during the summer.

With the stalemate unbroken, I felt we were fast approaching a crossroads. The usefulness of U.S. "good offices" between the parties was about exhausted; soon we would have to put forward an American proposal in an effort to break the deadlock. We could not allow the stalemate to continue because of the risks it posed to Sadat and to our interests in the Middle East.

When I met with Dayan, I pointed out that Sadat needed greater specificity about what would happen at the end of the five-year transitional period, and pressed him for Israeli agreement to withdraw at the end of the transitional period. Dayan replied that Israel could not agree in advance to any process that would require eventual Israeli withdrawal from the West Bank, even if it were assured that there would be no Palestinian state, and even if the Israeli Defense Forces could remain in designated security locations. Carter was unhappy when I reported this to him, and wanted to criticize the Israeli position publicly.

I recommended against it. While Dayan loyally represented his government's views, he was groping for a way to embrace the concept of an interim arrangement. He understood that peace between Egypt and Israel would be impossible until this central issue was addressed. He believed that we must find a way to defer the question of the final status of the West Bank while the parties experimented with self-rule in the West Bank and Gaza. There was obviously a big difference between deferring action—which was politically unrealistic—and devising specific arrangements for negotiating the final status of the area during the transition period. I asked Dayan to secure authoritative Israeli answers to two specific questions: Would Israel agree that at the end of the five years a decision would be made on the final status and sovereignty of the territories; and would Israel outline the mechanism by which this change would be negotiated? Dayan agreed to ask the Israeli cabinet to respond to these questions as soon as possible.

There was little change in the positions of the sides over the next two and a half months. After heated debate on Capitol Hill, the Senate approved the Middle East aircraft sale as we submitted it. This victory was important to the peace process and bolstered Egyptian and Saudi confidence in our determination to strengthen political and security relations with them despite powerful domestic opposition. At the same time, the president acted to defuse growing Israeli apprehensions about an administration tilt toward the Arabs. After the Dayan visit the president publicly declared that he believed a settlement for the West Bank should be along the lines of Begin's autonomy proposal—elements of which we were using in refining our transitional proposal. On May 1, during a brief Begin visit to mark thirty years of Israeli independence, Carter vigorously reaffirmed the American commitment to Israel's security. Begin responded warmly. In a meeting with Begin I emphasized that he should not conclude that we were endorsing his self-rule proposal, because we still believed it did not go far enough. Begin said that Israel would hold its claim of sovereignty in abeyance for five years, which was a long time, during which much could happen.

The Egyptians were disturbed at what appeared to be a shift toward Begin's views, but it was essential that we mute our public exchanges with Israel as we prepared to launch a major effort to bring Egypt and Israel back to the negotiating table. I urged the Saudis not to yield to intense pressure to break with Sadat. In this matter we were helped by congressional approval of the Middle East aircraft package.

THE THIRD PHASE: FULL AMERICAN PARTNERSHIP IN THE NEGOTIATIONS

Early in the summer of 1978 the Policy Review Committee met several times to coordinate our next steps. If the Israeli response to the two questions I had given Dayan in April was reasonably forthcoming, I believed we might be able to persuade Sadat to talk directly with Israel. However, based on further exchanges with Dayan, I was not optimistic that the Israeli cabinet would make the necessary decisions. In that case, our only option would be to offer American proposals. Our efforts to remain evenhanded by refusing to endorse Begin's proposals, as well as our success with the Middle East aircraft package, tended to reinforce the view that we had bowed to Arab oil pressure and were jeopardizing Israel's security for the sake of larger American strategic interests in the Middle East. Many argued that after the approved aircraft package the burden was now on the Arabs to make the next move.

In the midst of our deliberations, we received helpful news from Cairo. On June 15 the Egyptians gave us a West Bank proposal that significantly altered their previous position. They still insisted on Egyptian-Jordanian administration of the occupied territories during the transition period and the removal of Israeli settlements. They also rejected our suggestion of an Israeli military presence on the West Bank during the transitional period, although they spoke of mutual security arrangements "during and following the transitional period." Privately, however, Sadat told us that he could be "forced" to acquiesce to Israeli troops in the West Bank during the transition and to President Carter's Aswan formula on the legitimate rights of the Palestinians.

Shortly afterward, the Israeli government responded to the two questions. Its delphic reply sidestepped the central issue of what would happen after the five-year transition. The cabinet said that after the five-year experiment in self-rule, "the nature of the future relations between the parties will be considered and agreed upon" by Israel and the elected representatives of the West Bank and Gaza. Stripped of ambiguity, the reply meant that Israel would not now commit itself to withdrawal from the West Bank or to Palestinian self-determination at the end of the five years. I issued a public statement saying the United States felt that Israel had responded inadequately to the questions we had put to it.

On June 21, after considering the Israeli cabinet's reply, I sent telegrams to Cairo and Tel Aviv proposing that Sadat and Begin send their foreign ministers to London for a meeting on July 11 which I would attend. Although it would disappoint Sadat, we decided once more to hold off introducing American proposals until we were able to explore how the two sides' thinking had evolved.

Israel was ready to attend the talks, as it had been ever since Sadat unwisely broke off the political committee discussion in January. At first Sadat delayed in accepting our invitation; he was angry because on June 25 the Israeli cabinet rejected his West Bank proposal even before he formally offered it. Begin stated that Israel was simply reacting to public accounts of the Sadat proposal, and that his government would naturally consider the proposal when it was received through the United States. To overcome Sadat's reluctance to send Foreign Minister Kamel to the

London meeting, we took advantage of Vice-President Mondale's scheduled visit to Israel to carry letters to Sadat and Begin from President Carter, putting the invitation on a personal basis. Sadat agreed to the London meeting.

. . .

The two days of discussions, which were rescheduled for July 18 and 19 and for security reasons moved to Leeds Castle in Kent, produced no agreement on any of the proposals on the table. Nevertheless, these talks among Dayan, Kamel, and me were of critical importance.

Perhaps one of the most important outcomes of the Leeds conference was the fact that, for the first time in decades, the Israelis and Egyptians dined together.

At our first meal, the evening of our arrival, we were strictly separated according to national groups. The Israelis chose to dine together, the Egyptians with each other. Although either would have shared a meal with the Americans, we could not dine with one and not the other.

That night, after everyone had gone to their rooms, Gay and I decided that continuing in this way would only sharpen the existing differences and that henceforth we would take all our meals together.

This decision was greeted with some trepidation and suspicion by our colleagues. But after a very pleasant dinner the next evening, at which Israelis, Egyptians, and Americans were seated in sequence around the table, everyone making an effort to be friendly with his partners, the evening was pronounced a resounding social success.

The atmosphere of the conference improved markedly thereafter. Even if no dramatic breakthrough had been achieved, an acknowledgment of each other's humanity was not an unimportant result.

Privately Dayan asked me if there was any chance of leaving the final status of the West Bank and Gaza to be decided in the future, rather than at the beginning of the transition period. He believed that if this were accepted by the Egyptians there could be a breakthrough. This came as no surprise as I had concluded that the Israelis were not going to agree in advance to withdrawal or to the principle of Palestinian self-determination. I told Dayan that I would not rule out an arrangement such as he was suggesting. He then offered his personal opinion that if the Israeli peace proposals were accepted, Israel would be prepared to discuss the question of sovereignty at the end of the five years and that an agreement could be reached at that time.

In our face-to-face discussions, Dayan and Kamel set aside each side's formal proposals and simply talked about the practical problems of working out an interim transitional arrangement. They were making progress even if they could not agree on the language of documents. The solution that was emerging closely resembled the approach we had been developing since my August Middle East trip nearly a year before. Dayan and

Kamel spoke in terms of a five-year interim arrangement during which the Palestinian Arabs would be able to run their own affairs, with a final solution to be negotiated during this period by the involved parties, with the participation of elected Palestinian representatives. Kamel acquiesced in the necessity for special arrangements to protect Israel's security during the transition, signaling Egypt's recognition that Israeli forces would not have to withdraw completely during the transition.

At the conclusion of the Leeds Castle talks, Saunders and Atherton and I agreed that we had at last come to the point where the U.S. role would have to change. We felt that there was no use in continuing to try to mediate Egyptian-Israeli agreement on the general principles of peace. Therefore, while still in Britain, we began discussing the structure and elements of an American proposal for a comprehensive settlement, including arrangements for peace between Egypt and Israel and an autonomy process for the West Bank. The night before we left London, Saunders began drafting the document which, after many permutations, was to form the basis of the Camp David framework for a comprehensive settlement.

Initially, our intention was that the Leeds Castle meeting would be followed in about two weeks by presentation of the American proposal, possibly at the U.S. monitoring station in the Sinai. This did not materialize, however, because Sadat prevented it by reverting to his position of refusing to negotiate with Israel. One reason for Sadat's action was anger at the Israeli cabinet's public rejection of his confidential request for the return of the town of El Arish and Mount Sinai to Egyptian control as a goodwill gesture. A positive Israeli response would have given him a modest public relations cover for resuming bilateral negotiations. The more important reason, however, was Sadat's conviction that only shock tactics would keep the United States energized and the Israelis off balance. Also, he was under strong pressure from his advisers, who were worried by Arab perceptions that Sadat was steadily sliding toward a separate peace with Israel. With his characteristically dramatic announcement, Sadat lost the initiative to Begin in the struggle for Israeli and American public opinion.

After this setback, the president and I agreed in late July that I should attempt a "rescue mission" to the Middle East. Initial planning for this trip focused on two objectives: getting Sadat's agreement to resume direct talks on a basis acceptable to Begin, and shoring up Sadat's confidence in our overall strategy. Sadat had been waiting since his talks with the president in April 1977 for the United States to enter the negotiating process as an equal participant. The president had, for what he and I felt were sensible diplomatic and political reasons, put off that decision much longer than Sadat had expected. Sadat was beginning to wonder whether our insistence on Egyptian-Israeli negotiations as a necessary framework for introducing American proposals was merely an excuse to avoid the political problems of carrying out Carter's commitment to him.

As staff work on my trip progressed, the president and I and our colleagues continued to consider how to break the impasse. Just before I left, the president made a momentous decision: He would invite Sadat and Begin to a summit at the presidential retreat at Camp David. It was a daring stroke, which I warmly supported. Repeated trips to Middle East capitals, shuttle diplomacy, infinite variations of draft principles and "elements" of solutions had narrowed and shaped the issues, but it would be necessary to get all the principals meeting face to face for as long as would be necessary in order to reach the political decisions that could make a settlement possible. If we could get the parties to agree to a peace treaty between Israel and Egypt and an interim solution to the West Bank, the way could be open to the general Middle East peace that remained our fundamental objective. We prepared the necessary handwritten letters to Begin and Sadat.

On August 6 and 7, I went to Jerusalem and Alexandria to deliver the handwritten letters from Carter to Begin and Sadat inviting them to meet the president at Camp David, beginning September 5, to negotiate a framework for peace in the Middle East.

I met first with Begin in Jerusalem and he accepted immediately and enthusiastically. I stressed the need to move forward. I warned that if we did not seize this opportunity, there was great risk that the chance for peace would slip from our grasp. Begin was apprehensive about our intentions for Camp David, worrying that he would be caught between Carter and Sadat. Later he stated publicly that at Camp David the United States should continue to play an intermediary role and should not offer any proposals of its own. After our meeting, I was fearful that there might be a leak before I got to Egypt, but true to his word, Begin kept the matter almost to himself alone and I was able to extend the invitation to Sadat without a whisper of public knowledge.

Sadat was delighted that at long last the United States was prepared to undertake the role of "full partner." I used this phrase for the first time after my meeting with Sadat and it had a positive impact on the Egyptians. He responded that he would come to Camp David filled with optimism and willing to listen to the other side. But having finally reached the moment of truth, Sadat was not his usual ebullient self. The risks for him were enormous, as they were for Begin and for Carter; unless the summit was a success, Sadat could expect an outcry from the Arab world. If the conference was a failure, it could mean repudiation of his entire peace policy.

Despite our plea to the Arab and Israeli leaders that they come to Camp David with no preconditions, Begin announced on August 31 that Israel's position would remain that there would be no withdrawal to the

1967 borders and that Israel would continue military control of the West
Bank and Gaza under any interim arrangement. He also said that the de
facto annexation of East Jerusalem was nonnegotiable.

• • •

Immediately upon my return from the Middle East, we plunged into
intensive preparations for the Camp David summit. Not since Theodore
Roosevelt mediated the treaty negotiated in Portsmouth, New Hamp-
shire, that ended the Russo-Japanese War had an American president
even approached what Jimmy Carter was about to attempt. And when
we investigated that parallel, we found it dissimilar, for Roosevelt had
remained on Long Island and had not participated directly in the Portsmouth talks himself. Thus, there were scant precedents to guide us, and
a myriad of political, diplomatic, procedural, and protocolary arrangements to be planned, not to mention the substantive problem of preparing an American draft peace agreement that could bring the sides
together.

We concluded it would be difficult to stay in Washington and devote
the necessary uninterrupted attention to our preparations for the summit. Yet we could not be far from Washington. My dear friend and
mentor, Averill Harriman, provided us with a perfect solution by making
available to us the guest house on his and Pam's place in Middleburg,
Virginia. On August 11 my wife and I and Hal Saunders, Roy Atherton,
and Bill Quandt drove down to Middleburg for a stay of several days. It
was a perfect location in the beautiful Virginia countryside, lying at the
foot of the Blue Ridge Mountains, where we could be alone and saturate
ourselves in the sea of matters necessary to prepare for what we prayed
would be a successful summit. All of us knew that the course of Middle
East history hung on the outcome of Camp David. In Middleburg we
worked out the basic plans for the summit and the supporting, immensely detailed briefing books, which I subsequently discussed with the
president. We also examined at length all of the contingencies that might
arise at Camp David and the various options for dealing with them.
These preparations turned out to be invaluable because of the confidence with which they inspired us. Saunders also brought along the draft
accord he had started at the end of the Leeds Castle talks, which we
revised in light of recent developments.

The broad as well as the immediate objective of the administration's
strategy was still to find a way to achieve a comprehensive settlement
that we could recommend to all the Middle East parties. In addition, at
Camp David, I hoped we could reach agreement on a draft of an Egyptian-Israeli agreement that would form part of the comprehensive settlement. These two agreements would serve as guidelines for the next phase
of the peace process: negotiations of peace treaties and autonomy for the
inhabitants in the West Bank and Gaza.

As for the important question of the U.S. role, I was sure a U.S.-drafted document would be necessary. The positions of the two sides were so far apart that the differences could not be bridged, starting with their drafts. This difficulty could be circumvented by starting from a U.S. draft. I believed Sadat and his advisers would welcome a U.S. draft agreement as the surest way to make progress. Begin, despite his publicly declared opposition to American proposals, would also probably conclude that this approach would be the only way to get an agreement. Moreover, it would suit his negotiating style, which was to concentrate on the specific language of documents.

There were to be two mutually reinforcing American teams at the summit, of which I was the common member: the political group, headed by the president and including Zbigniew Brzezinski; the able White House press spokesman Jody Powell; Hamilton Jordan, Carter's imaginative and wise political strategist; myself, and on occasion, the vice-president and Harold Brown; and the group of experts, who met under my direction and included Saunders, Atherton, Quandt, Sam Lewis, and Hermann Eilts, our immensely talented ambassadors to Israel and Egypt respectively. These two groups worked in the closest harmony. The political group negotiated with the Egyptian and Israeli senior political figures, while the professional group maintained contact with the Egyptian and Israeli teams and provided expert advice, analyses of the sides' positions as they evolved, and draft formulations to bridge the differences.

Another important decision made prior to Camp David, with which all of us agreed, was to insist that everyone stay at the historical retreat in Maryland, without any visits to Washington or even to nearby Thurmont where the press was quartered. It was also agreed that Jody would be the press spokesman for all the parties and that nothing of substance would be said until the meeting was concluded. We had seen too often the damaging effects of press leaks on negotiations. We were determined to prevent this from happening at Camp David. Our procedures worked, and in my judgment, contributed substantially to the success of the negotiations.

•   •   •

As the summit began there were two sets of proposals on the table: Begin's Sinai and West Bank-Gaza self-rule proposals of December 1977, and Sadat's West Bank-Gaza proposal put forward before the Leeds Castle talks started and summarily rejected by Israel. On the second day of Camp David, the Egyptians presented a proposal framework for a comprehensive peace. Meanwhile, we had in our pocket a revised draft of Saunders' framework for a comprehensive settlement that he, Atherton, Quandt, and I had prepared in August.

The first two days of the summit were largely exploratory, focusing on the purposes of the summit and the differences in each side's proposals. Carter spent much of his time with Begin and Sadat, at first as a three-some, but increasingly in bilateral sessions as he saw that Begin and Sadat tended to stiffen in each other's presence. Carter's aim during the first few meetings was to establish a rapport among the three leaders. He sought to break down the mistrust and animosity between Begin and Sadat, and to impress upon them the overriding importance for all to reach agreement at Camp David. In fact, the communiqué released after the first few sessions had nothing to do with the substantive issues or negotiating differences, but dealt with the common aspirations for peace. Carter wanted at the outset to put the summit on a high plane, reflecting the deep religious faith and humane purposes of the three leaders.

I and the professional team also met separately with the Egyptian and Israeli delegations on Wednesday, September 6, to clarify both the Egyptian and Israeli proposals. These bilateral discussions continued on Thursday and Friday. They revealed all too clearly how far apart the two sides were on the basic issues.

Early Saturday morning, September 9, the president and our political team, after considering the lack of progress in closing the enormous gap between the two sides' proposals over the first four days, concluded that the time had come to turn to an American negotiating text. It was decided that by Sunday, when work resumed after the Israeli Sabbath, an American draft of a peace framework should be ready for discussion with Begin and Sadat.

About nine that morning I went to the lodge where the professional team was working and briefed them on the political team's decision. I told them the president would like a working draft by early afternoon. We had anticipated this request and by working most of Friday night, Saunders had revised the August draft framework to take into account the Egyptian and Israeli papers that had been tabled at the opening of the Camp David session. Brzezinski and I and the members of the professional team went over the revision until we were ready to discuss with the president a well-developed draft. The president joined us during the afternoon, and the draft was then put into final form.

In accordance with prior arrangements, we first reviewed our draft informally and separately with each delegation. Carter, Mondale, Brzezinski, and I had a lengthy session with Begin and his senior advisers on Sunday. Begin and his associates retired to study the draft that night, and the president, Brzezinski, and I met with them again on Monday morning to receive their reaction. The Israelis had crossed out all the language in the preamble drawn from Resolution 242, in particular the language dealing with the inadmissibility of the acquisition of territory by war. They also deleted references to the "Palestinian people," substituting "Palestinian Arabs," and inserted "administrative council" in place of "self-governing authority." They eliminated reference to a peace treaty to settle the final status of the West Bank and Gaza, substituting a sentence to the effect that negotiations would deal with "all outstanding issues after the transitional period." In the Jerusalem paragraph they struck out the sentence, "An agreement on relationships in Jerusalem should be reached in the negotiations dealing with the final status of the West Bank and Gaza." The Israelis flatly refused to discuss our proposed language calling for a freeze on settlements while negotiations were in progress. The document was rapidly revised, incorporating some of the Israeli changes and rejecting others. It was given to Sadat by the president later Monday morning. It retained the Jerusalem paragraph, but left the settlements paragraph blank while we continued to explore that issue with Begin and Dayan. The Egyptians gave us their comments and proposed textual changes early on Tuesday morning, September 12.

The Egyptian comments, as did Israel's, showed how far we had to go. The Egyptians, in essence, also wanted to rewrite our draft. They struck out the "West Bank-Gaza" heading, and inserted in its place "The Palestinian Problem." They also inserted references to the "legitimate rights of the Palestinian people." The Egyptian draft stated that Israeli settlements would be withdrawn from the West Bank and Gaza, and that at the end of the five-year transition period the Palestinian people would decide their own future. Their draft further provided that at the beginning of the transitional period, governmental authority would be transferred to Egypt and Jordan. Finally, the Egyptian draft provided that Arab sovereignty and Arab administration would be restored to "Arab" (East) Jerusalem.

It was clear that we were confronted with two sharply opposing points of view on the nature of Palestinian autonomy: The Egyptians saw autonomy as the precursor to Palestinian self-determination and Israeli withdrawal from the West Bank. The Israelis' view, as reflected in Begin's December 1977 home-rule proposal, was that autonomy meant a limited form of administrative self-government under circumstances in which Israel retained control over both the West Bank and Gaza. The tension between these two points of view was to persist through everything we did at Camp David, through the Egyptian-Israeli peace treaty negotiations later on, and during the Palestinian autonomy talks, which began in May 1979. The challenge for the Camp David negotiations was to marry those conflicting objectives, building on two initiatives—Sadat's Jerusalem initiative and Begin's self-rule proposal.

Our approach to this challenge followed two closely related tracks. On one, we sought to press Begin to go as far as he could go in accepting the general principles of withdrawal, the application of Resolution 242 to all fronts, and the pursuit of a comprehensive peace. On the other, we attempted to transform Begin's self-rule plan into a serious arrangement for "full autonomy"—Begin's own words as the talks proceeded at Camp David—for the Palestinian inhabitants of the West Bank and Gaza and to provide a mechanism for the ultimate resolution of the final status of the West Bank and Gaza by the end of the five-year transitional period.

On Tuesday, with these considerations in mind, we prepared an American working draft and presented it to both sides as the basis for further negotiations. The September 12 American draft was the negotiating text that led to the agreement—on the twenty-third version—on a framework for a comprehensive peace, the essence of which was the Palestinian autonomy process. It specified that both sides explicitly acknowledged that the principles of Resolution 242—withdrawal on all fronts in return for full peace and diplomatic recognition—should be the basis of a peace settlement. It recognized the legitimate rights of the Palestinian people and provided that an elected self-governing authority for the West Bank and Gaza be established. It also provided that elected Palestinian representatives be parties to any negotiations on the final status of the West Bank and participate in determining their own future. The draft included language that provided for a freeze both on new settlements and the expansion of existing ones in the West Bank and Gaza while negotiations were underway. It also contained a paragraph on Jerusalem providing that a "municipal council representative of the inhabitants of the city shall supervise the central functions in the city," and retained the sentence that the Israelis had deleted from our September 10 draft concerning agreement on relationships in Jerusalem.

The second week's discussions centered on the U.S. compromise draft. On Wednesday, September 13, the president and I in marathon sessions met with each of the parties to discuss the American text. These grueling discussions continued on into Wednesday night and most of Thursday. Either the president or I presided. There were frequent breaks while the delegations went back to Begin and Sadat to discuss compromise formulations, as we progressed through revision after revision. The focus was almost entirely on the West Bank-Gaza autonomy arrangements, Jerusalem, settlements, and related issues; the bilateral issues between Egypt and Israel seemed relatively simple by comparison.

As the week wore on, it seemed possible, even likely, that because of deep divisions over the principle of withdrawal, Resolution 242, the nature of Palestinian autonomy, and the future status of the West Bank and Gaza, and Jerusalem, we could not reach agreement on the comprehensive framework.

I remember vividly several times when the mood was particularly dark and gloomy telling the president that although the future seemed almost hopeless, this was like most negotiations, with their moments of euphoria and periods of depression and despair. We agreed that the goal of peace was too essential to let it slip from our hands. If we failed it would be a long time before such a summit meeting could be held again. We were determined to persevere and to succeed. During all of this Dayan was very helpful in the darkest moments in helping us thread our way through the thickets. When we faced impasses, he sought imaginative ways to overcome our problems. He was tireless, working far into the nights despite the fact that he was almost always in pain from a bad back that had been broken a number of years ago, and from wounds he had suffered in the 1967 war. Ezer Weizman, Israel's charismatic, bright, and swashbuckling defense minister, was also most helpful, as was Attorney General Aharon Barak. Barak, who is now a justice of the Supreme Court of Israel, is a most gifted lawyer and scholar, and a wise, sensitive, and humane man. He has a marvelous facility with words, coupled with a creative mind. He was indispensable in finding imaginative ways to overcome what seemed insurmountable stumbling blocks.

Early in the second week, Carter told the political team of his concern that in our preoccupation with the West Bank-Gaza complex of issues—the core of the framework for a comprehensive settlement—we had overlooked a chance to negotiate an Israeli-Egyptian peace treaty. He noted that not only did the differences on the Egyptian-Israeli bilateral issues seem less profound in this area, but also that the presence of Sadat and Begin provided a unique opportunity to negotiate a framework for a peace treaty between two of our closest and most dependable friends in the Middle East.

After intensive discussion among our team and with key Israelis and Egyptians, Carter sat down in his lodge to draft the framework of a peace treaty between Israel and Egypt. He discussed the draft separately with Begin and Sadat, and by the middle of the second week we were negotiating the language of this second agreement in parallel with our broader negotiations. At that moment there appeared to be only two major problems in the way of reaching agreement on the framework for an Egyptian-Israeli treaty. Israel wanted to retain settlements and military airfields in the Sinai, which Egypt adamantly opposed. And, more seriously, Egypt insisted that implementation of a bilateral peace treaty must be linked to progress on a comprehensive settlement, including withdrawal from the occupied territories and resolution of the Palestinian questions. The latter issue was crucial to Sadat so that he could demonstrate that he was not abandoning his Arab brothers. This linkage between a bilateral peace treaty and progress in the West Bank autonomy talks was to become a critical issue during the subsequent negotiations.

As the discussions continued through the second week the pressure began to take its toll. Begin commented, half in jest, that he felt he was trapped within the chain link fences and tall trees of Camp David. "It is beginning to feel like a concentration camp," he said. Sadat and some of his colleagues also felt confined on this heavily wooded mountaintop, which was so different from their native land. Yet the fact that we were all together in this beautiful yet isolated spot was important, for all of us

knew that there was no escaping the task before us. We had to face the
hard issues and make the difficult decisions. We were all in this together
and the fate of Egypt and Israel and peace in the region were at stake.

As the days passed, Sadat grew increasingly unhappy with Begin's
stance on the West Bank-Gaza and Palestinian issues. He chafed under
what he regarded as Begin's haggling over minutiae. Sadat believed that
the three leaders should agree on the elements of a just peace and let the
experts put this agreement into treaty language. Instead, he found himself faced daily with a series of confrontations.

Friday, September 15, was a fateful day. That morning I received word
from Sadat that he wanted me to come and see him in his lodge. When
I saw him, his face was clouded and his mood somber. He was clearly
deeply troubled, and not his warm and empathetic self. He asked me to
sit down and then told me he had decided he must go home, as there
was no hope that we could achieve an agreement. I struggled to persuade
him to stay, stressing the importance of our task and our responsibility
to our peoples and to world peace. I asked him to remember that it was
his courageous initiative that in large part had made it possible for us to
be here at all, and that history would treat us harshly if we failed. I urged
Sadat to think about what I had said while I went at once to inform
President Carter.

With a leaden feeling of despair, I crossed the road to Aspen Lodge,
where the president was staying. When I told him of my conversation
with Sadat, Carter was shocked, but remained cool and steady, saying
that he would go immediately to see Sadat. He said we could not let him
leave now, when we had come so far. He picked up the telephone and
told Sadat he was on his way over to his quarters. As he left the lodge my
heart and prayers were with him.

I must have sat for close to an hour in Aspen waiting for the president
to return. The minutes ticked by with agonizing slowness. It was like
waiting outside an operating room.

Finally, the door opened and the president came in. He said simply,
"Sadat will stay." It was as though the sun had burst through the clouds.
My spirits soared. I felt that the last big river had been crossed and that
we would reach our goal. I could turn again to the business of negotiating
the agreements.

Over the first ten days we had made considerable progress in shaping
the outlines of an autonomy process, although difficult issues had been
deferred. However, as of Saturday evening, September 16, we were still
at loggerheads over settlements and Jerusalem.

By Sunday morning the president and I believed we had reached a
major breakthrough in our discussions with Begin. On Saturday night,
the president and I met with Begin, Dayan, and Barak, who played a
crucial role in devising formulae that permitted agreement on a number
of critical issues. We met for close to six hours, talking into the hours of

Taken on the day after I was sworn in. I spent much more time in my small office, which adjoined this more formal room.

President Carter, Foreign Minister Gromyko, Ambassador Anatoly Dobrynin and I meet in the White House at the time of Gromyko's first visit to Washington in September of 1977.

Ambassador Malcolm Toon, Betty Toon, Mrs. Gromyko, myself, Foreign Minister Gromyko, Gay, and Ambassador Dobrynin at the Bolshoi Theater on our visit to Moscow in April of 1978. A performance of the *Nutcracker Suite* was especially sheduled for us that evening.

The opening of the SALT talks. I meet President Brezhnev for the first time in the Kremlin in March of 1977.

Meeting with Vice Premier Teng Hsiao-ping in the Great Hall of the People in Peking. I had previously met the Vice Premier in 1975 when I visited China as a private citizen. [UPI]

Foreign Minister Huang Hua at the Summer Palace during my trip to China in August of 1977 to begin discussions on normalization of relations between our two countries. [CHRISTOPHER OGDEN/ TIME]

Prime Minister Menachem Begin making a serious toast after dinner in the Knesset. Behind him are the famous Chagall murals.

An early meeting in 1977 with President Anwar Sadat in his residence outside Cairo.

Moshe Dayan and I chat in the garden of his home in Tel Aviv. Behind us are ancient Egyptian relics from Moshe's marvelous collection.

The President, Anwar Sada
Osama el-Baz and I meet i
Carter's study in Aspen
Lodge at Camp David.

Prime Minister Mustafa
Khahil, Foreign Minister
Moshe Dayan and I in
Hawthorne Lodge at Camp
David. This picture was
taken during Camp David I
when we were negotiating
the Egyptian-Israeli Peace
Treaty in February 1979.
[STATE DEPT.]

We meet with the
Israeli delegation
in Holly Lodge.
Around the table
from left to right
are: Aharon
Barak, Ezer
Weizmann,
Moshe Dayan,
Menachem
Begin, Jimmy
Carter, Cyrus
Vance, Zbig
Brezinski, Fritz
Mondale.

A thrilling moment as the heads of government sign the Camp David Accords in the East Room of the White House on September 17, 1978.

My last meeting with President Sadat in Washington, D.C., on his last trip to the United States before his tragic death.

Foreign Minister Roelof Botha, Secretary of State for Foreign and Commonwealth Affairs, David Owen and I meet in London in August 1977 to discuss Zimbabwe.

Co-leader of the Patriotic Front and leader of Zanu, Robert Mugabe, at the Malta II conference in Dar-es-Salaam in April 1978.

I meet with Tanzanian President Julius Nyerere at the State House in Dar-es-Salaam in April 1978.

Co-leader of the Patriotic Front and leader of Zapu, Joshua Nkomo, at the Malta II conference in Dar-es-Salaam.

Chancellor Helmut Schmidt makes a point as Vice Chancellor and Foreign Minister Hans-Dietrich Genscher and I listen.

President Giscard d'Estaing and I talking before dinner at the Elysee Palace in Paris at the time of the NATO meeting.

Secretary of State for Foreign and Commonwealth Affairs Peter Carrington says goodbye as Hodding Carter and I leave the Foreign Ministry in London in February 1980.

Foreign Secretary David Owen gives a dinner for members of the Western Contact group at Carlton Gardens (the Foreign Secretary's house). From left to right are: Canadian Foreign Secretary Donald Jamieson, French Foreign Minister Louis de Guiring, and West German Foreign Minister Hans-Dietrich Genscher.

I meet with the Shah in the Niavaran Palace in Tehran on my first visit to Iran in May of 1977. John Miklor, our chargé d'affaires, looks on.

The Iran task force in the Operations Center at the State Department in December of 1979.

President Carter, Vice President Mondale and I attend a service for the hostages in The National Cathedral.

the early morning. As we reviewed the text of the comprehensive peace accord, Carter again raised the question of Israeli settlement activities. Begin was adamant that he could not enter into an agreement with Sadat that restricted Israel's right to continue settlements in the West Bank. Begin finally said he was willing to give to President Carter a separate letter stating that Israel would establish no new settlements until the autonomy negotiations were completed. On that basis, we agreed to drop from the draft comprehensive accord our proposed language on a settlement moratorium. After the meeting I asked Hal Saunders to prepare a draft letter that Begin could give to Carter, reflecting our previous night's agreement on settlements. However, because of the Jerusalem issue, which consumed much of the next day, we were unable to get the settlements letter signed at Camp David. This, together with other agreed side letters, was sent to the Israelis for signature on Monday morning, after the Framework for Peace had been signed on Sunday evening before the TV cameras in the East Room of the White House.

Since presentation of our September 12 draft, we had been attempting to reach agreement on a paragraph on Jerusalem embodying common views, and a good deal of useful language was developed on municipal administrative arrangements covering such areas as public transportation, tourism, and the like. Begin, however, would not accept language implying that the future status of Jerusalem was an issue for negotiations or related in any way to the autonomy process. Sadat continued to insist on some symbol of Arab sovereignty in East Jerusalem. He suggested to us a "Muslim" or Arab flag of some sort over the Islamic holy places in East Jerusalem. Begin would not accept any Arab emblem, however generalized or remote, in East Jerusalem, nor would he agree that its Arab inhabitants could participate in the West Bank autonomy arrangements. When I raised the idea of a plain green flag to be flown at the Dome of the Rock Mosque on the top of the Temple Mount, the prime minister exploded, telling me that it was sacrilegious to suggest that any flag could be flown over the holy of holies, and that if we pressed the issue he would leave Camp David immediately. It was becoming clear that it would not be possible to reach any agreement on language covering the issue of Jerusalem.

When, on Sunday morning, it had become evident that no paragraph on Jerusalem could be drafted that would both satisfy Sadat and be acceptable to Begin, we decided to drop reference to the city from the comprehensive peace accord. Instead, we suggested that each party simply state its own national position on Jerusalem in side letters. The professional team drafted our Jerusalem letter later Sunday morning, setting forth the American position as expressed in statements in the United Nations in 1967 and subsequently that we considered East Jerusalem to be occupied territory and that we did not recognize Israel's 1967 annexation.

When Begin examined this draft letter it was about midday. He again threatened to break up the summit. Dayan came to the main lodge where many of our meetings took place, and we met in the billiards room. Carter, having been informed that something was wrong, joined us. Dayan looked grave and upset. He warned us that if we insisted on setting out in detail the American position on East Jerusalem, Begin would simply pack his bags and go home. We were very angry. Carter furiously demanded to know if Israel meant to tell the United States it could not even publicly state its own national position. Deeply embarrassed, Dayan explained that politically it was impossible for Begin to associate himself with an agreement in the context of which the United States explicitly stated that it did not recognize Israel's annexation of East Jerusalem. Dayan was a serious man whom we both trusted. It was clear to us that he saw this as a make-or-break matter. The question for us was whether to press the issue and perhaps lose all that had been achieved or to find another way to say the same thing in different words. This was a difficult decision, but in the end, with my support, Carter decided that while we would affirm that the American position remained as contained in statements before the United Nations, we would not insist on spelling it out.

It seemed that the last major issue had been settled. In midafternoon, around two o'clock or so, Carter had a final session with Begin to confirm Israel's agreement on the two accords. After returning from the meeting with Begin, the president called Sadat to his lodge.

I was not present when the two presidents met, but Brzezinski, Hal Saunders, and I arrived at the lodge just as the two men emerged from the study. Sadat was subdued, although he did not appear upset. He left the lodge immediately without speaking to us. I asked the president if we should prepare messages to world capitals announcing a successful outcome at the summit. Carter responded, "I was almost afraid to ask him, but yes, I think we have an agreement."

President Carter said he had told Sadat that the two peace accords were not perfect, particularly on the basic point of establishing clear linkages between an Egyptian-Israeli treaty, and a comprehensive settlement and the implementation of the autonomy process in the West Bank and Gaza. But he had assured Sadat that we would work with him to see that Israel faithfully fulfilled both agreements. Right to the last moment some of Sadat's advisers were still arguing that the agreements were slanted toward Israel's positions. But Sadat trusted President Carter and gave his consent.

The Camp David Accords

As we boarded the helicopter and flew back over the rich Maryland farmland stretching as far as the eye could see, I thought back over the long and, at times, bumpy road that had led to Camp David and the historic achievement just realized. My heart was filled with joy and hope, yet I knew that there were many obstacles ahead. A major step forward had been taken but in a sense we had only just begun. The negotiation of the Egyptian-Israeli peace treaty would be difficult when we had to face the gritty details. And the ensuing discussions on the Palestinian issues would be difficult beyond anything we had experienced so far. Nevertheless, a critical page had been turned in the Middle East and a new chapter was about to be written. Things would never be the same there again and the door to real peace for Israel and justice for the Palestinians had at last opened. I prayed we could lead them through it.

On Sunday evening, September 17, Carter, Begin, and Sadat signed the two accords in a glittering ceremony in the East Room of the White House. On Monday night, the president described the agreements to a joint session of Congress, with Sadat and Begin looking on.

The "Framework for Peace in the Middle East" invited the other Arab states to negotiate peace with Israel on the basis of Resolutions 242 and 338 and the principles and provisions of the framework. The core elements of this framework were the arrangements for transitional self-rule and for negotiation of the final status of the West Bank and Gaza. The final status of the West Bank and Gaza was to be determined in negotiations between Israel, Egypt, Jordan, and representatives of the Palestinian self-governing authority. These negotiations were to begin no later than the third year of the transition period—a point that was hotly debated at Camp David. The accords also set forth a second framework containing the principles governing the negotiation of an Egyptian-Israeli peace treaty.

The "Framework for the Conclusion of a Peace Treaty Between Egypt and Israel" provided that the parties would make a good-faith effort to conclude a peace treaty within three months—by December 17. Its key elements were: full withdrawal of Israeli forces from the Sinai to the 1967 border within three years; within nine months from the signing of the accords Israel would complete an interim withdrawal to the line running from El Arish in the north to Ras Muhammad in the south; at the time of the interim withdrawal normal relations would be established between Israel and Egypt. Provision was made for security zones, monitoring stations, and an international force to police the border and to ensure freedom of passage through the Straits of Tiran. The status of the Israeli settlements in the eastern Sinai was left unresolved, but in a side letter to the president, Prime Minister Begin undertook to put the future of those settlements to a free vote in the Knesset. President Sadat stipulated in a parallel letter to President Carter that this accord would be void if Israel did not agree to the removal of the Sinai settlements, and that Egypt would not begin negotiations until this assurance was obtained from Israel. Fortunately, the Knesset rapidly approved removal of the Sinai settlements.

In a similar exchange of side letters relating to the general framework, Sadat stated that East Jerusalem should be under Arab sovereignty, whereas Begin wrote that Jerusalem was "one city indivisible, the capital of the State of Israel." In a letter to Sadat, Carter said that the American position was that "stated by Ambassador Goldberg in the United Nations General Assembly on July 14, 1967, and subsequently by Ambassador Yost in the United Nations Security Council on July 1, 1969." Sadat also affirmed that Egypt would "be prepared to assume the Arab role" in the negotiations on the West Bank and Gaza. This was to assure Israel against the possibility that Jordan would refuse to join the negotiations. However, the agreed exchange of letters between Carter and Begin on a moratorium on Israeli settlements in the West Bank and Gaza during the autonomy negotiations never took place.

On Monday, all the side letters, except the one on the settlements moratorium, came back from the Israeli delegation signed. Saunders called Ambassador Dinitz to inquire about the missing letter, and was told Begin was redrafting it. When the redrafted letter arrived Monday afternoon, it referred to a moratorium during the negotiations for a peace treaty between Egypt and Israel, i.e., three months. It was not until then—after the accords had been signed and announced—that we realized the prime minister was not going to carry through on the understanding we had reached with him the previous Saturday night. Begin contended that he had agreed only to a moratorium during the peace treaty negotiations, which were to take three months, not the autonomy negotiations, which would require at least a year or more to negotiate. Since we had been discussing only the comprehensive accord and the autonomy negotiations during the Saturday night session, it is difficult to understand how Begin could have so totally misinterpreted what the president was asking. But that was his position and he refused to budge from it.

* * *

The Camp David accords rank as one of the most important achievements of the Carter administration. First, they opened the way to peace between Egypt and Israel, which transformed the entire political, military, and strategic character of the Middle East dispute. Genuine peace between Egypt and Israel meant there would be no major Arab-Israeli war, whatever the positions of Syria, Jordan, the PLO or the Arab rejectionists. Second, Camp David brought the Palestinian question to the top of the negotiating issues, and upon the conclusion of the Egyptian-Israeli peace treaty, it would be the single focus of the negotiating process. This was a significant advance from the virtual refusal of Israel at the outset of our peace initiative even to admit that there was a Palestin-

·ian issue. Third, although we failed to resolve the issues of Israeli withdrawal and Palestinian self-determination, Camp David created and
defined a process for the resolution of these issues in the future.

Some critics have charged that Camp David constitutes an abandonment of a comprehensive settlement in favor of a separate Egyptian-
Israeli peace. This view was widely held in the Arab world, but it did not
reflect the facts as we saw them. The Camp David accords reflected in
our judgment the outer margins of the possible at that time. A review of
the accords shows that Israel did recognize in writing that the Palestinians had "legitimate rights," and would be given "full autonomy." Israel
did commit to a process which, if faithfully implemented, would lead to
the establishment of an elected Palestinian self-governing body and the
withdrawal of the Israeli military government. Moreover, if the self-
governing body acted responsibly, the autonomy process could become
irreversible; that is, Israel could find it politically impossible, and from a
security point of view unnecessary, to continue the status quo or to assert
sovereignty after the transition period.

Until Monday afternoon we believed that Prime Minister Begin would
carry out his commitment to refrain from establishing any new settlements in the West Bank and Gaza during the negotiations required to
establish a Palestinian self-government. Tragically, and in my opinion at
least as much from his fear of Israeli domestic opinion as from any
misunderstanding of what President Carter had said, Begin altered his
commitment. And, as Begin came under increasingly strident attacks
from Israeli hawks, he insisted that he had agreed to nothing new, that
everything done at Camp David was consistent with his December 1977
self-rule plan, and that the Palestinians would have no more than limited
administrative autonomy. These statements caused untold damage and
weakened our position in explaining the benefits for the inhabitants of
the West Bank and Gaza as a result of the accords.

• • •

Our most immediate tasks were to try to keep the door open for Jordanian participation in the autonomy talks and to maintain Saudi support for Sadat. Accordingly, the president asked me to leave immediately
for Jordan and Saudi Arabia to explain the Camp David accords and to
answer any questions their leaders might have. I was also to seek their
direct support, which I was unlikely to get. King Hussein and Prince
Fahd were angry with Sadat, who had returned to Cairo without explaining to them what had been accomplished at Camp David and why. They
believed he had given them an explicit commitment before the summit
to negotiate a comprehensive settlement in which the rest of the Arabs,
including the Palestinians, could join, or at least support, without unacceptable political risk. Instead, they told me, most of the Arab world was
attacking Sadat and that no recognized Palestinian leader would be will-

ing to participate in the autonomy negotiations at this time. Both Hussein and Fahd said that Sadat had let them down by making a separate peace with Israel in exchange for the return of the Sinai.

They argued that Sadat's failure to explain neither his actions to the Arab world nor Begin's statements after Camp David proved that we had produced only a bilateral peace treaty. I argued insistently that much had been achieved and that the autonomy arrangements could lead ultimately to Palestinian self-determination. I reviewed in detail the benefits that could flow from the accords if they would seize opportunities presented by the agreement. They expressed disbelief that the Israelis would carry out the terms and spirit of the accords.

At the conclusion of my lengthy discussion with King Hussein he said he had additional questions he needed to have answered before he gave us his considered response. He promised to send them to us shortly. After my return to Washington, the president and I personally worked on our reply to King Hussein's questions. The president then personally signed the answers and sent Hal Saunders to Amman to deliver them to the king on October 16. Hal spent hours with the king's advisers and had two separate meetings with the king himself. Hal also met with Crown Prince Fahd and his advisers and with West Bank Palestinians. Unfortunately, he fared no better than I had.

Because the October 16 answers to King Hussein's questions so clearly represent the president's and my views immediately after Camp David, it is important to summarize them. The answers stated that under the Camp David accords, the final status of the West Bank and Gaza would be determined by negotiations among Jordan, Egypt, Israel, and representatives elected by the inhabitants of the area. These negotiations would start no later than the third year after the beginning of the transitional period. The outcome of the negotiations would be put to a vote of the elected representatives for ratification or rejection. Our view was that sovereignty ultimately resided in the people of the West Bank and Gaza, and that they would express their will on the final status of the area through that vote. In other words, the U.S. position was that the inhabitants of the West Bank and Gaza should participate in all the important steps which would determine the future of the area, including the question of sovereignty.

The answers pointed out that the accords provided that the powers of the self-governing authority during the transitional period would be negotiated among Israel and Egypt, and Jordan, if it would agree to join. The self-governing authority would thus be established by international agreement, and the powers of that body would be defined by the three states—not by Israel alone.

For reasons that have been explained, the accords did not mention Jerusalem; but our position, affirmed in Carter's letter to Sadat executed simultaneously with the accords, was that East Jerusalem was occupied territory. However, recognizing the special religious character of the city, we could envision a final status for it different from that of the West Bank. We believed that whatever solution emerged from future negotiations should leave the city physically undivided; provide for free access to the holy places of the three faiths; and assure the basic rights of all the city's inhabitants. We would support proposals that would permit the Arab inhabitants of East Jerusalem to vote in the elections for the self-governing authority, but we believed it unlikely that the powers of the self-governing authority could be extended to East Jerusalem during the transition period.

The accords did not mention settlements, although, as noted, we believed we had obtained a commitment from Begin to abide by a moratorium during the autonomy negotiations. The long-standing position of the United States on settlements was that they were contrary to international law and were an obstacle to peace. Our view remained that during the negotiations required to establish the self-governing authority, Israel should refrain from establishing any new settlements.

As to the future of Palestinian refugees living outside of the West Bank and Gaza, we believed that they should have the right to settle there if they so chose. We expected that the relationship between the self-governing authority and Palestinians living outside of the West Bank-Gaza would be taken up in the autonomy negotiations, and it was our position that no inhabitant of the West Bank or Gaza who accepted the Camp David framework should be precluded from voting in the elections for the self-governing body or from holding office because of his or her political affiliation.

Lest it be mistakenly concluded that our only interest in the framework provided by the Camp David accords was the establishment of a West Bank-Gaza autonomy arrangement, we pointed out in our response to King Hussein that the stated objective of the accords was "a just, comprehensive, and durable peace and durable settlement of the Middle East conflict through the conclusion of peace treaties based on Security Council Resolutions 242 and 338, in all their parts." We recognized that there were differing interpretations of Resolution 242 on the two sides, particularly on whether Resolution 242 required withdrawal on "all fronts." We said the United States would stand by its long-held position on interpretation of this matter: that 242 required withdrawal on all fronts.

11

THE MIDDLE EAST:
THE SINAI TREATY

THE BLAIR HOUSE TALKS:
NEGOTIATING THE PEACE TREATY

On October 12, 1978, the Egyptian and Israeli delegations assembled in Washington to negotiate the details of the Egyptian-Israeli peace treaty pursuant to the framework agreed to at Camp David. Also, they were to conduct parallel discussions on a joint Egyptian-Israeli "side letter" defining the arrangements for negotiating autonomy for the inhabitants of the West Bank and Gaza.

President Carter welcomed the delegations at the White House that morning. The gathering was in marked contrast to the beginnings of other Middle East negotiations over the previous five years. Unlike the small negotiating groups that had been involved in the shuttles of Secretary Kissinger in 1974 and 1975, the traveling teams that had accompanied me to the Middle East and New York in 1977, or the small parties that had come to Camp David, these two delegations on October 12 had full complements of diplomatic, economic, legal, and military experts prepared to write a complete treaty of peace. For that reason it seemed to those of us who watched the brief ceremony that the effort on which we were about to embark had a different, long-term character. The atmosphere was expectant and positive, although everyone present knew that hard work lay ahead.

We had considered a number of possible sites for the talks, but in the end we decided to base them in Blair House, the president's spacious and lovely guest house across the street from the White House. Although its physical facilities were not really suited to this use, comfortable offices were established for the delegates and a meeting room provided. The historic nature of the site added to the atmosphere of serious purpose, and it was assumed that the delegates would have other work space at the nearby Madison Hotel. Eventually, more and more of the working parties' meetings shifted to the hotel, which became known among the delegates as "Camp Madison."

After the president's welcome at the White House, the parties immediately walked across Pennsylvania Avenue to Blair House and got down to serious work. The pattern that evolved after I formally opened the negotiations was for me to meet with the ministers and the individual negotiating teams of experts at points where critical decisions were being discussed, while Roy Atherton, with a supporting group of his own, managed the talks on a day-to-day basis. The first step at the opening session was a request from the two parties that we provide a negotiating text. After Camp David, we had prepared a short draft treaty with annexes on the detailed political and military arrangements, and it was encouraging to have both sides ask us to put the draft on the table as a working document. This not only avoided spending time on trying to reconcile conflicting texts from the two delegations, but also sidestepped the classic problem of advancing an "American plan."

The parties arrived with the intention of finishing the work within the period agreed at Camp David—three months from the signing of the Camp David framework, December 17, 1978. Reflecting on Camp David and the reaction of the Arab world afterward, we knew that the most difficult political issue would be the relationship between the peace treaty and a comprehensive peace involving the other parties in the Arab-Israeli conflict. This issue would come up in a variety of ways, the most common being the Egyptian demand for linkage between implementation of the treaty and progress on arrangements for the West Bank and Gaza. It would also appear in questions pressed by the Israelis about the relationship of the peace treaty to Egypt's other treaties and agreements with Arab states. For the Israelis, the most difficult issues would involve giving up the oil resources of the Sinai, the abandonment of the Sinai settlements, and the details of the security arrangements.

As the treaty negotiations proceeded, our conclusion that linkage of the implementation of the treaty to the autonomy talks would be the most difficult issue proved correct. The Egyptians wanted "synchronization" between the two negotiations in order to respond to Arab criticisms that they were signing a separate peace with Israel. This took the form of Egyptian pressure for Israel to agree, in a side letter, to a specific date for completion of the autonomy talks and the holding of the elections for the self-governing body. The Egyptians insisted that the two be coterminous with the interim withdrawal from the Sinai, i.e., nine months after the peace treaty was signed. The Israelis were granitelike in their resistance to this demand and the debate over setting a goal or target date for completing the autonomy negotiations went on until the eve of the treaty signing in the spring of 1979.

The Egyptians also proposed a sequence of steps in normalizing relations—diplomatic recognition, opening of embassies, exchange of ambassadors, opening of consulates, and so on—to coincide with the stages of the Israeli withdrawal from the Sinai. The Egyptians felt that as well as providing leverage to ensure Israeli compliance with the withdrawal schedule, this sequence would stretch out treaty implementation so that it would take place parallel to the West Bank and Gaza autonomy talks. Conversely, the Israelis demanded establishment of full diplomatic relations, including the exchange of resident ambassadors, promptly upon completion of the interim withdrawal to the El Arish-Ras Muhammad line. The timing of the exchange of ambassadors became virtually an obsession with the Israelis. They understood what the Egyptians were trying to do and would not agree to anything that implied that implementation of the peace treaty was tied to progress on the Palestinian issues or the question of a comprehensive peace. For Israel, the peace treaty had to stand on its own base.

Another major question was Israel's demand that the treaty include an explicit provision specifying that Egypt's peace treaty obligations would take precedence over its defense agreements with other Arab states in the event of any future Arab-Israeli conflict. Israel argued that under international law an earlier international obligation would have priority over the peace treaty, and that Egypt had several defense agreements with other Arab states. Israeli legal advisers contended that, in the absence of such a clause, in a war between Israel and another Arab state with which Egypt had a treaty, Egypt would be empowered to honor its prior agreement. Therefore, the Israelis argued, Egypt had to state in unequivocal language that the Egyptian-Israeli peace treaty superseded any other international agreement.

As the negotiations got underway, the linkage issue was immediately contended. Israel strongly resisted the Egyptian demand for inclusion of language in the body of the treaty relating it to a comprehensive settlement. As in the case of linkage to the autonomy talks, the Israelis would not agree to anything that would condition complete fulfillment of the treaty to any act that was beyond the powers of Egypt and Israel to control. The Israelis feared that if the peace treaty were described as a step toward a comprehensive settlement, and a comprehensive settlement did not materialize, Egypt could denounce the treaty. Within a few days, however, an acceptable compromise seemed to be emerging. The compromise was a preambular good-faith commitment by both sides to solve the problems of a comprehensive peace and to deal with the Palestinian issue. This preambular language was to be the subject of tedious hairsplitting throughout the Blair House talks and beyond.

Progress was made on other issues as well. Israel offered to speed up portions of its interim withdrawal, and the Egyptian delegation agreed to the exchange of resident ambassadors upon completion of the withdrawal to the El Arish-Ras Muhammad line. On the priority of the treaty over other international obligations, the Egyptians appeared to understand the deep-seated Israeli concern and the two sides were actively searching for acceptable language. Some advance was also made in defining unilateral Israeli "gestures" (actions) in the West Bank and Gaza that would enhance Arab confidence in the seriousness of the negotiations. But overall, progress was slow. It was not until October 23, after Carter had personally intervened to help prevent threatened departures by both delegations and to halt semantic quibbling by both sides, that a tentative agreement was reached on the main issues, ad referendum to governments. The agreement did not include, however, the crucial side letter on the West Bank-Gaza, on which the delegations remained far apart. The Egyptian delegation satisfied the Israeli demand for a specific clause on the priority of obligations issue, and the Israeli delegation agreed to the insertion of language in the treaty preamble reflecting the continuing commitment of both nations to a comprehensive settlement.

Agreement was reached at such an early date because of the courage, skill, and determination of the negotiators on both sides, aided by the U.S. team. Particular credit must be given to the work of Dayan, Weizman, and Elyakom Rubenstein, Dayan's able assistant, on the Israeli side, and General Kamal Hasan Ali, Boutros Ghali, and Osama El-Baz, the extremely gifted negotiator on the Egyptian side. On the U.S. side Atherton, Saunders, and Quandt were most steadfast.

Sadly, however, both delegations proved to have gone further than their governments would accept. The next day, Boutros Ghali, the talented Egyptian minister of state for foreign affairs, reported that Sadat objected to several points, especially the language on priority of obligations, and insisted on reopening this and other issues. Israel's reaction was less negative; the Israeli cabinet approved the draft treaty "in principle," but also wanted some changes, particularly in softening the linkage language in the preamble. Dayan and other members of the Israeli delegation briefly returned home for consultations, and the Washington talks were delayed until they returned on October 26.

As had happened too often before, the negotiating climate was soured by fresh difficulties stemming from Israeli settlement activities in the West Bank. The Egyptians had been pressing us to work out an Israeli freeze on new settlements before the treaty signing, stressing the importance of this issue to the other Arab nations. While Cairo and Jerusalem were still considering the preliminary texts developed at Blair House, however, Begin announced plans for expansion of West Bank settlements. This step was contrary even to Begin's version of the Camp David accords. We were very angry, and I at once issued a public statement of regret. We privately tried to make Begin understand that such actions were endangering the negotiations, but he rejected our protests and insisted he had made clear at Camp David that Israel would continue to enlarge existing settlements even as it refrained from establishing new ones. Sadat was upset and Egypt promptly announced that it was considering bringing its negotiators home from Washington.

In this tense atmosphere, the delegations returned to the negotiating table. We were determined to resist demands from either side to reopen issues unless it was clear that a mutually agreeable solution existed. We could not afford to lose ground by debating agreed language all over again. Despite our best efforts, this proved impossible. Both sides insisted on reopening points on which agreement had already been reached.

At this point I rejoined the discussions, having just returned from SALT negotiations in Moscow. I began discussions with Ghali and Dayan about the West Bank and Gaza side letter. They had agreed that the letter would state the intention of the parties to begin negotiations on arrangements for establishing the Palestinian self-governing authority after the Sinai peace treaty was ratified. Sadat also wanted the letter to specify a timetable for the completion of the autonomy negotiations, which Dayan warned us Begin would refuse to do. Moreover, in an effort to show some visible gain for the Palestinians, Sadat proposed that if problems should arise about the West Bank arrangements, the autonomy process would be implemented first in Gaza, where the Egyptians believed they could influence local Palestinian leaders.

Over the next two weeks the negotiations plodded forward on the linkage language in the preamble, the priority of obligations clause, and a host of minor issues. The American team produced a steady stream of alternative formulations in an effort to close the gaps in the treaty text, while the Egyptians and Israelis exchanged versions of the West Bank and Gaza side letter with exquisitely obscure and minute linguistic changes. The Egyptians kept trying to pin the Israelis down to specific arrangements and time frames, while the Israelis resisted any phrase that could not be traced back to the Camp David language. The work was appallingly tedious, but day by day we inched forward.

During that period, on November 2, I briefly met with Begin in New York when he stopped on his way to Canada. We went through the treaty literally line by line. He was adamant that we must drop or weaken the language in the preamble about the commitment to a comprehensive peace. I tried to persuade him that the existing draft language was a major concession by Sadat, who had wanted a clause in the body of the treaty itself, but Begin was immovable. Begin also raised the idea of a large American loan to help Israel pay for the costs of withdrawing from the Sinai. I told him this could be decided only by the president and would, of course, require congressional approval. Importantly, Begin confirmed that even though Camp David called for Jordanian participation in the West Bank and Gaza negotiations, Israel and Egypt could proceed alone, if necessary.

One of the major reasons for the difficulties in the treaty negotiations was the increasing political problems Begin and Sadat faced at home. The attack on Begin from both right and left after Camp David did not abate. His critics argued that in agreeing to provide autonomy for the West Bank and Gaza, he had taken the first step toward an independent Palestinian state. Begin responded by stating he had not agreed at Camp David to anything that had not been previously approved by his cabinet in the December 1977 self-rule proposal; his announcement on settlements was meant to demonstrate that he was not compromising on the West Bank. Such statements intensified the difficult task of persuading the Arabs that the Camp David accords described a process that could lead to the fulfillment of "Palestinian rights" and a fair settlement between Israel and its neighboring Arab states.

I had realized after my trip to Saudi Arabia and Jordan in September that we would have to conduct a major informational effort in the Arab countries to explain what Camp David really involved. I asked the International Communications Agency and Hal Saunders to propose ways of getting across the message that whatever Begin might now be saying, Camp David was a significant advance from the original self-rule proposal. A number of video cassettes and instructional telegrams to area ambassadors were prepared, which centered on the clear differences between the self-rule proposal and the "full autonomy" agreed upon at Camp David. Key to this effort were our answers to the questions from King Hussein. As noted in the previous chapter, the president and I had decided to answer the questions in writing. Thus we could set out easily the American interpretation of what had been agreed, particularly on the meaning of full autonomy, and our view of the strategy for resolving the ultimate status of the West Bank and Gaza. To make our answers as authoritative as possible, they were signed by President Carter and delivered to Arab leaders by Hal Saunders. However, this highly visible and necessary effort provided ammunition to Camp David's critics in Israel.

The Egyptians made little effort to explain the Camp David accords. They did, however, in the context of the Blair House negotiations, make a strong plea for Israel to take what Boutros Ghali called confidence-building steps that would help improve the political atmosphere in the West Bank and Gaza and demonstrate to the Arabs that Israel intended to carry out in good faith its obligations under the accords. Like us, the Egyptians believed the Israeli settlement program was the single most damaging point in undermining the credibility of the Camp David process. They argued that Israel must make some gesture—such as freezing settlement activities, easing restrictions on political activity in the West

Bank, and withdrawing the military government—if there was to be any hope of persuading the other Arabs that Camp David had been a step forward.

Continuing differences of interpretation also plagued our attempt to make progress in the parallel West Bank and Gaza discussions at Blair House. The Israelis denied that there would ever be a referendum in which the Palestinians would participate, even though the Camp David accords explicitly provided that the agreement on the final status of the West Bank-Gaza would be submitted "to a vote by the elected representatives of the inhabitants of the West Bank and Gaza." We had told King Hussein that we interpreted this to mean that Camp David did "not preclude the holding of an election by the inhabitants of the West Bank and Gaza, after the conclusion of an agreement on the final status of the West Bank and Gaza, for the express purpose of electing representatives to whom that agreement will be submitted for a vote." Similarly, Begin now denied that there need be any withdrawal of the Israeli Defense Forces from the West Bank, although the Camp David accords specified that some Israeli forces would be withdrawn and the rest redeployed into a limited number of security locations. Dayan argued in the treaty talks that the Israeli military government could continue for a time even after the self-governing council had been established, whereas the Camp David accords stated that ". . . the Israeli military government and its civilian administration will be withdrawn as soon as the self-governing authority has been freely elected." And Begin declared that the self-governing authority would merely be an administrative body, whereas we insisted that the powers and responsibilities of the council were to be determined in negotiations, not by Israel alone.

Sadat became increasingly worried over these differences as well as over his inability to establish an explicit link between the peace treaty and an overall settlement. On November 5 the pan-Arab conference at Baghdad called on him not to sign a treaty with Israel and threatened an economic boycott of Egypt if he went forward. This deeply disturbed Boutros Ghali and the other Egyptian negotiators. On November 9, when it seemed the final major treaty drafting issues were close to solution, Sadat wrote Carter that he had to have a commitment about what was to take place in the West Bank and Gaza before he could sign the treaty. It was difficult to be sure how much the growing Egyptian concern about Cairo's isolation from the Arab world represented Sadat's personal feelings and how much those of his political advisers, but it was clear that Sadat was prepared to risk further delay in concluding the treaty in order to obtain meaningful commitments on autonomy.

Dayan and Weizman seemed reasonably confident that Israel could accept the nearly finished treaty text, but they were concerned at the persistent Egyptian demands for more detailed arrangements on the

West Bank and Gaza, and worried about how this would affect the Israeli cabinet's reception of the treaty.

Carter agreed with me that we must redouble our efforts on the West Bank and Gaza issue. On November 11 we gave the sides our redraft of the West Bank side letter, which we suggested should be from President Carter to Begin and Sadat, rather than a joint letter between the latter two. Our version did not have a timetable for the granting of autonomy —one of the chief Egyptian demands—but it committed Israel to begin negotiations one month after ratification of the peace treaty, with a target date of not later than the end of 1979 for holding an election for the self-governing authority. We also pressed the Israelis to be as forthcoming as possible on the "goodwill gestures" to improve the atmosphere in the West Bank and Gaza.

Sadat responded negatively. He also insisted on reopening the treaty language on the linkage between the treaty and a comprehensive settlement, the proposed resolution of the "priority of obligations" clause of the treaty, and other issues that had been tentatively resolved by the delegations. He sent Vice-President Hosni Mubarak to Washington to meet with us on November 16 to convey his concerns and his feeling that we were asking him to make all the compromises in the face of Israeli intransigence. Mubarak warned us that it was imperative for Sadat to link the peace treaty to Palestinian autonomy. If this were not done, he said, the positions of both Egypt and the United States in the Arab world would deteriorate. He emphasized that Sadat wanted an Israeli commitment to complete the autonomy talks and to withdraw the Israeli military government by January 1980. Mubarak said Sadat thought that autonomy should begin in Gaza first, as a confidence-building model for the West Bank and as concrete evidence of progress on the Palestinian issues. Carter and I argued to Mubarak that we must recognize how far Israel had come on the West Bank and Gaza question with its commitment to begin autonomy negotiations within one month after ratification of the treaty. We pointed out further that the autonomy negotiations would be in progress as Israel withdrew in stages from the Sinai, with final withdrawal to be completed in three years. Thus, as a practical matter, we said, implementation of the treaty and the phases of the autonomy process would be parallel proceedings. Carter urged Mubarak to recommend to Sadat that Egypt accept the treaty as it stood.

On November 21 Begin telephoned Carter to say that the Israeli cabinet had accepted the draft treaty—providing Egypt also agreed to it. He also said that Israel would not accept any timetable or target date for completing the autonomy negotiations or for holding elections, as Sadat was demanding. As far as Begin was concerned, the treaty negotiations were finished and Egypt should accept the language as it stood. Moshe Dayan told the press that the Egyptians "could take it or leave it."

We had reached a serious impasse. The treaty issues Sadat had raised, although difficult, were negotiable. The fundamental problem continued to be Sadat's determination to gain Israeli agreement to a specific time frame for granting autonomy to the Palestinians. Sadat wrote Carter on November 25 that he could not sign the treaty under the existing circumstances without breaking his pledge not to conclude a separate peace. He insisted the solution was for Israel to agree to a target date for the establishment of autonomy coincident with the completion of the interim withdrawal in the Sinai. Sadat also raised again the problem of the priority of obligations, complaining that as this language had evolved at Blair House, it had become offensively explicit in subordinating Egyptian agreements with other countries to the treaty with Israel.

After discussing these matters with Carter on the telephone, on November 29 Sadat asked us to deliver a letter from him to Begin, offering his personal proposal for completing the negotiations. In tough, sometimes harsh words, Sadat demanded that Israel soften the clause on priority of obligations. He proposed that he and Begin exchange letters committing themselves to begin negotiations within one month after ratification of the treaty, to hold elections for the Palestinian self-governing council by September 1979, and to inaugurate the self-governing authority within one month thereafter. Sadat added that if Israel would restore its earlier commitment to accelerate the phases of the interim withdrawal, Egypt would exchange ambassadors within one month after Israeli forces withdrew to the El Arish-Ras Muhammad line. Responding through us on December 4, Begin rejected Sadat's proposal and reiterated Israel's readiness to sign the current draft treaty without any change.

• • •

In the aftermath of the Sadat-Begin exchange, the president concluded that the only chance of making the December target date set at Camp David was to try shuttle diplomacy again. Although, as I mentioned earlier, we were at a critical point in the secret negotiations with Peking on normalization, and I was preparing to meet Foreign Minister Gromyko in Geneva just before Christmas on SALT, the president asked me to return to the Middle East in early December with a U.S. compromise package. My objective was to get the treaty signed as quickly as possible, as the longer the impasse dragged on, the stronger the antitreaty forces in both Israel and the Arab world would become. Even if the shuttle diplomacy failed, which seemed likely, the president felt that the fact of our having tried would bolster Sadat's confidence in our determination to persevere.

The compromise package we developed drew upon ideas suggested by Prime Minister Mustapha Khalil during a visit to Washington at the beginning of December. Mustapha Khalil was one of the most interesting men I was fortunate to know during my term as secretary of state.

Charming, wise, self-confident, honorable, and well organized, he was excellent to work with and became a warm and trusted friend.

We decided that although I would continue firmly to oppose any reopening of the treaty text itself, I would suggest to Sadat a proposed American letter on priority of obligations, embodying a U.S. legal opinion that Egypt would not be debarred by the treaty from coming to the aid of an ally who was the victim of an armed attack. A second interpretive note, aimed at Sadat's linkage problems, would declare that the treaty was being concluded "in the context of a comprehensive peace settlement in accordance with the provisions of the Framework for Peace in the Middle East agreed at Camp David." Finally, on the West Bank and Gaza timetable issue, I would tell Sadat we would support language in the side letter that elections would be held "not later than the end of 1979" for the self-governing authority—but as a good-faith target, not as a deadline—and the self-governing authority would be established within one month after the elections.

I went first to Egypt, arriving on December 10, to discuss the compromise package with Sadat. I gave him a handwritten letter from President Carter reaffirming his personal commitment to a comprehensive peace settlement. The talks, which lasted three days and most of the nights, were not easy. Sadat and his senior cabinet advisers believed they had already gone beyond what was politically wise in meeting Israel's concerns. After all that had happened since the Blair House talks opened on October 12, it was extremely difficult to get them to compromise once again. I stressed that we must find a way to close off the issues quickly. Sadat was deeply concerned about what was happening in Iran, and we agreed that peace between Egypt and Israel was vital for maintaining stability in the Middle East. Finally, Sadat said he would accept the treaty text as written, thus overruling his cabinet. Further, he agreed to our interpretive statements and the letter on the priority of obligations. On the West Bank and Gaza side letter, Sadat again reversed a previous cabinet decision and dropped his demand for a fixed date for the elections, agreeing that the target date would be not later than the end of 1979. Sadat would not yield on the exchange of resident ambassadors, which he now said would take place one month after inauguration of the self-governing authority. He reiterated his willingness to have autonomy begin first in Gaza.

From Egypt I went to Jerusalem, on December 13, to outline to Begin and his advisers the proposals Sadat had accepted. I began by warning them that President Carter and I sensed that the political conditions for peace between Egypt and Israel were eroding, and that there were growing dangers of instability in the entire Middle East. Begin and the cabinet were uncompromising. While I was en route to Israel, Carter publicly praised Sadat as "generous and responsive" to U.S. suggestions and urged Israel to show equal flexibility. This angered Begin and his cabinet, who argued that it was they—not Egypt—who had accepted the treaty drafted at Blair House. The Israelis were also upset by the way I presented the Egyptian position, saying that we agreed with it, which basically we did. Begin told me the position of the cabinet was that the proposals did not bring a peace treaty closer. The day I returned to Washington, having been suddenly called back by the president for the announcement of normalization of relations with the People's Republic of China, the Israeli cabinet issued a harshly worded statement critical of our "pro-Sadat" attitude regarding the compromise proposals. When informed of this statement as I flew homeward, my patience gave way, and I told the traveling press that it was the government of Israel that had prevented us from meeting the December 17 deadline.

• • •

Fortunately, despite this brinkmanship, neither Begin nor Sadat wanted to close the door on the chance for a settlement. Discussions with both sides resumed immediately. Just before Christmas I met Khalil and Dayan in Brussels, and in January, Roy Atherton and Herb Hansell went to Cairo and Jerusalem to work continuously on specific treaty language. Neither of these efforts produced any real change in either side's positions, but they kept the dialogue alive.

I told Carter I believed Begin and Sadat still wanted a treaty. The problem was that each, especially Begin, was under tremendous political pressure from domestic opponents of the process launched at Camp David. Moreover, the Iranian Revolution had made each side more cautious and fearful as they tried to assess the potential repercussions of events in Iran for their own countries. The fall of the shah had eliminated one of Israel's major sources of oil, leading to a dramatic stiffening of Israeli terms for giving up the Sinai oilfields.

Atherton and Hansell's efforts in Jerusalem on the "priority of obligations" issue showed that Israel was locked in on the proposals I had brought from Cairo. Sadat was also immovable. As far as he was concerned, the burden to move was on Begin. The question for us was how to get the sides talking again. Carter and I discussed the possibility of another Camp David-type summit, but with the sides so far apart on major issues, the risks were too great. We decided to try a second round of ministerial-level talks, to be held at Camp David, beginning on February 21.

Prior to the Camp David ministerial talks, Harold Brown made an important trip to the Middle East, foreshadowing a reshaping of American security policy in the region after the collapse of the shah's regime. The purposes of Brown's trip were to buttress local confidence in the United States as a reliable partner and to strengthen our security ties with the key states, such as Israel, Egypt, Saudi Arabia, and Jordan. The president asked Brown to make clear that we saw an Egyptian-

Israeli peace treaty as vital to ending the mutual isolation of two of our staunchest friends and thus permitting all of us to focus more attention on regional security. Brown was also instructed to explore ways of enhancing our ability to assist our friends, including the possibility of an increased American military and naval presence in the region and access to basing facilities.

Brown reported that while there was serious concern in the wake of the Iranian Revolution, there was neither panic nor any willingness to suppress local disputes, above all the Arab-Israeli conflict, in the interest of greater regional security cooperation. Brown concluded, as had I, that the main threats to the moderate states in the region came from internal political, economic, and social problems—often exacerbated by external forces—rather than from direct military aggression from the Soviet Union, a radicalized Iran, or the Arab rejectionists.

Brown recommended that we intensify our efforts to conclude an Egyptian-Israeli peace treaty as soon as possible. At the same time, he felt we must increase economic assistance while continuing to provide essential military assistance. Finally, he concluded we must find a way to enhance our military capabilities in the area without the necessity of establishing local American bases; that would be politically difficult for our Arab friends. Brown was clear that broader security cooperation would come only over time and in an evolutionary way. I strongly endorsed his assessment.

In the brief talks at Camp David, Prime Minister Khalil, Dayan, and I were unable to resolve the issues. Khalil had full powers from Sadat to conclude an agreement, while Dayan could only discuss, explore, and suggest ideas he thought Jerusalem might accept. The president and I quickly concluded that the ministerial talks were not going to work, and I asked Dayan to request that Begin join the negotiations with the Egyptian prime minister. Begin declined to deal with any Egyptian but Sadat, but said he would come to Washington to meet with the president. He was not enthusiastic about the visit, but to have refused the invitation would have openly ruptured his already tense relationship with Carter. For Begin, or any Israeli prime minister, to appear to be on such bad terms with the president of the United States would have been deeply disturbing to Israeli public opinion, already anxious because of the strains in U.S.-Israeli relations.

The Carter-Begin meetings on March 2–4 were among the most difficult the two leaders ever had, especially the first one on March 2. The president became more and more frustrated at Begin's insistence on debating every issue at length, and angry with his skepticism about Sadat's sincerity. Carter stressed the enormous strategic importance to the three countries, and to the stability of the Middle East generally, of concluding the negotiations and turning our attention to the growing turmoil in the region. He told Begin he did not believe any Arab state posed a threat to Israel in the immediate future, and he could not understand why Begin acted as though Egypt were somehow looking for an excuse to attack Israel. Carter said that Sadat had proven he wanted peace, and that as far as Carter was concerned, all Begin's problems about the language of our compromise proposals were inconsequential and an exercise in semantics. I could not but agree; as a negotiator I had tried innumerable formulations without success to meet Begin's concerns, and I told him I had exhausted my linguistic ingenuity.

After a further discussion on March 3, the atmosphere improved as Begin became somewhat less confrontational. Perhaps he felt matters had gone too far the previous day. He noted that he was not insisting Article VI (priority of obligations) meant that the peace treaty "prevailed" over Egypt's other treaties. Seizing on this opening, I suggested another formula for the priority of obligations clause, and we followed up the next day by giving Begin a new proposal. We agreed to drop the idea of a letter stating the U.S. legal opinion, to which Begin strongly objected, and instead, suggested an interpretative minute to be annexed to the treaty. The minute would read:

> It is agreed by the Parties that there is no assertion that this Treaty prevails over other Treaties or agreements or that other Treaties or agreements prevail over this Treaty. The foregoing is not to be construed as contravening the provisions of Article VI(5) of the Treaty, which reads as follows: "Subject to Article 103 of the United Nations Charter, in the event of a conflict between the obligations of the Parties under the present Treaty and any other obligations, the obligation under this Treaty will be binding and implemented."

Begin found this acceptable and said he would recommend it to his cabinet. Thus, for Egypt, Article VI was interpreted to mean that the treaty did not prevail over its other agreements. For Israel, however, this interpretation was declared not to contravene the binding nature of the peace treaty in the event of conflict with other obligations, subject to the right of collective security under the UN Charter. Of such are diplomatic compromises made; six months of negotiations to reach agreement with Begin on two contradictory statements in the same interpretation.

Although he also found merit in our new language for the West Bank and Gaza letter, which substituted the word "goal" for the phrase "target date" and related the goal to completion of the autonomy negotiations rather than to the elections, which were to be held "as expeditiously as possible," Begin made it clear that he could not agree to anything without going back to his cabinet for approval. On the problem of oil supply, he continued to insist that oral assurances were insufficient, and that Egypt must give Israel a written commitment to sell it the output from the Sinai oilfields after Israeli withdrawal. The president said we could not force Egypt to sell its oil and sought to reassure Begin by stating that the United States would guarantee Israel's petroleum supply if Egypt were to cut off Sinai oil. Notwithstanding, Begin still demanded that Egypt grant Israel preferential access.

At the end of these talks, Begin agreed to recommend our compromise language to the cabinet for an urgent decision, and he promised he would do his best to convince the cabinet to accept what had started out badly and turned out well. After a day of debate, the Israeli cabinet approved the new proposals.

Now, it was necessary to gain Sadat's acceptance.

CARTER'S TRIP TO THE MIDDLE EAST

After Begin's trip, we had several alternatives: to try ministerial-level talks again; to launch another round of shuttle diplomacy; to invite Sadat to Washington to hold a new three-power summit; or for the president to go to the Middle East. Most of the president's advisers, including myself, favored ministerial talks or another round of shuttle diplomacy. Although I knew he wanted badly to conclude the negotiations, for political if not for substantive reasons, I doubted Sadat would simply accept what we had been able to work out with Begin. This would mean going back to Begin. However, the president was convinced that only his personal mediation stood a chance of gaining the peace treaty. He decided that he would go to the Middle East. Carter's senior advisers finally supported his decision, while recognizing that it involved a major political risk for him if it failed.

The president's decision was a breathtaking gamble and an act of political courage. The unresolved issues made final agreement unlikely without further negotiating rounds. Failure in personal presidential diplomacy, coming on the heels of the fall of the shah, could have sapped the administration's political strength as we were reshaping our security policy in Southwest Asia and the Persian Gulf, as well as girding for a difficult ratification fight over the SALT II Treaty, which was certain to provoke a prolonged debate over U.S.-Soviet relations, our defense posture, and the strategic balance.

As Carter prepared to leave for Cairo, Sadat had not yet agreed to our ideas for resolving five major issues: (1) Egypt's demand for an interpretative note to the treaty, making clear that it was a part of the comprehensive settlement called for at Camp David; (2) Egypt's demand for a satisfactory solution to the priority of obligations problem so that it would be clear the treaty would not prevent it from honoring a defense agreement with an Arab state which was the victim of aggression; (3) Egypt's insistence that the letter on the West Bank and Gaza contain a target date for elections; (4) Israel's demand that Egypt exchange ambassadors one month after completion of the interim withdrawal in the Sinai; and (5) Begin's March 4 demand that Egypt formally agree to a multiyear commitment to sell Sinai oil under preferential arrangements.

We went first to Cairo on March 7 to explain to Sadat how we believed the five issues could be settled. He disliked some of the formulations we had worked out with Begin at the beginning of March, particularly the new softening of the timetable language in the West Bank-Gaza letter. Sadat wanted us to try again to get Begin to agree that autonomy could begin first in Gaza, and that even before the autonomy period began, Egypt be permitted to station "liaison officers" there as the symbol of an Arab presence. He was also not happy with the interpretative note to the effect that the treaty, although not to be construed in contradiction to the Camp David framework for a comprehensive peace, was to be fulfilled independently of the actions of any other party. On the interrelated issue of the exchange of ambassadors and Israel's accelerated interim withdrawal, he agreed the only sensible course was for each side to adhere to its original commitments, which had been withdrawn for political reasons. At this point, Sadat's attitude was that we had done our best with Begin, little more was to be expected, and the most important consideration was to get the treaty signed and the autonomy negotiations started. His mind was very much on Iran and the general threat to Middle East stability.

We flew to Jerusalem on the evening of March 10 to meet with Prime Minister Begin. The presidential party arrived at the Ben Gurion Airport, where we were greeted with an imposing reception complete with twenty-one-gun salutes and the ruffles and flourishes attendant on a presidential visit. Almost everyone of note in Israel was present. There was, however, a feeling of tension in the air. I was pleased to see a number of close friends and was particularly happy to have the opportunity to ride with Moshe Dayan and Sam Lewis on the long drive to Jerusalem. Gay rode in another car with Rachel Dayan, a charming lady who had become a close friend of ours.

On the way Moshe brought me up to date on recent events and we discussed the chances for a successful outcome. Both of us recognized that the obstacles were formidable. When we arrived at the outskirts of Jerusalem, the presidential party was greeted with the traditional ceremony of bread and salt. The party then separated into two groups. The president and Rosalynn went to a small dinner with the prime minister and Mrs. Begin, while the rest of us went to an informal dinner given by Moshe and Ezer at the King David Hotel, where the presidential party was staying.

Carter and Begin went right to work that night and got off to a shaky start. Once again Begin seemed to regard any change in matters we and Israel had agreed upon as American collusion with Egypt. Further, Begin said he could not sign a treaty before the Knesset approved it—which would take days. Carter had hoped to be able to conclude and sign the treaties during his trip, and was acutely disappointed at Begin's position.

The next morning, accompanied by Roy Atherton and Hal Saunders, I met with Moshe and his able assistant Ely Rubenstein at nine-thirty. Our discussion was general, covering the idea of a memorandum of agreement between the United States and Israel on the American politi- cal role as de facto guarantor of the treaty, the joint letter on autonomy, oil supply for Israel, and Article VI of the treaty, and finally, what had transpired in the meeting between Begin and Carter the previous night. I said that their meeting had not been helpful and stressed the point that a Knesset debate in advance of signing might produce a negative result. No one could predict what speeches would be made, what the impact of those speeches would be, and what the reaction to them in Egypt might mean for the treaty negotiations.

At about eleven o'clock the first of two meetings between the president and Begin, along with a host of advisers, was convened in the Israeli cabinet room. The talks went badly and there were sharp and angry statements on both sides of the table. No progress was made and the meeting broke up, to be reconvened at three P.M. When the sides met again, I offered suggestions for resolving the differences on Article VI and the West Bank and Gaza letter. Dayan and Deputy Prime Minister Yadin disagreed with them. After a short while we adjourned to meet again at five P.M.

At that meeting, in what was to have been the third session of the day, the president urged that we continue our efforts to bridge the differ- ences. However, Begin suggested that we stop for the day as he had to discuss the matters in dispute with his cabinet. On this note, the meeting broke up.

We were caught in a bind brought about by pressures of time and procedure. The president was demanding that all issues be resolved dur- ing his visit, and Begin was saying he could not act without the approval of his cabinet and the Knesset, both of which would have taken more time than was available. As Moshe Dayan pointed out in his recent book, *Breakthrough*, both sides "were not innocent of any mistakes."

That night there was a splendid dinner given for the president in the Chagall Hall of the Knesset. The setting was festive but the mood was one of weariness and anxiety.

That night after the dinner, the Israeli cabinet met from eleven-thirty P.M. to five A.M. We were to learn after the treaty had been signed that the cabinet made several decisions. First, they agreed to an Egyptian change in the wording of the interpretative note to Article VI of the treaty. Second, it was decided not to include any references to establish- ing autonomy first in Gaza in the joint letter, but if Egypt should propose it, to consider this matter in the autonomy negotiation. Third, it was decided to notify me that Israel was interested in buying from Egypt the total oil production from the wells Israel had drilled in the Sinai. If Egypt should fail to meet such a commitment, Israel would turn to the United States in accordance with the U.S. guarantee. As Dayan notes in his book, this was a combining of the Israeli request and the suggestion I had made that the United States be guarantor of Israel's oil supply. In addition, the Israelis moved toward a compromise on the issue of exchange of ambassadors.

These steps were constructive but clearly insufficient to bridge the gap between the parties, and I told Dayan so.

On March 12, the final full day of negotiations, Carter and his advisers met with Begin and what appeared to be the entire Israeli cabinet at ten-thirty A.M. The atmosphere was strained and gloomy. Compared to the risks of further delay the remaining issues seemed small, but the Israelis were in no mood for further compromise.

Both Carter and Begin were becoming testy. Time was running out, yet three major obstacles still remained. One was the Egyptian proposal that the parties agree to autonomy in Gaza first, if it should prove impossible to implement autonomy in both the West Bank and Gaza at the same time; the second was Egypt's unwillingness to give the kind of preferential access to Sinai oil that Israel wanted; the third concerned Sadat's desire to station Egyptian liaison officers in Gaza.

On beginning autonomy first in Gaza there was no give. On the third issue—Egyptian liaison officers—the president hammered on the point that this seemingly minor concession would help to bring about Gazan support for autonomy. This could also build confidence in the autonomy process among the West Bankers. Begin felt he was being pressured unduly and refused to budge. On oil supplies our proposal that Israel could receive its oil from Egypt through an American company was rejected as impractical and unacceptable as a matter of principle. We were deadlocked and the meeting adjourned to permit Begin and Carter to go to the Knesset, where they were to deliver speeches. The Knesset session was a stormy one with much shouting and hectoring of Begin by the Communists and some members of his own Likud party. The session was climaxed by the ejection of Geulah Cohen, a member of Begin's own party, from the chamber. Few of us had attended a session of the Knesset before, and we were astounded by the din and disorder. This made the worst sessions in the U.S. Congress look like models of parliamentary decorum.

When the session ended the Israeli cabinet went back into private session at two o'clock. At about four forty-five Zbig and I and our associates joined Begin and the Israeli ministers without President Carter. After the morning cabinet meeting, I had told the Israelis that I would not go to Cairo with their current proposals, as I knew I could not "sell" them to the Egyptians. The meeting got nowhere. Each side repeated its prior positions and we remained deadlocked. Finally, when it became clear that nothing new would emerge, we adjourned. Begin gave me a draft of a joint statement to be issued by him and Carter. I read it grimly. It tried to paper over the harsh reality that after the Camp David summit, the Blair House talks, the ministerial sessions at Camp David, my rescue mission to Cairo and Jerusalem, Begin's visit to Washington and the president's trip to the Middle East, we had failed to bridge the last narrow gap. I left for my hotel anguished that we had fallen short when we had come so close. The remaining three issues seemed so insignificant compared to the prize that could be seized with a little flexibility and imagination.

When I got back to the hotel I told the president that we were deadlocked. Carter was as depressed as I was. It seemed that his brave move to come to the Middle East had failed and we were going to return to the United States empty-handed.

I went to my room and told Gay wearily that it looked almost hopeless. I said we had to keep trying but it would take a near-miracle to save the day. I did not know that at that moment Dayan, with other ministers, had gathered a rump session of the cabinet without Begin to explore what could be done to find a way out of the box we were in.

The ministers agreed that our efforts should not be permitted to fail and that a further effort should be made. Some new ideas were offered on the oil supply problem. Dayan called Begin and suggested that he and another minister meet with me to see whether we could find a way out of the deadlock. Begin agreed but told Dayan to come alone.

I was sitting in my room pondering possible last-minute alternatives when the phone rang. It was Dayan calling to ask if he could come to meet with me. I told him I was delighted to hear from him and that he should come over immediately. When he arrived we sat down in my room for what was to be one of the crucial meetings in the Middle East negotiations. We talked for several hours. As Dayan rightly stated in his book, "We had had dealings with each other over quite a long period and I believe we had found a common tongue and mutual trust." I certainly shared that feeling.

On the Gaza issues he urged me to persuade the Egyptians that we should drop the idea of Gaza first and make no mention of Egyptian liaison officers in the West Bank and Gaza letter. He stressed that the Egyptians could propose advancing elections in Gaza ("Gaza first") at the autonomy negotiations. He also underscored that when Israel withdrew from El Arish and normal relations began, "any Egyptian could travel to Gaza on an Israeli visa, just as any Israeli would be able to go to Cairo on an Egyptian visa." I was prepared to accept Dayan's suggestion if we could reach an agreement on the oil supplies question.

Dayan said that he understood that the Egyptians could not agree at this time to sell Israel oil on a long-term basis and at a preferred price. When I heard this, I knew that we were approaching a breakthrough.

Dayan suggested that it would be wise to have the president invite Begin for breakfast. I called the president, who agreed to extend the invitation.

Dayan and I then turned to constructing the final pillars of the bridge. I asked Dayan what Israel could live with in terms of U.S. guarantees. He replied that it would be necessary for the U.S. oil guarantee to last for twenty years rather than the five we had offered. I said I felt we could move in his direction on this. Dayan said further that there must be a clause in the treaty stating that Israel had a right to buy oil directly from Egypt. He pointed out that without such a clause the Egyptian boycott would remain in effect. It would be difficult to do, but I felt we could draft language to meet his point and persuade the Egyptians to accept it. I so indicated to him, saying that I would, of course, have to discuss these matters with the president but that I was hopeful. When we shook hands at the elevator, I thanked heaven for Dayan and his patience, imagination, and courage.

I immediately called the president and told him that I believed we had crossed the bridge and that the end was at hand. I suggested to the president that we compromise on a fifteen-year duration for the U.S. oil guarantee and that we draft the treaty clause Dayan had requested. The president was overjoyed and said he would invite Begin and Dayan to join us for breakfast to try to clinch the agreement.

Hal Saunders, Roy Atherton, Sam Lewis, Mike Sterner, and I then set to work on drafting the new treaty clause. By early morning we had an acceptable draft, which we took to the president. He approved.

When I got back to my room, I looked for Gay. I found her reading across the hall wondering how things were going. I told her excitedly that I thought a breakthrough had been achieved. I was thrilled, yet apprehensive of the outcome of the breakfast. Until we had Begin's agreement, the issues were not settled.

The next morning I called Dayan at seven and asked him to join me in my room. He came right over and I gave him the draft of the oil provisions of the treaty. We had prepared it as an addition to Appendix C of the treaty. The draft said that the treaty and the appendix determined the establishment of normal economic relations between Israel and Egypt. It further stated that normal economic relations included the commercial sale of oil by Egypt to Israel and that Israel would have the absolute right to submit proposals for the purchase of oil which was not needed for Egyptian internal consumption. Finally, it specified that Egypt and concession owners would also receive proposals for the purchase of oil by Israel on the same basis and terms applicable to all potential purchases. I also told Dayan that we were prepared to extend the U.S. guarantee for fifteen years. That meant that if Israel was unable to purchase the oil it needed from other sources, the United States would supply it.

Dayan was very pleased and told me he had spoken to Begin about our talks early that morning. I said that we were scheduled to join the president and Begin at breakfast. We walked down the hall to the president's room, where Begin had already arrived. After some light, friendly talk we turned to the issues at hand. The president described our oil proposals, and Begin said he would take them to the cabinet immediately. We then turned to Gaza, and Dayan repeated what he had said to me the previous night about Israel's willingness to entertain a "Gaza first" proposal during the autonomy negotiations. Against that background, the president agreed to support the Israeli suggestion. The president then asked whether there could be unilateral steps taken on the West Bank to improve the atmosphere. Begin said that we should give the request to him in writing and he would consider it "sympathetically."

The president further stated that Dayan and I would negotiate a memorandum of agreement on the U.S. position in the event of an Egyptian violation of the treaty. In addition, Carter assured Begin that he would ask Congress for substantial financial assistance to help cover the costs of Israeli relocation from its Sinai military bases during the withdrawal, and pledged to continue discussions on the supply of additional military equipment. Begin agreed to our proposals, contingent upon unqualified acceptance by Sadat and approval by the Israeli cabinet.

As the meeting broke up the president said he would report the results of our discussions to President Sadat that afternoon and would call Begin and let him know the reception. There was a feeling in the room that we had crossed the last river, although we knew that the discussion with Sadat might be difficult.

At the farewell ceremonies at the airport, Begin said to the president, "You have succeeded." As I said good-bye to the prime minister and Dayan I was choked with emotion. It had been a long and hard journey but we were on the threshold of a historic accomplishment.

We arrived at the Cairo airport about four P.M. We were greeted by Sadat, Mubarak, and Khalil and moved immediately to the upstairs lounge in the main building, where a large table had been arranged for us. On one side of the table the president, Zbig, and myself were seated. On the other side were Sadat, Mubarak, and Khalil.

The tension was electric as Carter outlined to Sadat what had been agreed upon in Jerusalem. Khalil was openly unhappy with some of the results of our meetings. He described lucidly the basis for his objections. Sadat listened carefully and asked further questions of us. Finally, he said that he had made up his mind. He would agree to the final language of the interpretative notes contained in Appendix C of the treaty and would drop his demand that autonomy begin first in Gaza and that the West Bank and Gaza letter include reference to an Egyptian liaison official in Gaza. We came downstairs to the waiting room where Jehan Sadat, Rosalynn, Gay, and the rest of our party had been waiting anxiously for almost two hours. "We have agreed," the president told them, with Sadat smiling broadly beside him. Then, surrounded by us all, the president called Begin on the only telephone in the room, in a corner not far from where the press was hovering beyond the door. Begin confirmed the agreement, sealing the accord.

Surrounded by the onlookers, press and presidential party, Carter and Sadat moved to the microphone set up on the tarmac in front of Air Force One and Carter announced that the elements of the peace treaty had been agreed upon.

• • •

Begin and Sadat arrived in Washington on March 25 for the treaty-signing ceremony and to receive the West Bank and Gaza autonomy letter from Carter. Inevitably, there were last-minute hitches. For several days prior to Begin's arrival I had discussions with Dayan on the U.S.-Israeli memorandum of agreement (MOA), as well as on the oil supply agreement and the U.S. financial and military assistance package that had been agreed to in Jerusalem. The president also met Sadat and Begin to work out the precise details of the accelerated Israeli withdrawal from that portion of the Sinai containing the oilfields.

The final details concerning Israeli access to Sinai oil remained an issue right down to the end. They were not finally resolved until Sadat and Begin agreed in a meeting in the residence of Ashraf Gorbal, the distinguished and extremely able Egyptian ambassador in Washington. At that time Sadat guaranteed to the Israelis the right to bid for Egyptian oil at the world market price on a permanent basis, thus removing the last major stumbling block to the signing ceremony. We did go down to the wire on one or two minor details, such as the spelling of names of cities on the maps annexed to the treaty. Sadat asked Begin not to seek a written agreement on access to Egyptian oil. However, Dayan felt a document was necessary and requested me to get a letter from President Carter confirming the arrangement. I did so, but said it would not be delivered until the time of the signing of the treaty.

The signing took place on a beautiful sunny afternoon on the front lawn of the White House. All of official Washington was present and everyone was euphoric. The pageantry was memorable, and I shall never forget the moment when the final signature was placed on the documents. We had come to the end of a long, difficult, and successful journey; another, however, lay ahead—the autonomy talks.

Later that afternoon Moshe and I signed the MOA at my office in the State Department. Only a few of us were present, but this was an extremely important compact for future U.S.-Israeli relations.

That night there was a splendid dinner in a huge striped tent on the south lawn of the White House. Everyone was there and the event was festive and joyous. Yet we all knew that we faced many hard problems in the days ahead when we began the autonomy negotiations.

THE AUTONOMY TALKS

I shall not review the details of the West Bank and Gaza autonomy talks that followed. Instead, I think it more useful to discuss our aims for the autonomy talks and to analyze why the autonomy process stalled so quickly.

From the American point of view, the Israeli agreement at Camp David to negotiate full autonomy in the West Bank and Gaza bound Israel to a good-faith effort to comply with the timing goals and procedures. Carter and I, as well as Saunders, Atherton, Quandt, and all the fine Middle East experts who worked with us, had concluded that a single negotiation could not produce a settlement of the Palestinian problem. Thus, the Camp David approach represented to us a practical process for moving gradually and through concrete stages toward a final solution. Our intent was to create a procedure that could, if used seriously and conscientiously, lead to a Palestinian homeland while at the same time taking into account Israel's legitimate security concerns.

Some commentators have argued that whatever the Carter administration's intentions, the autonomy talks in reality merely provided cover for a separate Egyptian-Israeli peace and undermined the more fundamental American interest in a durable comprehensive settlement in the Middle East. I do not accept this interpretation. I recognize that some Israelis saw the goal of a bilateral peace treaty as the principal objective of the negotiations, as did some of the Egyptians whose chief priorities were the return of the Sinai and the creation of a state of peace between the two nations. This does not mean, however, that the leaders did not recognize the reality that there could be no just and lasting peace until the Palestinian issues were resolved. I believe a more accurate analysis would indicate that the procedures worked out at Camp David for bringing into existence a Palestinian self-governing body that would play a key role in negotiating the final status of the West Bank and Gaza provided a practical process within which the many complex issues could be resolved. We believed these procedures constituted the substance of self-determination while safeguarding the vital interests of Israel and Jordan. The fact was that it was not possible to offer the inhabitants of the West Bank and Gaza an immediate and free vote on what they would like their future to be. The roots of the conflict and the passions that had been engendered were too deep to be changed by the stroke of a pen. The result had to be achieved over time—the transitional period—and through a process of negotiation. And for any negotiation to succeed there had to be Palestinian participation. Since the Israelis would not sit down with the PLO, it became necessary to find a means, at least, for Palestinian participation from among the inhabitants of the West Bank and Gaza. The autonomy process provided the indispensable political basis and negotiating structure for resolving the Palestinian issue, which was the sine qua non for attempting to persuade the other Arab parties that the Camp David process could produce solutions compatible with Arab interests and dignity.

Why, then, did the autonomy process not lead to elections and a self-governing authority within the good-faith goal of one year? At most only the same level and intensity of leadership on all three sides that had characterized the peace process leading to Camp David and the Egyptian-Israeli peace treaty could have made the autonomy talks succeed in that period of time, and even that might not have succeeded. The odds that Israel and Egypt, without constant top-level American participation, could negotiate an autonomy arrangement were extremely poor.

Moreover, the political backlash in Israel to the giving up of the Sinai and particularly the Sinai settlements was such that it undercut the capacity of the Israeli leadership to take the bold steps that were necessary to achieve the goals set at Camp David. Neither were we able to persuade the key Arab nations and the Palestinian inhabitants of the West Bank and Gaza that we were serious about granting full autonomy as we had promised at Camp David. Israel's retreat from "full autonomy" and its unwillingness to declare a moratorium on the creation of new settlements struck an almost mortal blow to the hopes for success in the West Bank and Gaza. The chances for progress were also deeply hurt by the terrorist actions of the PLO, which continued to endanger Israeli citizens and lessen the chance for movement on the part of the Israeli leaders. The continuing unwillingness of the PLO to recognize the right of Israel to exist within secure and recognized boundaries added another strand to "the baffling cobweb of issues." Its intransigence on this matter made it virtually impossible to bring a Palestinian voice to the negotiations.

As a result, even the efforts of our extremely able Middle East negotiators, Robert Strauss and Sol Linowitz, were unavailing. Progress was made, but the key issues of water, land, security, settlements, and the questions of who would be permitted to vote and what the voting procedures would be remained insurmountable.

Other important obstacles to progress in the autonomy talks were the looming elections in both the United States and Israel. Not only did the elections take the time and attention of the leaders and their advisers away from the Middle East negotiations, but they also limited the flexibility of the leaders to make the courageous moves required for progress at the negotiating table. In addition, much of American attention was devoted to the hostage crisis. Consequently, as time began to run out, the negotiations ground to a halt.

The coincidence of the autonomy negotiations with highly urgent foreign policy and national security issues in 1979–80, and with elections in Israel and the United States, does not mean that the process established as a result of Camp David cannot succeed. The talks during the final eighteen months of the Carter administration laid the essential foundation for a possible long-term solution. It was clear, however, that as soon as the elections were over it would be essential to give top priority to the autonomy talks and to renew the flagging momentum. Experience has taught us that matters do not stand still in the Middle East. If momentum is allowed to flag, they begin to slide backward.

12

SOUTHERN AFRICA: HELPING TO SHAPE CHANGE

THE CARTER ADMINISTRATION came to office with mixed legacies from the previous administration's southern Africa policy. On the positive side, by 1976, Secretary Kissinger had set in motion important yet fragile negotiations aimed at resolving the Rhodesia and Namibia conflicts.

By January 1977, however, the previous administration's recent shift in its African policy had not significantly improved America's position with black Africa. Black Africans mistrusted the motives behind the shift in policy. Up to that time the Rhodesia and Namibia questions had been primarily the responsibilities of Great Britain and the United Nations, respectively. Neither the states that considered themselves the "front line" against white minority rule (Angola, Botswana, Mozambique, Tanzania, and Zambia) nor the black nationalist factions waging guerrilla war in Rhodesia and Namibia believed that the United States genuinely understood or cared about African problems except as they affected East-West rivalry. Black Africa suspected that the United States, which had supported the losers in the Angolan civil war, wanted to protect American and Western strategic interests through a strong Republic of South Africa shielded by a barrier of black client states dependent upon Pretoria's political, economic, and military support. It was clear from the outset that we would have to overcome this negative legacy of African suspicion if we were to play an effective role in Africa.

In no other aspect of foreign policy did our administration differ so fundamentally from that of our predecessors. President Carter and his principal advisers agreed even before he took office that American participation in resolving the conflicts in Rhodesia and Namibia and in seeking an end to apartheid in South Africa was vital. It was essential to demonstrate to the Third World our understanding of and willingness to take a leading role in dealing with their problems. We believed that if we could offer a credible alternative to armed struggle, change inevitably would take place in an arena in which the West could play an effective role in channeling the flow of events toward democratic institutions. If the only alternative for the Africans was civil war, our ability to influence events would be greatly reduced and that of the Soviets correspondingly increased.

Like the previous administration after its conversion, we recognized that identifying the United States with the cause of majority rule was the best way to prevent Soviet and Cuban exploitation of the racial conflicts of southern Africa. But our decision to break sharply with the policy of the past did not merely reflect concern about Soviet influence or revolutionary movements. We were committed to majority rule, self-determination, and racial equality as a matter of fairness and basic human rights. If the United States did not support social and political justice in Rhodesia, Namibia, and South Africa itself, Africans would correctly dismiss our human rights policy as mere cold war propaganda, employed at the expense of the peoples of Africa.

Our approach to southern Africa, however, was neither popular in Congress nor well understood by the American public. Many conservatives feared that we favored Communist-supported black guerrilla groups; some worked hard to compel us to support white-dominated solutions in Rhodesia and Namibia. Some liberals and American blacks, on the other hand, worried that we were overly cautious, too solicitous of the feelings of the political groups within Rhodesia, too anxious to keep in step with our Western allies, and unwilling to accept the political costs of exerting strong diplomatic and economic pressures on South Africa, the linchpin of white minority rule. However, in southern Africa, as in the Middle East, SALT, the Panama Canal Treaties, and other matters, such as human rights, President Carter was determined that we must do what was in our long-term national interest, and not what was politically expedient or good for his ratings in the public opinion polls.

RHODESIA

In November of 1965, refusing British demands for majority rule, Prime Minister Ian Smith unilaterally declared the colony of Rhodesia independent. At Britain's request and with the support of the United States, the United Nations imposed mandatory economic sanctions and an arms embargo on the rebellious colony. However, helped by South Africa and the Portuguese colonies of Angola and Mozambique, Rhodesia successfully evaded the impact of the sanctions. In 1972, despairing of British diplomatic efforts to negotiate majority rule, black nationalists under the charismatic Joshua Nkomo began a guerrilla war against the Smith regime. The war grew in intensity and new guerrilla groups were formed.

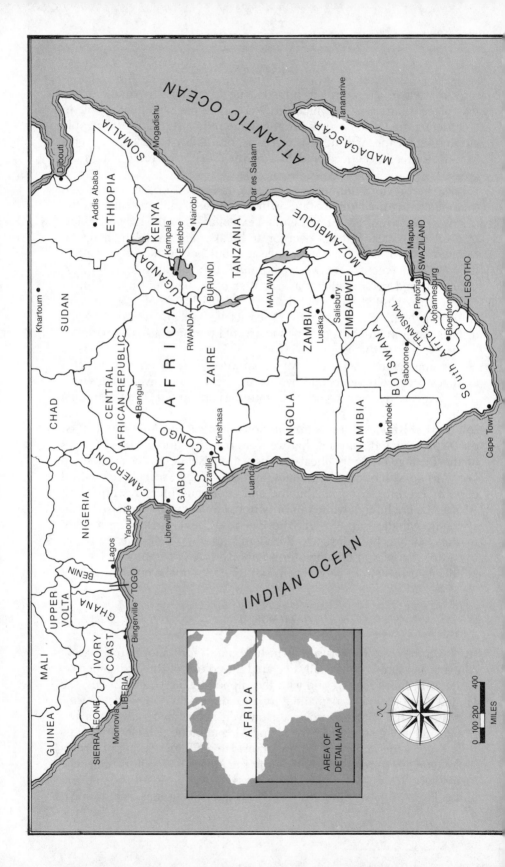

However, until 1974, the Rhodesian government forces had little difficulty holding their own against the poorly armed and ill-trained nationalist forces.

In 1975, the passing of the Portuguese African empire reshaped the political complexion of southern Africa. After Portugal announced its intention to withdraw its administration, civil war erupted in Angola among the contending guerrilla forces. In an ill-conceived attempt to prevent victory by the Marxist-oriented MPLA, the Ford administration put its weight and assistance behind the rival FNLA and UNITA factions. At the same time, South African combat forces supported UNITA in a campaign widely believed to be supported by the United States. To avoid defeat the MPLA asked for military assistance from the Soviet Union and Cuba. This gave the Soviets and Cubans a foothold in Angola which they still maintain. Cuban intervention with substantial combat forces proved decisive, and by the end of the year the FNLA and UNITA were forced to revert to guerrilla war. In January 1976, Congress, fearing a repetition of Vietnam, prohibited in the Clark Amendment further American covert assistance to the groups involved in the Angolan civil war. South Africa recognized the futility of the losing struggle against the now-dominant MPLA and began withdrawing its forces into Namibia.

The United States, hurt by association with South Africa, confronted the threat of collapse of its southern Africa policy and the prospect of a radicalized and expanded Rhodesian insurgency. In April 1976 in Lusaka, Zambia, in a dramatic bid to regain the initiative, Henry Kissinger announced American support for majority rule in Rhodesia and began work to convene a Rhodesia conference based on five general principles. These were: majority rule within two years; formation of an interim government; negotiations between the Salisbury regime and the black political groups on the powers and composition of the interim government; agreement of Britain and Rhodesia to enact enabling legislation; and the termination of UN sanctions. In September 1976, after obtaining only conditional Zambian and Tanzanian agreement to these principles, Kissinger, assisted by the South Africans, requested Ian Smith to announce acceptance of the principles as the basis of a peace conference. The principal black nationalist groups, however, rejected the five points, which had not been discussed with them, and demanded that the peace conference negotiate a rapid transfer of power to them.

With great skill, Kissinger succeeded in getting the parties to attend a conference at Geneva in December 1976; but a stalemate quickly developed over the two sides' fundamentally conflicting goals—Smith's determination to protect the privileged political position of the whites, and the black nationalists' demand for control of the country after a brief restoration of titular British legal authority. While appearing to accept the principle of majority rule, Smith hoped for a prolonged interim regime during which the whites would control the government and the security forces, and which would allow a slow transition to black majority rule with strong guarantees for the whites' political and economic power.

After the collapse of the Geneva conference, which broke down over the conflicting demands of each side for a dominant position during the transition period, Ivor Richard, the British chairman, attempted to break the deadlock by proposing a British commissioner to head the interim government while a council of black nationalists and whites drafted an independence constitution. On January 24, 1977, Smith rejected this idea and called for Rhodesian whites and moderate blacks to negotiate a settlement without British assistance or the participation of the guerrillas. This was Smith's "internal solution" strategy, in which he sought to split the black nationalists and negotiate a settlement with those he considered most amenable to a solution acceptable to the whites. He particularly hoped to entice Bishop Abel Muzorewa, head of the African National Council (ANC), Ndabaningi Sithole, who led a wing of the ANC, and Joshua Nkomo, leader of the Zimbabwe-Africa Political Union (ZAPU) guerrilla faction, into an internal settlement excluding Zimbabwe-Africa National Union (ZANU) leader Robert Mugabe, a professed Marxist but in fact a pragmatist.

The ANC had no armed forces and neither Muzorewa nor Sithole had joined the guerrilla struggle; ZAPU received limited Soviet assistance. Nkomo's main assets were a significant political organization inside Rhodesia, his standing as the first black liberation fighter, and the strong support of President Kenneth Kaunda of Zambia. Mugabe's larger and better armed ZANU, based largely in Mozambique and carrying the brunt of the war against Salisbury, was feared by Rhodesian whites as the most dangerous of the guerrilla groups. Mugabe's principal African supporters were President Julius Nyerere of Tanzania and President Samora Machel of Mozambique. Nkomo and Mugabe, although political and personal rivals, formed a shaky tactical alliance called the Patriotic Front, which was supported by the Organization of African Unity and by the critically important front line states as the legitimate representative of the Zimbabwean people. Because Muzorewa refused to join the guerrillas, and particularly because he was exploring the idea of an arrangement with Smith, the rest of Africa increasingly regarded him with suspicion.

The front line states provided the Patriotic Front with bases, political support, some material assistance, and advice. The Tanzanians, Zambians, and Mozambicans also often acted as diplomatic intermediaries between the Patriotic Front and the British and Americans. In this they were joined by the Nigerians. Although not a neighboring front line state, Nigeria carried great weight as a result of its size and economic strength and its powerful leadership under President Olusegun Obasanjo. The front line states unwaveringly supported the goal of black majority rule. They were prepared to back a continuing struggle to see it attained, although they wanted an early end to the conflict before it led to a wider war and perhaps a major East-West confrontation. As the struggle wore on, difficulties in their respective economies made them even more anxious to end the costly war.

The Carter Administration Policy Review

As we took office, I was worried that the armed black nationalist groups, impatient at the collapse of the Geneva negotiations, would seek more external aid in order to escalate the fighting. I wanted to act promptly to demonstrate our determination to play an active and important role. The president, Andrew Young, and others agreed that we should actively assist the British in negotiating the replacement of the illegal Smith regime through an internationally acceptable settlement that would end the war. Until we completed our own policy review and worked out a joint strategy with the British, we decided to endorse Ivor Richard's January proposal as a basis for negotiations. To prevent a slide toward intensified war, Carter wrote to the heads of the front line and other key black African states affirming our determination to seek a negotiated settlement. I asked South African Ambassador Roelof (Pik) Botha, who later became South Africa's foreign minister, to make clear to Smith that the United States would not support a white-dominated internal solution and that we intended to tighten sanctions against Rhodesia by asking Congress to repeal the Byrd Amendment. This was done in March, thus ending the exemption of Rhodesian chrome from our embargo. Confirming South Africa's interest in continuing negotiations, Botha told me Pretoria had been upset by Smith's rejection of Ivor Richard's recent proposal. He said, however, that his government would not pressure Smith to join a settlement unacceptable to the Rhodesian whites.

Our initial consultations in London in February of 1977 revealed that the British were deeply concerned about the worsening political and military situation in southern Africa, but would go no further on Rhodesia without active U.S. support. They told Andy Young, who as our ambassador to the UN was to play a key role in rebuilding African confidence in the United States, that only we could influence the South Africans and the front line states to persuade Smith and the guerrilla groups to resume negotiations. The British feared that if a serious peace process—which they believed they could not mount without American political support—did not get underway soon, African efforts to impose a mandatory economic embargo against South Africa, the main loophole through which Rhodesia evaded sanctions, would intensify. Britain could veto UN sanctions, but only at the risk of retaliation against Britain's growing economic interests in black Africa. However, to acquiesce in sanctions would cause damage to the large British economic stake in the Republic of South Africa. London was worried that we would not stand with them in opposing sanctions at this time. For my part, I had doubts about the effectiveness of the sanctions and agreed that the best way to avoid them was to breathe new life into the negotiating process. My objective was to put in place an effective strategy for avoiding an escalation of the conflict and to achieve a negotiated settlement and majority rule.

In our first discussion it was evident that the British Labour government wanted our support in putting forward new proposals. In February I told Ivor Richards we would work with them in drafting principles that could be discussed with the South Africans, the front line states, Smith, and the black nationalists to see if we could get sufficient agreement to reconvene the Geneva conference. Development of these principles and the overall Anglo-American strategy was delayed by the tragic and untimely death of Anthony Crosland, the British foreign secretary.

Tony Crosland was succeeded by Dr. David Owen, a brilliant and strong younger member of the Labour party, who was to become one of my close friends. Dr. Owen had already held a number of important ministerial posts, including secretary of state for the navy, minister of health, and minister of energy. His background in national security affairs was solid and extensive. A supple and penetrating mind was matched by courage and vision. Owen was, however, so quick and demanding of himself that he expected the same of others and often bruised the feelings of his colleagues in the Foreign Office. Nevertheless, he was a most effective and imaginative foreign secretary and continues today to be one of the bright lights on the British political scene. I found it both delightful and stimulating to work with him.

• • •

I believed that the path to breaking down Smith's obduracy and deflecting him from an internal settlement was through Pretoria. As long as Smith was convinced that in the last analysis South Africa would stand by him, he would avoid facing political and military realities. There was strong evidence that the South Africans—in contrast to their confidence and rigidity about their own internal situation—viewed the military situation in Rhodesia as ultimately hopeless and wanted a negotiated solution that would lead to a non-Marxist, black-ruled state. They believed that if negotiations failed, the guerrilla forces would turn to the Soviets and Cubans for the means to wage an all-out war. South Africa foresaw under those circumstances a hostile, Soviet-backed, radical black state on its northern border, probably with a substantial Cuban military presence. I believed Pretoria, properly handled, would support a negotiated settlement, so long as it was not imposed on the whites.

Because of deeply held convictions and our commitment to human rights and democracy, President Carter and I were not willing to seek political advantage by presenting opposition to Soviet influence or radicalism as the foundation of American policy toward Pretoria. The republic itself was part of the larger problem of instability in southern Africa because of its own political repression and racial discrimination. It would be necessary to make clear to the South Africans that we not only condemned apartheid, but wanted them to begin to evolve toward full political participation by all the inhabitants of the country. In March, Young, Brzezinski, and I began to work with Vice-President Mondale to prepare an authoritative statement of U.S. policy in southern Africa which he could make to South African Prime Minister Vorster. Mondale was concerned that Vorster would try to portray such a meeting as symbolizing a continuation of the previous U.S.-South African relationship unless he could declare unequivocally the administration's commitment to human rights and political justice in all of southern Africa, including South Africa itself. We agreed that our message must be worded so that South Africa could not misunderstand the attitude or intentions of the new administration. At the same time we sought no public confrontation with the South Africans. Indeed, it was understood that we would seek to present our views in such a way as to gain the South Africans' cooperation in dealing with regional problems without driving them into a rigid defense of the status quo.

As we consulted with the British and prepared for Mondale's meeting with Vorster, Smith continued to lay the groundwork for an internal settlement. On March 9 we learned that Bishop Muzorewa had decided to negotiate secretly with Smith with the aim of reaching agreement on an election open to all nationalists and under international supervision. Inasmuch as Rhodesian security forces would remain in control of the country during the election, there was no chance that the Patriotic Front would agree to Muzorewa's plan. Nevertheless, that Muzorewa was willing to break ranks with the other black leaders indicated that Smith might be able to conclude an internal settlement with a major black nationalist leader.

In a meeting with David Owen and me on March 10, the president agreed that we and the British would work jointly in preparing a new peace initiative for Rhodesia, with the aim of a negotiated settlement in 1978, if possible. We would try to convene a peace conference to draft a constitution for Zimbabwe (the African name for Rhodesia) and to negotiate the arrangements for a transition period of six months or less, during which a British caretaker administration would organize and conduct elections free from intimidation and open to all parties. In addition, a fund for Zimbabwe development financed by international contributions would be established to assist the new state. David Owen asked that we stand shoulder to shoulder with them as a full partner in our future efforts. The president agreed. The future would prove the soundness of this decision. Although Rhodesia was at heart a British problem, the failure to resolve the escalating conflict could affect us adversely. We were willing to be a full partner because the alliance would give us needed strength in dealing with our own Congress and greater combined leverage with the African parties.

Fortified by Carter's assurances of our direct participation, David Owen decided to broach the ideas we had discussed in Africa in early April. If he found sufficient agreement among the parties on the basic elements, Owen would call for a preparatory conference in Vienna during the summer. A constitutional conference in which we, as well as the British, would participate would then be held in London, followed by elections and, if all went well, independence in early 1978.

I met with David in London on April 1 to discuss his upcoming exploratory talks. He said that he was prepared to call the preparatory conference even if Smith refused to attend. He emphasized, however, that for political and tactical reasons, it was essential that the United States participate. He was candid about the nationalists' distrust of Britain and the necessity of our political weight and diplomatic assistance, although American participation in a constitutional conference for a British colony would be unprecedented.

I assured David that we would attend if this would help, and he could so inform the parties in Africa. I warmly wished him luck despite my concern that his plan was not yet sufficiently developed to get agreement from the parties. It contained no mention of how security would be maintained during the transition, how fair elections could be conducted, or what would be done about the Rhodesian or liberation forces in an independent Zimbabwe. In view of this, I decided not to endorse the specific plan in conversations with the Africans, but to emphasize that we strongly supported the effort to get negotiations started.

The outcome of the trip justified our caution. Although no one, not even Smith, rejected the proposals outright, the black Africans disliked the suggestion of American attendance at a constitutional conference, apparently fearing that the British would use our presence to deflect African pressures. The front line states also expressed concern that if the United States became too openly involved in the peace process the Soviets might try to insert themselves. The Africans also wanted greater specificity on how security would be maintained during the transition, suspecting that the British intended to rely primarily on the Rhodesian Army while keeping the liberation forces out of the country or confined to certain areas. Owen told the front line states and the Patriotic Front that the British would not proceed without U.S. participation. He was convinced that mere American support for a British lead would not be enough to move the parties. However, in discussions with Owen on May 6 in London, I persuaded him that in deference to African concerns we should drop the idea of American participation in a constitutional conference. We agreed instead that the United States would henceforth participate jointly with the British in consultations with the parties. Thus originated what came to be called the consultative group. The key members were John Graham, a senior British Foreign Office official, and Stephen Low, our ambassador to Zambia. The two formed a harmonious partnership over the next two years in conducting Anglo-American consultations with the parties in all phases of the negotiations. The Graham-Low friendship and rapport mirrored the warm friendship between David and me.

Mondale-Vorster Meeting

Vice-President Mondale met with Prime Minister Vorster in Vienna on May 19 and 20 to discuss our policy toward southern Africa. Mondale told Vorster that our future relations would depend on Pretoria's actions and attitude toward political and racial change in southern Africa, including the beginning of a progressive transformation of South African society away from apartheid. Mondale emphasized that we intended to vigorously assist British efforts to negotiate majority rule in Rhodesia, and would participate actively in the efforts of the United Nations to secure independence for the South African-controlled territory of Namibia. He underscored the fact that our policy was rooted in our view of human rights, and was not solely based on anti-Communism. Mondale told Vorster that we wanted good relations with South Africa and were prepared to work closely with them. He made clear, however, that failure to address seriously the political and racial injustices in Rhodesia, Namibia, and South Africa would mean that the United States would have to change its position of opposing mandatory sanctions against South Africa. He added that in the absence of significant progress in these three areas, there would be an inevitable deterioration in U.S. relations with South Africa.

Although Mondale's statement encompassed our overall policy toward South Africa, Vorster's response focused on South Africa's internal racial and political situation. Vorster asserted that Mondale was demanding the immediate imposition of "one man, one vote," which was not what Fritz had said. All of us knew that change in South Africa could not take place overnight and would be slow and painful. Mondale explained that the United States did not have a timetable or blueprint for change in South Africa and endeavored to make clear that because of our own racial experiences we viewed their problem with understanding. Unfortunately, Vorster chose to interpret our position as an attempt to intervene in their internal affairs and the meeting broke up on a bitter note.

Despite the chasm of disagreement on apartheid, Vorster's comments on Rhodesia and Namibia were restrained and positive. The South Africans were critical of Ian Smith and his regime and indicated they did not intend to back indefinitely the Rhodesian whites in a losing struggle. Vorster said that South Africa would "support Anglo-American efforts to get the directly interested parties to agree to an independence constitution and the necessary transitional arrangements, including the holding of elections in which all can take part equally so that Zimbabwe can achieve independence in 1978, and peace."

• • •

After the Mondale-Vorster meeting, the Anglo-American consultative group found Ian Smith adamantly opposed to the principle of universal suffrage unless there were specific legal protections and constitutional guarantees for the whites. He also wanted education and property qualifications on the right to vote in order to dilute the black electorate. If this were agreed, Smith would accept a transition period considerably briefer than the two years Kissinger had proposed. The Patriotic Front, on the other hand, vehemently opposed a constitution that provided special protections for the whites or that curtailed the voting rights of any black Zimbabwean.

When we received the report of these consultations in early June, I concluded that the Anglo-American settlement proposal would have to contain special arrangements for the whites if we were to bring Smith into a negotiation. I had in mind reserving a number of seats in the legislature, although fewer than the blocking vote Smith wanted, protection against amendment of the independence constitution for several years, and assurances that pension payments to retired white civil servants and military personnel would continue under majority rule. The British also favored these measures, and the first step was to work out with David Owen how to include them in the proposal we and the British were preparing. We would then resume discussions with the front line states and the South Africans, whose support of the proposal would be essential in gaining agreement from the black nationalists and the Rhodesians.

David Owen and I met in Paris on June 24. David was concerned about the Smith-Muzorewa contacts and by the lack of progress after his April trip, and wanted to return to Africa as soon as possible. I concurred that we should move rapidly, but urged him not to go until we were adequately prepared. He agreed that we needed to do more work among ourselves, particularly on the crucial question of how public order and security could be maintained during and after the transition period. David said that it would be politically impossible to get Parliament to approve the use of British forces in a peacekeeping role. He also felt that a UN peacekeeping force would not be acceptable to the white Rhodesians, many of whom did not trust the United Nations. He believed a force drawn from Commonwealth countries might be a viable alternative, but only if the Rhodesian Front, Smith's political party, agreed. We both believed that no country would be willing to provide peacekeeping forces if there was a significant risk that they would be drawn into serious fighting. We also believed that we could expect an international force to remain for a brief period, during which they would supervise and maintain the peace during elections. Underlying these difficulties was a serious problem. It concerned the roles of the Rhodesian Army and the guerrillas in the post-independence Zimbabwe defense forces. David felt that the liberation forces would have to predominate, but he believed that acceptable members of the Rhodesian Army should be allowed to join the independence forces. It would be difficult under the best of circumstances to integrate the liberation units into the national army, and the stabilizing presence of elements of the existing Rhodesian security forces, especially the well-trained and disciplined black troops, could be important.

After our discussions in Paris, the Anglo-American consultative group returned to Africa, only to encounter intransigence on all sides. Nkomo demanded that negotiations be solely among the Patriotic Front, Smith, and the British, thus excluding Muzorewa, Sithole, and other black nationalists. Nkomo, presumably speaking also for Mugabe, seemed willing to accept a Commonwealth peacekeeping force during the transition and acknowledged the necessity for elections. Smith was adamant that he would not accept any solution that turned over power to Nkomo and Mugabe after a short transition period. We felt that he was trying to develop a parallel negotiating track with Muzorewa and Sithole as a way of splitting the Patriotic Front by attracting Nkomo into a black majority government, leaving Mugabe isolated.

On July 23 Owen came to Washington for talks with the president and me on a joint settlement proposal, which was nearing completion. Owen emphasized, and we agreed, that he must be in a position to put a settlement plan to the parties as a joint U.S.-U.K. initiative. Carter had approved active U.S. cooperation with the British on Rhodesia, but he was not as current on the issues or the nuances of the parties' positions as he was with those of the Middle East or the SALT negotiations. However, he recognized the growing sensitivity of Congress to the Rhodesia issue, and stressed the importance of a fair and politically sustainable proposal. The president wanted our position to be based solidly on the principles of universal suffrage and free and fair elections open to all parties, blacks and whites. He wanted the proposal to be able to withstand attacks in Congress from either the Right or the Left as unbiased in favor of any group. Carter did not want to rule out in advance any fair solution that could gain international acceptance, even one proposed by Smith. He pointed out that Muzorewa had not chosen violence nor was he tainted with Communist backing. In terms of U.S. public opinion, Muzorewa was the most popular black nationalist and had strong support in Congress, especially in the Senate.

Owen told us he believed we were close to agreement with Smith and the Patriotic Front on the principles of universal suffrage and free elections. He stressed, however, that the key to the acceptability of our proposal was a workable solution to the security issues. The Patriotic Front's position was that it must dominate the security forces from the very beginning of the transition period on the grounds that its supporters and political cadres would otherwise be intimidated by the Rhodesian Army and police. The Patriotic Front, supported by the front line states, also demanded prior agreement that the Zimbabwe National Army would be based on the liberation forces and that the Rhodesian security forces would be disbanded. Smith clearly was unwilling to surrender total responsibility for law and order to the Patriotic Front, either during the transition or after independence. Owen said that there should be a place for the existing Rhodesian security forces in an independent Zimbabwe. What he had in mind was that elements of the Rhodesian Army would provide a barrier to Marxist influences in ZANU and ZAPU and a guarantee against a white exodus that could destroy the economic and administrative infrastructure of Zimbabwe before the black moderates could consolidate their control.

The president, Owen, and I were agreed. Owen would present a fair and balanced joint Anglo-American proposal. The main elements of the proposal were: a transition based on British authority and restoration of legality; a democratic constitution; genuine majority rule with protection for the rights of all individuals; and free and impartial elections under British supervision and international observation. We would not allow any of the parties to veto presentation of the plan. If Vorster failed to bring Smith to acceptance of our proposal we would put strong pressure on South Africa; conversely, if Smith cooperated and the nationalists balked, we would not stand in the way of a settlement that met our fundamental conditions. Owen agreed that we should first discuss the elements of the Anglo-American proposal with Tanzanian President Julius Nyerere, a highly intelligent and personally engaging man who was a major voice among the front line states, during his scheduled visit to Washington in early August. If Nyerere's visit went well, Owen would then introduce the proposal in September, after the August Rhodesian elections.

In the meeting with Owen and afterward, Carter showed considerable interest in whether an agreement between Smith and one or more of the major black nationalist groups might lead to an acceptable solution. Muzorewa was already engaged in secret negotiations with Smith. In our discussions with the president, Owen had referred to a long-standing British interest in promoting an accommodation between Smith and

Nkomo—who was thought to be more pragmatic and pro-Western than Mugabe. Dick Moose, whom we had just named assistant secretary for African affairs, and Tony Lake argued vigorously against the idea of U.S. support for any such secret deal because they believed it would not end the fighting but would severely damage our relations with the front line states. They were skeptical that Smith would ever surrender enough power to Nkomo to make it possible for him to break with Mugabe and run the risk of black civil war and universal African opprobrium.

While acknowledging the weight of Moose and Lake's arguments, neither the president nor I felt we should rule out acceptance of an internal settlement that provided for fair elections open to all and a genuine transfer of power to a government elected by universal suffrage. To do otherwise would contravene one of the guiding principles we had agreed upon with Owen: that we would not allow the external black nationalists, Nkomo and Mugabe, to block a settlement that met the basic tests of fairness. However, I agreed wholeheartedly with their advice not to support any move to divide the Patriotic Front. Although Nkomo was the senior black nationalist, his political base in Zimbabwe was the minority Ndebele tribal group, and his guerrilla forces were only a fraction the size of Mugabe's. In addition, such an internal settlement was unlikely to end the fighting, nor would it gain broad international acceptance.

Carter, Warren Christopher, and Dick Moose met with Nyerere on August 4 and 5, while I was in the Middle East. To the dismay of Christopher, Moose, and the other Africa experts present, the president announced that in private discussions he had agreed with Nyerere that the Zimbabwe National Army should be based on the black liberation forces, and that this should be an element in the Anglo-American proposal. In return, Nyerere promised to endorse the Anglo-American proposal, to try to persuade the other front line presidents to support it as well, and to extract from Mugabe and Nkomo an unequivocal commitment to the principle of fair elections open to all Rhodesians.

Nyerere's support of the Anglo-American proposal was a significant achievement, but gained at the cost of introducing what some of our advisers believed could prove to be a fatal flaw. On August 12, on my way back from the Middle East, I stopped briefly in London. Owen was visibly upset with the report he had received of the Carter-Nyerere exchange. I used a brief meeting with Nyerere at Heathrow Airport to support Owen's idea of balancing an eventual Patriotic Front-dominated independence army with use of the Rhodesian police to maintain order during the transition period.

Nyerere accepted a role for the Rhodesian police and followed through on his commitment to the president. By late August the front line states had endorsed presentation of the Anglo-American proposal to South Africa and Smith—although, with the exception of Nyerere, they had not given it unqualified approval. Importantly, the Nigerians also added

their support. However, in Pretoria, Owen found both Vorster and Foreign Minister Botha firm in their belief that negotiations would never get
started if we put to Smith a proposal containing the Carter-Nyerere
agreement. Owen stressed the role of the Rhodesian police in maintaining law and order, and tried to persuade Vorster that this concession had
been necessary to get front line support. Vorster, although reaffirming
that South Africa would see that Smith lived up to any agreement he
signed, refused to pressure the Rhodesians to accept the proposal.

* * *

On September 1, David Owen publicly announced the U.S.-U.K.
peace plan for Rhodesia and met Smith and his cabinet in Salisbury.
The elements of the Anglo-American proposal were: a transfer of power
from the Smith regime to a British-administered transition government;
a new constitution providing for universal suffrage and a bill of rights
protected from amendment for a period of time; an internationally supervised cease-fire; free and impartial elections; and arrangements for the
handling of all armed forces, including the establishment of an independence army based primarily on the liberation forces. In addition, it contemplated the negotiation of acceptable constitutional protections for
minority rights, including guaranteed representation in the independence legislature.

The day before the plan was offered, Smith's Rhodesian Front won
every seat in the parliamentary elections, thus eliminating any possibility
of the white moderates forming an effective opposition. Smith's ability
to pursue an internal settlement was greatly strengthened, and Owen's
reception by the triumphant Smith cabinet was openly hostile. Smith did
not reject our proposal out of hand. According to Andy Young and Dick
Moose, who had accompanied Owen to Africa, Smith was playing for
time to see whether anything would come from his contacts with Muzorewa and Sithole. Thus, we could expect him to continue talking. He
agreed to allow Field Marshal Lord Michael Carver, the British resident
commissioner-designate under the Anglo-American proposal, to come to
Rhodesia to discuss international security arrangements. Smith insisted,
however, that Carver's discussions with Rhodesian security officials
should not be taken to imply that Salisbury accepted the proposal.

Under pressure from the front line states and Nigeria, the Patriotic
Front made positive, if noncommittal, statements about our proposal.
Nkomo and Mugabe's real aim remained an immediate transfer of power
from Smith to the Patriotic Front during a quick transition, with only a
figurehead role for the British resident commissioner. Like Smith, they
were not persuaded they had fully played out their other options. From
their perspective, continued conflict might increase the likelihood that
Britain and the United States would pressure Smith and the South Africans to settle on terms favorable to the Patriotic Front before the Soviets

and Cubans were drawn in. This was a dangerous game. The longer Nkomo and Mugabe maneuvered, the more time Smith would have to negotiate an internal settlement with Muzorewa.

In the August talks with Nyerere, and subsequently in letters to other front line leaders, President Carter stated that should the Patriotic Front accept the Anglo-American proposal and Smith fail to respond favorably, the United States would support sanctions against South Africa as a means of pressuring the Rhodesians. Moreover, the British had agreed that jointly we would take measures to ensure that the transfer of power from Smith was genuine. The question in September was whether we had reached the point of declaring our support for, or even initiating, mandatory UN sanctions against South Africa.

On September 20, the Policy Review Committee concluded that while Smith had not accepted the Anglo-American proposal, he was still willing to negotiate. The time had not yet arrived to seek sanctions against South Africa in order to achieve our objectives in Rhodesia. The greatest utility of the UN sanctions power was in the threat of its application rather than its actual use. Furthermore, David Owen had repeatedly made clear that because of its enormous economic stake in South Africa, Britain could not support a UN embargo. I believed that it might become necessary to seek economic sanctions in order to achieve our objective but I felt that we should not do so as long as there was a prospect of serious negotiations.

The British commitment to the Anglo-American proposal began to waver after the Carter-Nyerere agreement. Owen's concerns were deepened by the Patriotic Front's failure to respond more favorably during his visit to Africa in September. Subsequently, I learned of secret contacts between Smith and Nkomo. On October 17, I sent Moose to London to reiterate to Owen that we must stick together on the basic principle of elections open to all the contending parties and based on universal suffrage. Even if against all expectations, Nkomo and Smith were actually to reach agreement, excluding Mugabe would lead to the nightmare of black civil war.

The Anglo-American Plan on the Defensive: The Internal Settlement Option

Events in southern Africa began to move rapidly in the fall of 1977. In the face of a strong challenge from the Afrikaaner far Right in national elections scheduled for late November, Vorster's government initiated a brutal crackdown on political dissidents in South Africa during September and October. In mid-September, Steve Biko, a leading black nationalist in South Africa, died in prison under circumstances suggesting murder, setting off an outburst of anger throughout Africa. On October 24, our Policy Review Committee concluded that the time had come for us to support a Security Council resolution imposing a mandatory arms embargo against South Africa. I also persuaded the committee to recommend to the president that we also be prepared to support a UN resolution calling on member states to review their economic relations with South Africa. I hoped such a resolution, which would not commit us to any specific punitive action, would serve as a further warning to the South Africans that the next step would be economic sanctions. A mandatory UN arms embargo resolution was unanimously approved by the Security Council in early November.

Later that month, Ian Smith announced that he intended to devise his own settlement proposal, and on December 2 he began negotiations between him, Muzorewa, and Sithole. At the same time Secretary-General Kurt Waldheim raised a number of problems about a UN peacekeeping role in Rhodesia. Then Kenneth Kaunda publicly disagreed with our proposal for free elections open to all parties. Although, with Nyerere's leadership, the front line states reaffirmed their support for the Anglo-American proposal, much lingering damage was done by Kaunda's statements.

As a result of these actions and domestic circumstances in the United States, we faced a difficult situation. The administration's Africa policies were coming under increasing criticism from the Right, which accused us of softness in handling both the Shaba crisis and the Somali-Ethiopian war. There was also great sympathy for the Rhodesian whites and Smith's internal settlement strategy. To stay on course, it was vital that we not lose control of events in southern Africa.

NAMIBIA

Since the mid-1960s the United States had supported the United Nations' decision to rescind the responsibility assigned to South Africa by the League of Nations for the former German territory of South-West Africa (Namibia). However, until the Portuguese withdrawal from Angola and the subsequent growth of Soviet and Cuban influence, little was done to implement that decision. South African military forces easily contained a small, sporadic guerrilla war carried on by the black nationalist South-West Africa People's Organization (SWAPO), led by Sam Nujoma.

The establishment of a revolutionary government in Angola gave SWAPO a source of political and military support, but more important, a base from which to carry on the war in Namibia. South African attacks against SWAPO camps inside Angola kept tensions high along the border and provided a rationale, beyond Pretoria's covert support for antigovernment Angolan insurgents led by Jonas Savimbi, for more than 20,000

Cuban troops who were brought into Angola to help counter South African combat forces which had been introduced into the civil war. By 1976, the Namibia problem, although of smaller dimensions, had joined the conflict in Rhodesia in posing a serious threat to stability and Western interests in southern Africa. Nujoma's small guerrilla bands presented no immediate threat to South African control of Namibia, but it was likely that with increased Soviet and Cuban training and material support, SWAPO would grow stronger, and more committed to a military solution.

In an attempt to realign American policy in southern Africa, Henry Kissinger wisely sought to initiate a negotiating process for Namibian independence. In January 1976, with U.S. support, the UN Security Council adopted Resolution 385, which called for an end to political repression and racial discrimination in Namibia, the release of political prisoners and the repatriation of exiles, free UN-supervised elections, and South African withdrawal. Kissinger then tried to get South Africa and SWAPO together in Geneva and, at one point in the fall of 1976, appeared close to success.

Shaken out of its complacency by the sweeping changes in the region since 1974, South Africa seemed ready to consider withdrawing from Namibia, although its preference clearly was the creation of a client state organized along racial and tribal lines. In discussions with Kissinger in September 1976, the South Africans agreed to a seven-point proposal for Namibian independence: 1) a Geneva conference would be held to negotiate a constitution; 2) the UN would participate as an observer; 3) South Africa would discuss its post-independence relationship with Namibia; 4) arrangements for elections would be negotiated; 5) any issue could be raised at the conference; 6) South Africa would accept a constitution negotiated by the various internal and external Namibian parties; and 7) the goal would be independence by December 31, 1978. Subsequently, as a gesture of good faith, South Africa gave the United States a private commitment to release a substantial number of political prisoners. SWAPO rejected the seven-point proposal.

At about the same time, South Africa was conducting in the Namibian capital of Windhoek a meeting of the tribal and ethnic-based Namibian political groups referred to as the "Turnhalle" conference, taking its name from the hall in which the meeting was held. The objectives of the conference were to seek a basis for a settlement and to build an internal counterweight to SWAPO. The effort of the South Africans and the small white Namibian minority to create an anti-SWAPO black and white coalition was facilitated by tribal fears of a SWAPO dominated by the people of the Ovambo tribe and dislike of SWAPO's radicalism. SWAPO refused to accept the legitimacy of the ethnic parties, and would not agree to negotiate with them. Nujoma's position was that SWAPO would only attend a conference with South Africa and the United Nations, and only if South Africa committed itself in advance to complete withdrawal and independence within nine months from the initiation of negotiations. Furthermore, SWAPO saw no need for elections, inasmuch as it considered itself the legitimate representative of the Namibian people and viewed the Turnhalle parties as either tribalists, South African puppets, or white racists.

When Kissinger's negotiating initiative stalled, South Africa intensified preparations for a settlement based on a coalition of the Turnhalle parties (called the Democratic Turnhalle Alliance, or DTA) as an alternative to an internationally negotiated and supervised independence process that would include SWAPO. Until the election of President Carter, South Africa may have believed the United States would eventually accept such an internal settlement because of its fear of Soviet exploitation of African nationalism to establish a foothold in southern Africa. South Africa expected to continue using Western economic, political, and strategic interests in South Africa to block United Nations actions, such as mandatory economic sanctions, that were aimed at forcing it to stop supporting the Smith regime in Rhodesia, to withdraw from Namibia, and to begin dismantling apartheid.

● ● ●

In January 1977, the prospects for a peaceful solution to the Namibian problem were dim. Nevertheless, even though the Namibia conflict was not as urgent or inflammable as the escalating war in Rhodesia, there were important reasons for revitalizing the flagging negotiations.

We were concerned not only with the issue of self-determination and the right of the peoples of Namibia to participate freely in the life of their country, but also we believed that a peaceful settlement in Namibia could be a step toward evolution within the Republic of South Africa. A successful pluralist society in Namibia could encourage those South African whites who were willing to move toward greater political, economic, and social equality.

In addition, although our views were never to be accepted by the president and Brzezinski—especially after the Shaba and Horn of Africa crises—Andy Young and I were in agreement that South African withdrawal from Namibia was necessary if we were to get the Cuban troops out of Angola. The more intense the conflict in Namibia became, the greater the risk that the South Africans would carry the war more deeply into Angola, thus increasing the possibility that the Cubans would be engaged directly in the fighting. If a Cuban-South African conflict spilled over into Rhodesia, as we believed it could, there would be a war along race lines in southern Africa in which we would be virtually powerless to prevent immense damage to American political, economic, and strategic interests.

Fortunately, President Augustinho Neto and the Angolan leadership recognized the dangers of a wider war and proved to be vigorous supporters of a negotiated solution. Because of Neto's influence with Sam Nujoma, I believed our interests would be well served by maintaining a close and cooperative relationship with Angola on the Namibia problem. Moreover, we had generally agreed at the outset of the new administration that we should seek to establish normal relations with all nations regardless of the fact that we had differing ideologies; hence, our initial contacts with Cuba, Vietnam, and the PRC, as well as Angola.

Carter was of two minds about Angola. His instinct was to work with the Angolans to help them reduce the insecurity problems that had caused the introduction of the Cubans into Angola and that now served to justify their retention. Our actions directed to reconciling the differences between Zaire and Angola at the time of the Shaba affair had served this very purpose. But politically Carter was sensitive to Cuban activities and the impact they would have at home if we appeared too soft in dealing with them. This led us to step back from the brink every time we came close to establishing diplomatic relations. The failure to normalize relations with Angola did not prevent us from essential contacts. We worked through the Angolan missions abroad, embassies of friendly countries in Luanda, and periodic visits by special American envoys, but these were awkward and less effective substitutes for sustained communication through embassies in Luanda and Washington. The unwillingness to normalize relations never made sense in terms of our objectives of getting the Cubans out of Angola and influencing Luanda toward moderate solutions to problems in which we had an important interest. In retrospect, it is clear that we should have acted quickly to normalize relations. Such a move would have enhanced our ability to negotiate with Luanda, and it would have been consistent with the principle of universality of diplomatic contacts.

Without a strategy for achieving Namibian independenc, the Western nations would soon be faced with the dilemma of how to respond to African demands for mandatory sanctions against South Africa. If there were no credible negotiating initiative, the Africans would be able to force a Security Council vote. We would then either damage our relations with black Africa by vetoing the resolution, which would be at odds with the Carter administration's Africa policy, or by approving it, destroy the negotiating process and harm important Western economic interests in South Africa, as well as set an undesirable precedent that might be used against our friends, such as Israel, in the future. I believed that if we were forced to apply economic sanctions, we might lose all hope of negotiating independence for Namibia. It was this conviction, as much as my concern over the political and diplomatic considerations, that led me to be more reluctant than some of my advisers to adopt a position on economic sanctions which would result in a deadlock.

The president and I agreed that the United States should actively support Namibian independence in accordance with the terms of UN Resolution 385. At an early date we also decided to work through the United Nations and in collaboration with our Western allies and the front line states. The vehicle for Western cooperation would be a body known as the "contact group." Andy Young suggested in January that representatives of the five Western members of the Security Council— the United States, Britain, France, West Germany, and Canada—meet regularly to coordinate strategy and develop plans for Namibian independence. We all felt that unity among the five would give us greater strength and lessen the chance of fragmentation of effort. We agreed to work with the front line states to bring Nujoma and SWAPO into serious negotiations, taking care to have one or more front line states present when the contact group met with SWAPO leaders. This would help to allay suspicion that we were trying to play the Africans off against each other. All contact group proposals were accordingly to be advanced jointly.

• • •

Andy Young's extraordinarily able deputy, Ambassador Donald Mc-Henry, became chairman of the contact group. Under McHenry's active and strong leadership, the group began consultations among the five Western members within weeks of our taking office. We briefly explored the possibility of convening a peace conference on the basis of the seven points Kissinger had worked out with the South Africans. However, expecting a changed attitude from the new administration, neither the front line nor SWAPO was interested. In late February, the South Africans also refused to reconfirm their commitment to the seven points because the Turnhalle conference they had initiated was nearing agreement on a program for electing a constituent assembly.

We agreed with Don McHenry that it was urgent to reach agreement among the five on a contact group proposal so that we could show the South Africans that there was an alternative to the Turnhalle process. In February and March, Don and his colleagues held intensive discussions with the South Africans and the front line states in New York in an attempt to develop the elements of an approach that would be acceptable to all parties. Contact with SWAPO was difficult, partly because its leaders were so frequently out of reach, but also because of its suspicions about our motives.

By late March, an approach along the lines of Resolution 385 was taking form. On March 19, however, the Turnhalle conference announced agreement on their own program for Namibian independence by December 31, 1978. The conference ruled out participation by SWAPO, thus eliminating any chance that their purpose could serve as the basis for either negotiations or a cease-fire.

By pressing forward with Turnhalle, South Africa created an instrument that gave it tactical flexibility in dealing with the contact group. The South Africans could, when it suited them, tell us the proposed solution to an issue had to be cleared with the Turnhalle parties. In this way they could control the pace of negotiations when it served their purpose. At the same time, the South Africans continued to build up the Democratic Turnhalle Alliance as a viable political opponent to SWAPO should UN-supervised elections eventually be held. For a considerable period, perhaps until the failure of the Rhodesian internal settlement, South Africa probably believed that under certain conditions—the presence of substantial South African forces, a short campaigning period to prevent SWAPO from strengthening its political base within Namibia, and continued South African administration of the territory—the Turnhalle coalition could actually defeat SWAPO in elections. Alternatively, if the conditions of an internationally supervised settlement proved unacceptable to South Africa, it could grant formal independence to Namibia in accordance with the Turnhalle program while retaining de facto military and political control.

On April 7, after the Western five reached agreement on a basic position, the contact group ambassadors presented an unprecedented joint aide-mémoire to Prime Minister Vorster in Cape Town. Consistent with Resolution 385, the Western proposal called for free elections open to all parties under United Nations supervision and control. The contact group warned Vorster that the internal settlement was unacceptable to the international community and that if South Africa did not agree to early negotiations for Namibian independence, the Western five would have to reconsider their previous positions in the Security Council. This signified, as Vorster readily understood, that the five would no longer oppose mandatory UN sanctions against South Africa. Vorster reacted sharply to the implied threat of sanctions, which he termed "obnoxious," and said he would not interfere with the Turnhalle process. However, he added that South Africa was willing to continue discussing the Namibia issue with the contact group.

After further consultations in New York, the contact group representatives, led by Don McHenry, returned to Cape Town for further discussions with Vorster on April 27. This meeting turned out to be unexpectedly constructive. The South Africans' changed attitude was, in the judgment of many, due to the united Western assertion that we would no longer prevent sanctions unless they began seriously negotiating for Namibian independence under international supervision. Vorster agreed not to implement the Turnhalle program, accepted the principle of elections for a constituent assembly to draft an independence constitution, and affirmed that all Namibians, regardless of political affiliation, could participate in the elections. He indicated that the United Nations could be involved in the elections and independence process through a special representative, although the latter's powers and role were left undefined.

At this stage the Western five's objective was South African acceptance of the main elements of a settlement. Ahead lay difficult negotiations regarding the nature of UN participation in the transition arrangements and in South African military withdrawal. The South Africans had made clear that they intended to retain administrative control of Namibia prior to independence and that the UN's primary function would be to monitor the election.

In early May, when the contact group briefed the front line states and SWAPO on the Cape Town talks with Vorster, the parties appeared satisfied with South Africa's commitment to hold UN-supervised elections and to suspend the Turnhalle process. All emphasized the importance of a dominant UN role during the transition, including providing a "substantial" peacekeeping force, and early and complete removal of South African military forces before elections. SWAPO's position was that the UN should assume de jure control of Namibia during the transition, and it also wanted Pretoria to declare publicly that it would withdraw under a schedule to be negotiated with SWAPO and the United Nations. SWAPO insisted it would have nothing to do with the Turnhalle parties. The front line and SWAPO continued to withhold endorsement of our approach, as they waited to see if the contact group could actually induce South Africa to agree to Namibian independence on terms that would be acceptable to SWAPO.

Vice-President Mondale's May 1977 meeting in Vienna with Prime Minister Johannes Vorster produced little progress on the Namibia question. Mondale reiterated the fundamental Western position that had been put to Vorster by the contact group on April 7. If there was no progress on Namibia and Rhodesia, the Western attitude toward South Africa would change.

Mondale sought to establish a common ground between the West and South Africa on Namibia by underlining the extent to which the sides agreed to key elements of Resolution 385. But when Mondale urged that an impartial UN interim control should replace South African administration during the transition period, Vorster responded angrily that he was personally committed to a Turnhalle-type interim authority and that it had been hard enough to agree that Turnhalle would not be the permanent solution. The South Africans regarded the UN as irremediably biased in favor of SWAPO. From Vienna on, it seemed clear that despite what Vorster had told the contact group, the South Africans intended to follow a two-track strategy: preparing the option of an internal settlement, while at the same time continuing to explore the possibilities for a wider solution. Vorster agreed with Mondale that discussions should continue, and plans were set in motion for a second round with the contact group in Cape Town.

The next session with the South Africans was held on June 8–10, 1977. Once again I was slightly encouraged by their attitude. After arguing that the proposed transitional administrative structure should draw upon the Turnhalle parties, the South Africans agreed to appoint a single, impartial administrator general to run the territory prior to independence. This implied that despite what Vorster had told the vice-president, they would refrain from establishing an interim government based on Turnhalle, at least for the time being. South African officials reiterated that a United Nations special representative could participate in the transition process in cooperation with the South African-appointed administrator general. They also, after refusing to accept the Resolution 385 standard of "supervision and control," conceded that the UN special representative would have to be "satisfied" that the transitional political process was fair and open to all parties. Still remaining, however, was the all-important question of South African military withdrawal. South Africa did agree in principle to a "phased" withdrawal. We urged that the withdrawal be completed by the date of independence.

The South Africans refused to be pinned down on the size and nature of a UN administrative and military presence. These arrangements would be critical in gaining front line and SWAPO confidence in our plan. The contact group began a detailed study of the functions the UN might perform in the transition period, looking particularly at ways to monitor effectively the political process leading up to UN-supervised elections. It had become clear that the group would have to do the bulk of such work because the United Nations was unwilling to begin substantive planning without formal African approval of our approach.

Another difficult issue that arose in the June talks was the status of the economically important port and enclave of Walvis Bay on the coast of Namibia. Walvis Bay was a territorial anomaly in that it had not been included in the League of Nations mandate of South-West Africa. South Africa's position was that Walvis Bay was not at issue, having legally been part of its national territory since 1910 and before that of Britain's Cape Colony since 1878. SWAPO was equally determined that whatever its colonial history, Walvis Bay must be part of Namibia. Neither side had shown the slightest flexibility on this issue. I asked the State Department legal adviser to work on the problem, as I was certain that eventually we would have to offer a bridging proposal, although I was determined that we should not attempt to finally dispose of the issue in the contact group settlement plan. If the independence negotiations had to resolve the status of Walvis Bay, on which the sides were diametrically and immovably opposed, our initiative could be destroyed.

At the June talks the South Africans asserted that it was time for the

Western five and the front line states to secure SWAPO's agreement to the points we had been discussing, and to a cease-fire. Because SWAPO mistrusted the Western five as well as the South Africans, I did not expect this to be easy. The contact group aimed for talks with SWAPO in early August. Even before that meeting, Vorster and Pik Botha grudgingly agreed to the appointment of Ambassador Maarti Ahtisaari, an experienced and respected Finnish diplomat, as the UN special representative once the Security Council gave Waldheim a mandate to prepare for UN participation. The South Africans made it clear that they would not agree to partial troop withdrawal without SWAPO agreement to a cease-fire. If SWAPO would meet this condition, Vorster said, he would withdraw some troops even before the elections.

After the front line states and SWAPO were briefed on the talks with the South Africans their skepticism remained high, but they were visibly impressed by how far the contact group had gotten. However, SWAPO refused to consider a phased South African withdrawal as a basis for agreeing to a cease-fire and continued to insist that all South African forces must leave prior to elections. Another problem was Waldheim's understandable caution about the UN political and peacekeeping role. He was reluctant to allow his staff to begin work on UN participation until he was confident the Africans would endorse the contact group proposal. Therefore, besides pressing the front line states to urge Nujoma to be more flexible, the contact group also had to forge ahead with contingency planning for the UN's activities. Carter was pleased with what the contact group had accomplished and kept urging that we push Waldheim and SWAPO harder.

In the meantime, the front line states persuaded Nujoma to meet with the contact group in New York on August 8. President Neto, who wanted to reduce the South African military threat to Angola, was particularly helpful. Tanzanian President Julius Nyerere added his arguments, as he was also doing with the Patriotic Front on the Rhodesia issue. In addition to being committed to majority rule, Nyerere was anxious to stop the fighting in Namibia and Rhodesia before it widened.

On August 5, prior to the talks with SWAPO, Carter and Nyerere had met in the White House and, in addition to their discussion of Rhodesia, also reviewed the Namibian negotiations. At Carter's request, Don McHenry described for Nyerere the settlement plan we intended to present to SWAPO. There was much in it that would be painful to SWAPO, and Nyerere's support would be crucial. McHenry said that the contact group would propose free elections open to all Namibian parties to elect a constituent assembly charged with drafting a nonracial constitution. A UN special representative would participate in the electoral arrangements and in all phases of the transition to independence. One of his tasks would be to ensure that repressive and restrictive laws and regulations that would impede fair elections were abolished or modified. Although not formally having powers of approval and disapproval over the actions of the administrator general, which South Africa would never concede, the special representative would have to be "satisfied" with all the arrangements for the elections. McHenry emphasized that as far as the contact group was concerned, this gave the special representative the right to reject anything he considered unfair or partial.

During the transition period, McHenry continued, a South African-appointed administrator general would supervise the interim government together with the UN special representative. All racially discriminatory laws would be abolished, and all political prisoners released and exiles allowed to return to their homes. South Africa would begin a phased withdrawal of its military forces, to be completed upon independence. McHenry pointed out that South Africa had not produced a withdrawal plan and was unlikely to do so until SWAPO agreed to the principle of a cease-fire. There would be a substantial UN presence, although its size and function had not been fully analyzed. He said that we were thinking in terms of a monitoring group of about 1,000, rather than a large peace-keeping force. Carter stressed that we did not expect Vorster to go any farther until SWAPO demonstrated its sincerity by positive movement.

Nyerere's response showed how far we had to go. He said the front line accepted the principles of elections and universal suffrage. But the crux of his and SWAPO's concern was how to guarantee that the elections would be free and fair when South Africa retained political control and a military presence in Namibia during the transition. Nyerere and SWAPO's answer was, he said, to enhance the UN role. Nyerere stated that the UN should assume de jure responsibility for governing Namibia during the transition, with an administrative staff to replace the South Africans and the local authorities. Furthermore, Nyerere insisted, the UN must provide a substantial peacekeeping force, and South Africa must withdraw substantially all of its forces. He added that the Africans would reluctantly acquiesce in a small South African military presence until independence as a face-saver for Vorster. Upon independence, however, SWAPO must take power from the United Nations, and not from South Africa. Nyerere assured us Nujoma would respect such an agreement. He said that if the front line states were genuinely convinced the UN would supervise and control the transition, they would urge SWAPO to accept our plan and abide by a cease-fire. Nyerere accepted Carter's point that SWAPO must show some flexibility if we were to continue serious negotiations with the South Africans. Nyerere added that the Africans would give Secretary-General Waldheim assurances against being denounced, but we had to convince Waldheim that we were fully committed and that our plan was practical. Waldheim feared, Nyerere said, that the United Nations would look ridiculous if we did not intend to carry through.

In talks three days later in New York, Nujoma accepted, as had

Nyerere, the principle of free elections, a UN-supervised transition, and a South African-appointed administrator general. He agreed in principle to a cease-fire once the transitional process had begun and proposed that SWAPO forces be confined to designated bases in Namibia under UN monitoring, a point that was to become extremely controversial at a later stage of the negotiations. He did not, however, accept the retention of a residual South African force confined to its base under UN observation until independence. He also insisted that Ahtisaari's authority be superior to that of the administrator general. While far from full agreement, this was the first real progress we had made with SWAPO on the basic elements of a settlement, and it was indispensable in convincing the secretary-general that the time had come to start serious planning for the UN role. However, as Nyerere had warned, SWAPO's acceptance of the overall principles of our approach was conditional upon our obtaining a specific plan for South African military withdrawal and the deployment of a large UN peacekeeping force. We had to move rapidly to address these problems because South Africa intended to transfer authority to an administrator general on October 1 and we wanted to get the UN to endorse our proposal and appoint Ahtisaari as special representative for Namibia as soon as possible.

During September, the contact group worked at a hectic pace, helping the UN staff develop plans for UN participation and preparing for what was hoped would be conclusive negotiations with South Africa and SWAPO. To accelerate the negotiations, the contact group ambassadors met Prime Minister Vorster and Foreign Minister Botha in Pretoria on September 22–23 to discuss a timetable for South African military withdrawal and the details of the UN role. The contact group hoped to follow this meeting with another meeting with Nujoma. To the dismay of all, the South Africans opened with a sharp turnabout from the April and June Cape Town talks. Botha called the plan for a phased reduction to a 1,500-man level a device to turn over Namibia to SWAPO terrorists. He said that between the contact group's proposal and reactivating the Turnhalle process, he had no choice but to take the latter. Botha insisted the South African forces would not withdraw until the Western powers provided watertight guarantees that the Cubans would not enter Namibia. Interestingly, in light of positions that were taken five years later, the South Africans did not raise the issue of the continued presence of the Cubans in Angola.

In what we were eventually to recognize was a South African negotiating technique, Vorster then entered the discussions and prevented a breakdown. Vorster dropped Botha's demand for assurances about Cuban forces, although he warned that South African forces would reenter Namibia if there were any "Cuban tricks," and proposed a reduction of South African troops from about 24,000 to 4,000 on independence day, too many to suit SWAPO, but a substantial step in the right direction. Vorster insisted that elections must be scheduled for March 1978, which SWAPO was certain to reject for the reason that it would give it insufficient time to organize and conduct a political campaign. He objected to the concept of a UN peacekeeping force, proposing that the UN provide only sufficient personnel to monitor the elections. This would almost certainly be unacceptable to SWAPO.

Vorster's reasons for raising these new difficulties may well have been related to Afrikaaner politics. He had scheduled national elections in October, and South African policy toward Namibia was, of course, a major political issue. This very likely also accounts for Botha's toughness at the beginning of the talks. In fact, as we well knew, the South Africans were engaged at that very moment in covert contacts with the Angolans to negotiate a pullback from the Angola-Namibian border. Our information was that these secret talks were going quite well. In avoiding an impasse in the Pretoria talks, I believe Prime Minister Vorster wanted to keep both options open, an international settlement and an internal settlement, while he took a hard public line for the benefit of the Afrikaaner electorate.

In any event, after the September talks I told David Owen that I felt we were getting close to agreement on most of the substantive issues of a settlement, although many details remained to be worked out. He agreed, and urged that we not wait until we had resolved every one of SWAPO's problems to present a comprehensive proposal to the parties. David was deeply concerned with the interaction of the Rhodesian and Namibian negotiations. The contact group, he argued, should not push the Namibia negotiations with South Africa so hard that Pretoria withdrew from the process. If they did, the Western powers would have no means for avoiding sanctions and our strategy for dealing with the more urgent Rhodesia issue could be damaged.

At the end of October, the contact group offered the parties a compromise proposal on the remaining issues: a token South African force of 1,500 men to remain in Namibia, confined to a single base and to operate under UN monitoring until independence; release of all political prisoners; a UN military presence of "some 2,000 men," the exact number to be determined by the circumstances; measures to neutralize the Namibian police and militia; and deferral of the Walvis Bay issue for negotiation after independence. Both South Africa and SWAPO objected to the compromise proposal, and the hope of rapid progress toward a Namibia settlement began to fade.

13

SOUTHERN AFRICA: RHODESIAN BREAKTHROUGH; NAMIBIAN STALEMATE

RHODESIA

The Demise of the Anglo-American Proposal

IN LATE 1977 David Owen and I decided to invite the Patriotic Front to Malta to discuss the Anglo-American proposal. Originally, the Malta talks were to have included all parties, but Smith, Muzorewa, and Sithole would not come. We decided to go ahead without them. Owen viewed Malta as a final effort to push Nkomo and Mugabe off their insistence on a transitional arrangement that would provide a dominant role for the Patriotic Front and their refusal to consider Muzorewa and Sithole as anything but Smith's puppets.

Owen feared that unless an all-parties peace conference was convened quickly, we would soon have to contend with an agreement between Smith and Muzorewa and perhaps other black nationalists such as Sithole, which would contain a formal commitment to majority rule but reserve disproportionate power to the white minority, making it totally unacceptable to the Patriotic Front and the front line states. Owen had repeatedly warned us that it would be politically difficult for Britain to oppose an internal settlement leading to a black government in Salisbury. The British could not long maintain sanctions under such circumstances even if the settlement failed to gain wide international support.

Owen's concerns mirrored my own, but I thought it unwise to view the Malta talks as the last hope for the Anglo-American proposal. Whatever happened at Malta, substantial negotiations lay ahead before a settlement would emerge. The existence of the proposal and our continuing talks with the parties kept the negotiating process alive and was vital in preventing the Patriotic Front from intensifying the war. In addition, if the Anglo-American initiative stalled we would have nothing to counter the increasing momentum toward an internal Rhodesian settlement. The mood on Capitol Hill was also changing. A solid majority in Congress still supported a balanced, nonideological approach toward the problems of southern Africa, but conservatives, building upon growing public concern about Soviet and Cuban activities in Shaba and the Horn, were gaining strength.

The talks at Malta from January 30 to February 1 did make some progress. The nationalist leaders, however, continued to demand that the Patriotic Front share power with the British resident commissioner in the transition. We were unable to convince them that we would not tilt our proposal in their favor or that their intransigence was eroding our ability to contain growing political pressures at home. Nevertheless, Nkomo and Mugabe took a generally positive attitude. They indicated a desire to continue negotiating on the basis of the Anglo-American initiative, and asked for another round of talks.

The Patriotic Front was anxious to continue the negotiations, partly because of its alarm over the talks in Salisbury. On February 15, 1978, Smith and the black leaders indicated they had agreed in principle on a program for "majority rule." In fact, it fell far short of genuine majority rule. Although constituting only about 5 percent of the population, the whites would retain 28 percent of the seats in Parliament and have the power to block changes in the constitution for ten years. The plan envisaged negotiations between the Rhodesian authorities and the internal nationalists on a new constitution, transition arrangements, the future army, elimination of racial discrimination, and elections. The formal agreement establishing an Executive Council to supervise the transition to a multiracial regime was announced in Salisbury on March 3, 1978, with elections for the black members of Parliament planned for the end of the year. During the interim, Smith would remain prime minister, and Muzorewa, Sithole, and Jeremiah Chirau, a tribal chief, would join the Rhodesian Executive Council.

The president cautioned Andy Young and me neither to support nor reject outright the March 3 agreement. Carter's instructions were not easy for Andy, who was convinced failure to condemn the internal settlement would undermine the gains we had made with black Africa since we took office. These gains were due, in substantial part, to Andy's tireless efforts to persuade African leaders of our seriousness about genuine majority rule. Andy's initial criticisms of Smith and Muzorewa's February 15 announcement had already created problems on Capitol

Hill by fueling perceptions that we were opposed to an internal settlement even before we knew its terms. The president's instincts were right. We could not endorse the internal settlement, but neither could we reduce our flexibility in future negotiations by publicly rejecting it.

Shortly after the March 3 announcement, Bishop Muzorewa told me that he had entered the Salisbury agreement as a pragmatic way to ease Smith out of power while preventing a massive flight of Rhodesian whites. Muzorewa acknowledged that the agreement was less than perfect from the black point of view, but he was convinced it would achieve the fundamental goal of an independent Zimbabwe under a black government by the end of the year. But Muzorewa implicitly conceded the weakness of his position when he evaded my questions as to whether he was prepared to meet with Nkomo and Mugabe to determine if they would participate in the March 3 agreement. Clearly Muzorewa feared competing politically with Nkomo and Mugabe and wanted first to consolidate his position as the black leader who had ousted Smith. He appeared confident that he could siphon off much of the fighting strength of ZANU and ZAPU, leaving Mugabe and Nkomo no alternative but to join the political process he had set in motion.

In hindsight, it is evident that we did not take Muzorewa seriously enough, partly because we knew a lasting settlement depended on bringing in the guerrillas (Mugabe's and Nkomo's forces), partly because we doubted that Smith could persuade him to join a settlement, and partly because we underestimated his ambition to lead Zimbabwe to independence and his conviction that the internal settlement was a significant, if necessarily limited, step along that road. Because we had focused so much attention on Mugabe and Nkomo, Muzorewa doubtless concluded we would exclude him from any significant role in a settlement. This mistake allowed Smith virtually a free hand in convincing Muzorewa to join the internal settlement.

The March 3 agreement severely complicated our ability to maintain the Anglo-American initiative. Public opinion in the United States and Britain welcomed the Salisbury agreement, foreshadowing growing political difficulties in maintaining UN economic sanctions against Rhodesia as the Salisbury parties moved toward elections and a black majority government. After the March 3 announcement, both moderate and conservative senators introduced resolutions urging the administration to give serious consideration to the Salisbury agreement. We feared that if the Congress were to remove sanctions and accept the internal settlement, the United States could again find itself unwillingly aligned with South Africa and a pariah regime in Rhodesia. Our Africa policy would be shattered, with the Soviets and Cubans picking up the pieces. The stakes in finding an acceptable solution were high.

Although we and the British remained formally committed to the Anglo-American proposal, from mid-February 1978 on we began moving toward a strategy which married acceptable aspects of the internal settlement with the basic principles of the Anglo-American initiative. After the February 15 announcement by Smith, the Policy Review Committee concluded that we must build a bridge between the Patriotic Front and the Salisbury parties, drawing the former into the settlement process, while reducing the danger of protracted civil war. We decided that the Anglo-American proposal should remain on the table as a vehicle for negotiations, but above all as a standard against which the fairness of a final settlement could be measured. We felt strongly that whatever solution emerged must conform to the fundamental principles of the proposal.

Meanwhile, the British government was under growing pressure to extricate Britain from the Rhodesian quagmire. David Owen's faith in the Anglo-American proposal was waning, and he was increasingly drawn toward the idea of building upon the internal settlement. He saw in it both an opportunity and a danger. If a way could be found to broaden participation in the Salisbury agreement—by which Owen meant including Nkomo—and to modify it sufficiently to make it acceptable to African opinion, it might provide the basis for an early settlement. On the other hand, even if the Salisbury agreement failed to gain international support, once elections were held there would be heavy pressure from Parliament to recognize the new black government and finally have done with the Rhodesian millstone around Britain's neck. Owen was acutely sensitive to the harm this outcome would do to British and Western interests in Africa and the strains it would place on U.S.-U.K. relations.

Against this background, Owen concluded that he must intensify his efforts to bring Nkomo and Smith together. While we were kept informed of these efforts, we maintained our distance from them. In my view, the British were overestimating Nkomo's political assets. Nkomo himself was a realist about Mugabe's strength and Smith's long-range intentions, and as he was to prove at independence, he was prepared to subordinate personal ambitions to the larger goal of an independent Zimbabwe. Owen argued that we must find some way of prodding the Patriotic Front into negotiations with Salisbury before the security situation in Rhodesia deteriorated to the point where it was out of control. With misgivings, I agreed to secret British attempts beginning in late June to arrange an exploratory meeting between Smith and Nkomo. This risky plan was strongly opposed by Dick Moose and Tony Lake, but I agreed to give it a try on the condition that it was understood that Nkomo's purpose would be to see if his talks with Smith could be broadened to include Mugabe. I also insisted that this approach must proceed in parallel and be consistent with our continued negotiations on the basis of the Anglo-American proposal. I emphasized that the United States would not be a party to splitting the Patriotic Front.

On March 14, to the anger of Nkomo, Mugabe, and the front line states, we and the British abstained on an African-sponsored UN resolution condemning the Salisbury agreement. On March 10, we and the British had jointly announced our intention to try to persuade the various factions to attend an all-parties conference on the basis of the principles we had put forward in the Anglo-American proposal, that is, free and fair elections open to all and a transition to majority rule and independence. This enabled Andy Young to explain our abstention on March 14 on grounds that while we considered the Salisbury agreement inadequate, we wanted to avoid actions that would harden the positions of the parties as we pressed for an all-parties conference. The Patriotic Front promptly denounced us for failing to stand up for our proposal—the proposal the Patriotic Front's own inflexibility had done so much to undermine.

Ironically, our critics in Congress never took note of our repeated refusals to accede to the demands of the front line states and the Patriotic Front to give the latter a dominant role. To do so would have made a travesty of our firm commitment to a process open to all parties. In fact, the critics on Capitol Hill for the most part were at best only partially informed, usually by Smith's representatives, and unwilling to listen to explanations of our policy.

• • •

To prepare the way for the conference, Owen and I decided to go to Africa in mid-April to meet separately with the Patriotic Front, the front line states, the Rhodesian Executive Council, and the South Africans.

Our discussions with the Patriotic Front, which took place on April 14–15 in Dar es Salaam, were extremely difficult. Despite everything that had occurred since Malta, Nkomo and Mugabe still insisted on ignoring the changes in Salisbury. Mugabe had even begun to back away from the principle of internationally supervised elections open to all parties, and Nkomo refused to agree that the Rhodesian police could be primarily responsible for law and order during the transition period while the rival armed forces were confined to bases. Nkomo indicated that the police, as well as the army, must be based on the liberation forces, although he left the door open for admitting "acceptable elements" of both the Rhodesian security forces and police. Mugabe and Nkomo proposed that the Patriotic Front be guaranteed two-thirds of the seats on the interim Council of Ministers and wanted to narrowly define the powers of the British resident commissioner so that the commissioner could do little without the concurrence of the council. The only flexibility they showed was a willingness to negotiate the precise allocation of seats on the council, but as at Malta, they were adamant that the Patriotic Front must predominate. We warned Mugabe and Nkomo that Britain would never agree to administer such a biased transition arrangement, and we emphasized our opposition to the proposition that any single group should have a dominant position before free elections.

Owen and I had hoped to make progress with the Patriotic Front at Dar es Salaam so that in Pretoria we would be in a better position to persuade the South Africans to press Smith, Muzorewa, and the new Executive Council to attend an all-parties conference. When I cabled my report on the Dar es Salaam meetings to the president he became angry, and at his request I protested sharply to Nyerere and the other front line presidents about the nationalist leaders' intransigence.

When we arrived in Pretoria on April 16, the South Africans were in a quandary. They doubted that the Salisbury agreement would stop the guerrilla war or that it would prevent increased Soviet and Cuban contacts with the liberation forces, or even that it would gain international recognition and produce an end to sanctions. They were therefore anxious for us to continue our efforts to work out a settlement before the situation on the ground deteriorated further. On the other hand, Botha did not want to jeopardize Smith's chances of achieving an internal settlement. Their position was, as it always had been, that South Africa would see that Smith lived up to whatever he agreed to, but that they would not force him into any agreement.

The following day Owen, Young, and I flew to Salisbury to meet with the Executive Council. Our purpose was to urge the Rhodesians to attend an all-parties conference. This was my first visit to Rhodesia and I was impressed with the beauty of the countryside and the fertility of the land. I thought how tragic it was that this potentially strong and rich country was being wasted by civil war.

Because of mutual concerns about the deteriorating security situation, we stressed to Smith and the others the growing danger of an escalation of the war. Owen and I emphasized that our basic objective was to create a situation in which all Rhodesians, white and black, could participate in free and fair elections for a new government. In response, Smith and Muzorewa pressed us to support the internal settlement as satisfying our basic demands for democratic elections and majority rule. They were evasive about an all-parties conference, saying only that they would consider it. Later, after I returned to the United States, Muzorewa issued a statement ruling out negotiations with the Patriotic Front, and the Executive Council voted against attending an all-parties conference.

Driving back to the airport, our cars received a shower of eggs from a group of Sithole supporters. It did no damage but revealed the degree of heat that our visit had engendered.

As time went by, Muzorewa was becoming even more determined than Smith not to negotiate with the Patriotic Front. He expected to be leader of Zimbabwe by 1979 and was confident that once he acceded to power many of the rank-and-file guerrillas would choose peace rather than fight a black government. In early May, the Executive Council announced unconditional amnesty to all guerrillas who laid down their arms and returned to Rhodesia. I doubted Muzorewa would be receptive to negotiations with the Patriotic Front until he recognized that the Salisbury agreement would not produce international recognition.

The Debate Over Sanctions

With the emergence of the Rhodesian Executive Council and the scheduling of elections for majority rule, we were forced to turn much of our attention to fighting increasingly powerful congressional and public pressures to lift sanctions against Rhodesia. The struggle in Congress began in the spring and continued through a long hot summer. The proposal for an all-parties conference and the continuing talks in Africa enabled us to deflect all antisanctions efforts until July, when Senator Jesse Helms, the leader of the pro-Smith forces in the Senate, introduced legislation to suspend temporarily U.S. sanctions against Rhodesia as a demonstration of support for the internal settlement and the forthcoming elections. Helms' proposed measure received significant support. To many members of Congress, our unwillingness to endorse the Salisbury agreement suggested that we favored negotiating for the Patriotic Front the victory it could not win on the battlefield. Our steadfast refusal to accede to Mugabe and Nkomo's demands at Malta and Dar es Salaam should have convinced any fair-minded person of the fallacy of such a conclusion. However, Smith's supporters in Congress were painting a simplistic picture of an embattled multiracial, anti-Communist Executive Council under attack by a Communist-supported, radical Patriotic Front, and this was increasingly difficult to counter.

I told the Congress that we must remain neutral; that if we supported one side or the other there would be no chance for a negotiated settlement. Our course must be to insist that a solution involve all parties and be reached through free and fair elections open to all Rhodesians. Short of this, I argued, there would be no lasting peace. With the midterm elections approaching, many centrist and liberal senators and representatives, facing strong conservative challenges, did not want to hear complex explanations of our long-term strategy for a fair and durable solution in Rhodesia. It was evident that we would have to bend or face a mandated termination of sanctions.

Warren Christopher worked closely with the senators who supported our Africa policy to find a way to continue sanctions while not ruling out their termination if our basic tests of fairness were met. After intensive discussions, senators Jacob Javits and Clifford Case of the Senate Foreign Relations Committee devised an acceptable compromise. Sanctions would be lifted by December 31, 1978, if the president determined that the Rhodesian government had demonstrated its willingness to attend an all-parties conference and a new government had been installed following free, internationally supervised elections. (The Case-Javits amendment, which became law in September, gave us a sound basis for maintaining sanctions, at least until the internal elections were held.)

Our difficulty in turning back the Helms amendment and the necessity of accepting the Case-Javits substitute illustrated the growing difficulty of holding to a balanced African policy. As the sentiment of the country moved to the Right in angry frustration at the seemingly insoluble economic problems at home and growing turbulence abroad, there was an erosion of confidence in the administration's leadership. Within the executive branch there was also a perceptible hardening of attitudes.

The Smith-Nkomo Fiasco

In August, the Nkomo-Smith contacts exploded in our face. Luckily, we came out of the episode without irreparable damage.

During the summer the Rhodesian Executive Council continued to argue about attending an all-parties conference. Muzorewa and Sithole were keenly disappointed that the amnesty program attracted only a few liberation fighters and disheartened by the failure of their supporters in the United States to end sanctions. Smith, also disenchanted with the meager results to date of the internal settlement and facing demands from his own military to end the war while the Rhodesian forces were still able to cope with the guerrillas, was casting about for a new strategy to avoid an all-parties conference. We believed that some Rhodesian military leaders were seriously considering revoking Rhodesia's unilateral declaration of independence and asking the British to resume responsibility for the country. In response to Owen's probing, in late June, Smith asked for a meeting with Nkomo. Nkomo and President Kaunda of Zambia, who was close to Nkomo, expressed interest, and Owen conducted delicate and secret discussions with Smith, Kaunda, Nkomo, and the Nigerians to arrange a meeting in Zambia in August.

Although the Nigerians were brought into the discussions, the front line states, other than Zambia, were not to be made aware of the plans. I was deeply concerned about this decision, especially the exclusion of Nyerere. I stressed to the British my opinion that Nkomo and Kaunda's intention to proceed without Nyerere was a mistake.

According to reports I received, Nkomo insisted his only purpose in meeting Smith would be to work out a basis for a subsequent larger meeting that would include Mugabe. Tentative agreement was reached among the Africans involved that if the Smith-Nkomo discussions were fruitful, the Nigerians would attempt to persuade Mugabe to attend a second meeting with Smith to negotiate a new settlement to replace the Salisbury agreement. In great secrecy, Nkomo met Smith on August 14 in Zambia under the auspices of Kaunda and in the presence of Joseph Garba, the effective and talented Nigerian foreign minister. Owen cabled me that he understood Smith had promised to cede "full power" to Nkomo prior to elections. Owen's information was that Nkomo had responded that he must involve Mugabe and that Nigerian President Obasanjo would try to arrange that he enter the discussions later in the month. However, the planned second meeting involving Mugabe never took place.

Muzorewa and Sithole, seeing an opportunity to discredit Nkomo and anxious to block Smith from downgrading their roles in the internal settlement, leaked word of the August 14 meeting. When news of the meeting became known, the Nigerians and Zambians were embarrassed and Nyerere was outraged. Charges of betrayal, bad faith, and duplicity filled the air. I doubt that Smith ever intended to satisfy Nkomo's demand to negotiate the demise of the Salisbury agreement. Although he doubtless hoped Nkomo would join the internal settlement, Smith's more realistic aim probably was to play on Nkomo's and Mugabe's strong mutual dislike in the hope of driving a wedge between them. To restore his image, Nkomo became flamboyantly bellicose, boasting in September about ZAPU's shooting down a Rhodesian civilian airliner and the ghastly murder of survivors of the crash.

• • •

Paradoxically, the setbacks of August and September briefly revived the flickering prospects for an all-parties conference. The front line presidents, fearing fragmentation of the Patriotic Front, reiterated their support for an all-parties conference and endorsement of the Anglo-American proposal. Smith, with the Nkomo option gone and the internal settlement having failed to stop the fighting, began to look more seriously at how the Case-Javits amendment might be used to terminate sanctions and strengthen the Executive Council's position vis-à-vis the Patriotic Front. The diplomatic battleground again shifted to the United States.

On October 4, over vigorous African protests, we decided to permit the Executive Council, which had been invited by a number of conservative senators, to visit the United States. Had we refused to allow Smith and the others to come, their supporters in the Senate would have been in a much stronger position to launch a new attempt to terminate sanctions. If they came they might well discredit themselves. The hard political reality was that we were on the defensive regarding the internal settlement.

British Ambassador Peter Jay and I met Smith and Sithole in my office on October 9 for a very blunt exchange. I told Smith, who said his position was unchanged, that he and the other parties to the Salisbury agreement were heading for an all-out civil war. I urged him to consider attending an all-parties conference. He refused. Evidently he still believed he could make the Salisbury agreement work and defeat the Patriotic Front but needed time to win the struggle for public opinion in Britain and the United States.

One way to gain time was to appear to comply with the spirit, if not the precise letter, of the Case-Javits amendment. So, three days later, on October 12, brushing aside Muzorewa's objections, Smith told the Senate Foreign Relations Committee that the Executive Council would attend an "adequately prepared" all-parties conference. Subsequently, he confirmed this in a meeting with Under Secretary of State David Newsom. Muzorewa acquiesced on October 21. Smith's move shifted the burden to the Patriotic Front.

While the Executive Council was still in the United States, the Rhodesian Army launched large-scale attacks against guerrilla bases in Zambia and Mozambique, thereby assuring that the Patriotic Front would resist urging from the front line states to attend an all-parties conference. Playing into Smith's hands, Nkomo and Mugabe stated there could be no conference while they were under attack.

In mid-November, having been unable to complete negotiations on the independence constitution, the Executive Council postponed the holding of internal elections until April. This postponement gave us a few months' grace on the problem of sanctions.

In early December, British Prime Minister James Callaghan sent Sir Gledwyn Hughes as his personal emissary to the various Rhodesian parties to assess the prospects for a peace conference. Hughes found both sides intransigent on conditions for attending a conference, and uninterested even in discussing the substantive differences. Even before Hughes presented his report, it was obvious there was little hope of an all-parties meeting in the near future.

· · ·

On January 17, 1979, after receiving Hughes' negative assessment, Callaghan formally announced to the House of Commons that he had decided the necessary conditions for calling an all-parties conference did not exist. I agreed with this conclusion. It was urgent, however, that something be done to revive the negotiating process before the internal elections, which were just around the corner. Without some new strategy, we would soon face a showdown with Congress over sanctions and recognition of the new Rhodesian government. If we lost, the result would be a wider war and probable expansion of Soviet and Cuban influence.

Within the administration, and with the British, a searching reappraisal was begun. We clearly needed an approach that would take account of the changed situation in Rhodesia while enabling us to maintain our position that the internal settlement was deficient and would not bring peace. The Anglo-American proposal was no longer an adequate basis for defending our policy in Congress. The establishment of a black majority government in Salisbury after the April 20 elections, coupled with the Executive Council's October 1978 stated willingness to attend an all-parties conference, would give the opponents of sanctions grounds to assert that the internal settlement had fulfilled the requirements of the Case-Javits amendment. We faced a most difficult dilemma: To simply stand fast on the Anglo-American proposal and to fight to maintain sanctions would reinforce perceptions that we favored the Patriotic Front. But to recognize the internal settlement and to lift sanctions would identify us with a regime I was certain could neither end the war nor produce a stable government.

The elements of a more flexible approach, and one that would improve our support in Congress for maintaining sanctions, were developed in early April. We examined the following possibility: If after the April elections, the Rhodesian authorities would accept the principle of free, internationally supervised elections, and a new or significantly amended constitution, and if the Patriotic Front refused to negotiate on that basis, we would not oppose the lifting of sanctions by the Congress. On the other hand, if the Patriotic Front would agree to negotiations and impartial elections and the Rhodesian authorities refused to participate, we would declare our intention to maintain sanctions. If we followed this course, it would eliminate the perception that the Patriotic Front had a veto over our sanctions policy, and it would be a powerful message to Mugabe and Nkomo to come to terms with the changed realities within Rhodesia.

A critical factor in deciding future American strategy was the British national elections scheduled for early May. All serious political movement on the Rhodesian scene had stopped while the parties awaited their outcome. Our Policy Review Committee concluded that in anticipation of a presidential determination on sanctions under Case-Javits in June, we should make no outward change in our current policy until we could consult with the new government in London. It appeared that the Conservatives would replace the Labour government, and the Conservative attitude on Rhodesia appeared to differ sharply from that taken by the Labour party. Margaret Thatcher, the Conservative leader and probable new prime minister, reputedly favored recognition of the internal settlement, if the Rhodesian elections were certified free and fair by Conservative party observers, and an end to sanctions. If that were the result, it would be impossible to continue American sanctions.

The Rhodesian elections for the 72 black seats in the new 100-member Parliament ended on April 21, with an estimated 64 percent of the electorate participating. As expected, Bishop Muzorewa's African National Congress won a majority. Muzorewa would be the prime minister of the new state, to be called Zimbabwe-Rhodesia, when the government was installed on June 1. Despite complaints of irregularities by a disappointed

Sithole, the Conservative party observer mission reported that the elections were as free and fair as could be expected under the circumstances. Nonetheless, the Nigerians, the front line states, the Patriotic Front, and most African countries denounced the elections as a sham. On April 30 we, the British, and the French abstained on a UN Security Council resolution condemning the elections as illegal.

On May 3, Margaret Thatcher became the new prime minister and Lord Peter Carrington the new foreign secretary. Peter Carrington was a wise and experienced man who had previously served under a Conservative government in a number of key governmental positions, including those of First Lord of the Admiralty (secretary of the navy) and secretary of state for defense. I had first met Peter when he was First Lord and I was secretary of the army. I had a very high regard for him and was sure that he would be a strong and dynamic foreign secretary. Although I had not had a chance to talk to him about Rhodesia, David Owen had told me that Peter was generally supportive of the Labour party's policy concerning Rhodesia.

There was rejoicing in Salisbury, as Smith and Muzorewa anticipated radical changes in British policy and an end to Zimbabwe-Rhodesia's isolation. Salisbury's elation was premature. Prime Minister Thatcher made a number of positive statements about the internal settlement, but there were enough qualifications in what she and Carrington said to make us believe that their objective was to alter and broaden the Salisbury constitution in order to make it acceptable to the Patriotic Front. If so, this was a strategy we could support, so long as it led to fair elections open to all parties under impartial supervision.

I met Carrington in London on May 21 to discuss a number of foreign policy matters, particularly Zimbabwe-Rhodesia. Carrington explained that Prime Minister Thatcher's attitude was markedly different from her predecessor's. Her goal, he said, was to return Rhodesia to legality and international acceptability. He warned that she would not fight to continue sanctions when Parliament reviewed them in November. However, Carrington recognized that British decisions on Rhodesia would affect Britain's relations with us, black Africa, and the British Commonwealth, which was scheduled to have a heads of state meeting in August in Lusaka, Zambia.

I told Carrington that we, too, recognized that a major change had taken place in Rhodesia, and that the president was considering conditional acceptance of the April elections; for example, sanctions would be lifted if the Salisbury authorities took certain steps to overcome the deficiencies of the internal settlement. What we had in mind, I explained, was a revision of the Zimbabwe-Rhodesia constitution; progress toward an all-parties conference, without giving the Patriotic Front a veto over whether such a conference should occur; and elections under international supervision to ratify the amended constitution and choose a new government. I described frankly the political situation in Congress, namely that there was a majority in the Senate for ending sanctions, although I thought we still had enough support in the House to block sanction-lifting legislation for a while. I stressed, however, that the president had to take an evenhanded approach; while we were not going to let the Patriotic Front set our policy, neither were we going to accept the internal settlement as sufficient.

Although I made clear that our future approach had not yet been finally determined, Carrington was dismayed by the specific conditions we were considering as the price for terminating sanctions. I sensed that he wanted maximum flexibility over the next weeks to steer British policy in a moderate direction. Just before my meeting with Carrington I had received a message from my friend the dynamic Australian Foreign Minister Andrew Peacock, which he also sent to Carrington, stressing the importance of negotiations between the internal and external black nationalists. Peacock and his prime minister, Malcolm Fraser, were seriously concerned about the damage a confrontation between Britain and black Africa would do to the Commonwealth.

Carrington urged that we find a more general way to justify a presidential decision to maintain sanctions under the Case-Javits amendment. We wanted to help Carrington in his difficult task, consistent with our own political requirements, and I agreed that Dick Moose and Tony Lake, who had accompanied me, should discuss various options with Carrington's associates. Their discussion showed that the British hoped the president would keep sanctions under review without identifying specific preconditions for lifting them.

After the talks with Carrington I put two options, specific versus general conditions, to the president on May 30. Clearly, it would be more difficult to maintain sanctions if we did what Carrington wanted. Even so, I felt we would have a reasonable chance of defeating a sanctions-lifting bill in the House because of the strong support being given us by Congressman Stephen Solarz, the astute, hard-working chairman of the Africa Subcommittee of the Foreign Affairs Committee.

The president chose the option favored by Carrington. By not specifying the conditions that would satisfy our requirements for lifting sanctions, our task was made more difficult. The 1978 congressional elections had led to the defeat of several liberals, and the conservative mood in the country was deepening. The president risked a major and politically embarrassing defeat, but it was the best way to give the British vital maneuvering room and maintain pressure on both sides to negotiate a lasting solution. It was a courageous decision.

The president announced his decision not to terminate sanctions on June 7. I testified before the House Foreign Affairs Committee on June 12, explaining that while we recognized that progress had been made toward majority rule, the Salisbury government had failed to meet fully either of the Case-Javits conditions. I reminded the committee that even as the Executive Council was declaring its willingness in October 1978 to attend an all-parties conference, Rhodesian planes were bombing Patriotic Front camps in Zambia. I also pointed out that the April 20 elections were based on a constitution approved only by the white electorate and that reserved disproportionate authority to the white minority. I also stressed that ". . . no party should be allowed a veto over a fair political solution. No party will be allowed a veto over our own policies. We would give our full support to fair arrangements and to genuine efforts toward political accommodation, even if some parties refused to cooperate."

We were victorious in the House, thanks to the skillful leadership of Congressman Solarz in working out a compromise. The compromise set November 15, 1979, as the termination date for sanctions unless the president found this would not be in the national interest. The narrowness of the victory, however, made clear that time was running short. For the rest of the year we would have to fight continuously to prevent passage of legislation lifting sanctions before November 15.

With the election of the Conservative government in London, the American role in seeking a peaceful settlement of the Rhodesian conflict changed markedly. At the request of David Owen, we had been full partners with the British, not only in shaping strategy, but in face-to-face negotiations with the parties. Thatcher and Carrington had a quite different conception of the Anglo-American relationship regarding Rhodesia. They consulted closely with us as their diplomacy unfolded, but they clearly considered the main responsibility for a solution to be Britain's. We were fully prepared to step back and support the British in their leading role, but I emphasized to Carrington that we could not agree to merely changing the Salisbury constitution in the hope that the front line states would accept it and bring along the Patriotic Front. A revised constitution would be an extremely important step, but we remained committed to the basic principles that had underlain our policy from the outset—internationally supervised elections open to all parties, participation by all Rhodesians in the political process, and a lasting settlement.

The Breakthrough: Peace in Rhodesia

The credit for the final negotiation of Zimbabwe's independence properly belongs to the British, principally to the skillful diplomacy of Peter Carrington, and I shall only briefly summarize the key events. However, it is only proper to point out that the final settlement was fully consistent with the Anglo-American proposal. Further, in my judgment the successful resolution of the Rhodesia issue in the Lancaster House Conference would not have been possible without the substantial progress that had already been made with the Patriotic Front and the front line states prior to the British elections. For this, credit must go to David Owen and Jim Callaghan.

The breakthrough on Rhodesia came at the Commonwealth Conference in Lusaka in August 1979. Lord Carrington had carefully prepared the way by sending Lord David Harlech to Africa in June and July to prepare a report for Prime Minister Thatcher. Harlech's consultations led him to conclude that the front line states and Nigeria were ready to push the Patriotic Front into dealing with the regime in Salisbury, and that Muzorewa, having reluctantly accepted the fact that neither Britain nor the United States was prepared to recognize his government, was ready to consider changes in the Zimbabwe-Rhodesia constitution. Harlech favored a conference to amend the existing constitution, rather than negotiation of an entirely new settlement. Harlech's report had a major impact on Prime Minister Thatcher's decision to offer to convene a constitutional conference at Lancaster House in London. Until Carrington and Harlech persuaded Thatcher that continued negotiations were essential to protect Britain's African and Commonwealth interests, we and the British Foreign Office feared the Lusaka conference might blow up over Rhodesia.

We strongly supported Carrington's efforts in our discussions with a depressed and disappointed Muzorewa in mid-July. In consultations with the British, we were told that their aim was to develop a consensus among the parties before the Lusaka meeting. The consensus would support a constitutional conference with the Salisbury authorities on one side and the Patriotic Front on the other. I judged that Muzorewa would participate in the conference if he were convinced that international recognition and termination of sanctions lay at the end of the road.

At Lusaka, Prime Minister Thatcher and President Nyerere established a genuine rapport. In conceding that the Muzorewa government had to play a role in a settlement, Nyerere signaled an African willingness to accept the importance of the changes in Salisbury. For her part, Thatcher affirmed that Britain remained committed to establishing black majority rule before granting independence to Rhodesia, and that the existing constitution would have to be amended to remove the reserved white powers. Australian Prime Minister Malcolm Fraser also played a powerful role in moderating the differences and keeping the discussions focused on how to resolve the issues.

The evening of August 5, Thatcher, Nyerere, Kaunda, and Fraser reached agreement on a communiqué that spelled out the basis for a settlement. The heads of government declared that the aim must be genuine black majority rule, that the Salisbury constitution was defective in this respect, and that all parties must be involved if the conflict was to end. They agreed that a settlement must provide safeguards for minorities and that there must be free and fair elections under British authority and Commonwealth supervision. Britain undertook to invite the parties to a constitutional conference. Finally, implementation of a settlement would involve a cease-fire and an end to sanctions.

On August 14, after the Commonwealth Conference had ended, Carrington announced that Britain would invite the parties to attend a conference at Lancaster House in London to amend the Zimbabwe-Rhodesia constitution, arrange a cease-fire, and define the arrangements for elections. Muzorewa immediately accepted, and after a few days, Mugabe and Nkomo announced they would also attend. Carrington's strategy was to focus first on amending the constitution and only then to turn to the contentious problems of a cease-fire and the electoral arrangements. He wanted to keep the negotiations moving as rapidly as possible to build momentum and keep the parties from trying to wait each other out.

Although the United States did not participate, we were kept closely informed, and throughout the conference, we made our views known to the British and to the individual parties when necessary. We supported Carrington's strategy of postponing the problem of integrating the various forces into a national army until after a new government was elected, but we insisted that each side be treated equally in the cease-fire arrangements. The British were somewhat disposed to impose more stringent confinement restrictions on the liberation forces than on the Zimbabwe-Rhodesia Army. Our insistence that the same rules apply to all forces was a crucial element in Mugabe's willingness to accept a cease-fire and the concentration of ZANU military units under Commonwealth observation. Another contribution that was also important in gaining Nkomo's and Mugabe's acceptance of the British constitutional proposals was our promise to seek significant economic assistance from Congress for an independent Zimbabwe.

In late October, Carrington wisely proposed that during a short transition period all executive and legislative powers be placed in the hands of a British governor general, thus obviating the need for complicated balancing of power among the parties during this interval. Muzorewa responded favorably to the transition arrangements, but the Patriotic Front balked at leaving the Zimbabwe-Rhodesia Army and police intact under the authority of the British governor general. Carrington asked me to intervene with the front line to put pressure on Mugabe and Nkomo, which I did. One of our most important contributions throughout the Lancaster House Conference was to vouch for British sincerity and impartiality with the suspicious Africans. Throughout the Lancaster House negotiations the skillful work of our gifted ambassador in London, Kingman Brewster, and his assistant, Gibson Lanpher, was of the greatest importance in maintaining our contacts with all sides.

Negotiations on transition arrangements were completed in November along the lines of Carrington's proposal. They were modified to provide for more equal treatment of the two sides' military forces. Negotiations for a cease-fire began on November 22. Prior to that, we had a minor tactical difference with the British over the lifting of sanctions, which later became a rather serious irritant in our otherwise excellent collaboration with London.

One trying incident occurred in September when I received a call from Peter Carrington urging me to take steps with the Congress to recall two of Senator Jesse Helms' aides, John Carbaugh and James Lucier, from London immediately. Carrington said that they had been interfering in the Lancaster House negotiations and were making promises to Smith and Muzorewa on behalf of the U.S. Congress that were endangering the negotiations. I immediately went to Capitol Hill to meet with Frank Church, the chairman of the Senate Foreign Relations Committee, and with Jack Javits, the ranking minority member. I told them of my conversation with Carrington and asked that they meet promptly with Helms and secure the return of Carbaugh and Lucier forthwith. They wanted me to obtain a written communication from Carrington about the two aides to present to Helms. I agreed to do so. When I reached Carrington by telephone, to my surprise he said that for domestic political reasons it would be impossible for him to give us a written statement that would become public. I reported this to Church and Javits and urged them to press Helms anyway, as the situation was too important and too urgent to tolerate this outrageous activity. I met subsequently with Helms, who said he would be willing to call his aides back immediately and discipline them if they had been acting improperly. Unfortunately, we were unable to get from the British the hard facts necessary to take disciplinary actions.

On November 14, pursuant to the Solarz compromise legislation, the president made a finding under the Case-Javits amendment that it would not be in the national interest to remove sanctions prior to the arrival of a British governor general in Salisbury and the beginning of the process leading to impartial elections. The British had preferred, in order to increase pressure on the Patriotic Front, that we simply declare our intention to terminate sanctions as soon as the governor general arrived. The president and I believed, however, that this would have been inconsistent with our long-standing position that the commencement of a process for free and fair elections was a precondition for ending sanctions. Our decision was warmly received by the front line states and the Patriotic Front, which were still worried that if sanctions were terminated before elections, the Rhodesian authorities would find excuses to postpone or avoid them.

The cease-fire negotiations ran into serious trouble in early December, threatening to bring down the whole agreement. In a daring move to prevent a breakdown, Carrington dispatched Lord Christopher Soames to Salisbury on December 12 to assume control as the British governor general, even though an agreement had not yet been reached on the cease-fire. The British were convinced that the Patriotic Front was stalling in order to strengthen their forces in Zimbabwe-Rhodesia, and feared that Salisbury would launch strikes into Zambia and Mozambique. Carrington wanted us to join them in lifting sanctions immediately in order to strengthen Soames' hand.

We told the British that the dispatch of the governor general did not meet our requirements for terminating sanctions. With some grumbling about our "self-created" difficulties, the British arranged that upon Soames' arrival the election process would begin. An election commission was established, voter registration procedures were promulgated, and assurances were given that all parties could campaign freely. With these steps taken, the president issued an executive order on December 16 terminating American sanctions against Rhodesia. On December 21, the parties signed the Lancaster House agreement. Elections were conducted on February 27–29, 1980, culminating, much to the surprise of many and particularly the South Africans, in the designation of Robert Mugabe as the first prime minister of Zimbabwe on March 11. Zimbabwe became formally independent on April 18.

After all the bitterness and rivalry of the preceding several years, perhaps the most remarkable and encouraging aspect of the final settlement was the statesmanship displayed by the African leaders. Muzorewa agreed to step down as prime minister and test his political strength in free elections. Mugabe and Nkomo swallowed their repugnance of Smith and the Rhodesian Front and agreed to reserve twenty seats in the new legislature for the white minority. They also agreed that the independence army would be an amalgamation of the Rhodesian and liberation forces. In fact, the first commander of the Zimbabwe National Army was the former chief of the Rhodesian armed forces. Joshua Nkomo accepted Mugabe's electoral triumph and participated as a junior partner in the governing coalition. Nkomo, the grand old man of the Zimbabwe nationalist movement, had long aspired to the mantle that had fallen on Mugabe's shoulders, yet he refused to subject his country to further strife. The spirit of reconciliation extended as well to Mugabe, who surprised friends and critics alike by his moderation toward the white minority and the existing economic and political structure of Zimbabwe. Shortly before independence, Mugabe expressed appreciation to the United States for its role in bringing peace to Zimbabwe and said he looked to us as an ally rather than an opponent. This auspicious beginning raised hopes for a stable, moderate, nonracial society in Zimbabwe. As time has moved on, however, the situation in Zimbabwe has become more fragile. Nkomo and Mugabe have had a falling out and sporadic terrorist events have taken place. I continue to hope and believe that despite these difficulties, the bright promise for Zimbabwe's future will not be lost.

NAMIBIA

After the stalemate at the end of 1977, the South Africans told us that while they did not rule out further discussions of the contact group's October proposal, they had decided to schedule Namibian elections for June 1978. Although the contact group was holding together well, the British and the French seemed tempted to go along with an internal settlement. President Carter was irritated at SWAPO rigidity and also intermittently showed interest in an internal settlement to gain Namibian independence. Dick Moose and Don McHenry argued for renewed contact group activism to overcome the differences between South Africa and SWAPO, and urged me to persuade Owen and the others to press ahead for another round of talks with the parties on our settlement initiative.

The contact group agreed that our central problem was South Africa's ability to raise a steady stream of new issues. On the other hand, SWAPO's pretensions to a preferred position prior to elections was a serious obstacle. We were confident that if the front line states were satisfied we could attain genuine independence for Namibia, they would in the end persuade Nujoma and SWAPO to accept a reasonable agreement.

The contact group decided to invite South African and SWAPO representatives to New York for "proximity talks" in February 1978. To add political weight it was agreed the Western foreign ministers would act as intermediaries between the two sides. In order to sharpen the focus of the proximity talks, the contact group put its proposals in writing, despite the risk that texts would lead to semantic haggling.

The main features of the revised proposal were: a phased reduction of South African forces to 1,500 men who would be confined to designated bases under UN observation; withdrawal of South African troops would not begin until a cease-fire policed by UN military forces had taken place; the cease-fire would be followed by a four-month period of political campaigning, supervised by the UN special representative, which would culminate in UN-supervised elections for a constituent assembly. This new body would have the responsibility for drafting a constitution for Namibia in time for full independence by December 31, 1978. Both sides would release all political prisoners and allow them to return to Namibia.

The proximity talks began in New York on February 11. Pik Botha was waiting to see whether SWAPO would prove inflexible, as it had before. The front line states had succeeded, however, in persuading Sam Nujoma to moderate his uncompromising stance, and Nujoma withdrew his demand that the authority of the UN special representative be superior to that of the South African-appointed administrator general. Even more significant, Nujoma finally agreed to allow 1,500 South African troops to remain in Namibia through the elections, although he insisted that SWAPO units be allowed to concentrate at designated points, under UN surveillance, on the same basis as the South African forces. Nujoma also demanded that South African troops be confined to a single base in southern Namibia, away from the main center of SWAPO strength in Ovamboland. He proposed that the UN Transition Assistance Group (UNTAG) number no fewer than 1,000 observers and that the peace-keeping force be at least 5,000 strong, far more than South Africa was likely to accept. Nujoma also declared that SWAPO's demand that Walvis Bay be included in an independent Namibia was nonnegotiable.

The South Africans made a dramatic countermove. They abruptly withdrew Foreign Minister Botha from the proximity talks after West German Foreign Minister Hans-Dietrich Genscher bluntly warned him that Western support for further sanctions would be unavoidable if Pretoria was not forthcoming.

In March, shortly after the New York proximity talks, the black leader of the Democratic Turnhalle Alliance was assassinated, provoking outrage in Namibia and South Africa. Those South Africans who were pressing for the Turnhalle process were greatly strengthened. At that moment, it seemed increasingly likely that in both Namibia and Rhodesia the white citizens would choose settlements based on internal black political groups rather than internationally supervised elections. The dangers of this growing tendency underlined the urgency of continuing the contact group initiative, however poor the prospects for early progress. After further discussions in New York with South African and SWAPO representatives, we decided the group should go to South Africa with a "clarified" proposal. All of us in the Western five agreed that we could not tolerate further delays. After the next round, the group would put its settlement proposal into final shape and seek a Security Council mandate for UN involvement.

The contact group presented its proposal to the South Africans in late March so that it could be tabled in the Security Council on April 10. The proposed compromises were: (1) The South African-appointed administrator general would retain control of the Namibian police, who would be accompanied in their duties by UN observers; (2) the UN special representative would determine the size of the monitoring group and peacekeeping force he would need to accomplish his mission; South Africa would be consulted on the national composition of the UN force to ensure that it was not drawn primarily from nations avowedly sympathetic to SWAPO; (3) the contact group would take into account the wishes of the constituent assembly chosen during the UN-supervised elections if it asked that South African forces remain in Namibia after the elections; and (4) South African forces could be concentrated at two bases in northern Namibia, rather than in the south as SWAPO had demanded.

In this proposal the contact group had made a major effort to meet South African concerns, and it seemed that we had made a substantial stride forward. In mid-April Vorster agreed in principle to our proposal, subject to further discussions of certain points, as well as to our stated intention to declare to SWAPO that the issue of Walvis Bay would be negotiated only after independence. Even though Walvis Bay was not mentioned in our proposal, I thought the latter point would be important in persuading Nujoma that we had made an advance on our earlier suggestion to "defer" the issue. Since we were not going to "clarify" our proposal again, we presented the contact group plan to the Security Council.

In conditionally accepting our proposal, Vorster and Botha had clearly indicated they would not delay establishment of an interim government while waiting for us to satisfy SWAPO on the UN role and the location of South African troops. Therefore, it was important that SWAPO not delay the process, especially after South Africa announced its formal acceptance on April 25. We urged Nujoma not to react prematurely to our plan or to South Africa's acceptance, and the front line states and Nigeria backed us up. The Western five intended to stand firm.

Don McHenry and I met with Sam Nujoma and Nigerian Foreign Minister Joseph Garba on April 27 to underscore this point. Nujoma was angry because he felt we had unfairly boxed SWAPO in by presenting the proposal to the Security Council and getting South Africa to accept it before obtaining SWAPO's full concurrence. Before meeting us he had told the front line states that SWAPO could not accept the arrangements we had just negotiated with Vorster and Botha. The front line states refused to support his stand. Nujoma told me that while he would not reject the proposal, he intended to seek substantive changes.

Nujoma argued that we had, in effect, conceded the predominance of the administrator general over the UN special representative by giving him control over the Namibian police. He asserted that in return for SWAPO's concession in agreeing to the residual 1,500-man South African force, those troops must be confined to a single base in southern Namibia. If these forces were merely a face-saving gesture to Vorster, he asked, why was it necessary for any to be in Ovamboland? Finally, Nujoma said that the Western five must support SWAPO's position on Walvis Bay and include it in the contact group proposal.

Garba tried to stop Nujoma's effort to force new negotiations with the contact group. He made it unmistakably clear that the key black African states wanted SWAPO to help us place South Africa in a position where it would have to say yes or no to a fair Western proposal. Nujoma was surprised at Garba's intervention, and for a short while I thought Nigerian and front line pressure might carry the day. But in the end Nujoma released a long list of demands for changes in the contact group proposal.

On May 4, while the front line states and Nigeria were bringing further pressure to bear on Nujoma, South Africa launched a large-scale strike on a SWAPO base at Cassinga, deep inside Angola, asserting that SWAPO was massing for a new offensive. The Angolans, who were making an exceptional effort to dissuade Nujoma from blocking the contract group proposal, were furious. Nujoma immediately broke off the talks in New York and returned to Angola. SWAPO declared that as far as it was concerned, the negotiations were off indefinitely. The Western five supported a Security Council resolution condemning the raid, but the larger question on my mind was whether South Africa was sincere about trying to negotiate an acceptable settlement. Given the size of the attack and the prior intelligence work and military planning required, it seemed that Pretoria must have been preparing the raid even as Vorster was agreeing to our clarified proposal. Andy Young, Don McHenry, and Dick Moose were thoroughly skeptical of Pretoria's intentions.

Julius Nyerere had managed to get the front line states and SWAPO to agree to a summit in Luanda in June. I hoped he could use that meeting with Nujoma to reduce SWAPO's objections to the contract group proposal to manageable proportions. I did not want to risk substantive changes that would require more negotiations with the South Africans, nor was I willing to alter our position on excluding Walvis Bay. However, to meet SWAPO halfway, I thought the Western five could build on Tanzania's suggestion of a Security Council resolution supporting SWAPO's historical, geographical, and ethnic claim to Walvis Bay, although not endorsing its legal position, which my legal adviser, Herb Hansell, said was not juridically defensible. We would ask the front line states to lean heavily on Nujoma to accept the overall position we had worked out.

As we were working on this approach, Vorster announced on May 24 in Cape Town that South Africa would begin preparing for a December election of a Namibian constituent assembly. These elections, he said, would be held regardless of what SWAPO's position on the Western settlement plan might be. At this point it looked as though the negotiations might collapse. However, after the Luanda summit, Nyerere urged us not to give up hope, saying that despite Nujoma's lengthy list of demands, SWAPO's only irreducible problems were the location of South African troops during the preelection period and the status of Walvis Bay. He advised us to try again to persuade the South Africans to concentrate their forces in the south, away from Ovamboland and SWAPO's camps in southern Angola. Nyerere had persuaded SWAPO to meet in Luanda with the contact group to try to resolve the differences on Walvis Bay and the location of the South African troops. He was determined not to see the group fail, as he was convinced that our proposal was fair.

In a meeting in Paris on June 14, the foreign ministers of the group agreed that we would continue our effort. We agreed that the most we would do was to urge the South Africans to concentrate their forces at one rather than two bases. On June 22 South Africa refused this request, claiming that it amounted to a "substantive" revision of our proposal. The South Africans also warned us that the negotiations would be terminated if we changed our position on Walvis Bay.

The contact group meeting with SWAPO and the front line states in Luanda was a turning point. Since the views of Angola, Nujoma's principal supporter, would be critical, McHenry visited Luanda on June 22, prior to the meeting with SWAPO. He stressed the benefits an international settlement that removed South African forces from Namibia would confer on Angola. I followed this up with a personal letter to the Angolan foreign minister.

In Luanda, McHenry and his Western colleagues took a strong stand that we could not accept SWAPO's demand that the issue of Walvis Bay be resolved in the basic settlement, but would support the Tanzanian idea of a Security Council resolution calling for post-independence negotiations and affirming that Walvis Bay should be an integral part of Namibia. As for SWAPO's concerns about South African bases, we would not agree to reopen this point with South Africa but were prepared to urge Waldheim to augment the peacekeeping force to satisfy SWAPO that it was large enough to monitor all South African bases adequately. The front line states supported our position. Indeed, the Angolans insisted that the meeting not adjourn until SWAPO agreed to the group's proposal.

Encouraged, I reported to the president on July 12 that McHenry and the contact group had scored a breakthrough. Under heavy front line pressure, SWAPO agreed to our position on both the issues of troop location and Walvis Bay, on the condition that we support a Security Council resolution affirming that Walvis Bay should be reintegrated into Namibia after future negotiations. When we informed the South Africans of the Luanda breakthrough, they were extremely upset, claiming that the contact group had aligned itself with SWAPO after persuading South Africa to agree that Walvis Bay should be the subject of post-independence negotiations. SWAPO continued to complain about certain aspects of the settlement proposal, but I believed the Angolans and Tanzanians could keep Nujoma from backsliding. We seemed close to success.

On July 27 the Security Council endorsed the contact group's plan and the resolution on Walvis Bay. Four days later the South African cabinet decided to accept our settlement proposal conditionally, reserving the right to reject any arrangement relating to the UN role and restating South Africa's position on Walvis Bay. The way was at last clear for Waldheim to send his special representative to Windhoek to prepare a preliminary report on how the United Nations would implement its supervisory and monitoring role. This report was to be completed in

August, and it seemed possible that our goal of UN-supervised elections for Namibian independence by year's end could be reached.

•   •   •

On August 6, UN Special Representative Ahtisaari and a staff of experts arrived in Windhoek to begin work. They met with the appropriate South African administrative, police, and military authorities to assess their personnel needs. Based on Ahtisaari's findings, Waldheim advised the Security Council late that month that UNTAG would require 1,500 civilian administrative, elections, health, and other technical professionals to supervise the work of the administrator general, and nearly 400 police and 7,500 UN troops to monitor the security provisions of the settlement. The South Africans reacted sharply to the size of the peacekeeping force, having envisioned a force of no more than one or two thousand men.

Contact group efforts in September to alleviate South Africa's concerns were unsuccessful, and it refused to accept Waldheim's report. The South Africans variously argued that the UN was partial to SWAPO, that South Africa could not agree to anything without the concurrence of the participants in the Turnhalle conference, and that Nujoma's acceptance of the Western proposal and Waldheim's report were ambiguous and untrustworthy. Another difficulty involved the crosscurrents of Afrikaaner politics. On September 20, Vorster formally rejected Waldheim's recommendations for implementing the UN's role under the contact group's settlement plan, stating that they went far beyond what South Africa had accepted in negotiations with us. That day he also announced his resignation as prime minister, ostensibly because of poor health but also because of his involvement in a political scandal. His deepening political problems had set off a power struggle in the ruling Nationalist party.

At the beginning of September Pik Botha abruptly broke off discussions on Namibia in New York and returned to South Africa to make an unsuccessful bid to succeed Vorster. While in Pretoria, Botha told the contact group that the decision to hold internal elections in Namibia was nonnegotiable. He also said, however, that the constituent assembly would be able to make its own decisions about the future, thus leaving the door open for the Turnhalle Alliance itself to agree to an international settlement open to SWAPO and to further elections under UN supervision.

On September 28, Defense Minister Pieter W. Botha, a determined opponent of concessions on Namibia, was named by the Nationalist party leadership to succeed Vorster.

On September 29, the Security Council adopted Resolution 435, which endorsed Waldheim's report on Namibia and authorized him to make arrangements for the transition and elections. The African and nonaligned states made clear that they expected the Western five to support sanctions if South African compliance was not immediately forthcoming. We were now faced with a decision we had hoped to avoid. Should the United States support mandatory economic sanctions against South Africa and call upon our Western partners to fulfill the declaration we had made jointly in Cape Town in April 1977?

My advisers strongly urged that we seek a decision from the president that the United States be prepared to support and initiate sanctions if necessary. Failure to do so under existing circumstances, they warned, could destroy our successful efforts to rebuild the American position in black Africa. They recommended that we seek approval of carefully limited punitive measures of precisely stated duration and aimed directly at South African cooperation on Namibia.

After the Security Council's action on September 29, my contact group colleagues and I agreed that subject to approval by our governments, we would go to Pretoria in October to meet with the new prime minister. Before that meeting, our staffs would meet to work on our plans for those talks and what we should do afterward in the event of failure.

The president convened the National Security Council on October 6 to review our entire southern Africa policy, including the question of sanctions. He agreed that, failing positive moves by South Africa, the time had come for direct pressure. As planned, he directed that I, together with the other foreign ministers of the group, should go to Pretoria in mid-October. During that visit, I would seek a private meeting with Prime Minister Botha to give him a personal handwritten letter from the president. In the letter, Carter would offer to receive the prime minister in Washington for discussions on how South Africa's international standing could be improved, providing Pretoria reversed its negative September 20 decision. As a further inducement, the foreign ministers would offer to seek SWAPO's agreement to schedule UN-supervised elections for the spring of 1979 and to reduce the UN peacekeeping force to 3,500 combat troops plus 1,500 support personnel.

If Botha failed to respond positively to these proposals, the United States would be prepared to support sanctions, but only after we assessed the results of the Pretoria talks. Moreover, in order to avoid a confrontational atmosphere, we would not announce our intention to proceed with sanctions in the absence of a satisfactory response.

The Western five foreign ministers met in New York and agreed to assemble a group of experts to prepare a range of actions we could take if events went badly. Don McHenry and his contact group colleagues worked virtually without stop for two days, drawing up a list of possible sanctions and assessing the impact of each sanction on South Africa and on us, so that we could judge their effectiveness as well as their costs. None of the participants favored a total UN economic embargo, and the British in particular doubted that any measures the group's political leadership would be willing to adopt would have much effect on South Africa. Those steps that would have the greatest impact on the South Africans would, obviously, cause us significant economic loss, especially Britain. The actions that were most likely to be adopted dealt primarily with restrictions on landing rights for South African civil aircraft and Pretoria's access to export financing from Western sources.

We made the long journey to Pretoria in mid-October, stopping en route at Ascension Island for refueling. Ascension Island, which resembled the landscape of the moon, had been the staging area for the rescue operation in Stanleyville in the mid-1960s and was to serve a similar function for the British fleet in the Falklands War of 1982. Unfortunately, our mission was not to enjoy the same degree of success as those two.

On October 16–18 the five foreign ministers met with Prime Minister Botha and Pik Botha in Pretoria for extremely difficult talks. My colleagues and I decided to keep the meeting at the political level to minimize the chances of a stalemate over details, and we therefore excluded staff from most of the talks. This caused a good deal of concern among the experts, who feared that the foreign ministers, in their anxiety to keep the negotiating process alive and to avoid sanctions, would not press the South Africans hard enough. However, the shared judgment of the foreign ministers was that at stake was the entire Western strategy of patiently forcing South Africa to move step by step toward a settlement by resolving its legitimate concerns. It was essential that we convince the new South African government to continue working toward an acceptable settlement. The alternative was a bitter confrontation with Pretoria, collapse of the negotiations, and intensification of the guerrilla war.

The Pretoria discussions covered the whole array of outstanding issues arising from Waldheim's report, but the central problem was South Africa's intention to ignore Resolution 435 and proceed with the December internal elections in Namibia. Neither President Carter's letter, which I delivered privately to Prime Minister Botha after informing my colleagues of its contents, nor the concerted arguments of the five foreign ministers budged him from his determination to hold the Namibian internal elections as scheduled and to establish an interim administration based on them. We indicated that the Western governments would support elections within seven months of South Africa's agreement to implement Waldheim's plan, even though SWAPO would want a longer interval. We also emphasized that none of the five governments recognized SWAPO as more than one of the several Namibian political parties, and said we would insist that it compete in elections on an equal basis with the others.

Prime Minister Botha would go no farther than to agree that after the December elections South Africa would seek to persuade the newly elected leaders to participate in new elections under UN supervision.

After a quick consultation with leaders of the DTA, he informed us that talks between the administrator general, the authorities elected in December, and Special Representative Ahtisaari could begin on the modalities of an election, including a firm date.

At the conclusion of the Pretoria talks, we and the South Africans issued a communiqué containing Prime Minister Botha's agreement to these points. In a unilateral statement, the South Africans declared they would not withdraw their forces without a total cease-fire. Finally, they demanded that elections under UN supervision be held on a fixed date regardless of whether a cease-fire existed and whether South African troops had been withdrawn. We countered with our own statement which declared that if violence threatened to delay the elections, the matter should be brought promptly to the Security Council and to the Western five so that they could take appropriate action. We emphasized that no party could unilaterally delay holding the UN-supervised elections.

After Pretoria, the focus of negotiations shifted to the United Nations. The SWAPO representatives in New York rejected the Pretoria proposals and demanded that the Security Council vote mandatory sanctions. On October 31, SWAPO's demand was seconded by the key African states. Young and McHenry, supported by the contact group, managed to persuade the Africans to postpone presentation of a harshly worded resolution declaring the internal elections null and void and warning of sanctions if they were conducted. On November 13, the Africans insisted on putting the resolution to a vote in the Security Council, forcing the Western five to abstain. Our position was that the contact group's proposal was still alive. To demonstrate the administration's seriousness, President Carter had signed legislation on November 10 restricting the Export-Import Bank in financing trade with South Africa.

Western credibility with the African states was damaged by this vote. On November 25, Pretoria informed the United Nations of its intention to proceed with the December elections in Namibia. In New York on November 27, I warned Pik Botha that South Africa should not assume we were going to continue to resist attempts to impose mandatory sanctions if South Africa failed to comply with UN Resolution 435. He insisted that South Africa was still willing to cooperate, providing its concerns about Waldheim's report were resolved. I stressed that South Africa had to show some sign of progress if we were to avoid another sanctions resolution in the Security Council.

Two days later the president also met with Botha. Carter criticized the South Africans for having got themselves into a box with their insistence on going ahead with the December elections, and said we wanted to see what could be done to preserve the negotiating process. He emphasized that South Africa must indicate at once a willingness to implement the UN plan. Failure to do so, he warned, would inevitably lead to sanctions.

Carter reiterated his willingness to meet Prime Minister Pieter W. Botha, but not until South Africa indicated its readiness to comply with Resolution 435. He underlined the growing risks of increased Soviet involvement if the negotiating process failed.

Our sharp warnings evidently had some impact on the South Africans. In a meeting with Waldheim on November 29, Foreign Minister Pik Botha declared Pretoria would "recommend strongly" to the winners of the December elections that they accept Resolution 435 and agree to new elections seven months after the introduction of UNTAG. In addition, Botha said, South Africa would retain full authority in Namibia after the elections. Thus, the December victors would not form an interim government. Botha insisted this was as far as South Africa would go.

As Botha had indicated, on December 22, after the Democratic Turnhalle Alliance won nearly all of the seats in the constituent assembly elections, the new Namibian leaders announced agreement "in principle" to UN-supervised elections. They declared, however, that the constituent assembly could not agree to a reduction in the South African military presence prior to a complete cease-fire. Under these circumstances, David Owen and I agreed that we should not let the existence of the constituent assembly become a reason to apply sanctions or abandon our settlement plan, and I urged Waldheim to treat the South African response as a positive reply and to continue preparations for UN participation. I was determined that we should leave no stone unturned in preventing the negotiations from collapsing, leaving no option to the Africans but intensified conflict and greater dependence on Soviet and Cuban military assistance.

Pressing the UN Plan

UN Secretary-General Waldheim agreed to press ahead with the UN plan for implementing Namibian independence, although he was understandably disheartened by the events of November and December. However, under continuing pressure from Angola and Zambia, SWAPO decided in early January 1979 to stand by its acceptance of the UN plan. That same month Waldheim sent Special Representative Ahtisaari to consult with Foreign Minister Botha. Once again, the South Africans appeared to agree to the main elements of the UN role, but raised new issues that prevented implementation. South Africa rejected SWAPO's demand that its units within Namibia be concentrated in designated locations. The strange positions of the two sides can be explained by SWAPO's desire to hold a piece of Namibian land, however small, even at the risk of exposing its forces to South Africa. Conversely, rather than allow SWAPO to gain in negotiations what it could not win in the war, South Africa refused to agree that SWAPO units should go to assigned

locations during a cease-fire despite the obvious military advantages this
would give Pretoria should fighting resume. Botha also declared that
before a cease-fire could begin and UNTAG arrive, SWAPO must accept
UN monitoring of its bases in Angola and Zambia. SWAPO instantly
and vehemently rejected international monitoring, although it declared
its readiness to have Angolan and Zambian forces keep its bases under
observation.

Foreign Minister Pik Botha agreed to come to New York on March 16,
and at my urging was accompanied by a delegation from the Turnhalle
parties. I assured him they would have the same access to the contact
group as SWAPO.

These talks failed to resolve the remaining issues, which, from the
South Africans' side at least, centered on some form of international
observation of SWAPO bases in Angola and Zambia. We persuaded the
latter governments to agree that the UN could establish liaison offices in
their countries to coordinate Angolan and Zambian monitoring of
SWAPO bases. SWAPO agreed to UN liaison officers in Angola and
Zambia, but the South Africans rejected this as an inadequate substitute
for UNTAG forces in those countries. Moreover, although SWAPO continued to insist that its forces must remain in Namibia in bases during a
cease-fire, Foreign Minister Botha told us South Africa would not agree
to this, even if the guerrilla forces were monitored by the UN.

After the March proximity talks, we continued to pursue the idea of
stronger Angolan and Zambian assurances that they would effectively
police the SWAPO bases in their countries, in cooperation with UN
liaison officers. The South Africans steadfastly insisted they were bound
by the views of the internal parties, who feared SWAPO infiltration during a cease-fire unless adequately monitored by neutral forces. Despite
these problems, the South Africans maintained that they and their Turnhalle associates wished to resolve the remaining differences so that the
UN plan could be implemented.

On May 14, the South African administrator general proclaimed the
constituent assembly to be the Namibian national assembly, able to leg-
islate everything short of independence. At the same time, the South
Africans indicated their willingness to work out an international settlement. In July, we suggested a demilitarized zone along the Namibia-
Angola border, patrolled by UNTAG personnel, as an alternative to
international monitoring of SWAPO external bases. But after the unproductive exchanges of February and March 1979, the negotiations, although continuing for the remainder of the Carter administration, were
essentially stalemated.

·   ·   ·

Unfortunately, we did not succeed in bringing about Namibian independence. Nevertheless, I believe that the establishment of a negotiating

framework for the Namibian question was important for U.S. and Western interests. The existence of the process, the determined efforts of the contact group to move it forward, and the real, if incomplete, progress that it produced were essential to rectify the damage done to Western relations with sub-Saharan Africa over prior years. Without the Namibia negotiating process—together with the Zimbabwe settlement—the United States would have no workable strategy for improving its relations with black Africa and blocking the spread of Soviet and Cuban influence in southern Africa.

Considering the backsliding that followed September 1979, it would be easy to conclude that South Africa is not serious about negotiating Namibian independence, particularly under international supervision. Although I am still uncertain whether South Africa is serious about reaching a negotiated solution, I have not given up hope that it may prefer a solution that would gain international acceptance, end the drain on South African lives and resources, and afford it a chance to end its isolation.

For the future, we should press ahead on the basis of Resolution 435 and the contact group plan. At the present stage of negotiations, it is self-defeating to seek to condition implementation of a settlement, as is being done, on Angola's commitment to terminate the Cuban presence prior to the departure of South African troops. The removal of Cuban forces will come in the natural course of events after South African withdrawal, but not before.

We must not give up. A way must be found to convince South Africa that it can accord full independence and majority rule to Namibia without jeopardizing the security of South Africa or the safety of the Namibian whites and non-SWAPO blacks.

Change was and is sweeping through Africa, and those who identify with it will be able to influence its direction. If it is the Soviet Union that is perceived as a supporter of African aspirations, Moscow will be able to exploit change for its own purposes. If the United States stands for democratic, peaceful, and just change, we will be able to help shape and guide the change in ways consistent with our values and interests. That is the essence of what the Carter administration sought to do in Namibia and Zimbabwe.

14

THE SHAH FALTERS

THE CARTER ADMINISTRATION'S basic approach to our relations with Iran was similar to those of other post-World War II administrations. Relations between the two countries had grown closer during the Nixon-Ford years as military cooperation increased. Iran was seen as the major force for stability in the oil-rich Persian Gulf. Its military strength ensured Western access to gulf oil and served as a barrier to Soviet expansion. Its influence in the Organization of Petroleum Exporting Countries (OPEC) made it important to the American economy. Although our assessment of the importance of Iran and our approach to our relations with it were in some ways similar to those of prior administrations, there would be marked differences in the way in which we conducted our bilateral relations, particularly as regards arms sales and human rights.

In January 1977, Iran seemed to be an increasingly powerful nation on the road to modernization under the authoritarian rule of Shah Mohammed Reza Pahlavi. Since his famous "White Revolution" of the 1960s, the shah had sought to modernize Iran, and Presidents Kennedy and Johnson had supported him in his program of social and economic reform. There had been progress despite opposition from the fundamentalist Islamic clergy and the landed class who felt their interests were threatened. But economic growth and a facade of Western institutions obscured the narrowness of the shah's political base and the deep internal problems of a traditionalist society in transition. The economic changes brought about by the White Revolution had not been accompanied by real political change.

In the early 1970s, a complex interplay of factors began to divert the shah from his experiment. The modernization of the 1960s had significant political, economic, and military elements, but in the 1970s the shah concentrated almost single-mindedly on industrial development and a military buildup of abnormal proportions. His decision to build Iran into a regional military and economic giant arose in part from doubts about America's post-Vietnam will in security matters. The shah's determination that Iran must assume more responsibility in the gulf coincided with the adoption of the "Nixon Doctrine" which envisioned key regional states as surrogates for American military power in preserving order and blocking Soviet inroads. In 1972 President Nixon determined that Iran should be permitted to acquire virtually any American conventional weaponry the shah deemed necessary. Iran was seen as the logical replacement for receding British power in the Persian Gulf. A well-armed, pro-Western Iran would make an American military presence unnecessary, and Vietnam had rendered it politically unfeasible. Few foresaw the dramatic rise in oil revenues that would enable Iran to purchase huge quantities of very costly military equipment.

Iran welcomed the opportunity to play a role as regional great power and policeman of the gulf. The shah had a strong sense of the past glory of Persia and resented his country's former subjugation by foreign powers. He was acutely aware of Iran's vulnerability in a region of immense oil wealth and political instability. Moreover, as he often pointed out, Iran lay directly in the path of historic Russian expansionism. Building up Iran's military strength suited his aspirations and met his security concerns.

The shah recognized that Iran's greatest natural resource, petroleum, would be exhausted well before the end of the century. By making maximum use of the petroleum bonanza, he could finance a modern and economically diversified industrial economy capable of sustaining a prosperous and secure Iran after the oil was gone. Although the reforming impulse of the 1960s never entirely disappeared from his mind, the shah became absorbed by the challenges of creating a modern economy.

The Nixon and Ford administrations placed great emphasis on building up the shah as a regional guarantor of stability, and on trying to persuade him to moderate his support for higher oil prices. They became less attentive to political development as a necessary accompaniment to industrialization. There was little effort to consult with Iran about its military spending and defense needs and their relationship to social and economic development. Without constant American interest and encouragement, the impetus of the 1960s toward political reform waned.

During this period, the U.S.-Iranian relationship was not without significant problems. Despite the regional security cooperation, there was considerable U.S. concern in Congress in 1975 and 1976 about the pace and scope of the Iranian military buildup. The shah's ambitions appeared to go beyond ensuring Iran's security and maintaining stability in the Persian Gulf. The Ford administration concluded, however, that the basic policy of supporting Iran's political and military role in the region was sound.

The other major strain arose when, prompted by U.S. legislation requiring greater attention to human rights violations by recipients of

American military and economic assistance, the Ford administration began to express apprehension about the shah's harsh treatment of political dissidents. Because the Nixon and Ford administrations had in large part deferred to the shah's sensitivities about contacts with his political opponents, American knowledge of the nature of the opposition was sketchy. The dissenters appeared to consist of Westernized secular politicians (grouped around the old social democratic National Front coalition), religious fundamentalists, leftist radical students and intellectuals, and the small Tudeh (Communist) party. But the opposition did not appear to pose an immediate threat to the shah.

• • •

Carter, Brown, Brzezinski, and I recognized the importance of Iran in Persian Gulf security matters. Nevertheless, we were also determined to hew to our position on human rights and to our goal of restraining the sale of American weapons. Congress's growing concern about human rights was increasingly reflected in legislative restraints on the transfer of military equipment to Third World nations. It was clear that it would be hard to maintain public support for our strategic relationship with Iran if the shah failed to pay more attention to human rights. I was aware that the shah would be anxious about our policies on these two matters. Neither the president nor I, however, believed that the maintenance of a stable relationship with Iran precluded encouragement of improvement in its human rights policy and the development of a practical method of identifying and meeting its military needs.

Quite clearly, Carter's emphasis on human rights in the election campaign and the early days of the administration disturbed some of our allies and friends whose human rights records were poor. In major speeches in 1977, Warren Christopher and I sought to explain the universality of our concern. Neither the president nor I wished to use human rights as an ideological weapon, but rather as a basic element of our foreign policy.

We applauded and supported the measures the shah was beginning to take to improve human rights; he already had begun to curb SAVAK (the Iranian intelligence and security service) in its use of extralegal measures to control subversion, and he was working to strengthen judicial and police procedures for dealing with political opponents. He also appeared to be contemplating modest political liberalization in an attempt to reach the more moderate elements of the secular opposition, thus bringing them into association with the imperial regime. These measures, while overdue, were important, and they received our support.

Human rights did become a source of some discord between the shah and the administration, although a good deal less than has been suggested. Consistent with our convictions and with legislative requirements, we continued to protest excesses of Iranian security forces. The shah himself was eager for Western, especially American, approval and support. Contrasting our commitment to human rights with the attitude of the previous administration, the shah apparently worried that many in the Carter administration, particularly President Carter, considered him a tyrant. The shah also was disturbed by the hostile treatment he received in the American press and from some members of Congress. Although a sophisticated observer of the United States, he doubtless found it difficult to believe that the Carter administration itself was not behind a good deal of the harsh criticism of him. His concerns were exacerbated when, after mid-1977, the new U.S. ambassador, William Sullivan, began to question some long-held basic Iranian tenets, especially the economic and social ramifications of Iran's enormous expenditures on arms. An outstanding career diplomat, Sullivan, with our backing, was determined to improve our knowledge of the Iranian political scene, which had lagged since the 1960s.

The shah's anxieties about the political implications of our human rights policy were intensified by his awareness that we were carefully reviewing all aspects of our arms transfer policy. The Persian Gulf was a particular focus of attention. Iran alone accounted for about half of the $8 billion in annual American military sales. The shah was fearful that we would change our arms supply relationship in ways that might be harmful to Iran's foreign policy and its security interests.

The shah's concerns were based on a misunderstanding of our views about U.S.-Iranian relations. We decided early on that it was in our national interest to support the shah so he could continue to play a constructive role in regional affairs. The shah had provided important economic assistance to countries in the area and had been helpful in reducing tensions in Southwest Asia. Iranian forces had aided the pro-Western ruler of Oman to defeat an insurgency backed by the leftist regime in Aden. Furthermore, Iran was a reliable supplier of oil to the West, and its exports were critical to our NATO allies and Japan. The shah had refused to join the 1973 Arab oil embargo or to use oil as a political weapon. He was also Israel's primary external source of oil. At the same time, however, the shah was a strong advocate of higher OPEC oil prices since he needed the revenues to finance Iran's purchase of military equipment and industrial modernization. Otherwise, there was considerable harmony between the shah's policies and our regional interests.

· · ·

There had been no American ambassador in Iran since Richard Helms left at the end of the Ford administration. The president felt, therefore, that I should visit Tehran to explain the president's views to the shah and put our human rights and arms sales policies in proper perspective.

As I prepared to leave for Tehran in early May of 1977, some urgent decisions needed to be made on pending Iranian requests for arms, primarily expensive advanced aircraft. The president decided to honor prior sales commitments to Iran, but he wanted me to make clear to the shah that consistent with our objective of reducing U.S. arms sales, we must develop a better way of determining Iran's future military needs and how they could best be met.

I met the shah on May 13 in the Niavaran Palace in Tehran. He was an intelligent, quiet, yet imperious man. Though he was seemingly decisive, I had a vague feeling that he was insecure. I opened the meeting by delivering a presidential invitation to visit Washington in November. The shah was delighted. After an exchange of pleasantries we turned to business. The shah sketched the strategic situation in the region. His primary worries, he said, centered on Soviet ambitions in Africa and the Middle East. He was concerned that Moscow, facing eventual energy shortages, sought to control the oil resources of the Middle East. We discussed strategies for containing such action and the shah's plans in this regard. I also explained our plan for denying the Soviets opportunities to increase their influence by working with the regional parties to help bring about solutions to the threatening conflicts in the Middle East and southern Africa. In this connection, we talked at length about U.S. plans for reconvening the Geneva Middle East Peace Conference. The shah warmly endorsed our approach and promised to do all he could to support a just settlement of the Arab-Israeli dispute.

I emphasized that we wanted to continue our military supply relationship with Iran, and I informed the shah that the president had decided to go ahead with the pending sale of 160 F-16 advanced fighter aircraft, despite the serious political problems this would pose with Congress. We would also, I told him, seek congressional approval of his request for the sophisticated and costly airborne warning and control (AWACS) aircraft. The shah was relieved and did not focus adequately on my admonition that we must put our sales of arms to Iran on a more orderly basis. I warned him that we almost certainly would not buy for our air force the type of F-18 aircraft that he wanted, thus ruling out the sale of F-18 aircraft to Iran. He was unperturbed, but emphasized the importance of regional air superiority and requested an additional 140 F-16 fighter aircraft beyond the 160 we had already agreed to deliver. I told him we would take his request under consideration.

Turning to the most sensitive topic, I pointed out that human rights were not only an important part of the American tradition, reflecting our nation's origin and values, but also internationally recognized principles enshrined in the Universal Declaration of Human Rights and the UN Charter. I stressed their importance as a key element of our foreign policy. I emphasized that the president was committed to reaffirming the primacy of human rights as a national goal. I noted that our attention to this issue applied to all nations. We were encouraged by the steps Iran recently had taken to improve the treatment of prisoners, I said, and welcomed the shah's intention to permit visits by international human rights organizations to verify the improvements. The shah responded by tracing his policies back to Cyrus the Great and sought to defend the Iranian human rights record. He said that his regime was under attack from within by Communists and assorted fellow travelers and that there were limits on how far he could go in restraining his security forces. He warned that if Iran were to slip into civil strife, only the Soviet Union would stand to gain. He had no objection to our human rights policy, he said, as long as it was a question of general principle and not directed at him or did not threaten his country's security.

I noted the shah's familiarity with international issues far afield from Iran. More striking was his resigned air about matters that depended on his personal decision. Later, Sullivan and other Americans who knew him confirmed my impression that the shah had a strong fatalistic streak.

Upon my return to Washington, President Carter issued Presidential Decision Memorandum 13 (PD-13) declaring that arms transfers would henceforth be used as an *exceptional* instrument of U.S. foreign policy. In addition, a dollar ceiling would be imposed on worldwide sales, exempting only our NATO allies, Australia, New Zealand, Japan, and Israel. We did not mention Iran. Announcement of this new policy rekindled the shah's fears that we did not value our relationship with Iran. Ambassador Ardeshir Zahedi complained to me that the exclusion of Iran from the list of exempted countries showed that the president considered Iran to be of no significance. In reply I drew Zahedi's attention to the provision of PD-13 which said that we would give special consideration to friendly countries that "must depend on advanced weaponry to offset quantitative and other disadvantages in order to maintain a regional balance." I asked him to reassure the shah that the president was indeed committed within limits to meet Iran's special needs. Zahedi agreed to relay these assurances and said he thought they would remove any misunderstandings.

· · ·

On July 7, the president formally notified Congress of his intention to sell Iran seven AWACS aircraft (containing some of the most advanced electronics equipment available to the U.S. Air Force). The subsequent debate in Congress and the administration's handling of this controversial issue became a major test in convincing the shah that the president was serious about continuing a special security relationship with him.

An intensive U.S. Air Force study in the fall of 1976 had concluded that seven to nine AWACS would give Iran an adequate air defense system against any regional threat short of a Soviet attack. From a military point of view, the value of the AWACS in strengthening Iran's security was clearly established. Most senators and congressmen accepted in principle the importance of the U.S.-Iran security relationship, although a vocal minority regarded the shah as a brutal dictator who should not be given any U.S. support. The great cost, over $1.2 billion, and the sophisticated technology of the AWACS united many normally friendly members of Congress with the critics in challenging the sale. The debate on Capitol Hill centered on several concerns: congressional protests at the size of the sale on the heels of PD-13; the risk of compromising AWACS' sensitive equipment; the necessity of keeping a large number of Americans in Iran to train the Iranians to operate and maintain these planes; and the question of Iran's political stability after the shah.

Former senator John Culver, a good friend, a marvelous advocate, and a fine legislator, led the attack on the AWACS sale. More than anything else, it was his blunt criticisms that convinced me we had underestimated the depth of congressional concern and the strength of the opposition. Quite soon after we had submitted the sale to Congress for review, I realized that we were facing a possible defeat.

The concerns raised by Culver and other opponents had been studied thoroughly in drawing up the terms of the sale. In testimony before the Congress, we explained our view that the AWACS aircraft would fill an important defense requirement and would strengthen our relations with Iran at a time when we were trying to persuade the shah to moderate increases in oil prices, which were causing major dislocations in the international economy. After a difficult three weeks, it became painfully clear that we were fighting a losing battle. We faced almost certain defeat unless we could find some way to meet congressional objections. A way out was provided by Senator Hubert Humphrey, chairman of a key subcommittee of the Foreign Relations Committee. I had known the senator for many years and admired and liked him greatly. He was a wise and skillful legislator with a large generous heart. I had turned to him often over the years for advice and counsel. Never was he too busy to drop what he was doing and help, whether it was night or day. When he died in 1978 the Senate lost a magnificent leader and a great American. Humphrey suggested that we withdraw the proposed sale and, after further consultations with the shah, resubmit it with a number of assurances that could win over enough supporters.

On July 28, we withdrew the proposal from Congress temporarily in order to negotiate additional assurances with the shah and to prepare for round two. The shah regarded the additional security precautions as humiliating, although in reality they were largely cosmetic, and he threatened to cancel his request. He eventually agreed to the new arrangements so that the package could be resubmitted in September, but he continued to smolder at the attacks on him and his regime in Congress and the American press.

Even with the new assurances, the second round was extremely difficult. Senate opponents staked their case primarily on human rights and
the risk of loss or compromise of highly sensitive communications and
cryptological equipment. The strength of the Senate opponents forced
us to concentrate on the House of Representatives to prevent passage of
a concurrent resolution disapproving the sale. Only Carter's continuous
personal intervention through meetings with the House leadership and
his repeated telephone calls to key congressmen enabled us to get the
sale through. The effect of this summer-long fight was, perversely, to
shake the shah's confidence in the United States as a dependable ally.
He missed the more open access to U.S. military equipment he had
enjoyed in the early 1970s, and he resented the public criticism.

•   •   •

The shah's state visit to Washington was scheduled for November
15–16, a little over a month after the AWACS sale cleared the Congress.
While it was expected that the president and the shah would have a *tour
d'horizon* befitting the heads of two powerful nations, we had three concrete objectives:

- to convince the shah of the president's firm commitment to the U.S.-
  Iranian special relationship;
- to secure the shah's agreement to a systematic arrangement for pro-
  jecting Iran's defense needs and our ability to meet them; and
- to elicit a commitment from the shah that he would take a moderate
  and sympathetic position on oil prices at the December OPEC meeting.

The bruising AWACS battle had shown how important it was to avoid
such debates in the future. The shah was still pressing his request for 140
additional F-16 aircraft and other major items of military equipment. We
had to make him understand that the administration must take into
account domestic political realities. Our task was to achieve a realistic
understanding with him without reviving his perennial doubts.

The shah arrived at the White House on November 15. Unruly crowds
of both hostile and friendly demonstrators set up a clamor outside the
gates. During the welcoming ceremony on the White House lawn, a
scuffle broke between the two groups gathered on the Ellipse to the south
of the White House lawn. The fight was ultimately broken up with tear
gas. Clouds of gas drifted over the small group of dignitaries assembled
to hear the brief remarks of the two leaders. As the television cameras
rolled, the president, the shah, their wives, and the onlooking officials
coughed, daubed at their eyes with handkerchiefs, and hastened into the
White House to escape the stinging fumes. These demonstrations, after
several years of relative quiet among the large Iranian student population

in the United States, perhaps foreshadowed the resurgent opposition to the shah that was to dominate the following year in Iran. In hindsight, some analysts of the revolution were to call attention to these demonstrations as one of the early signs of the ferment that was to produce the revolution.

Despite the president's embarrassment about the tear gas incident, our discussions in the cabinet room went well. As was the custom, the shah first gave his views on a broad range of global issues. He was a disciple of the "grand design" school of interpretation of Soviet actions in Africa, the Middle East, and elsewhere. I did not share his belief in such a carefully worked out design for Moscow's adventurism, believing that it was founded more on capitalizing on targets of opportunity. We all agreed the most sensible and effective means of coping with the Soviets was to remain militarily strong while working to remove the conflicts on which Soviet influence thrived. Carter assured the shah that we were maintaining our own military strength and were treating the Soviets warily. The president said that he hoped the Soviets would recognize our mutual interests in limiting the competition, and he explained our approach of closing off Soviet opportunities by supporting peaceful change in southern Africa and a settlement of the Arab-Israeli conflict.

Carter stressed the punishing impact of increased oil prices on the industrial economies, especially Europe, and pressed the shah to support a price freeze at the December OPEC meeting. The shah concurred that the Western economies were hurting and that in the long run this was bad for Iran. He agreed to urge OPEC to "give Western nations a break," and said he would work for a price freeze. He correctly pointed out that this was only a palliative, and that some longer term plans were needed to deal with the energy crisis. He spoke of his concern about international financial stability because of the vast sums of money that were passing into the hands of some oil producers who, he believed, did not know how to manage it for the benefit of the world economy.

Carter, recounting the difficulty of the AWACS fight, explained that managing the U.S.-Iranian arms supply relationship would be easier if Iran would reduce its arms requests. He suggested that the two countries should jointly look at Iran's long-term defense procurement plans. The shah responded that his requests were based on a careful calculation of Iran's requirements. He insisted that 140 F-16s and 70 F-14s were necessary to complete his air defense plans. Reluctantly, the president agreed to consult with Congress, but he warned the shah not to underestimate the difficulty of gaining congressional approval of another large aircraft sale so soon after the narrow AWACS victory. Carter emphasized repeatedly the importance of closer cooperation to avoid damaging debates in the Congress. The shah promised to have his military leaders prepare a list of Iran's projected equipment needs to help our planning.

The shah left Washington encouraged by his conversations with the president, and we received from the embassy in Tehran glowing reports of his new mood of confidence and satisfaction.

• • •

President Carter paid a brief visit to the shah in Tehran on December 31 and January 1, 1978, during transit between Europe and India. As he had indicated in November, the shah presented Carter with a staggering military shopping list totaling more than $10 billion worth of items ranging from warships to radios. It was during this visit that Carter made his extemporaneous New Year's toast to Iran as an island of stability. At the time, it seemed just the usual effusiveness typical of such occasions, and certainly not markedly inconsistent with the prevailing intelligence and academic estimates about the internal situation in Iran. The president's words would come back to haunt us during the Iranian crisis.

On our return to Washington, defense experts began an intensive review of the shah's shopping list, the external threats to Iranian security, and the process by which the two countries might best consult on Iran's defense needs. It soon became clear that most of the military and foreign policy professionals, both in the State Department and the NSC staff, were strongly opposed to questioning the shah's military equipment requests. Despite this resistance, an excellent analysis of Iran's security situation and defense needs was completed under the direction of Leslie Gelb and his staff in the State Department's Politico-Military Bureau (PM).

I had hoped this study could become the basis for an objective American evaluation of the shah's requests, and that future arms sales decisions could be made in the light of our own assessment of Iran's defense needs. As it was, we were almost entirely dependent on the shah's unilateral judgments about his force requirements. There was little agreement, though, even within State, on how to proceed. Everyone accepted the need to manage sales more rationally, but there was no consensus on how to respond to the shah's December requests or how to structure the mechanism for U.S.-Iranian consultations. Almost everyone agreed that Iran should not be exempted from the PD-13 constraints on arms sales, yet most believed it would be very difficult for us to tell the shah what his own military needs were. Several argued that with careful phasing the shah's requests could be met without unduly distorting our global military assistance program or compromising the PD-13 ceiling on the dollar value of arms transfers. A few thought we should use the requested sale as leverage to induce the shah to move faster in improving human rights.

Gelb and Ambassador Sullivan, who was also participating in the discussions, suggested a plan to establish a joint consultation arrangement that would keep discussions in a military-to-military channel. There would be ongoing technical discussions between the American Military

Assistance Advisory Group in Tehran and the Iranian military, but under the overall supervision of our ambassador. In this way we would inject needed policy oversight into the arms supply relationship while avoiding a perception in the shah's mind that we were altering or downgrading the basic security relationship. This solution was considerably less than the broad consultations on Iran's defense policy and posture that I wanted, but under different circumstances it could have been a first step toward a better mechanism for managing arms sales.

• • •

In the first half of 1978, sporadic demonstrations in Iran grew more frequent. Inflation, corruption, repression, and a declining economy appeared to be the underlying causes of the protests. However, the magnet that drew the dissidents together was the religious opposition to the shah. In 1963, the shah had crushed an opposition movement led by Ayatollah Ruhollah Khomeini, the ultraconservative leader of the Shi'ite Islamic sect, who was fiercely dedicated to the overthrow of the Pahlavi dynasty. The shah had the ayatollah exiled to Turkey and later to Iraq. In January 1978, in Qom, the main Islamic teaching center, police fired on religious demonstrators who were angered by an attack on Khomeini in the government-controlled press. Several people were killed in the Qom riots, including some members of the clergy.

More protests soon followed. Thus began a series of events that gathered force until they became a tidal wave sweeping away the monarchy.

Excessive use of force by the police played into the hands of the mullahs (religious leaders), who were demanding that Khomeini be allowed to return to Iran. As protests escalated to demonstrations and rioting, the poorly trained police continued to overreact. This produced a lengthening list of "martyrs." Because of the Shi'ite practice of commemorating martyrs forty days after their deaths, the violence tended to peak in forty-day cycles. Increasingly, the demonstrations took on a xenophobic, anti-Western, anti-American, and anti-Semitic character. I was sufficiently disturbed at the intensity and diverse makeup of the anti-regime demonstrations to report to President Carter on May 10 that the incidents amounted "to the most serious anti-Shah activities in Iran since 1963."

The shah faced a serious dilemma in trying to maintain control. The more forcefully his police suppressed disorder, the stronger became the mullahs' ability to arouse new protests. The shah concluded that engaging the urban middle class in the political process was the best way to separate the secular social democratic opposition from the religious fundamentalists and the radical leftists whose aims were antithetical to the more moderate, nonestablishment politicians. The shah refused either to halt the political liberalization measures he had adopted in 1977 or to crack down ruthlessly on the opposition.

While in Washington for an arms policy review in June, Sullivan told us the shah faced a long, rough period ahead, but that he should be able to weather the storm until the Iranian economy improved and his liberalization program began to draw off some of the opposition. Sullivan was uneasy about the growing power of the clergy, however, and wanted to establish contacts with the religious opposition. He said he had been warned against this by the imperial court. It was vital that we know what was going on, and I told him that he should meet with low-level figures to find out more about the nature of the opposition.

Relative calm was restored in Iran in June and July, and Sullivan returned to the United States on home leave. Over the summer, the State Department, the CIA, and the Defense Department intensified their analyses of the Iranian situation, and Bill Sullivan vigorously stepped up the embassy's reporting on the opposition. The intelligence community was still relatively confident that the demonstrations did not pose a substantial threat to the shah, although some of my colleagues were becoming increasingly concerned about the long-term implications if the widespread unrest was not soon brought under control.

It was becoming clear that the antiregime demonstrations were being orchestrated by the fundamentalist wing of the clerics, whose dominant figure was the charismatic Ayatollah Khomeini. So rapidly was his stature growing that even nationalist politicians who deeply opposed the idea of an obscurantist Islamic republic were drawn increasingly into the orbit of his influence. Many, including middle-of-the-road clerics who disliked the extremism of Khomeini, and who would have been content with a constitutional monarchy and a parliamentary democracy, were forced to echo Khomeini's demand for the abolition of the Pahlavi dynasty in order to maintain their credibility as opponents of the autocracy.

The shah's promise in early August of open parliamentary elections in June 1979 did not spark the hoped-for shift of secular political leaders toward the regime, nor did further measures to ease press censorship and restrictions on freedom of speech. The shah was under intense pressure from military hawks and civilian advisers alike to discontinue his policy of political liberalization and crush the demonstrations with unrestrained force. The shah insisted, however, that liberalization was the only means of dividing the opposition and broadening his political base. At the same time, he felt it important to use maximum restraint in maintaining public order if he was to break the cycles of violence. Although the State Department's Human Rights Bureau objected, we approved a request in late August for the immediate shipment of crowd-control equipment, including tear gas.

It would not be correct to assume from the foregoing that prior to September the situation in Iran was a subject of daily concern to the president or me. We were reassured by the judgment of the ambassador, the experts in the State Department, the CIA, and other agencies and foreign governments that even though he might be required to make political compromises that would dilute his power, the shah was not in serious danger. In August, the president and I were preoccupied with the forthcoming Camp David summit. Immediately after Camp David, I had to go to the Middle East. Much of October and November was spent on the Egyptian-Israeli negotiations at Blair House. We were making a strenuous effort to conclude the SALT negotiations and advance the normalization negotiations with China. Nevertheless, by the beginning of September, I had become worried by the violence of the demonstrations in Iran and the failure of the shah's liberalization measures to win over the secular opposition.

• • •

While the president and all of his top foreign policy and defense advisers were involved in the Camp David summit, a crisis was reached in Iran. On September 8, the shah declared martial law in a number of cities that had been centers of unrest. In clashes between the military and the demonstrators, a large number of demonstrators were killed, presaging a new spate of demonstrations and strikes. From all reports, the shah was depressed by his inability to restore order and uncertain what he should do next. Warren Christopher called me at Camp David to recommend urgently that the president talk with the shah. I urged the president to do so, and Carter telephoned him on September 10 to reaffirm our support and to find out how the shah planned to restore order. Sullivan reported that Carter's call had temporarily rallied the shah, but his vacillation quickly reappeared.

While I was still at Camp David, Christopher also met with Ambassador Zahedi, who had just returned from Tehran. Warren reaffirmed our support and urged moderation in enforcing martial law. Zahedi blamed the Communists for the increasingly well-organized character of the demonstrations and raised the absurd suspicion that we were plotting with the opposition to overthrow the shah. Christopher emphatically denied this ugly allegation. We had no solid information on Soviet involvement in the demonstrations, although the Communists doubtless were attempting to take advantage of the turmoil. It appeared that the snowballing unrest in Iran was not the product of Soviet or local Communist manipulation, but a massive outpouring of pent-up economic, political, religious, and social forces. The shah's failing self-confidence was the main reason I hesitated to recommend that Sullivan get in touch with the most important opposition leaders at this stage. The president and I feared, under the circumstances, that such conversations might further weaken the shah's confidence and feed his fears that we were attempting to position ourselves with a successor regime.

At the beginning of October the new Iranian foreign minister, Amir Khosrow Afshar, told me in New York that the shah was determined to press ahead with his political liberalization program in order to undercut the secular opposition and divide it from Khomeini. I assured him that we strongly supported this effort. He alluded to continued rumblings in Iran that we were supporting the opposition. I scotched this childish rumor, explaining that our embassy was in contact with secondary figures in the opposition in order to better understand what was happening.

Later in October, the shah announced a number of highly visible development projects in housing, education, and agriculture, and granted a number of generous wage settlements to stop a rash of strikes in key sectors of the economy. The concessions to the strikers boomeranged, however, leading to more strikes, including a strike in the critical oil industry. The shah informed us that in order to finance these measures, he was curbing his ambitious nuclear reactor construction program and was cancelling major military purchases, including the pending request for F-16 and F-14 aircraft. We agreed that these steps were prudent.

•   •   •

When I returned from SALT talks in Moscow at the end of October, the shah was at a crossroads. Martial law had failed to stop the demonstrations and strikes, which were reducing the economy to near chaos. Oil production had fallen from 6 million to little more than 1 million barrels per day, causing the government to lose most of its foreign exchange earnings. The October high-visibility measures and veiled hints to moderate opposition politicians that they might have a role in a new government evoked no response. The shah was still unwilling to give unequivocal assurances to the opposition that he would share enough of his political power to make it worth the risk of associating themselves with the regime. An attempt to silence Khomeini by persuading the Iraqi government to expel him backfired. The ayatollah went to Paris, where he gathered around him an entourage of religious and political supporters and made full use of the excellent communications facilities available in Paris to control the demonstrations in Iran. On October 24, after Sharif-Emani's conciliatory measures failed, the shah told Sullivan and British Ambassador Anthony Parsons that he was considering either a military government or a civilian coalition cabinet, including some members of the opposition. Although he did not put it directly, clearly the shah wanted to know if we would support a military government.

In the State Department, some of my colleagues told me that in their view the events of September and October meant the shah's autocratic reign was over. They said that the only questions now were how much power the shah must relinquish, and to whom. They saw two primary contenders, the generals and the secular political opposition, although they recognized that antiregime forces ranging across the political spectrum were drawing closer to the Islamic clergy. They made a strong case against U.S. support for a military government, pointing out that Ambassador Sullivan was opposed to increased military involvement in the political arena. The Iranian military, they argued, had been discredited by recent events and had shown no capacity to govern or to rally public support. Still, they saw the shah as the only figure capable of leading a transition to a new regime, although one in which his power would be markedly reduced. They further believed we should encourage the shah to persevere in his efforts to foster political liberalization.

These arguments were powerful and persuasive, but in my judgment we were operating with too limited an understanding of Iranian political realities to give such far-reaching advice to the shah at this time. I felt that the shah, who had been on the throne more than thirty-seven years, was the best interpreter of the political possibilities open to him, but none of us was fully aware of the extent to which the shah had lost touch with Iranian politics. In retrospect, I have wondered whether the shah had received some further diagnosis from his doctors about the progress of the cancer that later killed him, which may have increased his fatalism and passivity.

The candid views of my advisers were, of course, known to the White House as well. Zbig concluded that the State Department had given up on the shah and was "soft" on a military solution to the crisis. In a situation quite different from the close and harmonious cooperation on the Middle East—although some of the same people were involved in both—an estrangement grew up between the White House and my key advisers.

In December I learned from George Ball, who had come to Washington at our request to conduct a special review of the situation in Iran, that Brzezinski had opened up his own direct channels to Tehran and had carried on discussions with Ardeshir Zahedi without the knowledge of anyone in the State Department. This, I believe, contributed to the shah's confusion about where he stood and to his inability to decide what to do. I immediately went to see Brzezinski. I told him that I had heard from an impeccable source that he was communicating directly with the Iranians and that this was intolerable. He denied the accusation. I told him that I believed otherwise and that I wished him to come with me to see the president. The president met with us and I told him what I had learned. He asked Zbig if this was true. Zbig denied it. The president then asked that he be supplied with copies of all communications between the White House and Tehran. That was the last I heard of the matter, but the back-channel communications stopped. This was, to say the least, a painful experience.

On November 3, the shah called the White House to ask the president's views on a military government or an attempt to form a coalition government. We were faced with an agonizing decision. It was clear that the shah's strength was disintegrating. We decided that we should send a message instructing Sullivan to go to the shah and assure him that we supported him "without reservation" in the crisis. We would not attempt to tell the shah how to deal with his own internal political problems, but would stress our confidence in his judgment about the composition of a new government and assure him that we would back whatever decision he made. For Sullivan's personal guidance, we added that if the shah's decision was to turn to the military we would strongly prefer a military government with the shah to one without him. Without his unifying presence as a focus for its loyalty, the army might rapidly splinter into warring factions.

Shortly after this message was dispatched, events in Iran reached a climax. As a tremendous wave of violence shook Tehran, the British embassy and a number of other buildings were burned. On November 6, in a limited resort to the military option, the shah replaced Prime Minister Sharif-Emani with General Reza Gholam Azhari, chief of staff of the armed forces. The Azhari government, however, was military in name only, with most ministries headed by civilians. Azhari moved immediately to try to restore order. At the same time he sought to conciliate the opposition by arresting several former government and SAVAK officials. He also instituted measures against government corruption. Simultaneously the shah announced an investigation into the finances of the royal family.

On November 9, Sullivan sent a message that brought home how far the political situation had disintegrated. While he believed we had no real alternative but to continue supporting the shah, Sullivan urged that we begin "thinking the unthinkable." What should the United States do if the shah and the military proved unable to govern and the regime collapsed? Sullivan's message corroborated the analysis of some State Department advisers, but caused consternation in the White House. There was a brooding fear that any action that implied we did not expect the shah to survive would contribute to his paralysis of will and stimulate the opposition to increased violence.

In mid-November, our State Department advisers urged a clearer policy to protect U.S. interests as best we could in the face of certain and imminent change. By that point, several were beginning to doubt that the shah could remain even as a figurehead in a parliamentary democracy. They judged the likely outcome of the crisis to be either a military junta with the shah as a symbol of legitimacy or a military coup without him. An alternative was a civilian government, supported by the military, in an Islamic republic. A final possibility was a complete collapse and resulting chaos. Most believed that we should immediately begin positioning ourselves to adjust to an Iran without the shah. In addition, echoing arguments urged with increasing force by Sullivan, they suggested that if the shah could not bring himself to deal with the moderate opposition, we should seek an accommodation between the military, as the strongest pro-Western force, and the Islamic clergy, as the dominant political force in the country.

Pressures from the White House to encourage the shah to use the army to smash the opposition were becoming intense. I shared the judgment of Sullivan and my other advisers on Iran that such a move would be wrong, because it was likely to lead to disintegration of the army, which was more than 50 percent conscript. Still, I did not believe that we should abandon the shah or promote an arrangement between the generals and the religious hard-liners while there was still a chance that the shah might succeed in reaching an agreement with responsible members of the opposition on an orderly transition to a constitutional monarchy. On November 22 I cabled Sullivan that we must offer the shah our frank advice in helping him try to put together a new civilian government. I emphasized again that we could not make the decisions for the shah. Sullivan was to assure him we were making crystal clear to the opposition that the United States continued to support him. I told Sullivan to make sure that the embassy staff underlined this fact in any contacts they had with the opposition.

Sullivan said that he understood our frustration and concern, but that we must recognize that the shah had decided he must remain in the background while his supporters attempted to bring the moderate opposition into a coalition government. Sullivan said the shah wanted to convince the moderate secular politicians that he had abandoned his imperial role and was prepared to be a constitutional monarch. Sullivan added that the shah simply did not believe our statements of support.

As I have mentioned, in early December, at the suggestion of Treasury Secretary Michael Blumenthal, who has just returned from Tehran, the president asked George Ball, former undersecretary of state during the Kennedy and Johnson administrations, a wise and good friend of mine, to undertake an objective review of the situation in Iran and make prompt recommendations on a U.S. course of action. In addition to his own widely based sources, Ball drew heavily on Hal Saunders and our staff for briefings. I was confident he would offer realistic, sensible advice.

On December 13, the Special Coordinating Committee met to hear Ball's conclusions. I was in the Middle East and Warren Christopher represented the State Department. Ball said that the shah was finished if he did not act immediately to cede real authority to a civilian government. Supported by Christopher, Ball recommended that we try to convince the shah to make a dramatic public announcement that he was turning over power to a civilian government, retaining only his position as head of the armed forces. Brzezinski and Brown argued that we should not move so fast or try to give the shah such detailed advice.

Brzezinski urged Carter not to accept Ball's recommendations. As it turned out, the president did not accept the advice of either Brzezinski,

Ball, or the State Department. Instead, he determined that we should not be so blunt with the shah, and he directed that we first assess the shah's attitude before pushing him to relinquish his political power. Carter also directed that we get the shah's approval before talking to moderate opposition leaders about a compromise solution. The president clearly recognized, however, that we had passed the point of unreservedly supporting the shah, and he was beginning to think in terms of advising him to compromise.

As waves of demonstrations shook Iran during the first half of December, coinciding with the Shi'ite holy month of Moharram, which is characterized by mourning and extreme emotion, the shah continued to vacillate about how much power he should give the secular opposition if they agreed to join a coalition. On December 13, Sullivan reported that he had had a "long somber session" with the shah about discussions with opposition political leaders. The shah had talked with National Front politicians Shapour Bakhtiar and Gholam Hossein Sadiqi, and planned to meet Karim Sanjabi, leader of the National Front. Adding that he had little hope for these conversations, the shah outlined three options: to keep trying to form a civilian coalition government; to "surrender" to the opposition by leaving the country after appointing a regency council; or to form a military junta that would apply an iron fist policy of harsh repression. The shah said that he feared the iron fist could lead to disintegration of the army and Iran.

In Washington, Sullivan's report laid bare deep differences between Brzezinski and me as we contemplated the possibility of the fall of the shah. Zbig appeared to see a military coup, preferably in support of the shah, as the only hope of protecting American interests. I strongly advocated a political solution with the shah remaining as constitutional monarch if possible, but without him if necessary, coupled with efforts to preserve the Iranian military as an institution. While I did not rule out eventual support for a military government whose purpose would be to restore order and end the bloodshed, I did not believe the United States should make such a fundamental decision for Iran, which is precisely what the shah was attempting to get us to do. The iron fist was wrong on two counts. First, the Iranian Army, more than 50 percent conscript, could not make it work. Second, support for the iron fist would be antithetical to what I believed the Carter administration stood for. The president refused to give American blessing to the iron fist.

By the end of December, I had little hope that even an English-style monarchy was possible. The shah's concessions since August, too little and too late, had not shaken the religious and political opposition's determination to end the monarchy. The shah's best chance, his conversations with Sadiqi, had failed to produce agreement because the shah was still unwilling to share enough power with a coalition government to split the moderate nationalists off from the Khomeini followers. Although we continued to support the shah, I had concluded that our central objective should be to preserve, if we could, the integrity and cohesion of the armed forces. This would be needed for the dangerous transition to a new Iran without the shah. With almost desperate urgency, Sullivan recommended that we immediately open communications with all the politically significant groups inside Iran in a last-ditch effort to reach agreement between the shah and the opposition before the army disintegrated. I supported this view.

Sullivan reported on December 26 that the shah had again discussed the idea of a regency and questioned whether we would support a policy of brutal repression. This cable brought matters to a head in Washington. On December 28, I and my staff prepared a draft telegram instructing Sullivan to tell the shah unequivocally that the United States would not support the iron fist option and that we believed he must move swiftly to establish a new civilian government to replace General Azhari. The draft cable instructed Sullivan to say that we did not believe either of the shah's options, his departure or brutal repression, could resolve the crisis.

This cable reflected my fear that under pressure from his advisers, the shah would try to crush the opposition in a showdown. I wanted to act immediately to disassociate the United States from such a mistake. It was important that we not be identified with an almost certainly unsuccessful action, and that we attempt to dissuade the shah from destroying the army in a vain effort to save his throne. The United States had to be able to deal with a successor government so that our common national interests in a stable, non-Communist Iran could reemerge after the turmoil. I wanted also to authorize Sullivan to talk immediately with responsible political elements in the government, the opposition, and the military. The aim of these discussions would be to urge establishment of a civilian government with firm military support that would restore order and guide Iran from autocracy to whatever new regime the Iranian people themselves decided upon, whether constitutional monarchy or Islamic republic.

Brown, Brzezinski, Turner, Schlesinger, Aaron, and I met in the White House situation room December 28 to discuss guidance for Sullivan. My views were contained in the draft cable. Brzezinski argued strongly for a message of complete support for the shah. Brown, Schlesinger, and Turner were against active U.S. involvement with the opposition in trying to build a viable coalition. After discussion it was clear that there was no support for my draft cable. We finally reached agreement on a message that emphasized that we continued to prefer a moderate civilian government. "But," the draft read, "if there is uncertainty either about the underlying orientation of such a government or its capacity to govern, or if the Army is in danger of becoming more fragmented, then a firm military government under the Shah may be un-avoidable."

I went alone to Camp David that afternoon to discuss with the president the message we had prepared. He acknowledged the dangers of the shah's continuing flirtation with the iron fist and the probability that his presence in Iran would prevent any understanding between the moderate opposition and the military leaders. Carter and I then worked out together the following change in the draft message after reference to the danger of the army becoming more fragmented: ". . . then the Shah should choose without delay a firm military government which would end the disorder, violence and bloodshed. If in his judgment the Shah believes these alternatives to be infeasible, then a regency council supervising the military government might be considered by him." The shah could not fail to see from this message that we would support a military government only to end bloodshed, but not to apply the iron fist to retain his throne. I immediately dispatched the message to Sullivan.

15

THE STORM BREAKS

ON JANUARY 2, the shah told Ambassador Sullivan that he had decided to appoint Shapour Bakhtiar, a prominent figure from the old National Front coalition, as prime minister. The shah was highly skeptical of Bakhtiar's chance of winning support, but he wished to give the civilian government alternative every possible chance before turning to either of the other alternatives. Since he had refused to give Bakhtiar control over the Defense Ministry, the military budget, or senior military appointments, he had every reason to doubt the new prime minister's ability to win over the secular opposition.

The shah told Sullivan he did not believe the iron fist would work because the strikers would sabotage the economy. In any event, he said, he could not order the bloody repression of his own people. Sullivan and the shah then discussed the regency council alternative. The shah indicated that he had agreed with Bakhtiar that after swearing in the new cabinet he should leave the country for a rest while the new prime minister attempted to bring the political situation under control. The shah said that although he would make a public statement to that effect, he would not set a date and would depart only if things quieted down enough for him to do so without the country and the army slipping into chaos. Speaking from instructions, Sullivan told the shah he would be welcome in the United States, and also conveyed an invitation from President Sadat to come to Egypt.

Sullivan reported that in his opinion the shah was stalling, trying to keep his options open. This could be fatal for Bakhtiar's efforts, because Bakhtiar's only hope was to convince the opposition that the shah had relinquished political power, which Bakhtiar was now in a position to share. Sullivan warned that the shah's procrastination was inevitably pushing him toward the regency option, and that by then it would be too late for Bakhtiar or any other moderate political solution.

The next day, January 3, Sullivan sent for my "eyes only" a personal message in which he said that for the United States the "moment of truth" had arrived in Iran. He reported that all the moderate elements in and out of the government agreed that the shah must leave the country at once. He said, however, that a group of military officers were urging the shah to forget Bakhtiar and apply the iron fist. Other Iranian generals were hinting at a coup to depose the shah if he did not make some clear decision within the next few days. I agreed with Sullivan's conclusion that American interests, as well as those of Iran, required that the shah leave immediately. The problem, as Sullivan observed, was that the shah would depart Iran only if he was advised to do so by the president. Sullivan emphasized that if the president intended to offer this advice, it must be done at once. If not, we could anticipate a military coup within a few days.

On January 4, the president and his advisers met to discuss Sullivan's assessment. We agreed that Sullivan's advice should be accepted. I immediately sent Sullivan a message from the president which was intended to end the shah's hesitation and to strengthen the chances of Bakhtiar being able to broaden his cabinet. It said that we supported the decision to establish a civilian government under Bakhtiar and his effort to preserve the independence, stability, and integrity of Iran. It also said that the president concurred in the shah's intention to leave Iran under a regency council, and assured him that he would be welcome in the United States. The president concluded by stressing the importance of the military leadership remaining united and in control of the armed forces. Sullivan was instructed to make this latter point directly to the military leaders.

The next day I followed up the president's message with a cable to Sullivan to make sure that he fully understood the president's intentions. I told him that, assuming Bakhtiar was indeed a moderate pro-Western nationalist, we preferred a civilian government under a regency council while the shah temporarily absented himself from the country. We wanted Bakhtiar to have the support of a united Iranian military, but we believed that the military must have contingency plans should the civilian government prove unsuccessful. I stressed to Sullivan that the purpose of those contingency plans should be to restore order.

Iranian military unity had become absolutely vital. After discussing alternatives with Harold Brown, General David Jones, and me, the president decided that we must have on the ground in Tehran an American military man working directly with the Iranian military leadership. His function would be to ensure that the military made sensible, realistic plans to hold the armed forces together, supported the constitutional processes, and was prepared to prevent a total collapse. The officer selected was General Robert Huyser, then deputy to Alexander Haig, supreme allied commander in Europe. Huyser, who was personally known to many of the senior Iranian generals, arrived in Tehran on January 5.

Sullivan was justifiably perturbed at his unheralded appearance and angrily demanded that Huyser be instructed to coordinate with him. This was done. In my message I emphasized that Sullivan and Huyser were to do everything possible to induce the Iranian military to support a pro-Western civilian government capable of restoring order and economic production. However, if the government were on the verge of collapse, we would understand the need for contingency plans and actions to end disorder, bloodshed, and violence.

On the evening of January 5, Sullivan met with the shah to discuss the president's message. The shah was still pessimistic about Bakhtiar's chances for success. He reaffirmed his intention to leave Iran, but was still vague about the timing.

Sullivan told the shah that we had heard reports from military officers that they had set up a "board" which planned to take the shah into protective custody and prevent his departure while they "cleaned up" the country. Sullivan noted that the officers had requested our cooperation, and he asked the shah whether he knew of this board and had approved its plans. The shah replied that it had been set up at his suggestion to do the necessary contingency planning for military actions in the event Bakhtiar failed. He dismissed as nonsense the idea of its taking him into custody, pointing out that he soon would be out of the country. He agreed that we should work with the military and warned that unless the generals received total U.S. support, the contingency plans would not work. The shah also said that on January 6 Bakhtiar would be named prime minister, and the shah would reaffirm his intentions to name a regency council and then depart.

Huyser found the generals in a state of confusion. They were growing increasingly disillusioned with the shah, and several expressed an interest in attempting to contact Khomeini and the religious forces. Some of the generals told Huyser that they believed the anticommunism of the military and the religious leaders could give them common ground. Sullivan's reports agreed with Huyser's, and Sullivan added that the generals wanted us to contact Khomeini directly to persuade him to give Bakhtiar a chance to establish order after the shah's departure and to prevent Communist and other radical leftist groups from exploiting the chaos. Sullivan's argument was that as long as the shah had left the country, Khomeini would surely prefer to have a cohesive, effective army to ensure Iran's external and internal security during the political transition to an Islamic republic. There was evidence that Khomeini intended the formal structure of government to remain in the hands of secular politicians while he and the clergy shaped and guided the revolution into fundamentalist Islamic channels.

I agreed with Sullivan's assessment of the situation. On January 7, I recommended to Carter, who was then attending the Guadeloupe summit meeting of Western leaders, that I be authorized to open a direct channel to Khomeini in Paris. My plan was to do this through Ambassador Theodore Eliot, a very able retired senior Foreign Service officer. Eliot, with previous experience in Iran and Afghanistan, agreed to go to Paris to see Khomeini, and a message was being prepared for him to take with him. I wished Eliot to urge the ayatollah to give Bakhtiar time to restore order before he returned to Iran. We knew Khomeini had a healthy fear of the army and was strongly anti-Communist. I hoped that he could be persuaded by the prospect of a military coup and the danger of Communist exploitation of a clash between the army and the mullahs to remain in Paris long enough to give Bakhtiar some breathing room. I emphasized to Carter that the purpose in contacting Khomeini was not to negotiate, but to convey a message that unless he allowed Bakhtiar time to form a viable government, the Communists might seize the leadership of the radical Left.

The president rejected my recommendation. He feared that such a step would be taken to mean we had abandoned the shah and were prepared to go outside the constitutional process to reach an understanding with Khomeini. In his opinion, such a perception would destroy Bakhtiar's slender chances and possibly split the military leadership as well. After a long discussion on January 10 with Mondale, Brzezinski, Brown, Powell, Aaron, and me, Carter decided to telephone President Valéry Giscard d'Estaing to ask that the French government urge Khomeini to give Bakhtiar an opportunity to restore order, although he agreed that the French should say this also represented American views. At that meeting, it was decided that Huyser should remain in Tehran to encourage the military to support Bakhtiar, while Sullivan would reaffirm to Bakhtiar that he had our support. Sullivan was to advise the shah that the United States believed he should appoint a regency council and leave Iran promptly. Our instructions to Sullivan and Huyser about planning for a military government in the event the civilian government failed were reaffirmed.

Brown and I sent the necessary messages to Huyser and Sullivan through our separate channels that day. Giscard agreed to approach Khomeini as Carter had requested. Sullivan reported on January 12 that he had carried out his instructions, and that the shah had said he would leave on January 16, after Bakhtiar was formally installed as prime minister. Sullivan said Washington must accept the fact that the shah probably would never be able to return to Iran and should concentrate all its efforts on helping Bakhtiar to hold the military together. Sullivan again recommended urgently that we attempt to bring about an accommodation between the military and Khomeini.

On January 13, I spoke to Sullivan on the secure telephone and assured him that the president and I understood his concern about the consequences of a conflict between Khomeini and the military. Sullivan reported that Brzezinski was trying to get General Huyser to push the military into a coup attempt. I told Sullivan that he and Huyser should understand clearly that a military coup should be discouraged, and that neither he nor Huyser should be misled by any unauthorized communication. Sullivan and Huyser were in an extremely difficult position, and Newsom and I did our utmost in daily telephone conversations to answer any questions they might have about U.S. policy.

• • •

On January 16, the shah left Iran—not for the United States but for Egypt. Evidently he believed that he should remain as close as possible to Iran in order to be able to return quickly should the military succeed in restoring order. This decision further reduced Bakhtiar's chances of persuading the moderates that he was free of the shah's influence and able to act independently.

I continued to press Sullivan's suggestion of facilitating an understanding between Khomeini and the military. By this time, Khomeini's representatives in Tehran and the military were already in contact with each other. The president agreed. On January 16, using an informal channel we had opened to a member of Khomeini's entourage, Warren Zimmerman, chief of the embassy political section in Paris, met with Ibrahim Yazdi, a secular politician with close ties to the Islamic clergy who had emerged as the ayatollah's interlocutor with Westerners, and who was a naturalized American citizen. As instructed, Zimmerman emphasized that Khomeini's sudden return could provoke a confrontation with the military. Yazdi's questions suggested that Khomeini wanted to avoid a clash with the military. He implied that although Khomeini would resist an attempt by the army to save the monarchy, the ayatollah was not opposed to military actions to preserve the army's cohesion and integrity.

In the meantime, Sullivan's reports made clear that the army leadership was demoralized. It had no realistic plans and was probably incapable of holding itself together for more than a few weeks if it actually did try to seize power. Huyser found little difficulty in persuading the generals to support Bakhtiar and the constitutional process. He was cautiously optimistic about the leadership capabilities of certain generals, but did not disguise the immense strains. However, in Sullivan's blunt estimation, the army was a "paper tiger."

In a personal message to me, Sullivan described Bakhtiar as a determined, even quixotic man playing a high-stakes game and not amenable to American advice. The military, while willing to support Bakhtiar as the legitimate head of government, was not prepared to back his threats. The generals were moving toward a position of neutral guarantor of the constitution and public order, while continuing their secret, but so far unproductive, meetings with Ayatollah Mohammed Beheshti, Khomeini's main representative in Tehran.

On January 22, Sullivan and Huyser jointly asked for a reexamination of U.S. policy. They warned that with Khomeini's apparently imminent return, the two major anti-Communist forces in Iran, the army and the clergy, were at the point of tearing each other apart. In particular, Huyser asked that he be authorized to inform the military that the United States would not support a coup and that should Bakhtiar fail, the army should maintain its integrity and attempt to negotiate an understanding with Khomeini.

The message confronted Washington with a traumatic dilemma. Sullivan and Huyser's arguments were compelling, and they had a far better sense of the rapidly changing political realities in Tehran. However, their strategy would almost certainly mean the prompt collapse of Bakhtiar, as both the military and Khomeini would conclude that we had abandoned hope that he could succeed. In a tense discussion with Brown, Brzezinski, and me, the president decided to follow a middle course. On January 23, Sullivan and Huyser were instructed to seek Bakhtiar's and the military's concurrence in a U.S. approach to Khomeini through the Paris Zimmerman-Yazdi channel. The message to Khomeini urged the ayatollah to allow his representatives in Tehran to reach an understanding with the military and the Bakhtiar government on a process in which all could participate in reshaping the Iranian political system. Zimmerman was also instructed to make clear to Yazdi that the United States was urging both the government and the military to reach agreement with Khomeini's representatives. Zimmerman was to reiterate that Khomeini's return before such an understanding was reached could lead to confrontation between the non-Communist forces, which could only end in disaster for Iran.

At the same time, Huyser and Sullivan were told that their request to inform the army that the United States would not support a coup was denied. Huyser was to continue to advise the military on contingency planning, but also to make clear that Khomeini's return was not in itself a cause for implementing the contingency plans. Sullivan had made it absolutely clear in his messages to me that any attempt to block Khomeini's return or to arrest him on arrival would sweep away Bakhtiar and destroy the military.

Bakhtiar and the military leaders agreed to our approaching Khomeini. Zimmerman met Yazdi on January 23. Yazdi carefully noted down the message to convey to Khomeini. Four days later he gave Zimmerman Khomeini's response—a combination of threat and olive branch. Khomeini warned that if Bakhtiar or the army tried to oppose him, it would be harmful to American interests in Iran. On the other hand, if they did not interfere, he would quiet things down. He went on to say that many of our concerns about his attitude toward relations with the United States would be resolved when we saw the provisional government he intended to name to guide Iran to an Islamic republic. Yazdi explained that this meant the United States would be able to deal with the provisional government, and mentioned Mehdi Bazargan, a highly respected pro-Western democratic political figure, as the probable provisional prime minister. Khomeini concluded that he intended the country's future to be decided by the Iranian people.

Reports I had received from Clark Clifford, who was in contact with the National Front politicians grouped around Khomeini, supported the thrust of the ayatollah's message. Clifford's interlocutors indicated that Khomeini intended to set up a government drawn from moderate secular politicians, with the Islamic clergy remaining in the background as the guiding political and spiritual force of the revolution. Karim Sanjabi and his colleagues had evidently reached an understanding with the ayatollah that the National Front would have a leading role in the provisional government. The National Front representatives seemed confident they would be able to keep the revolution in democratic channels, but stressed that we should disassociate ourselves from Bakhtiar soon because he was going to disappear very quickly.

In Iran, overt anti-American incidents were increasing. The nonofficial American population was beginning to stream out of the country, and I decided we must also reduce the nonessential official community. On January 29, I instructed Sullivan to order the immediate departure of all military and civilian employees not absolutely necessary for the functioning of the American mission, and all dependents. Sullivan was also to advise the American business community to accelerate its departure. He and his staff took charge of organizing the mass exodus. A task force under the chairmanship of David Newsom coordinated the Washington end of this massive effort, and between December and March we successfully evacuated more than 45,000 Americans without loss of life.

Meanwhile, Bakhtiar was rapidly losing confidence that he could handle Khomeini. An attempt to promote a face-to-face meeting with the ayatollah collapsed, and Bakhtiar realized he would be deposed if he attempted to block Khomeini's return. On January 29, Bakhtiar told Sullivan he would let Khomeini enter Iran unimpeded. Bakhtiar's tactic at this point was, as he put it, to let Khomeini "drown in mullahs." His hope was that the religious opposition would break into competing factions and Khomeini's charismatic appeal would evaporate once he was physically present in Iran. This was a strategy of desperation, and despite our continuing public pronouncements of support, it was obvious that Bakhtiar had little time left. Our only chance of preventing a clash between the conservative forces was to press harder for an understanding between the military and the religious and secular opposition forces arrayed around Khomeini.

The case for actively urging the parties to negotiate an understanding was impeded by Brzezinski's determined opposition to direct contacts with the ayatollah, despite the fact that both Bakhtiar and the military wanted our help in working out an arrangement with Khomeini, and by his persistent arguments to the president that we advise the Iranian military to seize power. In my judgment, we had delayed too long in urging the shah to take decisive steps to form a regency council, appoint a coalition government, and leave. Now we were tying ourselves to the Bakhtiar experiment beyond the point where there was any chance of his participating in a new regime. As Sullivan put it, the United States had become "identified with evaporating institutions." Sullivan's conclusion was that Khomeini had won a revolution, and that Washington was still not accepting that fact and adjusting to it.

On February 1, Khomeini's arrival in Tehran was greeted by multitudes of supporters. For several days Bakhtiar attempted unsuccessfully to negotiate with Khomeini. On February 5, after Bakhtiar failed to persuade the military to prevent the Khomeini groups from setting up a parallel government, Khomeini appointed Mehdi Bazargan as provisional prime minister. We thus found ourselves in the extraordinary situation of attempting to deal with two governments—Bakhtiar's constitutional but disintegrating government, and Bazargan's, representative of the real political power in the country. On February 6, we sent Sullivan a message reiterating that we supported Bakhtiar as the legal head of government. Sullivan—by this time Huyser had left—was instructed to encourage the military to stand with Bakhtiar in order to increase his chances of preserving the constitutional process in his bargaining with Bazargan. However, we did authorize Sullivan to work informally with Bazargan on such matters as the safety of Americans and arrangements for evacuation of U.S. personnel should that become necessary.

On February 9, I warned the president that the strains on the military were leading to fragmentation, lack of discipline, and growing anti-Americanism. Sullivan reported that Tehran was chaotic, with fighting between loyal military units and rightist and leftist bands, which were obtaining arms from disintegrating army units. The long-feared crisis within the military erupted on February 9, when units in air bases outside Tehran rebelled against their officers and gave their allegiance to Khomeini. The Imperial Guard, the most loyal troops available, were sent to crush the uprising. The rebellious air force units were joined by heavily armed revolutionary "militia." In heavy fighting the Imperial Guard forces began to dissolve and some of the troops apparently joined the mutineers. Fighting spread rapidly.

On February 11, as the military disintegrated, Bakhtiar resigned and went into hiding. The army leaders, recognizing the futility of further resistance, ordered their troops into barracks.

The next day the building housing the armed forces high command and the American Military Assistance Advisory Group came under violent attack. In a harrowing drama, Sullivan and his staff struggled successfully to extricate the American military advisers from the fighting. Meanwhile, David Newsom called Sullivan from the White House situation room to ask for an assessment of the chance for an immediate coup. Sullivan, under the immense strain of trying to save the Americans, gave a colorful, but unprintable, reply.

• • •

The pressing question for Washington after the departure of Bakhtiar was whether to open diplomatic relations with the Bazargan provisional government. Bazargan named to key positions a number of moderates, including Yazdi as deputy prime minister and Sanjabi as foreign minister, and informed us that the provisional government wished to continue relations with the United States. On February 12, instructions were sent to Ambassador Sullivan to maintain contacts with the new government pending a presidential decision on the question of relations. At this point, we had two immediate concerns: preventing sensitive military and intelligence equipment from falling into unfriendly hands; and the safety of the American citizens.

Sullivan and the American military advisers were already working closely with the provisional government and the Iranian military to protect the critical equipment and installations. The cooperative attitude of Bazargan's government was indicative of the political moderates' strong desire to continue a military relationship with the United States and their healthy concern for Iran's external security. The safety of the embassy staff was a problem of greater urgency. The embassy's military protection had been withdrawn when the Bakhtiar government collapsed, and gangs of armed, hostile, and uncontrolled youths were roaming the streets. Moreover, in the increasingly open struggle between the Mujahedin, a neo-Marxist Islamic faction, and the Marxist Fedayeen, there was danger that one or both would attack the embassy in an effort to provoke a confrontation that would undermine the Bazargan government. It was essential that Sullivan work out satisfactory security arrangements with Bazargan and Yazdi.

Fortunately, Sullivan was able to secure quickly a commitment from Yazdi to protect the embassy, because on February 14 a nightmare came true. That day, a Fedayeen band assaulted the embassy, and after the Marine guards withdrew behind clouds of tear gas, seized the ambassador and the reduced staff, but not before they managed to destroy the classified files and communications equipment.

At the same time, rebels in nearby Afghanistan kidnapped Ambassador Adolph Dubs. In a surreal scene, virtually every senior official from the Near East bureau jammed into the State Department operations center, which had the quickest communication with both places. In one corner, one group sought to coordinate negotiations in Kabul to secure Dubs' release; in another corner, a second group struggled to keep in touch with Sullivan in Tehran. Officials moved to and fro between chattering wire service tickers and jangling telephones while the operations center staff struggled to keep abreast of the dozens of urgent telegrams spewing from high-speed printers.

For a time it seemed that we would secure Spike Dubs' safe release after prolonged negotiation with the rebels, but were almost certain that some Americans would be killed in Tehran during the attack on the embassy. Instead, the courage and coolness of Bill Sullivan and his staff enabled them all to escape, thanks to the timely arrival of Yazdi and pro-Khomeini forces. In Kabul a reckless assault by Afghan government forces on Spike Dubs' kidnappers led to his tragic death. Sullivan had deliberately and calmly ordered the Marines and embassy staff not to resist the Fedayeen, who had hoped to provoke a bloody shoot-out. It was a display of courage and professionalism for which I felt the deepest admiration.

• • •

On February 16, we announced that the United States would maintain normal diplomatic relations with the new regime. Relations clearly would be difficult as the provisional government struggled to establish its authority over the factions that were contending violently for dominance. As the Iranian revolution passed through its successive stages, our national interests in this strategic country required that we maintain a presence even though our relations with the new regime would necessarily be limited. We believed that over time U.S. and Iranian interests in a strong, stable, non-Communist Iran should permit a cooperative, if far less intimate, relationship to emerge.

Sullivan reported that despite Yazdi's success in freeing the embassy staff, the writ of the provisional government did not run far. Groups of heavily armed young men of various religious, political, and ideological persuasions were roaming the streets, fighting each other, pursuing suspected remnants of the imperial regime, and meting out summary "revolutionary justice." All professed allegiance to Khomeini, but a vicious, confused power struggle was in progress, with the Tudeh and other radical leftist factions apparently on the losing end.

The Iranian armed forces were in disarray. Many senior generals had fled, gone into hiding, or were under arrest. I advised President Carter that it was important for us immediately to do what we could to support Bazargan and the moderates to whom Khomeini had entrusted the formal reins of government. Sullivan was instructed to call on Bazargan for the first time on February 21 to assure him, and through him, Khomeini, that the United States accepted the revolution and did not intend to intervene in Iran's internal affairs. Sullivan said that the United States was prepared to continue an arms supply relationship with the new government. He also protested the summary executions and the widespread violations of human rights that were taking place.

In March I made one of the most distasteful recommendations I ever had to make to the president. It was that the shah, who had left Egypt for Morocco, be informed by our ambassador in Morocco that under the prevailing circumstances it would not be appropriate for him to come to the United States. Had he immediately accepted our original invitation after he left Iran on January 16, there might have been no strong adverse reaction in Iran, assuming he kept a low profile and made no statements about returning to Iran. However, our support of Bakhtiar had inflamed Iranian paranoia about American intentions. Further, in an effort to consolidate his power and focus the energies and hatreds of the warring factions on an external enemy, Khomeini began demanding the return of the shah to face revolutionary justice. Both U.S. interests in establishing a modus vivendi with the new Iranian government and the safety of the Americans in Iran dictated that the shah should not be allowed into the United States at this time.

On March 17, the shah was informed of the president's decision. He reacted calmly and merely requested our help in finding another place of exile. Apparently he had put aside any thought of returning to Iran and had turned to the problem of finding a secure refuge. Although his affairs were being handled mainly by private representatives in the United States, we undertook to contact a substantial number of countries on his behalf. Eventually we were able to secure a temporary safe haven for him in the Bahamas, and finally, after considerable negotiations, in Mexico. Throughout these efforts, the administration was under considerable pressure from some of the shah's friends in America, including David Rockefeller, Henry Kissinger, John McCloy, and others, to admit him to the United States. We respected their sincerity and shared their concern, but we repeatedly explained to them the difficulties and dangers such a course of action would pose for U.S. interests and, perhaps, the lives of the embassy staff. Although the shah wished ultimately to come to the United States, reports from our embassy in Tehran supported our judgment that he should not now be permitted to enter this country.

In mid-April, Chargé d'Affaires Charles Naas (Sullivan had left Iran on April 6) cabled that Khomeini was stepping up his attacks against the United States and that most of the irregular security force had been withdrawn from the embassy. Several thousand Americans still remained in Iran. Both they and the embassy staff would be in danger if the shah came to the United States.

In response to an appeal by the shah and after consulting with Naas, we decided to allow the shah's children to attend school in the United States. When Naas discussed this matter with Bazargan, the prime minister agreed that it should cause no problem, although he reiterated his warning about the dangers of admitting the shah himself. The president determined that the empress could come to the United States for medical treatment, if necessary, but not to reside with the children. In permitting the empress to enter even temporarily for medical treatment, we would be skirting dangerously close to confirming suspicions in Iran that the United States still supported the shah. Humanitarian concerns, however, demanded that we do whatever we could to help his family, as long as American lives and national interests were not subjected to unacceptable risks.

In May a new impasse arose in our relationship with Iran. The brutal treatment of officials of the former regime had been extended to ethnic and religious minorities. We strongly protested these acts and tried to expedite the emigration of Iranian Jews and others from Iran. On May 17, the Senate passed a resolution condemning these human rights abuses. Khomeini then increased his attacks on the United States. In consternation, the provisional government withdrew its approval of Walter Cutler, whom we had nominated to replace Ambassador Sullivan. We refused to withdraw Cutler's nomination and informed Bazargan that U.S.-Iran relations would be conducted in Tehran at the level of chargé d'affaires. On June 18, Bruce Laingen arrived to replace Naas.

• • •

The fall of the shah will provide a rich field for scholarly study. Much time will pass before a reasonably objective analysis of the collapse of the imperial regime can be made. However, in view of the false charges that the shah was undermined and brought down by the Carter administration's human rights policy or by our alleged failure to counter Soviet-inspired subversion, I would like to make some personal observations that may contribute to that eventual assessment.

In my opinion, the fall of the shah was a textbook example of a clash between Western modernization and traditional religious, economic, and social structures. Exacerbating the resulting strains on Iranian society were the massive inflow of oil revenues after 1973 and the shah's decision to accelerate Iran's industrialization and build up its military power. The impact of this drive on Iran's traditional patterns was shattering. The sudden influx of wealth also gave rise to pervasive corruption and profound economic dislocation.

I do not believe the clash between modernization and tradition inevitably required the termination of the Pahlavi dynasty, and certainly not the establishment of a xenophobic religious autocracy. Had the shah not lost his awareness that the drive for economic and social modernization must be accompanied by the creation of democratic political institutions, the tragedy might have been averted. In deference to the shah's changed priorities, the Nixon and Ford administrations failed to encourage him to maintain a balanced modernization program as President Johnson had done. By the time the Carter administration resumed American support for political as well as industrial and military modernization, eight years had been lost, and massive fissures already had appeared in critical sectors of Iranian political, economic, and social structures.

By the mid-1970s, the shah himself had become more conscious of the widening gulf between his modernization efforts and the values and interests of traditional Iranian society. As the Carter administration came to office, the shah already was looking for new ways to address key political questions, although hesitantly. He accepted our endorsement of his liberalization efforts as a counterweight to those advisers who opposed his plans to broaden political participation. He did so, I believe, because of a sense of the monarchy's growing isolation from the political forces at work in Iran and not, as some have asserted, out of deference to our human rights policy. Without doubt the shah wanted to be perceived by us as a progressive, humane reformer. He was extraordinarily sensitive to popular Western portrayals of him as a dictator kept in power by repression and force. As he made clear to us on several occasions, he did not object to our strong commitment to human rights as long as the policy was not applied in such a way as to undermine Iran's political stability or security. The shah wanted Western, especially American, approval, but in my opinion he did not reach his conclusions on political liberalization because of human rights pressure from the Carter administration.

Nor do I ascribe the fall of the shah to a grand Soviet design to destroy the American security system in Southwest Asia and to open a path to the Persian Gulf. The Soviets have always sought whatever advantage they could from turmoil and instability. However, as Afghanistan and Poland were later to demonstrate, they have accorded extreme importance to stability on their borders. Over the years Moscow had reached a modus vivendi with the shah, seeing in him a force that could control resurgent Islamic fundamentalism. One must always bear in mind atavistic Russian fears of Islamic revival stirring the rapidly growing Muslim ethnic minorities in the Central Asian Soviet republics into opposition to Communist control. Khomeini was probably as disturbing to Moscow as he was to Washington.

• • •

A difficult question is whether there was anything the United States could have done to influence the direction of the Iranian Revolution during November and December of 1978 and early January of 1979. My answer is, perhaps—had we been willing at the outset to make fundamental decisions for the shah, enabling him to overcome his hesitation to find a way of sharing power with his adversaries. But even then it may have already been too late, for the forces that unleashed the revolution were deep-seated and long in the making.

There were divisions within the religious opposition that the shah could have exploited. Initially, Khomeini did not control the more moderate elements of the Shi'ite clergy. Moreover, not until late November or perhaps the Moharram demonstrations of early December had the political moderates fallen totally under his sway. By that point, and probably earlier, the shah had no option but to find a way to transfer power peacefully to acceptable elements of the opposition. But the moment for the shah to commit himself dramatically to a devolution of authority through a constitutional monarchy passed quickly after the massive demonstrations of December 1978. As late as the end of December, the United States still might have been able to help the democratically inclined opposition and the military to play a more influential role in shaping the revolution.

But the administration could not overcome its internal policy divisions. We dissipated our potential influence by trying to breathe life into the imperial constitution rather than seeking to mediate an understanding among the army, the political establishment, and the Khomeini-controlled opposition. By early February, our only sensible course was to attempt to come to terms with the revolution.

• • •

The removal of Iran from the ranks of American allies and its control by an unfriendly regime was a blow to our political and security interests in Southwest Asia. Strategically, the loss of the intelligence collection stations in northern Iran caused a temporary diminution of our ability to gather information on Soviet nuclear forces. This caused us difficulties during the Senate consideration of the SALT II Treaty. Although the outcome of the Iranian Revolution was, of course, far from apparent in 1979–80, the disintegration of the shah's regime without a stable, pro-Western successor potentially opened the door to the eventual establishment of a government susceptible to Soviet influence and harmful to our interests in the gulf. Should this occur, the consequences for the global balance between East and West would be significant.

The rapid reemergence of the historic antagonism between Iraq and Iran and the subsequent choosing of sides accentuated divisions in the Arab world. The fall of the shah thus produced no new anti-Western, anti-Israeli, radical Islamic coalition. However, fed by statements of political opponents of the Carter administration, many of our friends in the region professed to be anxious about American will and constancy. The potential impact on the confidence of Anwar Sadat, the Saudis, the gulf states, and King Hussein was worrisome, but Harold Brown's trip to the region in February 1979 revealed concern but no sense of panic among the moderate states about either Soviet intentions or the disappearance of the shah. Our friends wanted continued discreet political and military support, but no splashy deployment of American military power which could exacerbate their internal political difficulties. The states of the region wanted American policy to be tailored to their individual political and security situations. They did not and do not want an artificial and unworkable anti-Soviet "strategic consensus."

The greatest immediate damage to American interests was in the economic sphere. Between 1979 and 1981, oil prices tripled, due in part to the collapse in Iranian production. The shock of renewed OPEC price increases magnified existing strains on the international economy and contributed to sharpening inflation in the United States. This was somewhat counterbalanced by steadily falling Western demand for oil as a result of a worldwide recession and increased conservation by consumers. By 1981–82, even with Iran and Iraq locked in war and with reductions in OPEC production, an oil glut had begun to bring down prices. The economic problems caused by the drop in Iranian oil production were short-term—although they were a major factor in Carter's defeat in November 1980.

At this writing, an evaluation of the long-term consequences of the shah's fall cannot be made. That will depend on what happens in the power struggle that is likely to follow the death of Khomeini. If a durable, non-Communist regime emerges, it is probable there will be an improvement in U.S.-Iranian relations based on our common interests in a secure, united, and prosperous Iran. If, however, Iran slides into civil war, the temptation will exist for the Soviet Union to fish in the troubled waters. This may seem illogical in light of their experience in Afghanistan. But we cannot forget their hypersensitivity to instability on their borders. If this should happen there would be grave danger of a U.S.-Soviet confrontation.

16

THE SALT DEBATE

THE SALT II RATIFICATION DEBATE

On June 22, 1979, four days after President Carter and Brezhnev signed the SALT II Treaty in Vienna, it was submitted to the Senate for advice and consent to ratification.* Like all treaties, it would need the approval of two-thirds of the senators present and voting. As in the case of the Panama treaties in 1977, voting for SALT presented substantial political risks to many senators who might otherwise have hailed it as the greatest foreign policy achievement of Carter's presidency. It had become the catalyst of a broadening conservative challenge to détente.

The Senate Foreign Relations Committee opened hearings on July 9 led by Chairman Frank Church and the ranking Republican member, Jacob Javits. The hearings launched a great national debate that focused not only on the terms of the treaty, but on a much broader range of issues: the nature of the U.S.-Soviet relationship; the role of nuclear arms control in U.S. foreign policy; trends in the military balance; the adequacy of our defense capabilities, programs, and spending; the will of the West to protect its interests; and finally, the nature and scope of U.S. national interests.

I have no doubt that the Salt II Treaty was and is in the national interests of the United States and its allies. Nor do I believe that failure to ratify the treaty was due to "fatal flaws" in the treaty. Even those who led the attack against the treaty and its so-called flaws chose to abide by

* The SALT II Treaty (with a termination date of December 31, 1988) was submitted to the Senate together with the Protocol, lasting until December 31, 1981, 98 Agreed Statements and Common Understandings relating to the provisions of the treaty and its protocol, a Joint Statement of Principles and Basic Guidelines for SALT III, a Memorandum of Understanding on an agreed data base on strategic offensive arms, and an exchange of statements by presidents Carter and Brezhnev on the Backfire bomber.

its terms once they assumed office. The record of the congressional hearings shows that opponents of the treaty failed to prove their case. Ratification was blocked because the opponents were successful in creating political linkage between the treaty and the problem of restraining Moscow's attempts to expand its influence.

In condemning linkage as applied to arms control, I want to make clear that I do not suggest that all linkage is unsound. To the contrary, I believe that linkage in other areas, such as economic linkage for specific trade policy purposes, is philosophically correct and sensible. If we have items of trade that are important to the Soviets, this can give us valuable leverage in restraining their activities. This leverage will not override their national security interests, but it can be helpful in giving the Soviets incentives to act with greater restraint abroad, as well as facilitating trade agreements. Linkage in the case of nuclear arms control rests on a different base. There the agreement itself advances our own security and thus outweighs any advantage that might come from denying the other party the benefits of the bargain.

The driving force behind much of the opposition to SALT II came from the ideological Right, which supported reflexively almost any argument against the treaty, however unsound. For some, the fact that the treaty was with the Soviet Union was enough to make it suspect. More damaging, however, was the linkage argument and the fact that it was advanced by some former officials, such as Henry Kissinger and Alexander Haig. I was especially saddened by Henry's position, since he had contributed much to achieving the SALT II agreement. Even as they guardedly supported the treaty as contributing to American interests, they legitimized the fallacy that the United States could use the treaty to punish the Soviet Union for actions in areas that were unrelated to the strategic balance. Many of the critics seemed to forget that three administrations had negotiated the treaty, and had done so out of a cold assessment of American security interests, and not as a reward for good behavior on the part of Moscow.

The arguments for linkage that were advanced during the debate gave some senators in the center, who were fearful of the rising conservative tide, an intellectually defensible ground for withholding their support until Moscow "got the message" that it could not have the SALT II Treaty unless it acted with greater restraint in the global competition. It seems self-evident that a nation will enter into an arms control agreement only when the agreement enhances its security, and not as a reward for good behavior on the part of the other nation—particularly when the behavior could rapidly change after the agreement is signed. But this logic, unfortunately, is less than persuasive in the atmosphere of an approaching political campaign.

Another difficulty was the merely lukewarm support of some liberal and moderate senators, who might have been SALT's natural supporters.

They were disappointed that the cuts were not greater, and they spoke of SALT II as little more than a license to continue the arms race. Understandably, they were also concerned at signs that both sides intended to proceed under the treaty with a new generation of nuclear missiles, including such technologically advanced systems as the MX, Trident II, and cruise missiles, each of which would mark an escalation in the qualitative competition. But they were experienced individuals and should have recognized that arms control is a long and difficult process, which can often move forward only in modest steps. Arms control is not for the short-winded or the faint of heart. I understood that their statements were only an opening position, which they hoped to use in extracting commitments from the administration about the objectives of SALT III. But they failed to reckon with the fact that their words would be taken up by hard-line opponents and used to block ratification.

Another important factor in the SALT debate was the political standing of the Carter administration. In the second half of 1979 our political strength was less than during the Panama treaties debate. For a variety of reasons, our strength had eroded. Our foreign policy accomplishments were marred by a perception of an inconsistent and divided administration. In those crucial months of 1979, the SALT II Treaty faced an uphill political struggle.

On the positive side, however, the treaty had much in its favor. First, SALT enjoyed a powerful base of popular support which could be mobilized. Second, the treaty was supported by the Joint Chiefs of Staff, who had actively participated in its negotiation. Third, the treaty was endorsed by our NATO allies, whose security interests it directly affected. Finally, the treaty was a substantial improvement over the SALT I Interim Agreement. It was a carefully balanced package whose net effect was to impose useful limits on Soviet forces while leaving the United States free to pursue the strategic options that the Joint Chiefs of Staff considered essential.

I believed that when it came time to vote, we could get the required 67 votes.

On July 9, the Senate Foreign Relations, Armed Services, and Intelligence committees began extensive hearings which lasted throughout the summer. Scores of witnesses, proponents and opponents, official and private, testified. The hearing record for the Foreign Relations Committee alone totaled six volumes.

Significantly, in the first phase of hearings, few serious critics contended that the treaty should be rejected outright—a tacit acknowledgment of the strong public support for the SALT process. Opponents initially centered their arguments primarily on four alleged flaws or deficiencies in the agreement, which they said needed to be rectified either through amendments to the treaty or through conditions placed in the Resolution of Ratification. The critics claimed:

• The negotiating compromises were weighted in favor of the Soviet Union, particularly in permitting it to retain its 308 launchers of heavy land-based missiles, while banning them for the United States, and in not counting the Backfire medium bomber under the 2,250 aggregate ceiling. This was not true, as the evidence presented to the Senate demonstrated.

• Soviet compliance with the treaty could not be verified by our intelligence resources, and the ambiguous language of some provisions gave Moscow too much latitude to interpret the treaty in ways harmful to the United States. Again, this was not so. The treaty was adequately verifiable.

• The treaty and its protocol contained provisions that could impede American defense cooperation with our NATO allies and set an adverse precedent for negotiations on cruise missiles in SALT III. This was also false, as was demonstrated by the unanimous support of our NATO allies.

• We had failed to negotiate sufficiently deep cuts, especially in land-based missiles with multiple warheads (MIRVed ICBMs). From the conservatives' viewpoint this, together with the Soviets' 308 heavy missiles, would eventually give Moscow a dangerous superiority in the most accurate and powerful strategic weapon in each side's arsenal. To some liberals, the modesty of the reductions signified that the treaty was not arms control but merely a codification of the arms race. Although all of us would have liked deeper cuts we had gone as far as we could at the time.

A contention heard more and more frequently once it became clear that attacks on the treaty were not hitting home was that the United States had failed to keep pace with the Soviet Union in both nuclear and conventional forces because it had been lulled into complacency by the SALT negotiations. It was suggested that we faced a strategic "window of vulnerability" which would not be closed until new ICBMs, such as the MX, could be deployed in the late 1980s. The charge that the SALT process had caused complacency in Congress and among the electorate was coupled with the argument that SALT II should be held in "abeyance" until Congress remedied the alleged inadequacies and committed the United States to sharp increases in the defense budget. Related to this was the false claim that the Carter administration had deliberately held back major strategic programs, such as the MX, Trident II, and cruise missiles, in order to facilitate the SALT negotiations.

As with the Panama treaties, a principal element of the opponents' strategy was to press for radical changes in the SALT agreement that would require Soviet acquiescence or a renegotiation of basic terms of the treaty. Such changes would either kill the treaty or require its reopening. Reopening the treaty to seek greater concessions for the United States would expose us to reopening by the Soviet Union of vital issues that had already been resolved in our favor.

The case for the SALT Treaty was made in a series of appearances in July before the Senate Foreign Relations and other committees. Harold Brown, General David Jones, the Joint Chiefs of Staff, Stansfield Turner, Ralph Earle, and I were the principal witnesses. Our goal was to explain why the treaty advanced our security, and correct the fallacies and misinterpretations about SALT that had arisen since 1977. It was important for us to show that even though the agreement was an intricate web of mutual adjustments, the United States would be more secure with the treaty than without it. We sought to dispel the notion that the Senate's choice was between an ideal, unattainable agreement and the treaty that had been negotiated, as its opponents were trying to do. Further, it was necessary to counter the argument that because the final agreement was not as far-reaching as the March 1977 comprehensive proposal I had taken to Moscow, it represented a concession to the Soviet Union, and less than real arms control. In March 1977 we had attempted to make a quantum leap forward and the Soviet Union had shown itself unready to take such a huge step. Yet, critics ever since had tried to make our comprehensive proposal the standard against which any agreement must be measured.

We believed the best way to answer questions about the treaty was to explain what it did and did not do, and what the strategic situation would be with and without it.

First, unlike SALT I, the SALT II Treaty established equal ceilings on strategic missiles and bombers for both sides—2,400 at the outset, to be lowered to 2,250 by December 31, 1981. The Soviets would have to destroy some 250 operational weapons systems to reach the 2,250 aggregate ceiling; without SALT, they could deploy at least 3,000 missiles and bombers by 1985. On the other hand, the United States would not have to destroy any operational weapons to get under the 2,250 ceiling. The treaty also held both sides to 1,200 MIRVed ICBMs, and within that total each side was limited to 820 land-based MIRVs.

If the SALT Treaty were not approved, we estimated the Soviets could field by 1985 as many as 1,800 MIRVed missiles, including more than 920 land-based ones. The 1,320 combined ceiling on heavy bombers carrying air-launched cruise missiles and MIRVed missiles was of no practical value to the Soviet Union because of the mix of their forces. The United States, however, with its advanced air-launched cruise missile program, would be able to deploy 120 ALCM-armed heavy bombers before having to decide whether to reduce any MIRVed missiles to stay under that ceiling.

We carried over from SALT I the freeze on the construction of new launchers for heavy land-based missiles. This prevented the Soviets from deploying more than their existing 308 heavy missiles. As Harold Brown and I testified, we decided to drop our demand for reductions in heavy missiles after concluding that a limit of 820 on MIRVed ICBMs would do just as much to alleviate our ICBM vulnerability problem. Moreover, that approach was negotiable. It was asking too much of SALT to expect it to bring about a reduction of heavy land-based missiles; this would have required a drastic restructuring of the Soviet strategic force, which emphasized ICBMs over the technologically more complex sea-based missiles in which we had such a marked advantage. The Joint Chiefs of Staff had been clear during the negotiations that they did not want heavy missiles. They preferred the smaller but more powerful MX missile.

Far more important for our security than a meaningless "right" to build heavy missiles which we did not want was the so-called "fractionation" limit we had negotiated. This prohibition on increasing the number of warheads on both sides' missiles meant that the Soviets could not exploit the enormous lifting power of their heavy land-based missiles by adding more than 10 warheads. With 10 set as the maximum on the SS-18, our MX would carry as many warheads as the largest Soviet missile. Without this freeze, we believed the Soviets could deploy 30 or more on each SS-18 and, as well, increase the number of warheads carried on their lighter missiles, the SS-17s and 19s. The one permitted new Soviet ICBM would also be limited to 10 warheads.

The treaty would hold the Soviets to some 10,000 to 12,000 warheads by 1985, roughly equivalent to us. Without it, they could conceivably have as many as 20,000. Of course, we could expand our warhead totals at least as much as they could, although this would be very costly. Brown estimated that by 1985, without SALT, spending for strategic forces would have to be at least $30 billion more than would otherwise be the case. The freeze on warhead fractionation was one of the most significant achievements of SALT II and pointed the way to curbing the race in qualitative improvements of weapons.

I had expected the issue of verifying Soviet compliance to be one of our most serious problems during the ratification debate. Verification is a complex matter, involving some of the most secret and esoteric aspects of U.S. intelligence collection. It involves both political and technical judgments. The political leadership must make an assessment of the verifiability of an agreement after weighing a range of factors, including each side's monitoring capabilities, political and military incentives for the other side to attempt significant cheating, the risks of detection, and the ability to respond rapidly and effectively with compensating programs in the event the other side cheats. Verification makes use of our technical capabilities to monitor Soviet strategic activities. This is done by satellites and other intelligence means.

Although some of my colleagues worried that the absence of a total ban on telemetry encryption would damage the treaty's ratification prospects, I believed we could show that it was adequately verifiable without a total ban. The loss of the collection stations in northern Iran in February 1979 was a serious setback, both in the sense of temporarily impairing our ability to check Soviet compliance with certain SALT limitations and in its impact on key senators, such as John Glenn, who had become the Senate's leading expert on monitoring. However, Harold Brown testified that although it would take more than a year to recoup all the intelligence capabilities lost in Iran, the Soviets would need far more than a year to carry out any significant clandestine testing program.

I strongly supported increased spending for our intelligence collection programs. This would improve our SALT monitoring capabilities, as well as our overall knowledge of Soviet strategic activities. One of SALT's most significant contributions to strategic stability was the measures it required of each side to facilitate the other's access to information about its strategic forces. Of particular importance were the prohibitions against deliberate concealment of strategic forces, and including by encryption of any telemetry relevant to SALT limitations and interference with reconnaissance satellites and other monitoring capabilities. Without the treaty our capability would be blunted, and our task of following Soviet strategic activities would be far more difficult.

Brown, Turner, the Joint Chiefs of Staff, and I were in agreement that the treaty was adequately verifiable. This did not mean that we believed U.S. intelligence could monitor Soviet compliance with every one of the treaty's limitations with 100 percent confidence. That was technically impossible and unnecessary. As Brown stated:

> . . . there is a double bind which serves to deter Soviet cheating. To go undetected, any Soviet cheating would have to be on so small a scale that it would not be militarily significant. Cheating on such a level would hardly be worth the political risks involved. On the other hand, any cheating serious enough to affect the military balance would be detectable in sufficient time to take whatever action the situation required.

As for the short-term protocol limits on cruise missiles, we had determined at the outset that SALT must not foreclose NATO's essential options. At the time of the SALT hearings, we and our allies were moving rapidly toward a decision to strengthen NATO's long-range theater nuclear forces with ground-launched cruise missiles and the new Pershing II ballistic missile. Some of our allies were concerned that the protocol would establish a negotiating precedent for limits on cruise missiles beyond the terminal date of the protocol. I had obtained Soviet Foreign Minister Andrei Gromyko's explicit concurrence that this would not be the case. During the treaty hearings the Soviets reaffirmed this position to a Senate delegation to Moscow headed by Senator Joseph Biden.

I found disturbing the charges of some opponents of the treaty that allied endorsements of it were ingenuous and politically motivated. The allies strongly supported the SALT Treaty, and in my testimony I emphasized that failure to ratify the treaty would be extremely damaging to their confidence in us. Approval of the treaty would, I said, demonstrate to our allies that the United States could properly manage its strategic relationship with the Soviet Union.

One of the strangest aspects of the 1979 SALT debate was the ostensible consensus between liberals and conservatives in favor of deep reductions, and their joint condemnation of the treaty for having failed to attain them. Reductions were and obviously are important, but they are not the sine qua non of significant arms control.

One of the most important objectives of nuclear arms control must be improved survivability of delivery systems, both missiles and bombers. Progress in achieving greater survivability of weapons can be as important to our survival as large reductions. Failure to deal with the problem of the vulnerability of major elements of each side's deterrent forces could lead both superpowers into a hair-trigger, launch-on-warning posture that would be highly dangerous in a crisis. Thus, depending on many other variables, deep reductions may or may not contribute to strategic stability, and other objectives may be of equal or even greater importance.

The real choice for the Senate was: Are we better off with *this* treaty than with no treaty? My answer was unequivocally, yes, but let us ratify this treaty and get on with negotiating further reductions and tighter qualitative controls in the next phase (SALT III).

By the time the first cycle of hearings was finished and the Senate began its August recess, there was little doubt that the momentum favored the treaty. Every facet of the agreement, the protocol, and the principles for SALT III had been thoroughly explored and legitimate concerns answered. That proponents had prevailed over the skeptics was reflected in a shift in the thrust of the debate away from the treaty's provisions toward more subjective questions concerning the administration's ability to deal with the Soviet Union, linkage, defense budgets, and trends in the military balance. Henry Kissinger's July 31 testimony in support of the treaty but calling for increased defense spending, a new strategic doctrine emphasizing American capabilities to attack Soviet strategic forces, and a Senate condition making further SALT negotiations contingent on Soviet international restraint pointed to the main directions in the next round.

In our final appearance before the August recess, Harold Brown and I reiterated the administration's firm commitment to NATO's goal of an annual 3 percent increase after inflation in defense spending. In view of past difficulties we as well as earlier administrations had had in getting congressional approval of our full defense budget requests, I welcomed the consensus emerging from the SALT debate for a more substantial defense effort. However, conservatives were seeking to make the SALT Treaty hostage to an administration commitment to go well beyond the agreed 3 percent level. Just before the August recess, senators Sam Nunn, Henry Jackson, and John Tower of the Armed Services Committee wrote to President Carter asking for increases of at least 4 or 5 percent.

At the beginning of August it seemed to me that the outlines of a ratification "bargain" were taking shape. The president approved the MX missile deployment in June, and by August, studies of a mobile basing scheme were far advanced. If Carter would decide to deploy the MX in a mobile basing mode, agree to an increase in the defense budget, and acquiesce in several conditions acceptable to the administration in the Resolution of Ratification, he would satisfy many of the critics. The president would have responded to their concerns about ICBM vulnerability and stilled doubts about his commitment to a strong defense. Moderates and many conservative senators would ease their political concerns through the stated conditions to the treaty. The likelihood of Senate approval of the treaty in the late fall or early winter was reasonably good, though still not certain.

There was considerable discussion about how far the administration should or could go toward meeting the demands of defense-minded senators, such as Sam Nunn, without distorting our budget priorities. In my judgment, existing strategic weapons deployments and ongoing programs were in line with the basic requirements of deterrence and essential equivalence. The vagueness of the demands for more defense spending was evidence that the critics were having difficulty identifying major strategic programs where more money could usefully be spent. I felt there was little the United States could do to accelerate the main strategic and theater nuclear programs, which were already preferentially funded. I believed additional expenditures should be made on conventional forces, and should be used primarily to upgrade combat readiness and improve equipment maintenance, hardly the stuff of which headlines are made. The president was unwilling to be stampeded into spending more for defense than the planned 3 percent. He wanted a careful analysis of where additional resources could be used, and considerable work to this end was done during and after the August recess. Carter made it clear that we would spend more where need could be demonstrated, but not simply to gain votes for SALT.

Regarding conditions to ratification, the president and all his senior advisers were unanimous that no amendments or Senate conditions equivalent to amendments to the agreement could be accepted. Despite contrary opinions that were being bruited about by some treaty critics, we had little doubt that the Soviet leadership would reject any such changes. I believed that we could accept some understandings in the Resolution of Ratification, as we had done during ratification of the

Panama treaties, when these amounted to unilateral clarifications, interpretations, or declarations of U.S. policy that would not require Soviet
agreement or acknowledgment. Since they might open the floodgates to
amendments, this was risky. But it could be vital in winning the votes of
influential senators. It had been evident for some time that we needed
virtually a full-time political strategist to direct the ratification debate. I
was delighted when in June the president appointed Lloyd Cutler, a
brilliant Washington attorney and a close and valued friend of mine for
many years, to take on that task. If anyone could guide the treaty
through the Foreign Relations Committee, and on the Senate floor,
without the imposition of conditions that would kill it, it was Lloyd.

THE SOVIET BRIGADE IN CUBA

As the Senate SALT hearings progressed over the summer, another issue
slowly developed within the intelligence community and then burst dramatically on the political landscape. Once again the Soviet-Cuban connection diverted attention from more important questions and hurt us.
This was the belated "discovery" by the intelligence agencies of a Soviet
combat brigade in Cuba. When this was made public, it provoked a
political storm and delayed Senate consideration of the treaty long
enough for it to be overtaken and shelved as a result of the Soviet invasion of Afghanistan.

Because of Cuban military involvement in Angola and Ethiopia and
the Mig-23 flareup of late 1978, feelings about Cuba and its relations with
the Soviet Union ran high in the administration. In April 1979, Brzezinski had asked the intelligence agencies to reanalyze available information
about Soviet military activities on the island. In May, Brown also had
begun to express concern about stepped-up Soviet military activity in the
Caribbean and had urged that we consider a broad range of political,
military, and diplomatic countermeasures. I was uneasy. Knowing the
domestic political volatility of anything having to do with Cuba, I had
little doubt that any issue involving it would be distorted. As a nation,
we seemed unable to maintain a sense of perspective about Cuba, and
tended to inflate Castro's influence. Ironically, we had been in direct
contact with Cuban leaders for some time through highly secret channels and had made modest progress in alleviating certain bilateral problems relating to political prisoners, refugees, and better family access by
Cuban-Americans.

On July 17, Florida Senator Richard Stone alluded in a public hearing
on the SALT Treaty to the threat that Soviet combat troops in Cuba
would pose. Later, he called on the administration to come forward with
what it knew about any Soviet combat personnel based on the island.
Stone wanted to know whether such forces would constitute a violation

of the understandings we had with the Soviet Union, dating from the 1962 Cuban missile crisis and after, regarding Soviet military presence in Cuba. He was evidently well informed about the intelligence community's ongoing review of information on Soviet military activities in Cuba. Stone requested and was given a detailed classified intelligence briefing on July 24. He showed particular interest in whether we had information about a Soviet brigade command structure in Cuba. That afternoon he wrote to the president referring to such a possibility.

On January 27, 1978, during consideration of the Panama treaties, Carter had written Stone that, ". . . it has been and will continue to be the policy of the United States to oppose any efforts, direct or indirect, by the Soviet Union to establish military bases in the Western Hemisphere." Carter's letter had been important in gaining Stone's vote for the Panama treaties. It is possible that the Florida senator, currently struggling for reelection, saw a similarly firm Carter response to his question concerning the possibility of Soviet combat forces in Cuba as a way to reduce the political liability he had incurred by that vote. On July 25, Stone met with Vice-President Mondale and strongly urged that the administration take firm action. Stone argued that Soviet combat forces in Cuba would constitute a basic violation of a 1970 refinement of the 1962 understanding. He contended that the Soviets must be challenged or they would conclude they could violate agreements with us, such as SALT, without serious risk. Mondale ordered intelligence activities directed at Cuba stepped up in the hope that we could get a clearer picture of what was involved.

What had piqued Stone's interest in July was accumulating evidence, turned up in the intensified intelligence analysis Brzezinski had ordered, that there might be a Soviet unit of approximately brigade size and structure in Cuba. However, available data were ambiguous and fragmentary. It was not yet possible to determine whether any of the several thousand Soviet military personnel who had long been in Cuba in a training capacity were organized into a "combat" force. In a report on July 26, I was informed that the most the intelligence community could conclude was that there was a Soviet ground force unit in Cuba. The intelligence analysts were not prepared to say whether it was a combat force, a training structure for Cuban forces, or a facility for Soviet development and testing of tropical combat tactics.

The facts at that point were: neither the 1962 Kennedy-Khrushchev understanding banning offensive nuclear weapons or delivery systems from Cuba nor the 1970 prohibition on Soviet submarine bases covered Soviet ground forces; Soviet military personnel had been advising and training Cuban forces since at least 1962; as far as the intelligence community could tell there had been no substantial increase in the Soviet military presence; there were reports of some Soviet combat, as distinguished from logistical or administrative, personnel; and there was evidence, as yet inconclusive, that these combat troops might be organized as a brigade. On July 27, at the request of the White House, I wrote to Senator Stone that there was "no evidence of any substantial increase of the Soviet military presence in Cuba over the past several years or the presence of a Soviet military base."

At the end of July we found ourselves in a most difficult position. The Senate SALT hearings would soon be recessed for several weeks. Rumors of a Soviet brigade in Cuba were spreading, but there was doubt such a brigade existed. The intelligence experts could provide no solid information on size, composition, purpose, or even how long it might have been in Cuba. Senator Stone, a Foreign Relations Committee member with an intense interest in Cuba, had seized the issue. Stone had stated in closed-door discussions that if there was a Soviet combat unit in Cuba, the administration must deal with it resolutely.

I agreed that the presence of a Soviet combat brigade in Cuba would be a serious matter and would have to be made an issue in our bilateral relations with Moscow. On July 27, even though intelligence on the brigade was still inconclusive, I had Marshall Shulman meet with a senior Soviet embassy official to warn them that the presence of a combat unit in Cuba would inflame U.S.-Soviet relations at a critical moment in the Senate debate on the SALT II Treaty.

The brigade matter escaped the headlines through the month of August. Meanwhile, intelligence surveillance of the island was further augmented. On August 25, my staff reported that the intelligence was now sufficient to conclude that there was a Soviet motorized rifle brigade in Cuba, and that it had recently participated in field maneuvers as a combat unit. The unit, they said, consisted of some 2,000 to 3,000 men and appeared to have been in Cuba since at least 1975 or 1976. Its precise mission was still uncertain.

My judgment was that it was highly unlikely that the Soviets would agree to withdraw the brigade, if this became a public issue. Moreover, we would not be on solid ground in claiming the brigade violated the understandings on Cuba, since they did not cover Soviet ground forces. While past American administrations had frequently complained about the numerous Soviet military personnel on the island since 1962, none had made their presence an issue of compliance with the understandings. Given the intense political interest in Cuba, there was no doubt this new intelligence would be leaked very quickly. Little time remained for diplomacy to defuse the issue before it became a "crisis." Unfortunately, Soviet Ambassador Anatoliy Dobrynin was on leave in Russia, and I did not want to try to deal with such a sensitive question through second-level Soviet officials. I asked our ambassador in Moscow to urge Dobrynin's immediate return to Washington.

On August 28, my staff, in close consultation with the NSC, developed a plan to brief by telephone key members of Congress. We would outline the recent intelligence and tell them that we had lodged a strong protest with the Soviets underlining our serious concern. On August 29, Under Secretary David Newsom called in the Soviet chargé d'affaires. Newsom said that we were aware of the brigade and requested an explanation of its presence. He emphasized the harm it could cause to U.S.-Soviet relations unless quickly resolved.

On August 30, as planned, the calls to the Senate and House leaders were made. We explained the facts and that we had just learned a well-known defense journal with close ties to the intelligence community had this information and might publish it within a few days. All reacted calmly, except for Senator Frank Church. Church was in Idaho, fighting for his political life against a powerful assault by strident right-wing political action groups which were focusing largely on his alleged softness on defense and his support for the SALT Treaty. Church was being embarrassed by a news clip of a trip he had made to Cuba in which he was pictured with Fidel Castro.

Church's reaction, Newsom told me, was that revelation of the existence of a Soviet brigade would "sink SALT." Church then called me and said he believed it essential that someone in authority make the information public immediately, before it was leaked in some distorted form without any explanation or clarification. I told him that we did not intend to make any statement until we had more information. He asked me what would happen if he made a statement. I told him that it would be harmful, but I acknowledged to him that he was the only one who could make the decision. My expectation was that Church would say nothing, and that there would be no public discussion.

This proved to be incorrect. That same evening, Senator Church broke the story and called on President Carter to demand that the brigade be withdrawn immediately. A few days later he added that SALT probably could not be ratified unless the Soviets agreed to remove the brigade. Thus, before we had a chance to pursue quiet diplomacy, a hard line on the brigade had been drawn. There were others who echoed his call for linking the SALT Treaty to removal of the brigade. Church postponed resumption of the SALT hearings and asked me to appear before the Foreign Relations Committee on September 5 to discuss the brigade.

From my point of view, the brigade was an important issue that demanded a satisfactory resolution, but it was not sufficiently serious to warrant a "crisis" atmosphere, and definitely not a reason to interfere with the ratification of the SALT Treaty. Nevertheless, in the political climate of late 1979, a rational separation of the brigade issue and SALT was not possible. The president and I agreed that a firm but realistic stand was necessary.

I hoped that we still might be able, through Dobrynin, to persuade Brezhnev and Gromyko to take some helpful steps, such as removing the command structure and heavy weapons from the unit. If they would do so, we might resolve the brigade issue without fatally damaging SALT ratification.

Before leaving for Capitol Hill on September 5, I held my regularly scheduled press conference. In preparation for it, I discussed with my staff how to handle the inevitable question: "What are you going to do about the Soviet combat brigade?" To preserve negotiating flexibility while conveying seriousness, I decided to respond that we would require a change in the status quo.

When asked the question at the press conference, I replied, "I will not be satisfied with the maintenance of the status quo." My reply sounded stronger than I intended, and was widely interpreted to imply that we would demand removal of the brigade. What I meant was that changes in the armament, structure, and function of the brigade could allay our concerns about its combat capability. Later I met with the president, who agreed that the formulation I had used was consistent with our discussions. But in hindsight, I regret not having used words less open to misinterpretation.

That afternoon I went before the Senate Foreign Relations Committee and testified at length on the issue of the brigade. After that appearance, the committee agreed to resume its SALT hearings while I pursued discussions of the brigade issue with the Soviets. This was welcome news. We wanted the ratification struggle concluded before the end of the year, if at all possible.

Throughout the next three weeks, I met half a dozen times with Dobrynin and twice with Gromyko to discuss unilateral Soviet measures that would alter the status quo and resolve our concerns. I was unsuccessful. At the same time, I and others in the administration pressed the intelligence community to provide answers to further questions about the brigade, particularly its exact mission and how long it had been in Cuba. There were disturbing discrepancies in what the various agencies had been reporting, and it seemed increasingly possible that the brigade had not been surreptitiously inserted into Cuba recently. Closer examination of records revealed that earlier American administrations had known of Soviet ground units in Cuba and had not regarded them as worth concentrated intelligence surveillance. In 1962 the president and his advisers had wanted the ground units removed along with the missiles and the bombers. However, they did not press the matter, and the ground units remained. The more resources the intelligence community devoted to the brigade matter, the farther back in time information about it went—eventually all the way to 1962. Appallingly, awareness of the Soviet ground force units had faded from the institutional memories of the intelligence agencies. It was a very costly lapse in memory.

By late September it was evident that the unit in question had almost certainly been in Cuba continuously since 1962. Part of the damage done by the brigade issue was the misleading initial impression that it had been secretly introduced into Cuba only a few years before in a new and defiant Soviet challenge to our interests in the Caribbean. Much was made of this until, by mid-September, intelligence reports made clear it had been present in Cuba well before 1975.

The newly unfolding facts did not resolve all our problems. I proposed in the talks with Dobrynin and Gromyko that the Soviets remove the brigade headquarters, heavy equipment, and weapons, and discontinue its field exercises. They refused, insisting that it had been in Cuba unchanged in its function as a training unit for over seventeen years. They said it had nothing to do with the 1962 understanding, and that the United States had no right to request any gesture from Moscow. However, on September 27, Brezhnev wrote to Carter affirming that the unit in question was a "military training center," and that the Soviet Union had "no intention of changing its status as such a center in the future." The Soviets deemed this assurance a significant undertaking, not required of them by the Cuba understandings, which we could use to close off the issue.

After a second meeting with Gromyko on September 27 in New York, I concluded that the Soviets would not do more.

Lloyd Cutler and Hedley Donovan suggested that we recommend to the president that he invite a group of senior statesmen to meet with us to appraise the evidence and either verify or question the initial conclusion of the intelligence community that the brigade was a recent strengthening of the Soviet forces in Cuba. These men could also advise us as to what we should demand of the Soviets in terms of a change in the status quo, and whether we should link further efforts on SALT ratification to a satisfactory resolution of the brigade issue.

I agreed with Lloyd and Hedley's suggestions, and we recommended this course of action to the president, who concurred. The panel of Wise Men included a broad cross-section consisting of sixteen former Republican and Democratic senior State, Defense, CIA, and White House officials.* The panel met at the White House on September 29 and 30.

After receiving briefings from a number of adminstration officials, including myself, the group, although not unanimously, came to the following general conclusions. First, that they were highly skeptical that the brigade had recently been moved into Cuba. They concluded that the discovery of the brigade was in fact the rediscovery of the brigade that had been there since 1962, and that in reporting the incident they had mistakenly interpreted it as a new development. Second, that the brigade posed no threat to the United States. Third, that our response

* George W. Ball, McGeorge Bundy, Clark Clifford, Roswell L. Gilpatric, W. Averell Harriman, Nicholas deB. Katzenbach, Henry Kissinger, Sol Linowitz, John J. McCloy, John A. McCone, David Packard, William Rogers, Dean Rusk, James R. Schlesinger, Brent Scowcroft, and William Scranton.

should be measured and that we should accept minor changes in the status quo as satisfactory. And fourth, that we should not link SALT and the brigade issue. This advice was most helpful to the president and to me in shaping our response.

After the meeting, I recommended to the president that, in addition to announcing Brezhnev's September 27 assurances, we should also take a number of measured unilateral actions. These included increased surveillance of Cuba, increased economic and military assistance to Caribbean nations, and a larger regional U.S. military presence. I urged that these steps be announced publicly in connection with the brigade issue and not aimed at the overall U.S.-Soviet relationship. I told the president, as did Lloyd Cutler, that I favored treating the problem as a serious but isolated incident. My strong advice to the president was that we put the brigade issue behind us quickly and move on to the ratification of SALT. Letting the brigade matter drag on was doing serious damage to relations with our allies and friends, who were feeling that we had lost our sense of proportion. On October 1, the president spoke to the nation along the lines we had discussed.

After the president's address the brigade matter faded rapidly, although it lingered as a problem in the ratification debate. Politically, the administration had been seriously hurt by the episode.

THE SALT HEARINGS RESUME

The resumption of the SALT hearings was initially overshadowed by the brigade issue and my meetings with Gromyko. The positions of the first round of hearings were reversed. Some opponents now seemed more anxious to push the treaty to a vote; proponents, disturbed by the Cuba brigade stalemate, were more cautious, weighing the political risks to the treaty and to themselves. Senatorial and public interest in the hearings waned, and the once-crowded committee sessions were only sparsely attended. The debate turned sharply toward U.S.-Soviet political and military competition. Sensing a reversing of the momentum, conservatives intensified their efforts to tie the fate of the treaty to a major American military buildup.

From the start of the administration I had favored a prudent increase in defense spending and, together with Harold Brown, had pressed the president hard to agree to the 1977 NATO commitment to an annual 3 percent increase in defense spending above inflation. The NATO long-term defense program, the MX, the air-launched cruise missile and Trident submarine and missile programs, and the emerging alliance plan for theater nuclear weapons represented a comprehensive, balanced, and sustainable strategic plan. But now, in late 1979, suddenly to escalate defense spending and accelerate major weapons programs would, I felt, fuel the perception that we did not have confidence in our plan for maintaining the military balance. Conservatives would point to it as proof that we had not been doing enough on defense. Whatever increases we agreed to would not be sufficient to satisfy them. Liberals and some moderates would see such a move as an attempt to "buy" ratification of the treaty and a surrender to conservative pressures.

The Foreign Relations Committee hearings concluded on October 10 with an appearance by Harold Brown and me in closed session. Ever since the July hearings, pressure had been intensifying to postpone a Senate vote on the treaty until after the administration had presented the fiscal 1981 defense budget. Late in September, Gerald Ford had called for deferring a vote on SALT until Congress had approved a 5 percent real increase in 1981 defense spending. With the Republican party now joining the call for more spending on the military, the treaty had little chance unless the moderates could point to an increasing defense budget to justify supporting SALT. Before Brown and I appeared before the Foreign Relations Committee the president decided to take the unprecedented step of previewing the 1981 defense budget and five-year defense plan two months ahead of schedule. The preview would show the administration was firmly committed to a 3 percent real increase in defense expenditures, even if additional funds had to be requested from Congress to reach that level. If we could manage this defense budget preview well, it would still be possible to have a Senate vote before the end of the year.

President Carter also faced an extremely difficult decision on the basing plan for the MX. The military planners had recommended a plan for moving 200 MX missiles on launcher vehicles randomly among 4,600 widely spaced concrete shelters in valleys in Nevada and Utah. In August and early September, as we listened to the briefings on the proposed basing plan, it was apparent that neither the president nor most of his senior advisers felt comfortable. Tremendously expensive, politically controversial, and technically complex, it would be difficult to explain and defend. As one observer remarked, it would be the largest construction project in human history, dwarfing the pyramids of Egypt.

The plan, however, was the best of the several options we had examined, and for many reasons it was important that the president not delay a basing decision. On September 7, Carter approved this basing system. I supported his decision. I had long felt, since the 1977 cancellation of the B-1 bomber, that ratification of the SALT II Treaty would be unlikely without a firm administration commitment to the MX program.

Reassured by Carter's commitment to preview the defense budget and the MX basing decision, on October 16 the Foreign Relations Committee began to debate a draft Resolution of Ratification. Over the next three weeks, the committee adopted more than twenty conditions to ratification, but no amendments to the treaty. One, a reservation introduced by Senator Church, required that "prior to the exchange of the instruments of ratification, the President shall affirm that the United States will assure that Soviet military forces in Cuba (1) are not engaged in a combat role, and (2) will not become a threat to any country in the Caribbean or elsewhere in the Western Hemisphere." I believe that Church, a man dedicated to controlling and reducing nuclear weapons, had come to regret having linked the SALT Treaty so categorically to removal of the Soviet brigade. This reservation was an attempt to give the president flexibility to make the required affirmation based on unilateral U.S. measures, without Church's having to retreat entirely from his earlier stand.

There were many other reservations, understandings, and declarations in the committee's resolution, some of which would be bitter pills for Moscow to swallow. But in my opinion, none posed an insuperable obstacle to ratification. Several dealing with verification that were introduced by Senator Glenn were valuable clarifications, and most of the remainder were laudable reaffirmations of U.S. determination to maintain strategic equivalence, continue defense cooperation with our allies, and pursue more substantial reductions and limitations in SALT III. Sustained by an irreducible majority on the committee determined not to accept "killer amendments," senators Church and Javits skillfully deflected proposals that would have made the terms of ratification unacceptable to Moscow.

On November 9, by a vote of 9 to 6, the Foreign Relations Committee approved the Resolution of Ratification. Ten days later, the committee published a massive 551-page report on its exhaustive examination of the SALT II Treaty. This excellent report concluded that:

> . . . ratification of the SALT II Treaty, subject to the conditions the Committee has recommended, would make a positive contribution to American security and foreign policy interests, provided that the United States also vigorously undertakes necessary measures to maintain deterrence and essential equivalence, improve theater nuclear and conventional capabilities where needed, and enhance its intelligence capabilities. Conversely, the Committee believes that rejection of the Treaty, either directly by vote of the Senate, or indirectly through Senate action requiring renegotiation of some of its terms, would be contrary to our nation's security and foreign policy interests: It would strain the coherent functioning of the NATO Alliance; it would destabilize our relationship with the Soviet Union during a period of great potential international turbulence; it could require even higher defense expenditures for strategic forces; and it could result in a significant degradation in our intelligence capabilities.
>
> The Committee believes that the Treaty cannot be sent back to the negotiating table to seek greater concessions from the Soviet

Union without also reopening fundamental issues resolved in favor of the United States and thus running a significant risk that there will be no agreement in the near term. It is the Committee's judgment that this Treaty is better for the United States at this point than no Treaty at all. The Treaty is a compromise of interests reached over seven years of painstaking negotiations, and the Committee is persuaded that this bargain should now be sealed so that the two Parties can move promptly to the follow-on negotiations, which provide the best prospect for achieving the stringent limitations and deep reductions which were not achieved in SALT II.

The treaty reached the floor several weeks later than we had hoped, but Majority Leader Robert Byrd, who had come out strongly for the treaty on October 24, still thought a vote could come before the Christmas recess. However, as so often in its turbulent history, SALT II once again fell victim to external events.

17

IRAN:
HOSTAGES ARE TAKEN

SINCE THE REVOLUTION, our relations with Iran remained badly strained, but our diplomats in Tehran had gradually expanded their contacts with the Bazargan government. A number of common interests gave us a basis for developing contacts with some parts of the government. Businessmen needed to return to Iran to pick up interrupted work, and both governments wished to scale down and sort out the residue of a huge military purchase program. Also, hundreds of Iranian students wanted to return to the United States to continue their studies. This required the reopening of our consular facilities in Tehran.

Our limited aims were to maintain access to Iranian oil and to gradually develop improved relations with the new government. We knew this would not happen quickly since we were in the midst of continuing revolution. The prodemocratic secular nationalists were clearly having difficulty holding their own against pressures from the clergy to erect a theocratic, authoritarian state.

As the power struggle mounted, we remained watchful, doing what we could to stabilize relations with the new government. In August, for example, we agreed to resume the limited supply of spare parts for the American-made military equipment used by the Iranian armed forces. We also exchanged intelligence with one or two members of the Bazargan government. This was done discreetly, since any contact with American intelligence officers could endanger our Iranian interlocuters. Although the number of American officials in Iran had been drastically reduced after the February 14 attack on our embassy, a staff of about fifty (formerly about 1,400) remained. Their duties were to maintain contact with the new government and provide Washington with current analysis of the bitter political struggle for control of the revolution.

As relations slowly became more businesslike, embassy and consular staffs were increased to about seventy people. The physical security of our chancery building had been strengthened since the attack on February 14. Our staff could hold out now for at least two or three hours, sufficient time for government forces to arrive, and for the destruction of secret files and sensitive communications equipment. In September, following our persistent protests throughout the spring and summer about the Iranian guard force that surrounded the compound, the Iranian government finally replaced them with uniformed police.

In the fall of 1979, the Iranian Revolution was far from over. There was widespread resistance by such dissident ethnic groups as the Kurds, with whom the government was waging a civil war. Every faction seeking to dominate the revolution harbored paranoid fears of residual "pro-shah" forces in the country and suspected that the United States would try, as it had in 1953, to restore the shah to his throne. Those vying for power fell into two broad categories: the secular nationalists who wanted to erect a modern Iranian state, and the Islamic clerics who wanted to rid Iran of "corrupting" Western influences and establish an Islamic state. There was little unity within either of these wings of the revolution. The secular nationalists were split into a moderate democratic group led by Bazargan, and a second group, which included Abolhassan Bani-Sadr, and which shared at least some of Khomeini's Islamic ideals. To the left were extreme factions who coalesced in shifting alliances aimed at establishing a radical, Marxist Iran. The clerics were also split, between a moderate wing grouped around Ayatollah Kazim Shariat-Madari and a much larger, more powerful Islamic fundamentalist wing led by Khomeini's lieutenants. The ultimate arbiter in the contest for power was Khomeini.

As we tried to establish a businesslike relationship with the new leaders, we also began to explore ways to strengthen regional security. There were a number of Special Coordinating Committee meetings through the summer and fall to review U.S. security policy in the Persian Gulf. Brown, Brzezinski, and I agreed that we should move promptly to bolster our defense ties and military capabilities in the region. Harold Brown and I recommended several important measures to the president in August. The program included enhancing our capabilities to deploy rapidly ground, air, and naval forces into the area, to conduct joint military exercises with friends and allies, to increase moderately our permanent presence (mainly through naval deployments in the Indian Ocean) and to initiate more substantial security consultations with key states in the region.

In addition, the president approved actions by us to gain access to local ports and airfields during a crisis (including expansion of air and naval facilities on the tiny British-held island of Diego Garcia), and to pre-position combat equipment for support of American ground forces. All of this preceded the Soviet invasion of Afghanistan. These steps stemmed not from the invasion of Afghanistan, as some have suggested, but rather from the turmoil in Iran. The hostage crisis and the Soviet invasion of Afghanistan simply accelerated measures already under way.

• • •

In late December of 1978, when the shah had first talked about leaving Iran, we had instructed Ambassador Sullivan to tell him he would be welcome to come to the United States. Instead of coming to the United States, he dallied in Cairo and Morocco to show his displeasure with the United States. He was encouraged in this by Ambassador Zahedi. Had the shah come to America at that time, the tragic events that followed might have been different. After the occupation of our embassy on February 14, 1979, however, we concluded that if we were to leave American officials in Tehran, admitting the shah might jeopardize their safety. It was therefore President Carter's difficult duty to send word to the shah, who was then in Morocco, that he should not come to the United States. Staff studies pointed out that if the shah were permitted to come to the United States, it would be seen by most Iranians as an indication that we intended to restore him to the throne and overturn the revolution. The studies suggested that Americans in Iran might be taken hostage to be held against his return to Iran to stand trial.

We accepted the conclusions of the report but decided that should order and government authority be restored in Iran, it might then be possible for the shah to come to the United States. In July, we weighed the possibility of admitting him, but Bruce Laingen, our able chargé d'affaires, advised that it was unsafe to do so under the existing circumstances. Laingen advised that it might be feasible to admit the shah when the internal power struggle was resolved, but until then there was a great risk that his admission might be used by anti-Western forces as a lever to gain control of Iran. Laingen urged that the problem of the shah's admission be deferred while the United States continued to seek improved relations and until a stable constitutional government was formed. We agreed.

Further study of the shah's plight and its relationship to the direction of the Iranian Revolution continued in August. We were becoming concerned that the shah's stay in Mexico—where we had helped him to find temporary residence—might not be extended beyond October.

In September, Laingen briefly returned to the United States for consultations, and the question of whether and when political conditions in Iran would allow us to admit the shah was again discussed. Once again, we judged that the time was not ripe.

On September 28, however, a virtual bombshell exploded. Under Secretary David Newsom was told by David Rockefeller's office that the shah was seriously ill and might ask to come to the United States temporarily for medical reasons. When queried about the possible Iranian reaction to receiving the shah under those circumstances, our embassy replied that with the power of the mullahs growing, admission of the shah, even on humanitarian grounds, might provoke a severe disturbance.

We did not yet know the nature of the shah's illness when I met with the new Iranian foreign minister, Ibrahim Yazdi, at the United Nations on October 3. When asked by him whether we had any intention of admitting the shah, I told him that we did not rule out admitting him at some point. My intention was to test Yazdi's reaction to the prospect that the shah might have to come to the United States for medical treatment. Yazdi was noncommittal. The main thrust of our discussion involved Iranian complaints about the United States, the nature of our bilateral relations, and our position on the Bazargan government. I told him that we recognized and accepted both the revolution and the new government and were doing nothing to destabilize Iran, as he charged early in our conversation. I told him we were prepared to deal with Iran in the future on the basis of friendship and mutual respect. He listened attentively but again was noncommittal. Later, while he was still in New York, other State Department officials met with him at length to discuss the straightening out of Iran's military assistance accounts.

On October 18, David Rockefeller's staff told us that the shah's condition was worsening and that his illness could not be properly diagnosed and treated in Mexico. They emphasized that the possibility of cancer could not be ruled out. Two days later we were informed that he was suffering from malignant lymphoma, which he had been concealing for several years and which was no longer responding to chemotherapy. Rockefeller wanted to bring him immediately to Sloan-Kettering Hospital in New York. The State Department medical director, Dr. Eben Dustin, whom we had sent to Mexico to examine the shah, concurred in the diagnosis and in the urgent need for treatment at medical facilities in the United States.

Thus, on October 20, we were faced squarely with a decision in which common decency and humanity had to be weighed against possible harm to our embassy personnel in Tehran.

Before leaving that day for an important meeting in South America, I discussed with Warren Christopher my views on what we should recommend to the president. Following my guidance, on October 20 Warren sent a memorandum to the president which proposed that we:

> Notify Prime Minister Bazargan in Tehran of the Shah's condition and the humanitarian need for his hospitalization in the United States.
> Unless the Iranian Government's reaction is strongly negative—in which case I would consult you again before proceeding—to inform the Shah that we are willing to have him come to New York, but ask that his household in Mexico be kept intact pending further developments. (Lopez Portillo informed the Shah on October 19

that the Shah may return to Mexico following medical treatment
here.)

Allow the Shah to come here for treatment as arranged by David
Rockefeller.

Prepare to respond to press public inquiries with a statement that
the Shah is being admitted for diagnostics and evaluation on humanitarian grounds and that no commitment has been made as to
how long he can remain.

Carter approved these recommendations, which were designed to minimize the dangers as much as possible. The president and his senior
advisers were unanimous that we should go as far as possible to help the
shah if we were convinced the Iranian government could and would
protect the embassy. Carter tentatively decided that if we received a
satisfactory reaction from the Iranian government, we would admit the
shah.

On October 21, Laingen met with Bazargan and Yazdi to describe the
shah's condition and his need for treatment. Laingen reported they had
assured him the embassy would be protected, although they warned of
probable hostile demonstrations and feared that our bilateral relations
would be harmed. They suggested ways of handling the public aspects of
the shah's admission, which we took to indicate they believed the security problem was manageable. One official also wanted an assurance that
neither the shah nor his entourage would engage in political activities
while in the United States. This assurance was obtained from the shah,
and we immediately communicated it to the Iranian government. The
next day additional police were sent to guard the embassy.

When Laingen's report was received, the president made the final
decision to allow the shah to enter the United States temporarily. The
shah arrived in New York on October 22, and his first operation was
performed on October 24. The Iranian government, in announcing the
shah's arrival, stated that he was "terminally ill," a move that we interpreted as an effort to ease the reaction in Iran.

The initial public response in Iran seemed to bear out our assessment
that the Iranian government could maintain control of the situation.
There were large demonstrations, but protection around the embassy
was good. Khomeini himself at first merely threatened to bring suit in
the United States demanding the return to Iran of the shah's fortune.
On the other hand, most Iranians, including some members of the government, displayed strong suspicion about the seriousness of the shah's
illness and the necessity that he be treated in the United States. Meanwhile, medical reports indicated that the shah had only a fifty-fifty
chance of living another eighteen months.

By October 30, however, the mood in Iran had begun to change for
the worse. That day the government, frightened by hostile crowds, requested extradition of the shah for trial. November 1 seemed to be a

critical day. Khomeini called on students to increase their anti-U.S. activities in order to force us to return the shah. That same day, the government successfully diverted a massive demonstration away from the embassy. However, Khomeini evidently decided to align himself with the mob rather than the government, and Bazargan's and Yazdi's authority was seriously undermined.

At this critical moment both Bazargan and Yazdi were at the independence celebrations in Algiers. To my surprise, Brzezinski, who was a member of the American delegation to Algiers, met with them. He later told us that the meeting had been held at the Iranians' initiative. That, unfortunately, made no difference to the political consequences. The meeting was used by the militants in Tehran to charge Bazargan and Yazdi with being too inclined toward the United States. Their meeting with a high American official at the very time that massive anti-shah demonstrations were sweeping Tehran made Bazargan and Yazdi vulnerable to attack by extremists who wanted to purge the government of its secular and sometimes pro-Western elements. By the time they returned to Iran, both men's authority had been greatly weakened.

• • •

On Saturday night, November 3, at about 8:30 P.M., I arrived back in the United States from Korea, where I had gone to represent the president at the funeral of President Park. Shortly after 3:00 A.M. on Sunday morning, November 4, I was awakened by Arnie Raphel, my special assistant, with the terrible news that our embassy compound in Tehran was under attack from a street mob. Raphel had just been called by the State operations center and told that Ann Swift, a political officer in the embassy, was on the telephone describing the actions of the mob of about three thousand people who had broken into the compound. Alerts were being sent to the White House situation room, the Defense Department's National Military Command Center, the watch centers of all the intelligence agencies, and key State Department officials. The operations center, Raphel said, had been able to patch through Swift to Hal Saunders and two other officials, Sheldon Krys, executive director of the Bureau of Near Eastern and South Asian Affairs, and the acting director of Iranian Affairs, Carl Clement, at their homes. Saunders had taken charge of attempts to get through to Iranian government authorities to demand help. I told Arnie I would leave immediately for the department and that he should meet me there.

While I was dressing, Saunders continued to receive Swift's accounts of the mob's actions. During the next two hours, Swift remained in touch with Washington from her post in the ambassador's outer office in Tehran. Before I arrived at my office, Saunders and Laingen had ordered the destruction of classified material and the visa stamps to prevent their falling into Iranian hands. Once in the department, I started to receive frequent reports from the steadily growing group of political, security, and antiterrorist experts Saunders had begun to assemble in the operations center as he relayed instructions through the watch team. We all prayed they would be able to withstand the mob until help came from the Iranian government. We knew that no embassy could hold out for long without help from the host government.

A few minutes before 5:00 A.M. Washington time, Ann Swift told Saunders that some of the mob were reaching the upper stories of the chancery and had captured and were threatening to kill several Marine guards. Some of the staff, including four members of the Marine guard, had been taken prisoner, as the guards fought with tear gas to keep the attacking crowd from breaking into the ground floor of the chancery. Swift said the remaining staff (some seventy to eighty people, including Iranian employees) was going to surrender before the mob began to harm the captives and to cut through the vault door with an acetylene torch. With smoke from the ground floor beginning to reach the top floor, and fearing harm to the captives, Swift and the other senior officers had no alternative. At 4:57 A.M. phone contact with the embassy ceased. Shortly after 5:00 A.M. Swift said to her colleagues, "We are going down," and they started down the stairs to surrender.

Appeals to Iranian officials through Swift and Bruce Laingen, who chanced to be in the Foreign Ministry when the attack began and who was informed of the assault over his car radio after he left the ministry, had failed to bring a rescue force. Bruce, along with Victor Tomseth, the political counselor, and Michael Howland, a security officer, returned immediately to request help from Foreign Minister Yazdi, who had just returned from Algiers and was on his way to his office.

Contact with the compound continued for about half an hour after the staff on the second floor opened the door to the attackers. Elizabeth Koob, who was working in another building away from the compound, was still able to get through to the operations center by phone for some hours after the compound fell. She remained in contact with a few staff members who were still locked in the communications vault and reported that they were still destroying secret documents and coding equipment. At 5:30 A.M., Koob said she had just been told that they had completed the destruction. Communications with Koob stopped. That was the final contact with the compound.

A few moments after communications with the compound ended, David Newsom called from the operations center and said it was all over. I phoned President Carter, but he had already been informed by Zbig. We arranged to meet later, and I turned back to getting a task force set up in the operations center.

I learned later that the staff in the consulate building was able to escape from the compound by a side street. Five of them were able to reach the Canadian embassy, where they were given refuge. They were later joined by our agricultural attaché. Weeks later they were to escape with the gallant help of the Canadians.

Establishing a task force was standard procedure in any significant international crisis that involved Americans or U.S. interests, and did not in itself mean that we had concluded freeing the captives would be a lengthy process. Although everyone recognized that seizure of the embassy staff was an extremely serious matter, the general expectation throughout the day and even into the next was that their release would be obtained within a few hours once the Iranian authorities intervened, as they had done on February 14 under the leadership of Yazdi.

No one realized how completely responsive the mob was to religious extremists, or understood the fact that Bazargan's and Yazdi's political authority had been diminished. Yazdi remained in his office with Laingen and his colleagues until 8:30 P.M. He made some effort to get help but to no avail. Yazdi left, saying he had to attend a meeting of the Revolutionary Council.

* * *

On November 4 sixty-three Americans in the embassy were seized by the militant students. Three more, including Bruce Laingen, were incarcerated at the Foreign Ministry, and several others went into hiding.

Thus began an agonizing time for our countrymen and our nation. The Iranian government was disintegrating. While the embassy was still under siege, Laingen demanded that Yazdi help to end its occupation. After it had surrendered, we were able to open a direct telephone line to Laingen. He reported that Yazdi was upset. There was, however, little the foreign minister could do. He seemed to sense that he was losing control and that his orders would not be carried out. We also contacted the Ayatollah Behesti, but taking his cue from Khomeini, he too supported the militants. On November 6, the Bazargan government collapsed and power shifted to the religious leaders and their secular allies. Instead of replacing the government leaders, Khomeini gave full political authority to the Revolutionary Council, a body of clerics and militants, which had been acting as the guardian of the revolution.

In Washington, devising an effective strategy to secure the release of the hostages was made more difficult by our sparse knowledge of the political dynamics in Tehran. It was obvious that real authority resided with Khomeini.

The ayatollah's exact involvement in the taking of the hostages may never be known. Whatever his role, however, it seems clear that by the end of October he had decided to give his rhetorical support to the mobs. I felt that Khomeini was a charismatic and ruthless leader who was not one to row upstream. He preferred to move with the current of public opinion. After the takeover of the embassy, it became apparent that some of the Islamic figures in the revolution may have designed the seizure as a means of weakening the secular government. The student captors of the hostages later told some of the hostages that their purpose in seizing the chancery had been to mobilize popular support for the Islamic elements of the revolution and against the secular authorities. They had expected the takeover to breathe new life into the sagging revolutionary spirit and to last only a few days. To their surprise, their action exceeded their wildest expectations. The militants soon found themselves riding a tiger they could not or did not wish to control.

Probably, it was not until Khomeini saw the hysterical mob reaction and sensed the hostages' potential for uniting the warring factions against a hated foreign enemy that he decided to use them as a rallying point for bringing about a new Iranian state. He appeared to recognize that secular politicians, not the clergy, would have to administer an Islamic republic, but this, he felt, should be done only under the direction of the religious leaders. Before Khomeini could be sure that the delegation of administrative responsibility would not jeopardize the Islamic purity of the revolution, it was necessary to crush the independence of the secular nationalists, including those represented by Bani-Sadr.

Even though our understanding of the forces at work in Iran was limited, we understood that Khomeini alone had the power to free the hostages. Therefore, on November 5, we recommended to Carter that he send an emissary to Khomeini. Warren Christopher suggested Ramsey Clark, a former attorney general with good contacts among the religious leaders, including Khomeini, and William Miller, an ex-Foreign Service officer who had served in Tehran and spoke Farsi. Both were willing to go. Their primary task was to obtain the release of the hostages, but they would also listen to whatever Khomeini and the other leaders had to say about future relations with the United States. I agreed. Carter approved the recommendation, and Clark and Miller left on November 6 aboard a U.S. Air Force 707. Through Bruce Laingen, who had remained in the Foreign Ministry, and with whom we still had contact, we obtained Iran's agreement to allow them into the country.

On November 7, as Clark and Miller changed planes in Turkey because the Iranians would not permit a U.S. military aircraft to enter their air space, they received word that Khomeini had denied them admission and had decreed that no Iranian official could meet with any representative of the American government. It is difficult to say for certain what caused this turnabout, but it is likely that it was at least partly due to the announcement, as Clark and Miller were en route, that they were emissaries of the president. This was a bad mistake. Had their mission been kept unofficial and out of the spotlight, Khomeini might have received them. No one knows what the result of that might have been. Probably nothing—but perhaps it would have made a difference.

In retrospect, it seems probable that the Clark-Miller mission represented the last chance to get the hostages out before they became pawns in the Iranian power struggle—if indeed they were not already so by November 7. After that, it was evident that freeing the hostages would be a long and painful process, although we had no way of knowing at that point how terribly long it would turn out to be.

From the outset of the hostage crisis, we sought to develop a political strategy and a set of fundamental principles to guide us in freeing the hostages in a manner consistent with national honor and our vital interests. After receiving a pessimistic assessment on November 6 from the Joint Chiefs of Staff on the feasibility of a rescue operation, the idea was dropped. Nevertheless, contingency planning was permitted to go forward so that we would have options for a rescue operation if we learned the hostages were about to be harmed. On November 20, an additional carrier task force was sent to the Indian Ocean to join the one already there.

We believed that the hostages were pawns in a power struggle and valuable only as long as they were unharmed. Although we felt they were probably in no immediate physical danger, we were deeply concerned about the conditions of their captivity and the unpredictability of their captors and the emotional crowd that marched daily in the streets outside our embassy compound. These factors, and a judgment that U.S. military action would only stimulate the Shi'ite fervor for martyrdom, were the major reasons behind an early decision to use patient diplomacy and concerted international pressure rather than force.

Concurrently, the president decided that we would pursue two goals: protection of the nation's honor and interests, and the safe release of the hostages. We would not return the shah to Iran, offer any apology for past American policies or actions, or permit the hostages to be tried. To gain these objectives, we would follow a dual-track strategy:

• We would open all possible channels of communication with the Iranian authorities to determine the condition of the hostages and give them aid and comfort, to learn the Iranians' motives and aims in holding them, and to negotiate their freedom.

• We would try to build intense political, economic and legal pressure on Iran through the United Nations and other international bodies, increase Iran's isolation from the world community, and bring home to its leaders in Tehran the costs to the revolution and to Iran of continuing to hold the hostages in violation of international law.

Implementation of this strategy began almost immediately after it became clear that neither Bazargan nor Yazdi would be able to free the hostages. On November 9, the cessation of all shipments of military parts and equipment to Iran was ordered. On November 13, imports of Iranian oil were banned. On November 14, a key measure, freezing Iranian assets held in American banks and their foreign branches, was put into effect. We had been debating for several days whether to impose such a freeze, when in the early morning hours of November 14, Iran announced that it would withdraw all its deposits from our banks for the purpose of weakening the dollar. About 4:00 A.M. I was awakened by a call from Secretary of the Treasury G. William Miller, who had received word of the Iranian announcement. We quickly agreed that we should immediately put the freeze into effect. President Carter concurred and at 8:10 A.M. he signed the necessary papers. The freeze gave us important leverage; it was ultimately to play an important part in bringing about the release of the hostages. Congress strongly supported our actions.

Carter also leaned toward breaking diplomatic relations immediately. I advised against this because I believed it would needlessly close off a line of communication with Tehran, and perhaps endanger the hostages by inciting Iranian fears that we were preparing for military action. I saw little to be gained from gestures that would only aid in stirring up mass hysteria in Iran.

Once it became clear that Bazargan and Yazdi would not be able to carry out their commitment, we immediately went before the United Nations Security Council, which unanimously condemned the brutal seizure and demanded the immediate return of the hostages. At first it seemed that these moves might engage the Iranians in a dialogue, but this possibility dimmed as the revolution became more violent. To augment the action of the Security Council, and to demonstrate to the world that the United States was exhausting every peaceful remedy in the international storehouse, we also brought an action against Iran in the International Court of Justice. We were aware that Tehran would probably ignore an order from the World Court to release the hostages, but a ruling that Iran had violated international law would increase world pressure and deepen Iran's isolation. In mid-December, in an unprecedentedly rapid decision, the International Court issued a preliminary finding in our favor. There was an outpouring of condemnation of Iran by virtually all governments.

Within a matter of days after November 4, we had opened indirect and informal channels to Iran. Among them was a channel to the PLO. The PLO proved helpful in persuading Khomeini on November 17 to order the release of thirteen female and black hostages. The thirteen arrived in Washington on November 22. Through them and other sources, we gained information on what was happening in Tehran and the captors' barbaric treatment of some of the hostages. The publicity spurred intensified condemnation of Iran, and by early December it led to some improvement in the conditions under which the hostages were being held.

The first significant diplomatic avenue to be opened was through the United Nations. On November 14, I met secretly with Secretary-General Kurt Waldheim in New York to discuss how the UN might help, despite the fact that the Security Council actions had not produced any results. Hal Saunders and I left from a secluded part of Andrews Air Force Base for New York and rode from the Marine Air Terminal in New York to

Kurt Waldheim's house on Sutton Place in a yellow cab rather than the usual State Department car. There we met with Kurt and Rafeeuddin Ahmed, Kurt's *chef de cabinet*, who was a wise and helpful adviser throughout the hostage crisis. By that time we were already aware of the divisions within the Revolutionary Council. Secular nationalists, such as Bani-Sadr, and some religious pragmatists were reportedly looking for a quick end to the crisis before irretrievable damage was done to Iranian economic and political interests. Unfortunately, however, the Revolutionary Council had no authority over the captors, who would obey only Khomeini. Since we could not reach the ayatollah, we had no choice but to try to work through the Revolutionary Council.

Waldheim suggested that he invite Foreign Minister Bani-Sadr to New York for discussions on the hostages with the Security Council. I agreed to meet with him in private. His recent statements had indicated that Iran's basic conditions for freeing our people were a return of the shah's assets, an end to alleged U.S. interference in Iran, and an apology for our past "crimes" against Iran, which we were not prepared to do. On November 17, I gave Kurt a statement containing four points which, while they underwent some evolution, remained the heart of the American position throughout the almost fifteen agonizing months of the crisis:

1. We required release of all personnel held in Tehran.
2. We suggested the establishment of an international commission to inquire into allegations of violation of human rights in Iran under the previous regime.
3. We indicated that the courts of the United States would be available to the government of Iran to hear its claims on the assets it believed had been illegally taken out of Iran.
4. We proposed an affirmation by the governments of Iran and the United States of their intentions to abide strictly by the Declaration of Principles of International Law Concerning Friendly Relations and Cooperation among States in Accordance with the Charter of the United Nations, and by the provisions of the Vienna Convention on Diplomatic Relations.

The planned meeting with Bani-Sadr never materialized. He was suddenly dismissed from his post as foreign minister on November 28 and went into temporary eclipse until he reappeared as president of Iran in January 1980. He was replaced as foreign minister by Sadegh Ghotbzadeh, who, though also a secular nationalist, was close to Khomeini.

At the time the black and female hostages were released, there was talk in Tehran about putting some of the remaining hostages on trial as spies. We privately sent through intermediaries a stern warning that trying or harming the hostages would have grave consequences for Iran. But because of Bani-Sadr's dismissal, we could never be sure whether the message reached him. Carter repeated the warning on December 7 in a meeting with families of the hostages, and through a leaked account of that meeting, the message appeared in the *New York Times*. A number of options were examined, including blockading Iran's ports and mining its waters. Even amid the chaotic conditions in Tehran, the Iranians understood that our restraint was not limitless.

By the end of November, President Carter's political standing had risen dramatically. The public and Congress strongly supported the president's restraint in dealing with the crisis, as well as his firmness in refusing to capitulate to Iran's demands for extradition of the shah and for an apology. We sought to keep Congress and the American people fully informed about our efforts to secure release of the hostages, while naturally protecting the confidentiality of our indirect channels to Iranian leaders. The news media kept an intense spotlight on the crisis.

In hindsight, I believe it was a mistake for us not to have played down the crisis as much as possible, particularly after it became evident that freeing the hostages would be a long, slow process. The more we declared our fear for their safety and our determination to leave no stone unturned to gain their freedom, the greater their value became to Khomeini and the Islamic extremists. Obviously, we could not have kept the hostage crisis out of the nightly television news, even had we wanted to do so, but we made a mistake by contributing unwittingly to Iran's exploitation of the nation's heartfelt anxiety by letting it appear that the hostages were the only concern of the U.S. government. I share the responsibility for this mistake, since I did not advise the president against it. On the other hand, we must also recognize the fact that the glare of publicity may have helped to save their lives. In any case, we had very little choice but to treat the hostage problem as a major national issue.

This said, I am still convinced that the basic strategy of restraint, escalating international pressure, and diplomacy adopted in the first days of the crisis was right and consistent with the honor and interests of the United States and the safety of the hostages. In the end it proved successful, even though the president and the administration were wounded by it.

The month of December was dominated by intense efforts to exert massive international pressure on Iran. On December 4, the UN Security Council adopted Resolution 457, which called on Iran to release the hostages immediately and requested the secretary-general to lend his good offices in mediating a solution. When Iran rejected that resolution, Carter directed that we expel all but a handful of Iranian diplomats from the United States and that we begin consultations with our allies on the imposition of economic sanctions.

The Soviets supported Resolution 457 and told us privately they were urging the Iranians to comply with it. Moscow took a legally correct position on the hostages, though it was clearly seeking to exploit the situation to its advantage. We protested strongly about inflammatory radio broadcasts to Iran from the Soviet Union, warning Moscow that its actions in the crisis would affect American attitudes for a long time to come. By that time U.S.-Soviet relations were spiraling downward and little help was to be expected from the Soviet Union.

Immediately after the December 4 vote, we had started plans for obtaining allied support for strong economic measures against Iran. Financial and political experts were dispatched to Europe for preliminary discussions about the kinds of sanctions we might jointly impose. Despite the allies' sympathy for our plight, they strongly disagreed with us on the advisability of imposing stringent economic and diplomatic sanctions. Although we would push them, I was not optimistic about their willingness to face significant economic loss or risk political damage in the gulf before we had fully exhausted the possibilities of Waldheim's mediation.

In my talks with the NATO foreign ministers in December, I described our policy of restraint and the contacts we had had with Iran. I said that there were limits to the United States' patience and that a continuing stalemate would become intolerable. I stressed that the president was determined to apply strong economic pressure on Iran to make it more responsive to a negotiated solution. In private meetings, without aides, I warned that if diplomacy and economic measures were not successful—and they could not be without determined international support—we faced the alternative of military force. I urged that in the interests of avoiding such a situation, fraught with incalculable consequences for everyone, the allies join us in strong sanctions. My entreaties received ambiguous responses. All indicated a willingness to take limited economic steps against Iran if mediation and diplomacy failed, but agreed to only a few measures that would have an appreciable impact on the Iranian economy. Several allies said that for legal and domestic political reasons, they could do little without a binding Security Council resolution imposing sanctions on Iran.

On December 18, after my return from Europe, Carter accepted a recommendation by the Special Coordination Committee that we propose in the UN Security Council that all states ban military sales to Iran, prohibit new financial credits, cut off or sharply reduce all air and rail links, and apply a trade embargo on everything but such things as food and medicine. In light of the worsening situation in Afghanistan and our confrontation with the Soviets on this issue, we recognized that Soviet support for our resolution was unlikely. We decided to proceed anyway, because even if the Soviets and their friends on the Security Council vetoed or abstained, the resolution still might be used by our allies and friends as a legal basis for sanctions. As disappointed as I was, I still hoped that the allies would join us in sanctions once it became clear that we had at least nine votes in the Security Council in favor of sanctions.

• • •

Just before I left for Europe for consultations on Iran, we had received word that President Omar Torrijos was prepared to invite the shah to Panama. This was a potentially significant development. The shah's departure from the United States would deprive Iran of one of its main pretexts for continuing to hold the hostages. I didn't think that his departure would in itself resolve the crisis, but it could bolster those in Tehran who were trying to gain Khomeini's approval to free the hostages before serious harm befell the Iranian economy and the international standing of the revolution. While I was still in Europe, Warren Christopher, with my approval, recommended to the president that we move immediately to take advantage of Torrijos' offer.

On October 19, 1979, Joseph Reed informed David Newsom that Mexican President José Lopez Portillo had told the shah he could return to Mexico following his medical treatment in the United States. We requested confirmation of this in a message to our embassy in Mexico City on October 21. Telephonic confirmation was received from our chargé d'affaires the next day. Assurances were also received that the shah's household in Mexico would remain and that members of his family could stay in Mexico. On November 29, twenty-five days after the seizure of the hostages, we were stunned by the Mexican government's decision not to renew the shah's visa.

Why President Lopez Portillo reneged on these assurances is a matter for speculation. It seems highly likely, however, that, shaken by the sudden, sharp confrontation between the United States and the Iranian revolution, the Mexican government decided that the situation had so substantially changed that it would no longer honor its promise to the shah and its assurances to us.

We turned to Lloyd Cutler to carry out the delicate task of approaching the shah about going to Panama. On December 14, in a meeting at Lackland Air Force Base in Texas, where the shah had gone after his treatment in New York, Cutler reached agreement on the terms of the shah's stay in Panama. In the so-called "Lackland Understandings" we promised to provide the shah with medical assistance from U.S. facilities in Panama, as well as advice on security, although his protection was to be the responsibility of the Panamanian government. We assured the shah that we would continue to help him find a permanent refuge and would not characterize his presence in Panama as permanent. It was agreed that his children could remain in the United States and that the empress could visit them. Finally, the understanding stated that:

> The Shah's departure from the US does not preclude his returning here, but there is no guarantee that he may return. If he asks to return because of a medical emergency, we will favorably con-

sider his request. If he asks to return for nonmedical reasons, we will consider his request but can make no commitment whatsoever at this time.

On December 15, the shah left for Panama.

In the final ten days of December we conducted intensive discussions with members of the Security Council on the text of our proposed resolution. Carter wrote Brezhnev a personal message requesting Soviet support. The Soviets refused.

On December 31, a week after the Soviets had mounted the invasion of Afghanistan, the Security Council passed Resolution 461 by an 11–0 vote, with four abstentions, including the Soviet Union. The resolution set January 7, 1980, as the date when the Security Council would reconvene to adopt sanctions, if by that time Iran had failed to comply with the resolution of December 4 calling for release of the hostages. In failing to apply sanctions immediately, Resolution 461 underlined the disagreement between the allies and us. The Europeans, Japan, and other friends did not want to leave us in the lurch, particularly since they feared we might strike out at Iran, but none of them wanted to risk a long-term disruption of their Persian Gulf trade and oil links.

Despite the limitations of Resolution 461 and the political and security implications of the Soviet move into Afghanistan, in the final days of December the diplomatic track, which had been blocked since mid-November, reopened, and UN Secretary-General Waldheim completed his plans to go to Tehran to meet with the Iranian leaders.

18

THE RUSSIANS
INVADE AFGHANISTAN

AFGHANISTAN: A TURNING POINT IN U.S.-SOVIET
RELATIONS

THE LANDLOCKED, mountainous, poverty-stricken country of Afghanistan, inhabited by fierce and courageous tribesmen, has long been prey to stronger powers. Its people have striven to maintain a precarious independence by ferocious resistance and a delicate political balancing act. When the British withdrew from the Indian subcontinent in 1947, Afghanistan balanced uneasily between East and West, accepting aid from both the United States and the Soviet Union. The United States, having few interests in Afghanistan, maintained only a limited diplomatic presence and a small economic aid program. The Soviet Union overshadowed Kabul, which was careful not to offend its giant neighbor to the north.

This situation, which left Afghanistan as a buffer between the Soviets and areas of U.S. interest to the south (e.g. Iran and Pakistan), lasted until April 1978. Radical leftists in the army, in a bloody coup, overthrew the civilian government of President Mohammed Daoud (who himself had toppled the monarchy some years earlier) and killed Daoud.

Although the officers who overthrew Daoud were from the far Left, we had no evidence of Soviet complicity in the coup. Within a few days, Nur Mohammed Taraki, head of a pro-Moscow political faction, emerged as the leader in Kabul. The Soviets asserted that Moscow was surprised by the coup and by the emergence of Taraki as president, prime minister, and secretary general of the party.

After consultations with the Iranians about their security concerns, we informed Taraki that we would continue diplomatic relations with his regime. We reminded him of our long-standing support of Afghan independence and its nonaligned foreign policy. Iran and most of our European allies recognized the new government the same day. Taraki assured us that he intended to follow an independent course of action and asked for economic assistance. I concluded that our best chance to maintain a measure of influence in Kabul was to continue limited economic aid. To cut off all assistance or refuse recognition would almost certainly weaken our position in Kabul.

We were worried about the destabilizing effect of the coup on Afghanistan's neighbors, particularly Iran and Pakistan. We believed that the new regime's first priority would be to consolidate its own position. But there were substantial risks that the government in Kabul would seek eventually to undermine the government in Pakistan.

We sent Under Secretary of State David Newsom to Kabul in July to discuss economic assistance. He returned with a pessimistic assessment of the new regime's capabilities and intentions. He believed, however, that the political situation was still fluid and that it would be a mistake for us to halt economic assistance and lose the prospect of any influence in Kabul. We decided to continue several programs and to watch the situation closely.

During the remaining months of 1978 and into 1979, we received reports of widespread opposition to the Taraki regime and increasing armed resistance by tribal groups. The Afghan Army, riven with disaffection, was performing poorly and losing control of the countryside. Afghan exiles in Pakistan were calling for a general religious uprising against the Taraki government. The Soviets, who had signed a friendship treaty with Afghanistan in December 1978, were faced with the fact that Kabul's authority outside the major cities had collapsed. Moscow stepped up its military aid and dispatched more military advisers to shore up the crumbling Afghan Army.

As previously recounted, in February 1979 our ambassador, Adolph Dubs, was killed. With the security situation becoming ever more dubious, we refused to replace Dubs or to authorize new aid to Afghanistan.

By the middle of 1979, there were unmistakable signs of Soviet dissatisfaction with Taraki, who was ignoring Moscow's advice. In March, Foreign Minister Hafizullah Amin, a moving force in the April coup, was made prime minister. Even with the help of Soviet arms and military advisers, however, Kabul was unable to suppress the growing opposition. In July, Amin also became the de facto minister of defense and took control of the struggle against the insurgents.

On September 16, 1979, President Taraki was mortally wounded and several of his supporters were killed in a confused shoot-out during what appears to have been a palace coup. Taraki's death was announced officially on October 19, and he was replaced by Amin, who Moscow no doubt hoped would be more effective in prosecuting the war. However, the Soviets seemed to be unable to find a way to quell the insurgency. Amin proved to have a mind of his own, and the Soviets became increasingly dissatisfied with his inability to attract popular support. Eight thousand miles away, we saw the Soviet political and military stake increase as central authority and public order disintegrated.

Trying to Preserve a Balanced Policy

Assisting moderate governments in the Middle East and the Persian Gulf was a major element of the administration's policy. It underpinned our arms supply relationship with the shah, our decision in 1978 to sell advanced aircraft to Saudi Arabia, and our efforts to shore up Middle East stability by bringing peace between Israel and the Arabs. Ever since Harold Brown had gone to the gulf, in February 1979, we had been working to augment our military power in the region and strengthen our security ties with Saudi Arabia and other moderate states. Afghanistan and the continuing disorder in Iran were threatening the Persian Gulf security system. There was a danger of a vacuum into which Soviet power would spread toward the Indian Ocean and the Persian Gulf.

In looking back, I think we should have expressed our concerns more sharply at the time of the April coup that brought Taraki to power. There were reasons why we did not protest more vigorously. Although there was little question that the Taraki government would make itself responsive to Moscow, there was room for doubt about whether the Soviets had planned the coup or were involved in its execution. And there was reason to think that the strong Afghan nationalism of Taraki, and even more of Hafizullah Amin, might keep Afghanistan from becoming a Soviet satellite. After Newsom's trip to Kabul we concluded that our interests would best be served by letting Afghanistan continue its traditional balancing act between East and West. The United States had few resources in the area and historically we had held the view that our vital interests were not involved there. Moreover, our friends in the region had adopted a wait-and-see attitude. There was no disposition on their part to add to the instability by supporting opponents of the Marxists in Kabul. Although we were contacted from time to time about coup plots, my advice was that we not get involved.

By the late summer of 1979, it was evident that the Kabul regime was unable to pacify the tribal insurgents, who were motivated by regionalism, anti-Soviet nationalism, and Islamic fundamentalism. And it was clear that Afghanistan was becoming almost totally dependent on Soviet military aid. The Islamic character of the resistance to the government was doubtless deeply disturbing to the Soviets. The visit of the commander-in-chief of Soviet ground forces, General Ivan G. Pavlovskiy, to Kabul in August evidenced Soviet anxiety over the worsening situation. The Pavlovskiy mission stayed until mid-October.

By that time, the question was not whether the Soviets would become more actively engaged in the Afghan civil war, but what form their larger involvement would take. Most intelligence analysts thought it more likely that Moscow would significantly increase its military assistance and training of the Afghan Army and assume greater operational control of the war than commit its own combat troops.

In November and December, both the White House and the State Department were preoccupied with the Iran hostage crisis and other issues we were pursuing with the Soviets—particularly Kampuchea and southern Africa. The accumulating intelligence on Soviet activities received less top-level attention in the U.S. government than would otherwise have been the case. Also, there were background news stories coming out of Washington to the effect that there was a possibility of some form of U.S. military action against Iran. I felt this unwise. U.S. military presence in the area would make a collapse of the Kabul regime more dangerous for the Soviets and thus enhance the possibility of Soviet intervention. In addition, a U.S. military move in Iran might diminish international reaction to a Soviet invasion, as the Anglo-French attack on Egypt had done in the Suez crisis in 1956.

Initial administration contingency planning focused on a range of political and diplomatic measures. We began regular consultations with our allies and other states to keep them apprised of unfolding events and to start preparing a concerted political response to tightening Soviet control over Kabul. Through Pakistan and others we sought to keep the Iranians informed of what was happening and to convince them that the hostage crisis was diverting world attention from Soviet subjugation of a neighboring Moslem state. During November and December we warned the Soviets on several occasions.

By early December, intelligence was accumulating that contrary to earlier estimates, the Soviets were building up substantial forces on the Afghan border and were deploying some combat units in and around Kabul. On December 20, we received information that elite Soviet paratroops had moved into Afghanistan, and that it was likely additional forces would follow. On December 25, Soviet troops poured in. Amin was murdered and his government overthrown. The Soviets alleged that they had come in at his request. This was patently false. Rather, it appears that they were responsible for his death. Thus began the brutal invasion and attempt to subjugate the courageous Afghanis which continues to this day.

The most significant question for us was the nature of our response. Related was the question of why Moscow had elected to intervene massively with its own combat forces rather than increase its advisers and military assistance. Two theories were advanced within the administration. One suggested that Moscow had concluded that merely propping up the existing regime offered no long-term answer to the threat of fundamentalist Islamic resurgence. Should this occur, it could infect other Moslem states and weaken Soviet influence in the region, as well as increase Moscow's concern about its own Central Asian Moslem population. Rather than continue to limp along, this theory held, the Kremlin had decided to replace the Amin regime with a more compliant one and to intervene directly with sufficient force to guarantee the new regime's survival and push the insurgents back into remote areas. If this was the case, Moscow's objectives were primarily local and related directly to perceived threats to its national security.

The second theory, a more global one, postulated that the Soviets had calculated that their relations with the United States were deteriorating so badly that they had nothing to lose in moving decisively to liquidate the Afghan problem and improve their strategic position in Southwest Asia. Soviet pessimism, it was argued, was augmented by their paranoia about a U.S. "tilt" toward China and their fears of a NATO military buildup. By consolidating their position in Afghanistan, it was suggested, the Soviets would be in a position to exploit events in Iran. They would also be able to exert strong influence and pressure on both Pakistan (a long-time American ally and friend of China) and India as a counter to American moves into the Indian Ocean and Persian Gulf.

My view was that Moscow had acted as it did for a number of reasons. Its immediate aim was to protect Soviet political interests in Afghanistan which they saw endangered. Some Soviet leaders saw Amin as a nationalist Communist who did not listen to Soviet advice and was stumbling into a disaster. They feared that the regime would be replaced by a fundamentalist Islamic government and that this would, in turn, be followed by a spread of "Khomeini fever" to other nations along Russia's southern border. Other Soviets believed that they should seize this opportunity to position themselves more favorably with respect to China and Pakistan. Moreover, the downward spiral in U.S.-Soviet relations had released the brakes on Soviet international behavior. If, as is likely, Moscow had decided by late December that the SALT Treaty was in deep trouble, that access to American trade and technology was drying up, and that the dangers of American–Chinese–western European encirclement were growing, it probably had concluded that there was little reason to show restraint in dealing with a dangerous problem on its border. I am not suggesting that the Soviets would not have acted had relations with us been better. But it is possible that had there been more to lose in its relationship with the United States, the Soviet Union would have been more cautious. Finally, the Soviet leadership badly miscalculated not only the extent of the military resistance they would encounter, but also the strong reaction of the Islamic nations and the world community. Above all, they made a disastrous miscalculation about the reaction of the United States. In sum, there were both local and global pressures pushing the Soviets in the same direction.

The administration's response, hammered out in intensive high-level meetings between December 27 and January 2, was strong and calculated to make Moscow pay a price for its brutal invasion. Our fundamental objective was to bring about the withdrawal of Soviet forces. But recognizing that this might not be attainable for a long time, Carter directed that we should "make Soviet involvement as costly as possible." He also directed that we strengthen our position in the Persian Gulf and Southwest Asia. At the same time he agreed with his advisers that we should not link further action on SALT ratification to Afghanistan. However, he felt that it would not be possible to ratify the treaty in the current climate.

On January 3 the president requested Majority Leader Robert Byrd to defer Senate consideration of the treaty. To ameliorate the impact of this action on our European allies, and to strengthen the possibility of ratifying the treaty in the not-too-distant future, Carter asked Byrd to keep the treaty on the Senate calendar of pending business rather than return it to the Foreign Relations Committee.

The president announced that we would take no action contrary to the terms of the treaty pending ratification, so long as the Soviets did the same. This prevented the unraveling of restraints on the strategic competition at a time of high tension.

The president also directed that we strengthen our security ties with Pakistan, and improve our relations with India. It was agreed that a high-level mission would be sent to Islamabad to consult with the Pakistanis on military cooperation and that Clark Clifford would be sent as an emissary to India. If we could reach agreement with Pakistan on the terms of an assistance package, we would seek congressional approval to waive the legal prohibition on military aid to Pakistan. At the same time, we would reaffirm our nuclear nonproliferation policy and press Pakistan to provide acceptable guarantees that it would not develop a nuclear weapon.

The president also approved a number of measures to impress upon Moscow that there would be no quick return to "business as usual," as was the case after the Russian invasion of Czechoslovakia in 1968. The most important of the sanctions that were imposed was the embargo on new grain sales to the Soviet Union. No other measure was as costly to the Soviet Union or as clear a demonstration that the United States was prepared to accept significant sacrifices to impose a price for aggression. Other sanctions included stopping the sale of high-technology equipment, such as computers, restricting Soviet fishing privileges in American waters, postponing the opening of new consulates in Kiev and New York, and withdrawal from the 1980 Olympics in Moscow. A number of cultural and technical exchanges were also cancelled, and the presumption was established that future high-level meetings would also be cancelled unless there were strong reasons for not doing so. I fully supported these sanctions.

• • •

Differences over the direction of U.S.-PRC relations had resurfaced even before Afghanistan. Concerned about Harold Brown's proposed visit to Peking, I had sent Carter a memorandum on September 18, 1979, cautioning against a "tilt" toward China. Vice-President Mondale had previously discussed with the Chinese a valuable broadening of our relations in Peking, but over my objections, he had also proposed that the secretary of defense visit China later in the year. I advised Carter that

> . . . at certain points U.S.-PRC global or strategic interests will be parallel, and we will find ourselves working closely together in the UN or elsewhere in pursuit of common objectives. But this does not mean we should move into a military security relationship with China, for there is an element of finality in moving toward an alignment with China.

I believed that Brown's trip was planned for at the wrong time. The Cuba-Soviet brigade furor was at its height, and a visit by the American secretary of defense to Peking was bound to be perceived in Moscow as related. I felt that establishing military ties with China was an inappropriate and ineffective counter to the brigade issue.

The president had rejected my recommendation that Brown's trip be postponed until a time when there would be less chance that it would be perceived in Moscow, Peking, Tokyo, and NATO capitals as an anti-Soviet move. As planning had continued, it became apparent that I was alone in my desire to maintain our longstanding policy of evenhandedness between the USSR and the PRC on the transfer of dual-use technology, although before the Afghanistan incursion, Carter had agreed that we should not offer to supply arms or military equipment to China.

On December 17, the president once again chose balance and restraint in our policy toward China, although the temptation to proceed in the direction suggested by Brown and Brzezinski was surely strong. He determined that we should pursue our relations with China within the following guidelines:

• There would be no U.S. arms sales to China at this time.

• There would be no military relationship with China at this time.

• We had no desire to provoke a Sino-Soviet conflict or to manipulate Sino-Soviet tensions for tactical benefit.

The Soviet move into Afghanistan changed the picture. On January 4, 1980, just before Brown left for Peking, the president decided to offer

China nonlethal military equipment and reaffirmed an earlier decision to seek special treatment for China on high-technology transfers. I was worried that the offer to sell China nonlethal military equipment was the first step along the road toward providing offensive weapons.

In Peking, however, the Chinese proved more wisely hesitant than we were. Brown found a near convergence between the United States and China on broad strategic interests, but he also discovered that the Chinese leaders were wary of being used as a counterweight in the U.S.-Soviet geopolitical rivalry. I was not surprised.

• • •

The clearest expression of American determination to protect our national interests in the Persian Gulf region was the president's State of the Union message in January of 1980. Carter presented a practical program of actions to strengthen regional security and to deter further Soviet expansion. These actions included: reaffirming our 1959 security agreement with Pakistan; accelerating development of a rapid deployment force; increasing spending for conventional forces; encouraging closer security cooperation with friends and allies; and proposing legislation to reinstitute registration for the draft. I would have preferred that we reinstitute the draft, and I suggested that this would send the Soviets the clearest message of our determination. These, as well as other actions, represented a sustainable response to the invasion of Afghanistan and supplemented the more punitive measures we had taken immediately after the invasion, such as the grain embargo and the Olympics boycott.

I helped draft the president's State of the Union message, and in general I believed it to be a good statement of our policy. It made clear that although the United States would shoulder a major share of the military burden and provide the essential leadership, the defense of Western and regional security interests must be a cooperative effort. Our friends and allies, whose interests in open access to the gulf were at least as great as ours, should contribute to the common goal of increased security.

• • •

The Afghanistan problem highlighted tensions between the United States and our allies over the problem of responding to Soviet challenges outside Europe. We saw Afghanistan as significant for the West in two important ways: To begin with, it was the first example since World War II of Soviet military occupation of a non-Communist-bloc country. The security interests of the West dictated that we act cohesively and promptly to demonstrate to the Soviets that such behavior was not an acceptable part of the East-West competition. Second, the invasion moved Soviet ground and air forces several hundred miles closer to the gulf and the West's jugular vein of oil. Even if some allies did not fully agree that Afghanistan set a dangerous precedent for Soviet aggression in other areas, common Western interests dictated that we all contribute to strengthening the security of the oil fields and access to the Persian Gulf.

Our European allies and Japan agreed in principle that we must deter further aggression, and they supported limited sanctions and diplomatic actions, such as a strong condemnation of the Soviets in the United Nations. However, insofar as trade sanctions and export credits were concerned, they refused to take strong steps.

Several of our allies were prepared to take some measures to help strengthen security in the gulf. For example, we worked out with Great Britain an expansion of the naval and air facilities on the island of Diego Garcia in the Indian Ocean. A number of our allies, including Britain, Germany, Italy, and France, collaborated with us in an international financial consortium to assist Pakistan. But some of the allies were reluctant to increase their own defense spending and military capabilities in Europe to compensate for American military forces redirected to the Persian Gulf and Indian Ocean region. Several argued that we could do more for overall Western interests in the gulf by finding a solution to the Palestinian problem.

Another major factor inhibiting a strong allied response was the deferral of the SALT II Treaty and the prospect of an intensified nuclear arms race. On December 12, the alliance adopted a dual strategy for maintaining a stable nuclear balance in Europe: at a joint meeting of the NATO foreign and defense ministers, it was decided to deploy 572 intermediate-range weapons (U.S. Pershing II ballistic missiles and ground-launched cruise missiles) capable of striking targets in the Soviet Union; at the same time, it was agreed that the United States should offer to negotiate limits on U.S. and Soviet intermediate-range nuclear weapons, preferably in SALT III. The arms control aspect of this so-called two-track approach was politically essential to contain expected internal opposition to the proposed deployments within most of the member countries. It was agreed that limiting the deployment of intermediate-range weapons on both sides could prevent an unrestrained arms race in Europe, a race which would drain off resources better directed at building up NATO's conventional forces.

Maintaining an arms control dialogue between the United States and the Soviet Union was a critical part of the alliance's strategy for preserving the nuclear balance in Europe. With the ratification of the SALT II Treaty, limitations on and reductions in Soviet intercontinental weapons would have been in place and the West could have moved quickly to broader negotiations, including, for the first time, intermediate-range nuclear forces as well as intercontinental weapons. This was politically and militarily important to our allies.

There was another question that haunted alliance discussions in the wake of Afghanistan. The vigorous steps we had taken immediately after the invasion, followed by the broader political and military strategy outlined in the president's State of the Union speech, caused uneasiness in Europe and Japan. Many felt that the United States was about to swing sharply back into the cold war. In my discussions with the British, French, and Germans in late February, I encountered serious concern that the administration's reaction to Afghanistan was exaggerated and threatened to wreck the framework of East-West relations. Upset at what they viewed as inadequate consultations on a common Western approach before we announced far-reaching punitive steps, some felt we had adopted a confrontational strategy without taking European interests into account; having done so, we were now unfairly criticizing them for inadequate cooperation and support.

There were grounds for the allies' complaint—although I believe they should have given greater consideration to the need for rapid, decisive actions in the face of the Soviets' blatant aggression. But it is also true that, shocked at the speed and vigor of our reaction, they had concluded that we were moving farther away from a balanced policy than I and, I believe, the president intended. I assured the Europeans that the Carter administration was not going to dismantle the structure of détente or cut off communication with the East. I said that we believed the steps already taken were a firm and sufficient response and no new punitive measures were required. I emphasized that the arms control dialogue must continue because it was in the interests of the Western nations to do so. Moreover, I said, we would seek approval of the SALT Treaty as soon as we thought there was a chance it could be ratified.

One of the lessons to be learned from Afghanistan is the importance of giving a clear forewarning of what we viewed as unacceptable behavior, both as a deterrent to Soviet aggression and to prepare our allies and the American public for swift and firm counteractions.

The allies' concern over our reaction to Afghanistan pointed to a potentially serious divergence between the United States and its European partners over what constituted a balanced policy toward the Soviet Union. Because of their geographical propinquity to the Soviet Union and their understandable desire to protect the concrete gains of détente, our allies were reluctant to react as strongly as we did. Rather than risk the stability so slowly and painfully won in Europe, they preferred to leave to the United States the task of deterring Soviet adventures outside of Europe. This came perilously close to the mistaken idea that détente and western European-Soviet relations can be isolated from events elsewhere. Some allied leaders understood the fallacy of this thinking, but the central issue remains unresolved.

On the other side of the coin we must recognize that we are but one member of an alliance. In an alliance, there must be consultation among all the members. And we must understand that consultation is more than merely listening to what one's fellow members have to say. We must be willing not only to discuss matters thoroughly in advance, but also to adjust our position in order to achieve a unified alliance position. If we do this, we will remove an important cause of the strains that now beset the alliance.

U.S.-western European relations and the cohesion of NATO would be seriously damaged if two distinct views on how to treat the Soviet Union should begin to separate us. If the alliance is to remain the foundation of Western security there must be basic agreement on the nature of our global objectives and on the collective responsibility of the West to protect its interests. There must also exist a willingness on the part of all parties to participate as equal partners in the development of alliance policy.

•   •   •

Any American administration is a coalition of individuals with diverse viewpoints, and the Carter administration was no exception. Before Afghanistan, these differences, though sharp at times, were containable at the cost of not having a truly coherent policy. Afterward, however, it became increasingly difficult to hold the coalition together.

Of the president's advisers, I believed most strongly that we should strive for a balanced policy toward the Soviet Union and should avoid violent swings between trust and hysteria. I agreed that we must be strong, steady, and consistent, and that we needed both carrots and sticks to manage the relationship wisely. I was also of the view that how we conducted our relations with the Soviet Union in the next few years would be the most significant test of our judgment and our capacity for leadership.

Afghanistan was unquestionably a severe setback to the policy I advocated. The tenuous balance between visceral anti-Sovietism and an attempt to regulate dangerous competition could no longer be maintained. The scales tipped toward those favoring confrontation, although in my opinion, the confrontation was more rhetorical than actual.

In late January, I urged the president to communicate with Brezhnev to impress upon the Soviets that their action in Afghanistan threatened the very basis of U.S.-Soviet relations. Troubled and angered by the course of recent events, he declined to do so. With his permission, on February 8 I wrote to Gromyko warning that there was a high risk that each might miscalculate the actions of the other. I pointed out that the relationship between our two countries was the most critical factor in determining whether the world would live in peace, and that the series of events culminating in Soviet actions in Afghanistan had brought us to a fork in the road. I said that it was vital that both of us give sober consideration to the implications of the current situation for each side's interest in the maintenance of world peace. I went on to say that despite the differing political convictions of our countries, and because of the inherent competitive interest between us, we had sought to establish common rules of behavior that would reduce the risk of conflict. This, I said, would not be possible unless both of us recognized the need to act with restraint in troubled areas. I emphasized that it should be evident that the withdrawal of Soviet military forces from Afghanistan was necessary to restore a sense of stability to the region, and pointed out that the United States had vital interests at stake in the Persian Gulf region. I closed by saying that if there was restraint on both sides and respect for the independence and territorial integrity of the states in the region, our respective interests need not lead to confrontation, and requested that he indicate to us Soviet intentions in both Afghanistan and the region.

I also sought Carter's approval to meet Gromyko in March to reinforce this message and to reopen a dialogue between us. The president again refused. I then suggested that Marshall Shulman be sent as a special emissary to meet with Brezhnev in an attempt to reestablish a dialogue, but this too was turned down.

In a somber meeting with Ambassador Dobrynin on March 21, I urged him to make Moscow understand there was no prospect of improving our deteriorating relations until its leaders grasped the seriousness of Afghanistan. I underlined that the president and I remained committed to controlling nuclear weapons and did not want to see this essential part of the East-West framework destroyed. I told Dobrynin that we wanted to pursue frank talks and I asked him to pass on to Gromyko my suggestion that he and I get together in April or May. However, it was left to Edmund Muskie, my successor, to reopen the channels of communication with the Soviet leadership in his meeting with Gromyko on May 8 in Vienna.

• • •

A question troubling Congress, the allies and the American public in the spring of 1980 was whether the Carter administration had a coherent view of the international situation, a sense of global strategy, and consistent policies and objectives. At the root of this concern was confusion at the apparent sharp contrast between our foreign policy goals and priorities before and after Afghanistan.

In response to requests from Congress for a clear exposition of the administration's overall strategy, I appeared before the Senate Foreign Relations Committee on March 27 to offer a comprehensive statement of U.S. foreign policy. Although I did not know it at the time, this was to be my final opportunity as secretary of state to define and explain America's foreign policy and its role in a changing world. To allow for comparison of that statement with my October 24, 1976, memorandum to candidate Jimmy Carter on my views on what his foreign policy should be, I have included the full text of both in the appendix to this book. However, I would like to quote from my March 27 testimony.

Some have argued that a strong response to Soviet military growth and aggression is overreaction. But to disregard the growth of Soviet military programs and budgets . . . or to explain aggression as a defensive maneuver . . . is to take refuge in illusion.

It is just as illusory, and just as dangerous, to believe that there can be a fortress America or that the world will follow our lead solely because of our military strength. America's future depends not only on our growing military power; it also requires the continued pursuit of energy security and arms control, of human rights and economic development abroad.

As we look to the 1980s, our first obligation is to see the world clearly.

We confront a serious and sustained Soviet challenge, which is both military and political. Their military buildup continues unabated. The Soviet Union has shown a greater willingness to employ that power directly, and through others. In that sense, Afghanistan is a manifestation of a larger problem, evident also in Ethiopia, South Yemen, Southeast Asia and elsewhere.

The world economic order is undergoing a dramatic change. An energy crisis has rocked its foundations. Economic interdependence has become a daily reality for the citizens of every nation.

At the same time, the assertion of national independence has reshaped the political geography of the planet. There is a profusion of different systems and allegiances, and a diffusion of political and military power. Within nations, we see an accelerating rise in individual expectation.

These challenges require a full American engagement in the world—a resolve to defend our vital interests with force if necessary and to address potential causes of conflict before they erupt.

Can we say that our security is more threatened by the growth of Soviet military power or by the strains we can foresee in the international economy? By the prospect of nuclear weapons in the hands of additional nations or by the prospect of social and political turmoil in many regions of the world?

The hard fact is that we must face each of these and other challenges simultaneously. Clearly, our interests do collide in particular circumstances. There will be no escaping the difficult task of weighing our interests against each other, moving each forward whenever possible.

Our course in the world must be defined by a mix of interests, sensibly balanced, meeting always the central imperative of national security for our country and our people. No simple slogan or single priority can answer in advance the dilemmas of the coming decade.

I had hoped the March 27 hearing would spark a serious discussion in Congress, the press, and inside the administration about the way the United States should conduct itself in a world in which the many complex problems are not susceptible to solution by simple answers or the use of military power alone. I was convinced that the main lines of our foreign policy remained valid and would stand up well under a searching cross-examination. But televised hearings do not encourage such debate. The senators were more interested in the events of the moment, such as the grain embargo and energy. Senator Si Hayakawa carried this one step further by pressing me on the burning issue of collecting traffic fines from Iranian students in Washington.

19

RESIGNATION

BEFORE THE INVASION of Afghanistan, our strategy toward Iran was to exert increasingly heavy political and economic pressure until the advantages to Iran of holding the hostages were outweighed by the costs. Afghanistan did not invalidate this broad approach, but it did compel us to proceed with greater care so as not to drive Iran into the arms of the Soviet Union. The risks were not high, because of Khomeini's antipathy to communism and Iran's fear of Russia. Still, they could not be ignored, and that was one of the dangers underlying my opposition to threatening Iran with military action.

Afghanistan also had an effect on the secular pragmatists such as Bani-Sadr and Ghotbzadeh. The more realistic members of the Revolutionary Council seemed interested in ending the crisis soon so that Iran could turn its attention to its external security and its internal economic problems.

Khomeini's role and objectives in the hostage crisis remained unclear. Interestingly, even he did not seem to have total freedom of action. The fact that he was using the hostages to consolidate his control of the revolution indicated that his power was not absolute. We could not be sure of the degree to which he shared the Revolutionary Council's concern over Iran's international isolation, growing rift with Iraq, and vulnerability to Soviet political and military coercion. By year's end, however, we were reasonably confident that Khomeini's endorsement of the occupation of the embassy was primarily to strengthen the revolution and to manipulate the players in the struggle for power.

The first step toward serious negotiations began with Secretary-General Waldheim's trip to Tehran on January 1, 1980, pursuant to Security Council Resolution 461, to see whether he could break the stalemate. By this time the Iranians were demanding that they be given an international forum in which they could publicly air their grievances against the shah and the United States and justify their seizure of the hostages. After discussing with the president how we might turn this demand to our advantage, I gave Waldheim a new statement of our position on December 31. Our position was that we would not block a public inquiry once the hostages were released, and that we were prepared to work out the arrangements for such a hearing in advance of the freeing of the hostages. We reasoned that an agreement to set up an international tribunal to hear Iranian grievances could be portrayed by the secular pragmatists in Iran as satisfying the country's political requirements, and would in turn give us leverage to negotiate the hostages' release.

The five points in the statement I gave Waldheim were:

1. All U.S. personnel must be released from Iran prior to the institution of any international tribunal.

2. The United States is prepared to work out in advance of a release a firm understanding on arrangements for the airing of Iranian grievances before an appropriate forum after the hostages have been released.

3. The United States will not object to Iranian suits in U.S. courts to recover assets allegedly taken illegally from Iran by the former shah.

4. The United States will affirm jointly with Iran its intention to abide by the Declaration of Principles of International Law Concerning Friendly Relations and Cooperation Among States in Accordance with the Charter of the United Nations, and the provisions of the Vienna Convention on Diplomatic Relations. The United States accepts the present government of Iran as the legitimate authority in Iran and reaffirms its view that the people of Iran have the right to determine their own form of government.

5. The United States is willing, once the hostages are safely released, to seek in accordance with the UN Charter a resolution of all issues between the United States and Iran.

Waldheim left for Tehran with our five points in his pocket. However, when he arrived in Iran he ran into a storm. He was physically threatened and treated badly. I feel that he handled himself very well under extremely difficult conditions, and I will be everlastingly grateful to him for all he did over many months to help bring about the safe return of all the hostages.

While he was in Tehran, the Iranians sought to twist Waldheim's statements into suggesting that the commission could begin its work before the release of the hostages. I made it clear this was unacceptable. Although Waldheim's visit to Tehran was not immediately successful, the Iranians did become interested in the idea of an international commission, and it eventually became the core of the release plan worked out in the following weeks.

On January 7, Waldheim's negative report on his trip to the Security

Council reopened the question of sanctions. After a brief delay to consider an Iranian proposal to establish an international commission of inquiry—unacceptable because it did not provide for prior release of the hostages—we pressed for a sanctions vote on January 12. The Security Council meeting ran late into the evening. The council chamber was packed and the tension was acute. Some of the representatives had not received their instructions when the meeting opened and we waited anxiously for word to reach them from their capitals. The final vote was 10 to 2 with 2 abstentions. China did not participate. The lone veto was cast by the USSR.

Despite the veto, we declared that the United States would impose sanctions. We asked our allies to join us. Several of them told us that they could not do so without a binding UN resolution. Since the Iranian presidential elections were scheduled for January 29, the allies asked us to refrain temporarily from imposing sanctions and to wait until we could find out whether the new government would enter into serious negotiations.

We reluctantly agreed to their request. Although it was unlikely, we hoped that elections would produce an Iranian leader with power to make binding decisions. But we were upset. Although some of our allies faced legal difficulties because of the lack of a binding UN resolution, we felt they could have found a way to act if they had chosen to do so. Because the imposition of strong sanctions was vital to our strategy of increasing pressure, we were determined to impose them as soon as possible, with or without allied participation.

After the January 12 vote, we received indications through our indirect channels that the Afghanistan invasion had stirred the interest of some of the Iranian leaders in a sign from us that would help them move Khomeini toward a resolution of the crisis. That day, Carter approved sending the Iranians, through Waldheim, a fuller statement of our position:

> 1. The safe and immediate departure from Iran of all U.S. employees of the Embassy in Tehran and other Americans held hostage is essential to a resolution of other issues.
> 2. The United States understands and sympathizes with the grievances felt by many Iranian citizens concerning the practices of the former regime. The United States is prepared to work out in advance firm understandings on a forum in which those grievances may subsequently be aired, so that the hostages could be released with confidence that those grievances will be heard in an appropriate forum after the release has taken place. The United States will not concur in any hearing that involves the hostages. The United States is prepared to cooperate in seeking through the auspices of the UN to establish such a forum or commission to hear Iran's grievances and to produce a report on them. The U.S. Government

will cooperate with such a group in accordance with its laws, international law, and the Charter of the UN.

3. The U.S. Government will facilitate any legal action brought by the Government of Iran in courts of the United States to account for assets within the custody or control of the former Shah that may be judged to belong to the national treasury of Iran by advising the courts, and other interested parties, that the U.S. Government recognizes the right of the Government of Iran to bring such claims before the courts and to request the courts' assistance in obtaining information about such assets from financial institutions and other parties.

4. Once the hostages are safely released, the United States is prepared to lift the freeze of Iranian assets and to facilitate normal commercial relations between the two countries, on the understanding that Iran will meet its financial obligations to U.S. nationals and that the arrangements to be worked out will protect the legitimate interests of U.S. banks and other claimants. The United States is prepared to appoint members of a working group to reach agreement on those arrangements.

5. The United States is prepared to appoint a representative to discuss with Iranian representatives the current threat posed by the Soviet invasion of Afghanistan and to recommend to their governments steps that the United States and Iran might take in order to enhance the security of Iran, including the resumption of the supply of military spare parts by the United States to Iran.

6. The U.S. Administration is prepared to make a statement at an appropriate moment that it understands the grievances felt by the people of Iran, and that it respects the integrity of Iran, and the right of the people of Iran to choose their own form of government. The U.S. Government recognizes the Government of the Islamic Republic of Iran as the legal government of Iran. The United States reaffirms that the people of Iran have the right to determine their own form of government.

These six points formed the basis for the ultimate resolution of the crisis and release of the hostages in January 1981.

• • •

In mid-January, our attempts to initiate negotiations were hampered by the absence of a direct means of communicating with Iranian leaders. In Iran, there was chaos, and there was no one but Khomeini with power to make decisions. However, during January, we opened a new channel to Tehran that allowed us to revive the idea of an international hearing linked to release of the hostages, which brought us close to success in March.

In January, Jordan, Carter's chief of staff, was contacted by Panamanians whom he had come to know during the ratification of the Panama Canal Treaties. They told him that Christian Bourget, a French lawyer, and Hector Villalon, an Argentinian businessman living in Paris, who had close associations with members of the Revolutionary Council, wished to meet with someone in the administration.

I was skeptical. But we were determined not to leave any stone unturned. The president and I agreed that Jordan, accompanied by Hal Saunders, should meet secretly with the two lawyers in London on January 18 to hear what they had to say.

On their return from London, Saunders and Jordan told me they were convinced that the two lawyers provided a channel of communications worth pursuing further. Bourget and Villalon indicated a willingness to act as intermediaries in working out a scenario for the release of the hostages. They told Jordan and Saunders that the new Iranian president, who was to be elected at the end of the month, would be forced to compete with the religious hard-liners and would have limited authority. They confirmed that we would have to help create a more favorable atmosphere in which the secular nationalists and religious pragmatists might try to persuade Khomeini that the hostages had become a liability. The president and I agreed that the contacts with the two lawyers should continue. A second meeting took place in Jordan's White House office on January 25, and more detailed discussions were held later in Bern and Paris. On January 24, Carter accepted the unanimous recommendation of his senior advisers that sanctions be deferred while we tried to work out a release scenario through Bourget and Villalon. At the same time, we decided to press ahead in seeking condemnation of Iran at a forthcoming conference of Islamic nations.

We developed a series of five interrelated steps for controlling the program of action at each critical point; any Iranian failure to comply would allow us to stop the process without compromising our basic position:

• In step one, we would inform Bani-Sadr, who appeared to be the likely winner in the presidential runoff elections, and Ghotbzadeh that we were prepared to begin a series of reciprocal moves. We would indicate readiness to allow Waldheim to appoint a UN Commission of Inquiry to hear Iran's grievances, provided the Iranians would request it as a means to achieve an early end to the crisis and would state in writing that the commission would be able to see each of the hostages. This was a significant gesture on our part, since it meant the commission would go to Iran before the hostages were freed. The Iranians' request would be designed to indicate that they too were working toward an arranged scenario.

• In step two, once Iran had formally requested the commission, Waldheim would appoint the members and define its mission as "fact-finding," to distinguish it from a judicial tribunal called to render judgment on the United States. The commission would not leave for Iran until the Iranians announced, in the name of Khomeini, that the commission would be allowed to see each of the hostages.

• Step three had to do with the ongoing Iranian attempt to extradite the shah from Panama. Ghotbzadeh had been pursuing this ploy, and the Panamanians had seemed to have some interest in a staged extradition proceeding as a way of helping the Iranian moderates. We would not permit anything that might lead to the arrest of the shah, and there would be no extradition.

• Step four was a set of interlocking constraints on the actions of the commission. After holding private discussions with Iranian authorities, the commission would announce that it was prepared to return to New York to report to the Security Council on Iran's grievances. At the same time, the commission would tell the Revolutionary Council that the hostages were being held under inhumane conditions. Khomeini would then order the hostages transferred to a hospital, under the joint control of the Iranian government and the commission. It would be made clear that the commission would not report to the Secretary-General until the hostages were removed from control of the militants.

• In step five, the commission would report to the Secretary-General, recommending that the United States and Iran form a joint commission to deal with bilateral problems, including the freeze on Iranian assets. Khomeini would "pardon" the hostages, and in conjunction with a Shi'ite religious period in March, expel them. We would not participate in the joint commission until the hostages were free.

After negotiations with the lawyers in Bern on February 9 and 10, this arrangement was accepted in principle by the Revolutionary Council and, we were told, by Khomeini himself.

I briefed Waldheim on the plan and he agreed to help. By mid-February the stage appeared to be set, and on February 13 the plan was put in motion by the Iranians with a message to Waldheim indicating approval of the idea of a Commission of Inquiry. There was a momentary hitch when Iran's request for the commission failed to relate it to the release of the hostages. This omission was corrected. There was, however, a second hitch on February 20. As the commission was assembling in Geneva, the Iranians sent a message to Waldheim authorizing the commission to come to Tehran but misstating the commission's terms of reference. After talking to Waldheim, the president gave him the consent of the United States for the mission to proceed to Iran, on the understanding that Waldheim would reconfirm the original terms of reference. Waldheim did so.

On February 17, Waldheim named the five members of the commission: Ambassador Andres Aguilar of Venezuela and Ambassador Mohammed Bedjaoui of Algeria, cochairmen; Presidential Assistant Adib Daoudy of Syria; Harry W. Jayewardene of Sri Lanka; and Louis-

Edmond Petitti of France. Bani-Sadr followed suit on February 19 when
he announced publicly that Khomeini and the Revolutionary Council
had approved the commission and had invited it to Tehran.

After Waldheim and I had outlined the procedure to Aguilar and Bedjaoui, the commission members gathered in Geneva and flew to Tehran
on February 23. As they were en route, however, warning signs were
raised in Tehran. Khomeini announced that the hostage issue would be
decided by the Majlis (parliament), which would not be elected until
March 14. The ayatollah's announcement was a significant departure
from the plan and raised doubts as to whether Khomeini had actually
agreed to it. More than that, it tended to confirm the view that he
intended to hold the hostages until all the main institutions of an Islamic
state were in place. If so, this meant that securing release of the hostages
would not be possible until the Majlis had organized itself, a prime minister was selected, and a cabinet named—a process that could take
months. We could not, of course, be certain that this was in fact Khomeini's intention. And even if it were, we still might gain a significant
easing of the conditions under which the hostages were being held and
hasten the day of their freedom if we could get them out of the hands of
the militants and under the control of the Revolutionary Council.

We confronted a difficult choice, whether to call a halt, or proceed to
see if Bani-Sadr and Ghotbzadeh could at least get the hostages under
their direct control. We decided to continue.

The commission began its work of collecting information on Iran's
grievances against the previous regime and past U.S. actions. But in
another failure to follow the arrangement, the militants refused to allow
the commission to visit the hostages. We received word from Bourget
and Villalon that Bani-Sadr and Ghotbzadeh were maneuvering desperately to persuade Khomeini to order the transfer of the hostages from
the embassy compound to the Foreign Ministry. On March 6 it appeared
that the pragmatists in the Revolutionary Council had gained the upper
hand when, having failed to gain a clear sign of support from Khomeini,
the militant students grudgingly announced they would relinquish the
hostages to the government. Failing to move decisively, Ghotbzadeh
merely declared the government's intention to take custody of the Americans.

Waiting tensely in Washington, we were keenly aware that until
Khomeini spoke, the government's authority was shaky. On March 8 I
reported to the president that the Revolutionary Council had issued a
statement that the militants either had to give up the hostages to the
government or allow the commission to meet with them. It looked as
though Bani-Sadr and Ghotbzadeh were going to comply with the plan.
Accommodations for the hostages were prepared in the Foreign Ministry, where Laingen, Victor Tomseth, and Michael Howland were still
being held. However, our information was that Bani-Sadr was being

strongly opposed in the Revolutionary Council by clerical hard-liners and their secular allies.

Tragically, Bani-Sadr and Ghotbzadeh waited too long to act. On March 10, Khomeini finally chose sides and publicly instructed the militants at the compound to prevent the commission from seeing the hostages until it had issued a report on Iran's grievances and until the Iranian people had, in some unspecified way, approved it. Correctly inferring from this that the government did not have Khomeini's support, the militants reneged on their March 6 announcement. Thus blocked, the commission could go no farther. Refusing Ghotbzadeh's appeal to stay, the members departed from Tehran the next day.

I met with the commission members on March 12 at the UN headquarters in New York, and found them in disagreement: Some believed that they should have remained a few more days to give Ghotbzadeh another chance to pull the arrangement back together. Others felt that the Iranians were too deeply divided, the government too paralyzed by fear of the militants, and the secular wing around Bani-Sadr too weak for the commission to do its part. One thing seemed clear. Khomeini would ride the strongest current and would not risk his authority as leader by supporting the secular leaders' efforts to end the crisis until at least the new government was fully in place. Some of the commission members believed that Khomeini's transfer of responsibility for the hostages to the Majlis was intended to bring Bani-Sadr and Ghotbzadeh to heel and affirm his authority over the Revolutionary Council. However, Bani-Sadr hoped to gain substantial support in the Majlis, and some members of the commission felt there was a chance that the commission would be asked to return to Tehran. They said Bani-Sadr intended to try to resolve the crisis within the next fifteen days.

The members were uniformly critical of the "evidence" offered to support Iranian grievances. They said the Iranians had largely ignored the commission's fact-finding function until near the end of its stay. It appeared that Iranians of all factions were less interested in airing their complaints against the shah and the United States than in using the hostages to serve political ends.

Some of the members expressed the belief that had Ghotbzadeh acted at once after the militants' March 6 announcement agreeing to give up the hostages to the government, the militants would have turned over the hostages to the government then and there.

Because Bani-Sadr seemed to have more authority than Ghotbzadeh, and because he had indicated that the two weeks after the Majlis elections could be decisive, I advised that we try to keep the plan alive.

Immediately after the commission left Tehran, Ham Jordan and Hal Saunders returned to Bern for another secret meeting with Bourget and Villalon, in which they worked out the following revised scenario:

• After the March 15 elections, Villalon would carry a message from

President Carter to Bani-Sadr that would state that despite public demands for stronger measures, the United States was prepared to continue its policy of restraint for a few more days in order to allow the commission to go forward with its work. The message would say that we would regard transfer of the hostages to government control as evidence of Bani-Sadr's willingness to end the crisis and release them.

• The commission, in private messages to Bani-Sadr and Ghotbzadeh, would indicate it would not complete its report before seeing all the hostages, but that it was ready to return to Tehran to resume work when informed of the date for visiting them. The commission would suggest the period of March 21-25.

• The commission would return to Tehran after the government took custody of the hostages, and after Bani-Sadr had agreed that the commission would be able to announce it had come to complete its mission and declared that in accord with Khomeini's wishes, all evidence and documents relating to Iran's grievances would be made available to the commission.

• The commission would visit each of the hostages, inform the Revolutionary Council that its report to the Security Council would have little credibility unless the hostages were freed, and request Iran to set a date for release. The commission would assure the Revolutionary Council that its report would be released on that same day.

Prospects for the revised plan were slim. The second round of voting for the Majlis had been postponed indefinitely because of charges of fraud. The formation of a parliament, confirmation of Bani-Sadr as president, and the selection of a permanent government would be delayed at least several more weeks.

The shah's sudden departure from Panama also had reduced the chances that the revised scenario might work. He had become upset with the talk of extradition, which we would not have permitted, and with his treatment from the Panamanians. On March 23 he left for Egypt, where he remained until his death on July 27.

After the discussions in Bern, Bourget and Villalon sought Iran's agreement to the revised plan and received a positive response. Once again, it appeared that Bani-Sadr would try to take control of the hostages. We decided to take the first step. On March 25, Carter sent a letter to Bani-Sadr demanding that the hostages be transferred to the government immediately or the United States would be forced to take "additional non-belligerent measures that we have withheld until now."

This was not an empty threat. On March 22, the president directed us to prepare to take several actions: impose formal economic and trade sanctions; conduct a census of financial claims against Iran; and expel all Iranian diplomats. He asked me to prepare a message to our allies requesting them to break diplomatic relations and institute sanctions by a fixed date. I was also to warn them that the alternative was military action. I was worried where this was leading us. Discussions about a range of military actions were accelerating. They included a naval blockade and mining of Iranian ports. Within the White House there was growing impatience with the diplomatic approach. Increasingly, I heard calls for "doing something" to restore our national honor. Carter himself was losing faith that the strategy worked out in November and December could produce positive results. He was angry about our allies' hedging on sanctions and putting strong political pressures on Iran.

On March 26, the president wrote to prime ministers Thatcher, Trudeau, and Ohira, Chancellor Schmidt and President Giscard d'Estaing outlining his decisions on sanctions and asking for their support. We called in their ambassadors to stress the importance of making the Iranians understand the gravity of the situation. We warned them that without active support from our friends, unilateral actions more severe than those the president had described to their heads of government would be forthcoming.

The ambassadors' initial reaction was quite negative. They complained about lack of consultations and expressed grave reservations about the consequences if we should resort to force. Except for a strong positive response from Trudeau, the formal replies to Carter's letter echoed what we had heard from the ambassadors—strong endorsement of our diplomatic approach and counsels of restraint.

Again the arrangement broke down, this time with a profound impact on the president's attitude. A bogus letter from Carter to Khomeini purporting to admit to past U.S. interference in Iran was fabricated and made public in Iran. (We still do not know who did this.) We immediately disavowed the forged letter, but in a foolish attempt to deflect extremist pressures on himself, Bani-Sadr released two confidential letters Carter had sent to him.

On March 31, we learned that Bani-Sadr intended to make yet another attempt to take control of the hostages. The president and his senior advisers gathered in the White House in the early morning hours of April 1—the morning of the Wisconsin primary—to await a new message from Bani-Sadr which we had been informed would be coming through the Swiss embassy.

When the communication arrived, it simply said that Bani-Sadr had announced that his government would take over the hostages if the United States would promise to cease its "propaganda" and drop all financial claims against Iran. Given all that had gone wrong in March, this was a shaky assurance at best, and I advised Carter against taking it at face value.

*   *   *

On April 7, the president broke diplomatic relations with Iran and unilaterally put into effect the economic and political sanctions that the

Soviets had vetoed on January 12. I began an intensive effort to persuade our European and Asian allies to join us. In meetings with their ambassadors, I stressed that American patience was wearing thin and that the president was determined to gain the release of the hostages one way or another. However, not until April 22, only two days before the rescue attempt, did they agree to apply sanctions on May 17 unless decisive progress had been made by that date.

As I noted earlier, the president had decided soon after the hostages were seized that all peaceful means to secure their freedom would be exhausted before the use of force would be considered. At the same time, very closely held military planning went forward to enable us to act promptly should any of the hostages be harmed or seriously threatened. Political oversight and coordination of this military planning on the civilian side was handled by Brzezinski and Brown.

At the end of March, as we were attempting to resurrect the release scenario, Carter approved a recommendation, with which I concurred, that an intelligence probe be carried out in Iran to gather information in case a rescue operation should prove necessary. Carter, Mondale, Brzezinski, Brown, Jones, and I met at Camp David on March 22 to discuss the hostage crisis. We discussed a wide variety of options, including the use of military force. I expressed my opposition to the use of any military force, including a blockade or mining, as long as the hostages were unharmed and in no imminent danger. In addition to risking the lives of the hostages, I believed military action could jeopardize our interests in the Persian Gulf and perhaps lead Iran to turn to the Soviets. Even if Tehran did not seek support from Moscow, Khomeini and his followers, with a Shi'ite affinity for martyrdom, actually might welcome American military action as a way of uniting the Moslem world against the West.

My judgment, based on what we had observed in March, was that the hostages would be freed only when Khomeini was certain all the institutions of an Islamic republic were in place. It was unmistakably clear that the secular pragmatists did not have sufficient power or influence with Khomeini to resolve the crisis themselves. Our only realistic course was to keep up the pressure on Iran while we waited for Khomeini to determine that the revolution had accomplished its purpose, and that the hostages were of no further value. As painful as it would be, our national interests and the need to protect the lives of our fellow Americans dictated that we continue to exercise restraint.

I also believed strongly that the hostages would be released safely once they had served their political purpose in Iran. I found support for this conclusion in what had happened in two similar cases where Americans were held hostage. These were the Angus Ward incident, involving the seizure of our consular staff in Mukden at the end of World War II, and the case of the USS *Pueblo*. The Ward case had many similarities to the seizure in Iran, as is clear from the memorandum of the Joint Chiefs of Staff to President Truman recommending against the use of military force. I had sent a copy of this memorandum to the president shortly after the hostages were taken.* I was convinced that as time passed the chances of physical harm to the hostages diminished.

Following the meeting at Camp David there was no indication that a decision on the use of military force was imminent.

On Thursday, April 10, I left with my wife for a long weekend's rest in Florida. On Friday, April 11, in my absence, a meeting of the National Security Council was hastily called to decide whether a rescue operation should be attempted. Warren Christopher attended as acting secretary of state. He was aware of, and shared, my strong views against the use of military force in Iran, but he was not fully briefed on the rescue operation, which had been kept a tightly held secret. Christopher properly declined to take a position on the rescue mission and argued that there still remained important political and diplomatic options to consider before we resorted to military force. But he was isolated. Everyone else at the meeting supported the rescue attempt, and President Carter tentatively decided the mission would be launched on Thursday, April 24.

• • •

When I returned to Washington late Monday afternoon, Christopher informed me of the meeting. Stunned and angry that such a momentous decision had been made in my absence, I went to see the president very early the next morning and spelled out my strong objections to the rescue mission. As I recall it, we talked for about forty-five minutes. The president said that the decision had been a very difficult one for him to make —the hardest since he had become president. He said the arguments that I made were telling and asked me if I wished to present my views to the National Security Council. I thanked him for giving me the opportunity to speak to the other members of the council, and we agreed to hold the meeting in the cabinet room as soon as we completed our meeting with Begin, who was in Washington for consultations.

I returned to the State Department to work on my notes for the NSC meeting. I thought not only about the rescue mission, but also about my ability to continue as secretary of state if the president affirmed his determination. I had disagreed with policy decisions in the past, but accepting that men of forceful views would inevitably disagree from time to time, had acquiesced out of loyalty to the president knowing I could not win every battle. The decision to attempt to extract the hostages by force from the center of a city of over five million, more than six thousand miles from the United States, and which could be reached only by flying

* For the text of the memorandum, see appendix.

over difficult terrain, was different: I was convinced that the decision was wrong and that it carried great risks for the hostages and our national interests. It had to be faced squarely.

The members of the NSC gathered shortly after we finished the meeting with Begin. The president stated that I had disagreed strongly with the decision made on Friday and had asked to present my views. He then turned to me.

I pointed out that we had made substantial progress in gaining allied support for effective sanctions. Having exerted heavy pressure on our allies to impose sanctions, for us to suddenly use military force without prior warning to them would look as if we had deliberately deceived them.

I pointed out further that the formation of the Majlis, to which Khomeini had given jurisdiction over the hostage crisis, could be a major step toward a functioning government with whom we could negotiate in Iran. As for the hostages, I continued, our intelligence was that they were in no physical danger and were in satisfactory health. We had recently received a report from the Red Cross doctors who had examined them. Moreover, even if the raid were technically successful, the mission was almost certain to lead to a number of deaths among the hostages, not to mention the Iranians. The only justification in my mind for a rescue attempt was that the danger to the hostages was so great that it outweighed the risks of a military operation. I did not believe that to be the case.

I reminded the group that even if the rescue mission did free some of our embassy staff, the Iranians could simply take more hostages from among the American journalists still in Tehran. We would then be worse off than before, and the whole region would be inflamed by our action. Our national interests in the whole region would be severely injured, and we might face an Islamic-Western war. Finally, I said there was a real chance that we would force the Iranians into the arms of the Soviets.

No one supported my position and the president reaffirmed his April 11 decision.

The days between Tuesday, April 15, and Sunday, April 20, were ones of deep personal anguish. I talked with Gay, Warren, Dick Holbrooke, Tony Lake, Sol Linowitz, Arnie Raphel, my special assistant, and Peter Tarnoff, on whose judgment and wisdom I depended greatly. I felt that I must resign. As good friends, they offered arguments pro and con, but as we talked I became more certain than ever that this was a matter of principle on which I should resign. I recognized that the president was in political trouble, and I wished I could stand by him. But by Thursday, April 17, I knew I could not honorably remain as secretary of state when I so strongly disagreed with a presidential decision that went against my judgment as to what was best for the country and for the hostages. Even if the mission worked perfectly, and I did not believe it would, I would have to say afterward that I had opposed it, give my reasons for opposing it, and publicly criticize the president. That would be intolerable for the president and for me. That day, I told Carter I would have to resign if the mission went forward. He urged me to stay and told me I could explain later that I had opposed the attempt on principle, but he refused to countermand the decision.

On Monday morning, April 21, I sadly wrote out a formal letter of resignation, which I had discussed with Gay the night before. I delivered it to the president in the map room of the White House that afternoon. It was one of the most painful days of my life, as I am very fond of Jimmy Carter. We had become close friends, and I was torn at having to leave him in this time of trouble. With great sorrow I handed him the letter. He started to put it away. I asked him to read it. He did, and then slowly put it in his pocket. He said we would have to talk again. I told him that I wanted to make it clear that I would resign whether or not the mission was successful. I agreed to his request not to make my resignation public until after the rescue attempt, and to remain in my position until the mission was completed. It was clearly understood that my decision was irrevocable, whatever the outcome of the rescue operation. Over the next three days I offered whatever advice and help I could to make the operation a success.

On the afternoon of the rescue attempt, I was in the situation room at the White House chairing a meeting when, at about five o'clock, I was handed a message saying that the president wanted me to join him immediately. I hurried upstairs to the president's small study just off the Oval Office. He was seated at his desk; in the room were Fritz, Harold, Zbig, Warren, Jody, and Hamilton. Carter said that the mission had been aborted. In a way I felt a sense of relief, as no one had been injured. I joined Fritz on the couch as the president outlined the reasons for canceling the mission. Then there was silence.

A few minutes later, we began to wrestle with what to say to the public and how best to inform the Iranians about what had happened, since they would soon find the abandoned helicopters we would have to leave behind. Notification was necessary to lessen the possibility of harm to the hostages. Suddenly the red phone rang. The president picked it up and listened. He paled visibly. It was David Jones at the Pentagon reporting the tragic news that a helicopter had collided with one of our C-130 aircraft loaded with men on the ground at the landing site in the desert. Jones said that there were casualties and that the situation was very serious. About twenty minutes later, Jones called again to say that several of our servicemen had been killed in the collision. We were stunned and grief-stricken.

As the shock began to wear off, we returned to the subject of informing the Congress and the nation. At about 7:45 P.M. we moved to the cabinet room. The president remained in his study to make a checklist of actions to be taken. Shortly after 8:00 he rejoined us. We spent the next three hours discussing the notification of the families of those who had been killed, the families of the hostages, and congressional and foreign leaders, preparing the text of a press statement, and determining when we could safely make a public announcement. It could not be done until all of the rescue team was out of the area, but it had to be done as soon as possible. In order to protect the hostages from retaliation, we had to make clear that the mission was not part of an all-out invasion. At about midnight, the president authorized us to make the announcement at 1:00 A.M. and to start immediately to inform the congressional leaders.

I returned to the State Department with Warren and began the difficult task of informing Senator Robert Byrd, Speaker Tip O'Neill, Minority Leaders Senator Howard Baker and Representative John Rhodes, and other congressional leaders of the disaster. Only Senator Byrd had had any inkling of the mission. All the leaders were deeply saddened and many were very upset. By the time I finished, it was close to 2:00 A.M. Bone tired, I returned home with a heavy heart and told Gay what had happened.

Over the next several days, I waited for the president to pick my successor and announce my resignation. On Sunday, April 27, Carter told me that he had selected Senator Edmund Muskie. Although I had recommended Warren Christopher, who was superbly qualified, as my successor, I was pleased with the choice, as I had been a great admirer of Ed for many years. I could understand that the president might wish to make a break with the past.

On the morning of April 28, I met with the president in the Oval Office. We talked briefly and he gave me his letter accepting my resignation and stating that he respected the reasons for my decision. On leaving his office, I met Hamilton in the outer room. I wished him well and asked him to take good care of the president, who would need help at this difficult time.

Hodding Carter and I rode back to the State Department together. We discussed the press conference I would hold later in the morning to announce the resignation. It was a sad moment and not the way I had wanted to end the work we had begun in January 1977 when we had forged what I believed, and still believe, was a foreign policy worthy of a great nation.

After lunch, I called my staff together to tell them of my resignation and to ask them all to stay. A number of them had already told me they wished to leave. I told them that our country and the president needed their help and that they should stay.

Lloyd Cutler, who had only learned about the mission the Friday before it took place, told me he also intended to resign, and I urged him not to do so. He was indispensable to the functioning of the White House, and it was vital that he and Warren Christopher remain.

The next afternoon Gay and I stood side by side in my office while our friends in the department came to say good-bye. It was a heartrending time for both of us. At about four o'clock, we went to the lobby of the main entrance where Kenneth Blakely, the president of the American Foreign Service Association, had thoughtfully gathered a host of colleagues and friends. Gay and I were overwhelmed. I made a short speech of thanks for all they had done to help me, then with Gay on my arm, moved slowly through the throng and out the front door to our waiting car.

20

HARD CHOICES

THIS BOOK HAS BEEN about managing the foreign affairs of our country
in times of great change, about setting priorities and striving not to be
diverted by the agendas of others, about living in a practical world that
compels hard choices. This does not suggest that the affairs of state
should be reckoned without regard for principle. To the contrary, it
requires that our goals and priorities be infused with our inherited values
and principles. It requires that we recognize what can be done and what
cannot be done. It requires that we be idealistic, not ideological, and
that we be unafraid to admit past mistakes and take prudent chances. It
compels us to recognize that it is not a sign of weakness to negotiate
compromises that are in our interest, and that in trying to achieve too
much too fast, the best can become the enemy of the good.

More specifically, looking to the future, we must recognize that we
can no longer afford an American foreign policy that is hostage to the
pressures of the moment or that swings widely at the start of every new
administration. We must choose policies for the long run and ask ourselves as we do what the shape of the world of the 1990s will be.

There is no doubt that we and many other nations will continue to
face the Soviet Union as competitor and potential adversary, since we
and the Soviets have sharply different social and economic systems based
on different values, and divergent views of our respective interests in the
world. We still will bear the heavy burden of maintaining a strong military defense. There will still be an Atlantic Alliance, seeking as its first
task the security of western Europe and North America. We will continue to look to Japan as our principal friend and partner in East Asia,
while we continue trying to draw China into the outside world. And we
will still seek to provide for our own economic security and prosperity in
a competitive world, and to help manage a global economy.

But much will be different in the 1990s. Exploding populations, greater
economic competition among and within the industrialized and devel-

oping worlds, increasing pressures on the global environment, religious and cultural revivals, and conflict in some parts of the world that are relatively peaceful today—all will create an environment of even greater danger. There are two looming, inescapable facts. First, more nations will possess nuclear weapons. Second, economic expectations, particularly in the Third World, will inevitably outrun the possibility of fulfillment.

TRANSITION AND CHOICE

In the past, we have faced challenges in East-West relations. We will have to adapt ourselves to a world in which we can rarely act alone, a world in which we must nurture different attitudes, skills, and sources of power and influence.

• • •

What instruments of foreign policy do we need for the latter part of the 1980s and the 1990s? How should we face the traditional problems confronting us as a superpower? And how must we deal with the new agenda of issues and problems?

Two sets of challenges confront us: the traditional issues that fit within the pattern of international life developed since World War II, and a second set of new issues arising from factors that are just beginning to appear on the horizon. We cannot deal with either in isolation. We must deal with both in a coherent and integrated fashion.

I will start with the more traditional issues and then turn to the more cloudy, yet real, world of the future.

We must begin by revitalizing our national strengths—military, economic, political, and moral.

STRENGTH FOR THE 1980s: THE MILITARY DIMENSION

The United States must continue to maintain sufficient military strength to meet the power of the Soviet Union and a range of other contingencies. That issue now seems past debate. The real debate has hardly begun: not only *how much* we should spend on our military forces but also *what* we should spend it on.

Our most critical preoccupation must be with preserving deterrence and preventing the holocaust of a nuclear war that could end civilization. Nothing during the next two decades is likely to alter that fact. We must maintain strategic nuclear forces that will enhance deterrence while avoiding those weapons likely to reduce stability and invite the very conflict we seek to prevent. We must have a nuclear doctrine that itself will reduce the risks of war and forgo speculation about the possibilities of fighting a so-called limited nuclear war—speculation that only increases the risks of conflict. And we must couple this with serious efforts to make progress on balanced and verifiable arms control agreements that will reverse the upward spiral of the nuclear arms race.

As we modernize our nuclear forces, we must choose what meets our real needs. We should maintain our triad of nuclear forces with Poseidon and Trident submarines, land-based missiles, and long-range bombers— all supplemented by up-to-date command, control, and communications. Proceeding with the obsolescent B-1 bomber is a waste of money. We would be far better off to accelerate the development of the Advanced Technology Bomber as an effective long-term replacement for our B-52 bombers armed with cruise missiles.* We must also reexamine whether the MX missile should be deployed. We must examine our needs for conventional military forces. Where are we most likely to be challenged? Who is likely to join us? What kind of combat are we likely to face? What types and quantities of military forces will best meet these requirements? As we look to the late 1980s, conventional force deficiencies are obvious. We have been preoccupied with strategic forces and the challenge of Soviet strategic power almost to the neglect of conventional force readiness, training, maintenance, and adequate supply.

We need to increase our ability to project conventional forces abroad, whether to maintain open sea lanes to Europe and Japan and to the vital Persian Gulf, or to be able to back up treaty commitments, or to have an option for limited engagement abroad, should this be required to protect our vital interests. But we must not interpret an increase in conventional military power as a license for militarizing our attitudes toward difficulties in the outside world, for becoming ourselves perceived as part of the problems rather than their solution, or for radically altering our conventional force commitments on the European continent.

Substantial improvement in our conventional defenses in Europe is long overdue. We have the know-how and the capability to develop new weapons and tactics, providing greater flexibility and punch. What we need is the wisdom and the political will to make necessary decisions. This would reduce our dependence on both battlefield and intermediate-range nuclear weapons in Europe. It was Western inferiority in conventional forces that led to a NATO strategy of potential reliance on nuclear weapons in the European theater. Improvement of conventional defenses and consideration of a shift in NATO strategy must be coupled with a renewed effort to reach agreement with the USSR on parity of conventional forces in Europe. This is not a pipedream. My discussions

---

* This aircraft is also called the "Stealth" bomber because it is almost invisible on a radar screen.

with Soviet leaders indicate that a substantial opportunity now exists to negotiate with the Soviet Union on this. We should make a determined effort.

This is the context in which we should consider the recent proposal by four distinguished former U.S. officials for a doctrine of "no first-use" of nuclear weapons. That is clearly a desirable long-term goal, but it can only be achieved—in concert with our European allies—if it follows rather than precedes the realization of genuine parity in conventional forces in Europe that makes a true nonnuclear defense possible. Doctrine should not be changed until there is a viable alternative to put in its place.

At the same time, we must examine again how we raise our military forces. Conscription lost its credibility during the Vietnam War, partly because it was judged unfair, more because the ends of the conflict were rejected, not just by those young men called to serve, but by a significant portion of the American people. Effectiveness argues increasingly for a return to the draft—following the example of most of our NATO allies. Fairness argues for a method of deciding who serves that is seen to be fair and that takes us beyond reliance in any branch of service upon young Americans who are unable to get decent jobs elsewhere. Military service should be only one part of a national service program that calls young people from all economic, social, and educational strata.

Military strength is vital and it cannot simply be measured by the dollars we spend, but by the quality and effectiveness of our forces. But military power is not the only measure of our strength, even though we sometimes let it become the coin by which we judge our power and influence. Most important, we cannot—as we are doing now—jeopardize the basic strength of our domestic economy by failing to check inflationary defense spending unrelated to our interests and the military capabilities we need to protect those interests.

INCREASING STRENGTH THROUGH ARMS CONTROL

The 1970s began as a hopeful time of seeking to place limits on both strategic and conventional military arms. It was not based on unfounded idealism but on practical realism—the knowledge that the burgeoning of military forces would make conflict more likely or, if it occurred, more costly in human life. The 1980s risk becoming a lost decade for arms control, unless we and the Soviet Union relearn the lesson understood for nearly two decades by every U.S. administration, as well as by the American people: that our security can and must be genuinely advanced by vigorous pursuit of arms control agreements—comprehensive, far-reaching, balanced, equitable, and verifiable.

All this has been well known for many years. Yet the basic lesson of the nuclear age bears repeating: the two superpowers—and all other countries—are in the same boat and will survive or founder together. Neither the United States nor the Soviet Union can provide for its own security against nuclear holocaust unless it also helps to provide that security for the other. Neither can seek a decisive nuclear advantage without the risk of provoking an attack in which both would be destroyed.

In short, the most basic security for the superpowers—security from nuclear war—cannot in the final analysis be dominated by competition. Their security must be based on an unparalleled degree of cooperation. It must be common security.

It would be unconscionable to lose the chance to negotiate firm limits on strategic arms and progressively to reduce them, either because we undervalue these efforts or because we link them to other developments in East-West relations. Arms control agreements are either in our interest and should be pursued, or they are not and should not. We must not lose that chance because we are unable to understand that national strength and security can both be enhanced at the bargaining table as well as in the arsenal. If we do, we will enter the 1990s less secure than we are now.

Both in the United States and in western Europe, public concern about nuclear issues is reaching an all-time high, in part because the Reagan administration did not stake out a clear and negotiable position on strategic arms control. The proposal for a nuclear freeze, led by senators Edward Kennedy and Mark Hatfield, has become a rallying point for public discontent. Its merit lies primarily in helping to deepen public knowledge and political involvement in these issues. Its primary result should be to stimulate the administration to reassert U.S. leadership in arms control, with a positive commitment to strategic arms reduction talks and a genuine effort to pursue a far-reaching and comprehensive agreement with the Soviet Union.

Strategic weapons are not the only appropriate focus for arms control negotiations. In Europe, we should continue efforts both to reduce the level of military forces on both sides and to shift the kinds and positioning of armaments from offensive to defensive. For example, a battlefield nuclear-weapon-free zone could be created in central Europe along the lines recently suggested by the Independent Commission on Disarmament and Security Issues.* In limiting or preventing conflict, arms con-

---

* In Europe, both sides deploy large numbers of so-called battlefield nuclear weapons, many of which are stored in forward sites close to the line dividing East from West. These weapons, numbering in the thousands, are themselves a source of anxiety. They could well become a source of instability. If tensions rose in Europe, there would be military pressures to delegate command responsibility over their use before a conflict began. And if war did begin, the pressure from both commanders to use these weapons before they were overrun would be almost irresistible. In either case, the risk of nuclear conflict would go up without measurably increasing the strength of deterrence.

trol can also be a critical adjunct to our national strength and effectiveness in other parts of the world. In particular, we should revive efforts to regulate and limit the expanding trade in conventional arms, beginning with the now-shelved talks between the United States and the Soviet Union.

DOMESTIC ECONOMIC VITALITY

We need to rebuild our economic base at home, to achieve sustained economic growth, and to integrate better our foreign policy and domestic economy.

Our relative economic strength in the world has inevitably declined, partly because industrial nations shattered by war have been rebuilt and have prospered, and partly because other countries have either made the difficult climb into the modern economic world or possess scarce but vital natural resources. But we have also contributed to our relative economic decline by living off our economic capital, as we have let our plant and equipment in key industries deteriorate, as we have shifted increasingly to a service economy, and as we have neglected essential research and development for both military and civilian uses. We have lagged behind many other nations both in the rate of rising productivity and in adapting to a world in which competition for political power and influence is increasingly in the economic realm.

It is essential that we reduce inflation without causing massive unemployment. That we increase productivity, ensure development of our human capital, promote technology through increased research and development, increase energy development and conservation, modernize our capital stock, and create new economic arrangements among business, labor, and government. These are indeed matters of national security; they extend beyond consideration of whether or not we prosper in the global economy.

One economic issue—inflation—fundamentally affects all the rest. This complex and seemingly intractable problem must be attacked at its roots. A first and indispensable element of a comprehensive anti-inflation program should be an incomes policy that will hold both prices and wages in check while longer term, more basic measures have time to take

---

The commission proposed the creation of a battlefield nuclear-weapon-free zone. This zone would begin in central Europe and eventually extend to the northern and southern flanks of NATO and the Warsaw Pact. All nuclear weapons would be withdrawn 150 km, the effective range of battlefield weapons, from the central front. Within that zone of 300 km, no nuclear weapons could be based, stored, or exercised. To guarantee compliance on both sides, on-site inspections would be permitted on a challenge basis. Of course, battlefield nuclear weapons could be reintroduced in a crisis or conflict. But the zone could build confidence that might help prevent a crisis. Further, it would serve as an example of an alternative to automatic increases in the numbers and quality of nuclear arms.

effect. An incomes policy should involve both business and labor and should be even-handed. There are many ways to implement an incomes policy, ranging from quite rigid to quite flexible. My own experience as a lawyer involved in business matters over thirty-five years leads me to favor a tax-based incomes policy (TIP) that rewards those who remain within targeted levels and penalizes those who do not.

We will need far better organization in the federal government, and between it and private industry, to relate domestic and foreign economic policies to one another—e.g., agriculture, energy, foreign aid, trade, export promotion, management of the dollar, and coordination of economic policies among the industrialized states. We can no longer talk of foreign and domestic problems as though they were in different worlds. They must be seen and solved together. There no longer is a single U.S. economy, but rather a world economy in which various U.S. industries, sectors, and regions must compete with overseas counterparts.

POLITICAL WISDOM

America's strength will also depend on the political bonds of our society and on the wisdom of our leaders and citizens in preparing themselves for the challenges that lie ahead.

For several years, confidence in our national institutions has been eroding—in part because of Vietnam and Watergate—and because of chronic economic difficulties, in part because of a lack of public trust in our government, and in part because of a widespread sense that Washington has been out of touch with American reality. There can and must be remedies that will restore popular confidence in our government's ability to perform, both at home and abroad, up to the level of the expectations of the American people. But the radical surgery in domestic spending practiced by the Reagan administration is not the answer. Identifying the federal government as the basic problem, rather than as an institution in need of change, like any other, only sows confusion. Cutting back too drastically on social programs, especially education, reduces the human capital that is a key element of national strength. Harking back to a past that may never have existed can be misleading and destructive.

The American people's confidence in government is essential for national strength. It can only be restored by a four-fold process: scrapping government programs and regulations that don't work or serve our needs, and making sure that those that remain are as effective as possible; placing government functions at those levels most accountable and responsive to our people wherever possible; telling the truth about our domestic economic circumstances and the real nature of the challenges we face abroad; and finding new ways to enlist the support of the American people—through the Congress and just plain listening to what people are saying. Understanding the realities of the outside world will be crucial. We must be able to deal creatively with issues that require more subtlety, imagination, and deftness in light of our relatively diminished military and economic power.

MORAL POWER

We Americans are at our best when we are true to ourselves. To be strong as a nation, we must come to grips with our commitment to social justice at home, and we must ensure that our foreign and defense policies abroad measure up to American values and beliefs, rather than measuring them only in terms of our most narrowly defined national interests. In fact, championing human rights is a national requirement for a nation with our heritage. A responsiveness to the needs of people in less-developed nations is a national interest. And the pursuit of peace and of ways to reduce the causes of conflict is a national interest for a nation that sponsored the Marshall Plan, helped bring Japan from defeat to one of the world's leading democracies, and helped to diminish conflict between Egypt and Israel. Without this moral strength, it would be impossible for any president to call upon the American people for the sacrifices which from time to time must be made.

• • •

Against this background of national strength, what are the immediate problems we face abroad? Traditional foreign policy issues will require us to exercise wise leadership for the years ahead—in East-West relations, the Atlantic Alliance, our partnership with Japan, drawing China into the outside world, peacemaking in places like the Middle East, helping to manage the global economy, and in helping to open up areas of opportunity for nations in the developing world.

EAST-WEST RELATIONS

What kind of relations will we have with President Yuri V. Andropov and with the next generation of Soviet leaders? Will both our nations be plunged deeper into the cold war? Will there be opportunities to mitigate some of the most dangerous aspects of our rivalry? Do we see only confrontation ahead?

As new Soviet leaders come to power, they will bring with them not only the attitudes that have been shaped by their character, quality, and background, but by the options that our policies present. Soviet interests will be the critical factor. But we in the West can influence the directions the Soviet Union will take, to some extent. We are not left without choices or influence.

The first element of Western policy toward the Soviet Union must be durability—the capacity of successive allied governments to follow a more consistent expression of Western interests that extends beyond national elections or changes in public mood. If we want Soviet leaders to understand what we expect of them in mutual relations, they must have some capacity to predict our attitudes and behavior.

The second element of Western policy in East-West relations must be the closeness of our partnership with like-minded states, beginning with those in western Europe. None of the Western nations will profit if we permit divisions to open, as happened in the Afghanistan and Poland crises. We will disagree on some particulars because our interests are not always identical. But the United States and its allies must demonstrate that they can work together so that their actions will have a stronger political impact and demonstrate to Soviet leaders that there is no value in trying to separate us.

Third, we and our allies must maintain the military forces required to meet Soviet challenges, both in Europe and elsewhere if need be. The Soviet Union must have no opportunity to test us militarily or to exploit military advantages politically. It is never easy to strike a balance between sufficient military power and excessive reliance on military instruments, but the Western alliance must be able to make those judgments. And the Soviet leadership must know that we are prepared to pay the price for security.

The West has advantages over the Soviet Union, for example, our far better ability to adapt to change both at home and abroad, our more efficient economies and greater freedom from the dead hand of bureaucracy, and the fact that we are linked together by choice rather than compulsion.

Fourth, we in the West must begin again to distinguish those areas of East-West relations where there is no room for compromise from those areas where mutual agreement is possible. We must lead a new generation of Soviet leaders to understand where our vital interests lie—e.g., along the central front in western Europe, in the Persian Gulf, in Northeast Asia, and in other areas of the globe where Western interests are significantly engaged. And all nations must recognize that foreign intervention in Iran can have dangerous international consequences.

During the last decade, a major factor in the deterioration of East-West relations was the Soviets' lack of restraint in exploiting local conflicts, in the hope of expanding their influence. When an opportunity does come for more sensible management of U.S.-Soviet relations, it will be important to find ways to increase that restraint. While it is not feasible to develop across-the-board "codes of conduct," we can seek practical limitations in specific regions of the world where both countries have an interest in keeping political competition from reaching explosive levels.

By the same token, there is positive, long-term value for us in seeking regional limits on arms or superpower involvement, whether in Europe through mutual and balanced force reduction talks, or in parts of the developing world, as was approached tentatively during the 1970s with regard to the Indian Ocean. There is value in creating incentives for the Soviet Union to become more economically engaged, though with due care concerning the transfer of militarily significant technology. And there is value in building a Soviet stake in East-West relations that can temper Moscow's behavior, if not the character of its long-term ambitions. The West cannot and should not seek to make up for basic Soviet economic failures. But to the extent that Soviet leaders are prepared to begin the long process of demilitarizing their economy in favor of civilian needs, we should be prepared to encourage it.

We and our allies must continue talking with the Soviet Union. There can be no excuse for halting communications, especially in times of tension when clarity about each other's intentions is vital to stability and peace.

Much of what happens in the world in the years ahead will depend upon Soviet willingness to recognize and accommodate to the impact of change in eastern Europe and elsewhere—and to do so sooner rather than later. We can provide incentives. We can help make clear to Soviet leaders that we do not seek to roll back Soviet control of eastern Europe, to gain greater influence for ourselves, and that a larger degree of self-determination for the nations of eastern Europe need not be a threat to their security. And we must continue to emphasize the process that began with the Helsinki Final Act to enhance security in Europe, to promote East-West cooperation on a reciprocal basis, and to insist upon a growing Soviet recognition of basic human rights.* Yet the Soviet Union itself will have to make the most critical choice of all—whether it wishes to live productively with other nations or to force upon us continuing confrontation. We must be prepared to respond effectively to either Soviet choice.

In the West, we must think of our relations with the Soviet Union in terms of decades, not simply from year to year. Our long-term purpose must involve making clear to present and future Soviet leaders that we are prepared to have a constructive relationship with a Soviet Union that does not seek to dominate other countries and that accepts a responsible role in the world.

There can and will be no respite from the West's careful management of East-West relations, no let-up in the need for Western strength, no slackening in the need for vigorous pursuit of mutual and balanced re-

---

* The final act of the conference on security and cooperation held in Helsinki, Finland in 1975, attended by 35 nations, including the United States and the Soviet Union.

ductions in both strategic and conventional forces. We have a responsibility to go halfway in seeking agreement with the Soviet Union where our interests coincide. The world is too small for us and the USSR to permit a drift back to cold war or worse.

THE ATLANTIC ALLIANCE

For more than thirty years, support for the Atlantic Alliance has been the cornerstone of U.S. foreign policy: hence the Marshall Plan, NATO, the Organization for Economic Cooperation and Development (OECD), U.S. support for the European Community, and the complex web of relations among our nations. It is inconceivable that anything will happen during this decade or in the next to lessen the importance of western Europe to the security and prosperity of the United States. East-West relations in Europe may improve, thereby opening up opportunities to ameliorate some basic tensions. There may be a new burst of effort in developing European unity including, in time, the creation of a defense community to parallel the others. But the ties between western Europe and the United States will remain as vital for both sides as they are now. American retreat from Europe would be utter folly.

At the same time, the Atlantic Alliance is now changing in profound ways, requiring significant adjustments. The allies will need to create new ways of doing business with one another, including a greater sharing of responsibilities and the power of decision.

In working to preserve America's partnership with Canada and our European friends and allies, we must first understand the nature of the changes taking place:

• Our European allies, geographically pinned to the central front, increasingly view East-West relations in terms somewhat different from the United States, with its more global view. This has already become a source of growing tension across the Atlantic. But if all of us are prepared to face these differences realistically, we can also create practical and sustainable policies for dealing with the Soviet Union and the states of eastern Europe—in terms not of ideology but of real Western interests. The potential transformation of East European states during the next decade will require the Western allies to show particular sensitivity and subtlety and to coordinate their policies closely.

• The United States now needs greater support from its allies in meeting challenges elsewhere in the world where we have common interests, such as the Persian Gulf. But to gain allied support, we Americans must also be prepared to share the process of decision much more effectively than ever before.

• Recently, tensions have been growing within the alliance over the best means of relating to nations of the developing world. Part of this tension stems from the failure of the United States to keep pace with most European states in the share of national wealth transferred to developing nations. European states and Japan also tend to see the Third World in regional terms, while we tend to globalism. But the greatest difficulty is our disagreement with our Western partners over the extent to which change in many parts of the developing world stems from internal factors, and the extent to which the Soviet Union and its allies play a determining role, or at least are able effectively to exploit discontents. The United States must not make the critical mistake of seeing every conflict in the developing world as East-West confrontation.

• Economically, we and our Atlantic partners find ourselves increasingly strained in seeking harmony in our policies. There is growing tension among us caused by reduced rates of growth, by slowing increases in productivity, and by more intensified competition for third-country markets. Domestic economic policies of our various nations increasingly risk being in conflict with one another, as each seeks to minimize inflation and unemployment, sometimes without sufficient regard to the impact of such efforts on other member states. We might permit this new competitiveness to divide the alliance and increase the practice of beggar-thy-neighbor policies. But instead we can and must find means to work more closely together in solving common problems and in relating domestic economic management in any one country more effectively to the requirements of all.

• A younger generation of Europeans and Americans knows less about one another and has less instinctive understanding of one another's problems and the demands of alliance than has been true of any other generation since the Second World War. The successor generation on both sides of the ocean has not been brought effectively into the Atlantic partnership, so that its basic purposes can be understood and nurtured. We can allow this trend to continue with growing estrangement across the Atlantic. Or we can work together to ensure that the essential elements of alliance can be extended, revised, and passed on.

The Atlantic Alliance has been unique in history. It has far exceeded expectations at its birth—both in the time it has survived and prospered and in the range of its effectiveness in tying nations and peoples together. We have nothing to fear in the inevitable changes taking place. Efforts to stand still would surely fail. Only by adjusting to change and by looking for new opportunities can the alliance be as relevant for the late 1980s and 1990s as it has proved to be in the past.

JAPAN

Our relationship with Japan has long taken second place to our emphasis on the Atlantic Alliance. This has reflected our greater strategic preoc-

cupation with security on the European continent, the structure of our
economic relations, and basic cultural affinities. Increasingly, however,
we must look to Japan as a key partner of equal importance—not so
much for purposes of security, though they are real, but because of the
growing significance of international economic issues for our nation's
prosperity and the effective conduct of an overall foreign policy. Japan
is not alone in becoming more important to us; it is representative of the
entire Pacific basin.

The United States is now clearly a full-fledged economic power in the
Pacific, complementing our strategic role. As a result, during the next
decade we will focus a growing part of our interests and concerns west-
ward on East Asia rather than eastward on Europe.

Japan's growth and development since the Second World War continue to be remarkable. So too is its growing ability to assume new and
common responsibilities within its region. We are tempted to translate
these facts into pressure on Japan to become a major military power,
thus relieving the United States of some of the burden of providing
significant naval forces in the western Pacific. In the years ahead, however, the United States must take great care to distinguish calling on
Japan to increase its military spending, which is desirable, and playing a
security role, which would be a serious error. Four key facts underlie
this urge for caution: the unique provisions of Japan's constitution, residual memories in much of East Asia (including Japan) about its role in
World War II, a relatively smaller though growing security problem in
East Asia and the western Pacific compared with that in Europe, and the
critical need for Japanese efforts in both regional and global economic
development.

In promoting common interests, therefore, the United States and its
other industrial-state partners should place more emphasis upon what
Japan can do economically rather than militarily. Japan will need some
defense increases to help protect the Home Islands as the United States
and, I hope, some of its European allies, takes on new security burdens
—most prominently in the Persian Gulf, where Japan also can support
security by playing a political and economic role. But within its own
region, Japan should concentrate on helping to promote the common
economic well-being of all the Pacific basin countries. It has already
begun cooperating with the Association of South-East Asian Nations
(ASEAN) and has significantly increased its foreign economic assistance.
Japan's economic role can also be extended to other areas of collective
importance to the West: for instance, it is already providing economic
support to Pakistan, Turkey, and Egypt.

We should help draw Japan even more effectively into the triangular
economic and political relationship which includes the United States and
western Europe—where U.S.-Japanese and U.S.-European relations are
well developed but European-Japanese relations lag far behind. Today,

we must deal with real problems of Japanese competitiveness in industrial-state markets, not through penalizing Japan for its higher rates of productivity, but by encouraging Japan to open up its markets and to undertake the efforts suggested here to compensate for our continued shouldering of most of the common western Pacific security burdens. Tomorrow, Japan too will increasingly feel the winds of competition, especially from the emerging economic powers of South Korea, Taiwan, and some of the ASEAN states. Along with the United States, its interests will grow in working for cooperative economic arrangements throughout the Pacific basin.

Mutual trust must be the essence of our relationship with Japan. As we take major political or economic steps, it is no longer possible for us to engage in "shocks" to Japanese expectations for close and effective consultations. U.S.-Japanese relations must be a true partnership in politics, economics, and security.

CHINA

Elsewhere in East Asia, the U.S. relationship with the People's Republic of China may continue to be one of the most difficult but vital conundrums in U.S. foreign policy. This still-young relationship must be developed slowly, steadily, and persistently. In dealing with China, the United States must in particular adopt policies that can remain consistent over many years, surviving changes in U.S. administrations. Normalization, which took so long to achieve, is not irreversible. To be sure, Taiwan continues to be a significant economic partner of the United States and the well-being of its people remains important to us. But we cannot consider Taiwan "another China," whose ties with us can be played off against those we have with Peking. We must not try to turn back the clock.

Defining what role China will play in East Asia and elsewhere is not something we either can or should try to do. Several years must pass before the long-term directions of China's fairly recent involvement in the outside world become clear. In some areas, however, U.S. and Chinese interests can proceed in parallel, as has been true recently in Southwest Asia and in the search for continued stability in Korea. It is in our interest that China's emergence proceed in ways that can mutually reinforce our own concern for security and stability—especially in East Asia—and that can build upon economic opportunities for our two nations and others in the region. But we must not overestimate our ability to influence China's future role—beyond following the general prescriptions here—both on our own and in close collaboration with allies like Japan.

China and the United States are friends, not allies. During the rest of this decade and into the next, many U.S. and Chinese interests may prove to be similar, but they will surely diverge in important areas. Circumstances do not warrant, nor do our interests counsel, moves toward formal U.S.-Chinese security ties, joint military planning, or the sale of offensive weapons. Moves to cross these thresholds could stimulate unrealistic Chinese expectations, create unnecessary fears on the part of other Asian friends, and invite paranoid reactions from the Soviets. The West may face less of a direct Soviet military threat because of Moscow's concern with China—although that proposition is debatable. But we must not slide into believing that we can somehow play a "China card" against the Soviet Union. For us to try to manipulate either nation against the interests of the other would be to run great risks of our becoming embroiled in their tensions and conflicts, thus undermining our efforts to manage relations effectively with both.

PEACEMAKING

The United States will have a vital interest in continuing to play the role of peacemaker. For the foreseeable future, the Middle East will be a primary and necessary focus of our attention. Despite real success in the Camp David accords and the Egyptian-Israeli Peace Treaty, the Arab-Israeli conflict is far from settled. The Palestinian question continues to fester and a comprehensive peace eludes our grasp. Lebanon is overrun by the presence of foreign troops and is still at risk.

In the Middle East, we have no option other than to play our part as a full and active partner and deeply engaged mediator seeking constantly to resolve the conflict at the peace table. Our interests, our loyalties, and our experience all require the United States to continue shouldering the major part of that burden, even if other outside states can eventually serve as trusted interlocutors. Inevitably, we will also need to help guarantee agreements emerging from the laborious process of making peace.

Elsewhere, we will also continue to have major interests in peacemaking. We have often found that we do best when we share the task of promoting peace with other nations. Peace came to Zimbabwe because Britain and the United States were able to work with all the African nations of the region. So, too, it may be possible to help resolve the problems of Central America by working with our Latin American neighbors, some of which—like Mexico—have indicated a willingness to play a leading role.

THE INTERNATIONAL ECONOMY

As part of our traditional role in foreign policy, we now face escalating demands for effective management of the global economy by the nations of the world. Competition will increase across the board—for expanding exports (and increasingly for restricting imports), for securing raw materials, for gaining capital, and for shifting the burden of domestic economic adjustment to other nations. Nor will these problems be limited primarily to that fraction of the global economy dominated by the industrialized states. In terms of the tools and policies we need for economic management, distinctions between developed and developing nations will steadily disappear.

For the United States, adjusting to a world ever more preoccupied with these issues will be particularly difficult. Only recently have we become fully engaged in the global economy, in the sense that the world beyond our shores now has a greater direct impact than ever before on our domestic economic policies and on the lives of all Americans, in food, fiber, fuel, the changed role of the dollar, and the rising percentage of our GNP bound up in foreign trade.

It will be vital for us to change some of our basic attitudes about the global economy and our role in it. We must, for example, recognize that an increasing amount of our trade each year is carried on with developing countries. So too we must change a number of our economic practices, to focus even more on our role in foreign trade. At some point, for example, we must review carefully the application of our antitrust laws to the foreign operations of U.S. companies, an area where some of our major competitors have significant advantages over us. Both government and the private sector must promote U.S. exports more vigorously. And in the next decade, we may want to review the role of the dollar as the world's reserve currency.

Furthermore, we and others will need to strengthen the classical institutions for managing the global economy—including the IMF, the World Bank, the OECD, Multilateral Trade Negotiations, the GATT, the regional development banks, and a host of United Nations bodies. We will need to refine and develop recently established institutions, like the Seven Nation Economic Summit.* These annual summits still do far too little to help coordinate the domestic economic policies of the industrialized nations. Nor do they yet provide an effective forum for consultations on vital political and security questions that often are inseparable from the global economy. And they do not yet deal adequately with issues that tie developed and developing nations together. In addition, management of the global economy may require new institutions —e.g., to help developing nations exploit their domestic energy resources, as has been proposed by the World Bank.

With every day that passes, it is becoming more obvious that the conduct of international economic diplomacy demands our coming to terms with complex North-South relations. Developing nations, individually

---

* The Seven Nation Economic Summit includes Britain, Canada, France, West Germany, Italy, Japan, and the United States.

and collectively, are increasingly vital to our own well-being at home. They are now our fastest growing markets abroad and take more U.S. exports than do the European Community and Japan combined. Our economy depends heavily upon the raw materials we import from the developing world—almost 100 percent of our tin, 90 percent of our bauxite, all of our natural rubber, and nearly 40 percent of our petroleum. For American workers, growing markets in the developing world mean jobs—today about 800,000 in the manufacturing sector alone. For American farmers, developing-world markets are critical. They consume about one out of every three acres of U.S. farm production.

Today there is only one OPEC; tomorrow there could be other groups of developing-country exporters, although, with the exception of natural gas, none could expect the market concentration found in oil. Newer institutions like ASEAN will have a rising impact on our economic and political relations with developing countries and will require an enlightened response from the United States and other industrial nations. In general, our ability to trade effectively with developing states will increasingly depend on our willingness to respond wisely to their interests and concerns.

We also share an interest with developing countries in narrowing the combustible disparity between wealth and poverty. We share an interest in striking an even balance between the burgeoning demands of more people for a better life and the immutable reality of limited resources. And we share an interest in achieving a steady and more equitable rise in standards of living without destroying our planet in the process.

We must therefore base our actions toward the developing world not only on our genuine humanitarian concern for the harsh conditions of life that face hundreds of millions of our fellow human beings, but must also ground them in the inescapable proposition that peace and prosperity for ourselves, now and for the future, relate directly to the strength of our relations with the developing nations.

In the decade ahead, major international negotiations will focus on striking a North-South bargain, covering all aspects of economic relations and involving a wide range of countries. That goal will likely prove to be overly ambitious, but that does not remove the need for industrial states to be sensitive to the desires of developing nations to participate more fully in the decisions and benefits of the global economy. Developing countries must have a greater chance to join and be deeply involved in critical international institutions. They must have greater access to resource transfers, whether through trade, investment, balance of payments support, better terms of trade for primary products, or development assistance. In food and energy, the ties, tensions, and potential opportunities will be particularly important, calling for new means of doing business.

In general, the United States can advance and protect its interests in a sound global economy by following six key principles:

- We must recognize that economic interdependence is no longer just a slogan, often honored in the breach, but a reality of international life;
- our domestic economy must adjust to meet new and insistent demands of the international marketplace;
- the prosperity of all nations—developed and developing alike—will depend upon renewed commitment to liberalized trade, even when domestic pressures for protectionism obscure the profound risks of slowed growth in global trade;
- we must coordinate U.S. domestic economic policies with those of other nations, especially in the industrialized world, to place emphasis on sharing opportunities for growth and prosperity instead of hardship and difficulty;
- openness and mutual benefit must characterize our economic policies toward developing nations, to reflect our growing dependence on them for raw materials and markets, and in some cases to help keep them stable and independent as well; and
- the United States must again become an active and supportive partner in the key multilateral development and financial institutions.

A New World

The issues discussed above all reflect the pattern of international life since the Second World War. But other developments are now on the horizon that will profoundly affect the way the world works in the late 1980s and into the 1990s. All of them could produce some basic challenges to the existing order. Some will affect the structure of security, some will affect the global economy, and some will critically influence the ability of individual people to direct their own lives. Not all of these developments are new; but all do fit within a framework requiring fresh thought and effort on the part of the United States and many other nations and institutions.

New Factors in Security

For nearly four decades, issues of international security have been basically shaped by the post-World War II system. In major respects, this system is dominated by U.S.-Soviet rivalry. It depends on sets of alliances sponsored by the superpowers. It has so far been able to survive the limited shocks from changes and developments, the end of colonialism, the weakening of some alliance bonds, the emergence of Sino-Soviet tensions, the rise of conflict in the Third World, and shifts in the global economy.

In many areas, however, the basic system of international security faces challenge from developments that cannot readily be contained within existing patterns of behavior. Several developments are important, and will become more so in the future:

- the increasing capacity of many nations to build nuclear weapons and the greater likelihood that some will actually do so;
- the burgeoning trade in conventional arms to Third World nations, intensifying both the risk and the nature of conflicts;
- the increasing chance of armed conflict within or between nations in many parts of the developing world, risking not only regional instability but also escalation involving nations of East and West;
- the growth of terrorism, deriving from a wide variety of factors and threatening nations in virtually all parts of the world; and
- the rise of militancy based on religious and cultural revival.

While these developments are most intense in the Third World, their impact is not limited to it. Nuclear tension and conflict anywhere would be of universal concern. Third World conflict that risks spreading cannot be ignored. Internal conflict for the purpose of political and social change often risks drawing in outside powers, either to exploit internal tensions or to deter the involvement of other outsiders. Terrorism has become a living reality, even in the heart of nations fully protected against traditional military threats. And, particularly in the Middle East, religious and cultural trends can pose threats to the interests of outside states, at times even confounding their ability to comprehend what is happening—much less to deal with it effectively.

All these developments will impose severe demands on the United States, requiring special tools of foreign policy. The first need is for better understanding of national, cultural, religious, and ethnic aspirations. This will tax our educational system and the training of our professional diplomats and policymakers.

Second, we need to investigate more deeply the sources of conflict— national rivalry or ambition, the sting of poverty, or profound differences of outlook on the nature of society, especially as between some developing nations and the West.

Third, we must be even more sensitive to the individual character of different nations in the Third World, resisting the temptation to categorize or to lump together whole regions with diverse cultures or historical experiences.

Fourth, we must impress on developed nations the need to restrict their actions in the Third World, if they are to avoid becoming embroiled in situations that cannot be contained or that could jeopardize everyone's interests. Stopping nuclear proliferation requires a stronger international regime to contain uncontrolled spread of the plutonium economy and other transfers of the ability to make nuclear weapons. So, too, the world's arms suppliers need to show far greater caution in balancing the perceived value of the transfer of conventional weapons against the increased risks of conflict.

This effort to limit conflict in the Third World can only work if done in concert with Third World nations. Forbearance in acquiring either nuclear or conventional armaments will not happen unless individual developing countries can fulfill key national interests by other means: whether through regional balances, outside guarantees, effective peacemaking, or—most difficult of all—through amelioration of internal economic difficulties that sometimes prompt ambitions for military power. Even so, nations seeking nuclear or conventional military power simply for purposes of national aggrandizement may do so despite concerted efforts to dissuade them. Although this problem has no enduring solution, outsiders can help to offset or to isolate such developments.

New Factors in the Global Economy

Many important trends in the global economy are already clear, but many go beyond our traditional understanding.

• Each day, there are over 200,000 new mouths to feed in the world, and each year 27 million. By the year 2000, the world will have an additional one and a half billion people—more than the entire growth in the world's population from the birth of Christ through 1950.

• Ninety percent of that increase will be in the developing world. Indeed, by the year 2000, 8 out of every 10 people will live in those nations. Their median age will be about 19. Mexico City will exceed 30 million people; Calcutta, 20 million; and Cairo, 17 million.

• If we do not reverse existing patterns, many of the resources we need to meet these mounting human needs will disappear. The world's critical forests, which, among other things, provide the primary fuel for 2 billion people, are being destroyed at the rate of 50 acres a minute. At that rate, they will be cut in half by the year 2000.

• The world's base of farmland is declining. In North Africa alone, a quarter of a million acres dries into desert each year. Every year, a million acres of farmland in the United States are being converted to urban use.

• Pressures on the world's supply of fresh water are also compounding the problem of producing enough food to feed its people. Even in the

United States we are seeing the results of poor planning. Globally, the growing shortage of water is likely to become a major concern later in this decade.

• At the moment, we are enjoying a respite from the constant rise in oil prices. But the oil glut is only temporary, in part caused by recession in much of the developed world. We will see this cycle repeated in the future. Especially in nonrenewable resources, the long-term trend is for energy scarcity, although the United States and other nations do have sources of untapped fossil fuels, of which U.S. coal is an example. Meanwhile, most Third World nations have had little relief. With the severe oil price increases of the 1970s, their external debt has skyrocketed. Many of them are unable to meet their basic energy needs because of increased costs and, thus, their economic, political, and social progress is hobbled.

• In general, the world's natural resources and ecosystems are under greater pressure than ever before in history. This pressure will continue to escalate, thwarting the hopes of billions of people in the developing world for better lives. The quality of life in the developed world will not escape unharmed.

• • •

None of these developments have obvious answers. Too many of them have been barely investigated, with not much done beyond an inventory of the damage already incurred and that likely to take place in the next few years. The need for effective responses is not limited to economics; it also extends to the overall fabric of international relations and prospects for an orderly evolution of global politics.

These developments also impose on us the need to end the retreat from multilateralism currently being led by the United States—e.g., our diminishing support for the international financial institutions, particularly the World Bank, in which we have traditionally played a major role. As the world becomes more interdependent, we must recognize the limits of bilateralism and the importance of multilateral approaches to problems that transcend international boundaries. Halting the spread of nuclear weapons, managing the world's resources sensibly and fairly, preserving an environment that can sustain us—these problems do not derive from any single nation, nor can any single nation working alone resolve them. Wherever possible, we must practice a new kind of diplomacy, an inclusive diplomacy of working together with others to achieve common goals. Such multilateral efforts are time-consuming and complex, but they can often be more productive than going it alone.

Critical to this effort are the United Nations, the international financial institutions, and regional institutions such as the Organization of American States, the Association of South-East Asian Nations, and the

Organization of African Unity. These organizations can often provide the most effective setting for resolving international disputes and for broadening the realm of international cooperation, but regrettably they do not enjoy sufficient public support in our nation today. Like other organizations, they have shortcomings, but the fact remains that they provide an indispensable mechanism for solving problems we cannot hope to solve alone.

Where we are dissatisfied with these institutions, we should seek to reform them. Where we see weaknesses, we should try to strengthen them. We will chart a lonely and misdirected course if we neglect them.

NEW FACTORS IN HUMAN DEVELOPMENT

Finally, during the next several years, we and other nations will be tested in added ways as new developments impinge upon the lives of individual men, women, and children. For example:

• The world has entered a new era of mass migration. More refugees have fled their homes in recent years than at any other time since the great upheaval brought on by the Second World War. From Southeast Asia, Afghanistan, Cuba, the Horn of Africa and elsewhere, a great flood of people is seeking refuge from conflict or oppression. No civilized nation can turn its back on their plight. Responsibility for offering refuge and opportunity should be widely shared.

• In the United States, we are undergoing an influx of immigrants from Mexico and elsewhere in Latin America that is beginning to rival the great movement of peoples here during the nineteenth century. In significant measure, our linguistic and cultural frontier is no longer on the Rio Grande. More than ever before, these developments require us to focus on our place and role in this hemisphere. It will rival our traditional preoccupation with Europe and our newer interest in East Asia.

• In many parts of the world, especially in a wide range of developing countries, the pace of internal political and social change is quickening. We must react sensitively to this inevitable process of change, avoiding indifference on the one hand and, on the other, overreaction to events that may go against our interests in the short term. Our own national traditions suit us for the task. Building on our experience as a pluralistic nation, we must also learn to work effectively in an increasingly pluralistic world.

• Most importantly, in recent years the worldwide demand for human rights—political, social, and economic—has intensified. In the United States, we have benefited from our commitment to human rights since the founding of the Republic. Often in our history we have been willing to champion these rights abroad. Particularly with the firm commitment of the Carter administration, we have also begun to understand that promoting human rights is a major national interest, not to be dismissed when other needs arise.

In pursuing a human rights policy, we must also understand the limits of our power and wisdom. We could defeat our goals either through a rigid attempt to impose our values on others or a doctrinaire plan of action. Where we are determined to act, our means range from quiet diplomacy in its many forms, through public and forceful pronouncements, to withholding of assistance. Wherever possible, we should use positive steps of encouragement and inducement. We should give our strong support to countries working to improve the human condition, and should act in concert with other countries through international bodies. In the end, deciding whether and how to act in the cause of human rights requires informed and careful judgment. No mechanistic formula will produce an automatic answer.

In shaping our relations with developing countries, as with others, we must maintain our commitment to human rights progress. This commitment derives not only from our nation's values, but also from a practical judgment born of experience. We know that governments that respect the basic rights of their citizens, that can adapt to change, and that are able to hear and reconcile the divergent views of their people will be more stable friends and partners over the long haul.

This does not mean we should try to impose our values or form of government on others. It does mean we should support efforts to move away from arbitrary and oppressive governance. And we must seek to do so before the ties between a government and its citizens erode, with resultant suffering and turmoil.

•   •   •

Predicting the course of future events is difficult.

During the next decade, it is unlikely that we will find easy answers to major questions. Our wisdom, imagination, and leadership will be severely tested. We will find increasingly that we must work with other nations to achieve our goals and to coordinate, as never before, our foreign and domestic concerns. We are likely to find that in many areas of foreign policy, our basic frame of reference is shifting, sometimes subtly, sometimes with dramatic force.

We must therefore prepare ourselves for what may come by constantly probing for new understanding, by educating ourselves and the coming generation in the realities of the world and our place in it, and by developing the national strength, skills, and relationships with others that can help us meet the future with confidence.

This is a national task. Solutions to the many problems that will face us will not come from one political party, or from the government alone, or from Americans of only the Left or Right. All Americans must share the responsibility—the executive branch, the Congress, the media, the schools and universities, business, labor, farmers, the professions, and countless millions of individual Americans.

We should not fear the future. Despite the uncertainties, the prospect of sometimes painful change, the new stresses placed on global politics and economics, we can help to shape the world of tomorrow. We can see tomorrow as merely an extension of today and erode our ability to adapt to and influence new circumstances. Or we can see what lies ahead as another opportunity to use our immense strengths and talents to provide better lives both for our own people and for others. The choice is ours, but it must be made early in this decade if we are to play our necessary role in the next.

· · ·

I once heard a Tasmanian folk tale that I shall never forget. In the beginning, the story goes, the sky was so close to the earth that it blocked out all the light. Everyone was forced to crawl in the darkness collecting with his hands whatever he could find to eat.

But the birds of that land decided that if they worked together they could raise the sky and make more room to move about. Slowly, with long sticks, they lifted the sky. The darkness passed and everyone could stand upright.

To each of us it sometimes seems that our sky is dangerously close. We live under the shadow of nuclear weapons. Deep divisions and conflicts between nations pose a constant danger. Millions of our fellow men live lives of grinding poverty. But I believe that if we work together, we too can lift the sky and make more room for all to move about—with dignity and in peace.

APPENDIXES

Appendix I

OVERVIEW OF
FOREIGN POLICY ISSUES AND POSITIONS *

The following memorandum rapidly surveys, if not all the trees in the foreign affairs forest, at least the clumps of trees. The risk in such a process is that sight of the forest may be lost. I start, therefore, with a broad statement of the themes that should, I think, make up the primary elements of the foreign policy of the Carter Administration.

(1) In its dealings with the Soviet Union, the United States will keep itself strong, and will stand resolutely firm to protect key United States interests. At the same time, the new Administration will continue to direct its efforts toward the objective of a further reduction of tensions between the two countries.

—Although of central importance, US/Soviet issues will not be permitted to so dominate our foreign policy that we neglect other important relationships and problems.

(2) The new Administration will bring a new sensitivity, awareness and priority to the vast complex of issues clustering around the relationships between the industrialized and the unindustrialized world, and the new set of global issues that are emerging, such as energy, population, environment, and nuclear proliferation.

(3) The United States will continue in international forums its unwavering stand in favor of the rights of free men and, without unrealistically inserting itself into the internal operations of other governments, to give important weight to those considerations in selecting foreign policy positions in the interests of the United States.

(4) In its conduct of its foreign policy, the new Administration will proceed with gravity, not flurry; will not try to do everything at once or solve all the world's problems; and will keep its mind focused on long-term general objectives, not just the crises of the moment.

(5) The new Administration will accept the necessity to make the Congress and the American people joint partners in foreign policy matters. To do so, the President will assume major public leadership on foreign policy matters, and make a major investment in educating the public to perceive the difference between its long-term interests and its short-term interests, and the difference between the interest of the nation as a whole and the

* In October 1976 I prepared this memorandum setting out specific goals and priorities for a Carter foreign policy should he be elected.

interests of particular subconstituencies and interest groups within the United States.

These are pervasive general foreign policy themes. But a President will not always have the luxury of setting his own agenda and his own timing. Unforeseen crises will occur, demanding instant reaction. And the new Administration will inherit several deep-seated, impacted sore spots (e.g., Mid-East, Korea, Greece-Turkey-Cyprus, Panama) that will require prompt attention, as appears in later pages.

At the outset, it may be useful to give a thumbnail sketch of the political landscape in which the issues facing a new Administration are rooted, since that context will affect the foreign policy options available to the President, both in terms of constraints and opportunities. After setting this background, I will discuss the highest priority issues on a regional and functional basis.

I. Political Context.

Western Europe is emerging from the serious recession which has affected both policies and politics for the last several years. However, the role of the various parties and coalitions in power is thin or shaky in most countries.

In Britain, the Labor Government is faced with very serious economic problems and mounting political problems. Trade balances are off, inflation has not been brought under control, and the Labor Party is fighting to keep itself in office.

In France, the government has a paper-thin margin, and it is being forced to abandon many of the reform proposals which it had put forward. In the meantime, the left is growing stronger, and there is a real possibility that we may see a socialist prime minister within the foreseeable future.

In West Germany, although the economy is good, Schmidt has just squeaked through a close election and has a very shaky political base from which to govern.

Moving to the Iberian Peninsula, we see in Portugal a more stable situation than seemed possible a short while ago. However, the political margin of the government is narrow. Spain has been moving slowly toward the center, but civil strife remains a real possibility.

Italy has gotten through its recent elections, but again the political margins are precarious. A form of sharing of political power has evolved in the agreement worked out between the Communists and the Christian Democrats. The Italian economy remains, however, in serious condition, and it is not clear that the Christian Democrats have the strength or leadership to stay in power.

In Yugoslavia, Tito is past 80 and the problem of transfer of leadership may well soon present very difficult and complex problems, both within and without Yugoslavia. Some observers predict the likelihood of direct Soviet intervention. I would doubt this and believe attempts at subversion more likely.

Greece and Turkey are glaring at each other across the Aegean, and both governments have fragile political bases.

Thus, the principal actors in Western Europe are all faced with the problem of very thin political margins which will make it difficult for them to take any bold actions, and one can anticipate that their individual and collective actions will be cautious and careful. The questionable concept of Euro-communism—libertarian nationalist communism—further clouds the Western European picture with the uncertainty it portends for the future.

In the Middle East we find a similar situation arising out of the continuing conflict in Lebanon, with the resultant disputes among the Arab states it has produced, and the small political margin of the Rabin government. One must conclude that neither side in the Israeli-Arab dispute is likely to undertake any major new initiative without leadership from without, and the possibility of a resumption of military actions remains real.

In Eastern Europe, the situation varies country-by-country. Most of the countries have been suffering from the high cost of Soviet petroleum and raw materials. This has increased the tensions between the Soviet Union and the East European countries, especially Poland, East Germany and Hungary. Poland is in the throes of an economic crisis and is faced with an explosive situation among its workers. On the other hand, most of the East European nations appear anxious to expand trade with the West in order to increase credits to cover the East European trade imbalance. On the foreign policy scene, Romania is the most independent in formulating its own course of action.

In Africa, the problems of Rhodesia, Namibia and South Africa consume the lion's share of the attention of those in the southern half of the continent. The book is still unwritten as to how the Kissinger initiative will come out and what problems it will leave on the plate of the new Administration. The problems arising from the Angolan conflict are receding into the past, and the recent Kissinger initiative has somewhat tempered the losses suffered by the Angolan misadventure. The black Africans, however, will be watching carefully to see whether we really mean what we have been saying recently about black majority rule.

Elsewhere in Africa, the dominant issues will relate to economic and social problems—those involved in the so-called North-South dialogue. We can anticipate that these pressures for resource transfers and greater assistance to the developing nations will continue and, indeed, may become one of the two or three dominant issues in the next five to ten years. On the non-economic side, mention must be made of the Territory of the Affars and the Issas, the last remaining European colony in Africa. That Territory will realize independence this year, and it is possible conflict may break out at that time. The importance of this area is due to its geographical location on the Horn of Africa, and Soviet interest in establishing a base in the area.

Turning to Russia, we see an aging leadership with the two senior members of the government in ill health. In addition, Soviet economic growth has slowed and the Soviets have failed to meet some of their most important 5-year plan objectives. This failure has been exacerbated by bad harvests. I would expect the Soviets to continue to pursue their own policy of détente and to place progress in the SALT talks high on their agenda. They are also likely to press for most-favored-nation treatment and an expansion in the US-Soviet trade relations. The problems of human rights will continue to be a thorn between us. In sum, I anticipate that we will see the Soviet Government's actions continuing generally along current lines and characterized by caution. This does not mean, however, that we should not anticipate Soviet attempts to probe and extend their influence outside Europe.

The recent transfer of leadership in China has not yet taken firm roots, and it is too early to predict whether it will last. This uncertainty cannot fail to affect its foreign relations. I believe that China will not embark on an expansive foreign policy in the foreseeable future. It will rather concern itself mainly with sorting out its domestic—political and economic—problems. Insofar as US-China relations are concerned, I would expect no marked deviation from past policy.

Japan remains the most important country for us in the Far East. Japan is our second largest trading partner, with whom we have a long-standing security treaty. However, the Japanese are in political turmoil arising, in part, from the Lockheed scandal, which has greatly weakened the Liberal Democratic Party. It is possible that the Liberal Democratic Party itself will be driven from power in the next two years. Insofar as US-Japanese relations are concerned, they will continue strong and the Japanese will be watching to see how we proceed in our relations with their Asian neighbors. I would expect Japan to continue to participate more actively in the world councils and to expand its contacts with the West.

Southeast Asia is still embroiled in the aftermath of the Vietnam war and in the process of sorting out competing influences in the area. We should anticipate a number of local problems, increased progress toward Southeast Asian regionalism, and a continuing competition between the Soviets and China for influence in the area. Because of this competition, we may find Vietnam seeking to improve relations with the United States in order to provide itself with a balance wheel. Malaysia and Thailand will continue to present difficult security problems stemming from domestic economic, social and ethnic dissatisfaction.

On the Indian sub-continent, Mrs. Gandhi has strengthened her hold on the reins of political power and appears entrenched, despite some opposition to her authoritarian governance. India, however, remains plagued with serious food problems which could result in famines, as in neighboring Bangladesh. In Pakistan, Prime Minister Bhutto has consolidated his political authority and is making some progress in improving relations with India. Although the scene is more stable than in the recent past, there are continuing tensions, particularly as regards Bangladesh. Overall, the key to the future in the Indian sub-continent lies in the development of Chinese-Russian relations and the effect of that relationship on the Chinese-Indian equation.

In Latin America, we are faced with the consequences of our long neglect and the residue of resentment stemming from past paternalism. This has contributed in part to the new stance which the Latin American countries have taken in striking out on their own, and the increasing role they are playing in world councils. We face the North-South issues most directly here in our own backyard. The problems of the Latin American countries vary and cannot be treated in a lump. Most immediately, we face the problem of the Panama Canal negotiation, which will require a decision in the very near future.

In closing, mention must be made of Canada, where tensions with our neighbor on the north continue to mount and the relations between our two countries continue to sour. This becomes increasingly important as we face a renewal of the energy crisis without an energy policy. This relationship cannot be permitted to continue to fester without unacceptable detriment to the US. It will, however, do so unless we mount a serious effort to re-examine our whole relationship and work out a better understanding between us.

In sum, the foregoing sketch indicates that throughout most of the world we see potentially high tensions and limited political tolerance arising from the narrow political bases and transfer-of-leadership situations which exist in a number of important nations. There remain the festering sores of the Middle East, the dispute between Greece and Turkey, the problem of Cuba, the North-South differences, and other global issues—all of which cry out for leadership.

Although most of the issues I have talked about are geographical, perhaps the most difficult set of problems are the global issues, i.e., energy, food, population, nuclear proliferation, North-South disputes, environment, etc. These issues cannot be resolved on a bilateral basis, and it will require strong leadership and perhaps new institutions to cope with them.

It is difficult to see, however, where this leadership will come from, as most of the traditional leaders are constrained in what they can do.

This raises the question of the United States and what role it can play in world affairs. With a President and Congress of the same party, the government will have a strength which it has not had in the past. In addition, a majority of the people appear to have crossed a watershed following the Vietnam war and the recession of the early 1970's in terms of their views of foreign affairs and the role the US should play. A recent survey indicates that the vast majority of the American people believe that "the United States has real responsibility to take a very active role in the world." Sixty-two percent of the people reject the idea that since the US is the most powerful country in the world, we should go our own way in international matters. In short, "The American public is ready to support an active, responsible, sacrifice-demanding foreign policy, if it can be demonstrated that the national interest will be served thereby."

II. Regional and Functional Issues.

A. US-SOVIET RELATIONS.

Although of importance, US-Soviet issues should not be permitted to so dominate our foreign policy that we neglect relationships with our allies and other important issues, as has been the case in the past. Our principal goal must be to bring about continuing reduction of tension, coupled with fidelity to our principles and national interests. The most critical issues which will face the new Administration in the first six months are set forth below.

The first issue is whether the President should participate in a "get-to-know" meeting with the Soviet leadership within the first three months. I recommend that this be put off for at least six months on the basis that the first meeting with the Soviets should be one with a carefully prepared agenda and an anticipated substantive product. The President should not feel that he is being immediately put on test, as was the case with President Kennedy.

I believe it will be possible to set up the first meeting around a discussion of the strategic issues and, hopefully, to conclude a SALT II agreement. In this connection, the first question which is raised is whether we should seek an agreement extending the interim SALT agreement for an additional year, in order to give us more time to deal with the matter. I think this would be a mistake. We have until October 1977 to reach a SALT II agreement, and I believe it is important to keep the pressure on both ourselves and the Soviets to conclude such an agreement.

The only critical issues remaining in the SALT negotiation are how to deal with the Soviet Backfire and the US Cruise missiles. These are difficult issues, but not beyond resolution. I would recommend that the issues of these two weapons systems not be bypassed, as some have suggested, and that they be included in the SALT II package, either directly under the Vladivostok ceilings or by a separate side agreement executed at the same time as the SALT agreement on the items which have already been agreed to. The resolution of this issue within the US Government must be attacked immediately upon your taking office, and useful work on this problem can be done in advance of inauguration.

During the first six months of the year, further work can be done on developing a possible agenda for SALT III, which could be part of summit discussions in the fall of 1977.

A fall summit meeting need not be limited to SALT issues. Should an early attack be made on the most-favored-nation problem—which is of great importance to the Soviets—and on the elimination of the Jackson Amendment? I believe the trade question need not be addressed at an early date. It is wise to use this item for a bargaining lever and to keep the cat on their back for a while. Insofar as food is concerned, I believe we should deal with the Soviets on a businesslike basis and eschew the use of food as a political weapon.

I will not attempt to sketch the agenda of the items which would be appropriate for the first summit meeting, as there will be sufficient time to develop such a program.

B. WESTERN EUROPE.

Turning to Western Europe, the issues which call for early attention include the establishment of contact with European leaders, developing concrete ideas with respect to methods of closer cooperation with our European allies, improvement of NATO's strength, and working cooperatively to develop an agenda and method of dealing with the North-South issues now being discussed in CIEC.

With respect to possible summit meetings with European leaders, I would recommend that you not make a trip to Europe during the first three to six months, but that you extend an invitation to major European leaders and others to visit Washington to see you.

Early attention must be directed to concrete suggestions which may be put forward in your discussions with major European leaders as to how one might improve the coordination and cooperation with our allies and the European Community. I suggest that we should not give our European colleagues a proposed plan on which we expect them to sign off. To do so would be to repeat the errors of the "Year of Europe." Our approach should be low-key and should be worked out in conjunction with the European leaders. We must avoid the appearance of forcing our views down their throats.

It is important, in my judgment, to suggest at a very early stage a review of our NATO forces, force structure, deployments, and equipment. This will indicate our interest in Europe and the importance of maintaining a strong, lean and effective NATO force. It will be a difficult task because of the disparate views of the allies on many of the issues which will be raised. Studies should be started immediately after the election to provide the shape of proposals that could be introduced at the first NATO ministers' meeting.

It would appear that the CIEC discussions are about to founder. It is possible that this will happen before you take office. It is also possible, however, that the December CIEC meeting will be put over until after the inauguration in the hope that new leadership may be able to breathe life into these discussions. It is, therefore, a matter of highest priority that a study be instituted immediately after inauguration to determine the general framework of the US approach to the social and economic problems encompassed within the CIEC discussions. In my judgment, it would be a grave mistake to let the North-South dialogue fall apart. It is in the interest of both the developed and developing countries to come to grips with these terribly difficult problems. It must be done, however, on a realistic basis and not overload the circuits or raise unrealistic expectations on the part of the developing world.

Other less important items are the development of our approach to Eurocommunism and the posture to be taken in the MBFR negotiations on mutual balance force reductions. With respect to the latter, I would recommend that we continue the status quo by not changing the NATO offer at this time. This can, for the immediate future, await progress in the SALT discussions. If that course is followed, this would dictate that we treat with the tactical nuclear weapons problem by holding back on withdrawal of tactical nuclear weapons in the immediate future.

A subdivision of the issues relating to Western Europe is the Greek-Turkish conflict. This issue is of major importance, as I believe it is time urgent. Greece and Turkey came dangerously close to military confrontation in August of this year when Prime Minister Caramanlis almost took military action against the Turkish vessel Seminik. In addition to the problems of the Aegean (which include air, sea-bed resources, and sovereignty disputes), there are, of course, the continuing problems of Cyprus.

Prime Minister Demirel has a very thin majority in the legislature and is under constant attack for any Greek-related action which appears to be soft. Similarly, Caramanlis is under continual attack from the moderate opposition and from the left, led by Andreas Papandreou. Thoughtful observers in both countries indicate that, unless progress is made promptly toward resolution of these differences, unwise and dangerous action may be undertaken by either Caramanlis or Demirel.

In my judgment, it is necessary for the United States to undertake a careful initiative in acting as a mediator, along with the European Community and perhaps Romania. There have been clear indications from the Greeks that they would welcome such a course of action, and suggestions from the Turkish that they might also be prepared to go along with such an initiative. There is obviously risk, but the risks on the other side are also great. A new initiative merits very serious consideration.

C. MIDDLE EAST.

We have a vital interest in the maintenance of peace in the Middle East. Our interest arises from our commitment to the independence and security of Israel, our needs and those of our allies for Middle Eastern oil, our national interest in maintaining friendly and cooperative relations with the Arab states and with Iran, and the danger of military confrontation with the USSR in the region. At present, Arab-Israeli negotiations are on the back burner. The Arabs are having too much trouble among themselves and the problem of Lebanon continues to loom large and almost insoluble. It is clear, however, that the time for negotiations will come again. In that event, the US enjoys the confidence of both states and is best suited to undertake a new initiative.

With respect to the Arab-Israeli dispute, I continue to believe that we should nudge the situation along, but not take any strong initiative in the first several months, which should be devoted to quiet diplomacy directed to building a base for resumption of serious settlement discussions. Ultimately, I believe we should urge the parties to reach a general settlement to be carried out in stages. The settlement would involve the Arabs' agreeing to normalization of relations with Israel in exchange for return of most of the territories occupied by Israel in 1967. It would also involve various guarantees and assurances among the parties and from others.

In reaching such an agreement, the US should enlist, at an appropriate time, the aid of the Soviet Union. During the first several months of your Administration, I believe the Administration should consult with Congressional leaders and leaders of American groups especially concerned with US policy toward Israel. In this connection, it is important to enlist a small and thoughtful group from the Jewish community, which would include men like Phil Klutznick and Morris Abram.

I do not foresee the need for any immediate decision on the question of further military assistance to Israel. You may be faced, however, with demands from some of the Arab countries to counter the recent arms shipments to Israel. At this moment, I do not know enough about the facts to reach a confident conclusion on the matter. I believe, however, that it may be necessary to provide defensive arms to one or two Arab countries to balance the situation.

D. US-CHINESE RELATIONS.

As mentioned above, China is in the throes of the transfer of power to new leadership under a government headed by Chairman Hua Kuo-feng. It is too early to say whether his government will last, but it would appear that it has the support of the military, which is essential to survival.

I believe it is important to indicate at an early stage that the new Administration stands behind the ultimate goal of normalization of diplomatic relations, as you have indicated in a number of statements during the campaign. Further, I believe it is important to move to a new degree of cordiality and understanding with the Chinese. To this end, I believe that early contact should be made with the Chinese Government, and that one or more visits at a level below the President should be undertaken.

I believe it would be a mistake to entangle the President in this situation at too early a date. It would be better to send the Secretary of State to China to talk about a wide range of issues and to begin to get a better understanding of the Chinese view and give them a better view of the thinking of the new Administration. This would give the right signal and would, I believe, be met receptively by the Chinese.

The issue of "normalization" is very complex and must be approached with caution. It is essential that before any steps are taken the negotiating record be carefully examined. At this time we do not know what promises and commitments have already been made, as the negotiating minutes have been kept secret. In the meantime, I would see no reason to alter the current arms sales policy to

Taiwan. As I have previously indicated, in the long run I feel we clearly should move toward total normalization, but I do not think we have to rush. Mao is now dead, and it is unclear how much flexibility the new government will have at the outset. Our plan should be measured and careful.

In any discussions with the Chinese, we should, of course, discuss, in addition to the subject of normalization, the question of what China would be prepared to do with respect to preserving stability in the Korean Peninsula, expansion of trade with the US, resolution of unsettled US claims, and expansion of cultural and other private contacts between our two countries.

E. JAPAN AND KOREA.

Japan is the anchor of our foreign policy in the Far East and one of our core allies. The Nixon shocks are beginning to recede into the past and our relationships with Japan have improved. The Japanese are, nonetheless, puzzled about our future relationship. This uncertainty is exacerbated by their internal political difficulties. You have stated repeatedly the importance of the US-Japanese relations in your campaign, and early steps should be taken to underscore your commitment to strong and improved relationships.

In this connection, the question arises as to whether you should make a trip to Japan to meet with the Prime Minister early in the first six months. I recommend against this. I think you should maintain the position that for the first six months you will remain in the US and devote yourself to the task of getting on top of the various domestic and foreign problems that face a new President. Because of this, I would suggest that you extend an invitation to the Prime Minister to come to the US some time during the first six months, in the same way you will have done with the major European leaders.

There are no immediately pressing trade or other foreign policy problems which require resolution prior to such a get-together meeting.

Korea remains a trouble spot which can explode at any moment. In my judgment, it is doubtful that any lasting solution can be achieved until President Park and Kim Il Sung are no longer in office. Notwithstanding, I believe the US should continue to work toward a six-power conference which would deal with the long-range problems of this divided country. In the meantime, the most important issues will concern troop withdrawals, military and economic assistance and human rights.

With respect to the question of withdrawal of US troops, I believe that this issue must be addressed with great care because of the way the rest of the world will perceive it. It must be discussed in advance with both the Japanese and the South Koreans, and it would be a mistake to prepare a specific timetable for withdrawal and present it to them for their approval. On the other hand, I believe that it is correct to work toward the withdrawal of US ground forces on a phased basis.

Military and economic assistance can be dealt with in the normal way, recognizing, of course, that they are inter-linked with US troop deployments.

The problem of human rights will remain a very difficult one. We must continue to make clear to the Korean Government at the highest level that this is a matter of deep concern to us and that failure to make progress in this area erodes support for South Korea. I would not recommend that we threaten to cut back on military or economic aid. I think we must first test what straight and forthright statements of our position to President Park will produce in the way of action on the part of the ROK Government. If this does not work, we should apply a variety of lesser pressures, such as cutting off various forms of cooperation other than military and economic aid. One specific step which should be taken is to end South Korean intimidation of South Korean citizens and Americans of South Korean descent in the US.

F. VIETNAM.

In my judgment, Vietnam presents an opportunity for a new initiative. This initiative would involve the sending of a special Presidential envoy to Hanoi, as well as to Laos and Cambodia, to discuss the issue of MIA's. During the visit to Hanoi, the special emissary would probe Hanoi's intentions and would be authorized to say that the US would be prepared to put to the Congress a program of humanitarian assistance in such areas as housing, health and food, once there was an accounting for MIA's. If a favorable response were received, a Presidential statement on the beginning of such negotiations could involve the announcement of an appointment of a prominent American special envoy (such as Averell Harriman, who is highly respected by the Vietnamese).

This would be the first step along the road to normalization of relations. I believe that such a goal would be in the interests of both countries. The Vietnamese are trying to find a balance between over-dependence on either the Chinese or the Soviet Union. It is also to the interest of the US that Vietnam not be so dependent. The Vietnamese have indicated during the Paris Peace Talks their desire for establishing a friendly and constructive relationship with the United States. From the standpoint of the United States, this would give the US an opportunity to have more influence with a nation which obviously will play an important part in the future development of Southeast Asia. Such a relationship might be able to help move that development along a peaceful course, as opposed to a military course.

G. INDIAN SUB-CONTINENT.

Although problems in this area may be thrust upon you by future events, I see only one issue at this time to which you should give early attention. That issue is whether we should proceed with the building of an additional facility at Diego Garcia in the Indian Ocean. I do not have all the facts relating to this issue, but on the basis of what I now know, I favor not halting construction unilaterally. There is some risk that Bahrein may soon ask the US to close its base there, which would leave us without a facility in the Persian Gulf-Indian Ocean area. The Diego Garcia base would give us more leverage with respect to the now greater Russian deployment in the area and would permit more rapid reinforcement in the region than is currently possible.

H. AFRICA.

A number of diplomatic issues with regard to Africa will arise during the first year of the new Administration. They include our relations with Zaire and Nigeria, and, more particularly, possible sales of sophisticated conventional arms to both countries and to Kenya. These issues do not have to be faced immediately but should be studied promptly.

The problems of Southern Africa, however, are more pressing and will probably require action within the first three months of a new Administration. First are the issues which relate to the current Kissinger initiatives in Southern Rhodesia and Namibia. With respect to Southern Rhodesia, the proposed Kissinger formula is fraught with pitfalls which I will not attempt to sketch. It is clear, however, that the new Administration will probably be faced with a decision on the implementation of the Kissinger plan. Among the available possibilities, I would recommend that the US be prepared to modify the Kissinger proposals to make them more acceptable to the Africans, should that prove to be a stumbling block, and use our leverage on South Africa and Southern Rhodesia to gain acceptance. This should be coupled with letting the British take the lead, as they appear to be willing to do.

With reference to Namibia, it appears that it will not be possible to make any real and lasting progress without inclusion of the SWAPO in the discussions of an ultimate solution. At this time they are not included in the negotiations. On the specific steps to be taken by the US, judgment does not have to be made until the situation is clarified by events happening between now and January.

The long-range problem will continue to be South Africa. On the specific issues of immediate importance, I believe that we should return to the strict policy of the Kennedy and Johnson years on sale of arms and military equipment to South Africa. If the US decision has not been taken with respect to the Transkei by inauguration day, I believe we should not recognize the Transkei in a *de jure* sense, but should find a way of dealing with it *de facto*. Further, we must continue to make clear to the South Africans and to the world our strong abhorrence of apartheid and violation of human rights in South Africa.

We must continue to shore up the "front line countries" and move toward closer relations with Angola and Mozambique. In this connection, an early visit by the Assistant Secretary of State for African Affairs to Southern Africa would be important.

I. LATIN AMERICA, PANAMA AND CUBA.

I agree with the conclusion in the Latin America issue paper that Latin American countries are striking out on their own in a way inconceivable a few years ago. This has taken place both in the world arena and in bilateral contexts, and has been encouraged by the emergence of growing cadres of technocrats and by a residue of resentment and hostility stemming from historic patterns of US paternalism and neglect. Lastly, I agree that Latin America, as a powerful and prosperous member of the Third World, will play a major role in the evolution of the international economic order.

In determining what overall approach can best secure the positive cooperation of the Latin American and Caribbean states in dealing with major global issues and what relative priorities a new Administration should give to our interests at stake in the hemisphere, I favor a course of action which would treat Latin American nations in the same fashion as we treat nations in other areas of the world. More specifically, where we have matters of bilateral interest they should be treated bilaterally, and global issues should be dealt with in multilateral forums.

I am persuaded that we must move away from the concepts of a "special relationship" or an "inter-American community," which have been rejected by Latin American leaders and evoke memories of past paternalism. Each country in Latin America has always been unique. These countries have become more differentiated as economic development has advanced at different rates. Henceforth, the US should give serious diplomatic attention, on the basis of negotiations conducted between equal sovereign powers, to the countries which lie to our south. Problems of a bilateral character can especially be predicted in our dealings with Mexico, Brazil, Argentina and Chile.

I also support the suggestion that the President or the Secretary of State make a major policy address defining the overall approach of the new Administration to Latin America early in the new Administration. The speech should stress the President's personal interest and set forth fundamental principles which would act as guidelines for the future.

Panama is a very critical issue in terms of future relations with Latin American nations. What we do or do not do with respect to the negotiation of a new treaty will be watched very carefully throughout Latin America. From the standpoint of both security and continued smooth operation of the Canal, I believe it is necessary to work out a new treaty which is acceptable to the Panamanians. With respect to the objections that are often raised, I believe that: (1) the Panamanians have as much interest as we in keeping the Canal running safely and smoothly; (2) the Canal being Panama's single most valuable economic resource, the Panamanians have a greater stake than we do in its profitability; and (3) the Canal is vulnerable to being damaged by the simplest, unsophisticated weapons—one small bomb or dynamite charge exploded in Gatun Lake Dam could put the Canal out of commission for one to two years. Accordingly, I believe it would be safer to enlist Panama's cooperation than to end up in conflict, which would endanger the operation of the Canal.

I fully recognize that the issue is charged with emotion and that the political situation in the US Congress is very difficult. I do believe, however, that we must make the effort to negotiate such a treaty if we are to develop proper relations with Latin America.

In addition, it must be noted that the US is largely committed as a result of the negotiations to date. To move backward would be viewed by many as reneging on our commitments and would run the risk of conflict. Accordingly, I believe that the new Administration should not interfere in the negotiations which will be going on between now and the change of administration, but should keep itself closely informed. Thereafter, the new Administration must face up to completing the negotiations and carrying the battle to the Congress.

With respect to Cuba, I believe the time has come to move away from our past policy of isolation. Our boycott has proved ineffective, and there has been a decline of Cuba's export of revolution in the region. In addition, most Latin American nations have already renewed diplomatic and economic ties with Cuba. As indicated in the issues paper, a high Cuban official has recently indicated that his government would be willing to take mutual steps leading to "resumption of relations" with a Carter Administration early in the next year. It was suggested that a partial lifting of the embargo of food and medicine would be followed by an appropriate Cuban response—the release of eight or nine American prisoners.

I believe that this presents an opportunity for a constructive new initiative and I favor option number 3 in the issues paper. That option suggests that we indicate quietly to the Cubans that the President is prepared to lift the embargo of food and medicine if Cuba will make an appropriate response and avoid escalating tensions with regard to Southern Africa and Puerto Rico.

J. ARMS CONTROL, PROLIFERATION AND ARMS TRANSFERS.

I have already discussed the next steps in the SALT negotiations. With respect to a nuclear test ban, I recommend that despite the problems with the Threshold Test Ban Treaty and the Peaceful Nuclear Explosion Treaty, we should not withdraw these treaties from Senate consideration. The Threshold Test Ban Treaty does place significant limits on further Soviet high-yield testing, and the withdrawal of the treaties would risk losing the limit now obtained and seriously undermining Soviet-American relations. I do not believe this approval of these treaties would impede the initiation of negotiations with the Soviet Union for a comprehensive test ban treaty.

With respect to the CTB, I believe that we should go forward with the negotiations as outlined in your speech before the United Nations. I believe that there is substantial support in the country for this move, and that it will be possible to muster support from the Joint Chiefs. This will not be an easy task, but I think it is substantially aided by the fact that we are dealing with a 5-year treaty, rather than one without term. The negotiation of such a treaty would be a major step forward in the arms control field and would have positive spill-over effects in the area of non-proliferation.

Turning to the question of proliferation, I believe several actions should be initiated in the first six months. First, there should be a reaffirmation of our policy of refusing to export uranium enrichment and plutonium reprocessing facilities and technology. Second, it should be stated that the new Administration intends to defer decision on the issue of developing a plutonium reprocessing plant in the United States. These two steps should be coupled with diplomatic action which can be commenced at the meetings with the leaders of major allied countries when they come to the US. At those meetings, you may wish to urge their participation in an agreement among the supplier countries to institute a moratorium on the sale of reprocessing and uranium enrichment facilities and technology. In addition, diplomatic efforts to enlist new signers to the Non-Proliferation Treaty must continue.

With respect to arms transfers, I believe the new Administration should start a major review of US arms transfer policy even before it takes office. Immediately upon your taking office, a statement should be made that there will be no new negotiations with respect to arms transfers pending the completion of this review.

In addition, a separate study should proceed in parallel which would examine the various unilateral, bilateral and multilateral steps which might be taken in the arms transfer field. I recognize that there is legitimate basis for public skepticism about the possibility of progress in the arms transfer field because of our inability to affect the conduct of other arms manufacturing countries. Nonetheless, this is an extremely important area which vitally affects our foreign policy, as well as the peace of the world, and deserves new and imaginative thinking and effort.

K. INTERNATIONAL TRADE NEGOTIATIONS.

There are several pressing issues in this area which must be addressed during the first six months of a new Administration. The first concerns the US position in the negotiations under the General Agreement on Tariffs and Trade (GATT) —the so-called Tokyo Round. The options run from deferring everything to driving ahead to complete major elements of the negotiation in 1977. I believe we should choose the middle ground, i.e., aim for an early 1977 agreement on relatively non-controversial items.

This option would maintain momentum in the negotiation and would realize certain limited objectives by resolving the easier issues. This would clear the field for a more fundamental examination of the tougher issues, and would also give the Congress something relatively easy to ratify. This option has no major disadvantages. The other two options present major difficulties.

Another important issue concerns the coordination and management of US trade policy. In this area, I support the conclusion that no single department's jurisdiction can encompass national economic and interdependence issues, since they cut across virtually all departments and are essentially Presidential. Thus, I favor a White House based office for the coordination of foreign economic policy. As to the location of such coordination within the White House, I believe it should rest in the office of the Assistant to the President for National Security Affairs. It should probably be vested in a deputy assistant. The size of the staff should be as small as possible—two to four individuals.

With respect to the question of organization for trade policy, I strongly favor continuation of the current system—coordination by the President's Special Representative for Trade Negotiations. This operation worked well on the Kennedy Round and has strong Congressional support. In addition, it is understood by domestic interests and other countries' trade negotiators. Each of the other options presents too many problems.

Another item which must be faced very early in 1977 is the position of the new Administration with respect to the Multi-Fiber Textile Agreement. The new President will have to indicate whether the US will pursue the policy of the current Administration, which is to renew the agreement essentially unchanged, or to adopt a different course. I recommend that the new Administration reserve its position while the textile situation is reviewed. A decision should be accompanied by a restatement of US support for multi-textile understanding on the textile trade. As suggested in the issues paper, deferring the decision would make it possible for the Administration to link the textile negotiations with general negotiations on trade. In addition, a policy review would make it possible to determine whether a useful trade bargain could be struck with the developing countries. There is no major disadvantage.

L. ECONOMIC ASSISTANCE.

Here again, the new Administration will be faced with immediate and difficult budgetary and political questions. As you know, economic or so-called development assistance falls into three categories: US bilateral economic development programs administered by AID and the Peace Corps, and multilateral development programs, which receive US funding through the World Bank, regional banks and various United Nations agencies. A second category is political economic assistance. A third category is straight humanitarian or relief assistance. There is also military assistance, which has often been bracketed with, but in fact is not, development assistance.

The first question is who should receive economic assistance. Here, I believe that we should continue to make economic assistance available to both the least-developed and the middle-level countries, as it is at present. I believe it would be unwise to adopt a rule that only very poor countries will receive US bilateral economic assistance. Not the least important of the several advantages favoring this suggestion is the fact that the other course of action would make most Latin American countries ineligible for development aid.

A second issue is whether economic assistance should be denied to countries that flagrantly violate human rights. Current aid legislation prohibits economic assistance to those who violate human rights, unless the President can demonstrate that such aid gets to the poorest people. The issue is whether this escape clause should be tightened. It would be a mistake, in my judgment, to do so. Conditioning economic assistance on such a policy would appear to be an intrusion into the internal affairs of the recipient countries. In addition, it would appear to be saying that in order to show our sympathy for the poor, we are withdrawing the aid designed to improve their wellbeing.

Another key question is whether economic assistance should be multilateral or bilateral, or both. I believe it should be both. We should provide capital aid increasingly through the regional development banks, while continuing to rely on bilateral channels for more technical assistance. The regional development banks are generally considered to be efficient in handling multilateral aid. However, assistance can be provided more efficiently on a bilateral basis.

Finally, I believe that economic assistance should be increased. There is an international target of .7% of GNP. Other countries are taking the target seriously and some have reached it. I am not suggesting we should attempt to go to .7%. We are currently at about .25% and should do more. Moreover, the capability of aid-delivering agencies to help host countries develop useful projects has improved over the years, while the amount of human deprivation has continued to increase.

Budgetary decisions will have to be made with respect to Fiscal 78 Budget on the funding of economic assistance programs for the next two years. The amounts involved are very large. I would recommend the so-called lower option (2-a) contained in the Development Assistance issues paper, which would provide for authorization of $3.65 billion, an appropriation of $1.26 to $1.87 billion. I think it would be impossible to get anything higher through the Congress, and even this option will be difficult to achieve. However, we must meet our obligations. Failure to do so in a responsible manner could shake the international institutions, resulting in setbacks to their current lending programs and projects. The critical item with the Congress will be the amount of the appropriation, rather than the authorization.

M. RELATIONS WITH DEVELOPING NATIONS.

Whether we like it or not, one of the most important and difficult issues which will face the new Administration is the question of our relations with the developing nations. The developing nations have found that they can achieve political leverage by operating in concert and have made it a central focus of their foreign policies under the rubric of a demand for a "new international economic order." The developing countries' goals in this area affect trade, commodities, investment and technological transfer, monetary reform, and aid.

Our relations with the developing countries are important because without their participation and cooperation, we, as well as they, may find it most difficult to grow and prosper. They now constitute a majority in most international bodies in which global problems are dealt with. While the developing nations may not be able to force action, they can block it.

As you know, the current Administration had opposed requests from the developing countries for change in international economic systems for a number of years. This policy was changed in the speech of the Secretary of State at the 7th Special Session of the United Nations General Assembly in September 1974. Since then, however, little of significance has been accomplished, and we face the danger of increased tensions if the ongoing discussions and negotiations come to naught.

The current outlook is gloomy. The dialogue at CIEC appears to be going nowhere. The UNCTAD meeting last spring ended without important accomplishment and little progress is being made in other areas such as Law of the Sea, food, commodities, and debt rescheduling.

Insofar as the US public is concerned, surveys would indicate that the country is ambivalent. People feel that we should help the less fortunate, but they feel, at the same time, that our aid is not getting to the poor people who really need it, and that we are taxing the American people, including the poor, to assist the well-to-do and rich in other countries. I believe, however, that our people will support a policy which they feel is practical and is properly directed toward alleviating suffering and deprivation in the developing world. More public education is needed, and it will have to come in large measure through Presidential leadership.

Among the available options concerning our overall approach to the problem, selective functional cooperation with the developing nations makes the most sense. If we chose this course of action, the US would agree to discuss in good faith all the issues being raised, looking where possible to strike bargains where gains for both sides can be assured, but refusing to agree to proposals which we believe are economically unsound or politically unacceptable. This would serve to diffuse the danger of growing confrontation between the North and the South. It would also put the US in a position of leadership it has not had since the early 1960's.

Turning briefly to specific issues, the first key issue is trade. What the next President does about the Tokyo Round is extremely important. If you follow the course of action suggested earlier in this paper, I believe you will be on solid ground. The problem of commodities is incredibly complex. The preferred solutions will vary among different commodities and positions will vary among the developing countries. The use of buffer stocks should be approached with caution. Perhaps more can be done quickly by increasing US strategic stockpiles in the metals area, than can be done by the use of buffer stocks. Attempts to hold prices on raw materials at artificially high levels do not make sense. But it is true that volatility of commodity prices is to many countries an obstacle to economic development.

I have already commented on the question of development assistance and it need only be noted further that after trade, concessional aid is the single most important issue you will have to address from an economic standpoint in the North-South relations.

Space does not permit adequate discussion of international debt service by developing countries. Suffice it to say that the better-off developed countries do not need it and fear that it would jeopardize their credit standing. The debt issue, thus, comes down to the poor countries. Of the total amount owed, two-thirds is owed by India, Pakistan and Egypt.

With respect to monetary reform, the issue concerns the developing nations' claim that they do not receive a fair deal from the IMF because of their lack of voting weight. This in turn relates to the question of special drawing rights, which are allocated on the basis of IMF quotas, which are in turn a rough indicator of the financial importance of the member country in the world economy, and thus of each member country's need for international reserves. In this connection, consideration should be given to the possibility of permitting raw materials such as copper, tin, etc., to be used as reserve currencies.

Further, with respect to the question of the oceans, we have the problem of the stalled Law of the Sea Conference. It is currently stalemated primarily on the issue of deep sea mining. Here I believe that we must take a new initiative if we want to restore vitality to the negotiations. A possibility worth pursuing is a fleshed-out version of Secretary Kissinger's most recent suggestion, i.e., a two-track approach involving mining by both private interests and the public "Enterprise." Under this approach, the US and other individual countries would provide the necessary technology and know-how to the Enterprise.

With respect to food, the basic answer is increased food production in the developing countries themselves. Accordingly, there should be increased emphasis in both bilateral and multilateral efforts on increasing the developing countries' production of food. It will, however, take many years to increase food production in the poor countries. Therefore, in the meantime, it will be important to establish and maintain sufficient grain reserves in the developed countries to meet recurring needs in the developing countries.

Finally, we must continue to work on the population problem, which is inextricably linked with the problem of food and social and economic progress.

In light of the foregoing, the first and most crucial task is to develop a coordinated strategy for dealing with the various issues presented. They cannot be dealt with on a piecemeal basis. Therefore, as soon as key appointments have been made, a task force should be formed to develop such an integrated strategy under a tight time schedule—two to three months. This should be done in coordination with key members of the Congress.

N. ENERGY.

Energy is not a foreign policy problem, although it has foreign policy implications. The basic question is: How do we supply our energy requirements through the year 2000? This must be answered by promptly enacting a comprehensive energy program. There is also the larger question of meeting the energy needs of other nations, which is currently being addressed in the CIEC meetings. There again, people are waiting to see what the US is going to do and are looking for US leadership.

In December of this year the OPEC countries will again meet to decide the question of oil prices. The best available information indicates that the price rise will be between 10% and 15%. I believe it will be about 15%. I do not believe that the public or, indeed, the Administration have faced up to what the effect of a

15% price increase will be. I think it will have a substantial adverse effect on the economy.

I recommend that immediately after the election you institute a full-scale review of energy policy with a tight time schedule—two months. The matter has already been studied to death and it should be possible to complete the job within that time. At the time of the announcement of the study, contact should be made with Congressional leaders to lay the groundwork for early passage of an energy program.

In addition, I would recommend that quiet contacts be made with the Saudis and the Iranians early in 1977 to exchange views and to attempt to begin to move toward a better understanding of each other and a more cooperative relationship. This should be done whether or not there is a 15% price hike.

O. THE UNITED NATIONS.

The United States now finds itself isolated in the United Nations on a great many issues. A number of these—Southern Africa, the Middle East, and the question of a new international economic order—are of major importance. On these, as well as other important subjects, the US often faces a Third World coalition whose common positions are frequently difficult for us and the other developed nations to accept. I agree with the statement in the UN issues paper that views expressed in the UN on these issues are not irrelevant and do affect the bilateral foreign policy behavior of states. We cannot afford to remain in an isolated position in dealing with these and other matters. As the issues paper suggests, "To the degree the UN remains an inhospitable forum for the US, UN debates and resolutions will adversely affect US foreign policy."

Our present state of isolation has come about in large part by reason of our neglect and the downgrading of the United Nations during the last eight to ten years. This can and must be corrected. The first steps have been taken by the US in the recent appointment of Ambassador Scranton, who is highly regarded within the UN.

Now that most of the bilateral problems that have consumed an undue share of our attention are behind us, the stage is set for a new Administration to concentrate more on the multilateral problems of the future, and the United Nations is an excellent platform from which to state and debate our views on these matters. Multilateral issues are going to become increasingly important to the US and the world community, and we should not only play a part but accept a leadership role. We must, therefore, address ourselves promptly to completing the reorientation of our stance and policy toward the UN and couple this with the appointment of an outstanding Permanent Representative and staff.

P. DEFENSE.

There are many important defense issues. Space precludes treating each of them. There is, however, one overriding question which has highest priority—what to do about the Fiscal 1978 defense budget request and the related 5-year budget plan. These two documents are well advanced in their preparation and reflect the policies of the current Administration. It is essential that a transition team be put into the Pentagon as soon as possible after the election to begin work on these documents, as the Budget must be submitted to the new Congress fifteen days after it convenes.

The same group should also begin work on the Secretary of Defense's posture statement, which is probably also in an advanced state of preparation. This is a major undertaking as both documents are complex and require a great deal of background knowledge. It would be most useful if the transition team could include not only defense experts, but someone who has previously served in the Bureau of the Budget.

In addition, various studies on key defense issues should be initiated. The most important are strategic policy, manpower policies, and combat readiness. The latter study should be done quietly, as it would be harmful to create the impression that our combat readiness is in bad shape. I am, however, concerned about the state of our combat readiness in Army, Navy and the Air Force. A number of military officers have spoken to me recently about their concern in this area and feel that this is a matter of urgency. It would be easy to put together a very good team to draw up the necessary guidelines for the study, and it would receive the enthusiastic support of senior and responsible military officers. Similar detailed guidelines should be prepared for each of the other studies.

Q. ORGANIZATIONAL ISSUES.

Organizational issues surrounding foreign policy questions must be considered under two separate headings—national security issues, and other foreign policy issues.

1. *National Security Issues.*

The first issue concerns the procedure for channelling advice to the President and for developing Presidential decisions. Here, I would recommend a combination of two of the suggested options. The principal method would be through a formal system for reviewing policy options similar to that now in use. That system starts with a national security study memorandum; the response to that memorandum is an option paper with an analysis of the problem, followed by a discussion of pro's and con's of various options. The President then reaches a decision, either with or without a National Security Council meeting, depending upon the importance of the issue. Following a decision, a memorandum is issued reporting the decision and assigning responsibility for implementation. The system is particularly suited to those issues where the President needs to make a single, major decision and can control the timing of that decision.

This option would be combined with a system whereby in certain cases the President will deal directly with an *ad hoc* group including the Secretary of State, Secretary of Defense, National Security Advisor, and such others as the President may wish to include in the decision-making process.

The second major issue concerns the allocation of basic responsibility in national security-foreign policy affairs. Among the various possibilities, I personally favor the option that would assign to the State Department a pre-eminent role. I do so because nothing is more essential than that military instruments be always seen as means of, and not ends of, foreign policy. To the extent possible, therefore, I believe the policy leadership role should be assigned to the Secretary of State. In practice, however, I believe it must be recognized that this system cannot be made to work without special supporting machinery. The domestic political constituency of the Defense Department is vast and very powerful; that of the Department of State is almost non-existent. That situation cannot be changed. I, therefore, support the maintenance of a strong office of the Advisor to the President on National Security, and of an NSC structure that operates under his chairmanship and under the wing of the President, thus bringing to bear the political clout of the President.

In any event, there must be a cooperative effort in dealing with national security matters, and there must be the closest cooperation between the Secretary of State, the Secretary of Defense, the National Security Advisor, and others involved in national security policy-making.

The success of this choice of options is largely dependent upon the quality of the senior officials in the Department of State, and in their ability to operate as a team, both within the Department and in working with other elements of the national security apparatus.

2. Other Foreign Policy Issues.

More and more, the foreign policy agenda is being taken up by issues that lie outside, or only touch upon, the field of national security. The most obvious examples are questions of international economic policy (trade, monetary systems, credits, etc.), but they are not limited to economic issues (e.g., pollution, communications, law of the sea, etc.). In most, if not all, cases, these issues of the new foreign affairs agenda bear directly on the interests of major domestic constituencies—farmers, labor, exporters, etc. In some cases, they directly involve the immediate interest of all citizens, as consumers or otherwise. The oil-energy controversy is the most striking example. These issues intermix domestic and foreign considerations.

How can the Government best work out its policy positions on these issues? The affected domestic constituencies should, and will, be heard. The Secretaries of Labor, Agriculture, and Commerce—and others—must play a part. The Department of State neither has the expertise nor the political leverage to deal with these intermixed domestic and foreign issues. The NSC is even less properly oriented for them. Yet the entire Cabinet is too large to be manageable, and on any given issue only a few Secretaries would be interested.

Only two options remain: (1) The White House can build up within its own staff a mini-replica of each of the Departments, and then thrash out these intermixed questions within the White House Staff. (The negatives to that approach are too obvious to require listing.) (2) On an issue-by-issue basis, the affected and interested members of the Cabinet can be brought together to deal with particular problem areas, with the Department of State the only continuing member always present. This second route is clearly the way to go. But to do so will require serious Presidential attention to the question of how the Cabinet can be effectively used. To make this new arrangement work, it will be essential, among other things, to create a small staff whose sole job it is to service the Cabinet itself, under the direction of a coordinating executive director.

Other reasons exist for developing new organizational tools for making better use of the Cabinet. But the new intermixed issues of domestic-foreign affairs will in time demand it.

Three other organizational issues of importance require comment:

1. INTERNAL ORGANIZATION OF THE STATE DEPARTMENT.

The morale and work product level of the Department of State are today in very bad condition. The new Administration should give priority to the task of revitalizing the Department, giving it a new and crystallized sense of mandate, and holding it to effective performance. This does not mean that the Department should be increased in size. It should, instead, be reduced. And it does not mean that it should be returned to pre-Kissinger patterns, as the bureaucracy would wish. The Department, and the processes of the Foreign Service, need complete overhaul to accord with modern conditions. That can only be brought about by a Secretary and Deputy Secretary who are resolved to bring it about—who genuinely see the importance of building up the effectiveness of the institution as an institution.

Unless this job is done, there is no possible way the United States can effectively implement diplomatic policies of any kind—and stave off diplomatic assaults—in the hundreds of bilateral and multilateral forums in which today we must continuously negotiate all around the world.

With respect to State Department organization, I believe that the Secretary of State should use a mixed approach, under which he would combine a strong team of line officials, balanced by an analytical staff serving the Secretary and his principal assistants. In my judgment, it would be a mistake to take either a strict line or staff approach, as some have suggested.

A further issue concerns the question of whether a substantial consolidation and clarification of responsibilities within the Department should be made. I believe that it should be made, but would suggest that it be done in a measured way.

2. THE INTELLIGENCE COMMUNITY.

Most would agree that the 1947 National Securities Act establishing the CIA is no longer an adequate framework for the conduct of American intelligence activities, and that changes are required. I concur with those who do not believe that the President's February 1976 Executive Order reorganizing the intelligence community is adequate. The new President should address himself to the problem of reorganization of the intelligence community at an early date. However, the problem is not so pressing that a decision has to be made in the first three months of an Administration. This will provide time to study the various alternatives and to come up with a well-thought-out plan that has a chance of adoption by the Congress. To this end, the study should be carried out in close coordination with the Congress.

3. RELATIONSHIPS WITH THE CONGRESS.

A major assignment lying before the incoming President will be the development of better working relationships with the Congress in matters of foreign policy. There is no way in which this can be done easily, and sometimes it will not be possible to do it at all. But much more effort will have to be made than in the past by the President and all Executive Branch officials who deal with foreign policy matters to maintain open channels of communication with the Congress, and to give reality to the process of Congressional consultation.

If this is not done, and done effectively, the result will simply be that the President will not be able to operate the nation's foreign policy in the interests of the nation. The real cost of poor Congressional relationships is not that the Congress stymies the President—though that cost is great. The intolerable cost is that if the President and the Congress are not working together, small special interest constituencies are enabled to pressure some local Congressmen and Senators into taking legislative action that ties the hands of the President, and subordinates the national interest of the United States to the particular interests of the subconstituency, or of a particular foreign country that cannot be tolerated.

With strong Presidential leadership, ways should and can be found to construct new and continuing organizational arrangements for regular consultation and communication between the White House and the Hill on foreign policy matters. Your party majorities in both Houses will provide you an unusual opportunity to develop these new, desperately needed organizational channels.

CR VANCE
October 24, 1976

Appendix II

MIDDLE EAST DOCUMENTS

U.S., U.S.S.R. Issue Statement on the Middle East

Joint U.S.-Soviet Statement[1]
Having exchanged views regarding the unsafe situation which remains in the Middle East, U.S. Secretary of State Cyrus Vance and Member of the Politbureau of the Central Committee of the CPSU, Minister for Foreign Affairs of the U.S.S.R. A. A. Gromyko have the following statement to make on behalf of their countries, which are cochairmen of the Geneva Peace Conference on the Middle East:

1. Both governments are convinced that vital interests of the peoples of this area, as well as the interests of strengthening peace and international security in general, urgently dictate the necessity of achieving, as soon as possible, a just and lasting settlement of the Arab-Israeli conflict. This settlement should be comprehensive, incorporating all parties concerned and all questions.

The United States and the Soviet Union believe that, within the framework of a comprehensive settlement of the Middle East problem, all specific questions of the settlement should be resolved, including such key issues as withdrawal of Israeli Armed Forces from territories occupied in the 1967 conflict; the resolution of the Palestinian question, including insuring the legitimate rights of the Palestinian people; termination of the state of war and establishment of normal peaceful relations on the basis of mutual recognition of the principles of sovereignty, territorial integrity, and political independence.

The two governments believe that, in addition to such measures for insuring the security of the borders between Israel and the neighboring Arab states as the establishment of demilitarized zones and the agreed stationing in them of U.N. troops or observers, international guarantees of such borders as well as of the observance of the terms of the settlement can also be established should the contracting parties so desire. The United States and the Soviet Union are ready to participate in these guarantees, subject to their constitutional processes.

2. The United States and the Soviet Union believe that the only right and effective way for achieving a fundamental solution to all aspects of the Middle East problem in its entirety is negotiations within the framework of the Geneva peace conference, specially convened for these purposes, with participation in its work of the representatives of all the parties involved in the conflict including those of the Palestinian people, and legal and contractual formalization of the decisions reached at the conference.

[1] Issued on Oct. 1, 1977, in New York.

In their capacity as cochairmen of the Geneva conference, the United States and the U.S.S.R. affirm their intention, through joint efforts and in their contacts with the parties concerned, to facilitate in every way the resumption of the work of the conference not later than December 1977. The cochairmen note that there still exist several questions of a procedural and organizational nature which remain to be agreed upon by the participants to the conference.

3. Guided by the goal of achieving a just political settlement in the Middle East and of eliminating the explosive situation in this area of the world, the United States and the U.S.S.R. appeal to all the parties in the conflict to understand the necessity for careful consideration of each other's legitimate rights and interests and to demonstrate mutual readiness to act accordingly.

TEXT OF AGREEMENTS SIGNED
SEPTEMBER 17, 1978

A FRAMEWORK FOR PEACE IN THE MIDDLE EAST AGREED AT CAMP DAVID

Muhammad Anwar al-Sadat, President of the Arab Republic of Egypt, and Menachem Begin, Prime Minister of Israel, met with Jimmy Carter, President of the United States of America, at Camp David from September 5 to September 17, 1978, and have agreed on the following framework for peace in the Middle East. They invite other parties to the Arab-Israeli conflict to adhere to it.

Preamble

The search for peace in the Middle East must be guided by the following:

—The agreed basis for a peaceful settlement of the conflict between Israel and its neighbors is United Nations Security Council Resolution 242, in all its parts.*

—After four wars during thirty years, despite intensive human efforts, the Middle East, which is the cradle of civilization and the birthplace of three great religions, does not yet enjoy the blessings of peace. The people of the Middle East yearn for peace so that the vast human and natural resources of the region can be turned to the pursuits of peace and so that this area can become a model for coexistence and cooperation among nations.

—The historic initiative of President Sadat in visiting Jerusalem and the reception accorded to him by the Parliament, government and people of Israel, and the reciprocal visit of Prime Minister Begin to Ismailia, the peace proposals made by both leaders, as well as the warm reception of these missions by the peoples of both countries, have created an unprecedented opportunity for peace which must not be lost if this generation and future generations are to be spared the tragedies of war.

—The provisions of the Charter of the United Nations and the other accepted norms of international law and legitimacy now provide accepted standards for the conduct of relations among all states.

—To achieve a relationship of peace, in the spirit of Article 2 of the United

* The texts of Resolutions 242 and 338 are annexed to this document.

Nations Charter, future negotiations between Israel and any neighbor prepared to negotiate peace and security with it, are necessary for the purpose of carrying out all the provisions and principles of Resolutions 242 and 338.

—Peace requires respect for the sovereignty, territorial integrity and political independence of every state in the area and their right to live in peace within secure and recognized boundaries free from threats or acts of force. Progress toward that goal can accelerate movement toward a new era of reconciliation in the Middle East marked by cooperation in promoting economic development, in maintaining stability, and in assuring security.

—Security is enhanced by a relationship of peace and by cooperation between nations which enjoy normal relations. In addition, under the terms of peace treaties, the parties can, on the basis of reciprocity, agree to special security arrangements such as demilitarized zones, limited armaments areas, early warning stations, the presence of international forces, liaison, agreed measures for monitoring, and other arrangements that they agree are useful.

Framework

Taking these factors into account, the parties are determined to reach a just, comprehensive, and durable settlement of the Middle East conflict through the conclusion of peace treaties based on Security Council Resolutions 242 and 338 in all their parts. Their purpose is to achieve peace and good neighborly relations. They recognize that, for peace to endure, it must involve all those who have been most deeply affected by the conflict. They therefore agree that this framework as appropriate is intended by them to constitute a basis for peace not only between Egypt and Israel, but also between Israel and each of its other neighbors which is prepared to negotiate peace with Israel on this basis. With that objective in mind, they have agreed to proceed as follows:

A. *West Bank and Gaza*

1. Egypt, Israel, Jordan and the representatives of the Palestinian people should participate in negotiations on the resolution of the Palestinian problem in all its aspects. To achieve that objective, negotiations relating to the West Bank and Gaza should proceed in three stages:

(a) Egypt and Israel agree that, in order to ensure a peaceful and orderly transfer of authority, and taking into account the security concerns of all the parties, there should be transitional arrangements for the West Bank and Gaza for a period not exceeding five years. In order to provide full autonomy to the inhabitants, under these arrangements the Israeli military government and its civilian administration will be withdrawn as soon as a self-governing authority has been freely elected by the inhabitants of these areas to replace the existing military government. To negotiate the details of a transitional arrangement, the Government of Jordan will be invited to join the negotiations on the basis of this framework. These new arrangements should give due consideration both to the principle of self-government by the inhabitants of these territories and to the legitimate security concerns of the parties involved.

(b) Egypt, Israel, and Jordan will agree on the modalities for establishing the elected self-governing authority in the West Bank and Gaza. The delegations of

Egypt and Jordan may include Palestinians as mutually agreed. The parties will negotiate an agreement which will define the powers and responsibilities of the self-governing authority to be exercised in the West Bank and Gaza. A withdrawal of Israeli armed forces will take place and there will be a redeployment of the remaining Israeli forces into specified security locations. The agreement will also include arrangements for assuring internal and external security and public order. A strong local police force will be established, which may include Jordanian citizens. In addition, Israeli and Jordanian forces will participate in joint patrols and in the manning of control posts to assure the security of the borders.

(c) When the self-governing authority (administrative council) in the West Bank and Gaza is established and inaugurated, the transitional period of five years will begin. As soon as possible, but not later than the third year after the beginning of the transitional period, negotiations will take place to determine the final status of the West Bank and Gaza and its relationship with its neighbors, and to conclude a peace treaty between Israel and Jordan by the end of the transitional period. These negotiations will be conducted among Egypt, Israel, Jordan, and the elected representatives of the inhabitants of the West Bank and Gaza. Two separate but related committees will be convened, one committee, consisting of representatives of the four parties which will negotiate and agree on the final status of the West Bank and Gaza, and its relationship with its neighbors, and the second committee, consisting of representatives of Israel and representatives of Jordan to be joined by the elected representatives of the inhabitants of the West Bank and Gaza, to negotiate the peace treaty between Israel and Jordan, taking into account the agreement reached on the final status of the West Bank and Gaza. The negotiations shall be based on all the provisions and principles of UN Security Council Resolution 242. The negotiations will resolve, among other matters, the location of the boundaries and the nature of the security arrangements. The solution from the negotiations must also recognize the legitimate rights of the Palestinian people and their just requirements. In this way, the Palestinians will participate in the determination of their own future through:

1) The negotiations among Egypt, Israel, Jordan and the representatives of the inhabitants of the West Bank and Gaza to agree on the final status of the West Bank and Gaza and other outstanding issues by the end of the transitional period.

2) Submitting their agreement to a vote by the elected representatives of the inhabitants of the West Bank and Gaza.

3) Providing for the elected representatives of the inhabitants of the West Bank and Gaza to decide how they shall govern themselves consistent with the provisions of their agreement.

4) Participating as stated above in the work of the committee negotiating the peace treaty between Israel and Jordan.

2. All necessary measures will be taken and provisions made to assure the security of Israel and its neighbors during the transitional period and beyond. To assist in providing such security, a strong local police force will be constituted by the self-governing authority. It will be composed of inhabitants of the West Bank and Gaza. The police will maintain continuing liaison on internal security matters with the designated Israeli, Jordanian, and Egyptian officers.

3. During the transitional period, representatives of Egypt, Israel, Jordan, and the self-governing authority will constitute a continuing committee to decide by

agreement on the modalities of admission of persons displaced from the West Bank and Gaza in 1967, together with necessary measures to prevent disruption and disorder. Other matters of common concern may also be dealt with by this committee.

4. Egypt and Israel will work with each other and with other interested parties to establish agreed procedures for a prompt, just and permanent implementation of the resolution of the refugee problem.

B. *Egypt-Israel*

1. Egypt and Israel undertake not to resort to the threat or the use of force to settle disputes. Any disputes shall be settled by peaceful means in accordance with the provisions of Article 33 of the Charter of the United Nations.

2. In order to achieve peace between them, the parties agree to negotiate in good faith with a goal of concluding within three months from the signing of this Framework a peace treaty between them, while inviting the other parties to the conflict to proceed simultaneously to negotiate and conclude similar peace treaties with a view to achieving a comprehensive peace in the area. The Framework for the Conclusion of a Peace Treaty between Egypt and Israel will govern the peace negotiations between them. The parties will agree on the modalities and the timetable for the implementation of their obligations under the treaty.

C. *Associated Principles*

1. Egypt and Israel state that the principles and provisions described below should apply to peace treaties between Israel and each of its neighbors—Egypt, Jordan, Syria and Lebanon.

2. Signatories shall establish among themselves relationships normal to states at peace with one another. To this end, they should undertake to abide by all the provisions of the Charter of the United Nations. Steps to be taken in this respect include:

(a) full recognition;

(b) abolishing economic boycotts;

(c) guaranteeing that under their jurisdiction the citizens of the other parties shall enjoy the protection of the due process of law.

3. Signatories should explore possibilities for economic development in the context of final peace treaties, with the objective of contributing to the atmosphere of peace, cooperation and friendship which is their common goal.

4. Claims Commissions may be established for the mutual settlement of all financial claims.

5. The United States shall be invited to participate in the talks on matters related to the modalities of the implementation of the agreements and working out the timetable for the carrying out of the obligations of the parties.

6. The United Nations Security Council shall be requested to endorse the peace treaties and ensure that their provisions shall not be violated. The permanent members of the Security Council shall be requested to underwrite the peace treaties and ensure respect for their provisions. They shall also be requested to conform their policies and actions with the undertakings contained in this Framework.

For the Government of the
Arab Republic of Egypt:

A. SADAT

For the Government
of Israel:

M. BEGIN

Witnessed by:

JIMMY CARTER

Jimmy Carter, President
of the United States of America

ANNEX

Text of United Nations Security Council Resolution 242 of November 22, 1967

Adopted unanimously at the 1382nd meeting

The Security Council,

Expressing its continuing concern with the grave situation in the Middle East,

Emphasizing the inadmissibility of the acquisition of territory by war and the need to work for a just and lasting peace in which every State in the area can live in security,

Emphasizing further that all Member States in their acceptance of the Charter of the United Nations have undertaken a commitment to act in accordance with Article 2 of the Charter,

1. *Affirms* that the fulfilment of Charter principles requires the establishment of a just and lasting peace in the Middle East which should include the application of both the following principles:

(i) Withdrawal of Israeli armed forces from territories occupied in the recent conflict;

(ii) Termination of all claims or states of belligerency and respect for and acknowledgement of the sovereignty, territorial integrity and political independence of every State in the area and their right to live in peace within secure and recognized boundaries free from threats or acts of force;

2. *Affirms further* the necessity

(a) For guaranteeing freedom of navigation through international waterways in the area;

(b) For achieving a just settlement of the refugee problem;

(c) For guaranteeing the territorial inviolability and political independence of every State in the area, through measures including the establishment of demilitarized zones;

3. *Requests* the Secretary-General to designate a Special Representative to proceed to the Middle East to establish and maintain contacts with the States concerned in order to promote agreement and assist efforts to achieve a peaceful and accepted settlement in accordance with the provisions and principles of this resolution.

4. *Requests* the Secretary-General to report to the Security Council on the progress of the efforts of the Special Representative as soon as possible.

Text of United Nations Security Council Resolution 338

Adopted by the Security Council at its 1747th meeting, on 21/22 October 1973

The Security Council
1. *Calls upon* all parties to the present fighting to cease all firing and terminate all military activity immediately, no later than 12 hours after the moment of the adoption of this decision, in the positions they now occupy;
2. *Calls upon* the parties concerned to start immediately after the cease-fire the implementation of Security Council Resolution 242 (1967) in all of its parts;
3. *Decides* that, immediately and concurrently with the cease-fire, negotiations start between the parties concerned under appropriate auspices aimed at establishing a just and durable peace in the Middle East.

FRAMEWORK FOR THE CONCLUSION OF A PEACE TREATY BETWEEN EGYPT AND ISRAEL

In order to achieve peace between them, Israel and Egypt agree to negotiate in good faith with a goal of concluding within three months of the signing of this framework a peace treaty between them.

It is agreed that:

The site of the negotiations will be under a United Nations flag at a location or locations to be mutually agreed.

All of the principles of U.N. Resolution 242 will apply in this resolution of the dispute between Israel and Egypt.

Unless otherwise mutually agreed, terms of the peace treaty will be implemented between two and three years after the peace treaty is signed.

The following matters are agreed between the parties:

(a) the full exercise of Egyptian sovereignty up to the internationally recognized border between Egypt and mandated Palestine;

(b) the withdrawal of Israeli armed forces from the Sinai;

(c) the use of airfields left by the Israelis near El Arish, Rafah, Ras en Naqb, and Sharm el Sheikh for civilian purposes only, including possible commercial use by all nations;

(d) the right of free passage by ships of Israel through the Gulf of Suez and the Suez Canal on the basis of the Constantinople Convention of 1888 applying to all nations; the Strait of Tiran and the Gulf of Aqaba are international waterways to be open to all nations for unimpeded and nonsuspendable freedom of navigation and overflight;

(e) the construction of a highway between the Sinai and Jordan near Elat with guaranteed free and peaceful passage by Egypt and Jordan; and

(f) the stationing of military forces listed below.

Stationing of Forces

A. No more than one division (mechanized or infantry) of Egyptian armed forces will be stationed within an area lying approximately 50 kilometers (km) east of the Gulf of Suez and the Suez Canal.

B. Only United Nations forces and civil police equipped with light weapons to perform normal police functions will be stationed within an area lying west of the international border and the Gulf of Aqaba, varying in width from 20 km to 40 km.

C. In the area within 3 km east of the international border there will be Israeli limited military forces not to exceed four infantry battalions and United Nations observers.

D. Border patrol units, not to exceed three battalions, will supplement the civil police in maintaining order in the area not included above.

The exact demarcation of the above areas will be as decided during the peace negotiations.

Early warning stations may exist to insure compliance with the terms of the agreement.

United Nations forces will be stationed: (a) in part of the area in the Sinai lying within about 20 km of the Mediterranean Sea and adjacent to the international border, and (b) in the Sharm el Sheikh area to ensure freedom of passage through the Strait of Tiran; and these forces will not be removed unless such removal is approved by the Security Council of the United Nations with a unanimous vote of the five permanent members.

After a peace treaty is signed, and after the interim withdrawal is complete, normal relations will be established between Egypt and Israel, including: full recognition, including diplomatic, economic and cultural relations; termination of economic boycotts and barriers to the free movement of goods and people; and mutual protection of citizens by the due process of law.

Interim Withdrawal

Between three months and nine months after the signing of the peace treaty, all Israeli forces will withdraw east of a line extending from a point east to El Arish to Ras Muhammad, the exact location of this line to be determined by mutual agreement.

For the Government of the
Arab Republic of Egypt:
    A. SADAT

For the Government
of Israel:
    M. BEGIN

Witnessed by:

JIMMY CARTER

Jimmy Carter, President
of the United States of America

ACCOMPANYING LETTERS [1]
[SINAI SETTLEMENTS]

SEPTEMBER 17, 1978

DEAR MR. PRESIDENT:

I have the honor to inform you that during two weeks after my return home I will submit a motion before Israel's Parliament (the Knesset) to decide on the following question:

If during the negotiations to conclude a peace treaty between Israel and Egypt all outstanding issues are agreed upon, "are you in favor of the removal of the Israeli settlers from the northern and southern Sinai areas or are you in favor of keeping the aforementioned settlers in those areas?"

The vote, Mr. President, on this issue will be completely free from the usual Parliamentary Party discipline to the effect that although the coalition is being now supported by 70 members out of 120, every member of the Knesset, as I believe, both on the Government and the Opposition benches will be enabled to vote in accordance with his own conscience.

Sincerely yours,
(signed)
Menachem Begin

The President
Camp David
Thurmont, Maryland

SEPTEMBER 22, 1978

DEAR MR. PRESIDENT:

I transmit herewith a copy of a letter to me from Prime Minister Begin setting forth how he proposes to present the issue of the Sinai settlements to the Knesset for the latter's decision.

In this connection, I understand from your letter that Knesset approval to withdraw all Israeli settlers from Sinai according to a timetable within the period specified for the implementation of the peace treaty is a prerequisite to any negotiations on a peace treaty between Egypt and Israel.

Sincerely,
(signed)
Jimmy Carter

Enclosure:
Letter from Prime Minister Begin (Letter at Tab A)

His Excellency
ANWAR AL-SADAT
President of the Arab
Republic of Egypt
Cairo

---

[1] Correspondence concerning the Israeli settlements in the West Bank and Gaza was not ready when these letters were released, as had been anticipated.

SEPTEMBER 17, 1978

DEAR MR. PRESIDENT:

In connection with the "Framework for a Settlement in Sinai" to be signed tonight, I would like to reaffirm the position of the Arab Republic of Egypt with respect to the settlements:

1. All Israeli settlers must be withdrawn from Sinai according to a timetable within the period specified for the implementation of the peace treaty.

2. Agreement by the Israeli Government and its constitutional institutions to this basic principle is therefore a prerequisite to starting peace negotiations for concluding a peace treaty.

3. If Israel fails to meet this commitment, the "Framework" shall be void and invalid.

Sincerely,
(signed)
Mohamed Anwar El Sadat

His Excellency JIMMY CARTER
President of the United States

SEPTEMBER 22, 1978

DEAR MR. PRIME MINISTER:

I have received your letter of September 17, 1978, describing how you intend to place the question of the future of Israeli settlements in Sinai before the Knesset for its decision.

Enclosed is a copy of President Sadat's letter to me on this subject.

Sincerely,
(signed)
Jimmy Carter

Enclosure:
Letter from President Sadat (Letter at Tab C)

His Excellency
MENACHEM BEGIN
Prime Minister of Israel

[JERUSALEM]

SEPTEMBER 17, 1978

DEAR MR. PRESIDENT:

I am writing you to reaffirm the position of the Arab Republic of Egypt with respect to Jerusalem:

1. Arab Jerusalem is an integral part of the West Bank. Legal and historical Arab rights in the City must be respected and restored.

2. Arab Jerusalem should be under Arab sovereignty.

3. The Palestinian inhabitants of Arab Jerusalem are entitled to exercise their legitimate national rights, being part of the Palestinian People in the West Bank.

4. Relevant Security Council Resolutions, particularly Resolutions 242 and 267, must be applied with regard to Jerusalem. All the measures taken by Israel to alter the status of the City are null and void and should be rescinded.

5. All peoples must have free access to the City and enjoy the free exercise of worship and the right to visit and transit to the holy places without distinction or discrimination.

6. The holy places of each faith may be placed under the administration and control of their representatives.

7. Essential functions in the City should be undivided and a joint municipal council composed of an equal number of Arab and Israeli members can supervise the carrying out of these functions. In this way, the City shall be undivided.

Sincerely,
(signed)
Mohamed Anwar El Sadat

His Excellency JIMMY CARTER
President of the United States

17 SEPTEMBER 1978

DEAR MR. PRESIDENT,

I have the honor to inform you, Mr. President, that on 28 June 1967—Israel's Parliament (The Knesset) promulgated and adopted a law to the effect: "the Government is empowered by a decree to apply the law, the jurisdiction and administration of the State to any part of Eretz Israel (land of Israel—Palestine), as stated in that decree."

On the basis of this law, the Government of Israel decreed in July 1967 that Jerusalem is one city indivisible, the Capital of the State of Israel.

Sincerely,
(signed)
Menachem Begin

The President
Camp David
  Thurmont, Maryland

SEPTEMBER 22, 1978

DEAR MR. PRESIDENT:

I have received your letter of September 17, 1978, setting forth the Egyptian position on Jerusalem. I am transmitting a copy of that letter to Prime Minister Begin for his information.

The position of the United States on Jerusalem remains as stated by Ambassador Goldberg in the United Nations General Assembly on July 14, 1967,[2] and

[2] For text, see Department of State *Bulletin* of July 31, 1967, p. 148.

subsequently by Ambassador Yost in the United Nations Security Council on July 1, 1969.[3]

Sincerely,
(signed)
Jimmy Carter

His Excellency
ANWAR AL-SADAT
President of the Arab
Republic of Egypt
Cairo

[IMPLEMENTATION OF COMPREHENSIVE SETTLEMENT]

SEPTEMBER 17, 1978

DEAR MR. PRESIDENT:

In connection with the "Framework for Peace in the Middle East," I am writing you this letter to inform you of the position of the Arab Republic of Egypt, with respect to the implementation of the comprehensive settlement.

To ensure the implementation of the provisions related to the West Bank and Gaza and in order to safeguard the legitimate rights of the Palestinian people, Egypt will be prepared to assume the Arab role emanating from these provisions, following consultations with Jordan and the representatives of the Palestinian people.

Sincerely,
(signed)
Mohamed Anwar El Sadat

His Excellency
JIMMY CARTER
President of the United States
The White House
Washington, DC

[3] For text, see Department of State *Bulletin* of July 28, 1969, p. 76. Footnotes added by the Department of State.

[DEFINITION OF TERMS]

SEPTEMBER 22, 1978

DEAR MR. PRIME MINISTER:

I hereby acknowledge that you have informed me as follows:

A) In each paragraph of the Agreed Framework Document the expressions "Palestinians" or "Palestinian People" are being and will be construed and understood by you as "Palestinian Arabs."

B) In each paragraph in which the expression "West Bank" appears, it is being, and will be, understood by the Government of Israel as Judea and Samaria.

Sincerely,
(signed)
Jimmy Carter

His Excellency
MENACHEM BEGIN
Prime Minister of Israel

[AIRBASES]

THE SECRETARY OF DEFENSE
WASHINGTON, D.C. 20301

SEPTEMBER 28, 1978

DEAR MR. MINISTER:

The U.S. understands that, in connection with carrying out the agreements reached at Camp David, Israel intends to build two military airbases at appropriate sites in the Negev to replace the airbases at Eitam and Etzion which will be evacuated by Israel in accordance with the peace treaty to be concluded between Egypt and Israel. We also understand the special urgency and priority which Israel attaches to preparing the new bases in light of its conviction that it cannot safely leave the Sinai airbases until the new ones are operational.

I suggest that our two governments consult on the scope and costs of the two new airbases as well as on related forms of assistance which the United States might appropriately provide in light of the special problems which may be presented by carrying out such a project on an urgent basis. The President is prepared to seek the necessary Congressional approvals for such assistance as may be agreed upon by the U.S. side as a result of such consultations.

(signed)
Harold Brown

The Honorable
EZER WEIZMAN
Minister of Defense
Government of Israel

THE EGYPTIAN-ISRAELI PEACE TREATY

TREATY OF PEACE BETWEEN
THE ARAB REPUBLIC OF EGYPT AND THE STATE OF ISRAEL

The Government of the Arab Republic of Egypt and the Government of the State of Israel;

PREAMBLE

Convinced of the urgent necessity of the establishment of a just, comprehensive and lasting peace in the Middle East in accordance with Security Council Resolutions 242 and 338;

Reaffirming their adherence to the "Framework for Peace in the Middle East Agreed at Camp David," dated September 17, 1978;

Noting that the aforementioned Framework as appropriate is intended to constitute a basis for peace not only between Egypt and Israel but also between Israel and each of its other Arab neighbors which is prepared to negotiate peace with it on this basis;

Desiring to bring to an end the state of war between them and to establish a peace in which every state in the area can live in security;

Convinced that the conclusion of a Treaty of Peace between Egypt and Israel is an important step in the search for comprehensive peace in the area and for the attainment of the settlement of the Arab-Israeli conflict in all its aspects;

Inviting the other Arab parties to this dispute to join the peace process with Israel guided by and based on the principles of the aforementioned Framework;

Desiring as well to develop friendly relations and cooperation between themselves in accordance with the United Nations Charter and the principles of international law governing international relations in times of peace;

Agree to the following provisions in the free exercise of their sovereignty, in order to implement the "Framework for the Conclusion of a Peace Treaty Between Egypt and Israel":

ARTICLE I

1. The state of war between the Parties will be terminated and peace will be established between them upon the exchange of instruments of ratification of this Treaty.

2. Israel will withdraw all its armed forces and civilians from the Sinai behind the international boundary between Egypt and mandated Palestine, as provided in the annexed protocol (Annex I), and Egypt will resume the exercise of its full sovereignty over the Sinai.

3. Upon completion of the interim withdrawal provided for in Annex I, the Parties will establish normal and friendly relations, in accordance with Article III (3).

ARTICLE II

The permanent boundary between Egypt and Israel is the recognized international boundary between Egypt and the former mandated territory of Palestine, as shown on the map at Annex II, without prejudice to the issue of the status of the Gaza Strip. The Parties recognize this boundary as inviolable. Each will respect the territorial integrity of the other, including their territorial waters and airspace.

ARTICLE III

1. The Parties will apply between them the provisions of the Charter of the United Nations and the principles of international law governing relations among states in times of peace. In particular:
   a. They recognize and will respect each other's sovereignty, territorial integrity and political independence;
   b. They recognize and will respect each other's right to live in peace within their secure and recognized boundaries;
   c. They will refrain from the threat or use of force, directly or indirectly, against each other and will settle all disputes between them by peaceful means.

2. Each Party undertakes to ensure that acts or threats of belligerency, hostility, or violence do not originate from and are not committed from within its territory, or by any forces subject to its control or by any other forces stationed on its territory, against the population, citizens or property of the other Party. Each Party also undertakes to refrain from organizing, instigating, inciting, assisting or participating in acts or threats of belligerency, hostility, subversion or violence against the other Party, anywhere, and undertakes to ensure that perpetrators of such acts are brought to justice.

3. The Parties agree that the normal relationship established between them will include full recognition, diplomatic, economic and cultural relations, termination of economic boycotts and discriminatory barriers to the free movement of people and goods, and will guarantee the mutual enjoyment by citizens of the due process of law. The process by which they undertake to achieve such a relationship parallel to the implementation of other provisions of this Treaty is set out in the annexed protocol (Annex III).

ARTICLE IV

1. In order to provide maximum security for both Parties on the basis of reciprocity, agreed security arrangements will be established including limited force zones in Egyptian and Israeli territory, and United Nations forces and observers, described in detail as to nature and timing in Annex I, and other security arrangements the Parties may agree upon.

2. The Parties agree to the stationing of United Nations personnel in areas described in Annex I. The Parties agree not to request withdrawal of the United Nations personnel and that these personnel will not be removed unless such

removal is approved by the Security Council of the United Nations, with the affirmative vote of the five Permanent Members, unless the Parties otherwise agree.

3. A Joint Commission will be established to facilitate the implementation of the Treaty, as provided for in Annex I.

4. The security arrangements provided for in paragraphs 1 and 2 of this Article may at the request of either Party be reviewed and amended by mutual agreement of the Parties.

ARTICLE V

1. Ships of Israel, and cargoes destined for or coming from Israel, shall enjoy the right of free passage through the Suez Canal and its approaches through the Gulf of Suez and the Mediterranean Sea on the basis of the Constantinople Convention of 1888, applying to all nations. Israeli nationals, vessels and cargoes, as well as persons, vessels and cargoes destined for or coming from Israel, shall be accorded non-discriminatory treatment in all matters connected with usage of the canal.

2. The Parties consider the Strait of Tiran and the Gulf of Aqaba to be international waterways open to all nations for unimpeded and non-suspendable freedom of navigation and overflight. The Parties will respect each other's right to navigation and overflight for access to either country through the Strait of Tiran and the Gulf of Aqaba.

ARTICLE VI

1. This Treaty does not affect and shall not be interpreted as affecting in any way the rights and obligations of the Parties under the Charter of the United Nations.

2. The Parties undertake to fulfill in good faith their obligations under this Treaty, without regard to action or inaction of any other party and independently of any instrument external to this Treaty.

3. They further undertake to take all the necessary measures for the application in their relations of the provisions of the multilateral conventions to which they are parties, including the submission of appropriate notification to the Secretary General of the United Nations and other depositaries of such conventions.

4. The Parties undertake not to enter into any obligation in conflict with this Treaty.

5. Subject to Article 103 of the United Nations Charter, in the event of a conflict between the obligations of the Parties under the present Treaty and any of their other obligations, the obligations under this Treaty will be binding and implemented.

ARTICLE VII

1. Disputes arising out of the application or interpretation of this Treaty shall be resolved by negotiations.

2. Any such disputes which cannot be settled by negotiations shall be resolved by conciliation or submitted to arbitration.

ARTICLE VIII

The Parties agree to establish a claims commission for the mutual settlement of all financial claims.

ARTICLE IX

1. This Treaty shall enter into force upon exchange of instruments of ratification.

2. This Treaty supersedes the Agreement between Egypt and Israel of September, 1975.

3. All protocols, annexes, and maps attached to this Treaty shall be regarded as an integral part hereof.

4. The Treaty shall be communicated to the Secretary General of the United Nations for registration in accordance with the provisions of Article 102 of the Charter of the United Nations.

ANNEX I

PROTOCOL CONCERNING ISRAELI
WITHDRAWAL AND SECURITY ARRANGEMENTS

Article I
Concept of Withdrawal

1. Israel will complete withdrawal of all its armed forces and civilians from the Sinai not later than three years from the date of exchange of instruments of ratification of this Treaty.

2. To ensure the mutual security of the Parties, the implementation of phased withdrawal will be accompanied by the military measures and establishment of zones set out in this Annex and in Map 1, hereinafter referred to as "the Zones."

3. The withdrawal from the Sinai will be accomplished in two phases:

a. The interim withdrawal behind the line from east of El Arish to Ras Muhammed as delineated on Map 2 within nine months from the date of exchange of instruments of ratification of this Treaty.

b. The final withdrawal from the Sinai behind the international boundary not later than three years from the date of exchange of instruments of ratification of this Treaty.

4. A Joint Commission will be formed immediately after the exchange of instruments of ratification of this Treaty in order to supervise and coordinate movements and schedules during the withdrawal, and to adjust plans and timetables as necessary within the limits established by paragraph 3, above. Details relating to the Joint Commission are set out in Article IV of the attached Appendix. The Joint Commission will be dissolved upon completion of final Israeli withdrawal from the Sinai.

Article II
Determination of Final Lines and Zones

1. In order to provide maximum security for both Parties after the final withdrawal, the lines and the Zones delineated on Map 1 are to be established and organized as follows:

a. Zone A

(1) Zone A is bounded on the east by line A (red line) and on the west by the Suez Canal and the east coast of the Gulf of Suez, as shown on Map 1.

(2) An Egyptian armed force of one mechanized infantry division and its military installations, and field fortifications, will be in this Zone.

(3) The main elements of that Division will consist of:

(a) Three mechanized infantry brigades.

(b) One armored brigade.

(c) Seven field artillery battalions including up to 126 artillery pieces.

(d) Seven anti-aircraft artillery battalions including individual surface-to-air missiles and up to 126 anti-aircraft guns of 37 mm and above.

(e) Up to 230 tanks.

(f) Up to 480 armored personnel vehicles of all types.

(g) Up to a total of twenty-two thousand personnel.

b. Zone B

(1) Zone B is bounded by line B (green line) on the east and by line A (red line) on the west, as shown on Map 1.

(2) Egyptian border units of four battalions equipped with light weapons and wheeled vehicles will provide security and supplement the civil police in maintaining order in Zone B. The main elements of the four Border Battalions will consist of up to a total of four thousand personnel.

(3) Land based, short range, low power, coastal warning points of the border patrol units may be established on the coast of this Zone.

(4) There will be in Zone B field fortifications and military installations for the four border battalions.

c. Zone C

(1) Zone C is bounded by line B (green line) on the west and the International Boundary and the Gulf of Aqaba on the east, as shown on Map 1.

(2) Only United Nations forces and Egyptian civil police will be stationed in Zone C.

(3) The Egyptian civil police armed with light weapons will perform normal police functions within this Zone.

(4) The United Nations Force will be deployed within Zone C and perform its functions as defined in Article VI of this Annex.

(5) The United Nations Force will be stationed mainly in camps located within the following stationing areas shown on Map 1, and will establish its precise locations after consultations with Egypt:

(a) In that part of the area in the Sinai lying within about 20 Km. of the Mediterranean Sea and adjacent to the International Boundary.

(b) In the Sharm el Sheikh area.

d. Zone D

(1) Zone D is bounded by line D (blue line) on the east and the international boundary on the west, as shown on Map 1.

(2) In this Zone there will be an Israeli limited force of four infantry battalions, their military installations, and field fortifications, and United Nations observers.

(3) The Israeli forces in Zone D will not include tanks, artillery and anti-aircraft missiles except individual surface-to-air missiles.

(4) The main elements of the four Israeli infantry battalions will consist of up to 180 armored personnel vehicles of all types and up to a total of four thousand personnel.

2. Access across the international boundary shall only be permitted through entry check points designated by each Party and under its control. Such access shall be in accordance with laws and regulations of each country.

3. Only those field fortifications, military installations, forces, and weapons specifically permitted by this Annex shall be in the Zones.

Article III
Aerial Military Regime

1. Flights of combat aircraft and reconnaisance flights of Egypt and Israel shall take place only over Zones A and D, respectively.

2. Only unarmed, non-combat aircraft of Egypt and Israel will be stationed in Zones A and D, respectively.

3. Only Egyptian unarmed transport aircraft will take off and land in Zone B and up to eight such aircraft may be maintained in Zone B. The Egyptian border units may be equipped with unarmed helicopters to perform their functions in Zone B.

4. The Egyptian civil police may be equipped with unarmed police helicopters to perform normal police functions in Zone C.

5. Only civilian airfields may be built in the Zones.

6. Without prejudice to the provisions of this Treaty, only those military aerial activities specifically permitted by this Annex shall be allowed in the Zones and the airspace above their territorial waters.

Article IV
Naval Regime

1. Egypt and Israel may base and operate naval vessels along the coasts of Zones A and D, respectively.

2. Egyptian coast guard boats, lightly armed, may be stationed and operate in the territorial waters of Zone B to assist the border units in performing their functions in this Zone.

3. Egyptian civil police equipped with light boats, lightly armed, shall perform normal police functions within the territorial waters of Zone C.

4. Nothing in this Annex shall be considered as derogating from the right of innocent passage of the naval vessels of either party.

5. Only civilian maritime ports and installations may be built in the Zones.

6. Without prejudice to the provisions of this Treaty, only those naval activi-

ties specifically permitted by this Annex shall be allowed in the Zones and in their territorial waters.

Article V
Early Warning Systems

Egypt and Israel may establish and operate early warning systems only in Zones A and D respectively.

Article VI
United Nations Operations

1. The Parties will request the United Nations to provide forces and observers to supervise the implementation of this Annex and employ their best efforts to prevent any violation of its terms.

2. With respect to these United Nations forces and observers, as appropriate, the Parties agree to request the following arrangements:

a. Operation of check points, reconnaissance patrols, and observation posts along the international boundary and line B, and within Zone C.

b. Periodic verification of the implementation of the provisions of this Annex will be carried out not less than twice a month unless otherwise agreed by the Parties.

c. Additional verifications within 48 hours after the receipt of a request from either Party.

d. Ensuring the freedom of navigation through the Strait of Tiran in accordance with Article V of the Treaty of Peace.

3. The arrangements described in this article for each zone will be implemented in Zones A, B, and C by the United Nations Force and in Zone D by the United Nations Observers.

4. United Nations verification teams shall be accompanied by liaison officers of the respective Party.

5. The United Nations Force and Observers will report their findings to both Parties.

6. The United Nations Force and Observers operating in the Zones will enjoy freedom of movement and other facilities necessary for the performance of their tasks.

7. The United Nations Force and Observers are not empowered to authorize the crossing of the international boundary.

8. The Parties shall agree on the nations from which the United Nations Force and Observers will be drawn. They will be drawn from nations other than those which are permanent members of the United Nations Security Council.

9. The Parties agree that the United Nations should make those command arrangements that will best assure the effective implementation of its responsibilities.

Article VII
Liaison System

1. Upon dissolution of the Joint Commission, a liaison system between the Parties will be established. This liaison system is intended to provide an effective

method to assess progress in the implementation of obligations under the present Annex and to resolve any problem that may arise in the course of implementation, and refer other unresolved matters to the higher military authorities of the two countries respectively for consideration. It is also intended to prevent situations resulting from errors or misinterpretation on the part of either Party.

2. An Egyptian liaison office will be established in the city of El-Arish and an Israeli liaison office will be established in the city of Beer-Sheba. Each office will be headed by an officer of the respective country, and assisted by a number of officers.

3. A direct telephone link between the two offices will be set up and also direct telephone lines with the United Nations command will be maintained by both offices.

Article VIII
Respect for War Memorials

Each Party undertakes to preserve in good condition the War Memorials erected in the memory of soldiers of the other Party, namely those erected by Israel in the Sinai and those to be erected by Egypt in Israel, and shall permit access to such monuments.

Article IX
Interim Arrangements

The withdrawal of Israeli armed forces and civilians behind the interim withdrawal line, and the conduct of the forces of the Parties and the United Nations prior to the final withdrawal, will be governed by the attached Appendix and Maps 2 and 3.

APPENDIX TO ANNEX I
ORGANIZATION OF MOVEMENTS IN THE SINAI

Article I
Principles of Withdrawal

1. The withdrawal of Israeli armed forces and civilians from the Sinai will be accomplished in two phases as described in Article I of Annex I. The description and timing of the withdrawal are included in this Appendix. The Joint Commission will develop and present to the Chief Coordinator of the United Nations forces in the Middle East the details of these phases not later than one month before the initiation of each phase of withdrawal.

2. Both Parties agree on the following principles for the sequence of military movements.

a. Notwithstanding the provisions of Article IX, paragraph 2, of this Treaty, until Israeli armed forces complete withdrawal from the current J and M Lines established by the Egyptian-Israeli Agreement of September 1975, hereinafter referred to as the 1975 Agreement, up to the interim withdrawal line, all military arrangements existing under that Agreement will remain in effect, except those military arrangements otherwise provided for in this Appendix.

b. As Israeli armed forces withdraw, United Nations forces will immediately enter the evacuated areas to establish interim and temporary buffer zones as shown on Maps 2 and 3, respectively, for the purpose of maintaining a separation of forces. United Nations forces' deployment will precede the movement of any other personnel into these areas.

c. Within a period of seven days after Israeli armed forces have evacuated any area located in Zone A, units of Egyptian armed forces shall deploy in accordance with the provisions of Article II of this Appendix.

d. Within a period of seven days after Israeli armed forces have evacuated any area located in Zones A or B, Egyptian border units shall deploy in accordance with the provisions of Article II of this Appendix, and will function in accordance with the provisions of Article II of Annex I.

e. Egyptian civil police will enter evacuated areas immediately after the United Nations forces to perform normal police functions.

f. Egyptian naval units shall deploy in the Gulf of Suez in accordance with the provisions of Article II of this Appendix.

g. Except those movements mentioned above, deployments of Egyptian armed forces and the activities covered in Annex I will be effected in the evacuated areas when Israeli armed forces have completed their withdrawal behind the interim withdrawal line.

Article II
Subphases of the Withdrawal to the Interim Withdrawal Line

1. The withdrawal to the interim withdrawal line will be accomplished in subphases as described in this Article and as shown on Map 3. Each subphase will be completed within the indicated number of months from the date of the exchange of instruments of ratification of this Treaty.

a. First subphase: within two months, Israeli armed forces will withdraw from the area of El Arish, including the town of El Arish and its airfield, shown as Area I on Map 3.

b. Second subphase: within three months, Israeli armed forces will withdraw from the area between line M of the 1975 Agreement and line A, shown as Area II on Map 3.

c. Third subphase: within five months, Israeli armed forces will withdraw from the areas east and south of Area II, shown as Area III on Map 3.

d. Fourth subphase: within seven months, Israeli armed forces will withdraw from the area of El Tor-Ras El Kenisa, shown as Area IV on Map 3.

e. Fifth subphase: within nine months, Israeli armed forces will withdraw from the remaining areas west of the interim withdrawal line, including the areas of Santa Katrina and the areas east of the Giddi and Mitla passes, shown as Area V on Map 3, thereby completing Israeli withdrawal behind the interim withdrawal line.

2. Egyptian forces will deploy in the areas evacuated by Israeli armed forces as follows:

a. Up to one-third of the Egyptian armed forces in the Sinai in accordance with the 1975 Agreement will deploy in the portions of Zone A lying within Area I, until the completion of interim withdrawal. Thereafter, Egyptian armed forces as described in Article II of Annex I will be deployed in Zone A up to the limits of the interim buffer zone.

b. The Egyptian naval activity in accordance with Article IV of Annex I will commence along the coasts of Areas II, III, and IV, upon completion of the second, third, and fourth subphases, respectively.

c. Of the Egyptian border units described in Article II of Annex I, upon completion of the first subphase one battalion will be deployed in Area I. A second battalion will be deployed in Area II upon completion of the second subphase. A third battalion will be deployed in Area III upon completion of the third subphase. The second and third battalions mentioned above may also be deployed in any of the subsequently evacuated areas of the southern Sinai.

3. United Nations forces in Buffer Zone I of the 1975 Agreement will redeploy to enable the deployment of Egyptian forces described above upon the completion of the first subphase, but will otherwise continue to function in accordance with the provisions of that Agreement in the remainder of that zone until the completion of interim withdrawal, as indicated in Article I of this Appendix.

4. Israeli convoys may use the roads south and east of the main road junction east of El Arish to evacuate Israeli forces and equipment up to the completion of interim withdrawal. These convoys will proceed in daylight upon four hours notice to the Egyptian liaison group and United Nations forces, will be escorted by United Nations forces, and will be in accordance with schedules coordinated by the Joint Commission. An Egyptian liaison officer will accompany convoys to assure uninterrupted movement. The Joint Commission may approve other arrangements for convoys.

Article III
United Nations Forces

1. The Parties shall request that United Nations forces be deployed as necessary to perform the functions described in this Appendix up to the time of completion of final Israeli withdrawal. For that purpose, the Parties agree to redeployment of the United Nations Emergency Force.

2. United Nations forces will supervise the implementation of this Appendix and will employ their best efforts to prevent any violation of its terms.

3. When United Nations forces deploy in accordance with the provisions of Articles I and II of this Appendix, they will perform the functions of verification in limited force zones in accordance with Article VI of Annex I, and will establish check points, reconnaissance patrols, and observation posts in the temporary buffer zones described in Article II above. Other functions of the United Nations forces which concern the interim buffer zone are described in Article V of this Appendix.

Article IV
Joint Commission and Liaison

1. The Joint Commission referred to in Article IV of this Treaty will function from the date of exchange of instruments of ratification of this Treaty up to the date of completion of final Israeli withdrawal from the Sinai.

2. The Joint Commission will be composed of representatives of each Party

headed by senior officers. This Commission shall invite a representative of the United Nations when discussing subjects concerning the United Nations, or when either Party requests United Nations presence. Decisions of the Joint Commission will be reached by agreement of Egypt and Israel.

3. The Joint Commission will supervise the implementation of the arrangements described in Annex I and this Appendix. To this end, and by agreement of both Parties, it will:

a. coordinate military movements described in this Appendix and supervise their implementation;

b. address and seek to resolve any problem arising out of the implementation of Annex I and this Appendix, and discuss any violations reported by the United Nations Force and Observers and refer to the Governments of Egypt and Israel any unresolved problems;

c. assist the United Nations Force and Observers in the execution of their mandates, and deal with the timetables of the periodic verifications when referred to it by the Parties as provided for in Annex I and in this Appendix;

d. organize the demarcation of the international boundary and all lines and zones described in Annex I and this Appendix;

e. supervise the handing over of the main installations in the Sinai from Israel to Egypt;

f. agree on necessary arrangements for finding and returning missing bodies of Egyptian and Israeli soldiers;

g. organize the setting up and operation of entry check points along the El Arish-Ras Muhammed line in accordance with the provisions of Article 4 of Annex III;

h. conduct its operations through the use of joint liaison teams consisting of one Israeli representative and one Egyptian representative, provided from a standing Liaison Group, which will conduct activities as directed by the Joint Commission;

i. provide liaison and coordination to the United Nations command implementing provisions of the Treaty, and, through the joint liaison teams, maintain local coordination and cooperation with the United Nations Force stationed in specific areas or United Nations Observers monitoring specific areas for any assistance as needed;

j. discuss any other matters which the Parties by agreement may place before it.

4. Meetings of the Joint Commission shall be held at least once a month. In the event that either Party or the Command of the United Nations Force requests a special meeting, it will be convened within 24 hours.

5. The Joint Commission will meet in the buffer zone until the completion of the interim withdrawal and in El Arish and Beer-Sheba alternately afterwards. The first meeting will be held not later than two weeks after the entry into force of this Treaty.

Article V
Definition of the Interim Buffer Zone and Its Activities

1. An interim buffer zone, by which the United Nations Force will effect a separation of Egyptian and Israeli elements, will be established west of and adja-

cent to the interim withdrawal line as shown on Map 2 after implementation of Israeli withdrawal and deployment behind the interim withdrawal line. Egyptian civil police equipped with light weapons will perform normal police functions within this zone.

2. The United Nations Force will operate check points, reconnaissance patrols, and observation posts within the interim buffer zone in order to ensure compliance with the terms of this Article.

3. In accordance with arrangements agreed upon by both Parties and to be coordinated by the Joint Commission, Israeli personnel will operate military technical installations at four specific locations shown on Map 2 and designated as T1 (map central coordinate 57163940), T2 (map central coordinate 59351541), T3 (map central coordinate 59331527), and T4 (map central coordinate 61130979) under the following principles:

a. The technical installations shall be manned by technical and administrative personnel equipped with small arms required for their protection (revolvers, rifles, sub-machine guns, light machine guns, hand grenades, and ammunition), as follows:

   T1—up to 150 personnel

   T2 and T3—up to 350 personnel

   T4—up to 200 personnel.

b. Israeli personnel will not carry weapons outside the sites, except officers who may carry personal weapons.

c. Only a third party agreed to by Egypt and Israel will enter and conduct inspections within the perimeters of technical installations in the buffer zone. The third party will conduct inspections in a random manner at least once a month. The inspections will verify the nature of the operation of the installations and the weapons and personnel therein. The third party will immediately report to the Parties any divergence from an installation's visual and electronic surveillance or communications role.

d. Supply of the installations, visits for technical and administrative purposes, and replacement of personnel and equipment situated in the sites, may occur uninterruptedly from the United Nations check points to the perimeter of the technical installations, after checking and being escorted by only the United Nations forces.

e. Israel will be permitted to introduce into its technical installations items required for the proper functioning of the installations and personnel.

f. As determined by the Joint Commission, Israel will be permitted to:

   (1) Maintain in its installations firefighting and general maintenance equipment as well as wheeled administrative vehicles and mobile engineering equipment necessary for the maintenance of the sites. All vehicles shall be unarmed.

   (2) Within the sites and in the buffer zone, maintain roads, water lines, and communications cables which serve the sites. At each of the three installation locations (T1, T2 and T3, and T4), this maintenance may be performed with up to two unarmed wheeled vehicles and by up to twelve unarmed personnel with only necessary equipment, including heavy engineering equipment if needed. This maintenance may be performed three times a week, except for special problems, and only after giving the United Nations four hours notice. The teams will be escorted by the United Nations.

g. Movement to and from the technical installations will take place only during daylight hours. Access to, and exit from, the technical installations shall be as follows:

(1) T1: through a United Nations checkpoint, and via the road between Abu Aweigila and the intersection of the Abu Aweigila road and the Gebel Libni road (at Km. 161), as shown on Map 2.

(2) T2 and T3: through a United Nations checkpoint and via the road constructed across the buffer zone to Gebel Katrina, as shown on Map 2.

(3) T2, T3, and T4: via helicopters flying within a corridor at the times, and according to a flight profile, agreed to by the Joint Commission. The helicopters will be checked by the United Nations Force at landing sites outside the perimeter of the installations.

h. Israel will inform the United Nations Force at least one hour in advance of such intended movement to and from the installations.

i. Israel shall be entitled to evacuate sick and wounded and summon medical experts and medical teams at any time after giving immediate notice to the United Nations Force.

4. The details of the above principles and all other matters in this Article requiring coordination by the Parties will be handled by the Joint Commission.

5. These technical installations will be withdrawn when Israeli forces withdraw from the interim withdrawal line, or at a time agreed by the Parties.

Article VI
Disposition of Installations and Military Barriers

Disposition of installations and military barriers will be determined by the Parties in accordance with the following guidelines:

1. Up to three weeks before Israeli withdrawal from any area, the Joint Commission will arrange for Israeli and Egyptian liaison and technical teams to conduct a joint inspection of all appropriate installations to agree upon condition of structures and articles which will be transferred to Egyptian control and to arrange for such transfer. Israel will declare, at that time, its plans for disposition of installations and articles within the installations.

2. Israel undertakes to transfer to Egypt all agreed infrastructure, utilities, and installations intact, inter alia, airfields, roads, pumping stations, and ports. Israel will present to Egypt the information necessary for the maintenance and operation of these facilities. Egyptian technical teams will be permitted to observe and familiarize themselves with the operation of these facilities for a period of up to two weeks prior to transfer.

3. When Israel relinquishes Israeli military water points near El Arish and El Tor, Egyptian technical teams will assume control of those installations and ancillary equipment in accordance with an orderly transfer process arranged beforehand by the Joint Commission. Egypt undertakes to continue to make available at all water supply points the normal quantity of currently available water up to the time Israel withdraws behind the international boundary, unless otherwise agreed in the Joint Commission.

4. Israel will make its best effort to remove or destroy all military barriers, including obstacles and minefields, in the areas and adjacent waters from which it withdraws, according to the following concept:

a. Military barriers will be cleared first from areas near populations, roads, and major installations and utilities.

b. For those obstacles and minefields which cannot be removed or destroyed prior to Israeli withdrawal, Israel will provide detailed maps to Egypt and the United Nations through the Joint Commission not later than 15 days before entry of United Nations forces into the affected areas.

c. Egyptian military engineers will enter those areas after United Nations forces enter to conduct barrier clearance operations in accordance with Egyptian plans to be submitted prior to implementation.

Article VII
Surveillance Activities

1. Aerial surveillance activities during the withdrawal will be carried out as follows:

a. Both Parties request the United States to continue airborne surveillance flights in accordance with previous agreements until the completion of final Israeli withdrawal.

b. Flight profiles will cover the Limited Forces Zones to monitor the limitations on forces and armaments, and to determine that Israeli armed forces have withdrawn from the areas described in Article II of Annex I, Article II of this Appendix, and Maps 2 and 3, and that these forces thereafter remain behind their lines. Special inspection flights may be flown at the request of either Party or of the United Nations.

c. Only the main elements in the military organizations of each Party, as described in Annex I and in this Appendix, will be reported.

2. Both Parties request the United States operated Sinai Field Mission to continue its operations in accordance with previous agreements until completion of the Israeli withdrawal from the area east of the Giddi and Mitla Passes. Thereafter, the Mission will be terminated.

Article VIII
Exercise of Egyptian Sovereignty

Egypt will resume the exercise of its full sovereignty over evacuated parts of the Sinai upon Israeli withdrawal as provided for in Article I of this Treaty.

ANNEX III

PROTOCOL CONCERNING RELATIONS OF THE PARTIES

Article 1
Diplomatic and Consular Relations

The Parties agree to establish diplomatic and consular relations and to exchange ambassadors upon completion of the interim withdrawal.

Article 2
Economic and Trade Relations

1. The Parties agree to remove all discriminatory barriers to normal economic relations and to terminate economic boycotts of each other upon completion of the interim withdrawal.

2. As soon as possible, and not later than six months after the completion of the interim withdrawal, the Parties will enter negotiations with a view to concluding an agreement on trade and commerce for the purpose of promoting beneficial economic relations.

Article 3
Cultural Relations

1. The Parties agree to establish normal cultural relations following completion of the interim withdrawal.

2. They agree on the desirability of cultural exchanges in all fields, and shall, as soon as possible and not later than six months after completion of the interim withdrawal, enter into negotiations with a view to concluding a cultural agreement for this purpose.

Article 4
Freedom of Movement

1. Upon completion of the interim withdrawal, each Party will permit the free movement of the nationals and vehicles of the other into and within its territory according to the general rules applicable to nationals and vehicles of other states. Neither Party will impose discriminatory restrictions on the free movement of persons and vehicles from its territory to the territory of the other.

2. Mutual unimpeded access to places of religious and historical significance will be provided on a nondiscriminatory basis.

Article 5
Cooperation for Development and Good Neighborly Relations

1. The Parties recognize a mutuality of interest in good neighborly relations and agree to consider means to promote such relations.

2. The Parties will cooperate in promoting peace, stability and development in their region. Each agrees to consider proposals the other may wish to make to this end.

3. The Parties shall seek to foster mutual understanding and tolerance and will, accordingly, abstain from hostile propaganda against each other.

Article 6
Transportation and Telecommunications

1. The Parties recognize as applicable to each other the rights, privileges and obligations provided for by the aviation agreements to which they are both party,

particularly by the Convention on International Civil Aviation, 1944 ("The Chicago Convention") and the International Air Services Transit Agreement, 1944.

2. Upon completion of the interim withdrawal any declaration of national emergency by a party under Article 89 of the Chicago Convention will not be applied to the other party on a discriminatory basis.

3. Egypt agrees that the use of airfields left by Israel near El Arish, Rafah, Ras El Nagb and Sharm El Sheikh shall be for civilian purposes only, including possible commercial use by all nations.

4. As soon as possible and not later than six months after the completion of the interim withdrawal, the Parties shall enter into negotiations for the purpose of concluding a civil aviation agreement.

5. The Parties will reopen and maintain roads and railways between their countries and will consider further road and rail links. The Parties further agree that a highway will be constructed and maintained between Egypt, Israel and Jordan near Eilat with guaranteed free and peaceful passage of persons, vehicles and goods between Egypt and Jordan, without prejudice to their sovereignty over that part of the highway which falls within their respective territory.

6. Upon completion of the interim withdrawal, normal postal, telephone, telex, data facsimile, wireless and cable communications and television relay services by cable, radio and satellite shall be established between the two Parties in accordance with all relevant international conventions and regulations.

7. Upon completion of the interim withdrawal, each Party shall grant normal access to its ports for vessels and cargoes of the other, as well as vessels and cargoes destined for or coming from the other. Such access shall be granted on the same conditions generally applicable to vessels and cargoes of other nations. Article 5 of the Treaty of Peace will be implemented upon the exchange of instruments of ratification of the aforementioned Treaty.

Article 7
Enjoyment of Human Rights

The Parties affirm their commitment to respect and observe human rights and fundamental freedoms for all, and they will promote these rights and freedoms in accordance with the United Nations Charter.

Article 8
Territorial Seas

Without prejudice to the provisions of Article 5 of the Treaty of Peace each Party recognizes the right of the vessels of the other Party to innocent passage through its territorial sea in accordance with the rules of international law.

AGREED MINUTES
TO ARTICLES I, IV, V AND VI AND ANNEXES I AND III
OF TREATY OF PEACE

ARTICLE I

Egypt's resumption of the exercise of full sovereignty over the Sinai provided for in paragraph 2 of Article I shall occur with regard to each area upon Israel's withdrawal from that area.

ARTICLE IV

It is agreed between the parties that the review provided for in Article IV(4) will be undertaken when requested by either party, commencing within three months of such a request, but that any amendment can be made only with the mutual agreement of both parties.

ARTICLE V

The second sentence of paragraph 2 of Article V shall not be construed as limiting the first sentence of that paragraph. The foregoing is not to be construed as contravening the second sentence of paragraph 2 of Article V, which reads as follows:

"The parties will respect each other's right to navigation and overflight for access to either country through the Strait of Tiran and the Gulf of Aqaba."

ARTICLE VI(2)

The provisions of Article VI shall not be construed in contradiction to the provisions of the framework for peace in the Middle East agreed at Camp David. The foregoing is not to be construed as contravening the provisions of Article VI(2) of the Treaty, which reads as follows:

"The Parties undertake to fulfill in good faith their obligations under this Treaty, without regard to action or inaction of any other party and independently of any instrument external to this Treaty."

ARTICLE VI(5)

It is agreed by the Parties that there is no assertion that this Treaty prevails over other Treaties or agreements or that other Treaties or agreements prevail over this Treaty. The foregoing is not to be construed as contravening the provisions of Article VI(5) of the Treaty, which reads as follows:

"Subject to Article 103 of the United Nations Charter, in the event of a conflict between the obligations of the Parties under the present Treaty and any of their other obligations, the obligations under this Treaty will be binding and implemented."

ANNEX I

Article VI, Paragraph 8, of Annex I provides as follows:
"The Parties shall agree on the nations from which the United Nations force and observers will be drawn. They will be drawn from nations other than those which are permanent members of the United Nations Security Council."
The Parties have agreed as follows:
"With respect to the provisions of paragraph 8, Article VI, of Annex I, if no agreement is reached between the Parties, they will accept or support a U.S. proposal concerning the composition of the United Nations force and observers."

ANNEX III

The Treaty of Peace and Annex III thereto provide for establishing normal economic relations between the Parties. In accordance therewith, it is agreed that such relations will include normal commercial sales of oil by Egypt to Israel, and that Israel shall be fully entitled to make bids for Egyptian-origin oil not needed for Egyptian domestic oil consumption, and Egypt and its oil concessionaires will entertain bids made by Israel, on the same basis and terms as apply to other bidders for such oil.

For the Government of Israel: M. BEGIN	For the Government of the Arab Republic of Egypt: A. SADAT

Witnessed by:

JIMMY CARTER

Jimmy Carter, President
of the United States of America

JOINT LETTER TO PRESIDENT CARTER FROM PRESIDENT SADAT AND PRIME MINISTER BEGIN

March 26, 1979

Dear Mr. President:

This letter confirms that Egypt and Israel have agreed as follows:

The Governments of Egypt and Israel recall that they concluded at Camp David and signed at the White House on September 17, 1978, the annexed documents entitled "A Framework for Peace in the Middle East Agreed at Camp David" and "Framework for the conclusion of a Peace Treaty between Egypt and Israel."

For the purpose of achieving a comprehensive peace settlement in accordance with the above-mentioned Frameworks, Egypt and Israel will proceed with the implementation of those provisions relating to the West Bank and the Gaza Strip. They have agreed to start negotiations within a month after the exchange of the instruments of ratification of the Peace Treaty. In accordance with the "Framework for Peace in the Middle East," the Hashemite Kingdom of Jordan is invited to join the negotiations. The Delegations of Egypt and Jordan may include Palestinians from the West Bank and Gaza Strip or other Palestinians as mutually agreed. The purpose of the negotiation shall be to agree, prior to the elections, on the modalities for establishing the elected self-governing authority (administrative council), define its powers and responsibilities, and agree upon other related issues. In the event Jordan decides not to take part in the negotiations, the negotiations will be held by Egypt and Israel.

The two Governments agree to negotiate continuously and in good faith to conclude these negotiations at the earliest possible date. They also agree that the objective of the negotiations is the establishment of the self-governing authority in the West Bank and Gaza in order to provide full autonomy to the inhabitants.

Egypt and Israel set for themselves the goal of completing the negotiations within one year so that elections will be held as expeditiously as possible after agreement has been reached between the parties. The self-governing authority referred to in the "Framework for Peace in the Middle East" will be established and inaugurated within one month after it has been elected, at which time the transitional period of five years will begin. The Israeli military government and its civilian administration will be withdrawn, to be replaced by the self-governing authority, as specified in the "Framework for Peace in the Middle East." A withdrawal of Israeli armed forces will then take place and there will be a redeployment of the remaining Israeli forces into specified security locations.

This letter also confirms our understanding that the United States Government will participate fully in all stages of negotiations.

Sincerely yours,

For the Government   For the Government of the
of Israel: Arab Republic of Egypt:

M. BEGIN   A. SADAT

Menachem Begin   Mohamed Anwar El-Sadat

The President,
The White House

Explanatory Note

President Carter, upon receipt of the Joint Letter to him from President Sadat and Prime Minister Begin, has added to the American and Israeli copies the notation: "I have been informed that the expression 'West Bank' is understood by the Government of Israel to mean 'Judea and Samaria'." This notation is in accordance with similar procedures established at Camp David.

LETTERS REGARDING EXCHANGE OF AMBASSADORS

March 26, 1979

Dear Mr. President:

In response to your request, I can confirm that, within one month after the completion of Israel's withdrawal to the interim line as provided for in the Treaty of Peace between Egypt and Israel, Egypt will send a resident ambassador to Israel and will receive a resident Israeli ambassador in Egypt.

Sincerely,
A. SADAT
Mohamed Anwar El-Sadat

The President,
The White House

March 26, 1979

Dear Mr. Prime Minister:

I have received a letter from President Sadat that, within one month after Israel completes its withdrawal to the interim line in Sinai, as provided for in the Treaty of Peace between Egypt and Israel, Egypt will send a resident ambassador to Israel and will receive in Egypt a resident Israeli ambassador.

I would be grateful if you will confirm that this procedure will be agreeable to the Government of Israel.

Sincerely,
JIMMY CARTER
Jimmy Carter

His Excellency
Menachem Begin,
*Prime Minster of the
State of Israel*

March 26, 1979

Dear Mr. President:

I am pleased to be able to confirm that the Government of Israel is agreeable to the procedure set out in your letter of March 26, 1979 in which you state:

"I have received a letter from President Sadat that, within one month after Israel completes its withdrawal to the interim line in Sinai, as provided for in the Treaty of Peace between Egypt and Israel, Egypt will send a resident ambassador to Israel and will receive in Egypt a resident Israeli ambassador."

Sincerely,
M. BEGIN
Menachem Begin

The President,
The White House

LETTERS FROM PRESIDENT CARTER TO PRESIDENT
SADAT AND PRIME MINISTER BEGIN

March 26, 1979
Dear Mr. President:

I wish to confirm to you that subject to United States Constitutional processes:

In the event of an actual or threatened violation of the Treaty of Peace between Egypt and Israel, the United States will, on request of one or both of the
Parties, consult with the Parties with respect thereto and will take such other
action as it may deem appropriate and helpful to achieve compliance with the
Treaty.

The United States will conduct aerial monitoring as requested by the Parties
pursuant to Annex I of the Treaty.

The United States believes the Treaty provision for permanent stationing of
United Nations personnel in the designated limited force zone can and should
be implemented by the United Nations Security Council. The United States will
exert its utmost efforts to obtain the requisite action by the Security Council. If
the Security Council fails to establish and maintain the arrangements called for
in the Treaty, the President will be prepared to take those steps necessary to
ensure the establishment and maintenance of an acceptable alternative multi-
national force.

Sincerely,
JIMMY CARTER
Jimmy Carter

His Excellency
Mohamed Anwar El-Sadat
President of the Arab
Republic of Egypt

March 26, 1979
Dear Mr. Prime Minister:

I wish to confirm to you that subject to United States Constitutional processes:

In the event of an actual or threatened violation of the Treaty of Peace between Israel and Egypt, the United States will, on request of one or both of the
Parties, consult with the Parties with respect thereto and will take such other
action as it may deem appropriate and helpful to achieve compliance with the
Treaty.

The United States will conduct aerial monitoring as requested by the Parties
pursuant to Annex I of the Treaty.

The United States believes the Treaty provision for permanent stationing of
United Nations personnel in the designated limited force zone can and should
be implemented by the United Nations Security Council. The United States will
exert its utmost efforts to obtain the requisite action by the Security Council. If
the Security Council fails to establish and maintain the arrangements called for
in the Treaty, the President will be prepared to take those steps necessary to

ensure the establishment and maintenance of an acceptable alternative multi-national force.

Sincerely,
JIMMY CARTER
Jimmy Carter

His Excellency
 Menachem Begin,
  Prime Minister of the
  State of Israel

APPENDIX III

Memorandum by the Chairman of the Joint Chiefs of Staff (Bradley)
to the Secretary of Defense (Johnson) *

WASHINGTON, 18 November 1949.

The following are the views of the Joint Chiefs of Staff in response to your oral question as to what might be done by the Department of Defense to assist the Department of State to extricate Mr. Angus Ward from his predicament in Mukden:

a. The Department of Defense can, at little risk and cost, assist the Department of State to extricate Mr. Angus Ward from Mukden by providing transportation by sea or air for a duly accredited Department of State representative to any point for which diplomatic clearance for the visit has been obtained;

b. Other military alternatives involve either threats by the United States Government, coupled with a present apparent intent to carry out the threatened action, or direct military action as may be necessary in the circumstance. In either of these two courses of action there are military implications of such deep significance that they should be examined in detail;

c. Mukden, the locale of Mr. Ward's confinement, is the seat of government for Manchuria, this government being subordinate to the Chinese Communist Government at Peking. According to intelligence sources, Mukden is also the headquarters of a Chinese Communist army;

d. In accordance with the rights granted under the Sino-Soviet Treaty of 1945,† the USSR has established operating facilities for submarines and for surface vessels at Dairen and Port Arthur. Considerable quantities of Manchurian goods are exported from Dairen by sea; lesser quantities of goods are exported from Manchurian ports in the Gulf of Chihli and in Korea Bay. There is no overt United States trade with Manchuria;

e. It is recognized that political considerations could affect the military considerations involved. Such political considerations would include the nature of the warning and the color of authority (United Nations or the duly recognized Chinese Nationalist Government) under which military action might be initiated. Regardless of the political considerations, however, there are, broadly speaking, only two possible courses of military action; namely:

(1) Forcible measures to remove Mr. Angus Ward from Mukden; and

(2) Military redress;

---

* Copy transmitted to the Under Secretary of State by the Secretary of Defense in his letter of November 21.

† Signed at Moscow, August 14, 1945; for text, see Department of State, *United States Relations With China* (Washington, Government Printing Office, 1949), p. 585, or United Nations Treaty Series, Vol. 10, p. 300.

f. The physical removal of Mr. Ward from Mukden would require the employment of military forces in sufficient strength to force a landing, either by sea or by air, to effect rescue, and to fight their way out of Manchuria or, alternatively, it would require covert operations for the removal of Mr. Ward from Manchuria after forcibly extricating him from custody. The strength of the military forces required to force a landing and overtly to remove Mr. Ward from custody must be adequate, from the inception of the operation, to insure its success under all contingencies, and such strength is probably greater than that presently available. The undertaking of such military action would involve a conflict with the civil forces in that area, and probably the military forces as well. Thus such action might well lead to open war with the Chinese Communist Government. Furthermore, failure of the USSR to become involved, particularly in view of Soviet strategic interests in Manchuria and the presence of USSR units in the Dairen-Port Arthur area, can be regarded only as a remote possibility. In view of the foregoing considerations, there is a likelihood that overt United States military action might lead to global war. It is understood that covert measures to remove Mr. Ward from Manchuria would probably require action beyond the capabilities of the covert strength available to the United States Government. In the case of either overt or covert action for the removal of Mr. Ward, there would be grave doubts as to whether he would be allowed to survive. Moreover covert action, even if successful, would not sustain the attitude of the United States with respect to the treatment of its consular representatives and other nationals, and might be construed as a tacit admission of Mr. Ward's guilt;

g. The second course of action; namely, redress, would involve the application of retortion, reprisal, or some form of sanction such as embargo or blockade;

h. Since there are no diplomatic representatives of the Chinese Communist Government in United States territory, simple retortion is not possible. Retortion, however, could be accomplished through the kidnapping by covert forces of one or more highly placed officials of the Manchurian Government. Even if such an operation were within the capabilities of United States covert forces, this action would establish a highly undesirable precedent in United States international relations and, by the very nature of its covert form, would fail to provide a clear-cut basis for the extrication of Mr. Ward without at least tacit overt approval by the United States of an unfriendly act carried out by covert forces. Furthermore, retortion of this nature might not alter the decision of the Manchurian Government to hold Mr. Ward rather than to negotiate an exchange. In addition, our covert action or our subsequent retortion might jeopardize the safety of other United States nationals in Communist China;

i. Reprisal would call for seizure or destruction of Manchurian property or that of its citizens. Since there is no Manchurian property in the United States or its possessions, acts of reprisal would have to involve military operations directly against Manchuria and this again would probably lead to war;

j. A United States embargo would be futile in the absence of Manchurian trade with this nation or with nations subject to our influence; and

k. Pacific Blockade. A pacific blockade is a blockade established by one or more states against the ports of another to enforce certain demands, without the intention of going to war. As a rule only vessels of states whose ports are blocked are seized. The United States has never been a party to a pacific blockade. It is generally conceded—

(1) That a pacific blockade is a legitimate means of constraint short of war.

(2) Those parties to the blockade are bound by its consequences.

(3) As a matter of policy it might be advisable to resort to pacific blockade in order to avoid declaration of war.

(4) That states not parties to a pacific blockade are in no way bound to observe it.

Currently British interests control the greater percentage of ships entering China ports. They would not be affected by a United States declaration of a pacific blockade.

l. Blockade. A blockade is normally employed only in time of war and its institution is commonly considered a belligerent act. It affects shipping regardless of nationality. Such blockade to be recognized would have to be effective. It would involve either coercion of or prior agreement with the British and might eventually necessitate the commitment of strength adequate to deal with the Soviet naval and air forces in the Far East.

In view of all the foregoing considerations, the Joint Chiefs of Staff are of the opinion that direct military action to assist the Department of State in extricating Mr. Angus Ward from his predicament might lead to war and would not of itself insure his timely and safe extrication. They do, however, point out that the Department of Defense can assist by supplying appropriate transportation for the accredited representatives of the Government to negotiate for Mr. Ward's release. Consideration might also be given to designating a military officer, such as the Commander of the Seventh Task Fleet, to negotiate locally for the release of Mr. Ward.

For the Joint Chiefs of Staff:
OMAR N. BRADLEY

Appendix IV

UNITED NATIONS RESOLUTION 435 (1978)
*Adopted by the Security Council at its 2087th meeting
on 29 September 1978*

The Security Council,

Recalling its resolutions 385 (1976) and 431 (1978), and 432 (1978),

Having considered the report submitted by the Secretary-General pursuant to paragraph 2 of resolution 431 (1978) (S/12827) and his explanatory statement made in the Security Council on 29 September 1978 (S/12869),

Taking note of the relevant communications from the Government of South Africa addressed to the Secretary-General,

Taking note also of the letter dated 8 September 1978 from the President of the South West Africa People's Organization (SWAPO) addressed to the Secretary-General (S/12841),

Reaffirming the legal responsibility of the United Nations over Namibia,

1. *Approves* the report of the Secretary-General (S/12827) for the implementation of the proposal for a settlement of the Namibian situation (S/12636) and his explanatory statement (S/12869);

2. *Reiterates* that its objective is the withdrawal of South Africa's illegal administration of Namibia and the transfer of power to the people of Namibia with the assistance of the United Nations in accordance with resolution 385 (1976);

3. *Decides* to establish under its authority a United Nations Transitional Assistance Group (UNTAG) in accordance with the above-mentioned report of the Secretary-General for a period of up to 12 months in order to assist his Special Representative to carry out the mandate conferred upon him by paragraph 1 of Security Council resolution 431 (1978), namely, to ensure the early independence of Namibia through free and fair elections under the supervision and control of the United Nations;

4. *Welcomes* SWAPO's preparedness to co-operate in the implementation of the Secretary-General's report, including its expressed readiness to sign and observe the cease-fire provisions as manifested in the letter from the President of SWAPO dated 8 September 1978 (S/12841);

5. *Calls on* South Africa forthwith to co-operate with the Secretary-General in the implementation of this resolution;

6. *Declares* that all unilateral measures taken by the illegal administration in Namibia in relation to the electoral process, including unilateral registration of voters, or transfer of power, in contravention of Security Council resolutions 385 (1976), 431 (1978) and this resolution are null and void;

7. *Requests* the Secretary-General to report to the Security Council no later than 23 October 1978 on the implementation of this resolution.

Appendix V

STATEMENT OF U.S. FOREIGN POLICY
BEFORE THE SENATE FOREIGN RELATIONS COMMITTEE *

Mr. Chairman, Members of the Committee: I welcome the opportunity to join with you in looking beyond immediate events to America's overall posture and purposes in the world.

For the past four months, our primary concern has been drawn to an area of immediate crisis—Southwest Asia and the Persian Gulf. Terrorism in Iran and Soviet aggression in Afghanistan have required concentrated attention.

But even as we address these current challenges, we must constantly place our response to specific events within our broader strategy. Our present actions must not only meet immediate crises; they must advance our long-term interests as well.

Over the past several years I have met with the Committee many times on specific elements of our foreign policy. These hearings offer an opportunity to consider America's wide-ranging interests, how they relate to each other, and our overall course.

I hope these hearings can also serve another purpose: to help crystallize broad agreement on the general course that best suits America's interests and needs in the coming decade.

I do not suggest that a full consensus behind a detailed foreign policy is now likely. In a world of extraordinary and growing complexity . . . a world in which our interests are diverse . . . we cannot escape choices which in their nature are the stuff of controversy.

But I do believe that despite differences on decisions we have made, and that we and others will make during the 1980s, our nation can now shape a new foreign policy consensus about our goals in the world—and the essential strands of our strategy to pursue them.

This consensus can be built around agreement on two central points:

First, the United States must maintain a military balance of power. Our defense forces must remain unsurpassed. Our strategic deterrent must be unquestionable. Our conventional forces must be strong enough and flexible enough to meet the full range of military threats we may face. As a global power, we must maintain the global military balance. Our strength is important to our own safety; to a strong foreign policy, free from coercion; to the confidence of allies and friends; and to the future of reciprocal arms control and other negotiations. Our

* Statement I made to the Senate Foreign Relations Committee on March 27, 1980. This was my final appearance before the Congress.

strength also buttresses regional balances that could be upset by the direct or indirect use of Soviet power.

The second central point is this: that our military strength, while an essential condition for an effective foreign policy, is not in itself a sufficient condition. We must nurture and draw upon our other strengths as well—our alliances and other international ties, our economic resources, our ability to deal with diversity, and our ideals. By drawing fully on these strengths, we can help shape world events now in ways that reduce the likelihood of using military force later.

A global American foreign policy can succeed only if it has both these dimensions.

Some have argued that a strong response to Soviet military growth and aggression is overreaction. But to disregard the growth of Soviet military programs and budgets . . . or to explain away aggression as a defensive maneuver . . . is to take refuge in illusion.

It is just as illusory, and just as dangerous, to believe that there can be a fortress America or that the world will follow our lead solely because of our military strength. America's future depends not only on our growing military power; it also requires the continued pursuit of energy security and arms control, of human rights and economic development abroad.

As we look to the 1980s, our first obligation is to see the world clearly.

We confront a serious and sustained Soviet challenge, which is both military and political. Their military build-up continues unabated. The Soviet Union has shown a greater willingness to employ that power directly, and through others. In that sense, Afghanistan is a manifestation of a larger problem, evident also in Ethiopia, South Yemen, Southeast Asia and elsewhere.

The world economic order is undergoing dramatic change. An energy crisis has rocked its foundations. Economic interdependence has become a daily reality for the citizens of every nation.

At the same time, the assertion of national independence has reshaped the political geography of the planet. There is a profusion of different systems and allegiances, and a diffusion of political and military power. Within nations, we see an accelerating rise in individual expectations.

These challenges require a full American engagement in the world—a resolve to defend our vital interests with force if necessary and to address potential causes of conflict before they erupt.

These hearings can help illuminate how best to order and serve the wide range of interests we have in a world grown increasingly complex.

In my remarks today, I will discuss eight central American interests for the coming years. Each is broad in its own terms. But I do not believe that any of these interests can be narrowed, much less disregarded, without doing damage to the others.

Our most basic interest, and first priority, is the physical security of our nation —the safety of our people. This requires strong defense forces and strong alliances.

It also requires that we and our allies firmly and carefully manage a second area of concern: East-West relations.

A third interest—controlling the growth and spread of nuclear and other weapons—enhances our collective security and international stability.

Fourth, we must confront the global energy crisis and strengthen the international economy, for doing so is central to our well-being as a people and our strength as a nation.

A fifth interest, peace in troubled areas of the world, reduces potential threats of wider war and removes opportunities for our rivals to extend their influence.

Our diplomacy in troubled regions, and our ability to pursue our global economic goals, are strengthened by pursuing a sixth interest: broadening our ties to other nations—with China, for example, and throughout the Third World.

The advancement of human rights is more than an ideal. It, too, is an interest. Peaceful gains for freedom are also steps toward stability abroad—and greater security for America.

And finally, we cannot disregard our interest in addressing environmental and other longer term global trends that can imperil our future.

Pursuit of each of these interests helps shape the kind of world we want to see. Each is important—as a part of this broader conception and because failure in one area can lead to failure in another.

Can we say that our security is more threatened by the growth of Soviet military power or by the strains we can foresee in the international economy? By the prospect of nuclear weapons in the hands of additional nations or by the prospect of social and political turmoil in many regions of the world?

The hard fact is that we must face each of these and other challenges simultaneously. Clearly, our interests do collide in particular circumstances. There will be no escaping the difficult task of weighing our interests against each other, moving each forward whenever possible.

Our course in the world must be defined by a mix of interests, sensibly balanced, meeting always the central imperative of national security for our country and our people. No simple slogan or single priority can answer in advance the dilemmas of the coming decade.

Nor can we define our security interests in ways that exclude any region. To do so could leave beyond the lines of our interest nations of genuine importance to our well-being or tempt others to believe that we were ceding to them new spheres of influence.

Certainly, we will always have regional priorities. As I shall discuss in more detail, by history, strategic location, and shared values, our allies in Europe and the Far East are central to our planning, as is our Hemisphere.

We have also, in recent years, responded to new dangers in a region of growing strategic importance: Southwest Asia and the Persian Gulf. Because of its present urgency and its relevance to our overall foreign policy, let me begin there.

Our first concern is the continued, illegal detention of Americans in Tehran. Rarely have our determination and our judgment been so severely tested as in our efforts to free them. We will not rest until all of our people are free. As long as their cruel torment continues, this matter will remain at the forefront of our national agenda.

We have pursued a policy of firmness and restraint. This is the most practical course consistent with our national honor and the safety of the hostages.

International condemnation of Iran, and the economic measures which have raised the costs to Iran of their illegal actions, are bringing home to Iranians the fact that the holding of the hostages is harmful to their interests and to the success of their revolution.

But divisions within Iran have prevented progress.

We continue to work toward a peaceful resolution of the crisis. The United States agreed to the U.N. Commission of Inquiry to hear Iran's grievances and to work for a resolution of the hostage crisis. We regret that the Commission was unable to carry out its full mandate in Tehran. But we continue to support its mission. We are prepared to see its work go forward as soon as positive conditions exist.

We are reviewing again our options in the event tangible progress is not now made.

There is only one question at issue here: the illegal detention of our diplomatic personnel and American citizens, in contravention of international law and practice. We accept Iran's revolution as a fact; we do not question the right of the Iranian people to determine their own future; we do not reject Iran's desire to bring its grievances to the attention of the world. But Iran must first live up to its fundamental responsibilities for the safety, well-being and release of the hostages.

Several broader conditions in the area also converge to demand our attention.

One is our direct interest in the Persian Gulf region. Roughly one-quarter of the oil we import comes from this area of the world. For our allies the proportion is higher—two-thirds in the case of Western Europe, three-fourths for Japan. Loss of this oil would create havoc not only in the world economy, but for the security of our alliances.

Our stake in the region, however, involves more than oil. Peace and stability in the area are critical to the future of our friends there, and affect the broader peace. Our strength and skill in supporting their independence will demonstrate to them and to others the constancy of our purpose in the world.

Another condition is the potential for turmoil and instability, caused by tensions between and within nations.

A third condition is the geographic accessibility of this critical region to the Soviet Union. The Soviet invasion of Afghanistan increases and dramatizes the potential threat to the security of nations there and to the world's free access to natural resources and shipping routes.

That is the fact whatever we may speculate about Soviet aims. For intentions cannot be known with certainty. Even if they could, intentions can change. Our response must be based upon Soviet capabilities and Soviet behavior. To respond firmly to these realities now is not to be apocalyptic; it is simply to be prudent.

Thus we are moving to deal with a new security situation. We have increased our own naval presence there and we are working with others on access to additional air and naval facilities in the region. We are consulting with others on steps to reinforce deterrence to any future Soviet aggression.

These steps serve an explicit and unmistakable purpose. As President Carter has said: "An attempt by an outside force to gain control of the Persian Gulf region will be regarded as an assault on the vital interests of the United States, and such an assault will be repelled by any means necessary, including military force."

We are also acting to impose a serious and sustained price for the aggression that is being committed against Afghanistan. The steps we have taken—on grain, on technology, on the Olympics, and in other areas—have two purposes.

First, by responding firmly to aggression, we seek to deter it elsewhere. To pursue business as usual in the face of aggression is to tempt new adventures or risk miscalculation.

Détente cannot be divorced from deterrence. To oppose aggression now is to promote peace in the future—to foster the conditions for progress in East-West relations. To assume that we can obtain the benefits of détente while ignoring the need for deterrence would be shortsighted and dangerous. To assume that détente is divisible, that aggression need be met only when it directly threatens one's own region, could encourage aggression elsewhere.

Deterrence requires sacrifice. The United States is willing to bear its share. It is vital that the burden of sacrifice be shared among all our allies—for the sake of peace, for the sake of our alliances, and for the sake of the public support which makes those alliances strong.

The Soviet invasion is not only a challenge to our interests but to those of our allies as well. While there should be a division of labor, it must be an equitable one.

We do not seek nor are we asking our allies to dismantle the framework of East-West relations. We do ask that they take measures designed to deter the Soviets from new adventures that could produce new crises. It is important that we and our allies stand together in our condemnation of aggression.

This firm stand also serves a second purpose: the withdrawal of all Soviet military forces from Afghanistan.

Western pressures do not stand alone. The Soviet actions have been swiftly and strongly condemned by the overwhelming majority of the nations of the world. The Soviets are facing a staunch, broadly-based Afghan resistance. These factors all combine to impose a continuing cost on the Soviets for their aggression.

We also support efforts to restore a neutral, non-aligned Afghanistan, with a government that would be responsive to the wishes of the Afghan people. With the prompt withdrawal of Soviet troops, we would join with Afghanistan's neighbors in a guarantee of true neutrality and of non-interference in Afghanistan's internal affairs.

Let me be clear that so long as Soviet forces remain in Afghanistan, the sanctions we have undertaken in response to the Soviet invasion will remain in force. We see no sign of Soviet withdrawal. The evidence is of a continuing build-up.

Let me be equally clear, however, that our intention is to remove the sanctions when Soviet troops are fully withdrawn from Afghanistan.

This would include the tighter criteria we announced last week governing exceptions from controls on high technology exports to the Soviet Union. However, the changes we have proposed in the list of items to be controlled would, if adopted by COCOM, remain in place; such changes were being considered even before the invasion of Afghanistan, as necessary to promote Western security interests and to reflect the state of Soviet technology.

Nor will we alter our firm position opposing participation at the Moscow Olympics. The February deadline has passed.

Our response to the immediate situation is part of our long-term strategy in the region, as we work with others toward a cooperative security framework. Our purpose is not to dominate any nation; our purpose is to help the nations of the region preserve their independence and build their strength, so that they can resist domination by others.

We advance this objective in several ways.

We are persisting in our efforts for peace in that broad region. A comprehensive settlement between Israel and her neighbors remains a paramount American goal. It would strengthen the security of Israel, to which we remain unshakeably committed. It would enhance the security of Israel's neighbors and the stability of the region as a whole.

In South Asia, mutual suspicions between India and Pakistan harm the security of both and heighten the regional danger. We will continue to support their efforts to resolve the issues dividing them. We seek good relations with both. Our assistance to either one is not directed at the other.

We are working with the nations of the region to foster their economic progress and political stability. The conditions inviting internal disorder cannot be remedied by military force. They can be met as governments move to meet the expectations of their people in their own ways and within their own traditions.

We are strengthening the basis for security cooperation in the region—through military assistance, through access to facilities, and through our increased presence. We have reaffirmed, in these new circumstances, our commitment to the 1959 Agreement of Cooperation with Pakistan. The nature of our economic and security assistance will depend both on Pakistan's assessment of its needs and our own resource capabilities.

Finally, we seek to improve our relations with nations throughout the area, wherever there is a basis of shared interests. Our diplomacy is grounded in support for the independence of others and respect for their traditions and concerns.

I have concentrated on our approach in this one area because of its immediate importance and because it illustrates a more general proposition: globally, as well as in this region, our posture must be to maintain our own and allied military strength while pursuing an active, affirmative diplomacy. Both serve the full range of our interests.

Our most fundamental interest is to maintain our security through an assured balance of military power.

For more than fifteen years there has been a steady growth in Soviet military programs and budgets. They have doubled their defense efforts over the past two decades. There is no sign of abatement in this trend.

During most of that same period our own efforts, in real terms, decreased. We have reversed this downward trend. For if it were to continue, the current overall balance in military forces would be dangerously altered.

The increases in defense spending that this Administration has proposed require sacrifice at a time of economic difficulty. They are sacrifices we must make now for the sake of our future security.

As we proceed, we should not underestimate our existing strength. We want no dangerous miscalculations of our power or our will.

Simple U.S.-Soviet force comparisons, for example, ignore the principles of collective security that are the core of our defense strategy. On the whole, our allies make a significantly greater military contribution than Soviet allies. Combined NATO strength rests upon an economic foundation more than twice the size of that of the Warsaw Pact. And our alliances also have a fundamental cohesion that is far less certain on the Warsaw Pact side.

A fair measurement of the balance must also account for the fact that the Soviets have fully one-fourth of their ground and tactical air forces deployed along their border with China.

More broadly, our purpose in the world is in basic harmony with the deep determination of nations around the world to defend their sovereignty. A purpose in conflict with nationalism—a quest to dominate and control others—presents far more difficulties and dangers, as the Soviets are learning from the nationalists in Afghanistan.

Most important, we are moving in an orderly fashion to anticipate and remedy the potential gaps in our defenses—strategic, theater nuclear and conventional. Our real defense programs are growing. Reinstatement of draft registration will advance our capacity for sharp increases in military personnel should a future crisis require it.

To portray an America standing immobile in the face of growing danger may be fashionable—but it also is patently false.

Our security begins with the balance of strategic forces. The Soviet nuclear arsenal constitutes the one credible, direct threat to the continental United States.

To effectively deter that danger we must have a capability for certain and appropriate retaliation to any level of attack. We must also maintain forces which are, and are perceived to be, essentially equivalent to those of the Soviet Union, to avoid the possible military or political consequences that an imbalance might bring.

These requirements—flexible response and essential equivalence—are advanced by our programs to modernize and improve the three elements of our triad of strategic force: the MX mobile land-based missile, the Trident submarine and missile programs, and the air-launched cruise missiles for our manned bombers.

Our security is also based upon collective defense. The security of our allies is synonymous with our own.

The Soviet Union, with its Warsaw Pact allies, has increased its capability to mount a heavy attack, with little warning, in Europe. To counter that danger, President Carter in 1977 recommended to NATO a Long Term Defense Program to improve allied capabilities in each of ten vital areas ranging from air defense to maritime posture. The program was adopted in 1978. It is being implemented.

Last December in response to Soviet theater nuclear modernization, the NATO ministers agreed to a plan for modernizing our theater nuclear forces while we seek equal negotiated limits on both sides.

These force improvements reflect a common perception in NATO of the growing threat to Europe—and a common determination to respond. I will not pretend that there is unanimity in the alliance on all international issues. But NATO is united on its central role, and the alliance is making progress to guarantee that its capabilities will be sufficient to meet its obligations.

We have security interests in Asia similar to those in Europe. We are committed to maintaining our strength in Asia.

Our close association and alliance with Japan reflect strong economic ties and shared security interests. Our defense cooperation is expanding. Japan's Self-Defense Forces are undergoing steady improvement. We have urged Japanese leaders to expand these programs, within the limits set by the Japanese constitution.

We attach great importance to our alliances with our ANZUS partners—Australia and New Zealand. We stand firmly behind our other security commitments in the region.

In response to the confirmed sharp buildup in North Korea, we are maintaining our strength in that area. At the same time, the strength of our South Korean ally is growing. Next year, for example, South Korean defense spending is expected to reach nearly six percent of its gross national product, compared to roughly four percent in the early 1970s.

Conclusion of a revised base agreement with the Philippines has been an important, positive development for the sustained defense of the region.

Our forces in East Asia not only reinforce our security commitments there; because of their mobility they help protect interests that we and our Asian allies share outside the immediate region, such as those in the Persian Gulf.

Our European and Asian alliances have long encompassed our major defense priorities. They do not, however, define the perimeters of our security interests. We must also be prepared to reinforce the capacity for resistance to aggression in areas beyond our alliances.

Let me take a few moments to address this important question.

With an inescapable stake in the health of the international economy, we cannot idly watch vital resources fall under the control of an outside force. Our interests require that we be able and willing to help others resist challenges to their sovereignty and to counter, in particular, a growing Soviet ability to project its power.

Our ability to project our power is unsurpassed. But improvements must be made. Enhancing the mobility of our Rapid Deployment Forces will be an important step forward. Plans for Maritime Prepositioning Ships and a new large cargo aircraft will further strengthen our ability to respond quickly when crises occur.

The confidence of our friends and our political influence in the world depend, in part, upon our military strength and our will to use it if necessary. We must be seen as fully reliable. Our strength must be perceived as fully sufficient to meet realistic threats.

Certainly there are limits to what we can and should do. We would undermine the confidence of our friends and allies through bellicose pronouncements or a posture that implied an interest in dominating other sovereign states. The use of American military force is not a desirable American policy response to the purely internal politics of other nations. As the President said in his State of the Union address, "our power will never be used to initiate a threat to the security of any nation or the rights of any human being."

No easy formula can determine in advance when we should use military force beyond our alliance areas. The proper response in each case must be a function of the importance and immediacy of the American and allied interests at risk; the source and character of the threat; the potential involvement of friends and allies within and beyond the region affected; the prospects for success and the potential costs of our involvement; and other factors.

Our system rightly gives responsibility to both the President and the Congress for committing our military forces to combat. To sustain such a commitment requires a firm public base.

Obviously, direct military involvement is not our preference. The best answer to outside pressure is indigenous strength. Sensible programs of security assistance and arms supply can help our friends build their own capacity to resist.

A policy which concentrated solely on our own military strength and failed to provide for legitimate security needs of our friends would be worse than short-sighted. It would be dangerous. For such a policy would increase the danger of conflicts and international confrontations that might be avoided if local security balances are preserved.

Let me emphasize, Mr. Chairman, that if we shortchange our programs of security assistance now, we will be shortchanging our own future safety. Such programs are not gifts to other nations; they are investments which serve our security interests as well as theirs.

As we fulfill the needs of defense and deterrence, our second interest is in fashioning a relationship with the Soviet Union in which our fundamental competition is bounded by restraint.

The Soviet invasion of Afghanistan and their adventurism in Africa and Asia have done real damage to this relationship and to the immediate prospects for a more peaceful world.

We are prepared to impose costs on aggression for as long as necessary. We will promote America's interests and values in all of our dealings.

But we seek no Cold War, no indiscriminate confrontation. It is not in our interest, even during a period of heightened tensions, to dismantle the framework of East-West relations constructed over more than a generation. Even if we could discount the direct implications of an unbounded competition for our own interests—and we cannot—our relations with our Allies and our credibility throughout the world would still call for a diligent, good faith American effort to sustain a framework for peace.

Thus, even as we have responded to Soviet aggression, we have also held to our formal obligations. We are denying specific benefits to the Soviet Union; but we have not abrogated formal agreements. Progress has been suspended; but when Soviet behavior allows, the door to a more stable and mutually beneficial relationship—a competition bounded by restraint and a regard for each other's interests—will be open.

Meanwhile, we should avoid framing our discussions of East-West relations in ways that suggest a false choice between extremes: between some utopian state of perfect détente on the one hand, or, on the other, a condition of implacable hostility. In fact, realism and safety require that we conduct relations in the continuum between those two poles. At times, there will be greater progress in areas of mutual interest. At others, as now, the adversarial elements in our relations will be prominent. There will always be elements of both.

In seeking to deter further aggression and pressing for an end to the invasion of Afghanistan, we are working to create the conditions that will enable us to return to building a more stable relationship.

A third and related area of emphasis is arms control.

Our interests have been well served by the arms control agreements to which the United States and the Soviet Union are parties. In 1963 we halted poisonous nuclear weapons tests in the atmosphere. The SALT I Interim Agreement froze the number of offensive strategic missiles when the Soviets were building up in that area and we were not. The Anti-Ballistic Missile Treaty headed off a potentially costly and destabilizing arms race in these defensive weapons.

In the same fashion, the SALT II Treaty would serve this country's paramount security interests.

We must all think through very carefully the consequences of a no-SALT world.

What would that world look like?

Without SALT there would be no agreed limit on the number of strategic systems the Soviets could build. They could easily reach a total of 3,000 delivery systems over the next five years, more than 700 beyond what the treaty allows.

Without SALT there would be no limits on the number of separate warheads each missile can carry. Each of the Soviet Union's heaviest missiles—the SS-18s—could theoretically deliver twenty or even thirty nuclear warheads, instead of the ten the treaty allows. On those 308 SS-18s alone, the Soviets could mount as many additional warheads as their entire strategic force holds today.

Without SALT our own defense planning would be seriously complicated. For example, the MX program would be more difficult to design and build, and less certain to achieve its purpose.

Without the treaty, our ability to monitor Soviet strategic forces—and thus evaluate Soviet capabilities—could be impaired, since there would be no constraints on the deliberate concealment of those forces.

Without the treaty, the likely increase in Soviet strategic capabilities would compel further defense expenditures that could compound our already difficult budget choices.

The security advantages of SALT II have been reinforced by recent events. At a time of increased tensions between the superpowers, effective mutual constraints on strategic arms become all the more important.

For these compelling reasons of security, we should move ahead with ratification at the earliest feasible time.

In the interim, it is most important that both sides continue to observe the mutual constraints of SALT I and SALT II. Our own strategic programs are consistent with those agreements. We will, of course, continue to review our strategic arms requirements with the Congress, and we will keep a close watch on Soviet actions to see that they are exercising a similar degree of restraint.

For the same reasons, we will continue wherever feasible to pursue balanced and verifiable arms control agreements at other levels—in the Mutual and Balanced Force Reduction talks, on antisatellite warfare, on banning nuclear weapons tests, on chemical warfare, and in other areas. The TNF negotiating offer remains on the table. And we have called upon the Soviet Union to pursue it with us.

None of these efforts is undertaken as a favor to others; each one serves the national security interests of the United States, as well as others.

Our willingness to seek restraint in strategic weapons reinforces other critical arms control efforts. In particular, we must be concerned about the spread of nuclear weapons. The technology is losing its mystery. Six countries have already carried out nuclear explosions. At least a dozen more could produce a weapon within a few years of deciding to do so. The risks in this progression are self-evident. Regional nuclear arms races have become a real danger. The presence of nuclear arms in volatile areas multiplies the chance that they will be used.

Thus, we continue to press for the widest adherence to the Nuclear Non-Proliferation Treaty. We are urging others to take necessary steps to bring the Treaty of Tlatelolco into full force. And we vigorously support the improvement and application of International Atomic Energy Agency safeguards.

In 1977 President Carter also initiated the International Nuclear Fuel Cycle Evaluation, to involve both producing and consuming nations in a joint search for ways to realize the benefits of nuclear power while limiting the risks that nuclear weapons will be developed. This was not a negotiation that resolved all differences; it was a technical study that illuminated problems and possible solutions. It has provided a better understanding of the economics, technology, and risks associated with the nuclear fuel cycle and it produced consensus on a number of middle-range goals. These include the possible value of an international regime to manage excess plutonium, stronger fuel supply assurances for consumers under effective nonproliferation controls, and conversion of research reactors from use of highly enriched uranium fuels.

Differences remain in many areas. But the essential task has been advanced by this common effort.

More countries will approach the nuclear weapons threshold in the decade ahead, some with uncertain intentions in regions of tension and conflict. The time remaining to reduce the appeal of nuclear weapons and to develop safer ways to address legitimate energy needs is slipping away. Our non-proliferation efforts are more vital now than ever before.

Fourth, it is plainly in our interest to act now to forestall a future energy disaster. For, quite simply, that is what we could face.

We now import some 40 percent of the petroleum we use. This year alone, the bill for these imports will come to some $90 billion.

That energy dependence fuels our inflation. It strains the dollar. It drains our balance of payments. It increases our vulnerability.

As much as anything else we do in the coming decade, our effort to gain control of our energy future—to conserve, to expand our own production, and to develop new and renewable fuels—will determine not only the quality of our lives at home but the strength of our position in the world.

We must also recognize the profound consequences of the global energy crisis for other consuming nations whose economic health affects our own.

Our allies are even more dependent than we on the production and pricing decisions of OPEC and on political events in oil producing nations.

The point is vividly illustrated by the plight of Turkey, which now spends 70 percent to 80 percent of all its export earnings to pay for oil imports. Because of a shortage of fuel, it is only able to keep its industry functioning at something less than 50 percent of capacity. It would be hard to exaggerate the strains that the energy crisis places on many nations such as this democratic and strategically placed ally.

The developing countries are even more burdened by the rising price of oil, the inflation it helps to fuel, and the debts it brings. This year, developing countries will spend on oil and debt servicing alone three times what they will receive in outside economic assistance from all the industrial democracies and the OPEC countries.

The United States has a direct stake in the economic vitality of developing countries. They are increasingly important as partners in trade—both as markets and sources of supply. And the political effect of their economic stagnation can have serious consequences for us—with major social disruptions, a reversal of progress toward democratic rule and human rights, and new openings for violence and radicalism.

In short, our economy and ultimately our security depend upon whether we can gain control over our own energy future, and whether the world economy can manage the hard transition ahead.

We have made some progress in the past few years. While our economy was growing last year, our oil consumption declined. The elements of a national energy policy are taking shape.

Continued progress at home will give impetus to our international efforts—working with other consumers for more stringent conservation, and developing new energy resources through World Bank financing and our bilateral assistance.

As we grapple with the energy problem, it is important that we not lose sight of our broader economic interests or jeopardize the real progress that has been made in the past few years to open and strengthen the international economy.

Despite the persistence of protectionist impulses in times of economic difficulty, the Tokyo round of trade negotiations was able to agree upon significant reductions in barriers to trade—a result which both improves our access to foreign markets and helps to curb inflation at home. Current economic strains must not erode this major achievement.

The global economic structure is being strengthened in other ways—through negotiation of commodity agreements, progress on the common fund, and more funding for the multilateral development banks.

The International Monetary Fund, in particular, has a key role in helping countries through this time of adjustment and also in recycling OPEC's enormous surpluses. To fulfill these vital missions, the increase in IMF quotas scheduled for later this year is essential. We also have a stake in assuring the necessary capital for the World Bank, the International Development Association, and the regional development banks.

Let there be no mistake. The years ahead will be trying ones for the international economy. The trend in oil prices is alarming. The OPEC countries will continue to run massive surpluses—estimated at over $100 billion for 1980—which means corresponding deficits for other nations. The developing countries will be hardest hit—and faced with the painful choice between stunted growth and deeper debt.

The steps we have taken only buy us more time. We must use that time to make fundamental adjustments in our energy consumption and production patterns. Our older industries must be streamlined and re-tooled to meet the inevitable challenge of a more open and competitive world economy. More investment must be earmarked for new product lines and advanced technology. For that is necessary to restore the balance in international commerce—and to assure future prosperity for the American people.

A fifth element in our global strategy is to help achieve peaceful resolutions of disputes in troubled regions of the world.

The task is an imposing one, and it is not without costs. It is always difficult to work for accommodations which cannot fully satisfy the demands of any side, because they must be accepted by all sides. We must be prepared for frustration.

But working for peace is directly relevant to our interests in collective security and the freedom of other nations from outside domination. Regional conflicts pose the danger of wider confrontations. Disputes between our allies—as in the case of Greece and Turkey—weaken the common defense. And as a magnet draws iron, Third World conflict seems to draw the interest of the Soviets, the Cubans, or others prepared to exploit disorder.

We can take satisfaction that real progress in the pursuit of peace has been made.

The 1979 peace treaty between Israel and Egypt is an historic achievement. We have no more urgent diplomatic priority than the effort to complete and broaden that peace so that Israel, the neighboring Arab states, and the Palestinian people will be able to live securely and with dignity.

Our immediate attention must be on the autonomy negotiations. Ambassador Linowitz has worked hard and ably to focus and accelerate the talks, which have now begun to center on the substantive issues that lie at the very heart of the negotiations—issues like security, water, and land. We have no illusion about the complexity and sensitivity of the problems that remain. But in this evolutionary process we have overcome seemingly intractable obstacles before.

The President has invited President Sadat and Prime Minister Begin to Washington for talks in April. They know that the Camp David process provides the best opportunity in thirty years to bring the security of peace to the Middle East. We cannot let it slip away.

There has also been an historic breakthrough in Southern Africa. The nation of Zimbabwe will soon become a reality, through the realism of the parties, the skill of British diplomacy, the commitment of other African states—and because of the constructive role played by the United States. The steadfastness of the Congress in resisting attempts to lift sanctions prematurely played a singificant part in assuring that bargaining and balloting, not bullets, are shaping Rhodesia's future.

I want to be sure the importance of this event is understood. We have a wide range of interests in Africa—security interests, economic interests, an interest in political cooperation on all global issues. In my judgment no policy could have served those interests better than our stalwart support for the principle of majority rule, with minority rights, in Rhodesia. And nothing could have weakened us more there than to waver in this crucial effort.

Peace and stability are at risk in other parts of the world—in the Eastern Mediterranean, in Southeast Asia, in Northwest Africa, in our own hemisphere. All of those cases have some bearing upon American interests. At the same time there are, of course, practical limits on what we—or any one nation—can do.

The nature of our involvement will vary—from support for the efforts of others, to mediation ourselves, to helping maintain a balance of forces if that is required to induce the parties to settle.

But in each case we are determined to employ the influence we have to develop workable alternatives to war.

We advance regional peace in another tangible way, by striving to limit the destructiveness of war when it cannot be prevented.

Since 1977 the United States has taken the lead in working toward negotiated limits on conventional arms transfers. While we remain convinced that such agreements can contribute to a safer world, we do not at this time foresee progress.

In the absence of agreed international restraint, we do not plan to reduce further the ceiling on our own arms transfers. But the other elements of our arms transfer policy continue to serve our interests.

Arms transfers must be based on assessments of U.S. foreign policy and national security interests. The policy has a dual effect:

To facilitate those arms transfers that clearly promote the security of the United States and our allies and friends, and

To restrain transfers that are in excess of legitimate defense needs, could promote regional arms races or increase instability, or otherwise do not advance U.S. interests.

In short, our purpose in supplying arms is security, not profit.

Sixth, we have an interest in building positive bilateral relations with all countries, wherever there is a basis of shared concerns.

Scores of new countries—and new centers of power—have emerged since the end of the Second World War. The international landscape—and thus the nature of diplomacy—has been altered fundamentally. Questions of direct importance to us are determined not in a few capitals, but among one hundred and fifty-five. Our access to resources and to defense facilities cannot simply be declared; it must be agreed. We seek positive relations around the world not because we have a compulsion to be liked, but because our interests and the well-being of our people are at stake.

This interest in a broad network of relationships is reflected in our international approach:

This Administration has worked especially hard to strengthen our core partnerships with our traditional allies. If there appear to be new strains among us, they flow principally from the fact that we are facing up to hard, new challenges together.

We often have an interest in working with nations whose ideologies are different from ours. In a diverse world our exact scale of values will be replicated rarely if at all. It would make no sense to limit our influence by refusing to pursue specific areas of shared interest with other nations because of broader disagreement.

This is why we oppose, in principle, country-by-country limitations on our aid and trade programs. Obviously we will not have such relationships when there is not yet a basis for cooperation—as is now the case in Cuba and Vietnam. But our diplomacy is undercut when such restrictions are cast in law.

The establishment of full diplomatic relations with the People's Republic of China illustrates the value of an open approach. It is, in its own terms, an accomplishment of historic importance—an achievement of economic as well as diplomatic meaning, global as well as regional significance. Normalization is not an end in itself. It is the beginning of continuing efforts to improve our relations with Beijing.

Similarly, we are working toward improved relations with the nations of Eastern Europe.

The pursuit of our interests also requires that we stress an inclusive form of diplomacy, in which all who have a stake also have a role and are encouraged to accept a share of the responsibility for hard decisions. Our diplomacy on Namibia and Zimbabwe is a case in point. Such multilateral efforts are time-consuming and complex. But building coalitions is a process that Americans, with our own pluralistic traditions, well understand. Abroad, no less than at home, on many issues it is the only way to achieve workable results.

Our interest does not require that others be like us or always side with us. We seek their willingness to find areas of mutual interest, or balanced compromise when our interests may clash. A quest for uniformity is not realistic, nor is it required. The Soviets may demand ideological purity; we can serve our interests in a world of diversity.

In this context, let me dispute the suggestion that in our dealings with the Third World we have to choose between two approaches: competing with Soviet ambitions in the Third World by seeing the developing nations primarily through an East-West prism, or dealing with the Third World primarily in terms of Third World problems. These are sometimes presented as exclusive options.

But the choice presented—between an interest in Third World concerns and a determination to counter Soviet inroads—is false. In fact, the two are twin strands in a single strategy. For the best strategy for competing with the Soviets is to address the practical interests of Third World countries themselves—not only their security concerns but their goals of economic and political justice as well.

It would be misleading, of course, to gloss over our real differences with developing countries on a wide range of issues. But we can bargain most effectively, to our mutual benefit, when they are confident that we share the goals of equitable economic growth and the political independence.

Certainly there have been painful disappointments and setbacks. But because we have supported those goals, our relations with most of the nations of Africa, Latin America and Asia are better than they have been for many years.

The seventh way in which we advance our interests in the world—indeed our long-term security—is through support for human rights.

When the two concepts—human rights and national security—are uttered in the same breath, it is often to express unavoidable conflict—a fundamental tension between the pursuit of the good and the pursuit of the practical.

I strongly reject the idea that there is a fundamental incompatibility between the pursuit of human rights and the pursuit of self-interest.

By this, I do not mean to say that there can never be a conflict between human rights concerns and security concerns. We cannot escape the hard decisions that must be made in such cases. We must constantly weigh how best to encourage the advancement of human rights while maintaining our ability to conduct essential business with governments—even unpopular ones—in countries where we have important security interests.

But the fact remains that over the longer term, our pursuit of human rights is not only generally compatible with our national security—it contributes to that security.

We know from our own national experience that the drive for human freedom has tremendous force and vitality. It is universal. It is resilient. And, ultimately, it is irrepressible.

Just in the past several years, we have seen that drive for a fuller voice in economic and political life gain new expression . . . in Portugal and Spain and Greece . . . in Nigeria and Ghana and Upper Volta . . . in Ecuador, Peru and the Dominican Republic . . . and elsewhere.

These countries make a compelling case for the proposition that the tide in the world is running toward human rights and that it is in our interest to support it.

The United States cannot claim credit for these developments. But we can find proof in them that our policy of furthering human rights is not only consistent with American ideals. It is consistent with the aspirations of others.

Our support for those aspirations enables us to regain the political high ground in competition for world influence. It stands in vivid contrast to the practices of the Soviet Union abroad, as Afghanistan demonstrates, and at home, as the internal exile of Andrei Sakharov again makes clear.

In short, our willingness to press for human rights progress gives credibility to our commitment to freedom. And it is that commitment which has always been one of America's most enduring strengths in the world.

Our support for human rights serves our interests in another way. As President Carter put it in his State of the Union address, "In repressive regimes, popular frustrations often have no outlet except violence. But when people and their governments can approach their problems together—through open, democratic methods—the basis for stability and peace is far more solid and enduring."

As the President suggested, divergent views cannot be long repressed without sowing the seeds of violent convulsion. And once the ties are broken between a government and its people, outside intervention cannot secure its long-term survival.

Thus it is profoundly in our national interest to support constructive change before such ties erode and the alternatives of radicalism or repression drive out moderate solutions.

How each society manages change is a matter for it to decide. We cannot and should not write social contracts for others.

But we can help others promote—in their own ways—peaceful and orderly reform.

We do that by clearly expressing our opposition to official torture, arbitrary arrest and other abuses of individual liberties. Whatever short-term quiet they may provide, they engender long-term bitterness.

We do it by reinforcing efforts to open economic and political institutions to broader national participation—so that they are better able to accommodate conflicting views and interests.

And we do it by focusing development assistance on helping governments meet the basic human needs of their people. In doing our part to meet the greatest moral challenge of our times—the plight of hundreds of millions of human beings who lack adequate food or health care—we are also addressing the root causes of instability. We must recognize, in the demand of these people for their basic human rights, that stability can only come through peaceful progress, not through a desperate effort to preserve the status quo.

Nowhere do we see more clearly the race between radical and peaceful change than in Central America today. And nowhere is our commitment to peaceful change more clearly tested.

In Nicaragua, our challenge is to join with others in the region to help the Nicaraguan people and government succeed in building a stable, healthy, democratic society out of the debris of dictatorship and civil war.

We cannot guarantee that democracy will take hold there. But if we turn our backs on Nicaragua, we can help guarantee that democracy will fail.

Failure to appropriate needed American aid has jeopardized our interests. It has weakened the position of the private sector, which would receive the majority of our assistance. It has made it more difficult for the Nicaraguan government to pursue a development strategy that includes important roles for both the public and private sectors. And it has played into the hands of the Cubans.

Those who are most concerned about the potential for radical revolution in Latin America and growing Cuban influence in the region should be the strongest supporters of our efforts to help Nicaragua build a better future.

Our essential challenge in El Salvador is similar. In October, reformist military officers overthrew a military dictator in order to forestall the outbreak of a violent and bloody civil war. The Revolutionary Junta of Government, which includes the Christian Democratic Party, is committed to peaceful, sweeping change. An impressive agrarian reform has already turned more than 224,000 hectares of land over to the rural poor. The ultimate success of the program will depend heavily on our ability to provide technical and economic assistance.

The dangers of the situation are clear in the tragic and despicable assassination of Archbishop Romero.

If reform fails, El Salvador will become a battleground between the radical left and the radical right.

A moderate solution is still possible. It is in our interest. We will pursue this interest by helping the government of El Salvador pursue progress.

In short, we pursue our human rights objectives, not only because they are right, but because we have a stake in the stability that comes when people can express their hopes and find their futures freely. Our ideals and our interests coincide.

Eighth and finally, we cannot define our interests so narrowly as to exclude from our immediate attention a series of other global trends that darken the horizon.

We face a world population that could double in the next generation, overwhelming our global resources; already, for example, the world's tropical forests are disappearing at a rate of 50 acres a minute. The world-wide flood of refugees displaced from their homes—some seven to eight million people today—is growing. The enormous international traffic in narcotics costs our society nearly $50 billion each year and destroys thousands of lives. The mounting wave of international terrorism strikes at the very heart of civilized order.

Imagine for a moment how different our world could be for our children if we do not address these problems now on an urgent basis. To relegate these matters permanently to the back burner of our foreign policy is to invite even more serious consequences for us in the future.

Thus we have increased our bilateral aid commitment in family planning. The United States is the world's leading donor in this area.

We have focused greater attention, and greater resources, on efforts to deal with such potentially harmful environmental trends as the shrinking global base of tropical forests and farmland and the creeping spread of deserts.

The United States has taken a leading role in relief and resettlement of refugees, particularly in Southeast Asia where the need has been most acute. Humanitarian considerations alone would compel our generous response. Our political and strategic interests reinforce that requirement. For massive refugee flows heighten tensions in regions already unsettled by political and military conflict. We must help friendly governments which are risking severe internal strains as they shoulder a growing refugee burden.

Wherever possible, we have strengthened our bilateral cooperation with governments striving to halt the production of narcotics within their borders.

The steps that we take now to address such global issues can prevent our being engulfed by them later.

But let me make a fundamental point here: on these—and on many of the other challenges I have discussed this morning—there can be no exclusively American solutions. There can only be international answers, or there will be no answers at all.

The blight of terrorism is an especially urgent case in point. No nation can defeat it alone. We have been working actively through the United Nations and other multilateral institutions to build an international consensus on the criminality of terrorist tactics. International conventions—on aircraft sabotage, hijacking, the protection of diplomats, and against the taking of hostages—play a crucial part. We need wider support for the principles that governments should not give in to terrorist blackmail and that both those who commit and those who support terrorism have to be punished. Every feasible step—unilateral and multilateral—must be employed.

In this and many other areas, the truth is that we cannot assure our future security without a framework for global cooperation on issues that affect many nations and many peoples.

That is why we have welcomed and supported the growing strength of regional associations such as the Organization of American States, the Organization of African Unity and the Association of Southeast Asian Nations.

And that is why we need to support, and continue to help strengthen, the United Nations and its affiliated institutions. It is a center of global politics. The collective expression of world opinion embodied in recent U.N. votes on Afghanistan and Iran demonstrate that our interests can be advanced there. In the Middle East and elsewhere its peace-keeping operations reduce tensions. On refugees . . . on the fight against hunger, illiteracy and disease . . . on strengthening international resistance to terrorism . . . and on other issues of importance to us, the United Nations is making a concrete contribution.

Certainly, there are limits to what international organizations can accomplish. But to dismiss them as irrelevant or inconsequential would be folly.

The simple fact is that we need them and they need our support. The institutions of international cooperation and international law are essential to the practical advance of our interests in the world.

Mr. Chairman, I know that no one is more acutely aware of the breadth and complexity of our challenge than the members of this committee. We face a broad agenda. It requires constant, hard choices among compelling yet competing interests. In a dangerous world, it requires a willingness to defend our vital interests with force when necessary—and a diplomacy of active and constructive engagement to reduce the dangers we may confront. It requires sacrifice—in resources for our defense and help for other nations, in reduced consumption of energy and efforts to control inflation. It will test our wisdom and our persistence.

We will be badly served if we fail to understand a world of rapid change and shy away from its complexity. The flat truth is that complex problems can seldom be resolved by simple solutions.

Some have said that we are trying to do too much. I say we cannot afford to do less, in our own national interest.

Some say that in trying to do too much, we have accomplished too little. I say that in strengthening our military posture . . . in reemphasizing and strengthening NATO . . . in negotiating the SALT II Treaty . . . in normalizing relations with China . . . in helping achieve peace between Israel and Egypt and a framework for a comprehensive peace in the Middle East . . . in advancing peace in Zimbabwe . . . in the Panama Canal treaty . . . in the successful Multilateral Trade Neogtiations and other improvements in the international economic system . . . in closer ties to developing nations . . . and in promoting human rights . . . in all these areas, I say we are on the right road, even if it is a long and difficult one.

Some say that in seeking peaceful change toward human justice in every area of the world, we encourage radicalism. I say that the world is changing . . . that human beings everywhere will demand a better life. The United States must offer its own vision of a better future, or the future will belong to others.

Some have said that the Executive and Legislative Branches cannot collaborate effectively on foreign policy. I say that the record over the past few years has been a good one.

Some say that America is in a period of decline. I am convinced they are wrong.

There is no question that the years to come present a somber prospect. Soviet challenge in Afghanistan and beyond . . . energy crisis . . . revolutionary explosions when expectations run ahead of progress . . . such current events are all too likely to be harbingers of the trends of the coming decade. This is the reality we confront.

But it is also a reality that our strength, military, economic and political, gives us an unmatched capacity for world leadership.

We can succeed—if we combine power with determination, persistence and patience.

We can make progress if we promote the full range of our interests, and use the full range of our strengths.

THE CHAIRMAN. Thank you very much, Mr. Secretary, for a splendid summation of American foreign policy objectives worldwide.

I want to take this opportunity to express my own appreciation for the collaboration that has existed between the committee and the administration, and the consultation and briefings that you have furnished in response to committee requests. I believe all members of the committee would join me in extending to you our appreciation for that kind of cooperation.

INDEX

on Soviet bases in West, 359, 362–64
on Soviet invasion of Afghanistan,
 389–90
special Iranian relationship promised
 by, 319–21, 326
State of the Union speech of (1980),
 391
Vance offered office by, 29, 33
at Vienna summit, 109, 111, 134–35,
 138–39
Wake Forest speech of, 99
see also Camp David accords; Camp
 David summit meeting; Egyptian-
 Israeli peace treaty negotiations
Carter, Lillian, 33
Carter, Rosalynn, 246, 251
Carter, W. Hodding, III, 34, 43, 82, 412
Carver, Lord Michael, 270
Case, Clifford, 290–91
Castro, Fidel, 131
Castro, Raul, 87
CENTO (Central Treaty Organization),
 125
China, U.S. relations normalized with,
 23, 32, 45–46, 75–83, 113–19
 agreement reached for, 109
 announcement of, 109–11, 113, 119
 Chinese conditions for, 76, 77, 82
 communiqué drafted on, 79, 82
 Congress in, 77, 83, 115–19
 Eleventh National People's Congress
  in, 79–80
 "hegemony" opposed in, 110–12
 inaccurate press reports on, 82–83
 negotiating scenario for, 115
 PRM-24 on, 76–77
 SALT II and, 116
 strategy for, 114–17
 Taiwan issue in, 75–83, 115–16
 U.S. conditions for, 76, 77–78, 81–
  82, 115
China, People's Republic of (PRC), 44,
 75–83, 113–22, 390–91
 arms sales to, 19, 113–14
 East Asia and, 427–28
 potential U.S. influence on, 427–28
 Soviet hostility toward, 23
 in Soviet-U.S. relations, 78, 102, 106,
  110–14, 116, 120–22, 428
 Soviet-Vietnamese friendship feared
  by, 120–21
 in UN Cambodian debate, 124–27
 U.S. security relationship with, 76–78
 Vietnam attacked by, 121–22, 133

Chirau, Jeremiah, 285
Christopher, Warren, 39–41, 94, 316,
 326, 412
 in Chinese relations normalization,
  116–19
 in Iran hostage crisis, 330, 371–72,
  382, 409, 411
 Panama Canal Treaties and, 151–56
 in Rhodesian problem, 269, 290
Church, Frank, 119, 153, 155–56, 300,
 349, 361, 365–66
CIA (Central Intelligence Agency), 129,
 136, 325–26
Clark, Ramsey, 376
Clark Amendment of 1974, 71, 259
Clement, Carl, 373
Clifford, Clark, 340, 389
Cohen, Geulah, 248
Conference on Security and Cooperation
 in Europe (CSCE), 22
Congress, U.S.:
 Angolan civil war and, 259
 Angola-Zaire conflict and, 89–92
 Byrd Amendment repealed by, 261
 Camp David accords presented to, 227
 Carter's relationship with, 157
 in Chinese relations normalization, 77,
  83, 115–19
 foreign policy and, 27–28, 395–97
 human rights and, 316
 Iran hostage crisis and, 380, 411–12
 Iranian military buildup and, 315,
  319–21
 Israeli invasion of Lebanon and, 208–
  209
 Israeli supporters in, 192–93
 Koreagate affair in, 127
 Middle East aircraft sales and, 205,
  319–21
 neutron bomb and, 67–68
 Panama Canal Treaties and, 115, 144,
  145–56
 Rhodesian issue in, 267–68, 285–97,
  300
 SALT II and, 47, 61–63; see also
  SALT II ratification debate
 Somali aid sought from, 88
 southern African policy and, 257
 South Korea and, 128–29
 treaty and agreement approvals of, 47n
 conventional forces, 32, 65–66,
  416–17
Cooper, Richard, 43
Crosland, Anthony, 262

Geneva Middle East Peace Conference
(proposed), 318
  Arab divisions over, 166–67, 171
  Arab preconditions for, 166
  cochairmen's joint statement on, 191–
    193
  Israeli proposal for, 182
  Palestinian representation at, 167, 171,
    182–83, 185–86, 188, 190, 191
  PLO and, 167, 171, 182–83, 185–86,
    188, 190
  procedures for, 170–73, 191
  progress toward, 171–72, 191
  Resolutions 242 and 338 as basis of,
    193
  Sadat's Jerusalem visit and, 194
  working paper on, 193–94
Genscher, Hans-Dietrich, 94–95, 303
Germany, West, 276–83, 302–12, 392
  neutron bomb issue in, 68–69, 93–96
  in Ogaden dispute, 72, 74, 85–86
  SALT II cruise missile limits and, 67
  SALT II nontransfer provision and,
    97–98
Ghali, Boutros, 235–39
Ghotbzadeh, Sadegh, 379, 398, 402–5
Giscard d'Estaing, Valéry, 114, 120, 337,
  407
Glenn, John, 119, 129, 355, 366
Gleysteen, William, 76, 82, 130
global economy:
  classical institutions in, 429
  management needed in, 428–29
  new trends in, 433–34
  Third World and, 429–31
Golan Heights, 159–60, 162, 169
Graham, John, 265
Gravel, Mike, 156
Great Britain, 89–90, 256, 392
  Chinese arms sales and, 113–14
  in Namibian problem, 276–83, 302–
    312
  neutron bomb issue and, 93, 96
  nuclear forces of, 66, 139
  in Ogaden dispute, 72–74, 85–86
  possible South African embargo and,
    261–62, 271
  Rhodesian problem and, 257, 260–71,
    284–89, 294–301
  SALT II and, 67, 97–98
  Smith-Nkomo agreement and, 268–69
  in UN Cambodian debate, 126
  U.S. missile sales to, 97–98
Greece, 144, 168

Gromyko, Andrei, 13, 132, 355, 362,
  394–95
  Middle East negotiations and, 191–92
  1981 meeting with, 17–21
  in SALT II, 53–61
  on Soviet African activities, 103
Gromyko, Mrs. Andrei, 18
Guadelupe four-power summit, 120

Habib, Philip, 42, 53, 73–74, 81, 82
Haddad, Saad, 208–9
Haig, Alexander M., 19, 350
Hansell, Herb, 83, 242, 305
Harlech, Lord David, 298
Harriman, W. Averell, 151, 218
Hart, Gary, 129
Hartman, Arthur, 42
Hatch, Orin, 155
Hatfield, Mark, 137, 418
Ha Van Lau, 123
Hayakawa, Samuel I., 397
Helms, Jesse, 290–91, 300
Helsinki accords, 54, 423
Heng Samrin, 124
Holbrooke, Richard, 29–30, 42, 126,
  410
  in Chinese relations normalization,
    76–83, 116–19, 121
  in Korean withdrawal problem, 128–
    130
  in UN Cambodian issue, 126–27
Ho Liliang, 79, 81
House of Representatives, U.S.:
  Appropriations Committee of, 67–68
  Foreign Affairs Committee of, 201,
    296–97
  Rhodesian sanctions upheld in, 297
Howland, Michael, 374, 404
Hua Guofeng, 80
Huang Chen, 75
Huang Hua, 79, 81–82
Hughes, Sir Gledwyn, 293
human rights policy, U.S., 28–29, 33,
  44, 421, 423
  action limited in, 436
  elements of, 46
  Iran and, 315–19, 343, 345–46
  Korea and, 127–28
  potentially negative effects of, 102
  quiet diplomacy preferred for, 46
  SALT II and, 46, 54–55
  worldwide demand for, 435–36
Humphrey, Hubert H., 320

Hussein, king of Jordan, 161, 169–71
  on boundaries, 169, 175–76
  on Cairo meeting participation, 198
  Camp David accords and, 229–31
  Carter's meetings with, 175–76, 201
  on Palestinian issue, 170, 176
  personal style of, 175
  on procedural issues, 171, 176
  on West Bank-Gaza transitional
    arrangement, 187–88
Huyser, Robert, 335–41
Hyland, William, 53, 56

ICBMs (intercontinental ballistic
    missiles), 47, 49, 51–52, 64, 67,
    97, 100, 103–5, 133–34, 351–54
Independent Commission on
    Disarmament and Security Issues,
    17, 418
India, 23, 201, 389
Indonesia, 124–27
Inouye, Daniel, 129
International Communications Agency,
    237
International Court of Justice, 378
international security, 23, 431–33
Iran, 179, 314–48, 368–83, 398–412
  American business departures from,
    340
  American Military Assistance Advisory
    Group in, 324, 341
  Americans attacked in, 341
  anti-American incidents in, 340, 341,
    372–73
  anti-regime demonstrations in, 324–31
  army in, 331, 334–41, 343
  AWACS sales to, 318–21
  Carter's trip to, 201
  civilian government recommended for,
    330, 334–41
  Communists in, 319, 326, 337
  crowd-control equipment sent to, 325
  economic concessions made in, 327
  Fedayeen in, 342
  Ford administration and, 315–16
  human rights in, 315–19, 343, 345–
    346
  Imperial Guard in, 341
  importance of, 314
  increased violence in, 329–31
  as Islamic republic, 336, 339, 376,
    408
  Khomeini-military contacts in, 336–41
  Majlis in, 404

martial law declared in, 326–27
martyrs in, 324
military cohesion in, 332, 333, 335–
    341, 343
military government for, 331–33
military-industrial development in,
    314–15, 317, 319–21
Mujahedin in, 342
petroleum resource of, 315, 348
police overreaction in, 324
post-Khomeini power struggle predicted
    in, 348
post-shah governments possible in,
    329–30
provisional government in, 341–45,
    369–75
regency council alternative in, 331–
    332, 334, 336
as regional power, 314–15
revolution in, see Iranian Revolution
Revolutionary Council government in,
    375, 378, 398, 403–6
SAVAK in, 316–17
shah opposed in, 316
shah's fall from power in, 136, 242,
    334–38, 345–48
shah's return demanded in, 372–73
Shi'ite Islamic sect in, 324, 347
Soviet involvement in, 326, 346
U.S. arms sales to, 315–24, 343, 368,
    377
U.S. intelligence sites in, 136, 342,
    347, 354–55
U.S. military liaison for, 335–41
U.S. relations with, see Iranian-U.S.
    relations
"White Revolution" in, 314
Iran hostage crisis, 17, 254, 373–83,
    398–412
  Afghan invasion and, 398, 400
  allied support sought in, 407–8
  Bani-Sadr in, 402–8
  Canadian embassy as refuge in, 374–
    375
  Carter and, 376–78, 380, 400–02,
    406–12
  Clark-Miller mission to, 376–77
  Congress and, 380, 411–12
  diplomatic relations broken in, 407
  forged Carter-Khomeini letter in, 407
  government control of hostages in,
    404–7
  indirect communication channels in,
    378, 380

530

conventional forces of, 32, 65–66, 416
cruise missiles and, 66–67, 106–7
defense spending increases and, 65–66, 364
dual strategy of, 392
flexible response strategy of, 68
High Level Group of, 65
intermediate-range missiles of, 96–97
long-term defense program of, 65–66
neutron bomb and, 68–69, 92–96
SALT II and, 66–67, 97–98, 351–52, 355–56
Soviet SS-20 missiles and, 64, 67, 97
summit meeting of, 65
theater nuclear forces (TNFs) of, 18–19, 64–65, 96–97, 98, 355
U.S.-Soviet arms control and, 392
Netherlands, 93, 96
Neto, Agostinho, 70, 89, 274, 280
neutron bomb, 67–69, 92–96
Newsom, David D., 42, 293, 338, 340–342, 361, 370, 374, 382, 385
New York Times, 380
New Zealand, 121, 123, 126–27, 319
Nguyen Co Thach, 122
Nicaragua, 136, 156
Nigeria, 260, 269–70, 291–92, 295, 304–5
Nimitz, Matthew, 43
Nixon, Richard M., 22, 23, 26, 33, 75
Nixon administration, 50, 345
    China and, 121
    foreign policy under, 21
    Iran and, 315
    Panama Canal negotiations under, 141
Nixon Doctrine, 315
Nkomo, Joshua, 257, 260, 268–71, 284–95, 301
    Lancaster House conference and, 299–301
    Mugabe's victory and, 301
    on Patriotic Front as sole negotiator, 267
    Smith's contacts with, 271
North Atlantic Council, 53
North-South relations, *see* Third World
nuclear weapons:
    first-strike capability with, 50
    flexible response strategy for, 68
    "no first-use" doctrine for, 417
    see also SALT I; SALT II; SALT III; *specific weapons*
Nujoma, Sam, 272–76, 280–82, 302–6

Nunn, Sam, 129, 153, 357
Nyerere, Julius, 260, 268–69, 280–82, 292, 298–99, 305

Oakley, Robert, 123
Obasanjo, Olusegun, 70, 260, 292
Ohira, Masayoshi, 407
oil embargo (1973), 23, 160–61, 166
Oksenberg, Michel, 76, 79, 82, 116–19
Oman, 317
O'Neill, Thomas P. ("Tip"), 412
Organization of African Unity (OAU), 73, 74, 260, 434–35
Organization of American States (OAS), 434–35
Organization of Petroleum Exporting Countries (OPEC), 23, 314, 321–322, 348
Orlov, Yuri, 103
Owen, David, 262–70, 284–95, 297–298, 302, 311
    Anglo-American Rhodesian plan and, 267–70, 284–87
    Namibian problem and, 283
    Nkomo-Smith solution sought by, 287, 291–92
    Rhodesian exploratory talks of, 264–65
    on Rhodesian security problem, 266–267

Pakistan, 389, 392, 426
Palestinian issues, 160–64, 166, 169–70, 172–73, 176–78, 201, 213
    see also West Bank-Gaza; West Bank-Gaza Autonomy Talks
Palestinian Liberation Organization (PLO), 160, 162–63, 176–77, 254, 378
    reconvened Geneva conference and, 167, 171, 182–83, 185–86, 188, 190
    Resolution 242 and, 163, 171, 177, 188–89
    Sadat's Jerusalem visit and, 194–95
    on U.S.-Soviet joint statement, 192
Panama, 140–57, 382–83, 403
    canal dispute in politics of, 145, 157
    DeConcini reservations and, 154–56
    financial payments demanded by, 146–147
    shah in, 382–83, 403, 406
Panama Canal:
    crisis in (1964), 33, 140–41